The New Institutional Economics of Markets

The International Library of Critical Writings in Economics

Founding Editor: Mark Blaug

Professor Emeritus, University of London, UK
Professor Emeritus, University of Buckingham, UK

This series is an essential reference source for students, researchers and lecturers in economics. It presents by theme a selection of the most important articles across the entire spectrum of economics. Each volume has been prepared by a leading specialist who has written an authoritative introduction to the literature included.

Wherever possible, the articles in these volumes have been reproduced as originally published using facsimile reproduction, inclusive of footnotes and pagination to facilitate ease of reference.

For a full list of published and future titles in this series
and a list of all Edward Elgar published titles, visit our website at
www.e-elgar.com

The New Institutional Economics of Markets

Edited by

Eirik G. Furubotn

Honorary Professor of Economics
and Co-Director, Center for New Institutional Economics
University of Saarland, Germany
and Research Fellow, Private Enterprise Research Center,
Texas A&M University, USA

and

Rudolf Richter

Professor Emeritus of Economics
and Director, Center for New Institutional Economics,
University of Saarland, Germany

THE INTERNATIONAL LIBRARY OF CRITICAL WRITINGS IN ECONOMICS

An Elgar Research Collection
Cheltenham, UK • Northampton, MA, USA

Published by
Edward Elgar Publishing Limited
The Lypiatts
15 Lansdown Road
Cheltenham
Glos GL50 2JA
UK

Edward Elgar Publishing, Inc.
William Pratt House
9 Dewey Court
Northampton
Massachusetts 01060
USA

A catalogue record for this book is available from the British Library

Library of Congress Control Number: 2010927655

Mixed Sources
Product group from well-managed
forests and other controlled sources
www.fsc.org Cert no. SA-COC-1565
© 1996 Forest Stewardship Council

ISBN 978 1 84720 983 2

Printed and bound by MPG Books Group, UK

Contents

Acknowledgements

The editors and publishers wish to thank the authors and the following publishers who have kindly given permission for the use of copyright material.

American Economic Association for articles: Dennis W. Carlton (1986), 'The Rigidity of Prices', *American Economic Review*, **76** (4), September, 637–58; Avner Greif (1993), 'Contract Enforceability and Economic Institutions in Early Trade: The Maghribi Traders' Coalition', *American Economic Review*, **83** (3), June, 525–48.

Berkeley Electronic Press for article: David P. Baron (2002), 'Private Ordering on the Internet: The eBay Community of Traders', *Business and Politics*, **4** (3), 245–74.

P. Bernholz for his own article: (1993), 'Constitutions as Governance Structures: The Political Foundations of Secure Markets: Comment', *Journal of Institutional and Theoretical Economics*, **149** (1), 312–20.

Blackwell Publishing Ltd for article: Paul R. Milgrom, Douglass C. North and Barry R. Weingast (1990), 'The Role of Institutions in the Revival of Trade: The Law Merchant, Private Judges, and the Champagne Fairs ', *Economics and Politics*, **2** (1), March, 1–23.

Elsevier for article: Walter W. Powell (1990), 'Neither Market Nor Hierarchy: Network Forms of Organization', *Research in Organizational Behavior*, **12**, 295–336.

Northwestern University School of Law for article: Ian R. Macneil (1978), 'Contracts: Adjustment of Long-Term Economic Relations Under Classical, Neoclassical, and Relational Contract Law', *Northwestern University Law Review*, **72** (6), November–December, 854–905.

Oxford University Press for articles: Anthony T. Kronman (1985), 'Contract Law and the State of Nature', *Journal of Law, Economics and Organization*, **1** (1), Fall, 5–32; James M. Acheson (1985), 'The Maine Lobster Market: Between Market and Hierarchy', *Journal of Law, Economics and Organization*, **1** (2), Autumn, 385–98.

University of Chicago Press via Copyright Clearance Center's Rightslink Service: Vernon L. Smith (1962), 'An Experimental Study of Competitive Market Behavior', *Journal of Political Economy*, **LXX** (2), April, 111–37; Harold Demsetz (1969), 'Information and Efficiency: Another Viewpoint', *Journal of Law and Economics*, **XII** (1), April, 1–22; Phillip Nelson (1974), 'Advertising as Information', *Journal of Political Economy*, **82** (4), July–August, 729–54; Oliver E. Williamson (1979), 'Transaction-Cost Economics: The Governance of

Contractual Relations', *Journal of Law and Economics*, **XXII** (2), October, 233–61; L.G. Telser (1980), 'A Theory of Self-enforcing Agreements', *Journal of Business*, **53** (1), January, 27–44; Benjamin Klein and Keith B. Leffler (1981), 'The Role of Market Forces in Assuring Contractual Performance', *Journal of Political Economy*, **89** (4), August, 615–41; Yoram Barzel (1982), 'Measurement Cost and the Organization of Markets', *Journal of Law and Economics*, **XXV** (1), April, 27–48; Roy W. Kenney and Benjamin Klein (1983), 'The Economics of Block Booking', *Journal of Law and Economics*, **XXVI** (3), October, 497–540; Joel M. Podolny (1993), 'A Status-based Model of Market Competition', *American Journal of Sociology*, **98** (4), January, 829–72; Avner Greif, Paul Milgrom and Barry R.Weingast (1994), 'Coordination, Commitment, and Enforcement: The Case of the Merchant Guild', *Journal of Political Economy*, **102** (4), August, 745–76.

C. Woodruff for his own article: John McMillan and Christopher Woodruff (2000), 'Private Order Under Dysfunctional Public Order', *Michigan Law Review*, **98** (8), August, 2421–58.

S.Woodward for her own article: Armen A. Alchian and Susan Woodward (1987), 'Reflections on the Theory of the Firm', *Journal of Institutional and Theoretical Economics*, **143** (1), 110–36.

B.R. Weingast for his own article: (1993), 'Constitutions as Governance Structures: The Political Foundations of Secure Markets', *Journal of Institutions and Theoretical Economics*, **149** (1), 286–311.

In addition the publishers wish to thank the Library at the University of Warwick, UK, for their assistance in obtaining these articles.

Introduction

Eirik G. Furubotn and Rudolf Richter[1]

The objection essentially is that the theory floats in the air. It is as if one studied the circulation of the blood without having a body. Firms have no substance. Markets exist without laws … (Coase 1984, 230).

In approaching the literature on the 'market', it is important to keep in mind that modern mainstream economics gave no more than cursory attention to the market as an *institution*. The broader theory of the market was simply not given serious attention. Thus, as Coase pointed out, while microeconomic analysis dealt intensively with the determination of market prices, discussion of the market itself was virtually absent. In short, the post-war movement toward more formal theory reinforced the general tendency of the profession to interpret the market as simply a place where consumers and entrepreneurs met, exchanged commodities and, in the process, established prices. This perception was, of course, fully consistent with the standard neoclassical model of a capitalist economy. The latter construct assumed the existence of a large number of perfectly rational individuals – with each endowed with a well-defined preference ordering and a bundle of goods. In this system, individuals knew that, by exchange, they could improve their welfare. Moreover, given zero transaction costs, they would be motivated to bargain with each other until they reached a Pareto-efficient exchange equilibrium. That is, they would proceed to a state of the economy in which no actor could improve his individual position without harming someone else.

In this neoclassical model of costless transactions, perfect foresight, and perfect rationality, there is no need for a specific market organization. It does not matter whether an individual trades only occasionally or professionally, whether he goes to the next street corner or sets up a whole network of trade relationships. This is the world of general equilibrium theory[2] in which each actor trades with everybody else for whatever commodity he wishes, and for all dates to come. Its order consists of the (abstract) elementary constitutional rules of:

(i)   private property,
(ii)   contractual obligations, and
(iii)   obligations from tortuous acts.

All these rules are guaranteed by a supreme authority (the state)[3], and constitute the legal basis for the *perfect market* of neoclassical microeconomics. The rules are ideal in the sense that they serve to coordinate the individual consumption and production plans of a mass of perfectly rational, self-seeking traders so that a Pareto-efficient allocation of all system resources can be achieved.[4] In effect, then, the order, or organization, of perfect markets is fully described by the elementary constitutional rules and their enforcement mechanism.

By contrast, the New Institutional Economics (NIE) envisions a much less perfect world than the one just considered. It presupposes the existence of positive transaction costs, the absence of a comprehensive set of futures markets, imperfect foresight, and the presence of boundedly rational economic actors. Conditions are such that specific markets and their characteristics are of definite interest. Some of the markets are formally established and organized like the London Stock Exchange, eBay, weekly town markets, and annual fairs. Others are informally, or semi-formally, established and set up by intermediaries, or by producers. Hence, institutions such as the automobile market or the real estate market appear. These specific markets can be conceived as privately formed and operated public goods that are based on sets of particular formal or informal rules (in addition to the elementary constitutional rules noted above). Some of the markets operating in an economy evolve spontaneously, however, such as the black market for US cigarettes in Frankfurt (Main), Germany after World War II, the 'Polish Market' in Berlin after the collapse of the Berlin Wall in 1989, etc.[5] But, in general, most specific markets are established, or 'made', by identifiable people (such as the producers of new products) even though they may contain spontaneous elements.

In what can be termed a 'neoinstitutional' system, an individual who plans to buy or sell a particular commodity necessarily faces two (interrelated) *institutional choice problems*. That is, he first has to choose (or establish) a specific market organization within which to undertake trade in the commodity; and, second, he must select, within that market organization, a specific *contract* (a contractual governance structure[6]) to utilize in conducting exchange with a trading partner. Both issues represent *non-market coordination problems*. The initial problem is that of coordinating individual plans among many suppliers and demanders; the second is a problem of coordinating individual plans between two parties – viz., a supplier and a demander. From the standpoint of the present collection of essays, the first coordination problem, as the choice of a 'market organization' within which traders are to do business, is the one to which significant attention will be given. The second organizational problem, the choice of the governance structure of an exchange contract is the subject of, e.g., Williamson's transaction-cost economics (which has, i.a., important application to the theory of the firm).

A central objective of the NIE approach is to consider the implications of given institutional arrangements for economic behavior. With respect to markets, a basic point often made by NIE writers is that the marketers' common goal is to lower their costs of transacting. This seems plausible at first thought but more has to be said because the assumptions of the NIE include (besides positive transaction costs) the idea that human agents are boundedly rational and have imperfect foresight. That is, we face the need to consider the effects produced by a number of variables, and it becomes difficult to determine which institutional arrangement is more 'efficient', or socially preferable, to another. For example, we might like to know which of two real existing markets, A or B, has the more desirable design features. But, unfortunately, it is difficult (if not impossible) to make such a judgment. Market A may be said to be superior to B because it economizes on transaction costs to a greater degree than B. On the other hand, market B may appear to be more adaptive to certain possible changes in the economic environment than A, and better suited to the cognitive limitations of its potential users. How to assess the relative significance of different institutional characteristics that cannot necessarily be reduced to a common measure obviously presents challenges. Arguably, however, the situation described is even harder to deal with if it is accepted that the ultimate aim of institutional structures is to generate utility (welfare) for a stipulated group of people (as the citizens of a given nation). For, insofar as a change in, e.g., market arrangements tends to bring about change in a system's economic/social outcome, some individuals are likely to gain and others to lose. That is, some people may feel better off with option A and worse off with option B, while a different set of people in the system hold the reverse opinion. Then a social welfare problem exists. And since compensation of the losers by the gainers is normally not a practical possibility, any solution reached concerning the choice of A or B will be arbitrary – i.e., based on value-judgments and decisions on the relative 'deservingness' of the respective groups of people involved, or based on political power.

As was explained earlier, the organization of 'perfect markets' is fully described by the ideal of an *abstract legal order* – the elementary constitutional rules. When entering the more realistic world of the NIE, though, market organizations have to include, in addition, certain more concrete aids to trade. It is important to note, therefore, that a number of practical economic and social arrangements, which we now take for granted, had to be devised painfully over time in order to facilitate the effectiveness and growth of the market economy. These are things such as the common usage of money, common accounting of time, common units of measurement, common locations of trade (as local markets[7], an internet platform), the organization of the pricing mechanism (as auctioning, rigid prices cum advertising, wage bargaining between unions and employers). It is also true, of course, that any specific market order, or market design, has to find ways of dealing with certain basic activities of trade such as: search, inspection, bargaining, contract execution, control, and enforcement.[8] Moreover, the manner in which these basic functions are accomplished has great practical significance in the friction-filled NIE world. Hence, we shall be concerned with this literature.

Despite the efforts made by neoinstitutional economists to date, there is, unfortunately, no systematic theory of markets currently available that deals satisfactorily with the complete range of problems extant in an NIE world. What can be found, however, are explanations in the NIE manner of why, under certain circumstances, the basic activities of trade (noted above) are organized in one particular fashion rather than another. These arrangements deserve attention. Thus, a few prominent examples from this literature are reprinted in the present volume to illustrate this particular approach. It can be hoped, though, that the writings chosen point up certain fundamental theoretical issues in the field, and serve to increase understanding of how a deeper, more comprehensive institutional economic theory of markets may be developed.

In the interest of clarity and simplicity, the six elementary transaction activities of concern will be reduced to three categories. These are:

Part I.   *Precontractual Activities* (search and inspection)
Part II.   *Contracting* (price and contract formation)
Part III. *Postcontractual Activities* (execution, control, and enforcement).

The reprints presented in this collective volume, and our comments on the respective papers, will follow this classification scheme.

Part I   Precontractual Activities: Search and Inspection

Search and inspection are specific informational problems that require attention in an economic system having non-zero transaction costs. Stigler (1961) was the first to analyze the search for product prices. Subsequently, Nelson (1970) extended Stigler's approach to the search for information about product quality.[9] He noted that information about quality could be secured not only by way of search but also through experience, and that: 'Experience will be used when search becomes too expensive'. Accordingly, Nelson distinguishes between 'search goods' and 'experience goods'. Relative to this classification, typical search goods are cameras, furniture, china, glassware, and floor coverings. Typical experience goods are radios, television sets, tyres, batteries, automobiles, and bicycles.

Advertising as a vehicle for conveying information plays a role in the case of search goods, but personal inspection is also important (as, e.g., search for an apartment, a suit, a hat, etc.). Interestingly, misleading advertising is said to result in costs to the advertiser, for 'he suffers a decline in his credibility for future advertisements and pays the costs of processing non-buying customers' (**Nelson 1974**, Chapter 4, this volume). Therefore, 'consumers can have some confidence that the advertising of search qualities bears a close relationship to the truth'. Such confidence, however, is much less likely to exist in the case of experience goods: 'The major control that consumers have over the market for experience qualities is whether they repeat the purchase of a brand or not'. In short, consumers cannot expect much direct information from advertising concerning experience qualities. What they can get, though, is important indirect information: 'The consumer can learn that the brand advertises. I contend that this is the useful information that the consumer absorbed from the endorsement of announcers, actors, and others who are paid for their encomiums. These and other advertisements for experience goods have no informational content. Their informational role – beyond the relation of brand to function – is simply contained in their existence'. Advertisement for experience goods is of particular interest to neoinstitutionalists because advertising outlay can be interpreted as a means to save on transaction costs. Thus, the activity plays a part in explaining the creation of a market organization. Moreover, viewed in this way, advertising is not (necessarily) socially wasteful.

Relative to the question of inspection, two contributions from the informal New Institutional Economics literature are noted: a paper by **Barzel** (**1982**, Chapter 2, this volume), and one by **Kenney** and **Klein** (**1983**, Chapter 3, this volume).

Barzel (**1982**) argues that the problems and the costs associated with measurement pervade, and significantly affect, all economic transactions. Understandably, errors in measurement are too costly to eliminate entirely. We know that the values of equally priced items will tend to differ, and thus people will spend resources to capture the difference existing in valuation. Such resource expenditure, however, is wasteful, and it is hypothesized that traders can generally agree on methods that help to reduce this kind of resource use. A customer's random selection from an already optimally sorted commodity will serve to avoid the excessive expense of oversearching. For example, a mutual agreement among traders may be reached to suppress some readily obtainable information in order to preempt opportunities for excessive measurement. In practice, a variety of measures can be agreed upon that help marketers to lower measurement costs. As a result, there are product warranties, share contracts, brand names, vertical integration or simply suppression of information (like selling oranges in sealed bundles).

Kenney and **Klein** (**1983**) provide an interesting example showing how oversearching can be prevented. The case in question comes from the experience of the Central Selling Organization (CSO) of the DeBeers Group, which, at one time, sold most of the world's gem-quality uncut diamonds. The authors suggest that the cartel's selling organization contributed to a reduction of search cost by minimizing buyers' oversearching for information. The procedure utilized was as follows. Stones were sorted according to shape, quality, color, and weight in more than two thousand categories. Despite this, variations in the value of stones within each category were substantial. But to limit oversearching, stones of each category were sorted by DeBeers into imperfectly homogeneous categories and sold in preselected blocks to preselected buyers at non-negotiable prices. The dominant position of DeBeers in the world diamond market when this policy was in effect made it possible for such arbitrary rules to be enforced. Specifically, the monopolistic seller was able to insist that if buyers rejected the sales offer they were to be banned from any further dealings with DeBeers. Ostensibly, the policy was advantageous to buyers since it permitted buyers to maintain a long-term business relationship with DeBeers. And the relationship enabled buyers to earn rents whose present value was greater than the present value of the earnings stream they would otherwise achieve if they rejected sights of lower than average quality. 'Since these rents are lost if the buyer decides to reject a sight and is terminated from the list of invited buyers, a wealth-maximizing buyer will not generally reject sights ...'. While the logic here is easily grasped, the whole DeBeers system rests on monopoly power, and it is not clear that society would not gain from a more competitive market even if such change would lead to increased search costs.

Another way to help reduce search and inspection costs is for individuals to use personal contacts. Granovetter (1974/1995), for example, showed that personal contacts represented the method most widely employed by highly qualified people[10] to find out about jobs. Interestingly, the majority of those polled was only weakly tied to their contacts[11], and saw their contacts only occasionally or rarely. There are, of course, some strongly tied contacts, and direct or second and higher order ties, informal or formal relations, etc.[12] It is obvious that social networks facilitate search and inspection of the objects of exchange – or, as **Powell** (**1990**, Chapter 6, this volume)**,** argues – networks 'are particularly apt for circumstances in which there is a need for efficient, reliable information', and they 'are useful for the exchange of commodities whose value is not easily measured'. Central to these properties are reciprocal patterns of networks that are enhanced by long-term relationships. Powell does not share Williamson's belief 'that the bulk of economic exchange fits comfortably at either pole of the markets-hierarchy continuum'. This would, presumably, represent too mechanical a view. Rather, 'network forms of organization' should be seen as being the more general forms of organization – with 'markets and hierarchies' constituting only special cases. Be that as it may, Powell reports on interesting cases of market organization in: *craft industries* (construction, publishing, film and recording businesses), *industrial districts* or clusters (in Germany, Italy, Japan, and Sweden), *strategic alliances* (common in technology-intensive industries), and *vertical disaggregation* (such as the downsizing pattern in the Italian textile industry or the American automobile industry). To these cases, one could add as well *regional clusters* like Silicon Valley (Porter, 1998, ch. 7). The rationale for the network forms of organization is based, according to Powell, on three main factors: know-how, the need for speed, and trust. These elements are critical components of networks that further knowledge sharing – a practice typical of industries characterized by rapid technical progress (Richter, 2003).

The Maine lobster market offers a graphic example of the network character found in an implicitly agreed upon market organization. **Acheson** (**1985**, Chapter 1, this volume) gives a detailed description of this case. The actors involved are: lobster fishermen, lobster dealers and cooperatives, wholesalers, pound operators, trucking providers, retailers, restaurants, hotels, supermarkets, etc. Only a few vertically integrated firms exist (embracing units ranging from dealerships to wholesale operations). The actors noted are able to entertain mutually agreed upon, long-term vertical business connections. Normally, a fisherman will sell to only one dealer; dealers and cooperatives sell only to a small number of pound operators, wholesalers, etc. In this scheme, fishermen behave usually as price takers with dealers, who buy all of the lobsters their fishermen offer for sale. At the same time, restaurants, hotels, etc. want a steady supply of lobsters to come to them, and to be able to charge a fixed price for lobsters. These conditions represent the constraints with which dealers, cooperative managers, pound operators, etc. must contend in negotiating. They do this by contacting each other, vertically and horizontally, to exchange information and speculate on the way the market is going (e.g., by considering impending changes in the supply of lobsters and anticipated price changes). Acheson stresses that the way lobsters are bought and sold have strong relational features.[13] Individual identities matter on both sides of the market. In fact, the relationship between nearby dealers and wholesalers is some mixture of cooperation and competition. In other words, the situation described is a characteristic example of a market order understood as a system that involves mutual agreement among a multiplicity of people.

Another aspect of the trading functions of 'search' and 'inspection' (under conditions of positive transaction costs) is discussed by **Podolny** (**1993**, Chapter 5, this volume).[14] His analysis is concerned with quality competition among experience goods.[15] Product quality is said to be 'signaled' by the status of the producer in the market. Podolny defines 'a producer's status in the market as the perceived quality of that producer's products in relation to the perceived quality of that producer's competitors' products'. In short, producer's status is viewed as a signal of the underlying quality of a firm's product. Social relations mediate the link between quality and status. There is, however, only a loose linkage between a signal and its meaning; and, in consequence, quality shifts need not be realized immediately by consumers. Moreover, lags between quality shifts and the perception of quality changes by consumers are not only caused by technical impediments but, to a degree, also by the affiliations of consumers to social networks of brand users such as 'Mercedes drivers' or 'BMW owners'.

The core of Podolny's model is formed by three assumptions, which are coupled with his implicit assumption of positive transaction costs, and the idea that producers are boundedly rational profit maximizers. The basic assumptions are as follows:

(a)   Consumers cannot determine the quality of a product (i.e., an 'experience good') prior to its actual use or consumption.

(b)   The market status of a producer is taken to be a signal of quality on which consumers can and do rely for their decisions.

(c)   A producer's relations with others in the market mediate the linkage between status and quality. Such interaction creates inertial tendencies in the formation of exchange relations by biasing evaluation of the products. Quite simply, the ties existing between actors play a significant role in the formation of perceptions of quality.

An important economic consequence of a producer's position in the market network is that it affects his gross revenue and costs. Podolny argues that: 'For a producer of a given level of quality, additional status is most likely to translate into increased revenue, either in form of higher prices or greater market share'. Supposedly, then, for higher-status producers, advertising costs for attracting a given volume of business are lower. The same can be said for 'transaction costs' in the sense of convincing customers of the quality of the product. Finally, financial costs may also be lowered by an increase in status. And, in general, the presumption is that: 'the costs for a given quality output will be lower for the higher-status producer than the lower-status producer'. This conclusion is interesting but seems to be based on a special set of circumstances. Specifically, the notion appears to be that advertising becomes increasingly effective in producing higher status as the status level sought is raised, and that quality claims do not have to be supported by costly real improvements in product characteristics. These cost-benefit trends, though, are surely not inevitable.

It is true, of course, that the status of a firm is not fixed. With some effort, firms can shift their status positions within a market. Moreover, multimarket identity is not inconsistent with the dynamics of a status-based model. Thus, the incorporation of status processes into the understanding of market competition is well worth considering, and such action would provide a good basis for the development and extension of a sociological approach to markets. Finally, it should be noted that Podolny further illustrates his analytical themes by examining the pricing behavior followed by investment banks in the underwriting of corporate securities. The findings here provide empirical support for his status-based model of market competition.

The comments made above have attempted to introduce some of the current thinking found in the literature on search and inspection, and to show how ideas from the New Institutional Economics underlie such thinking. An important theme advanced by the exponents of neoinstitutionalism is that deviations from the ideal type of perfect market may lead to workable solutions to real-life market problems. For example, long-term personal relationships (i.e., implicit or explicit relational contracts) between buyers and sellers, and between competitors, can serve to facilitate the trading functions of search and inspection. In effect, traders here implicitly agree to a particular organization of search and inspection. Networks of relational contracts make this accommodation possible. Explanations of this sort are plausible but, like other findings of neoinstitutional analysis, they do not emerge from a precisely defined axiomatic construct comparable to that employed in general equilibrium theory. By its nature, the neoinstitutional world is more complex and fuzzy than the neoclassical world. Hence, specialized models developed from different sets of initial conditions are encountered.

Part II   Contracting: Price and Contract Formation

Markets, in the economic sense, can be understood as mutually agreed upon organizations designed to facilitate the exchange of private property rights among parties. From the perspective of the NIE, the way a market is organized is explained by the existence of positive transaction costs, and boundedly rational agents possessed of incomplete foresight. There is no ideal (or 'perfect') market organization that is able to serve as a benchmark for the determination of 'market efficiency' (as is assumed in neoclassical microeconomics). Moreover, what has to be recognized is that while the arrangements of a capitalist system protect private property from theft or physical change brought about by outsiders, property is not protected from changes in its market value. All private owners must bear market risk. Consequently, their property may be 'expropriated' by the legal actions of their economic competitors. As **Alchian**

(**1965**, Chapter 10, this volume) has put it: 'If I open a restaurant near yours and win away business by my superior service, you are as hurt as if I had burned part of your building'. For the owner who is harmed this is clearly a problem; and such market-risk effects may also be a problem for society in a 'neoinstitutional' world. That is, society may suffer if, lacking a comprehensive set of futures markets, the coordination of investment decisions cannot be accomplished effectively. For example, overinvestment in particular sectors may occur because, in a neoinstitutional economy, the price system does not represent a fully adequate signaling device. Each individual investor operates largely in ignorance of what other investors intend to do, and thus each can form the wrong impression of the profitability promised by his project. What may appear to be a good investment choice from an individual's point of view can turn out to be a disaster if many (noncommunicating) firms invest in the area simultaneously.

In theory, one alternative to this difficult situation would be to allocate resources through hierarchies rather than markets. Public instead of private ownership could be instituted. But, such policy would raise serious problems concerning how to control the public activities – inter alia, to avoid biased allocation induced by bribery. Alchian (1965) in his discussion of the pros and cons of private and public ownership, puts forward two reasons in favor of 'specialization of ownership' (i.e., private ownership). These are: (1) Concentration of rewards and costs *more* directly on each person responsible for them, and (2) Comparative advantage effects of specialized applications of (a) knowledge in control and (b) of risk bearing. As for (2a), the specialization in knowledge, Alchian's remark reminds one of Hayek's (1945) argument in favor of (capitalist) markets as opposed to Lange's (1938) idea of markets in a socialist economy. The second point (2b), ownership specialization in risk bearing, calls attention to the fact that people's attitudes toward risk differ: 'Exchange of ownership will reallocate risks among people, leading to greater utility in the sense that exchange of goods does' (**Alchian, 1965**).

Alchian makes clear, however, that his remarks are not to be understood as a general condemnation of public ownership. At the same time, he notes that one should keep in mind that 'the presence of one kind of relative deficiency does not justify a switch to another agency – which has other kinds of deficiencies.' In other words, it can be argued that while the price system in a neoinstitutional economy does not perform in the ideal way that the frictionless neoclassical model suggests, this fact does not justify the abandonment of market capitalism. Traditionally, neoclassical economists have focused their interest on the formation of prices on markets. The corresponding institutional framework of perfect competition is consonant with that of an auction. That is, traders agree explicitly to a public sale. They agree that an auctioneer will administer price negotiations between sellers and buyers according to an established rule (e.g., an English or Dutch auction). This implies a formally peaceful 'conflict' in the sense of Weber (1968, 38). The resulting competitive equilibrium price is illustrated by the intersection of a demand curve and a supply curve. And, significantly, this theory has been corroborated for the case of a double auction by **V. Smith** (**1962**, Chapter 12, this volume) in his famous experiment on competitive market behavior. It can be asserted, then, that if traders agree and are able to organize their market according to the conditions of perfect competition[16] (the classical ideal type of market organization), prices will converge to their competitive equilibrium (the intersection of the Marshallian Cross) even if the number of traders is small.

Of course, under the conditions of the NIE, such an arrangement among traders represents more a theoretical concept than a practical option. Obviously, the informational and other requirements needed to effectuate the scheme would be extraordinary and extremely costly. To organize all markets of an economy in the form of a commodity exchange or an organized stock market (where prices adapt to changes of demand or supply in fractions of a second) would demand an elaborate, strictly monitored and enforced institutional framework. Such a structure is just not feasible. What is found in the real world is a system in which most prices are administered. They are usually announced by one side such as the dealers in our example of the lobster market, or the producers in the case of producers' markets, and afterwards are kept constant for a time. As a result, prices are comparatively rigid – a phenomenon that characterizes all advanced economies. Yet, as **Carlton** (**1986**, Chapter 7, this volume) has shown, the degree of price rigidity differs greatly across industries. In some industries, the average price does not change for periods of well over one year, while, in others, the price changes quite frequently. One reason for price rigidity is found in the existence of 'menu costs' (or the costs of changing price labels). These costs are not negligible as has been shown by the work of such writers as Levy, Bergen, Dutta, and Venable (1997). Other reasons for keeping prices unchanged are said to be concern about the emergence of price wars, and the possibility of alienating customers (Blinder et al., 1998, 85). Differently expressed, the explanation could be said to lie with the price setters' desire to cultivate long-term relationships with their competitions and customers.

Interestingly, empirical work on rigid prices exploded during the last decade (Campbell and Eden, 2005). The motivation for this line of research, however, was not to support transaction cost economics but to prove the non-neutrality of money and, as a consequence, the effectiveness of an active monetary policy. It is true, of course, that 'rigid' prices are not permanently fixed and are changed from time to time. Although traders are not constantly changing prices, they may try to approach equilibrium prices by a weekly or monthly trial and error process. Thus, for example, Campbell and Eden (2005, 1) report that there is evidence that grocery stores 'extensively experiment' with their prices.[17] At the same time, there may also exist tacit price agreements among competitors as indicated by oligopoly theory. Moreover, suppliers may change their prices only after the announcements made by one firm – the price leader (Stigler, 1952, 234).

Representatives of the New Institutional Economics, such as **Alchian** and **Woodward** (**1987**, Chapter 9, this volume), argue that rigid prices are the result of a convention between sellers and buyers. Thus, these writers explain the practice of *posted prices* as follows: 'Posted prices, announced publicly and maintained until publicly revised, are prices at which the posting party will transact any amount. All parties obtain the same price; the price to a particular party could not be changed while all others were getting better prices'. The authors give as examples tuna and salmon fishing: 'where the fishing boats are reliant on a unique buyer-processor. Similarly, a fixed price guarantee occurs in many agricultural product markets where farmers plant crops relying on a unique buyer-processor'. Another reason for price rigidity is that, in long-term business relationships that require relationship-specific investments: 'opportunistic price changes (intended to effect a hold-up) are not clearly or cheaply distinguishable from price changes to which the parties would have agreed had the demand and supply environment been mutually foreseen' (**Alchian** and **Woodward 1987**). These explanations draw upon neoinstitutional reasoning. A key understanding here is that contractual relations develop between firms that are suppliers and those that are buyers (**Macneil**, **1978**, Chapter 11, this volume). Hence, a vertical form of cooperation can appear. That is, given specific investments on both the supply side and the demand side, a lock-in effect occurs; and, in this setting, quantity adjustments have much better incentive compatibility properties than do price adjustments. As Williamson (1985, 76) argues: 'price adjustment proposals involve the risk that one's opposite is contriving to alter the terms within the bilateral monopoly trading gap to his advantage.'

Of course, bilateral relationships between firms engaged in trade with each other do not constitute the only area in which price rigidity is utilized. The basic argument for rigidity could also be applied to the relationship between a seller and his many customers (i.e., the seller's clientele). All parties here may make specific investments. Then, with all locked-in to a degree, price inflexibility can be interpreted as a 'protection of the expropriable composite quasi-rent of dependent resources' (Alchian and Woodward, 1987). Similar arguments may be drawn upon to explain wage rigidities because the employment relationship is often a strongly relational contract with specific investments taking place in human and physical capital on both sides.

In contrast to the situation in neoclassical microeconomics, contracts in a neoinstitutional system are not considered as a means by which transacting parties fully define future performances and allocate risks of future contingencies (as in the Arrow–Debreu model). In a neoinstitutional context, such complete contracts are ruled out because the existence of transaction costs, bounded rationality, and limited foresight make their formulation prohibitively expensive. Thus, in cases of long-term relationships, it becomes rational not to specify contractually all elements of performance and, instead, to enter into cooperative exchange relationships that are able to adapt to unforeseen events.[18] For these cases, the term *relational transaction* (or contractual relation) was introduced in Macneil (1974). Contract, in the traditional legal sense of the word, relates to a *discrete* transaction. And in the model of perfect competition such transactions are assumed to take place in a social vacuum. Real-life transactions, however, are embedded in social relations. Macneil's premise emerges from his belief in the pervasiveness of 'relation' in the post-industrial socioeconomic world. Indeed, he says of 'relation' that 'its dominance seems constantly to be increasing' (Macneil, 1974, 694). Networks of contractual relations play an important role in market organization (as was illustrated in Chapter 1 of this volume by **Acheson's** essay on the Maine lobster market). In the lobster market case, market organization rested on the expectation of market participants that the existing exchange relations would be ongoing and continue into the future. As Macneil says: 'Such relational expectations, if firmly grounded in fact, assure "satisfactory" exchanges in the future without the need for present specificity, present communication or present measured reciprocity. A vast amount of economic activity is carried on at least partly on that basis' (Macneil, 1974, 718).

Note that it is possible to think in terms of a whole spectrum of different types of contracts as defined from a legal standpoint (Macneil, 1974, 738–40). At one extreme, we have the classical contract (regulating a discrete, one-time transaction), while at the other end of the spectrum we have relations or arrangements such as marriage and employment relations (Furubotn and Richter, 2005, 156f.). Contracts of the extreme 'relational' pole entail strong personal involvement, are long-term, and anticipate the possibility of trouble as a normal part of the ongoing association between the parties to the contract. Significantly, any difficulties or problems that do, in fact, arise are to be dealt with by means of cooperation and other restorational techniques (Macneil, 1974, 738–). Less complex than the twelve restorational concepts suggested by Macneil is his three-way classification of contracts. Here, he distinguishes among the classical, neoclassical, and relational categories of contract law, and this approach has relevance for the NIE and this collective volume. **Macneil (1978)** emphasizes the need to plan flexibility into long-term contracts, or to leave gaps in the planning that can be filled in as required. The justification for these provisions is that, with the increasing duration and complexity of contracts, it becomes too difficult and too time consuming to agree ex ante on how to respond to potential problems (as assumed in neoclassical contract law). In the long-term cases, of course, very different adjustment processes of an ongoing-administrative kind are needed that include internal and external dispute-resolution structures. Macneil's 'relational contract law', then, seems to be consistent with the neoinstitutional view of the economy since the latter envisions Knightian uncertainty, and questions the capacity of boundedly rational agents to establish optimal arrangements that will comport ideally with all the events that emerge in an ongoing system.

It was noted earlier that a key economic problem for neoinstitutionalists is to explain why one institutional arrangement (governance structure, order, or constitution) can be said to be preferable to another. But, despite the importance of this issue, a clear and unambiguous determination of the 'best' institutional structure cannot easily be made. Since major institutional reorganization will almost certainly bring about gains for some people and losses for others, value judgments must be involved, ultimately, in institutional choice (Buchanan, 1960, 111–116; Furubotn, 1987). But, apart from this matter, it is also arguable that the special conditions existing in a neoinstitutional system (i.e., positive transaction costs and decision makers having limited ability to acquire and process information) rule out the possibility of actual optimization in most cases of practical importance (Gigerenzer and Selten, 2001). In short, there is controversy in NIE circles about the extent to which certain formal mathematical concepts drawn from orthodox neoclassical theory can be adapted to the requirements of neoinstitutional analysis. Thus, Williamson, recognizing the uncertain future that is characteristic of a neoinstitutional environment, argues that: '… a governance structure obviously reshapes incentives. To focus entirely on *ex ante* incentive alignment, however, is a truncated way to study organization – especially if all complex contracts are unavoidably incomplete and if adaptation is the central problem of economic organization' (2000, 599). From this standpoint it is crucial to be able to *adjust* governance structure to the actual economic situations encountered over time by effecting 'a discriminating match, according to which transactions are aligned with governance structures so as to promote adaptation of autonomous and cooperative kinds' (2000, 599). In principle, then, the institutional solution adapted at any time can take the form of one of the extreme options (markets or hierarchies) or of any form falling within these limits.

Relational contracts are designed to offer agents some flexibility to deal with unforeseen events. Such contracts may be bilateral or multilateral (as, for example, bilateral cooperation between buyer and seller in a market exchange, or multilateral cooperation among all buyers and sellers within a market). These are joint actions involving two or more individuals. In the latter case, the term collective action is used in the literature. Collective action can be private (the market, the firm), or public (the community, the state). Recognizing this dichotomy, the New Institutional Economics operates at two levels of analysis. There is a macroscopic level that deals with what Davis and North (1971, 6) call the *institutional environment*, and a microscopic level that the same authors call *institutional arrangements*.

Williamson's (**1979**, Chapter 13, this volume) transaction-cost economics is concerned with the latter area.

Transaction-cost economics (TCE) suggests that by focusing on transaction costs, and seeking those arrangements, or governance structures, that economize on such costs, a decision maker is able to determine favorable organizational designs (Masten 1996, 4). Although this approach may tend to oversimplify the problem of institutional choice, transaction-cost economics does provide useful insights into the process of contracting. In particular, TCE emphasizes that since major frictional forces exist in a neoinstitutional economy, complete contracts, dealing with all conceivable contingencies, cannot be written. Inevitably, then, any contracts that are put forward will contain loopholes and, in consequence, there will be a need to revise or adapt contracts periodically to adjust them to conditions that were unforeseen initially. In principle, courts might be relied upon to enforce or modify contractual obligations, but actually this procedure tends to be relatively costly and inefficient. Particularly when transaction-specific investments are involved, and the hazards of 'ex-post' opportunism are faced, governance by court ordering will usually have to be supplemented, or even replaced, by private ordering. This line of analysis is of direct importance to the interpretation of works in the present collection because of the apparent practice of marketers to utilize relational contracts.

Williamson's TCE approach indicates that there is no black and white contrast to be made between 'markets' and 'hierarchies'. Also made clear is the fact that, in a neoinstitutional world, the concept of Pareto optimality has no applicability. **Demsetz** (**1969**, Chapter 8, this volume) emphasized the same point with respect to the *market failure* issue raised by public policy economists. He argues that the relevant choice in the real world is not between an ideal norm (Pareto efficiency) and an existing 'imperfect' institutional arrangement. Indeed: 'This *nirvana* approach differs considerably from a *comparative institution* approach in which the relevant choice is between [various] alternative real institutional arrangements' (1969). The core reason for the disparity noted is found in the assumptions made about the environment in which activity takes place. In a neoinstitutional world, decision makers are not idealized 'perfectly rational beings' but individuals who differ widely in respect to their abilities, initial resource positions, information endowments, risk preferences, and so on, and who face a great variety of constraints that limit their options. These obstacles are, for the most part, ineluctable and cannot be swept away by any simple means available to society. Nevertheless, individuals have motivation to undertake continuing search for better information and improved methods of decision-making. What is important in this kind of environment is what 'works', and therefore, diverse institutional solutions can be expected to emerge. Moreover, survival of diverse forms is possible because, even with competition, an organization need only be relatively efficient, rather than ideally efficient, to maintain its position in the system (Alchian, 1950).

Part III   Postcontractual Activities: Execution, Control and Enforcement

The functioning of any market, or market society, demands that a set of elementary constitutional rules be established together with a mechanism to enforce the rules. The key areas to be regulated would be: (i) the *property rights* of individuals, (ii) the procedures for the *transfer* of rights according to contractual agreement, and (iii) the *liability* of individuals for contractual obligations. The enforcement mechanism consists in the social sanctions in effect – which may be supplied by the traders themselves, by the organizers of specific markets, or by public bodies such as the city or state. Fundamentally, market economies depend on the support of a public authority in its capacity as legislator, administrator, and enforcer of the elementary constitutional rules of the game. In addition, public authorities play an important role in the creation of operational rules such as national (or international) agreements on the unit of account and means of payment, on the international calendar[19] and time zones,[20] on common measures and weights,[21] etc. Yet, the role of a public authority involves a contradiction. For, a state 'strong enough to protect property rights and enforce contracts is also strong enough to confiscate the wealth of its citizens' **Weingast (1993**, Chapter 23, this volume).[22] Hence, thriving markets require not only an appropriate system of constitutional rules: '… but a secure political foundation that places strong limits on the ability of the state to confiscate wealth' (ibid.). What is needed is a credible commitment by the state to respect private property and individual contractual obligations. But even though this is an old and well-discussed insight of the science of the state, it had little impact on the advice being offered by economists to the emerging democracies immediately after the breakdown of the Soviet Union and its allies. Apparently many of the economists 'doctoring the ailing economies of central and Eastern Europe' believed that the necessary institutional features of a free market would appear and 'be the automatic outcome of getting the prices right through elimination of price and exchange controls' (North, 1993, 12).

The central question of Weingast's paper concerns the limits that can be placed on the ability of the state to seize and appropriate wealth. He asks: 'What makes these limits credible, i.e., what makes them binding on political actors?' Weingast goes on to focus on the critical role of federalism for protecting markets in both England and the United States[23] and argues that federalism must have played a major role in protecting the growth of economic markets. In his response to Weingast's paper, **Bernholz (1993**, Chapter 15, this volume) argues that federalism seems to be neither a necessary condition for a free market economy, as the success of Hong Kong, Japan, France, and Taiwan demonstrates, nor a sufficient one '… if not combined with a strict division of power, as the example of modern England shows'.

The fact is, however, that the perfect constitutional state does not exist. In the real world of positive transaction costs, incomplete foresight and boundedly rational agents, there is no legal, administrative, or judicial perfection – and certainly no perfect control of governmental powers. Inevitably, formal institutional arrangements such as constitutions, laws, contracts, and charters are *incomplete*. They are to be completed (ideally) by 'community norms based on intense social interaction' (Aoki, 2001, XI ii), or 'private orderings' between the contractual parties (Williamson, 1983, 520). The problems involved are central to the new institutional economics.

The possibility that private ordering can take place has importance for neoinstitutional theory. And it is said that self-enforcement of contractual obligations is perhaps the most elegant form of private ordering. Its simplest manifestation is seen in simultaneous exchange. If the *quid* and the *quo* of exchange are separated over time and space, though, the type of self-enforcement found depends on the frequency of trade. Two extreme cases can be distinguished. These are: (a) Traders trade only once with marketers, or (b) indefinitely often with marketers. With respect to case (a), parties to non-simultaneous exchange can help themselves by conveying valuable assets such as hostages or collateral, or by unification with the other party (as in marriage or vertical integration). **Kronman (1985**, Chapter 19, this volume) exemplifies and discusses these three cases and others.[24] He warns that the existence of the state and its enforcement machinery does not make the three safeguarding techniques superfluous. In fact, we know that provision of collateral is a current method used for securing money loans. Apparently, 'the legal right to enforce a promise can reduce but never eliminate the insecurity associated with all temporally asymmetric exchanges ...'. But, of course, to use these techniques has its costs. 'Both hostages and collateral create their own forms of opportunism and are costly too ...' (**Kronman, 1985**).

In case (b), if traders trade indefinitely often with others, agreements can be enforced by the threat of breaking off the business relationship. Insofar as the system is assumed to be such that perfect rationality, perfect foresight, and zero transaction costs hold, detection of wrongdoing is *certain*. Therefore, rational actors, who will always desire to maintain profitable trade, have no choice but to avoid dishonest acts. One's reputation for honesty becomes an issue. The basic hypothesis of the model, as **Telser** (**1980**, Chapter 22, this volume) describes it, is '...that someone is honest only if honesty, or the *appearance* of honesty, pays more than dishonesty.' This statement, however, is a bit confusing because if merely the 'appearance' of honesty is possible, various dishonest strategies are conceivable – and decision makers are not 'perfectly rational.' In any event, the fundamental logic of this approach indicates that self-enforcing agreements will probably not work if, first, the sequence of transactions has a known end point (like an agreed upon marriage for two years). Presumably, the end point must at least be uncertain. Second, the expected horizon must be relatively long. The longer the expected horizon, the greater is the return to the parties from adherence to the terms of their agreement (**Telser, 1980**). Third, if the agreement must be played out under highly uncertain conditions, the situation is not conducive to self-enforcing contracts. This is so because the prospective gains to the principals are not clear, and their interest in collaboration is correspondingly dimmed.

From a technical standpoint, there is another issue connected with the role of uncertainty. The self-enforcement model is based on game theory, and thus requires very detailed information about what will eventuate over time. The informational requirements here are, of course, inconsistent with the basic NIE assumptions. Nevertheless, many theorists sympathetic with the aims of neoinstitutionalism are convinced that game theory represents an important tool kit for institutional economists provided there is awareness of its strong assumptions. Binmore brings this position out clearly:

> Game theorists believe that they can demonstrate formally how even the most selfish individuals will often find it in their own enlightened self-interest to cooperate with their neighbors in a long-term relationship. For this purpose they study the equilibria of repeated games. ... Little of what they have discovered in this area so far would have come as a surprise to David Hume (1739–40, bk. 3) who already articulated essential mechanisms some two hundred years before. However, these insights are now firmly grounded in formal models (1992, 21).

The point is that a repeatedly played game of conflicting interests (say a prisoner's dilemma game) can be transformed into a game of coinciding interests (in which the agents cooperate and achieve the efficient solution). Its solution is a Nash equilibrium of the recurrent (strategic) 'supergame' about the method of playing repeatedly a given 'underlying game' (here, the prisoner's dilemma game).

The question of how to interpret a multiplicity of equilibria in a game was addressed by Shelling (1960) with his focal-point concept. Schotter (1981) developed, starting from Lewis

(1969), what can be called the *institution-as-an-equilibrium-of-a-game* approach (Furubotn and Richter, 2005, 8). According to this view, an institution is defined as a salient Nash equilibrium of a recurrent 'supergame' about the way a given 'underlying game' is repeatedly played. It may be plausible to assume, then, that an efficient equilibrium is a salient Nash equilibrium – if we start from an unhistoric point 'zero'. But life is an ongoing process, and thus institutions are generally path dependent. A plausible 'salient' Nash equilibrium could then be the precedence – but this equilibrium need not be efficient. Since no actor has an incentive to change his strategy if no other does, an institution could conceivably persist in a 'bad' (inefficient) Nash equilibrium even though each single player would like to reach an efficient one. Such a set of events might explain the observed persistence of inefficient social structures (Eggertsson, 2005).

Self-enforcing contracts are of particular interest if the contractual terms relate to hard to measure product characteristics such as the 'taste' of a hamburger (**Klein** and **Leffler, 1981**, Chapter 18, this volume). In cases of this sort, 'market arrangements such as the value of lost purchases which motivate transactors to honor their promises may be the cheapest method of guaranteeing the guarantee' (1981). The fundamental theoretical result of the Klein–Leffler article is that market prices above the competitive level and the presence of non-salvageable capital are means of enforcing quality promises. The role of brand-name capital investments, which are 'sunk investments', thus becomes understandable: 'What assures high-quality supply is the capital loss due to the loss of future business if low quality is produced' (1981). The role for advertising can also be seen in this light. For,

> ... when consumers do not know the minimum quality guaranteeing price, the larger is the firm's brand-name capital investment relative to sales, [and] the more likely its price premium is sufficient to motivate high quality production. Competitive investment in brand-name capital is now no longer constrained to assets which yield direct consumer service flows ... For example: Luxurious storefronts and ornate displays or signs may be supplied by a firm even if yielding no direct consumer service flows. Such firm-specific assets inform customers of the magnitude of sunk capital costs and their supply of information about the quasi-rent price-premium stream being earned by the firm and hence the opportunity cost to the firm if it cheats (1981).

The authors repeat the argument by **Nelson (1974)** that advertising, by definition, provides valuable information to the consumer – namely, information that the firm is advertising (**Klein** and **Leffler, 1981**). The paper by Klein and Leffler, then, argues 'that consumers can successfully use price as an indicator of quality'. The authors refer in this context to the *informed* buyers who know of the existence of a gap between firm price and salvageable costs. In other words, consumers appreciate that the existence of a price premium gives them 'quality assurance'.[25]

One of the basic assumptions of self-enforcing mechanisms is that the misbehavior of players is public information (costlessly achieved), and that the threatened retaliations are sufficiently balanced (i.e., equally hurtful). However, in the real world, actors can be incompletely informed because of transaction costs, and the threat of retaliation may be unconvincing because of differences in the size or power of the actors involved. It is worth noting in this connection that although transaction costs and differences in size or power play no (essential) role in game theory, game-theoretic explanations of self-enforcement mechanisms are still applied to explain real-world situations that are characterized by costly information and power asymmetries. In such models, special institutions or organizations are assumed to provide low-cost information about each player's behavioral history and to coordinate community responses.

Numerous papers on self-enforcement mechanisms exist in the literature. Five significant examples of this writing are discussed in the following pages. The first three of these reproduced represent frequently quoted articles on certain historic institutions that served to encourage long distance trade – viz., the papers of **Milgrom**, **North** and **Weingast** (**1990**), **Greif** (1989, **1993**, Chapter 16, this volume), and **Greif**, **Milgrom** and **Weingast** (**1994**, Chapter 17, this volume). The fourth paper by **Baron** (**2002**, Chapter 14, this volume) describes one of today's most successful business innovations – the reputation mechanism of eBay's online market. The last paper by **McMillan** and **Woodruff** (**2000**) reviews systematically the different self-enforcing arrangements that exist under conditions of incomplete information.

Milgrom, **North** and **Weingast** (**1990**, Chapter 21, this volume) analyze the 'law-merchant' system of the Champagne Fairs of the twelfth and thirteenth centuries that introduced the special institution of the 'law merchants'. This approach involved the use of private judges drawn from the commercial sector who administered the *Lex Mercantoria* (a private code governing commercial transactions). The authors argue that, as trade communities grew larger, it became:

> … too costly to keep everyone informed about what transpires in all trading relationships, as a simple reputation system might require. So the system of private judges [the Law Merchants, LM] is designed to promote private resolutions of disputes and otherwise to transmit *just enough* information to the right people in the right circumstances to enable the reputation mechanism to function effectively for enforcement (1990).

Two techniques were used to save on information costs for traders:

(1)   A merchant could not enter the Fair without being in good standing with those who controlled entry, and any merchant caught cheating at the Fair would be incarcerated and brought to justice under the rules of the Fair. So anyone a merchant met at the Fair could be presumed to have a good reputation … .

(2)   Any party can visit the LM prior to finalizing a contract. At that time, for a cost …, the party can *query* the LM for the records of previous judgments about any other player'. The possibility that traders have of asking questions about the commercial history of trade participants had a second advantage. It:

(3)   … provides an opportunity for the judge to collect payments for his services even if no actual disputes arise. As applied to the Champagne Fairs, the local lord or his agents could appoint honest judges, register transactions, and tax them'.

The core version of the Milgrom–North–Weingast model 'is based on the presence of a special actor – a "judge" or "law merchant" (LM) who serves both as a repository of information and as an adjudicator of disputes.' The LM's authority includes the ability to award damages if the defendant is found to have cheated the plaintiff. But payment of the damage awarded is voluntary in the sense that there is no state to enforce payment. The authors argue that the LM system is a low-cost way for disseminating information about traders so that the person seeking information is not required to undertake widespread investigation. Moreover, the seeker need not know his party's whole history but merely whether there are outstanding judgments involving the party. In effect, then, the LM system is a centralized record keeping system. Finally, it should be noted that the honesty of the LM judges is explained as a consequence of their administering the *Lex Mercantoria* for a fee. They receive compensation for their services so 'that the LM business is itself valuable and [the] LMs may wish to maintain their reputation for honesty and diligence'. In short, arrangements are such that judges must remain (within limits) honest functionaries who cannot be bribed to falsify information about traders' misbehavior. The authors argue that the institution of the LM arose to make the reputation more effective by communicating information. And, seen from this perspective, it is plausible to say that the 'importance of state enforcement was not that it provided a means of enforcing contracts where one previously did not exist. Rather, it was to reduce [further] the transaction costs of policing exchange'.

The logic of the system just discussed is clear, but questions might be asked about the way in which the reputations of traders were established. That is, if information was accurate and local authorities allowed only merchants with good reputations to enter the Fair, there is at least some reason to ask why these honorable individuals would possibly change their behavior once admitted to the Fair and risk permanent exclusion.

In any event, Greif (2006) has pointed out that a very effective institutional arrangement, the 'community responsibility system' (CRS), permitted impersonal exchange without any knowledge about individual traders prior behavior. According to Greif, it was used widely in premodern Europe. Under this system, a major advantage existed because trade could take place safely and securely between merchants without the need of any knowledge of a trading partner's past conduct, or the expectation of future trade, or the necessity of reporting a trader's misconduct to others. The CRS mechanism worked because any local political/economic community (as city A) had significant interest in protecting its merchants' ability to trade with other communities (as B, C, ..., Z), and would lose this capacity (via retaliation by other cities) if it failed to safeguard the property rights of alien merchants or failed to enforce contracts impartially on their behalf. In other words, if an (alien) merchant from city B was wrongfully deprived of his rights by a merchant in city A, the political authorities of A would take action to ensure that the claims of the B merchant were satisfied. The authorities had incentive to act in this way since they wished to protect the interests of the total mercantile class in A to trade with other cities. As Greif says, this arrangement is worth considering because: 'The community responsibility system constitutes the missing link in understanding the institutional developments that led to the rise of impersonal exchange and modern markets' (2006, 232).

In thinking about this general area of research, it is important to understand that new institutional economic historians are not 'historicists' in the sense of Popper (1960). They do not suggest – as Karl Marx did[26] – that society will change 'along a predetermined path that cannot change' (Popper ibid.). Nor do they hope to test a universal law of history acceptable to science on the basis of the observation of a unique historical process. Historical processes, however, do consist of a series of recurring functional components,[27] such as the elementary functions of trade. And these elements may be reduced to testable hypotheses on organizational mechanisms (organizational templates) that underlie the working of specific economic institutions (as, e.g., the market). Economic theorists can proceed in this manner. And their theories are based, characteristically, on two types of hypotheses. The hypotheses involve: (i) human behavior and (ii) the institutional environment that influences behavior. An example of the latter is found in the conditions for 'perfect markets' noted by Stackelberg (1948) as:

'indifference concerning the location, time, quality, and personal properties of markets, commodities, and traders'.[28]

In this historical work, **Greif** (**1993**, Chapter 16, this volume) offers an example of a repeated merchant–agent game (the formal properties of which are reviewed briefly by Aoki (2001, 48–71)). Specifically, Greif examines the organization of a coalition, or economic institution, of Jewish traders, the *Maghribi*. These traders pursued complex, long-distance trade in the Mediterranian region during the eleventh century. Seeking efficiency and security, the Maghribi organized an informal principal–agent arrangement with which to conduct their affairs. In this construct, the traders were the principals and their employed 'overseas agents' were the agents. The latter accompanied the sea transport of goods, searched for buyers, negotiated and concluded purchasing contracts, monitored the transfer of goods, and secured payments. Under the conditions that prevailed, complete contingent contracts between the principals and agents were, of course, impossible because of the lack of foresight. Also impossible was the direct monitoring of the agents by the principals. And fraudulent agents could not be dealt with through court ordering. Nevertheless, despite these unfavorable circumstances, the Maghribi merchants were still able to devise a system that offered them some protection. This took the form of an agreement with the agents having the following provisions. The agents were to be, or become, members of an economic institution – the group of traders of the Maghribi. They could earn premiums for good behavior. But, if any agent deceived his principal just once, he was punished by being barred for life from any further assignments from the merchants of the Maghribi group. Moreover, if a fraudulent agent tried to become a principal (a merchant) himself, a Maghribi agent was free to deceive him. That is, no Maghribi tradesmen or merchants would punish the deceptive agent in the usual manner. Therefore, the would-be principal having a tainted record would soon be driven out of business. In this fashion, '… the Maghribi traders established a relationship between past conduct and future economic rewards. As a result, agents resisted the short-term gains attainable through deception …' (Greif, 1989, 881).

The papers discussed so far concern '… institutions used to overcome contractual problems among individual merchants active in long-distance trade.' Individual merchants, however, were not the only important parties. 'The rulers of the trading centers at which the merchants met and brought their goods were an important independent force. Trading centers needed to be organized in ways that secured the person and property of the visiting merchants.'[29]

Greif, **Milgrom** and **Weingast** (**1994**) interpret merchant guilds in the light of a repeated-game model which leads to the conclusion that guilds emerged to allow the rulers of trading centers to credibly commit themselves to the protection of the personal safety and property of alien merchants. The guilds centralized information about rulers' behavior and about disputes among merchants, and were able to use effective collective actions to apply sanctions against breach of promises by rulers (city governments). Basically, guilds provided merchants with both the leadership and the information transmission capability required for coordinated action. In theory, at least, they could decide when to impose a trade embargo and when to cancel it. Moreover, members were free to obtain information from guilds concerning disputes between their members and other traders. This kind of analysis of city-trader relationships, however, seems to be somewhat problematic. Modeling activity as equilibria of repeated games is not appropriate because of the differences in power that exist between city and foreign traders. Further, the interposition of a merchant guild, as the agency organizing communication and coordination between traders, does not necessarily lead to reputation equilibria. This is so because individual traders have no incentive to participate in the boycott of a city. To be effective, merchant guilds, like modern labor unions, have to be strong enough to force members to follow guild directives rather than to serve their individual interest. The authors do not deny that merchant guilds were cartels but maintain that they originally served as countervailing power centers against the rulers of trading centers (cities), and thus facilitated trade expansion. On the other hand, in the course of time, when larger political units emerged and took over the functions of merchant guilds, the guilds did not necessarily disappear but were transformed into monopolistic organizations that may have hindered the expansion of trade.

We know that self-enforcing agreements or, more generally, private ordering tends to develop not only in the absence of public order (as in medieval Europe) but also in the context of existing public order (in the 'shadow of the law'). The case of the private ordering in the eBay community of traders illustrates the latter situation. Different from the preceding examples, though, eBay's self-enforcement mechanism was designed by a visible hand – the founders and managers of eBay. The example reveals that the institution-as-an-equilibrium-of-a-game approach is employed by economists not only to explain past developments. In the eBay case just considered, it is applied to develop and justify ongoing business strategies such as that used by eBay.

Baron (**2002**, Chapter 14, this volume) gives a detailed description of the online auction market that is provided by eBay. As might be expected, the market in question is rather imperfect. Traders are anonymous and remote. Thus, buyers cannot examine the items before bidding, and have to pay in advance for items they have not inspected. On the other side, sellers have little recourse if a winning bidder refuses to pay. Despite such drawbacks, though, trade flourished in this market, and eBay turned out to be one of the true successes of the Internet. Presumably, success was based on the existence of *trust* among members of the eBay community of traders. Indeed, it is trust that represents eBay's principal asset: 'eBay's strategic focus is to support and expand this community'. The centerpiece of that support was a multilateral online reputation mechanism based on published reports describing the outcomes of actual transactions undertaken. It appears that this mechanism generated incentives similar to those in a long-term relationship between a buyer and seller. The mechanism, in fact, would seem to have many of the same features as the institution of law merchants – with the Internet serving the informational and reputation–accounting functions as well as facilitating dispute resolution. A community based on trust is, of course, vulnerable to (outright) fraud. Yet experience showed that fraud remained rare, and could be covered by insurance against fraud. Baron's general assessment of the eBay case is, therefore, that: '... the internet allowed an online reputation mechanism to support trust among anonymous traders, most of whom would not have repeated bilateral exchange. The reputation mechanism was multilateral and based on feedback provided by the parties to a transaction. This mechanism was the heart of eBay's strategy of building a community and sharing in the value created for its members'.

It has been said that: '... in communities where people hide behind their anonymity, private order, if it is to operate at all, must be organized' (**McMillan** and **Woodruff**, Chapter 20, this volume). This generalization concerning the private ordering of contractual relationships seems to be correct. History suggests that while private order organizations emerged during past millennia in quite diverse settings, all work in similar ways. That is: 'An organization such as a market intermediary (wholesaler) or trade association disseminates information about contractual breaches and coordinates the community's response to breaches. The usual sanction is to boycott the offender'. In their article, McMillan and Woodruff provide a systematic review of work done by economic historians on private ordering. The papers considered are based largely on the problem defined in prisoner-dilemma (PD) games, and on the results of a survey of the role of private ordering in former soviet-type economies. With respect to the game-theoretic material, they emphasize two ways to counter the self-defeating incentives of PD games. One is the law; the other is found in the repetition of PD games and the implied threat of retaliation. If the legal system functioned perfectly, contracts would never need to be self-enforcing. A frictionless legal system would always work at least as well as relational contracting. In practice, however, 'even when laws exist, their application and enforcement may not be cost effective or even possible'. It follows that, even in countries with functional legal systems, private ordering (the use of self-enforcing mechanisms) may complement or even substitute for public ordering. The advantage of private ordering is that the market participants are generally better informed about actual contractual issues than judges. '... They possess greater expertise in monitoring other participants conduct, ... their decisions can be more nuanced and ... they can consider information that cannot be introduced in court ...'. But it is also understood that there can be disadvantages of private ordering. These 'range from economic inefficiencies of exclusion and collusion to social costs of racial discrimination and criminal violence'.

McMillan and Woodruff define the formulation of contracts based on private instead of public or legal order as relational contracting. That is, they use the term (and concept) of 'relational contract' in a different sense than Macneil (1974) who first introduced the term as a way of viewing incomplete contracts.[30] The authors distinguish between bilateral and multilateral relational contracting – which they first discuss from the standpoint of spontaneous ordering. Bilateral spontaneous contracting in the authors' sense requires some degree of mutual dependence of the parties, and thus the threat of breaking off business relations (as in Telser's model) is ruled out. An example would be the 'clientalization' in Moroccan bazaars that arises because of a lack of an organized market for information. *Multilateral spontaneous contracting* may develop if community ties are strong enough so that the provision of information and the coordination of retaliation need no special organization. McMillan and Woodruff go on to discuss four other examples of this kind of spontaneous ordering. They find that private ordering becomes more difficult if information about breaches and coordinating responses to those breaches requires some definite organization. They speak of 'organizing private order', mentioning as examples for an organized private order the Law Merchants (**Milgrom, North, Weingast, 1990**) and the Merchant Guild (**Greif, Milgrom, Weingast, 1994**). After listing and discussing ten further examples of organized institutions, the authors conclude: 'The organized institutions divide along several characteristics. Some institutions provide only information, while others sanction their own members for failure to sanction defectors.'

Finally, McMillan and Woodruff give attention to the interaction that can occur between private and public order using the results of a survey taken in former soviet-type economies. 'The survey asked the managers about the ability of courts, other government agencies, or private parties to enforce contracts with customers and suppliers. Overall, just over two thirds (68%) of those surveyed said courts could enforce contracts with customers.' In addition, trade associations turned out to have a significant effect on business trust in Eastern Europe. 'Geographic distance adds to the complexity of relationships, making shipping, payment, quality inspection, and other issues more difficult.' Apparently, though, there is no evidence that courts on trade associations support long-distance trade. Instead, wholesalers provide useful assistance. In their summary, the authors repeat that: 'While private order fosters economic efficiency by making gains from trade realizable, it sometimes also harms efficiency by excluding new entrants from trading or by achieving price collusion.' And they end by saying that: 'Private order can usefully supplement public law, but cannot replace it.' One might add that a well functioning legal order is and remains the basis of a well functioning market economy.

Final Remarks

The argument has been made in the literature that there are two possible justifications for the use of conventional maximizing models in applied microeconomics (Thaler, 1991, 254). One justification, based on the familiar 'as if' position, is that maximizing models are good predictors. The other is that markets ensure that agents have to follow rational optimizing behavior in order to survive in a competitive economy. Practical experience, however, indicates that, in many situations, optimizing models fail to produce the good results claimed for them. Writers of the NIE School are, of course, particularly concerned with the limitations of traditional analysis. Hence, they assert that greater understanding of real-world economic behavior can come about only if attention is given to the roles played by transaction costs and bounded rationality in shaping events. These new assumptions, pertaining to economic 'frictions' and human cognition, are said to be 'crucial' because they represent assumptions on which the conclusions of microeconomic theory are 'sensitively' dependent (Solow, 1956, 65). Arguably, then, the NIE line of research is promising and can reasonably be expected to lead to more robust descriptive theory over time. Nevertheless, given the complexity of formulating a comprehensive model of a neoinstitutional system, work goes forward slowly. Indeed, at present, there exists no systematic new institutional economic theory of the market. On the positive side, though, the beginnings of such a construct are to be seen in the research that has been done in explaining how the basic functions of trade (search, inspection, bargaining, contract execution, control and enforcement) can be handled in a neoinstitutional world. Writings in this area have been featured in the present volume. And the hope is that, by presenting examples of this NIE literature and related works, readers will be able to gain greater insight into the true nature of the market problem.

Anyway, we have seen, the market is not just 'supply and demand determines the price'. To function properly, it demands a set of rules that regulate not only the price mechanism, but also the other basic functions of trade like search, inspection, contract execution, control, and enforcement. Independent of whether these rules evolved spontaneously or were made by identifiable people, they must be well designed and well implemented. As the present sub prime mortgage crisis illustrates, the quality and execution of these trading rules is vital for the functioning of the market itself (of the market as an organization). But the requirement poses a problem. Since the realization of an efficient institutional design for the market is difficult to accomplish, this fact may lead some observers to the conclusion that the only reasonable course of action for reform is to impose a set of highly restrictive rules on market operation. The thought here is, presumably, that only by strict regulation can the chaos and corruption engendered at times by market activity be checked. Opportunism and self-seeking behavior, however, are endemic to human society, and may be carried to counterproductive extremes in any system. Thus, from the standpoint of the NIE, there is danger of reform that goes too far and, through over-regulation, causes the loss of the flexibility and innovative potential, which market freedom promises. In short, the possibilities inherent in effective institutional design should not be underestimated. For the NIE, there is hope that cleverly conceived institutional arrangements can shape behavior and induce decision makers to undertake socially productive activity.

It should also be noted that another way to deal with Coase's complaint concerning the neglect of broad market theory would be to discuss specific market organizations as special arrangements designed to accommodate the six elementary functions of trade specified above. That is, consideration could be given to cases in which certain special purposes are served by market organization – as, for example, to facilitate trade in rare pieces of art (auction), in financial titles (stock exchanges), etc. But, unfortunately, no NIE studies of specific market organizations exist. To date, authors interested in neoinstitutional economics seem to be occupied with seeking the practical answers to problems of the *economics of information* (as in search), and, in particular, the problems related to *asymmetrical information* (as in cases of inspection and contract execution). Such work is undertaken with a critical eye on the *theoretic* answers of game theory (as in contract theory). But, regardless of the way one views these special lines of investigation inspired by game theory, the volume of this literature forthcoming (including the papers reproduced in this volume) indicates that game-theoretic material can hardly be neglected. If nothing else, the writings on the phenomena of self-enforcement and its relation to (temporarily) stable business relationships certainly demand attention. What is also significant, of course, is the fact that new institutional economists, unlike neoclassical theorists, reject the use of 'perfect markets' as the benchmark for evaluating the economic quality of markets (i.e., their 'efficiency'). Instead, they try to give reasons why so-called market 'imperfections', or deviations from the neoclassical ideal, may actually give rise to economic advantages. The development of this basic theme has real importance for the advance of descriptive economics, but it is clear that much more is to be done along these lines if the NIE model is to offer a serious challenge to the received mainstream doctrine.

Author note: Reprinted papers are indicated in **boldface** type.

Notes

1. Thanks go to *The Hoover Institution* at Stanford University and the *Private Enterprise Research Center* at Texas A&M University who aided our project by technical assistance. The Thyssen Foundation provided financial assistance for Richter.
2. Partial equilibrium theory of the market for one specific good is a component part of general equilibrium theory.
3. A simplification, cf. North (1990, 58)
4 Monopolies are irrelevant (Demsetz 1968, 61).
5. On the rise of open-air markets all over Eastern Europe in the 1990s see Sik and Wallace (1999); Karazman-Morawetz and Pilgram (1993) (quoted from Egbert 2007).
6. Williamson (1985, 32): 'Organize transactions so as to economize on bounded rationality while simultaneously safeguarding against the hazards of opportunism.' Since large numbers of contracts are incomplete, the parties to a contract must agree, either explicitly or tacitly, 'about the procedure

[the 'constitution'] that will be employed to deal with problems that may arise in the future' (Macneil 1974, 753).

7. Local markets are extended to large area markets ('nationwide' or 'global' markets).

8. As illustrated in Furubotn and Richter (2005, Ch. 7).

9. Nelson assumes that consumers already know where they can obtain each of the options open to them. Their information problem is to evaluate the utility of each option. He defines search to include any way of evaluating these options subject to two restrictions: (1) the consumer must inspect the option, and (2) the inspection must occur prior to purchasing the brand (1970, 312).

10. Professional technical and managerial workers of a Boston suburb.

11. Cf. Granovetter (1973) on the 'strength of weak ties.'

12. See the 'Social network conceptual toolkit' Smith-Doerr and Powell (2005, Fig. 1).

13. In the sense of Macneil (1978).

14. Though he mentions the term 'transaction costs' only in passing.

15. Podolny states: 'quality is, by definition, unobservable before the transaction'.

16. Traders are faceless strangers, traded products are perfectly homogenous, traders are perfectly informed on the good's quoted or traded price.

17. Campbell and Eden (2005) report that according to their study 'Increasing the difference between an item's price and the average price for the same item at other stores substantially raises the probability of a price change. However, the probability of changing a price close to average far exceeds zero, and most price changes occur with the original price close to average. In simple menu-cost models, extreme prices arise from the erosion of a fixed nominal price by other sellers' adjustments. Therefore, they are older than average. We find that most extreme prices are relatively young (less than a month old). That is, grocers deliberately select extreme prices, which they then quickly abandon. Taken together these results suggest to us that sellers extensively experiment with their prices.'

18. 'This includes internal and external dispute-resolution structures. At this point, the relation has become a minisociety with a vast array of norms beyond the norms centred on exchange and its immediate process' (Macneil 1978, 902).

19. The Gregorian Calendar was decreed by Pope Gregory XIII on 24 February 1582 by papal bull *Inter gravissimas* and slowly accepted by all trading nation states.

20. Based on Greenwich Time as suggested by an international congress 1889. It took a couple of decennia until it was globally accepted. Germany introduced the Central European Time in 1893.

21. The metric system was almost globally introduced in the 19th century. Exceptions among large states are England and the USA. Germany introduced the metric system in 1868.

22. Furubotn and Richter (1993).

23. He could have added 19th century Germany.

24. He adds as fourth technique 'hands tying' – 'giving one reputation in the community for your promise to perform' – which requires repeated exchanges on the side of the hostage giver. It belongs insofar to our second extreme.

25. On the game theoretic background see Fudenberg and Tirole (1991, 168 ff.) on 'Repeated games with varying opponents.'

26. 'When a society has discovered the natural law that determines its own movement, even then it can neither overlap the natural phases of its evolution, nor shuffle them out of the world by a stroke of the pen. But this much it can do: it can shorten and lessen the birth-pangs.' A formulation due to Marx in his preface to *Das Kapital*, Vol.1, July 1867 quoted from Popper (1960, 51).

27. For the 'functional' approach see Turner and Maryanski (1979).

28. Stackelberg (1948, 219 ff.): '*Keine räumliche, zeitliche, persönliche oder qualitative Unterschiede*' (Literally translated: No local, temporal, personal or qualitative differences).

29. Greif, Milgrom and Weingast (1994, 747), reproduced in this volume as Chapter 17.

30. Relational contracts, in the sense of Macneil, are contracts that do not try to take account of all future contingencies but are nevertheless long-term arrangements in which past, present, and expected future personal relations among the contractual parties matter (Macneil 1974, 753). Therefore, such contracts are, to a degree, *implicit, informal, and nonbinding*. Self-enforcement, in a concrete sense, plays an important role here (Furubotn and Richter 2005, 173).

References (not reproduced in this volume)

Alchian, A.A. (1950), 'Uncertainty, Evolution, and Economic Theory', *Journal of Political Economy*, **58**, 211–21.

Aoki, M. (2001), *Toward a Comparative Institutional Analysis*, Cambridge, MA: MIT Press.

Arrow, K.J. (1962), 'Economic Welfare and the Allocation of Resources for Invention,' in: A Report by the National Bureau of Economic Research, New York, *The Rate and Direction of Inventive Activity: Economic and Social Factors*, Princeton N.J.: Princeton University Press.

Binmore, K. (1992), *Fun and Games: A Text on Game Theory.* Lexington, Mass.: D. C. Heath.

Blinder, A.S., Canettie, E.R.D., Lebow, D.E. and Rudd, J.B. (1998), *Asking About Prices. A New Approach to Understanding Price Stickiness*, New York: Russell Sage Foundation.

Buchanan, J.M. (1960), 'Positive Economics, Welfare Economics, and Political Economy', in J.M. Buchanan (ed.), *Fiscal Theory and Political Economy*, Chapel Hill: University of North Carolina Press.

Campbell, J.R. and B. Eden (2005), 'Rigid Prices: Evidence from U.S. Scanner Data', Federal Reserve Bank of Chicago, Working Paper Series. *http://www.chicagofed.org/publications/workingpapers/wp2005_08.pdf*

Coase, R.H (1937), 'The Nature of the Firm', *Economica*, **4**, 386–405.

Coase, R.H (1960), 'The Problem of Social Cost', *Journal of Law and Economics*, **3**, 1–44.

Coase, R.H (1984), 'The New Institutional Economics,' *Journal of Institutional and Theoretical Economics*, **140**, 229–31.

Coase, R.H (1988), *The Firm, the Market, and the Law*, Chicago: University of Chicago Press.

Davis, L. and D.C. North (1971), *Institutional Change and American Economic Growth*, Cambridge, MA: Cambridge University Press.

Demsetz, H. (1968), 'Why Regulate Utilities?', *Journal of Law and Economics*, **11**, 55–66.

Egbert, H. (2007), 'The Culture of a Market: A Case Study of Open-air Horse Markets,' *Journal of Institutional and Theoretical Economics*, **163**, 493–502.

Eggertsson, T. (2005), *Imperfect Institutions: Possibilities and Limits to Reform*, Ann Arbor, MI: University of Michigan Press.

Fudenberg, D. and J. Tirole (1991), *Game Theory*, Cambridge, MA: MIT Press.

Furubotn, E.G. (1987), 'Privatizing the Commons: Comment', *Southern Economic Journal*, **54**, 219–24.

Furubotn, E.G. and R. Richter (eds) (1993), 'Symposium on New Institutional Economics; Recent Progress; Expanding Frontiers,' *Journal of Institutional and Theoretical Economics*, **149**, 1–362.

Furubotn, E.G. and R. Richter (2005), *Institutions and Economic Theory. The Contribution of the New Institutional Economics*, 2nd revised and extended edition, [1st ed. 1997], Ann Arbor, MI: University of Michigan Press.

Gigerenzer, G., and R. Selten (eds) (2001), *Bounded Rationality: The Adaptive Toolbox*, Cambridge: MIT Press.

Granovetter, M. (1973), 'The Strength of Weak Ties,' *American Journal of Sociology*, **78**, 1360–80.

Granovetter, M. (1974/1995), *Getting A Job. A Study of Contacts and Careers*, Chicago, 2nd edition, 1995.

Greif, A. (1989), 'Reputation and Coalitions in Medieval Trade: Evidence on the Maghribi Traders', *Journal of Economic History*, **49**, 857–82.

Greif, A. (2006), *Institutions and the Path to the Modern Economy: Lessons from Medieval Trade* (Political Economy of Institutions and Decisions), Cambridge: Cambridge University Press.

Hayek, F.A. (1945), 'The Use of Knowledge in Society', *American Economic Review*, **35**, 519–30.

Hume, D. [1739–40] (1969), *A Treatise of Human Nature.* Edited by E. C. Mossner. London: Penguin.

Karazman-Morawetz, I. and Pilgram, A. (1993), 'Ostgrenzöffnung als Gelegenheit – irreguläres Erwerbshandeln und seine Kontrolle,' pp. 147–68, in: Pilgram, A. (ed.), *Grenzöffnung. Migration und Kriminalität. Jahrbuch für Rechts- und Kriminalsoziologie 1993*, Baden-Baden: Nomos.

Lange, O. (1938), 'On the Economic Theory of Socialism' in O. Lange, F.M. Taylor, and B.E. Lippincott, Hrsg., *On the Economic Theory of Socialism*, Minneapolis, 57–143.

Levy, D., Bergen, M., Dutta, S., Venable, R. (1997), 'The Magnitude of Menu Costs: Direct Evidence From Large U.S. Supermarket Chains', *Quarterly Journal of Economics*, **112**, 791–825.

Lewis, D. (1969), *Convention. A Philosophical Study*, Cambridge, MA.

Macneil, I.R. (1974), 'The Many Futures of Contracts', *Southern California Law Review*, **47**, 691–816.

Marx, K. (1845), *Das Kapital*, 1. Bd., Juli 1867 [*Werke*, Bd. 23, p- 15 f.].

Masten, S.E. (ed.) (1996), *Case Studies in Contracting and Organization*, New York, Oxford: Oxford University Press.

Menger, C. (1883), *Untersuchungen über die Methode der Socialwissenschaften und der Politischen Oekonomie insbesondere*, Leipzig (Neuauflage Tübingen 1969).

Nelson, P. (1970), 'Information and Consumer Behavior', *Journal of Political Economy*, **78**, 311–29.

North, D.C. (1990), *Institutions, Institutional Change and Economic Performance*, Cambridge: Cambridge University Press.

North, D.C. (1993), 'Institutions and Credible Commitment', *Journal of Institutional and Theoretical Economics*, **149**, 11–23.

Popper, K. R. (1960), *The Poverty of Historicism*, London: Routledge & Kegan.

Porter, M.E. (1998), *On Competition*, Boston, MA: Harvard Business School

Richter, R. (2003), 'New Institutional Economics and Knowledge Sharing,' (39–48) in: E. Helmstädter (ed.), *The Economics of Knowledge Sharing. A New Institutional Approach*, Cheltenham, UK: Elgar.

Schelling, T.C. (1960), *The Strategy of Conflict*, Cambridge, MA.

Schotter, A. (1981), *The Economic Theory of Social Institutions*, Cambridge, MA.

Sik, E. and Wallace, C. (1999), 'The Development of Open-air Markets in East-Central Europe,' *International Journal of Urban and Regional Research*, **23**, 697–714.

Smith-Doerr, L. and Powell, W.W. (2005), 'Networks and Economic Life', (379–402) in: N.J. Smelser and R.Swedberg eds. (2005), Stackelberg, H. von (1948), *Grundlagen der theoretischen Volkswirtschaftslehre*, Bern: A. Francke Verlag.

Solow, R.M. (1956), 'A Contribution to the Theory of Growth,' *Quarterly Journal of Economics*, **70**, 65–94.

Stackelberg, H. v. (1948), *Grundlagen der Theoretischen Volkswirtschaftslehre*, Bern: Francke.

Stigler, G.J. (1952), *The Theory of Price*, rev. ed., New York: Macmillan Co.

Stigler, G.J. (1961), 'The Economics of Information', *Journal of Political Economy*, **69**, 213–25.

Thaler, R.H. (1991), *Quasi Rational Economics*, New York: Russell Sage Foundation.

Turner, J.H. and A. Maryanski (1979), *Functionalism*, Menlo Park, CA: The Benjamin/Cummings Publ. Co.

Weber, M. (1968), *Economy and Society: An Outline of Interpretative Sociology.* Edited by G. Roth and C. Wittich. Berkeley: University of California Press.

Williamson, O.E. (1983), 'Credible Commitments: Using Hostages to Support Exchange', *American Economic Review*, **73**, 519–40.

Williamson, O.E. (1985), *The Economic Institutions of Capitalism*, New York: Free Press.

Williamson, O.E. (2000), 'The New Institutional Economics: Taking Stock, Looking Ahead,' *Journal of Economic Literature*, **38**, 595–613.

Part I
Precontractual Activities:
Search and Inspection

[1]

The Maine Lobster Market:
Between Market and Hierarchy

JAMES M. ACHESON
University of Maine

1. INTRODUCTION

Owners of firms in the Maine lobster industry exist in a complicated social milieu. They have one set of ties with firms from which they buy and to which they sell lobsters, which I call vertical ties. They have other ties with firms at the same level of the market, horizontal ties. Both, I shall argue, are necessary for economic success in the industry, although they are used for very different purposes. This paper examines how members of the lobster industry use their ties; the reasons for their evolution; and the effect of this social system on the way prices are established in the industry.

The marketing system for lobsters in Maine is dominated by a large number of small, specialized firms which have developed long-term bilateral relationships. Fishermen, dealers, truckers, and wholesalers typically own their own small firms and buy and sell lobsters to each other. No vertically integrated firms have been developed which are involved in all phases of the business—from catching the lobsters to shipping them to distant markets. Yet the owners of these small firms do not act like the quintessential entrepreneur of the neoclassical model of economics, who responds only to market prices and buys and sells to the highest bidder with only economic optimization in mind. Rather, they buy and sell at the "established market price" to the same finite number of firms with whom they have developed ties. A fisherman ordinarily sells only to one lobster dealer; and the dealer usually sells only to a small number of pound operators, wholesalers, or other buyers. In this respect, the situation in Maine closely resembles the situation found in many other markets in the world where buyers and sellers have long-standing ties (Mintz; Geertz: 29ff.; Spoehr: 162ff; Wilson, 1980). However, there are differences as well.

The relationship between fishermen, dealers, and wholesalers is ambivalent. These people are dependent on each other, but a good deal of hostility pervades their relationships due to the ever-present threat of opportunism. It

Journal of Law, Economics, and Organization vol. 1., no. 2 Fall 1985
© 1985 by Yale University. All rights reserved. ISSN 8756-6222

386 / JOURNAL OF LAW, ECONOMICS, AND ORGANIZATION   I:2, 1985

takes very little for conflict to surface between fishermen and dealers. From the point of view of the fisherman, anyone connected with the marketing of lobsters is at least slightly suspect. Yet, ironically, the fisherman's response traditionally has been to form very close ties with one particular dealer—a man who, he often suspects, is part of a conspiracy to defraud him at every opportunity. The relationship between dealers, wholesalers, and distribution firms who regularly do business with each other is usually more businesslike and neutral, but even here suspicion abounds.

Owners of these lobstering firms also have many close ties with other nearby firms at the same level of the market. Dealers know other dealers in the area, and all of the wholesalers in a given city constantly exchange information. It is not at all uncommon for owners of firms in the lobster industry to have much more agreeable relationships with their close "competitors" than with the firms from which and to which they buy and sell.

2. GENERAL FEATURES OF THE MAINE LOBSTER INDUSTRY

In Maine, there are approximately 2,200 full-time lobster fishermen and another 7,000 part-time fishermen, who produce more lobsters than the fishermen of any other state or Canadian province. The lobster industry is an inshore trap fishery. Most lobster fishermen fish alone from gas-or diesel-powered boats ranging from 30 to 38 feet long. A typical fisherman might have between 300 and 600 traps.

Lobster fishing is highly territorial. To go lobster fishing, one must not only have a license but must be accepted by the group of men fishing out of a particular harbor. A fisherman ordinarily is allowed to go fishing only in the traditional territory of the "harbor gang" to which he belongs. Interlopers are strongly sanctioned, usually through the surreptitious destruction of their traps. These territories are relatively small, so that a fisherman is rarely more than ten miles from the mouth of his home harbor (Acheson, 1972; 1975; 1979).

Fishermen's activities and catches vary considerably over the annual round. The low point of the annual cycle are the mid-winter months. Lobsters are inactive at this time of year and fishermen are reluctant to go out in cold and stormy seas for small catches. Many do not fish at all during these months. Catches increase greatly in April, when lobsters become more active as the water temperature warms and they begin to migrate toward shore; fishermen set out more gear and pull their traps more often as the weather improves.

During the latter part of June and first part of July, catches again fall as lobsters begin to molt in large numbers; they become very difficult to catch. At this time, fishermen do not pull their traps often and devote a good deal of time to repairing equipment and painting their boats.

From the middle of August to the middle of November, catches increase as a new year's class of lobsters that have recently molted into legal size become available to fishermen and begin to migrate offshore. For most fishermen, this three-month period is intensely active.

Lobsters from Maine docks are distributed throughout the United States, Canada, Europe, and Japan through a complicated network of dealerships, pounds, wholesale firms, shippers, and retail distributors. Some of these firms buy and sell lobsters only in Maine or New England; others airfreight them all over the world.

Approximately 65 percent of all Maine lobsters are bought by the seventeen cooperatives and eighty-five small private dealers whose docks are found in every Maine harbor. There are three large vertically integrated firms, with headquarters in Boston, which own dealerships, trucking operations, lobster pounds, and wholesale operations. (These firms are not involved in fishing or the ultimate retailing of lobsters in distant markets.) An estimated 25 percent of the Maine catch is handled by these three firms together. Only an estimated 10 percent of the total Maine catch is sold to customers by fishermen directly.

There are dozens of small wholesale and retail firms in Maine and New England, along with innumerable small trucking operations. All these firms buy lobsters from dealers and cooperatives and sell them retail in their own local areas or wholesale to restaurants and hotels or wholesalers in distant cities.

In Maine there are also some 34 lobster pounds, usually enclosed portions of ocean inlets, where millions of lobsters are held off the market for a few months to take advantage of the seasonal price fluctuations. Some of the pounds are individually owned; others are the property of larger vertically integrated firms.

It is estimated that at least 70 percent of all lobsters are eaten in restaurants, hotels, clubs, or other institutions, although an increasing number are being sold to supermarket chains.

3. RISK AND UNCERTAINTY

Several factors combine to make the marketing of lobsters a risky and uncertain business. First, although there is a general pattern of cyclical changes in prices and catches, it is impossible to predict what prices will be even in the near future, and substantial price changes can occur unpredictably. Everyone in the industry is fully aware that catches and prices move inversely. The price generally comes to its annual peak during February and March when catches are at their annual low. The lowest prices of the year occur in late summer and early fall because lobster catches are high and demand is weakened by the exodus of tourists. However, every year sees substantial differences in prices and amounts caught. For example, in 1978

388 / JOURNAL OF LAW, ECONOMICS, AND ORGANIZATION   I:2, 1985

the highest price of the year was $3.90 and was paid at the end of February; two years later it was $3.65 and occurred during the fourth week of March. Between March and May, the price of lobster can drop anywhere from 40 to 60 percent. In some years, lobsters can be caught in some quantity until December; in other years there is a marked dropoff in abundance early in November. Sharp changes in price occur often and without warning. A fisherman can go out in the morning and be promised one price and return in the evening to find out that the morrow will bring a price 20 cents or even 50 cents less per pound.

A great deal of opportunistic behavior is characteristic of the lobster market. In the past, lying about prices and even cheating on poundage were common. More important, older fishermen present convincing evidence that dealers and wholesalers were involved in an active conspiracy to keep prices low. For example, fishermen in the central coast area say that in the 1930s and 1940s the three dealers on one peninsula were all brothers. They always paid at least a nickel per pound lower than fishermen received in harbors farther away from the Boston market, and the prices they paid were always identical. On occasion, if a fisherman got out of line, all three brothers would refuse to buy his lobsters as a means of sanctioning him. Outright lying and cheating are unquestionably less frequent today, due in great part to the advent of cooperatives. Nevertheless, sharp business practices are rife in the industry.

Since the marketing of lobsters is a full-time occupation, dealers and wholesalers know a lot more about the market than do the often part-time fishermen. They are loath to share information about sources of supply, prices, and potential buyers because they regard this as their stock in trade. There is no question that they use this differential knowledge to their own advantage on occasion. A common ploy is to delay giving a price increase as long as they can. They eventually will have to give the increase or face the prospect of losing the business of fishermen who will go elsewhere, but the temptation to delay is enormous, especially when it will take some time before fishermen find out about the situation. In the words of one dealer, "If the [ex vessel] goes up a nickel and I can hold off paying that for a week, I make an extra $800. That money is as good in my pocket as it is in theirs."

Nor are sharp practices and opportunism limited to the relationships between fishermen and dealers. They are found commonly in business dealings between dealers, wholesalers, pound operators, and truckers as well. Deception is far from unknown in the negotiations between such firms. There are many instances in which firms in the marketing chain will send a shipment to a distant wholesaler and have considerable difficulty in collecting their money. Occasionally, dealers have sold loads of lobsters to out-of-state truckers and found out later that the check they received was worthless.

Fishermen have a particularly jaundiced view of the marketing structure. One fisherman remarked, "It's a—crooked business." Many fishermen believe, like this man, that lobster prices are set by dealers and wholesalers who are in a conspiracy against them. Competetent observers of the industry would agree that some of the largest wholesalers have the ability to set prices. One employee of the National Marine Fisheries Service with long experience with the Maine lobster industry said, "When the biggest Boston wholesalers agree on a price, that is what the price is going to be all up and down the coast." Dealers and wholesalers, on the contrary, insist that lobster prices are set through negotiations and that the market is relatively competitive. While there is much evidence that the market is relatively competitive, the perceptions of fishermen unquestionably influence their behavior in important ways.

In order to operate in this kind of uncertain, unstable environment, people in the marketing chain establish sets of ties with others in the chain that serve to reduce risk and uncertainty.

4. DEALERS AND WHOLESALERS: NEGOTIATIONS AND AGREEMENTS

For all firms in the marketing chain the most critical ties are those between firms that buy and sell lobsters to each other. The number of firms with which a wholesaler or dealer has steady ties varies, depending on the size of the firm. It is not unusual for some small dealers to sell most of their lobsters to one wholesaling firm; and small wholesale houses may sell most of their lobsters to three to five customers. The larger wholesale and retail firms buy and sell to more firms, but still the number with which they regularly do business is relatively small.

These firms usually have an informal understanding that they will do business with each other over the long run. They do not ordinarily set up fixed obligations regarding the price to be paid. The price is the "going price" for that time of year—the exact price is left to negotiations. The most important part of such informal agreements is the understanding that the partners will continue to do business with each other at all times of year regardless of the supply. Such agreements are critical in helping to solve one of the pressing problems that everyone in the marketing chain faces, namely, how to get enough lobsters in time of scarcity (such as mid-summer and winter) and how to find markets for a vast overabundance in the fall months.

Dealers and wholesalers are caught between the expectations of fishermen and those of consumers. The fisherman demands to be paid for his catch on the day he catches it, regardless of how many or how few lobsters he brings in. Restaurants, hotels, and other institutions ordinarily want a steady supply of lobsters, and they want to charge a fixed price—in some part because of a reluctance to reprint menus. If dealers do not buy lobsters from fishermen during times of glut or cannot or will not supply their customers in times of scarcity, their fishermen and customers will seek out other dealers and wholesalers and may well not return. The strong bilateral ties between firms in the marketing chain go a long way toward solving this problem. In times of

390 / JOURNAL OF LAW, ECONOMICS, AND ORGANIZATION   I:2, 1985

scarcity, owners of firms know that the firms they have ties with will do their very best to supply them; dealers know that in times of glut "their" wholesalers will take as many lobsters off their hands as possible. In the words of one dealer, "It don't guarantee nothing; they just mean you get first preference. If the man is going to buy or sell to anyone, it will be with you if he possibly can."

In addition, firms with long-term bilateral ties know that the terms of an agreement are going to be kept. Delivery schedules will be adhered to and prompt payment will be received. These ties are clearly worth a good deal. Wholesalers and dealers are willing to forfeit short-run financial gain to maintain these ties in the long run.[1]

At the same time, there is suspicion and some hostility between firms up and down the marketing chain. Most agreements, once made, are carried out faithfully, but in the negotiations to establish an agreement one is always looking out for one's own interest. Firms that buy and sell lobsters to each other are dependent on each other; and yet their interests are not coterminous by any means. There is one thing that can never be counted on—accurate information on price. As one dealer said, "They will take you if they can. Your only protection is to know who you are dealing with. Even then you have to look out."

Firms in the same locality at the same level of the marketing chain have a very different but no less essential relationship with one another. If they are competitors for the same customers and sources of supply, they are often cooperative and depend on each other for accurate information. They work together because they face many of the same problems and operate in the same environment. The information they can get from each other concerning price is often far more accurate than what they can get from the people they buy and sell to, who, after all, have an ulterior motive for being deceptive.

Dealers and coop managers in any area know one another and are part of a tight network. They are constantly on the phone exchanging prices, sources of bait and fuel, and so on. In a similar fashion, the wholesale and retail firms in any city all know each other and exchange information about business regularly. The Portland and Boston dealers, as one man phrased it, "all have their heads together"; and the same could be said about the people in the Fulton Fish Market in New York.

Often more tangible assets are exchanged. Dealers and managers of cooperatives in a local area frequently sell each other bait and lend each other equipment.

---

1. I asked one small dealer if he would sell 500 pounds of lobster to a strange trucker who offered him 30 cents a pound in cash more than he would get from the wholesaler who currently buys his lobsters. He said, "I wouldn't do it. He wouldn't be around." He knew that the wholesaler would find another supply of lobsters if he reneged on their deal. It was not worth 30 cents a pound in the short run to lose that steady market. One only does business with firms that are going to be around, even if that means a short-term sacrifice. He also pointed out that no truck driver would pay in cash. This would mean that he would not be certain of payment until the check cleared.

The relationship between any two nearby dealers or wholesalers in a local area varies considerably. Sometimes bitter enmity exists, which usually finds its roots in faulty information or in one firm taking over markets or sources of supply belonging to another. Others are very friendly. In one Maine city, when a wholesaler's dock and establishment burned, he was able to move in with another wholesaler, an old friend. They shared the same office and conducted business from two desks on opposite sides of the room. The burned-out wholesaler also used some of his friend's storage tanks to store his lobsters.

Usually the relationship between nearby dealers and wholesalers is some mixture of cooperation and competition. The complex nature of the relationship is revealed in phone calls in which friendly jokes and accurate information are mixed with deceptive data and barbed comments.

Fishermen and dealers also enter into long-term arrangements to reduce risk. There is more ambivalence in the relationship, and the exchanges between them are different from those between dealers, wholesalers, and others in the marketing chain. The fishermen simply agree to sell all or most of their catch to "the man they fish for." The dealer, for his part, gives the fisherman a number of different benefits. He usually allows all the fishermen who regularly sell to him to use his dock free of charge. The dealer also supplies "his" fishermen with gasoline, diesel fuel, gloves, paint, buoys, and bait at cost or with only a small markup. Supplying bait causes dealers the most problems because it is such a critical item and supplies are irregular. Perhaps most important, a dealer gives all "his" fishermen a steady, secure market for their catches. Dealers always buy all of the lobsters their fishermen offer for sale regardless of how glutted the market might be.

Some fishermen have been able to gain workshop or storage space. Still others have arranged to get preferential access to bait in times of shortages. Sometimes dealers give some of their fishermen "interest-free" loans for boats, equipment, and traps. Usually such loans are given only with the provision that the fishermen will continue to do business with the dealer. Many of these loans are repaid by dealers taking a percentage of each day's catch. In a few cases dealers have even given some of their fishermen slightly higher prices for their catches. Ordinarily such "special" deals are kept as secret as possible.

The exact deal between the fisherman and the dealer is individually negotiated. The willingness of the dealer to give extra concessions to a particular fisherman depends in part on the length of time they have been doing business and the amount of trust built up between them. However, special deals and loans may also be given when the dealer wants to increase the number of fishermen doing business with him.

Fishermen and dealers have very different aims in their exchanges with each other. For the dealer, the most important consideration is to be able to secure a large and reliable supply of lobsters to satisfy customers who will go

392 / JOURNAL OF LAW, ECONOMICS, AND ORGANIZATION   I:2, 1985

elsewhere if their orders are unfilled. Since there is little price competition, the primary way for dealers to obtain a steady supply of lobsters is to attach as many fishermen to their firm as possible. From this perspective, low-cost gas and bait, dock space, and loans are being exchanged for a large, reliable supply of lobsters.

By agreeing to sell their lobsters to a dealer at the "established price" fishermen are in essence agreeing to give up their right to bargain about price in exchange for loans, bait, gas, dock space, and a certain market. Why do they give up the right to bargain with a man many are convinced will cheat them? The fact is that lobster fishermen are price-takers. They are not in a good position to bargain on price, and it makes little sense for them to schedule their fishing activities when price is highest. Agreeing to sell to a single dealer, in short, is a rational strategy. By giving up the ability to bargain (mainly nonexistent), fishermen are exchanging something of little practical value for other valuables.

5. NEGOTIATIONS, PRICES, AND MARKET POWER

On any given day, dealers and cooperative managers contact each other to exchange information and speculation on impending price changes, supplies of lobsters, and the way the market is going.

The price for which the dealer or cooperative manager sells lobsters is calculated in terms of the "boat price" (that is ex vessel price). A normal markup in 1984 was about 30 to 35 cents over the boat price, and this is what most dealers and managers try to get from their wholesalers.

Wholesalers will again set their selling prices in terms of a fixed increase over their buying price. Exactly what that selling price is depends in great part on the distance of the customer and the type of services the wholesaler is providing.

There is extreme pressure on any dealer or wholesaler to pay the same price others are paying for lobster in his local area at his level of the market. If he is paying a lower price than other dealers and coop managers in the local area, he will face some very unhappy fishermen who might switch dealers entirely. On the other hand, if he pays his fishermen more than other dealers, he often cannot pass on his increased costs to the firms from which he buys. Why should a wholesaler pay 15 cents per pound more for lobsters from this dealer when he can get it for less from others in the same area? As a result, dealerships in the same area usually have essentially the same boat price on any given day.

Negotiating a new price, dealers and wholesalers insist, is an uncertain business and one that takes a great deal of skill. One Portland dealer said, "I just go by the seat of my pants. I try to get what I think the market will bear. Sometimes I get the price I ask. Sometimes I don't." Successful negotiating depends on information, which is difficult and costly to obtain. Marketing lobsters is a full-time business.

The negotiations between dealers, wholesalers, and retailers involve an elaborate dance in which owners of firms seek to drive as hard a bargain as possible, consistent with maintaining long-term relationships with suppliers and buyers. It is common for individuals to withhold information from those with whom they do business in an effort to strengthen their negotiating position. Bluffing and deception, not to say outright lying, are not uncommon. Yet one does not want to be caught in too many falsehoods too often or to appear continuously calculative and grasping. This can cause a valued relationship to be severed. One negotiating ploy that is used with some success is to show that one is merely following the market. That is, the best way to get the price up or down is to be able to demonstrate that someone else is already buying lobsters at the desired price or is willing to sell them at that price. This puts pressure on the person with whom one is negotiating because everyone in the industry knows how important it is to be in accord with the market. Often several dealers or wholesalers in a city will agree to "hold out for a higher price" in the hope that they can do jointly what no single person can do on his own. If they all change the price at once, this spreads the onus. No single person has to accept the responsibility for raising prices, which may anger long-term trading partners. It is also apt to be more effective, since it sends a powerful message about changing market conditions. One small dealer said, "I try to build the price around me." By this he means that he tries to get other dealers, pound operators, and coop managers to change prices at the same time or even a little ahead of him.

Accurate information can usually be obtained only from a few nearby firms at the same level in the marketing chain. Much of the information about prices comes through the process of dickering itself and observing the negotiations of other firms. Thus, large firms, which have representatives on the phone constantly to dealers, pound operators, and marketing firms from Canada to Florida, have an edge in the negotiating process in comparison with small dealers who dicker with only one or two wholesalers at odd intervals. The smaller firms are fully aware that the largest firms have better data and watch them closely to get a sense of what is happening in the market.

Sometimes when an individual wholesaler or dealer jumps the price he pays for lobsters, the price change will reverberate up and down the coast and a new price will be "established." Without question, the most important factor involved in price jumps is the supply of lobsters. In the words of one wholesaler, "The reason the price jumps up is someone got short of lobster and hiked the price to get more." Others in need of lobsters follow suit.

There are no price negotiations between dealers and the men who fish for them. The dealer offers a boat price, and the fishermen are expected to accept it. They ordinarily do so, but not without some grumbling. A few fishermen

394 / JOURNAL OF LAW, ECONOMICS, AND ORGANIZATION   I:2, 1985

may be able to negotiate a special price, but even this is pegged to the daily boat price (for example, 5 cents more than the current boat price). Negotiations between dealers and fishermen mainly concern such matters as bait, loans, access to space, and other forms of differential treatment. Such negotiations do not occur on a daily basis.

The entire process by which prices are negotiated and changed is deliberately hidden from fishermen. No dealer or wholesaler is prone to give information on markets and sources to avoid unwanted competition. But they are especially reluctant to talk to fishermen. No dealer wants to admit to lowering prices. This always angers fishermen, who might go to another dealer.

Dealers have several ways of obscuring the way prices are changed and their role in the process. They tend to talk about price movements as if magical forces were responsible rather than human decisions. They often state that they merely take the prices that are set for them by large wholesalers. They often blame price changes on the largest companies. But no one clearly takes the initiative. As one fisherman put it, "When the price gets lowered, it's always someone else far to the westward who did it and the [dealers in his area] are forced to go along. Somehow you can never find out who the first one was that cut the price."

Although differential access to knowledge about markets strengthens the hand of dealers in negotiations with fishermen concerning price, there are real limits on the ability of dealers to cheat and strong pressures to pay the same boat price other dealers in the area are paying. Disgruntled fishermen can and do switch dealers. In addition, the advent of cooperatives has put special pressures on dealers to keep their prices competitive. If fishermen in an area are angered enough, they can form a cooperative which can put dealers out of business. This is the ultimate threat. Even if fishermen do not form cooperatives, the advent of cooperatives has given all fishermen—members and nonmembers alike—much more information about the market, which they can use in negotiations with dealers. Cooperative managers are hired by the fishermen to try to get as high a price as possible for the members. The price the cooperatives are paying for lobsters has become the standard by which all fishermen judge the prices they are receiving. According to one fisherman, "The main advantage of the coop is that it gives us a window into this dirty business." It is widely believed that since the cooperative movement gained momentum from the late 1940s on, fishermen have been receiving relatively better prices, but there is no hard evidence.

6. COMPETITION, OPPORTUNISM, AND MARKET POWER: FACTS AND FICTION

Many believe that the price of lobsters is controlled by a conspiracy of people in the marketing chain, who continually further their own interests at the expense of fishermen, and that the three largest Boston wholesalers literally set the price. Many fishermen are very hostile toward those in the marketing chain and will state with little provocation that they are continually being cheated. Other long-term observers of the industry would agree with them.

As one economist familiar with the industry points out, however, "It would be impossible for a single firm to continually fix prices. There are too many outlets for lobsters" (Wilson 1984). Statements of dealers and wholesalers and my own observations of negotiations would strongly reinforce this point of view.

Why do fishermen think they are being cheated when prices are really being set in an open market? In part, it is because the fishermen do not know much about the market given the secrecy involved. To some extent, the hostility and beliefs about price fixing have nothing to do with the objective facts about the market. Maine people are highly egalitarian; their dependency on dealers who always know so much more than they do about the market and are able to negotiate special deals with favored fishermen brings out the dark side of the Maine character, which finds voice in artful slander and hostility. But the whole problem cannot be explained in terms of ignorance and a cultural emphasis on slandering one's "social betters." Fishermen are acute observers of their industry, and the fact that so many are certain the market is being manipulated to their detriment underlines several important aspects of the lobster market. Some of the hostility and statements about "cheating" reflect more a sense of powerlessness and frustration among fishermen than they do objective insights into the nature of the market.

Moreover, a lot of smaller dealers and wholesalers are only too happy to perpetuate the idea that the largest companies set the prices in order to obscure their own role in the process. The largest Boston wholesalers are often among the first firms to make price changes and are watched like weathervanes by small firms, which helps to perpetuate the myth of their market power. More important, fishermen know that dealers and wholesalers spend a lot of time on the phone with each other making deals and "getting the price." They are aware that price changes can be started by one dealer or wholesaler, identified by name, and spread up and down the coast in a matter of days. In their view, this adds up to a rigged price. The facts are far more prosaic. The evidence is that the market is reasonably competitive, but price changes occur because of the well-advertised bidding activities of one or more firms known by name. Although impersonal market forces determine prices, they need to be activated. What is noticeable to fishermen is the seemingly arbitrary power of dealers and wholesalers to change prices at will. The gluts and scarcity of lobsters behing such changes remain obscure.

Finally, there really is petty cheating and opportunistic behavior. But while dealers do lie to fishermen, hold off paying price increases when they can get away with it, and so on, that is a far cry from being able to dictate the price regardless of gluts and scarcity in the market. Opportunism can exist in a

396 / JOURNAL OF LAW, ECONOMICS, AND ORGANIZATION   I:2, 1985

relatively competitive market, but local price variation and lagged responses do not necessarily indicate an ability to fix the level price. The highly personal way in which the market appears to operate nevertheless leads rational fishermen to strongly suspect that price fixing does exist.

7. LONG-TERM BILATERAL AGREEMENTS BETWEEN FISHERMEN AND DEALERS: NEITHER MARKET OR HIERARCHY

The Maine lobster industry is characterized by many small-scale fishing enterprises, dealers, and wholesalers who have long-term ties to each other. Yet prices are set in the main by competitive bidding. How should such a market be described and classified? In the past few years, Coase, Williamson (1975), and other economists concerned with the nature of elementary transactions have developed a body of theory that appears to be relevant to understanding this question.

These economists point out that exchanges take place along a continuum. At one end is a classical market. Trading here does not depend on the identity of the people involved and the relationship between the parties ends when the discrete transaction is complete. Price is the best source of information. At the other extreme are hierarchies, organizations in which parties to exchanges are in permanent relationships with each other, and transactions are regulated by administrative fiat—not the price mechanism. Large vertically integrated firms are one common type of hierarchy (Williamson, 1975). In these organizations several different departments do different productive processes under unified ownership.

Between markets and hierarchies are what Macneil calls "relational contracting" (1978). Here parties to exchanges are not part of a single organization but exchange goods and services with each other over long periods according to intricate and complicated formulas. Although price remains important, nonpecuniary values and personal relationships intrude.

The lobster market has elements of both the classical market and relational contracts. Although prices and quantities are responsive to classical supply and demand considerations, this is not an auction market. The way lobsters are bought and sold has strong relational features. Individual identities on both sides of the market do matter.

Why aren't sales made through classical market transactions? Alternatively, why isn't the industry organized into hierarchies (that is, large vertically integrated firms)? Why haven't dealers purchased boats and hired fishermen to run them, bought pounds and wholesaling and retailing outlets, so that both the production of lobsters and the marketing functions would be combined in one firm? Such firms should be more efficient in that they would automatically abolish all the transactions costs currently incurred in the elaborate, unfriendly dance between fishermen, dealers, and wholesalers.

There are three sets of social factors inhibiting firms from buying boats and hiring their own fishermen. First, it is very difficult for an owner to supervise a fisherman at sea. A man who hired a fisherman to operate his boat would almost certainly sustain higher than average costs of bait, fuel, maintenance, and trap losses. Second, the value placed on independence and the economic gains to be had make it unlikely that a highly skilled lobster fisherman would want to work for someone else. Third, and most important, lobster fishermen are highly territorial and the primary object in owning territories is to control the number of fishermen who are allowed to fish there. Any would-be entrepreneur who attempted to set himself up as a dealer and hire a number of fishermen would meet with stiff and certain resistance.[2]

Another set of constraints inhibits firms or cooperatives from acquiring a number of dealerships, wholesale houses, and retail outlets in distant cities. Distance combined with managerial problems are apparently the primary factors. Managing a dealership, pound, or wholesale operation takes a lot of skill, experience, and long hours. Good managers are difficult to hire since the type of man who can successfully manage a dealership for a big firm would prefer to own his own business. The managerial problem might be eased if the various dealerships, pounds, wholesale operations, and trucking headquarters were in the same location where they might be supervised from a central office. But they are not: dealerships are in Maine, but wholesale and retail outlets are in distant cities. There are three vertically integrated firms, but they have problems of coordination between the central office and widely scattered markets, pounds, and dealerships. These firms attempt to solve these problems by becoming silent partners of owners of dealerships and pounds.

The cooperatives experienced other problems when they attempted to integrate vertically. In the late 1970s the Maine Association of Cooperatives, "Big Mac," was formed to market the catches of all member cooperatives jointly in the hopes of being able to negotiate very favorable prices. Big Mac's joint marketing efforts failed after a few months due to severe internal conflict among member cooperatives. One of the primary problems was that truck drivers were hired as managers, on the grounds that they knew the city lobster markets. The idea that a competent manager for Big Mac might need to know accounting, finance, business law, and have personnel management skills did not suggest itself. Managing even a single cooperative is a formidable task (Fox and Lessa). Managing a number of cooperatives proved to be impossible.

Although the lobster market appears to be governed by classical supply and demand forces, this market also displays genuine relational features. The

2. A few vertically integrated firms are organized in Maine by people who own entire islands and all the fishing area off them. These island owners have been able to buy a small fleet of boats and hire fishermen to work for them. Arrangements vary considerably, but typically in such vertically integrated firms the owner provides his fishermen with a boat and traps. The fisherman provides his own fuel and bait. They split the catch evenly. But such vertically integrated firms are rare and occur only where a single man or family owns an island.

398 / JOURNAL OF LAW, ECONOMICS, AND ORGANIZATION I:2, 1985

identity of the parties does matter. Continuity is valued. Local information is important. It is not therefore correct to say that the parties to exchange in the lobster market are continuously meeting competition in a recurrent spot market. To annihilate the relational features in this market would be to introduce serious losses.

The possibility that very few markets are governed by wholly impersonal market forces is thus suggested. Whether or to what degree the economic analysis of "competitive" markets needs to make provision for dyadic ties is unclear. Further study of this matter is, however, suggested.

REFERENCES

Acheson, James. M. 1972. "Territories of the Lobstermen," 81 *Natural History* 60–69.
———. 1975. "The Lobster Fiefs: Economic and Ecological Effects of Territoriality in the Maine Lobster Industry," 3 *Human Ecology* 183–207.
———. 1979. "Variations in Traditional Inshore Fishing Rights in Maine Lobstering Communities," in Raoul Andersen, ed., *North Atlantic Maritime Cultures*, pp. 253–276. The Hague: Mouton.
Coase, Ronald H. 1937. "The Nature of the Firm," 4 *Economica* 386–405.
Fox, Catherine, and William Lessa. 1983. "Fish Marketing Cooperatives in Northern New England." New York Sea Grant Extension Publication, Cornell University.
Geertz, Clifford. 1978. "The Bazaar Economy: Information and Search in Peasant Marketing," 68 *American Economic Review* 28–32.
Macneil, Ian. 1978. "Contracts: Adjustment of Long-Term Economic Relations under Classical, Neoclassical and Relational Contract Law," 72 *Northwestern University Law Review* 854–97.
Mintz, Sidney. 1964. "The Employment of Capital by Market Women in Haiti," in Raymond Firth and B.S. Yamey, eds., *Capital, Savings and Credit in Peasant Societies*. Chicago: Aldine.
Spoehr, Alexander. 1980. "Protein from the Sea: Technological Change in Philippine Capture Fisheries." Ethnology Monographs no. 3, Department of Anthropology, University of Pittsburgh.
Townsend, Ralph, and Hugh Briggs, III. 1982. "Maine's Marine Fisheries: Annual Data 1947–1981." Maine–New Hampshire Sea Grant Program, University of Maine.
Wilson, James A. 1980. "Adaptation to Uncertainty and Small Numbers Exchange: The New England Fresh Fish Market," 11 *Bell Journal of Economics* 491–504.
———1984. Personal communication, unpublished.
Williamson, Oliver E. 1975. *Markets and Hierarchies: Analysis and Antitrust Implications*. New York: Free Press.
———. 1979. "Transactions-Cost Economics: The Governance of Contractual Relations," 22 *Journal of Law and Economics* 233–60.

[2]

MEASUREMENT COST AND THE ORGANIZATION OF MARKETS*

YORAM BARZEL
University of Washington and Hoover Institution

PEOPLE will exchange only if they perceive what they get to be more valuable than what they give. To form such perceptions, the attributes of the traded items have to be measured. Some measurements are easy to obtain; others pose difficulties. For example, determining the weight of an orange may be a low-cost, accurate operation. Yet what is weighed is seldom what is truly valued. The skin of the orange hides its pulp, making a direct measurement of the desired attributes costly. Thus the taste and the amount of juice it contains are always a bit surprising. The grower, more knowledgeable than the consumer, may gain by making the surprise an unpleasant one. The potential errors in weighing the commodity and in assessing its attributes permit manipulations and therefore require safeguards. The costs incurred by the transactors will exceed those under joint maximization.

A sampling of activities that arise solely because these costs are positive may hint at how costly the measurement of commodity attributes is.[1] Had product information been costless, warranties would disappear since attribute levels and defects could be effortlessly identified at the time of exchange; fancy packaging (unless valued for its own sake) as well as the *Consumer Report* and the Good Housekeeping Seal would be super-

---

* Steven Cheung should be credited with pointing out the importance of the "measurement problem." Thanks are due to Christopher Hall for his penetrating comments. I also received valuable comments from Keith Acheson, Armen Alchian, Steven Cheung, John Hause, Keith Leffler, and John McManus.

[1] A trifling episode dramatically illustrates how costly some measurements might be. In one of Eddie Bauer's sporting goods stores, sneakers were marked down to almost a third of the regular price after a single "defect" was found: their size markings were missing. (Thanks to Dean Worcester for the information.) Presumably, the cost to Eddie Bauer of measuring the sneakers' sizes, and perhaps of convincing consumers that nothing else was faulty, was perceived as more than half the retail price. The inducement required to compensate consumers for undertaking the measurement was obviously smaller than Eddie Bauer's cost, but still very substantial.

[*Journal of Law & Economics*, vol. XXV (April 1982)]

fluous, as would professional certification and recruiting efforts; and beautiful but rotten apples would fetch the appropriate price.

Virtually no commodity offered for sale is free from the cost of measuring its attributes; the problem addressed here is pervasive. "Market signaling" and "adverse selection" are seemingly instances of the general case. In both cases, the costs of measuring the attributes of individuals are high, and the resulting errors permit people to transfer wealth to themselves at a resource cost. Costly measurement is a factor common to these and various other instances where individual and joint maximization do not coincide.

The accuracy of measurement differs fundamentally from other valuable attributes. The presence of random errors introduces the opportunity for costly transfers of wealth. Of concern here are the effects of such behavior and the market arrangements that emerge to reduce the losses from the exploitation of the inaccuracies.[2]

THE NATURE OF MEASUREMENT ERROR

Consider a model adopting all but one of the Walrasian assumptions for a competitive economy; the exception is that product information is costly to obtain. Product information is defined as information on the levels of the attributes per unit of the commodity and on the actual amount contained in the nominal quantity. Measurements of these magnitudes are subject to error. The greater the variability of the measurement around the true value, the lesser the information about the commodity.[3]

Had product information been freely available, equally valued units would sell at the same price and, so long as choosing does not damage the commodity, a seller would not be harmed from allowing buyers to pick and choose. The seller then would have no incentive to constrain choice. It will be seen that when product information is costly, the seller may gain from imposing such a constraint.

The purchase of oranges when the desired good is fresh orange juice can illustrate the measurement problem. Suppose that oranges are identical in the quality of their juice, but the amount each yields varies; that the cost of squeezing oranges at the sellers' premises is prohibitive; that buyers and sellers are able to form estimates of the amount of juice any

---

[2] John C. McManus, The Costs of Alternative Economic Organizations, 8 Can. J. Econ. 334 (1976), takes a rather similar approach. Steven Cheung, A Theory of Price Control, 17 J. Law & Econ. 53 (1974), it seems, was the first to introduce the notion that markets are organized to minimize dissipation.

[3] Measurement is the quantification of information, and its use will facilitate in making the model operational.

orange contains and that the cost of greater accuracy is increasing. The amount of the attribute desired by consumers (and its price) then is subject to measurement error.[4]

Suppose further that numerous sellers sell the commodity. Each sorts it to as many classes as he wishes and then posts a price, say, in dollars per pound, for each class, permitting consumers to select any item provided they pay the posted price.

A consumer's periodic demand for the desired good is downward sloping, reflecting substitution within the period and the increasing cost of storage. The selection of a seller to buy from entails a fixed cost assumed to be so large that the entire period's quantity is obtained from a single bin of a single seller. After deciding which seller to patronize, a consumer will meet the period demand from that seller's offerings.

Had the units in the bin been identical and the amount of the desired attribute they contain known, the quantity purchased by a consumer would be determined by his demand for the attribute and by the price of the commodity. Had the units been varied, but not enough to justify *any* selection effort by the buyer, the quantity purchased would depend in part on the buyer's aversion to variability. At the going price for the commodity, the *expected* price for the attribute is determined, but the quantity obtained is subject to error. For now this effect of the error is abstracted from.

The quantity purchased in a particular period depends on the cost of selection in the following way. If, for instance, a buyer plans to buy only units estimated to be at the top quarter of the distribution, it is expected that four units will be inspected for each unit selected. The total cost of a purchased unit then is the sum of the posted price and the cost of inspecting four units. If, relative to its posted price, the commodity seems a better buy, so that the buyer plans to buy units from the top one-third of the distribution, then for every unit bought only three units will be inspected.

Thus, the interaction among the buyer's demand for the attribute, the buyer's cost of measuring the commodity, the posted price, and the estimated distribution of the attribute determines the amount purchased. That amount will increase as the demand for the good rises, as the cost of selection falls, as the posted price of the commodity falls, as the average quality increases, and, most important, as the *variability* of the commod-

---

[4] The assessment of how long a machine will last, the quality of a particular performance of a long-running play, and the cost of preparing a site for construction are a few additional examples of commodities that are difficult to evaluate or to measure, and thus their measurements are subject to error.

ity offered increases. The reason for the last result is that there is no added penalty for inspecting an exceptionally poor item, but there is an added gain to finding an exceptionally good one.

What are the constraints on the seller in posting his price? Buyers, it is assumed, make use of their past experience to predict the relationship between a seller's posted price and the distribution of his commodity. They will stop patronizing a seller who they determine has a high price relative to the distribution offered. This is the route by which competition from other sellers enters the model. Subsequent to a buyer's decision to buy from a particular seller, that seller faces a downward-sloping price function. To survive, however, the relationship between a seller's price and the quality of his offering cannot "exceed" that of other sellers too often.

How finely will a seller sort his commodity? Assuming that the cost of estimation increases with the accuracy of the estimate, suppose first that this cost is the same to the seller and to his buyers and that all buyers are identical in their aversion to variability. When the variability of the commodity offered at a given price is very low, buyers will forgo selecting and will take whatever is handiest. As variability increases, a point will be reached where selection will begin.

Under the assumptions here, sellers will sort the commodity to that break-even point in variability, that is, just finely enough to dissuade buyers from any sorting. When the seller effects such sorting, each item is measured *exactly* once. On the other hand, when buyers effect the measurement, each item will be measured *at least* once; some will be measured twice or more. Thus the net price—that is, price net of the cost of measuring—at which the commodity can be offered is lowest when the seller effects the measurement. Competition will force sellers to effect the measurement.

The conclusion that the seller will be the one to measure does not depend on the level of this cost so long as this cost is the same to buyers and to the seller. Whatever that cost is, the seller will always measure just finely enough to prevent buyers from measuring regardless of how averse to variability they are. The other side of the coin is that even when buyers do not value a better-sorted product, they will gain from measuring by getting the more highly valued units selling at a given price.

Suppose now that the buyers' cost of measuring is higher than the sellers', say, because a tax on measurement by buyers is imposed or because they are constrained in some way. It immediately follows that the sellers' level of sorting will fall to the new level that would just prevent buyers from any sorting. A striking feature of this result is that when the buyers' cost of measuring is increased, the net price they pay for the commodity, or for the desired attribute, will fall.

MEASUREMENT COST   31

Buyers perform their measurements in the market in two steps. In the first they estimate the distributions different sellers offer to decide from whom to buy; in the second they determine the properties of individual items. If the increase in buyers' cost applies only to the second step, then the analysis is complete. If, however, it applies to the first step also, a new problem arises.

If buyers' cost of determining what the distribution is is increased, a seller could more easily entice buyers to buy from him even when his merchandise is "overpriced." In that case, buyers must rely more heavily on their past experience or on some other proxy measure and less on assessing what they are offered on a particular shopping trip. The role of a seller's reputation, warranty, and so forth acquires, then, greater prominence. Constraining buyers' choice in that case will generate some gains but will also introduce new problems. Moreover, the imposition of such a constraint is unlikely to eliminate all measurement by buyers since buyers need to convince themselves that they do not receive worthless merchandise.

The earlier assumption that sellers' measurement cost is not higher than that of buyers seems satisfactory for single-attribute commodities. In reality, most commodities have numerous attributes whose levels vary across units. If a commodity is sorted by all its attributes, each unit may occupy a class by itself. If a commodity is not sorted so exhaustively, various buyers will find it worth their while to pick and choose by attributes that they value highly, but not ones by which the seller sorted the commodity. Whereas such sorting will generate a gain, it will be carried "too far" in comparison with the joint-maximization level.[5]

Because of the cost of measurement, the seller cannot capture the entire value of his merchandise had it been costlessly described. This was shown to be the case when the seller sorted to prevent consumers from any choosing. It is also the case when consumers engage in choosing, selecting items valued more than their price. Because of competition among consumers, however, they will be able to obtain the differential in value only by spending resources—those used on measuring the commodity and perhaps on rushing to the top of the line.

In the remainder of the paper, an attempt is made to determine whether particular market practices are designed to cope with the excess-measurement problem, and implications capable of refuting the hypotheses are derived. Some casual empirical observations are made, but no serious tests are conducted. The particular practices considered below are selected on the basis of their apparent "importance" or "interest."

---

[5] The buyer will sort to the point where an extra dollar's worth of sorting effort yields one dollar in value. Whereas the valued attribute is costly to produce, it is obtained by the buyer at a zero marginal charge from the seller.

An examination of some of the earlier considerations may facilitate in the derivation of hypotheses. A consumer who is convinced that he received a random selection from an optimally measured commodity will not use additional resources for measuring. This requires that trust is established, perhaps by acquiring brand names. The seller still has to select a method of selling to avoid excessive sorting. One such method is to raise the buyer's measurement cost. DeBeers's diamond "sights" seem a case in point. The approved dealers have diamonds chosen for them by DeBeers, and they are not allowed to pick and choose from different offerings.

A buyer's incentive for excessive measurement can also be lowered if he is compensated for items ultimately revealed to be of exceptionally low value, which may explain product warranties. The terms of exchange for warranted products depend on subsequent performance rather than relying entirely on measuring the commodity by the time of exchange. The arrangement, however, lowers the buyer's cost of the careless handling of the product. The severity of this problem depends on the nature of the commodity and on the contractual ability to curb abuse. Share contracts rely even more fully on subsequent performance and obviate the need for certain measurements at the time of exchange. Such contracts are expected, then, when the determination of the value of the exchanged property at the time of exchange is exceptionally costly.

The next four sections discuss product warranties, share contracts, brand names, and the suppression of information. Hypotheses are offered to explain these arrangements, and testable implications are derived. Later sections further expand the model and its applications to such diverse issues as vertical integration and futures markets.

Product Warranties

In every exchange, both the seller and the buyer will require some verification of the measurements of the exchanged goods: the seller to assure himself he is not giving up too much, the buyer to assure himself he is not receiving too little. The process of producing a commodity spans a period of time; the costs of measuring the attributes and of verifying the measurements will vary along the way and will be different for the buyer than for the seller. Which quantitites, then, will be measured, when, and by whom? The remainder of this section concerns measurement by the consumer at the time of consumption.

As a rule, measurement is by the seller, whether in advance or at the time of exchange. Quite often, however, measurement is automatic, or its cost is greatly reduced as the commodity is used. Therefore, substantial

MEASUREMENT COST 33

savings will result if measuring is left to the buyer to be performed at the time of consumption. A prevalent arrangement for vesting in the consumer the responsibility for certain measurements is that of the guarantee. Presumably, it is too costly for the seller to determine which of his products may have defects. The consumer, on the other hand, can obtain this information cheaply at the time of consumption.[6] In the absence of a guarantee, to avoid getting stuck with a bad item, the consumer will examine several to identify the one with the fewest defects. Given the expected cost of selection by buyers, the seller must price the items he sells below the expected valuation of the best unit; otherwise he will not be able to sell any unit. The differential between the price and the valuation of the units offered for sale is effectively left in the public domain, and buyers will spend resources to acquire it. Selling a commodity with a warranty is essentially a promise to provide one *good* unit at the going price. Thus, the warranty reduces the differential in value received by consumers for given payment and reduces correspondingly the attendant resource expenditure.

The fact that some new cars have numerous defects is not necessarily a sign of poor workmanship. The consumer may simply be more efficient than the seller in providing quality control. When no guarantee is offered, however, a buyer would inspect several cars before choosing one. This excessive examination is avoided when the product is guaranteed. A seller who guarantees his product, then, can raise his price not only by an amount equal to the expected cost of repair, but by a premium representing the cost to the consumer of a prior examination.[7] Guarantees are routine for new cars, but not for used ones. The apparent reason is that a new-car seller can relatively cheaply verify the measurement supplied by the buyer, which is not the case for used cars.[8]

When a warranty is too expensive to supply, two types of arrangements can be used to reduce excess measurement. One is a higher degree of

[6] The same consideration may explain certain return privileges. For such items as paint, tiles, and wool it may be difficult to match the items if a second purchase is needed. Since the consumer can measure his requirements most economically at the time of consumption, he is promised a refund for excess quantities of these goods he may buy originally.

[7] In his seminal "lemon" paper, George Akerlof discusses this role of warranties. See George Akerlof, The Market for "Lemons": Quality Uncertainty and the Market Mechanism, 84 Q. J. Econ. 488 (1970).

[8] The warranty is warranted only if buyers cannot easily exercise it even though they, rather than the seller, are at fault. The ability of one party or the other to abuse his position seems to correspond to Williamson's notion of "information impactedness," where "circumstances relevant to the transaction, or related set of transactions, are known to one or more parties but cannot be costlessly discerned by or displayed for others." See O. E. Williamson, Markets and Hierarchies 31 (1975).

quality control, which one would expect, for instance, with commodities designed for the tourist trade. The section on brand names continues this discussion. The other arrangement is to get the consumer to act as if his choice were random. The sale of used cars, where dealers often obliterate potential distinctions among cars, is, seemingly, a case in point. This issue is further developed in the section on the suppression of information.

SHARE CONTRACTS

Share contracts are often said to reflect the desire of the risk averse to moderate the effect of risk. Had this been their sole explanation, it would be refuted by the royalty payment to authors. The royalty contract between author and publisher stipulates that the author will receive a given share of the revenue from the sale of the book. Since the success of the book and the total revenue its sale will generate are not known when the contract is drawn, the author's income is uncertain. Had authors been paid a lump sum, their entire risk would have been shifted to publishers. Publishers are often diversified to start with, and thus paying a lump sum would increase the riskiness of their operations only moderately. The desire to reduce risk, then, would have generated the outright purchase of rights to books rather than the common royalty contract.

What else, then, could explain the sharing arrangement? In the royalty contract the share, or share structure, is set in advance, but the absolute amounts the two parties will receive are contingent on consumers' actual demand subsequent to publication. Because of the difficulty in predicting the ultimate success of the venture, the determination of the appropriate lump sum is expensive to reach. If publishers make competitive lump-sum bids, each of them will require some market research. Even the successful bidder's effort is excessive, since subsequently the information will emerge anyhow. Had publishers attempted to lower the cost by spending only a small amount on research, their bids would be subject to large errors, and the winning bidder might turn out to be a big loser.[9] By sharing, the need for market research is reduced and the error is largely limited to the sharing percentage, making the expected value of the royalty contract larger than the lump sum would have been.[10]

Share contracts are subject to incentive problems absent from lump-

---

[9] Their loss is similar to the loss to speculators in Hirshleifer's model. See Jack Hirshleifer, The Private and Social Value of Information and the Reward to Inventive Activity, 61 Am. Econ. Rev. 561 (1971). In that model, speculation is with respect to price; here, it is with respect to quantity.

[10] Similarly, owners of mineral rights usually do not sell their rights but rather agree to a share of the unknown revenues.

sum contracts and in this regard are more costly. For instance, the publisher will tend to advertise less than when he does not share added revenues with the author. The lesser the information problem, the more attractive the lump-sum arrangement; thus share contracts are expected to be more common with new authors than with established ones,[11] with the first editions than with subsequent ones, and with novels than with "how-to" manuals.

The sharing arrangement, then, makes some search less profitable. Market forces dissuade publishers and authors from acquiring prior information on the value of the traded property.[12] But because such acquisition would have been wasteful, the sharing arrangement is a more efficient solution.[13]

BRAND NAMES

Since consumption yields direct measurement, it is often advantageous to let consumers do the measuring, which may explain warranties and contracts as argued above. Consumers, however, can gain by understanding the value of the good, and it is often difficult to verify their measurements. On the other hand, at the time of transaction, measurement or verification may be rather costly.[14] How can costly measurement be avoided?

Suppose one wants to buy a six-pack of beer. To determine whether the beer is cold enough, he will touch one or two bottles, but not all of them. Similarly, if he looks for a rope of certain strength, he will test just a small segment. In both examples the procedure followed is not as innocuous as it may appear. The beer seller can reduce refrigeration costs if the easiest-to-reach bottles are coolest, and the rope maker can strengthen just the exposed end of the rope. When the buyer does not engage in a

---

[11] The more books an author publishes, the smaller the proportionate effect of risk from variability in the royalty income from any of the books. The risk-aversion model then implies that sharing, or royalties, will become more common as the number of books an author publishes increases, which is the opposite of this paper's prediction.

[12] See Yoram Barzel, Some Fallacies in the Interpretation of Information Costs, 20 J. Law & Econ. 291 (1977).

[13] Hashimoto hypothesizes that the Japanese wage-bonus payment is a sharing arrangement induced by the cost of evaluating a worker's contribution. He finds that the evidence conforms with this hypothesis. See Masanori Hashimoto, Bonus Payments, on-the-Job Training and Lifetime Employment in Japan, 87 J. Pol. Econ. 1086 (1979).

[14] Various contests and calls for bids are subject to a time limit. Presumably, the caller would wish to have all the materials assembled by a given time. The restriction imposed, however, is on the time marked on the posting, since this seems a much cheaper validation method.

more comprehensive test, he is implicitly trusting the integrity of the seller. But convincing others of one's integrity is a costly activity.

If the buyer is to buy without measuring every item, he has to be persuaded to rely on the seller's assertion of the prior measurement. In some instances, the seller will try to convince the buyer that his purchase will actually be "representative" of the lot; in others that the good is quite uniform and would not vary significantly from sample to sample. Uniformity is the subject of the remainder of this section; suppression of information is the subject of the next section.

A canner known to change the quality of peas (e.g., size, tenderness, sweetness) from one season to another will induce buyers to conduct a fresh, costly test every season. If, on the other hand, the canner is known to maintain tight quality control, much less testing is required. The canner's reputation, or brand name, serves here to guarantee that the product is, and will remain, uniformly good.[15]

The canner incurs costs in establishing reputation,[16] both in controlling quality to assure uniformity and in the maintenance of uniformity when external pressures would call for a change,[17] as any change endangers the canner's reputation, reducing the value of his brand name. Even a higher quality offered at the old price will cause problems by reinducing costly sorting. Thus, it is expected that when the seller's reputation is used to back the product, quality will fluctuate less than when the consumer is to measure it.

Product uniformity lowers the cost of measurement to the consumer. It is probable that to provide continuing uniformity, extensive measurement is required by the seller. However, a seller of established reputation can choose to measure at the cheapest point in the production process rather than at the time of exchange, as would be necessary if the buyer were to insist on verification of the measurement.[18]

---

[15] In an article on the growing and canning of peas, Susan Sheehan gives a detailed description of the extraordinary effort by Green Giant to guarantee product uniformity at all grades. See Susan Sheehan, Peas, The New Yorker, September 17, 1973, at 103.

[16] If it is easier to convince a consumer of the uniformity of a widely distributed product than of each of several narrowly distributed ones, horizontal integration is advantageous.

[17] This point was contributed by Levis Kochin. The pursuit of constant quality by Mars, a candy maker, is detailed in an article in Business Week (August 14, 1978, at 291). "One source of that mystique is Mars' fanaticism about the quality and freshness of its products. . . ." "While other manufacturers were . . . reducing the quality of their candy because of the price of sugar and cocoa . . . Mars [did not]." "[Mars] was the first candy manufacturer to date its products and to guarantee to take back and credit merchandise still on the shelf in four months."

[18] Brand name also involves "standards." Had the most desired characteristics of peas been easy to measure, the label of each can could have stated their amounts. A shopper then

When a buyer receives a bad unwarranted item, his money is lost. Thus, to gain the buyer's patronage the seller must persuade him that he himself will suffer a substantial loss if his product is found deficient. By backing the quality of the item with a brand name, a bad item sold under that name will tarnish the entire brand. The more likely the consumer is to encounter the brand in the future, the more severe the penalty he can impose on the seller and thus the less he has to worry about being cheated.[19] It is expected that the more difficult it is to measure commodities at time of exchange or to warrant them, the more extensive would be the brand under which they are sold. It is also expected, paradoxically, that a seller committed to compensate the buyer for defective products will sell relatively more defective units than a seller who makes no such commitment.

The Suppression of Information

The provision of uniform commodities would some of the time be too costly. A commodity may be defined as heterogenous if, when allowed, its consumers will spend resources on choosing among equally priced units. Thus, patrons line up for preferred seats in a single-price movie theater; produce and meat in a grocery store are routinely subject to selection; and prospective employers spend resources in recruiting among equally paid, but diverse, workers. As already noted, the competition for the high-valued items is a costly activity; spared of the added cost, a consumer would have offered more for the item.[20]

How much is a buyer who is not permitted to inspect and to choose willing to pay for a commodity? This depends on his guess of the quality of the unit handed to him, which, in turn, depends on how much he trusts the seller. He expects to be given an item from the low-quality end from a mistrusted seller. Suppose, however, that the seller is able to persuade the buyer that he is offering a random or a "representative" selection.

---

could choose his exact preference and uniformity would lose value. A consumer seeking uniformity would simply buy units having the same specifications. Thus the capability to measure implies the existence of "standards." These appear to be a substitute for brand name, and the usage of the two will be negatively correlated. It is expected that the fewer the dimensions of a commodity amenable to standardized measurement, the greater the emphasis on the brand name. Even for commodities that can be cheaply measured, however, brand name helps to assure that the measurements are correct.

[19] Klein and Leffler discuss the nature of brand names and particularly the "last-period" problem. Benjamin Klein & Keith Leffler, The Role of Market Forces in Assuring Contractual Performance, 89 J. Pol. Econ. 615 (1981).

[20] Precisely the same reasoning led to the conclusion that consumers will pay a premium (apart from those for risk reduction and for saving on the expected cost of repair) for commodities sold with warranties.

The buyer will have to submit to the choice effected by the seller, but the resource expense of duplicate sorting is bypassed. Thus, abstracting from risk aversion, he will be willing to bid up to his expected valuation.

Operating within the framework of competitive markets, it is argued that information on the quality of goods that inspection would have generated is deliberately suppressed.[21] On occasion, sellers may even offer buyers "a pig in a poke." There is no difficulty in opening the poke to inspect the pig. When trust can be created cheaply enough, trusting consumers will offer a higher average price for the entire batch when inspection is not allowed, and this arrangement will prevail. In some cases inspection might damage the commodity. In other cases, however, the arrangement is deliberately contrived at a cost of resources.

This may explain why apples are often sold in opaque bags filled in advance by the seller. The consumer spends less time per apple on inspection than when choosing them individually. He obviously will not buy the bag unless he believes that on average he gets a better buy; thus the seller's "fairness" becomes a factor in his decision. It is predicted that sellers catering to transient trade will sell a smaller fraction of their apples by the bag and will sort them into more uniform grouping than will sellers whose credentials are well established.[22]

The advantage of suppressing information may explain some of the practices associated with the selection of physicians by patients. As a rule, a physician has an immense edge over a patient in measuring the service delivered because of the complexity of medical problems and because of the great variability in outcome of a given treatment, even for a single person at different times. Since the patient's cost of measuring the service is much higher than the physician's, resources can be saved if physicians rather than patients engage in measuring. But how can patients be stopped from spending resources trying to identify the best buys? One way is to enhance even further the asymmetry in information between physician and patient.

Sellers of medical services, through the AMA, ADA, etc., spend a large amount of resources to persuade buyers to choose among physicians as if the choice were random.[23] Various measures taken by the AMA lower still further the return to measurement by patients. A high uniformity of skill among physicians is attained through the control of training, of qual-

---

[21] This parallels the argument that with the royalty-payment scheme, authors and publishers will abstain from collecting duplicate information on the value of a manuscript.

[22] The hypothesis could be tested by comparing the behavior of shopkeepers in resort areas during the tourist season with that during the off-season.

[23] The assumption of competition through free entry does not hold in this case. As will be shown presently, however, in at least one dimension the restriction on entry may prove to be efficient.

ifying examinations, and of admission to medical schools (where, e.g., large fellowships are less readily available than in other graduate programs). Not surprisingly, then, medical school graduates seem more uniform in ability than those in other professions.[24] Moreover, the gap between the training of nurses and physicians is so wide that only seldom would patients compare the services of the two.

Comparison among physicians also is discouraged. Physicians are constrained from criticizing one another, and until recently were not allowed to advertise and were severely restricted with respect to office signs, yellow-page entries, and the like. Additionally, price information is kept in low profile. Thus, a patient can compare physicians only by expedients such as word of mouth.

If the preceding hypothesis is correct, the following observations are implied: (1) The AMA would resist moves to make comparisons easier. (2) The easier it is for patients to measure a medical service, the looser will be its control by the AMA. (3) Income variability among doctors would be less than in other professions that require a comparable amount of training, such as law. Casual observations on the first two implications are in conformity with the hypothesis. The tenacious fight of the AMA against prepaid medical insurance is consistent with the first implication. The question as to whether to join such an insurance group itself requires comparison, and when a compensation schedule is provided, price comparison becomes easier.

With respect to the second implication, consider the distinction between acute and chronic medical problems. A person afflicted with a chronic problem gains experience which in time increases his ability to measure the service he receives. To that extent, he has a comparative advantage over someone with an acute problem. From this it is predicted that the treatment of chronic problems will be less tightly controlled by the AMA. This seems to be borne out by the fact that chiropractors, whose specialty is treating predominantly chronic ailments, are allowed to compete with physicians.

Vertical Integration

When production is specialized, the product will change hands before reaching the ultimate consumer. In this section, some of the problems associated with measuring the product in its intermediate stages are analyzed.[25] Home production is an extreme form of vertical integration.

[24] Medical societies also deny membership, and the right to practice, to physicians who prove "incompetent."

[25] Cohen's discussion of the firm is based, in part, on the difficulties in measurement. L. R. Cohen, The Firm: A Revised Definition, 46 S. Econ. J. 580 (1979).

Since all stages of production are carried out by a single person, the motive for excess measurement is absent but the advantages of specialization are lost. What role does the vertically integrated firm play regarding the problem of measurement?

Consider a production process requiring several workers. A firm employing these workers will incur the costs of contracting with them and policing their activities. These costs would be avoided if the process were divided among firms, each consisting of one worker who would buy the intermediate good from the one preceding him on the production line. He may also buy other needed materials and buy, or rent, the space and equipment he uses. These factors, combined with his own work, would enhance the value of the intermediate good which he subsequently would sell to the next man on the line.[26] If production is so organized, the problem of "shirking" disappears.[27]

At most points, however, the value of the intermediate product may be difficult to assess, and therefore its sale may be accompanied by excess sorting. Thus, costs are incurred also in the exchange among such firms. Sometimes the relationship between input and output is well understood. The change in input may then serve as a satisfactory proxy for the change in output value.[28] As will now be shown, the use of input as a proxy for output does not by itself necessitate exchange within a firm, though it is a condition for this form of organization.

Would separate one-worker firms be formed in a production process spanning the tasks of several workers where output is easily measured at the end points but not at others? If the first step is organized as a separate one-worker firm, its output has to be sold to the firm performing the next task. As asserted, it is more costly to evaluate that output directly than to

[26] During the 1860s, several major industries in Birmingham were composed of numerous one-man firms. See G. C. Allen, The Industrial Development of Birmingham and the Black Country, 1860–1927 (1929; reprinted ed. 1966).

[27] Jensen and Meckling analyze the problem of borrowing and of the associated policing when the amount of capital required for the efficient firm size diverges from what the entrepreneur can supply. For their analysis to hold, firm size has to be independent of what they call "agency cost." This would be the case if optimal firm size were an exogenous "technological" datum. It is suggested here that this size is itself economically determined. See M. C. Jensen & W. H. Meckling, Theory of the Firm: Managerial Behavior, Agency Costs, and Ownership Structure, 3 J. Fin. Econ. 305 (1976).

[28] Alchian and Demsetz state, ". . . Suppose a farmer produces wheat . . . with subtle and difficult quality variations determined by how the farmer grew the wheat. A vertical integration could allow a purchaser to control the farmer's behavior in order to more economically estimate productivity." A. A. Alchian & H. Demsetz, Production, Information Costs, and Economic Organization, 62 Am. Econ. Rev. 785 (1972). This statement comes close to the basic argument here. Alchian and Demsetz, however, do not make the crucial distinction between random and biased errors.

measure the value of the products entering the first step plus its additional inputs. Thus, to determine the value of the product it receives, the second firm will have to monitor the inputs of the first firm. So long as the transition to the third-step output can be measured cheaply, however, there is no clear advantage in integrating the first two steps.[29]

When inputs have to be measured at two successive junctures, a rationale for an integrated firm emerges. If the second firm is also a one-worker enterprise whose output is difficult to measure, the firm performing the third step will have to monitor not only the inputs in the second step but also the value of the product entering the first step and the inputs within the step. Thus, the inputs of the first firm have to be monitored by both the second and the third firm. Although the second firm could provide the third with its own evaluation of the first firm's inputs, it stands to gain from overstating the case. The third firm, then, would need to verify the figures in some way. The problem is obviously compounded as the number of steps increases. If a separate organization performs this function for all steps, the conservation of information is clear: There is no longer a need for each firm to monitor the inputs in all prior steps. It is hypothesized that this is a function of the "firm."[30]

In view of this explanation, the notion of residual payments so commonly associated with the firm obtains an entirely different interpretation. When output is easily measured directly, the contribution of a worker can be assessed by his output, and there is a strong incentive for him to become self-employed. At other times, output can be measured by inputs more cheaply than by measuring it directly. If output is measured by inputs, remuneration of inputs cannot be based on output. Employees of a firm are paid by inputs rather than by output not because of lack of "entrepreneurship," but rather because their input is measured more eco-

---

[29] Indeed, airlines employ engineers to inspect the airplanes assigned to them while they are being built by Boeing. Similarly, in other equipment contracts and in construction it is not uncommon that the buyer retains the right to inspect the production process.

[30] Coase pointed out two forces favoring organizing production by the firm rather than by the market. One is the cost of "discovering what the relevant prices are"; the other is "the costs of negotiating and concluding a separate contract for each exchange transaction which takes place on a market." R. H. Coase, The Nature of the Firm, reprinted in Readings in Price Theory 336 (1952). Suggested here is another force—the cost of measuring intermediate outputs which, it is argued, favors production within a firm. The motive for vertical integration suggested here resembles that offered by Klein et al. See Benjamin Klein, Robert G. Crawford, & Armen A. Alchian, Vertical Integration, Appropriable Rents, and the Competitive Contracting Process, 21 J. Law & Econ. 297 (1978). Their argument, however, hinges on small numbers; at the extreme, one buyer facing one seller. There is no restriction here on the number of either buyers or sellers. In Williamson's view also, small numbers are a necessary condition, since vertical integration "harmonizes interests" and reduces the hazard of cheating between firms (see Williamson, *supra* note 8, at 82).

nomically than their output; otherwise they would have become self-employed. Having employees bear the risk in output value through direct ownership has no desirable incentive effect and thus is of little purpose. When tasks are performed by employed workers, "shirking" becomes a problem and the entrepreneur is remunerated for his monitoring of inputs, which implies that he has to assume the risk of price and other fluctuations.[31]

Distinct firms will form and trade with each other at junctures where output can be readily measured, but where output is difficult to measure the different steps will be performed within the firm. Between the time that a commodity such as canned salmon leaves the manufacturer and the time it reaches the consumer, its physical properties and its value will have changed only slightly. Other goods such as produce and bread may change a great deal. The ownership of a commodity may not change at all between production and consumption, as is the case with home-grown vegetables, or it may change several times. It is predicted that ownership will change more frequently the less the commodity is subject to change. Thus, canned salmon is expected to change ownership more times than fresh salmon, powdered milk more than fresh milk, cookies more than fresh bread, and so on. A comparison, admittedly casual, of cookies and bread is in conformity with the prediction. Grocers buy the cookies they sell, but only rent shelf space to bakeries for bread sold through them.[32]

ERRORS OF PROXY MEASUREMENT

Often, the units by which a commodity is exchanged differ from those for which it is desired. For example, tires are measured by ply, size, and tread, whereas they are valued for strength, road-holding ability, and longevity; oranges are sold by weight, which includes the seldom-wanted skin. In this section, some of the problems that arise from the use of proxies are discussed.

Consider the tastiness of apples. Suppose that taste is extremely costly to measure and that it is correlated with color, which can be measured by the naked eye.[33] Color, then, is used as a measure of taste, and the market price of apples becomes a function of their color—the redder are Red

---

[31] This argument strongly parallels that of Alchian and Demsetz, *supra* note 28. Their "team production" output can be measured cheaply, but because of scale economies the output of a team member cannot. Team members, then, have to be policed and are remunerated according to their inputs.

[32] Coor's beer, which is more difficult to keep fresh because it has no preservatives, is supposedly monitored by that brewery more vigorously than do other breweries.

[33] John Umbect says (personal communication) that in Tangier, tangerines offered for sale are displayed on a branch with a leaf or two. The apparent reason is that a leaf is a better visual indicator of freshness than is the fruit itself.

Delicious apples, the higher is their price. Thus, an orchardist will optimize with respect to color.

When the proxy measure can be manipulated, here, too, people will redistribute income at the expense of resources. Suppose that a chemical fertilizer can enhance apples without affecting their taste. Abstracting from the asesthetic value of apples, if the consumer cannot discern whether the chemical has been used and obtaining that information is too costly, the orchardist will then apply the chemical.[34]

Since consumers ultimately value apples for their taste and not their color, had it been possible effortlessly to stop the use of the fertilizer, the cost of the extra reddening would have been avoided without incurring any other loss.[35] The use of the proxy seems wasteful—the apples are made "excessively" pretty. The proxy, however, is presumably used because the alternative of not using it is still more costly.

The use of the chemical will affect the relationship between color and value. Assuming diminishing marginal valuation, R_0 in Figure 1 is the original relationship between the two attributes. The application of a given amount of the fertilizer will shift the curve to the right to R_1. Apples of any given color are now valued less. Still, the redder an apple is, the tastier and more valuable it is. The shift in the curve, however, is not likely to be uniform. Rather, the redder the apples are to start with, the smaller is the shift. This is due to two factors, each of which is sufficient for the argument here. First, the originally redder apples are likely to gain less in value from a given increase in color. Second, a given dose of the fertilizer is expected to affect them less noticeably.

Thus R_1 is steeper than R_0. Given the cost and the error of measuring redness, the steeper relationship constitutes a reduction in the informational value of the color of apples. This is a force constraining the application of fertilizer, but it also guarantees that some amount will be used. To see this, assume momentarily that the relationships between redness and value and between redness and the amount of fertilizer are both linear. This means that R_0 and R_1 are parallel straight lines. If the return from the application of one unit of the chemical is positive, then a reapplication will yield the same return. Eventually, however, consumers would cease to employ color as a measure of taste. At this point, the return from its use in *any* amount will drop to zero. But as the use of the fertilizer is discon-

---

[34] A grower using the fertilizer need not be aware that his behavior is dissipating. He is informed by the market-price structure that consumers value redness, and that is what he is providing.

[35] Spence's "signal" is also a measurable attribute which is correlated with the "true" one and subject to manipulation. See M. Spence, Job Market Signaling, 87 Q. J. Econ. 355 (1973).

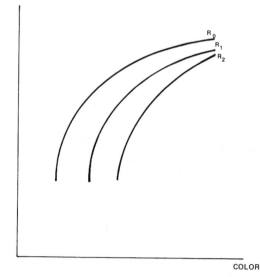

FIGURE 1

tinued, the relationship between color and value will be restored, returning us to the starting point of the cycle.[36]

When returns are diminishing, however, the dilemma disappears. In
Figure 1, R_2 represents the effect of a second dose of the fertilizer. The
return is lower because the effect on color is less than that of the first
dose, and also because an extra unit of color increases revenue less than it
did before, as R_2 is steeper than R_1. As more fertilizer is used, a point will
be reached at which the return from an extra dose is equal to its cost.

If the simplifying assumptions—that the fertilizer does not affect taste
and that color is valued only as a proxy for taste—are relaxed, the analysis grows more complicated but the logic remains the same. To the extent
that taste would be improved by the use of the fertilizer, dissipation is
decreased. If taste is affected adversely, but the correlation between taste
and color remains positive, dissipation will exceed the cost of the fertilizer. If taste is affected more than color, too little of the chemical will be
used; indeed, it will not be used at all if it does not alter color even though
it improves the taste.

Now, relaxing the second assumption, suppose that the color of apples
is valued for its own merit. In this case, the fertilizer will be applied apart
from its effect on taste, and it will be used beyond the point that would

[36] Rothschild and Stiglitz present another "no-equilibrium" result. Their setting is competitive insurance markets. See Michael Rothschild & Joseph Stiglitz, Equilibrium in Competitive Insurance Markets, 90 Q. J. Econ. 629 (1976).

have been dictated if color were merely a proxy for taste. The rest of the analysis remains unchanged.

The color of apples can undoubtedly be affected in other ways, such as the choice of harvest time, of storage temperature, and so on. Each of these methods will be used (and the information content of color function "degraded") to a point where the return equals the cost. The general principle is that maximization occurs with respect to whatever measures consumers use to determine market values. Presumably, the measures in actual use combine a high correlation with the desired ones while possessing high resistance to degradation.

Activities directed toward the market measures will, in general, be off the mark in terms of their effect on the "true" measures. Nevertheless, a grower who applies less of the fertilizer will find his revenue declining more than his cost since, given the assumptions here, he is unable to convince consumers that his less colorful apples are as tasty. This is an instance where the "bad" drives the "good" out of the market. Similarly, a consumer cannot gain by buying apples that are not as red as his own preferences dictate, since the price structure of applies of different shades of red is itself determined by consumers' valuation.

It is tempting to think that if a grocer would mark a bin of apples "ugly but tasty," and if the apples indeed proved flavorful, he could overcome the problem of the spurious measure.[37] The difficulty in convincing buyers that what looks unattractive may nevertheless be good is illustrated by the owner who spends resources to "beautify" the house he plans to sell in a way he did not feel was worthwhile when he was living there. Buyers are well aware of this common practice, but its survival demonstrates that the skin-deep treatment does affect their decisions. In the case of apples, the greatest benefits accrue to those growers able to convince consumers that they avoid the fertilizer while in fact using it. It is difficult to allay consumers' suspicions, since for each type of apple the redder it is the better it tastes.

Still, suppose that to a particular grower the cost of convincing consumers that no fertilizer was used is low enough.[38] It is predicted that on average the grower's apples will look less attractive, or rather, less red, than those grown with the fertilizer; that for given redness, the unfer-

---

[37] Safeway stores seem to harp on this theme when advertising their "Scotch Buy" brand as "It ain't fancy but it sure is good!" This brand, however, is backed by Safeway's own brand name. Two other examples (supplied by Marion Impola) of attempts to dispel mistrust are a seller's sign by his Kiwi fruit, "Ugly, but interesting," and Smucker's ad, "With a name like Smucker's, it's got to be good."

[38] If a growers' association can police its members more cheaply than consumers can police a grower, the association is expected to prohibit the use of the fertilizer. This restrictive practice actually promotes efficiency.

tilized apples will be more expensive; and that the unfertilized apples of a given taste will be cheaper, an implication that is easy to verify subjectively but not objectively.

Given the last implication, the unfertilized apples should drive the other apples out of the market. However, the cost of upholding the no-fertilizer claim will vary among consumers. It is expected, then, that both types of apples will continue to be provided. It seems plausible that the farther consumers are from the grower, the higher the cost of creating "trust." The notion that better Washington apples or California oranges will be shipped to the East Coast then applies to the better-looking, but not to the better-tasting, fruit.

FUTURES MARKETS[39]

The impersonality that characterizes markets in received models does not appear to hold for most actual markets, where the identity or brand name of transactors is essential to functioning. In "futures" markets, however, the trustworthiness of the parties is inconsequential, since apart from the enforcement role of the exchange there is no continuing relationship. The exchange certifies that the traded commodities meet the required specifications and that payment is forthcoming. Thus, the buyer need not worry about receiving defective merchandise and the seller does not have to spend resources to collect his pay. However, far from the accepted view, it appears that such impersonality is attained at high cost.

Suppose that the rate at which a good will deteriorate can be controlled. If the present price decreases as expected deterioration increases, the seller will spend resources to retard that process. Suppose, however, that measurement of the expected deterioration at the time the exchange is agreed upon is so costly that it will not be performed. Now, if the exchange is strictly by specifications, as in the futures trade, the prevention of deterioration will not occur since it will not be remunerated. On the other hand, in the spot market, where sellers operate under a brand name, deterioration will be controlled because a positive return is expected.[40]

This distinction may explain an otherwise puzzling phenomenon: Farm products traded in futures markets tend to be characterized as of "low-quality" or "garbage" grade.[41] How can such a term apply to a commod-

---

[39] An earlier analysis of these markets by Acheson and McManus is not unlike the one presented here. See K. Acheson & J. McManus, The Costs of Transacting in Futures Markets (August 1979) (unpublished paper, Carleton Univ.).

[40] Lindsay draws a similar distinction between government output that is evaluated strictly by specification, and private output, in which unspecified margins are (somehow) adhered to. See Cotton M. Lindsay, A Theory of Government Enterprise, 84 J. Pol. Econ. 1061 (1976).

[41] The costliness of measuring the protein content of wheat and the resulting allocation of

ity that meets all stipulated specifications? The answer may well be that other *non*stipulated attributes will be underproduced when the commodities are destined for futures markets. The levels of the valuable qualities could have been increased at a lower cost than their valuation except for the cost of measurement—which has prevented such action. For this reason, producers are not expected to plan to produce for the futures markets. Only when the commodity is found unsuitable for regular customers would they divert it toward the futures market.

Since commodities sold in futures markets are also sold in spot markets, two testable implications are suggested. First, the price in the spot market is predicted to be higher than that in the futures market for what appears, in terms of specifications, to be the same commodity. Second, specifications are expected to be more comprehensive in futures markets than in spot markets. Since brand name is already established in the spot market, some direct measurements can be dispensed with.

Uncertainty and Dissipating Behavior

Diminishing marginal utility of income implies that the more income varies around a given mean the less it is valued. The presumption that in reality the marginal utility of income is indeed diminishing is the basis for the accepted explanation of insurance, product warranties, and sharing arrangements that are said to reduce the uncertainty facing the individual. It was suggested, however, that warranties and sharing arrangements may be explained by a quite different force: the cost of getting reliable information about a good. This argument is now more generally related to the problem of uncertainty.

Some uncertainty is truly and entirely random; in most situations, however, opportunities abound for the human hand to affect the odds. A person facing an uncertain situation has reason to fear that if the odds are tampered with, they will not be in his favor. A used-car buyer who suspects that the salesman will attempt to saddle him with a worse-than-average car will take some countermeasures. Both the odds tampering by the seller and the protective steps by the buyer consume resources. The buyer, then, would pay a premium independent of any "risk aversion" to convert the uncertain situation into a certain one.

The risk-aversion model predicts that risk will be shifted toward the party for whom risk is less costly. The prediction here is that whoever is in a position to affect the odds will tend to assume the risk, though the two are not mutually exclusive. The payment of royalties rather than a lump

---

high-protein wheat to regular channels and low-protein wheat through impersonal channels is described by Carl L. Alsberg, Protein Content: A Neglected Factor in Wheat Grades, in 2 Wheat Studies of the Food Research Institute 163–76 (1926).

sum to an author, and particularly to a novice, tends to support the latter hypothesis.

The offering of warranties or of some other means to reduce uncertainty is itself costly. It is predicted that the more easily tampering can be detected and the larger the subsequent loss, the less frequently will a warranty be offered. Indeed, people are expected to expose themselves deliberately to detection to reduce the buyer's fear of being cheated.[42] It is predicted, though most tentatively, that well-established law firms will set fixed fees or fixed hourly charges rather than contingent fees more often than will less prestigious law firms. The highly reputable law firm having more of a reputation to protect is expected to monitor its members to provide clients with satisfactory service. To attract business, law firms of lesser reputation in effect offer insurance when they base their fees contingent on good performance.

CONCLUDING REMARKS

The problems and costs of measurement pervade and significantly affect all economic transactions. Errors of measurement are too costly to eliminate entirely. The value of equally priced items will differ, then, and people will spend resources to acquire the difference. Such resource expenditure is wasteful, and it is hypothesized that exchange parties will form such contracts and engage in such activities that reduce this kind of resource use. The customer's random selection from an already optimally sorted commodity will avoid the excessive expense. Thus, for example, it is expected that some readily obtainable information will be suppressed to preempt opportunities for excessive measurement.

Because inputs are sometimes the best available proxies for measuring output, vertical integration in the form of organizing output within firms can conserve some measurement costs. Measurement losses also can be lowered by other expedients such as share contracts and warranties. "Trust," "brand name," "repeat purchases," and the like also lower the need for costly measurements, though they are too costly to produce.

The fragments of evidence presented are only illustrative and should not be construed as a test of the model. Even the hypotheses offered are rather tentative; more thorough knowledge of the details of market organization are needed to make firmer predictions. They help to demonstrate, however, that the concept of "measurement" is operational and that the model based on it is capable of generating testable implications.

---

[42] The owner of a race track has less incentive to tamper with the results of a horse race when betting is on a parimutuel basis, which may explain the prevalence of that arrangement. In general, it seems that organizers of games of chance are rewarded not on the basis of their risk but of gross income. Sellers of insurance, on the contrary, subject themselves to substantial risk.

[3]

THE ECONOMICS OF BLOCK BOOKING*

ROY W. KENNEY   and   BENJAMIN KLEIN
California State University,   University of California,
Northridge   Los Angeles

I. INTRODUCTION

Block booking involves "the practice of licensing, or offering for license, one feature or group of features on the condition that the exhibitor will also license another feature or group of features released by distributors during a given period."[1] This contractual arrangement, common in the American motion picture industry from as early as 1916,[2] was declared illegal in two Supreme Court decisions, *Paramount Pictures*,[3] where blocks of films were rented for theatrical exhibition, and *Loew's*,[4] where blocks of films were rented for television exhibition.

The primary legal objection to block booking is that the practice "extends monopoly power." In *Paramount* the Supreme Court stated that block booking "adds to the monopoly of a single copyrighted picture that of another copyrighted picture."[5] Similarly, in *Loew's*, the Court asserted that a distributor cannot use the market power granted by the copyright in a "desirable" film to force exhibitors to license a second "undesirable" film, stating that "the antitrust laws do not permit a compounding of

---

*We gratefully acknowledge research support from the University of Chicago Law School Antitrust Project and from the Sloan Foundation Grant to UCLA for the study of contractual arrangements. We are indebted to Armen Alchian, Frank Easterbrook, Robert Hansen, William Jennings, George Miron, Kevin M. Murphy, John Sawyer, Finis Welch, and participants at Industrial Organization workshops at UCLA and the University of Chicago for useful comments on previous drafts and to Elizabeth Granitz and Robert Hansen for research assistance.

[1] United States v. Paramount Pictures, Inc., 334 U.S. 131, 156 (1948).

[2] Terry Ramsaye, A Million and One Nights: A History of the Motion Picture 750–51 (1926).

[3] United States v. Paramount Pictures, Inc., 344 U.S. 131 (1948).

[4] United States v. Loew's, Inc., 371 U.S. 38 (1962).

[5] Paramount, 334 U.S. at 156–57, quoting the district court.

[*Journal of Law & Economics*, vol. XXVI (October 1983)]

the statutorily conferred monopoly."[6] George Stigler has trenchantly criticized this extension-of-monopoly argument by asking the obvious economic question: Why can the distributor not collect just as much revenue by using his "market power" to set the price of the desirable film?[7] If the undesirable film is "overpriced," then the desirable film must be "underpriced."

Although the monopoly extension analysis makes no sense, a satisfactory alternative economic explanation has not been developed. The commonly accepted analysis is that block booking is a subtle form of price discrimination. This explanation dates back to the Aaron Director "oral tradition" at Chicago, where the block booking practiced in *Paramount* was considered similar to IBM's "tie" of tabulating machines and cards.[8] In 1956 Director published the hypothesis that block booking was a "method of charging different prices to different customers,"[9] but he did not formalize or test it. In 1963 Stigler applied the hypothesis to the Loew's case, presenting the theoretical argument in more detail together with some apparently confirming evidence.[10] Director and Stigler's price discrimination explanation for block booking has been widely, if uncritically, accepted[11] and has led to the general acceptance of price discrimination as a major economic motivation for "bundling."[12]

The price discrimination hypothesis assumes that films vary in their relative appeal across market areas. A distributor may find it difficult to

---

[6] Loew's, 371 U.S. at 52. Justice Goldberg also based his objection to block booking on a "market foreclosure" argument, stating that "[t]elevision stations forced by appellants to take unwanted films were denied access to films marketed by other distributors who, in turn, were foreclosed from selling to the stations." *Id.* at 48–49. This argument is clearly inapplicable to the Loew's case where the blocks together accounted for a small fraction of total television station programming. At the time of the case feature films constituted less than 8 percent of a typical station's programming. *Id.* at 47. In addition, since we are dealing in the Loew's case with films that had already been produced, the marginal cost of extending their use to TV stations was a very small portion of the total license fee. With such cost conditions it is difficult to see how one distributor could possibly set up a "barrier to entry" to another distributor.

[7] George J. Stigler, United States v. Loew's, Inc.: A Note on Block Booking, 1963 Supreme Court Review 152.

[8] International Business Machine Corp. v. United States, 298 U.S. 131 (1936).

[9] See Aaron Director & Edward H. Levi, Law and the Future: Trade Regulation, 51 Nw. U. L. Rev. 281, 292 (1956).

[10] Stigler, *supra* note 7.

[11] See, for example, Ward S. Bowman, Jr., Tying Arrangements and the Leverage Problem, 67 Yale L. J. 19 (1957); Lester G. Telser, Abusive Trade Practices: An Economic Analysis, 30 Law & Contemp. Prob. 488 (1965); and Robert H. Bork, The Antitrust Paradox: A Policy at War with Itself 377–78 (1978).

[12] See William J. Adams & Janet L. Yellen, Commodity Bundling and the Burden of Monopoly, 90 Q. J. Econ. 475 (1976).

BLOCK BOOKING   499

gauge this variation as closely as the buyers can and therefore sets uniform prices across markets for each film. If, however, films that are more highly valued in some markets are the less highly valued ones in other markets, distributors may increase their revenue by assembling films into blocks, which are priced uniformly. The prices set are "discriminatory" because, although there is only one price per block, the implicit price paid for individual films will vary across markets.

This simple price discrimination explanation for block booking, although ingenious, is inconsistent with the facts of *Paramount* and *Loew's,* for the prices of the blocks varied a great deal across markets. For example, evidence in *Loew's* indicates that an eighty-five-film package distributed to television stations by National Telefilm Associates sold for $700,000 in New York City and $1,600 in Lake Charles, Louisiana.[13] There were similar price differences in the theatrical exhibition contracts in the Paramount litigation, with a possible first-run exclusive showing rental fee of $150,000 and a last-run rental fee on the same film of only $10.[14] This large price variation undermines the uniform price assumption of the simple price discrimination hypothesis.[15]

One could rescue the price discrimination hypothesis by recasting it in terms of a uniform pricing formula rather than a uniform price per block.[16] If buyers' relative values on individual films vary across markets, and the distributor sets prices in each market according to a general "average value" pricing formula (for example, in the television case a price based on the advertising rates of stations in the different markets), then he will underprice some films in some markets and other films in other markets. However, if the demand for a block of films is more closely related to the factors in the distributor's pricing formula than are the demands for the individual films in the block, the distributor can capture a larger total revenue by block pricing. Block booking then appears to be a device which aids in the distributor's pricing decision and implies price discrimi-

---

[13] National Telefilm Associates, Exhibit 11, "Dream Features," Record at Exhibits 778, 803–06, Loew's 371 U.S. 38 (1962).

[14] Michael Conant, Antitrust in the Motion Picture Industry 72 (1960).

[15] Telser, *supra* note 11, at 493, notes that "[i]t takes a somewhat complicated mathematical analysis to state precisely the conditions that would make block booking more profitable than single pricing. Roughly speaking, block booking is more profitable if the variation of the revenue for the combination among cities is not too large." In a more recent article, Lester G. Telser, A Theory of Monopoly of Complementary Goods, 52 J. Bus. 211 (1979), he presents a formal analysis of the demand conditions under which tie-ins of complementary goods can be used by a monopolist to increase its return. But once again he assumes that prices are identical across markets, which makes the analysis inapplicable to the block booking cases.

[16] See Stigler, *supra* note 7.

nation across markets in terms of deviations of implicit individual film values from what would be given by the distributor's pricing formula.

Even this more subtle statement of the price discrimination hypothesis is inconsistent with the facts of *Loew's* and *Paramount*. The analysis implicitly assumes that prices are "set" by distributors rather than determined competitively. Yet in most markets there was more than one potential buyer of the distributor's product. The contract employed by distributors in *Loew's* granted one television station an exclusive right to broadcast the given group of films in each market area. In negotiating this contract distributors could and did in fact rely on competitive bidding among stations in each market to determine price. If, as Stigler assumed, the stations have more information about individual films values than the distributor, the distributor could just let this information be revealed by competitive auctions in multiple station markets. There is no reason for the distributor to set imperfect prices on the basis of estimated demand and hence no reason for block sales. Similarly, during the period covered by the Paramount litigation most cities had more than one theater that could potentially exhibit any individual film. These theaters could, in principle, compete with one another for exhibition rights to a film. There does not appear to be any reason for distributors to set uniform or formulaic rental fees.

To develop an explanation for block booking that *is* consistent with the facts of *Loew's* and *Paramount,* we first consider the arrangement employed by De Beers to market gem-quality rough diamonds. The basic economic forces are identical in all three cases. To economize on transaction costs a group of goods of individually uncertain and difficult-to-measure quality are average priced. Such block packaging can operate only if sufficiently high brand-name capital exists. Sellers are shown to choose the particular contractual arrangement that minimizes these brand-name costs in addition to other transaction costs.

II. DE BEERS

A. *The CSO Marketing Arrangement*

The Central Selling Organization (CSO) of the De Beers group markets most of the world's gem-quality uncut diamonds. Its share in 1980 was estimated at 80–85 percent, with total sales of approximately $3 billion.[17] However, only about 40 percent of the gems sold by the CSO come from

---

[17] Timothy Green, The World of Diamonds 65 (1981). Apparently much of the approximately 20 percent of gem-quality diamonds that are not marketed through the CSO is stolen merchandise. Michael Szenberg, The Economics of the Israeli Diamond Industry 14 (1973).

the seventeen mines owned or leased by De Beers.[18] The rest are purchased from independent mine owners under long-term (five to ten year) exclusive-dealing, monthly quota production contracts. If an independent producer's monthly output is higher than the particular quota fixed by De Beers for the month, the producer is required to stockpile the excess.[19]

Why do independent mine owners market through De Beers when it appears to be more profitable for them individually to expand production and sell their output on the open market? We suggest that the cartel enforcement mechanism that has prevented the deterioration of the CSO's dominance in wholesale diamond marketing is the efficiency of the CSO's selling practices. These cost savings, related to the minimization of buyer "oversearching" for information, appear to exceed any potential extra revenue to a diamond producer from marketing outside the CSO arrangement.

The details of the CSO marketing arrangement are important for understanding our analysis. Several million rough diamonds from all sources pass through the CSO's selling office each year. The CSO sorts these stones first by shape (six categories), then by quality (about seven categories), by color (about eight categories), and, finally, by weight, resulting in more than two thousand categories.[20] The variance in the value of stones within each category is nonetheless substantial. Independent producers are paid according to the number of stones of each category they provide, with the price of the stones in each category determined by the actual selling price received by the CSO during a representative period.[21] The long-term exclusive sales requirement, in addition to controlling total supply, prevents mines from searching through their output and selecting the best stones within each category for sale on the open market rather than through De Beers.[22]

The CSO's customers consist of approximately three hundred invited diamond traders and cutters. These customers are of two types: manufac-

---

[18] Green, *supra* note 17, at 64.

[19] Godehard Lenzen, The History of Diamond Production and the Diamond Trade 190 (F. Bradley trans. 1970).

[20] De Beers Consolidated Mines, The Diamond Mines of the De Beers Group 33 (1963); and Paul Gibson, De Beers: Can a Cartel Be Forever? 123 Forbes 45 (1939).

[21] Lenzen, *supra* note 19, at 190.

[22] Such selection would result in a negative externality on all other producers of stones in the particular category because compensation is related to average quality supplied by all. In addition to preventing such free-riding distribution effects, exclusive dealing saves the real resource costs of such "cherry picking." For a further examination of exclusive dealing as a mechanism to prevent wasteful preselection in a nonmonopsony context, see Edward C. Gallick & Benjamin Klein, Exclusive Dealing, Specialized Assets, and Joint Ownership: A Study of Tuna Fishing Contracts (Working Paper, UCLA, Dep't Econ. 1983).

turers who have their own cutting and polishing facilities and a few deal-ers in each cutting center in the world who supply small manufacturers.[23] Each customer is expected to buy regularly and, since average annual sales per customer are approximately $10 million, is screened to be financially sound.[24]

Each of the CSO's customers periodically informs the CSO of the kinds and quantities of diamonds it wishes to purchase. The CSO then assem-bles a single box (or "sight") of diamonds for the customer. Each box contains a number of folded, envelope-like packets called papers. The gems within each paper are similar and correspond to one of the CSO's classifications. The composition of any sight may differ slightly from that specified by the buyer because the supply of diamonds in each category is limited.

Once every five weeks, primarily at the CSO's offices in London, the diamond buyers are invited to inspect their sights.[25] Each box is marked with the buyer's name and a price. A single box may carry a price of up to several million pounds.[26] Each buyer examines his sight before deciding whether to buy. Each buyer may spend as long as he wishes, examining his sight to see that each stone is graded correctly (that is, fits the descrip-tion marked on each parcel). There is no negotiation over the price or composition of the sight. In rare cases where a buyer claims that a stone has been miscategorized by the CSO, and the sales staff agrees, the sight will be adjusted.[27] If a buyer rejects the sight, he is offered no alternative box. Rejection is extremely rare, however, because buyers who reject the diamonds offered them are deleted from the list of invited customers.[28]

Thus stones (*a*) are sorted by De Beers into imperfectly homogeneous categories, (*b*) to be sold in preselected blocks, (*c*) to preselected buyers, (*d*) at nonnegotiable prices, with (*e*) buyers' rejection of the sales offer leading to the withdrawal by De Beers of future invitations to purchase stones.

B. Oversearching

Because the De Beers sorting procedure implies a substantial variance in the value of stones within each quality category, stones within such

---

[23] Green, *supra* note 17, at 148. Given the fixed cost of traveling to London, it will not be economic for small manufacturers located in the cutting centers to deal directly with the CSO. In addition, as we shall see, it is economic for the CSO to limit the number and therefore the minimum size of customers.

[24] *Id.*

[25] Gibson, *supra* note 20, at 46.

[26] H. L. Van der Laan, The Sierra Leone Diamonds 95–96 (1965); and Gibson, *supra* note 20, at 49.

[27] Green, *supra* note 17, at 151.

[28] Szenberg, *supra* note 17, at 14.

categories therefore can be said to be average priced. Consumers faced with such a situation will have an incentive to search for undervalued goods and to find the exceptional values first. For example, consider a bin of oranges. If the oranges vary in quality but sell for a uniform price, each potential buyer has an incentive to inspect more oranges than he wants to buy, hoping to find those of unusually high quality (which are therefore undervalued). The problem is that the prices set by the seller for different qualities of oranges are not equal to market clearing prices and consumers will search out the higher quality oranges and leave the poorer quality oranges behind. A Gresham's Law type of phenomenon is created.[29]

The average price set by the seller is determined by his knowledge. Unless he is omniscient and costlessly knows the exact market value of each stone, we can expect buyers to search for the underpriced stones. While such prepurchase inspections consume real resources, they can be assumed to lead only to wealth transfers between consumers and the seller with no allocative effects.[30] The attempt by buyers to obtain an informational advantage over the seller can thus be labeled "oversearching."[31]

[29] Gresham's Law was originally applied to full-bodied metallic currency. The law stated that when both good (full weight) and bad (light, clipped, or sweated) coins circulate at par, the "bad coins will drive out the good." People will remove the "undervalued" fullbodied coins from circulation and use the metal for nonmonetary purposes (including foreign trade). This same effect occurs with the oranges. Early arriving shoppers will expend real resources to find the most undervalued oranges, and shoppers arriving late will find that the average quality of the remaining oranges has fallen. Note, however, that if consumers differ in their ability to search out different qualities and this ability is related to elasticity of demand, the bunching of different qualities together by the seller may be intentional price discrimination.

[30] We are assuming that price-adjusted high- and low-quality units of the good are perfect substitutes. For example, the quality of oranges may be measured solely in terms of amount of juice, and an average high-quality orange may yield twice as much juice as an average low-quality orange and sell for double the price. However, if one type of orange is preferred for a particular use (for example, juicing), some search would be socially valuable.

[31] Our analysis of excess search for quality information is equivalent to the Hirshleifer analysis of speculative oversearch, Jack Hirshleifer, The Private and Social Value of Information and the Reward to Inventive Activity, 61 Am. Econ. Rev. 561 (1971); to the analysis regarding the overinvestment in education as a screening device, Michael Spence, Job Market Signaling, 87 Q. J. Econ. 355 (1973); and, more generally, to the competition for the establishment of property rights, see Don Gordon, The Economic Theory of a Common-Property Resource: The Fishery, 62 J. Pol. Econ. 124 (1954); Steven Cheung, The Structure of a Contract and the Theory of a Nonexclusive Resource, 13 J. Law & Econ. 49 (1970); and Edmund Kitch, The Nature and Function of the Patent System, 20 J. Law & Econ. 265 (1977). In these cases, as in ours, the return to an investment is assumed to be purely distributive. Barzel has noted, in the spirit of our analysis, "The fact that many information situations have the potential for waste does not necessarily mean that waste actually occurs. If, in the aggregate, these actions produce a negative product, arrangements that successfully restrain them or reduce their impact will generate a positive return." Yoram Barzel, Some Fallacies in the Interpretation of Information Costs, 20 J. Law & Econ. 291, 292 (1977). In this context he discusses briefly the De Beers's selling practices and the supposed

Since buyers will have to examine the stones before they are cut (the exact placement of each flaw, chip, and inclusion must be discovered to determine the size of the largest finished gem that can be cut from each diamond), it may seem as if buyer inspection is necessary and hence Gresham's Law oversearching is costless. However, buyer search produces two costly effects: duplicative buyer inspections and induced increases in seller sorting.

The search for underpriced stones within a quality classification implies that some stones will be inspected and not purchased. Whether there is a social cost associated with persons' examining the quality of goods they do not then buy depends on the goods and buyers in question. When buyers have different tastes, duplicate inspections are necessary for each buyer to acquire the particular units that most closely satisfy his particular desires. Tastes vary considerably among people considering, for example, the purchase of a diamond engagement ring, and duplicate inspections are necessary for allocative efficiency.

In contrast, we may assume that each wholesale buyer places essentially the same value on rough uncut stones offered for sale by De Beers within the various quality categories. With a reasonable amount of search, all would agree very closely on the relative value of the different stones; they would agree on how to cut and set the stones and how long it would probably take to sell them (that is, on the inventory costs).[32] Because wholesale search is not necessary for the stones to go to the highest valuing ultimate user, and because whoever purchases the stones must inspect each closely no matter how much prepurchase inspection was done in the aggregate by other potential buyers, duplicate inspections in such a situation waste real resources.

On the other hand, very large stones weighing more than 14.8 carats, where presumably estimates of value vary considerably among buyers, are not included in the CSO sights. Instead of being sold on a fixed average-price basis, they are offered to particular buyers on an individual stone, negotiated-price basis. The buyers offered large stones are free to reject them without endangering their relationship with the CSO.[33]

---

gains which result from prepackaging of gems, *id.* at 304. Our analysis, which emphasizes the importance of prespecified buyers earning rents within a repeat-sale/brand-name enforcement mechanism, builds on his insightful work.

[32] Since the sight holders are purchasing stones for resale in fairly thick markets, the presumption that each values the same stones equally is reasonable. The hypothesis that the De Beers scheme is a method of interbuyer price discrimination, see, for example, Kenneth W. Clarkson & Roger L. Miller, Industrial Organization: Theory Evidence and Public Policy 244 (1982), is therefore highly unlikely to be correct. De Beers can neither take advantage of different consumer surpluses between buyers nor, in the long-run, appropriate the quasi rents between different-skilled cutters.

[33] Until his death in 1978, Harry Winston, a New York diamond dealer, was usually given the first opportunity to examine and purchase these stones. Green, *supra* note 17, at 152.

The attempt by buyers to discover underpriced stones would lead to lower total revenue to De Beers. After the buyer search, if underpriced stones within a classification were purchased and overpriced stones rejected, the CSO would be forced to lower its price to sell any of the remaining stones of lower than average quality—and buyer oversearching would begin again. To prevent this costly adverse selection process, the CSO could be expected to increase their initial classification effort. Increased expenditures on the quality sorting process would result in more accurate average prices, that is, a reduced variance in the value of stones within each quality classification, and hence higher total revenue received in the face of oversearching.

Oversearching will be eliminated entirely only if the seller is omniscient and can perfectly set the correct (market-clearing) price and buyers learn this. With any finite expenditure of resources by the diamond seller, gems will not be valued perfectly. Rather, gems will be categorized, with some remaining variance of quality within each classification. Therefore, some units of detectably different qualities will be offered at the same price and the potential for buyer oversearch remains.

More important, much of the quality search conducted by De Beers in attempting to set prices very accurately would be duplicative. Because the specific information required by the cutter to cut each stone optimally cannot be costlessly communicated by De Beers, we can reasonably assume that the cutter will have to examine the stone more closely no matter how much information De Beers collects in setting prices. Rather than engage in excessive quality search necessary to price each stone accurately, we can expect the CSO to adopt an alternative arrangement to minimize buyer oversearch. A marketing arrangement that prevented oversearching could increase the profitability of De Beers by the real resources they and their buyers expend on duplicate inspections.

C. Preselected Buyers Earning a Premium Stream

The CSO does not sell diamonds in average-priced quality classification bins through which buyers are permitted to search. Rather, the CSO assigns each sight of diamonds to a particular preselected buyer. However, if buyers could "freely" reject the sights they were assigned, they would accept only those they considered undervalued. The rejected sights would presumably have to be repriced at a lower level and assigned once again to another buyer, implying duplicative oversearch. In addition, De Beers would receive a lower price for its diamonds than the average of the value of all stones represented within each of its classifications.

Given that it is not economic for De Beers to spend the large amount of money that would be necessary to price sights perfectly, they must devise an alternative way to discourage buyers from rejecting their assigned sights. The CSO accomplishes this by pricing in such a way that buyers on average are earning rents the present discounted value of which is greater in almost all cases than the short-run profit that can be achieved by rejecting the sights of lower than average quality. Since these rents are lost if the buyer decides to reject a sight and is terminated from the list of invited buyers, a wealth-maximizing buyer will not generally reject sights, with the implied duplicative search, but will examine and purchase his own allotted sight.

This is analytically identical (but the transactors are reversed) to the Klein-Leffler case of a seller with a valuable reputation who is prevented from cheating a buyer.[34] In that case the seller receives a premium stream for the continued provision of high-quality goods to the buyer. In this case, the seller (the CSO) "pays" a premium to its buyers by selling diamonds at less than (costless-search) market-clearing prices. This premium serves to encourage the buyer to take low-quality goods occasionally. The payment of the premium is offset by savings in marketing costs, that is, the avoidance of oversearching, made possible by encouraging buyers to go along with the CSO's marketing scheme. The right to be on the CSO's list of invited buyers appears to be a valuable asset, the capital value of which is greater than any short-run incentive for buyers to search and reject overpriced sights.[35]

The CSO can minimize the costs of this arrangement by reducing the number of buyers on their list of invitees. This can be seen by assuming that the CSO intends to sell m stones each period forever. Let X_i equal the quality of the ith stone, measured in dollars. Assume further that the qualities of the stones marketed each period are identically, independently, and normally distributed random variables with means μ and variances σ^2:

$$X_1, \ldots, X_m \sim N(\mu, \sigma^2). \tag{1}$$

---

[34] See Benjamin Klein & Keith Leffler, The Role of Market Forces in Assuring Contractual Performance, 89 J. Pol. Econ. 615 (1981).

[35] Our argument is analogous to the economic rationalization for a manufacturer to have retailers earn a profit premium with the use of resale price maintenance and entry restrictions. See Benjamin Klein, Andrew McLaughlin, & Kevin M. Murphy, The Economics of Resale Price Maintenance: The Coors Case (Working Paper, UCLA, Dep't Econ. 1983). The existence of excess demand to be on the CSO list of invited buyers is evidence that presence on the list is a valuable asset. A number of qualified dealers have stated that they would like to be able to buy directly from the CSO. Van der Laan, *supra* note 26, at 98. De Beers does not sell this right to be an invited buyer for an initial lump-sum payment because of the additional "seller cheating" incentives that are created. (Intentional supply of low quality stones with buyer termination and resale of purchase rights by De Beers.) For further discussion of seller cheating see Section *E infra*.

Let P_i equal the price set by the CSO on the ith stone, such that

$$P_i = X_i - c + \epsilon, \tag{2}$$

where X_i equals the quality or "true" value of the ith stone to a buyer, determined after buyer inspection; c is a constant; and ϵ is a random variable distributed $N(0, \sigma_\epsilon^2)$. The expected premium to the buyer from acceptance of the CSO sale offer of the ith stone is $X_i - P_i$, or c.[36]

Consider two alternative marketing arrangements: (1) the CSO offers the m diamonds per period to m different buyers, that is, one stone per buyer, and (2) the CSO sells the m diamonds per period by offering $n(>1)$ stones per period to each of $j(<n)$ buyers, where $n = m/j$.[37] In arrangement 1, where each buyer is assumed to purchase one stone per period forever, the expected present discounted value to a buyer of remaining on the CSO list of invited buyers is

$$PV_1 = \frac{E(X_i - P_i)}{r} = \frac{E(c - \epsilon)}{r}$$

$$= \frac{c}{r}. \tag{3}$$

The capital cost to a buyer of rejecting an individual stone after examination and being blacklisted by the CSO is therefore c/r. Hence, a buyer will reject an individual stone if and only if

$$P_i - X_i > \frac{c}{r}. \tag{4}$$

Under arrangement 2, where each buyer is offered n stones per period forever, the expected present discounted value to the buyer of remaining on the CSO list of invited buyers is

$$PV_2 = \frac{nE(X_i - P_i)}{r} = \frac{nE(c - \epsilon)}{r}$$

$$= \frac{nc}{r}; \tag{5}$$

---

[36] Note that, more realistically, the expected premium is not a constant but is determined by past CSO behavior. Therefore, for example, if the buyer receives a stone where P_i is greater than X_i, the anticipated premium can be expected to fall. This will be discussed further in Section E *infra* when we consider the possibility of intentional deception by the CSO.

[37] We are not assuming here that the n stones are offered to the buyer on a "block" (single price, take it or leave it) basis. We want to consider only the effect of decreasing the number of buyers or, equivalently, the repurchase period. Section D *infra* considers the "blocking" question.

and a buyer will reject an individual stone if and only if[38]

$$P_i - X_i > \frac{nc}{r}. \tag{6}$$

It is therefore obvious that the expected number of stones rejected will be different for the two arrangements. The probability that a buyer in arrangement 1 will reject an individual stone is

$$
\begin{aligned}
P_r(1) &= P_r\left(P_i - X_i > \frac{c}{r}\right) \\
&= P_r\left(\epsilon - c > \frac{c}{r}\right) \\
&= P_r\left(\epsilon > c + \frac{c}{r}\right).
\end{aligned} \tag{7}
$$

The probability that a buyer in arrangement 2 will reject an individual stone is

$$
\begin{aligned}
P_r(2) &= P_r\left(P_i - X_i > \frac{nc}{r}\right) \\
&= P_r\left(\epsilon - c > \frac{nc}{r}\right) \\
&= P_r\left(\epsilon > c + \frac{nc}{r}\right).
\end{aligned} \tag{8}
$$

These rejection probabilities are represented by the cross-hatched areas in Figure 1. The CSO can decrease the probability that stones will be rejected (and hence duplicative quality inspection will occur) by (i) increasing expenditure on presale classification, and thereby decreasing σ_ϵ; (ii) by increasing the share of the marketing cost savings, the premium per stone, c, going to buyers; or (iii) by increasing the number of stones offered to each buyer per period n.

Decreasing the number of buyers (and hence increasing the number of stones each buyer receives per period) while keeping the expected premium per stone constant, raises the capital value to each buyer of remain-

---

[38] Expression (6) actually underestimates how much an individual stone must be overpriced in order for the buyer to reject it, since it excludes the lost premium on additional stones offered "this" period. It should more properly be considered the rejection point for the "last" stone offered in the current period. In addition, it underestimates the necessary overprice for rejection, because the expected value to a buyer of playing this game is greater than nc/r. Even if c equaled zero, buyers would obtain an expected return from the ability to reject, that is, from the ability to determine the last period. The expected value would be an average of the underpriced and slightly overpriced stones accepted before rejection; nc/r represents the total expected return given the absence of any rejection, which turns out to be our equilibrium condition.

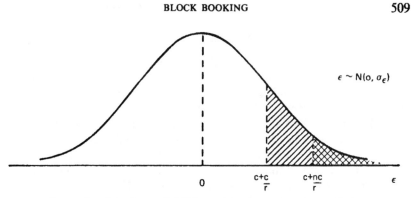

FIGURE 1.—Rejection probabilities, one versus *n* stones per period

ing on the CSO list of invited buyers. He is therefore less likely to reject any individual stone. Alternatively, for any given rejection probability the CSO can decrease the premium per stone as the number of buyers is also decreased. What limits this economizing process short of one or a few buyers the diseconomies of scale in cutting the stones. Given the fairly small scale of manufacture,[39] limiting the sale of rough diamonds to a few buyers would imply reselling of the stones before they are cut and hence oversearching.

Given the number of continuing buyers, the CSO wealth maximizing decisions concern (*a*) how much should be spent on categorizing and evaluating stones, thereby affecting the distribution of the actual values of stones around anticipated values,[40] and (*b*) how much of the total marketing cost savings should be shared with buyers by pricing stones at less than anticipated values. Given a particular sharing decision (that is, a given expected premium stream received by buyers), a greater categorization expenditure will reduce the variance of the value of stones and hence the number of stones rejected (and therefore the extent of duplicative searching). On the other hand, given a particular categorization expenditure and hence quality variance of price standardized stones, a greater share of the marketing cost saving that is passed on to buyers (that is, a greater price premium stream) will also imply fewer rejections and less duplicative searching.[41]

[39] For example, in 1961 the majority of people employed in the Israeli diamond cutting industry, which accounts for 30 percent of the world's output, worked in firms with thirty to ninety-nine employees. Szenberg, *supra* note 17, at 17, 60.

[40] The CSO "warranty" that gross classification "mistakes" will be corrected can be seen as a means of economizing on categorization expenditures in producing the desired underlying variance in stone quality within each stated classification.

[41] The premium per stone necessary to prevent rejection is quite small. Given the CSO physical classification process and the fact that mistakes are adjusted by the CSO, the

D. Block Selling

If the qualities of the individual stones within a classification are assumed to be independent, as seems reasonable, block selling does not generally decrease the incentive of buyers, each of whom is assumed to be receiving a given total number of stones per unit time and hence a given future premium stream, to reject stones. This can best be seen by continuing to assume that the CSO wishes to sell n stones per period forever to each of j buyers and, from equation (5), the present value to a buyer of remaining on the CSO list of invited buyers is nc/r, where c is the expected premium per stone. As we have seen, if an individual buyer is offered an individual stone, he will reject it only if it is overpriced by more than nc/r (eq. [6]) and the probability of this occurring is given by equation (8).

Alternatively, if the individual buyer is offered n stones this period at a block price of P_B, take it or leave it, the buyer will reject the package if and only if

$$P_B - n\bar{X}_B > \frac{nc}{r}, \tag{9}$$

where $\bar{X}_B$ is the average quality of a stone in the block. That is, once again a buyer will reject the package if and only if its price exceeds its total value by more than the present discounted value of the expected premium stream of remaining on the list of invited buyers. Since

$$P_B = n\bar{X}_B - nc + \Sigma\epsilon_i, \tag{10}$$

the probability that the block will be rejected by a buyer, pr (B), is equal to

$$\begin{aligned} \text{pr } (B) &= \text{pr}\left(\Sigma\epsilon_i - nc > \frac{nc}{r}\right) \\ &= \text{pr}\left(\Sigma\epsilon_i > nc + \frac{nc}{r}\right). \end{aligned} \tag{11}$$

That is, in order for rejection to occur, the total error of the n stones in the block must exceed n times the expected premium per stone plus the same critical capital value of the future premium stream value.

---

distribution of the value of stones within a category is not likely to be approximated by a normal distribution but rather by a distribution with much smaller tails and possibly a finite range. If, for example, the underlying distribution of an average value sight of $1 million is uniform between $.5 million and $1.5 million and there are ten sights a year, a premium per sight of only $5,000, or .5 percent of the average value, would be sufficient to prevent rejection of any sight if the interest rate were 10 percent. Only if a buyer underestimates the future expected premium stream or overestimates the quality deviation relative to the CSO estimates will a sight be rejected and the buyer be terminated by the CSO. We have not been able to find any examples of such buyer behavior and CSO punishment.

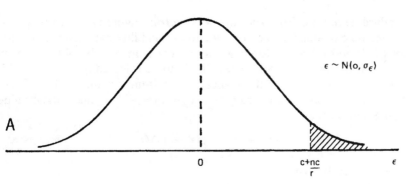

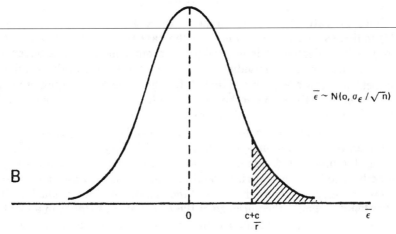

FIGURE 2.—Rejection probabilities, single stone versus block: *A*, single stone, equation
(8); *B*, block, equation (12).

To compare the single stone and block experiments more easily, equation (11) is rewritten in terms of the average error of stones in the block:

$$P_r(B) = P_r\left(\bar{\epsilon} > c + \frac{c}{r}\right), \tag{12}$$

and the rejection probabilities given by equations (8) and (12) are represented by the shaded areas in Figure 2.

Whether the block will be rejected more or less frequently is not obvious from examination of Figure 2. Although the standard error of the average random error of the stones included in the block is less than the standard error of the random error of an individual stone, the critical rejection value for the average error is less than that for the individual stone error. The question is whether $c + c/r$ in Figure 2B is more or fewer standard deviations from zero than $c + nc/r$ in Figure 2A. Because $\sigma_{\bar{\epsilon}} = \sigma_\epsilon/\sqrt{n}$, we can standardize our rejection probability expressions in equations (12) and (8) by multiplying the critical point for the block case by $\sqrt{n}$. That is, the block will be less likely to be rejected [$pr(1) > P_r(B)$] if and only if $c(r + n)/r$, the critical value from equation (8), is fewer standard deviations away from zero than $c(r + 1)/r$, the critical value from equation (12), or

$$\frac{c(r + n)}{r} < \frac{c(r + 1)\sqrt{n}}{r},\tag{13}$$

or, equivalently, when

$$r > \sqrt{n}.\tag{14}$$

Since the rate of interest is unlikely to be greater than $\sqrt{n}$, equation (14) indicates that it is generally not the case that the block will be less likely to be rejected. It is generally much more likely that a buyer will reject a block than an individual stone. The intuitiveness of this result can be seen as follows. We have assumed that the value of the future premium stream, nc/r, is the same in the case of both the individual stone and the block.[42] It follows that if this premium stream value is substantial, the probability of rejecting an individual stone must be essentially zero. If, for example, individual stones are priced at \$1,000 and nc/r is \$10,000, it is impossible that an individual stone will ever be rejected. Each individual stone by itself supplies such a small amount of information that a buyer will never reject solely on the basis of the individual observation.[43] On the other hand, because the variance of the *total* value of stones in a block is necessarily larger, the likelihood that a block will be overpriced by nc/r, and hence the probability of rejection, is necessarily larger.

Although not blocking appears to reduce the probability of rejection, it is far from obvious what such a selling arrangement would consist of.

---

[42] As we noted above, see note 38 *supra*, the lost premium stream resulting from rejection is identical in the two cases only if we consider the individual stone to be the last stone offered in the current period. However, we want to assume that the buyers in the two cases are offered the same number of stones each period to avoid the effect that increasing the number of stones per period, whether blocked priced or not, has on decreasing rejection probabilities. Therefore, in general, the value of the lost premium stream will be greater in the individual stone case than indicated in the text. (For example, if the stone is the first stone of the period we must add $(n - 1)c$ as the lost premium this period to the nc/r lost in the future.) Hence, modifying our analysis in this manner would reinforce our results—it would be even less likely that an "average" individual stone will ever be rejected.

[43] It appears that the CSO can continue to supply low quality stones without any danger of rejection. However, if the expected premium per stone is assumed more realistically not to be a constant but to be endogenously determined by past CSO behavior, the expected premium stream and critical rejection value will decrease over time.

Presumably, rather than one price being given for the entire sight, each stone would be individually priced. However, since there are thousands of very small diamond chips in many sights, in terms of increased transaction costs this would be analogous to putting a price tag on each kernel in a can of corn. As an alternative, at very little additional transaction cost we could certainly imagine separate prices on each individual diamond packet ("paper") in the sight.

How are the individually priced stones or packets in the sight to be offered to nonblock buyers? One obvious alternative would be a sequential presentation of the stones with rejection of any individual stone leading to immediate termination of additional sales in this and future periods. This arrangement is similar to what we have analyzed above and implies that an individual stone will be less likely to be rejected. For that reason sequential presentation increases the seller's potential to cheat buyers by supplying a nonrandom (overpriced) sample of stones. As opposed to block pricing, or the presentation of all of this period's stones before the buyer purchases any stones, buyers do not see the entire period's supply. A cheating seller can assume that buyers who would reject an entire period's package of stones if it were made available for them to inspect would initially accept some overpriced stones when they are offered and examined sequentially. As an extreme case, if the buyer's entire promised lifetime supply were sold in a block this period, then seller cheating would not be possible. With sequential pricing buyers are, in a sense, locked into past decisions regarding acceptance.

Although a theoretical framework of sequential search is "natural" to an economist familiar with the standard models of, for example, labor market search,[44] such a framework is difficult to consider as a realistic marketing alternative. The transaction costs of instituting such a sequential arrangement generally would be prohibitive. The idea of a produce man in a grocery store handing each customer individually priced oranges one at a time, or the CSO salesman's presenting a sight to each buyer one individually priced stone or paper at a time, is extremely counterintuitive. The marketing costs of such an arrangement would be so high as to make the suggestion close to nonsense.

A reasonable alternative definition of nonblock sales may be the presentation to the buyer of a package of n individually priced stones, where the buyer is not forced to accept the entire package on a take it or leave it basis. Buyers could be told that if they rejected any individual stone in the package they would not be invited in the future to purchase stones, but in

[44] S. A. Lippman & J. J. McCall, The Economics of Job Search (pts. 1,2), 14 Econ. Inquiry 153, 347 (1976).

principle they would not be facing a blocked marketing arrangement this period. Yet such a marketing alternative implies greatly increased costs of oversearching. If CSO priced each of the stones in a sight individually and let buyers search through their sights and reject any individual stones they wished to, such a nonblocked arrangement would increase the last period gains to a buyer rejecting stones and substantially increase rejection probabilities.

In terms of our previous framework, a buyer will reject a block if and only if it is overpriced by more than the future expected premium, or, rewriting equation (9),

$$\sum_i (P_i - X_i) > \frac{nc}{r}. \tag{15}$$

With separate prices a buyer will reject some stones if equation (15) holds, but also more generally, if

$$\sum_{(X_i - P_i)>0} (X_i - P_i) > \frac{nc}{r}. \tag{16}$$

That is, even if equation (15) does not hold, if the sum of the deviations of all underpriced stones in the package is greater than the capital value of the future expected premium stream, it will pay for the buyer to search through and separate out these stones and take his return now by rejecting the remaining stones in the package. Rather than increasing its categorization expenditures or the premium per stone it pays to buyers, the CSO prevents such increased rejection by demanding purchase or rejection of the entire sight.[45]

More generally, the exact manner in which this period's n stones are priced is not as important as the fact that this period's transaction is not isolated but rather is part of a long-term continuing relationship. The crucial element of the De Beers marketing arrangement is not the block price in the current period but the large block sale over time to prespecified buyers. A limited number of repeat buyers are promised n stones per period forever, on which they expect to earn a valuable premium per stone. These rents and the termination provisions established by the CSO encourage buyers not to search and reject any particular sight, whether the sight consists of an individual stone or of a larger

---

[45] Even if eq. (15) held and stones would be rejected whether block priced or not, there is no reason to permit a buyer who determined his entire sight was so significantly overpriced as to reject it then to select out and purchase the most underpriced stones in the package. This would merely transfer wealth from the CSO to last-period buyers before they are terminated.

subset of the promised total "lifetime" supply. While separate pricing of the *n* stones supplied in any period eliminates the conditional tie-in sale within that period, it is the temporal conditional tie-in sale between periods of seller selected stones that is essential for the marketing arrangement.

E. "Blind" Selling and Seller Brand Names

The CSO could prevent buyer rejection of sights and hence oversearching without any rent sharing (buyer premium) merely by prohibiting buyer search, that is, by completing the contracting process and demanding payment before the buyer has an opportunity to examine the stones. Although this may seem unusual, it is a fairly common marketing practice. For example, a seller of potatoes may prepackage and sell them in opaque bags. Because hiding the quality information eliminates the incentive for buyers to search, such a policy by the seller may be both profit maximizing and socially efficient.[46] More generally, some element of blindness is present in all transactions where buyers do not know fully every characteristic of the product being sold or where contract specification and enforcement is not perfect, that is, every transaction where buyers rely on seller brand names to some extent.

The problem involved in prohibiting all consumer prepurchase inspection is that it creates an increased incentive for the seller to cheat buyers and hence the necessity for increased brand-name capital. If goods are sold blindly, sellers can intentionally supply a very low quality product and earn an extra short-run profit. This extra profit occurs only for a short period of time because buyers that are so cheated will refuse to purchase on such terms from the seller in the future.

The "seller cheating" problem in the case of the marketing of diamonds is the intentional supply by the CSO of low-quality (overpriced) gems. When such cheating is detected, buyers will refuse to purchase from the CSO on the same basis. Therefore, cheating is prevented if the extra

---

[46] An example where a producer deliberately made prepurchase quality inspection more difficult can be found in FTC v. Adolph Coors Co., 83 FTC 32 (1973). Coors, a producer of beer with a limited shelf life, resisted a suggestion by the FTC that it open-date its product by marking each can with a packaging date. The additional cost of open-dating would be small, since each can was already marked with the packaging date in code. Coors's resistance may be rational because the open-dating would encourage inefficient search by prospective purchasers and the necessity for a sliding scale of prices or a costly dispensing mechanism. With the dates in code, purchasers are forced to take a "random" sample from the seller's shelves. In addition, open dating would "advertise" the beer's limited shelf life and possibly decrease consumer demand. See Klein, McLaughlin, & Murphy, *supra* note 35. In addition to preventing inefficient oversearch, blind packaging reduces search and hence the uncompensated damage to goods that occurs in the process.

short-run profit that could be earned by the CSO is less than the present discounted value of the cost savings of their marketing arrangement.[47]

Under blindness the capital value of short-run profit from intentionally supplying stones of a lower quality than anticipated is likely to be greater than the discounted value of the lost marketing cost savings after the selling arrangement collapses. While extreme forms of cheating, for example, placing gravel in packets and selling it as diamonds, could be prevented by explicit contractual specification of sale terms, the remaining short-run cheating potential is enormous. Given the CSO's imperfect classification process and somewhat subjective categories, the CSO's ability for short-run deception of blind purchasers of contractually specified grades of diamonds appears to be sufficiently high to prevent the use of blindness without some additional costly, firm-specific, nonsalvageable investments by the CSO.

Permitting prepurchase inspections reduces the CSO's short-run cheating potential but, as we have seen, makes it necessary to share the marketing cost savings of the CSO selling arrangement with buyers to prevent rejection of sights. For the CSO this is cheaper than the increased brand-name capital investment required under blindness. In equilibrium the present discounted value of the marketing cost savings net of the premium paid to buyers is greater than the lower short-run cheating potential under a system of buyer inspection.

The CSO can be thought of as possessing two distinct "brand names"—the expected discounted value of the net marketing cost efficiencies associated with their selling arrangement, which assures buyers that they will not cheat, and a reputation that it will share these marketing cost savings with buyers in the future, which prevents buyers from "cheating" them. De Beers's "monopolistic" return can be thought of as a normal return on these brand-name assets, and the likely economies of scale in creating these assets explain the stability of the marketing arrangement.

III. THE PARAMOUNT CASE

A. *The Economic and Legal Setting*

During the 1930s and 1940s, before the introduction and growth of television, movie attendance in the United States was substantially

---

[47] This is analogous to the mechanism used to prevent reverse franchisor cheating on franchisees by unfair termination. See Benjamin Klein, The Borderlines of Law and Economic Theory: Transaction Cost Determinants of "Unfair" Contractual Arrangements, 70 Am. Econ. Rev. Papers & Proc. 356 (1980).

greater than it is today.[48] On average, about five hundred feature films were produced yearly, with each of the eight largest motion picture distributors releasing between twenty-five and sixty films a year. The five "majors" named in the Paramount suit accounted for 73.3 percent of domestic film rentals in the 1943–44 season.[49] Distributors were fully integrated backward into production and partially integrated forward into theatrical exhibition.

Exhibition consisted of a series of separate runs over time, with contractually specified clearance periods between each run within designated geographical zones. First-run exhibition accounted for between 30 and 50 percent of total receipts, with later runs accounting for smaller and smaller fractions of revenues.[50] The last-run or neighborhood theater was the closest thing to television viewership today. While first-run theaters generally supplied a single feature program in elaborate surroundings for a variable period of time, often a few weeks, neighborhood theaters catered more to families and usually offered a program of double bills, shorts, and newsreels, changing their programs frequently, often twice a week. Of the approximately 18,075 theaters in operation in 1945, the eight largest distributors had an interest in 3,137, or 17 percent. However, their representation in first-run exhibition was large, controlling more than 70 percent of the first-run theaters in the nation's ninety-two largest cities.[51]

First-run admission prices were higher than later-run prices, with film licensing contracts specifying minimum admission prices for each exhibitor and run. Distributor-set prices combined with the geographically and chronologically separated exhibition schedules implied by distributor-set run and clearance terms created a fairly transparent marketing arrangement to facilitate price discrimination among consumers.

Film rental terms generally were stated in contingent form, that is, percentage of gross revenues for earlier run showings and flat fee per time for later runs. Percentage rental terms were generally stated as a simple fraction of admissions revenue until some dollar amount, or splitting point, after which the rental percentage would be increased. (Sliding per-

[48] Average weekly movie attendance peaked during the immediate postwar period (1945–48) at 90 million, a figure greater than half of the total U.S. population. By 1953, weekly attendance had dropped nearly 50 percent to 46 million, clearly reflecting the growth of television ownership. Recently the market has become even more limited in size and also in the age of customers. Weekly attendance in 1976 was about 18 million people, 74 percent of whom were under thirty years of age. Cobbett S. Steinberg, Film Facts 45–46 (1980).

[49] Conant, *supra* note 14, at 36. Current annual U.S. production is approximately two hundred films, Steinberg, *supra* note 48, at 43, and distribution is less concentrated.

[50] The actual number of runs depended on size of city, with, for example, eleven runs in the 1930s in Chicago and fewer runs in smaller cities. Conant, *supra* note 14, at 69–70, 155.

[51] *Id.* at 48–50.

centages of gross as a positive function of revenues—that is, multiple splitting points—sometimes existed.) Films were generally grouped in four or five categories or "classes" (determined largely by budgetary considerations) with different rental terms for each category. Percentage rental terms also declined with length of run and were sometimes specified to be lower for midnight shows.[52] Percentage rentals generally ranged up to a maximum of 50 percent, after the split point, for the first week and first run of the best films.[53]

Contracts between distributors and theaters for the exhibition rights to films typically covered a group or block of several different films. Since these "block-booked" contracts were made prior to the films' production, they were also said to be "blind sold." It is important to recognize that a common description of the usual block booking contract as an arrangement where "an independent exhibitor had to agree to license the distributor's entire yearly output of features or he could license none,"[54] is clearly an inaccurate description of the practice. Only in the case of the small, late-run neighborhood theaters was demand sufficiently large for the exhibitor to choose to license the entire annual stock of several distributors. More generally, early-run theaters, including those owned by producer-distributors, contracted on a block basis for the "best" films available from various distributors to fill out their annual schedules. Contracting for a distributor's entire schedule was therefore relatively rare.[55]

---

[52] See *id.* at 70; Howard Lewis, The Motion Picture Industry 191–200 (1933); and Brief for the United States, app. United States v. Paramount, for a description of the contracts.

[53] See Brief for the United States, app. United States v. Paramount. Gone With The Wind was licensed at the very unusual rate of 70 percent. See Motion Picture Films (Compulsory Block Booking and Blind Selling): Hearings on S. 280 Before the House Comm. on Interstate and Foreign Commerce, 76th Cong., 3d Sess. 542 (1940) (hereinafter cited as 1940 Congressional Hearings) (statement of William F. Rodgers). Today, film rental terms range up to 90 percent of gross, after deducting a contractually specified amount to cover exhibition costs (that is, the "house nut"). However, average film rental fees remain quite similar, with a 34 percent average rate paid currently (Steinberg, *supra* note 48, at 40); the average rate paid by the affiliated theaters to the eight distributor defendants was 27 percent, Brief of the Warner Defendants to the Supreme Court at 138, U.S. v. Paramount.

[54] Conant, *supra* note 14, at 77.

[55] Twentieth Century–Fox sold its entire output of fifty-two films in 1938–39 to less than 20 percent of their accounts. The bookings for the fifty-two films distributed by Paramount during the 1938–39 season ranged from 14,261 to 4,408 with a median of 7,855 (1940 Congressional Hearings, *supra* note 53, at 469, 584 (testimony of Charles C. Pettijohn and Hammond Woober, respectively). The Famous Players–Lasky Corp. (predecessor of Paramount) licensed their entire annual film output to only 4.6, 2.6, and 4.7 percent of the exhibitors they dealt with in 1922, 1923, and 1924, respectively. Lewis, *supra* note 52, at 158–59. Part of the confusion regarding the nature of the practice may be due to the fact that the original "trust" method of distributing films pre-1920 appears to have involved complete "program booking"; that is, the distributor's films were rented on an all or nothing basis. See Ralph Cassady, The Impact of the Paramount Decision on Motion Picture Distribution

Most exhibitors dealt with too many different distributors to exhibit all of each distributor's films, shorts, and newsreels.[56]

After an unsuccessful earlier attempt by the Federal Trade Commission to outlaw block booking,[57] in 1938 the Department of Justice brought a monopolization case against the industry and certain of its trade practices. In 1940 the government and the five major film distributors agreed to a consent decree that ostensibly eliminated block booking and blind selling. It required, among other things, that exhibition contracts be limited to five or fewer films and that every film be shown to exhibitors in each district prior to licensing.[58] Although the distributors followed the terms of the decree, the marketing of films remained largely unchanged. Exhibitors kept their designated runs, rented approximately the same number of films from each distributor as they had previously,[59] and almost never attended trade showings.[60]

The government reactivated the Paramount case in 1944 in an attempt to modify the decree. The district court's opinion, issued in 1946, required an end to minimum admission prices, "unreasonable" runs and clearances, and block booking and the institution of a system of competitive bidding film by film in each run, open to all theaters regardless of past

---

and Price Making, 31 S. Cal. L. Rev. 150, 154 n.30, 155 n.46 (1958). This "full-line forcing" method of distribution had vanished by the time of the Paramount litigation.

[56] The fact that exhibitors almost universally licensed films from more than one distributor is inconsistent with the hypothesis that block booking served the purpose of prevening exhibitors' free riding on the brand name of the distributor. While it is true that the brand name of the distributor was relatively more important to consumers than it is today, block booking does not appear to have served a purpose similar to the use by a franchisor of an exclusive requirements contract on an important input. Neighborhood theaters, changing their double bill programs twice a week, demanded more than two hundred films a year, or more than three times the annual output of the largest distributor. Hence exclusive input supply was impossible. However, this "brand name" analysis of block booking can explain the use of block-booking-type contracts by the television networks. Free riding on the audience flows between programs in the absence of block booking is demonstrated by the supply of substantially lower-quality programming by the affiliates (that is, lower audience ratings) when the block was broken by the FCC prime time access rule. See William Jennings, The Economic Effects of the Prime Time Access Rule (1983) (unpublished manuscript, Cal. State Univ., Northridge, Dep't Econ. 1983).

[57] FTC v. Paramount Famous-Lasky Corp., 57 F.2d 152 (2d Cir. 1932).

[58] United States v. Paramount Pictures Inc., [1940–43] Trade Reg. Rep. (CCH) at S56,072 (S.D.N.Y. 1940).

[59] For example, prior to 1940 the State Theater in Norfolk, Virginia rented almost all its films from Loew's and United Artists. After the decree in the 1943–44 season the same theater rented thirty-six of its thirty-eight films from the same two distributors. See Loew's Brief to the Supreme Court, app. 2 at xii, Paramount, 334 U.S. 131.

[60] See testimony of William J. Kemper, general sales manager, Twentieth Century–Fox, Supreme Court Briefs & Records, Paramount Trial record at 1178–79, 334 U.S. 131 United States v. Paramount, 66 F. Supp. 323 (S.D.N.Y. 1946).

status or affiliation. Blind selling was permitted, but exhibitors were given the right to reject 20 percent of films licensed if distributors chose not to offer prior trade showings.[61]

The Supreme Court affirmed in 1948 the lower court rulings on the illegality of the trade practices, including block booking, but reversed the lower court's competitive bidding requirement. The Court maintained that competitive bidding would necessitate detailed regulation of the industry to evaluate and monitor essentially incomparable bid terms. Instead, the Court directed the lower court to reconsider divestiture of theaters as a more workable remedy.[62] On remand the district court ordered the distributors to sell their theaters and, while not requiring a system of open competitive bidding, prohibited discrimination against small independent exhibitors in the licensing of films.

B. Prespecified Blind Buyers

Potential exhibitors during the period of the Paramount litigation contracted for their films blindly. Although they had some information about production budget estimates, likely writers, actors, and directors of each film title and the past year's gross rentals of the studio's films, they could not view the product they were purchasing. This is similar to the De Beers marketing arrangement where stones are ordered blindly. A major difference between De Beers and *Paramount* is that to economize on brand-name costs sight holders are permitted to check the quality of the diamonds they order before paying the CSO. Diamond buyers are, in principle, permitted to reject what they order while film exhibitors were not. Film rentals are fully blind, thereby increasing the short-run cheating potential and required brand-name capital of the distributor.[63] However,

---

[61] United States v. Paramount Pictures, 66 F. Supp. (S.D.N.Y. 1946). Paramount, 334 U.S. at 163.

[62] The Supreme Court also rejected competitive bidding on the grounds that such a system would place those exhibitors with "the longest purse," namely the defendants and the large circuits, at an advantage. Paramount, 334 U.S. at 164.

[63] Hammond Woober, general manager of Twentieth Century–Fox, recognized the brand-name mechanism when he testified at the 1940 Congressional Hearings in opposition to legislation that would have prohibited "blind" selling. He stated that "[t]here is a belief that we sell, as it is commonly expressed, a pig in a poke. In reality that is not the way pictures are sold. We sell pictures the same as other articles of merchandise are sold. If you are the owner of a Buick car and you paid a certain price for it, and the time comes to repurchase a car, you either place your confidence in the machine you own or you change the type of machine that you are going to buy and this is the way motion pictures are negotiated for." 1940 Congressional Hearings, *supra* note 53, at 585. The necessity for brand-name capital explains one of the sources of the apparent relative economies of scale in current film distribution, namely, that small independent producers generally distribute through a "major," and the fact that blind selling currently is utilized only by the majors. See David Lees & Stan Berkowitz, The Movie Business 135 (1981).

the fact that the film rental payment is contingent on quality supplied, that is, stated as a share of gross, reduces the distributor's short-run cheating profit and his necessary brand-name capital.

Film licensing in the 1930s was similar to the CSO marketing arrangement in another respect. Distributors did not conduct a competitive auction among exhibitors for blind films, but rather dealt with de facto prespecified buyers. Given the elaborate discriminatory marketing arrangement of runs, zones, and clearances, theaters in particular geographical locations were predesignated in terms of run and all theaters could not freely bid on all films without creating an extremely complex scheduling problem. During the selling season, which began each fall and continued over the next few months, hundreds of unproduced films were fitted into the schedules of thousands of theaters. Each theater generally dealt with the same distributors each year, contracting in advance for the following exhibition season, for approximately the same number of films rented in the current season. The rental of films by theaters, very far from a competitive auction, was closer to a continuing franchise relationship.[64]

Within this franchising environment it is unlikely that blind selling was employed to prevent prespecified exhibitors from searching to obtain an informational advantage over distributors. While films are average priced, oversearching does not appear to be important because distributors are much more likely than exhibitors to have information on the marketability of individual films. Prerelease screenings are not likely to supply much valuable information to an exhibitor. (If they did, the exhibitor would have a comparative advantage in production-distribution and should change his line of business.) In fact, as we have noted, when presale trade showings were required by court decree for a brief period of time, exhibitors did not attend them.[65]

Rather than preventing the buyer from taking advantage of an informational asymmetry, the primary purpose of blind selling appears to be substantial inventory-cost savings. Given the necessity of scheduling exhibitors months in advance of release, trade showings, while supplying little or no valuable information, would increase distribution costs substantially.[66] The main impact of the 1940 decree requiring such trade

---

[64] Explicit franchise agreements giving the exhibitor exclusive rights to license the distributor's films over a period of time, usually more than one year, were entered into with affiliated circuits. See Brief for Plaintiff, app. at 50–58, United States v. Paramount 334 U.S. 131 (1948); and 1940 Congressional Hearings, *supra* note 53, at 645 (Statement of R. H. Poole).

[65] Nonattendance may have been due also to exhibitors' fear of losing their valuable run designation if they attended such showings. But we have not been able to find any evidence to support the existence of such a threat by distributors.

[66] Hammond Woober testified at the 1940 Hearings that "each producing company would have to increase its inventory 50 to 100 percent to meet the requirements of the bill and that

showings appears to have been an increase in the inventory cost to distributors and an increase in the number of visits and hence the number of salesmen required to service exhibitor accounts.[67]

C. Block Booking

The *Paramount* marketing arrangement appears to differ from the De Beers arrangement in the absence of search by buyers for an informational advantage over the seller. Although films are average-priced, rejection of individual films from the group ordered and supplied does not appear possible. Sales are blind, and even if they were not, prerelease search, such as attendance at a trade showing, yields little valuable information. However, one point in the transaction process is completely analogous to the De Beers arrangement in terms of the ability and incentive of buyers to take advantage of an informational asymmetry.

After initial first-run results become available, the limited information conditions under which the licensing agreements had been made are altered drastically and a significant exhibitor contract-reneging problem is created. In particular, after the initial marketing results are available, the films are no longer blind and exhibitors have a potential informational advantage over distributors. Exhibitors could increase their return if they could select a subset of the originally licensed films to exhibit. This would be equivalent to the rejection after examination of overpriced diamonds in the De Beers marketing case. Rejection by an exhibitor of films contracted for creates scheduling problems, entails a costly recontracting process and rearrangement of the planned run scheme, and leads to lower average license fees on the distributor's total film output. Blocking was used solely as a way to prevent exhibitors from engaging in this postcontractual rejection of overpriced films.[68]

---

would require at least $100,000,000 to $200,000,000 of new capital. . . ." 1940 Congressional Hearings, *supra* 53, at 585.

[67] H. Huetting, Economic Control of the Motion Picture Industry: A Study in Industrial Organization 122–23 (1944 repr. 1971). Our analysis of blind bidding implies that both distributors and exhibitors would generally favor the practice. This appears to be consistent with the available evidence at the time. At the 1940 Congressional Hearings numerous independent theater representatives and owners voiced strong opposition to a proposed legislative end to blind bidding (and block booking). Support for the legislation primarily came from "disinterested" civic and religious consumer groups concerned about theater owners being "forced" to exhibit "immoral" films. The recent state legislative movement to outlaw blind-bidding arrangements, on the other hand, has been supported by exhibitor trade associations and is more difficult to explain.

[68] Postcontractual substitution of films by theaters within a zone also could prevent group and distributor maximization. For example, if two theaters in a particular zone are showing different films, say A and B, with weekly revenues of $1,000 and $200, individual exhibitor maximization may lead the second theater to substitute to film A from film B. This substitu-

Block booking existed as a means of enforcing contractual commitments and thereby preventing exhibitors from rejecting films after initial run results became available. If a theater owner attempted to refuse to exhibit a film licensed on a percentage of gross basis, the block contract defined the liquidated damages. Once an exhibitor contracted for a particular group of films within a category and a total price was agreed on, the blocked contract stated that refusal by an exhibitor to accept a particular previously agreed-on film would require the exhibitor to pay $1/n$th of the total agreed-on block price to the distributor.[69] Since the film of unanticipated low quality that the exhibitor would choose to reject will likely have a true value of less than $1/n$th of the package price, the liquidated damage block-booking clause can be viewed as a disguised penalty clause. Block booking, or the intentional overpricing of ex post unexpectedly poor quality films, can be thought of in this context as a way of enforcing blindness, effectively preventing exhibitors from searching out and rejecting the poorest-quality films after their first-run results become available.[70]

Block booking existed also in the sense of average pricing. Observers have generally described block booking as a practice where distributors systematically underpriced their good movies and overpriced their poor movies.[71] This ex post result occurs whenever anticipated quality within a

---

tion may lead to a reduction in joint weekly revenue below $1,200—say $1,000 ($500 at each theater). Distributors and consumers alike would seek ways to prevent this. If the contract were with an exhibitor in a one-theater town, postcontractual substitution would not be disruptive and hence would be permitted as long as rental fees were not reduced. 1940 Congressional Hearings, *supra* note 53, at 553 (statement of William F. Rodgers).

[69] Lewis, *supra* note 52, at 196; 1940 Congressional Hearings, *supra* note 53, at 430, 585 (Twentieth Century–Fox License Agreement and statement of Hammond Woober, respectively).

[70] In addition to this contractual mechanism distributors could have used a quasi-rent stream mechanism similar to that employed by De Beers to prevent rejection. By reclassifying the theater's run designation, distributors could reward or punish exhibitors. See Conant, *supra* note 14, at 61–69; and The American Film Industry 164 (Tino Balio ed. 1976). The magnitude of the theater owners' investment was dependent on run and, given the complex scheduling arrangement, generally not costlessly and immediately transferable to another distributor. See, for example, 1940 Congressional Hearings, *supra* note 53, at 714 (statement of William G. Ripley), at 643 (statement of R. H. Poole), and at 600–601 (testimony of Roy L. Walker), for evidence that an exhibitor's run assignment was considered a valuable right. It is interesting to note that of the 450 arbitration cases filed between 1941 and 1946 under the terms of the 1940 Paramount decree (which established a system of arbitration tribunals where independent exhibitors were permitted to bring complaints against distributors) more than 400 were related to clearance or run designation disputes rather than to contract disputes. See Conant, *supra* note 14, at 96; and Paramount, 334 U.S. 131, 1860 (1948).

[71] See, for example, Lewis, *supra* note 52, at 163; Bertrand Daniel, The Motion Picture Industry: A Pattern of Control 5–6 (1941). Conant, mirroring the explanation given by the court, notes that "[b]lock booking involved the transfer of monopoly power from popular

group cannot be measured perfectly ex ante and average pricing is employed. However, since most rental terms were set on the basis of actual performance of individual films ex post, why were more accurate pricing formulas not devised to minimize the extent of the average pricing present? The answer appears to hinge on the creation of optimal incentives for the supply of exhibition services.

D. *Optimal Incentives*

Flat lump-sum film rental fees appear to be the most efficient. The alternative, percentage rental contracts, entails two distinct costs—the costs of checking reported box office receipts and the costs of inducing exhibitors to supply optimum cooperative input levels. Since the costs of monitoring to assure accurate revenue reports by exhibitors are somewhat invariant to theater gross, flat rental fee contracts were generally used for the small, low-grossing, later-run theaters.[72] Flat rental fees maximize exhibitors' incentive to supply cooperative inputs such as local advertising, cleanliness of physical facilities, competent ushers and projectionists, the number of shows, length of run, and program design.[73] Many of these exhibition services have a significant but not easily measurable effect on total attendance. Even if the optimum level of services were known ex ante, their supply could not be contractually specified in a precise, enforceable manner.

Flat rental fees can solve the exhibitor incentive problem only if the fee is totally independent of performance. The lump sum cannot be determined ex post on the film's results, since knowledge of the formula on which such a payment is to be made would defeat its purpose of not influencing marginal incentives. The lump sum cannot even be a particu-

---

pictures and actors of great public preference to inferior pictures and unknown actors. Distributors charged less than the highest possible price for superior films and more for inferior films than if sold singly." Conant, *supra* note 14, at 79.

[72] See Conant, *supra* note 14, at 71; and Lewis, *supra* note 52, at 193–95 for a discussion of the magnitude of the monitoring of revenue receipts problem, including the problem of monitoring the monitors. Lewis concludes that "the rentals involved in many theaters were not large enough to warrant the expense involved in checking." *Id.* at 195.

[73] If the first or A film of a double feature bill was rented on a percentage of gross basis, the second or B film selected by the theater was required to be contracted for on a flat fee basis. Frank H. Ricketson, The Management of Motion Picture Theaters 194 (1938). To eliminate the incentive by exhibitors to rent lower than optimal quality B films, their flat rental fee was generally deducted from the gross before the sharing percentage was applied. This created an obvious contrary incentive on the part of the exhibitor to rent higher than optimal quality B films. Therefore some contracts contained a limit on the rental that could be deducted for the second feature. See, for example, Brief for the United States, app. at 127, United States v. Paramount.

lar amount per day because it would then distort incentives regarding length of run. The lump sum must be a one-time payment based ex ante on anticipated quality, related, say, to the film's production budget. Because film quality is so unpredictable, we would have a substantial variance within each anticipated quality/initial lump-sum payment classification. With such extreme ex ante average pricing, exhibitors would have the same desire to renege on contractual commitments by selecting individual films and rejecting others after initial results became available. However, since payment would presumably already have been made, reneging would not be possible.

Although flat rental fees maximize exhibitor incentives and minimize monitoring costs, they may not be optimal for two reasons. First, such an arrangement would require an increased amount of distributor brand-name capital. Given blindness, exhibitors must rely on the brand name of distributors to supply the optimum type and magnitude of film quality and promotional services. A distributor's ability to increase in the future the average lump-sum rental fees on its films if it supplies an exceptionally high level of services in the current period (and the necessity to lower its rental terms when supply is lower than anticipated) is an expensive policing mechanism. The brand-name capital required for the mechanism to work is large, because the short-run cheating potential on the part of the distributor is substantial. Quality is not easy to specify contractually ex ante, and there is a large random element in audience acceptance. Thus the exhibitor cannot know cheaply, even ex post, whether low quality has been supplied intentionally. A contingent payment arrangement, by decreasing the distributor's short-run cheating potential, economizes on the required brand-name capital costs.

The producer-distributor's incentive problem is completely analogous to the exhibitors' incentive problem. The distributor could rely on the brand name of the exhibitor alone to supply the optimum levels of cooperating inputs in the production process, but presumably the required exhibitor premium stream and specific capital investment are too large, and a contingent payment economizes on the required brand-name capital.

When both parties to a transaction must supply important inputs that cannot be prespecified cheaply by contract and when brand name costs are nontrivial, a sharing arrangement, while it creates potential moral hazard problems, may be the most efficient solution. In a world of imperfect foresight, measurement, and enforcement, some combination of specification, brand name, and disincentive costs will be associated with any contractual arrangement. The efficient solution entails choosing the particular arrangement that minimizes the sum of these transaction costs.[74]

A second factor, in addition to increased distributor brand-name costs, that may make a flat-fee arrangement nonoptimal is that exhibitor disincentives (and hence required exhibitor brand-name capital) do not vanish under lump-sum rental fees. Given the elaborate distribution system of multiple runs, early-run exhibitors renting films for a flat fee will have an incentive to exhibit the film for too long a period and interfere with profit-maximizing price discrimination. Theoretically, flat fees produce no distortions only when property rights are fully defined. In this case they are not; a theater owner deciding to exhibit a film for a longer period of time produces an externality on later-run theater owners who have purchased exhibition rights.[75]

An ingenious solution to this problem was the distribution contract with the large theater circuits. These circuits consisted of up to several hundred theaters under common ownership. The contract specified payment for licensed films based upon a percentage of the film's national gross (so-called formula deals). The circuit's actual success with the film did not affect the price paid,[76] so that the decreased average pricing of an accu-

---

[74] The contractual form and the particular share settled on will depend on the relative importance and contractual specifiability and enforceability of the cooperating inputs involved. When particular services are extremely large and not easily contracted for, flat fees may be the full-cost-minimizing solution (including transaction costs). For example, although first-run theaters generally rented films on a sharing basis, when the exhibitors supplied live entertainment, the films were often rented on a flat-fee basis. See 1940 Congressional Hearings, *supra* note 53, at 983 (statement of Austin C. Keough). Alternatively, theaters were sometimes able to deduct the cost of a stage show, up to some maximum amount, from the gross in calculating percentage rental fees. Brief for the United States, app. at 131. Exhibitor risk aversion, rather than transaction-cost minimization, is an alternative, not mutually exclusive, hypothesis for the presence of sharing arrangements. However, one should in general be hesitant to accept risk-aversion explanations for contractual terms. Risk explanations are logically equivalent to relying on tastes to explain behavior. They ignore the separate insurance market that may develop in response to such tastes and the fact that many similar sharing contracts are observed in situations where risk considerations alone would appear to imply lump-sum payments (for example, royalty contracts made by publishers with authors). If both parties to a contract can shirk, a partial sharing arrangement may be shown to be optimal under fairly general measurement and transaction-cost conditions within a risk-neutral environment. See Benjamin Klein, Kevin M. Murphy, & Ben T. Yu, Measurement Costs and Sharing Contracts (1983) (unpublished manuscript, UCLA, Dep't Econ.).

[75] Vertical integration of first-run exhibition may possibly be explained by the fact that it had the largest variability of run length, in addition to the largest amounts of other cooperating inputs. The distributors could have been expected to use their reciprocal transacting positions with one another to assure exhibitor performance in all first-run theaters. See Benjamin Klein, Robert G. Crawford, & Armen A. Alchian, Vertical Integration, Appropriable Rents, and the Competitive Contracting Process, 21 J. Law & Econ. 297, 305 (1978).

[76] Conant, *supra* note 14, at 74.

rate ex post contract was combined with the incentive structure of a lump-sum contract. Since these circuits had theaters in various runs, the problem of unnecessary holdovers between runs would be solved. Contractual arrangements similar to these formula deals are still used with the large circuits in England.[77]

Because these forces are likely to imply the use of a percentage of gross licensing arrangement, accurate ex post rental terms, as opposed to more approximate individual film average pricing (or blocking), would create severe exhibitor incentive problems. In particular, as the quality of an individual film increases, it is unlikely that the marginal rental percentage can likewise rise without disturbing exhibitor incentives. For example, consider a hypothetical case where it costs ten cents for the exhibitor to clean a theater seat and that it is worth twenty cents to the consumer to have the seat cleaned. If the film rental licensing fee is 50 percent (or lower) the seat will be cleaned. But if the rental fee of a higher-grossing film is raised beyond 50 percent the exhibitor will not clean the seat. Only if exhibitor services are supplied solely by a fixed cost, with no variable costs related to audience size, can the distributor increase the marginal rental percentage for higher-quality films without creating additional disincentives regarding the supply of exhibition services.

That block booking in the sense of ex post average pricing is related to exhibitor incentives is consistent with the fact that United Artists, which distributed films supplied by many independent producers and therefore required accurate measures of individual film values, licensed each film separately and extensively employed complex contracts with sliding rental percentages.[78] All distributors have now adopted similarly precise rental agreements. However, film licensing in England, which does not have the legal legacy of the Paramount decree, continues to have relatively simple contract terms with the maximum rate at 50 percent.[79]

E. Product Splitting

If the Paramount litigation was designed to encourage allocation of films by competitive bidding, it was unsuccessful. In the period immediately following the final decree, open competition occurred in perhaps several hundred cases out of approximately 15,000 or more potential

---

[77] U.K., House of Commons, Monopolies Commission, Films: A Report on the Supply of Films for Exhibition in Cinemas 12 (1966).

[78] Brief on Appeal of Appellant United Artists Corporation to the Supreme Court at 25, United States v. Paramount; and Brief for the United States, app.

[79] U.K., House of Commons, *supra* note 77, at 8.

selling transactions,[80] and these instances were arranged so that the distributors would avoid the risk of suit by disgruntled exhibitors.[81] Whenever possible distributors divided their films among competing theaters, either by assigning the films of a particular distributor or by assigning shares of the films of a particular distributor to competing exhibitors, with one exhibitor breaking the distributor's films into groups and the other distributor choosing first.[82]

This "product splitting" instituted by the distributors strongly supports our analysis. It was a natural reaction to the final decree, representing an obvious attempt by distributors to continue the de facto franchise relationship that existed with exhibitors during the 1930s and 1940s. However, given the radical changes that occurred in the film industry in the 1950s, it is difficult to understand why the practice persisted and remains fairly common today. In particular, the multiple-run scheduling considerations that required long-term exhibitor relationships largely disappeared with the introduction and growth of television. Film attendance, the number of theatrical films, especially B films, the number of theaters, and the number of runs declined dramatically. Price discrimination via second- and later-run exhibition is accomplished today primarily with cable and then network television release.

In addition, as we have noted, during the postdecree period, pricing of films moved from an average block regime to one where individual films

---

[80] Cassady, *supra* note 55, at 161. One general sales manager of a large distributor stated in 1956 that competitive bidding occurred in only 3.2 percent of the selling situations. Motion Picture Distribution Trade Practices, Hearings Before a Subcomm. of the Select Comm. on Small Business, U.S. Senate, 84th Cong., 2d Sess. 372 (1956) (hereinafter cited as 1956 Senate Hearings) (statement of Charles M. Reagan).

[81] As one company official stated, "The plain fact was that . . . [we] lawyers felt very keenly that the only way we could eliminate these endless legal disputes . . . was to have some system like competitive bidding which will afford the company an immunity. . . ." Problems of Independent Motion Picture Exhibitors relating to Trade Distribution Practices, Hearings Before a Subcomm. of the Select Committee on Small Business, U.S. Senate, 83d Cong., 1st Sess. 582 (1953) (statement of William Zimmerman). An antitrust division spokesman stated in 1953 that there were more than one hundred private antitrust suits pending against the major distributors, *id.* at 655 (statement of Philip Marcus). One company stated that it used competitive bidding only at the "specific request of one or more competing exhibitors or at the request of an exhibitor that he be licensed pictures on a run which had been formally licensed by his competitor." 1956 Senate Hearings, *supra* note 79, at 372 (statement of Charles M. Reagan).

[82] Cassady, *supra* note 55, at 164; James Gordon, Horizontal and Vertical Restraints of Trade: The Legality of Motion Picture Splits under the Antitrust Laws, 75 Yale L. J. 239, 240 (1965); Cassady at 165 and Gordon at 241 n.5 make extremely weak attempts to rationalize this practice. Film licensing in England consists of quite explicit product-splitting arrangements in the form of right of first refusal agreements by the two major exhibition circuits, ABC and Rank, each accounting for approximately one half of all first-run releases. U.K. House of Commons, *supra* note 77, at 15.

were priced more accurately by complex sliding percentages. Interfilm variances in the length of run and in grosses increased, and the predictability of the value of a given studio's annual output decreased. In this period exhibitors complained less frequently that they were forced to rent overpriced bad films in order to rent (presumably underpriced) good films and more frequently that distributors demanded excessive amounts for their better films.[83]

Yet as the industry and marketing arrangements have changed, product splitting has mysteriously survived. It is unlikely that a monopsonistic exhibition industry has imposed product splitting on reluctant distributors. Distributors initiated, and acquiesced in, the arrangement as an attempt to imitate the essential conditions, namely prespecified buyers, prohibited by the Paramount decree; and distributors could terminate it as easily by playing one exhibitor against another. Some exhibitors within each city are outside the split, and most split agreements include a provision for competition among alternative exhibitors if the distributor rejects the split designee. Alternatively, the distributor could bring suit against exhibitors who persisted against their desires for competitive bidding.[84] In cities where product splits are present, such distributor behavior is totally absent.[85]

Instead of monopsony, a likely rationale for product splitting is as a substitute for average block pricing in creating correct marginal exhibitor

[83] Conant, *supra* note 14, at 150.

[84] The argument that distributors might be reluctant to bring suit against exhibitors and damage their good will in continuing relationships makes little sense. There already exists a substantial amount of litigation between these parties concerning underreporting of receipts and other claims regarding contractual breach, and a large number of private antitrust actions. See Ralph Cassady, Jr. & Ralph Cassady III, The Private Antitrust Suit in American Business Competition: A Motion Picture Industry Case Analysis (Occasional Paper No. 4, UCLA Bur. Business & Economic Research 1964).

[85] Most litigation with regard to splitting has involved suits by exhibitors excluded from the split. See, for example, Viking Theater Corp. v. Paramount Film Distribution Corp., 320 F.2d 285 (3d Cir. 1963). There are a number of cases where distributors have claimed the illegality of product splits, but, as far as we know, these represent counteractions. For example, General Cinema Corp. v. Buena Vista Distribution Co., Inc., 532 F. Supp. 1244 (C.D. Cal. 1982) represents a counterclaim by Buena Vista against General Cinema's original claim that a minimum film rental based on a per capita charge represented illegal price fixing. (This contractual term appears to be designed to prevent exhibitors from underpricing admission and overpricing a complementary input, such as popcorn, on which no licensing fee is paid.) The court dismissed the original complaint and ruled on the counterclaim that General Cinema's participation in split agreements was per se illegal. This decision is contrary to most recent opinions. See, for example, Greenbrier Cinemas, Inc. v. Attorney General of the United States, 511 F. Supp. 1046 (W.D. Va. 1981), which represented an exhibitor's challenge to the Department of Justice April 1, 1977, change in policy regarding the legality of splits. Distributors are, however, cooperating with the Department of Justice in their most recent attack on the practice of splitting in Milwaukee, United States v. Capitol Service, Inc. Civil Action no. 80-C-407 (E.D. Wisc).

incentives. In nonbidding situations, including cities where product splits occur, distributors engage in renegotiation, that is, adjust rental terms downward if the film performs poorly.[86] This behavior would be extremely unlikely if distributors were facing exhibitors imposing an artificially low monopsonistic price. Renegotiation serves the purpose of mitigating the increased marginal disincentives regarding the supply of exhibition services created by the accurate, single-film, complex pricing schedule. Although the supply of exhibition services cannot be specified fully in an ex ante contractual manner, the distributor will presumably know ex post if the exhibitor "did a good job" and this will be reflected in the final adjustment.[87] Such renegotiation is not possible in bidding situations without violating the terms of the auction that the film go to the highest bidder, thus opening the distributor up to a discrimination suit by an exhibitor that submitted a failed bid.

Although the evidence is unclear whether the existence of a split depresses rental terms,[88] it appears to have an unambiguous effect on lowering guarantees—minimum, nonrenegotiable, up-front rental payments for the film run. Although complex sliding-percentage rental terms now price individual films more accurately, they do not set prices perfectly. Therefore, given the absence of block booking, guarantees are an alternative means of preventing exhibitors from reneging on contracts after initial poor attendance results become available. Money payments up front create the correct marginal exhibitor incentives regarding the supply of cooperating inputs, including run length and number of shows. The de facto long-term franchise arrangements with particular exhibitors implied

---

[86] See Cassady, *supra* note 55, at 176–77. Renegotiation only goes one way, namely, noncontractually required payments made by distributors to exhibitors.

[87] During the 1930s, renegotiation, although rarer and of a smaller magnitude, did occur when an entire block was, ex post, priced "unjustly." See Loew's Inc., 20 Fortune Magazine 25, 110 (August 1939); and 1940 Congressional Hearings, *supra* note 53, at 547. Contracts also contained provisions for reducing the percentages of gross in each price quality class if the aggregate receipts from films within that class fell below a contractually determined level. For example, for each film in the two highest percentage categories, if the theater did not earn a profit equal to at least one-third of the total film rental paid, the film automatically reverted to the next lowest category. Ricketsen, *supra* note 73, at 32–33; and Brief for the United States, app. at 131, United States v. Paramount.

[88] We would expect that a split would be accepted by a distributor only if rental terms are not lower. Charles M. Reagan, general sales manager and vice president of Loew's Inc., stated that ". . . we have indicated a willingness to eliminate competitive bidding whenever possible in situations where returns from the theaters are comparable by licensing our pictures on a split basis, that is, dividing our product between or among competitors," 1956 Senate Hearings, *supra* note 81, at 373 (statement of Charles M. Reagan). The evidence presented in United States v. Capital Service, Civil Action no. 80-C-407, indicates an unambiguously sharp decline in guarantees after the establishment of the split in Milwaukee (see exhibit GX9 and GX) but disagreement regarding the effect of the split on film rentals (see trial testimony of Ben Marcus and Irving Palace and exhibit DX509).

by product splitting with the possibility of distributor renegotiation reduce the necessity for such guarantees.[89]

IV. THE LOEW'S CASE

A. *The Economic and Legal Setting*

Many of the films produced during the 1930s and 1940s, covered by the theatrical exhibition contracts declared illegal in *Paramount* became the subject of new litigation as they were released by the major motion picture producers for television exhibition. Among the approximately 2,500 feature films made available for television by 1956 were major portions of the pre-1948 film libraries of MGM, RKO–Radio Pictures, Columbia, United Artists, and Warner Brothers.[90]

Distributors licensed feature films directly to local television stations. Each station renting a film received the exclusive right to air that film in its market area for some stipulated period of time. After a distributor announced the availability of a well-known library of films through advertisements in trade magazines (such as *Variety*) and direct mail advertising to local stations, the distributor's salesmen visited the stations offering a number of blocks of films. The contents of each block were named by the distributor, with each block consisting of a fairly representative subdivision of the entire library, and were uniform in composition throughout the country. Prices for the blocks were established by salesman negotiations with the stations in each market area, with the negotiating process often consuming several months.[91]

Not all license agreements covered distributor-selected blocks. Some stations were allowed to choose films from the entire library, cutting across the blocks. For example, only 113 of the 203 contracts made by Loew's and television stations between June 1956 (when they decided to release for television distribution their pre-1948 feature film library) and

---

[89] The common argument that guarantees are used as a means of reducing distributor's risk (see, for example, Film Studios Theater Retaliation against States Banning Blind Bids, Los Angeles Times, June 1, 1981, § 4, at 1, 3, 5) makes little intuitive sense given the relative asset positions of distributors and exhibitors, the ready access of distributors to more generalized capital and insurance markets, and the fact that they are used much less frequently in product splitting situations.

[90] United States v. Loew's Inc., 189 F. Supp. 373, 382 (S.D.N.Y. 1960).

[91] The description of a "typical" contracting sequence is a composite of testimony from the trial court case Civil Action no. 119–24, reproduced in Court Records and Briefs, Loew's, 371 U.S. 38. In particular see the testimony of Oliver A. Under, president of National Telefilm Associates Inc., *id.* at 5825–944.

March 1960 involved preselected packages of films or block booking.[92] Nevertheless, in 1957 the government brought six separate civil antitrust actions against the six major distributors of motion picture films for television (Loew's, C&C Super Corporation, Screen Gems, Associated Artists, National Telefilm Associates, and United Artists) alleging that refusal to license films on other than a block-booking basis violated the Sherman Act. As opposed to the Paramount litigation, there were no allegations of conspiracy.

The suits were consolidated and tried beginning in March 1960. The government demanded that the defendants be required to license feature films to television picture by picture and station by station. The district judge ruled that even one instance of refusal to license motion picture films other than by block-booking was a violation and granted injunctive relief.[93] The Supreme Court upheld the decision and imposed the government's desired remedy, although it permitted a distributor to refuse to offer for sale to one station an individual film that was part of a block of films over which negotiations were currently in progress with a competing station.[94] The effect of this reservation was to allow the distributors to continue their existing selling practices: trying to negotiate block sales but permitting deviations.

B. Contractual Cheating

One possible explanation for block sales is contractual cheating. Many films are made with contracts requiring compensation of actors, directors, writers, and investors out of the film's profits. When a block of films is rented, the distributor may attempt to hide profits on an individual film by allocating the rental receipts for the block arbitrarily among the individual films. If some films in the block are not profitable or do not contain profit-sharing clauses, producers and distributors could attempt to assign them the lion's share of the proceeds from the block's price and thereby reduce the contractually obligated profit-sharing compensation they must pay on the successful films.[95] However, this form of contractual cheating is

---

[92] The 113 block licenses included sixty-three contracts for the entire 723-film library, nine contracts for either preselected half of the library, thirty-six contracts for one or more of the three preselected groups of one hundred films, and five contracts for a group of sixty-seven films preselected by Loew's. Information about the Loew's contracts is from Court Record, Exhibits 626, Loew's Exhibit 21, Civil Action No. 119-24, Loew's, 371 U.S. 38. The information about the relative quantities of the various Loew's packages is found in Court Record at 675, 4869.

[93] Loew's, 189 F. Supp. 373 (1960).

[94] Loew's, 371 U.S. at 55.

[95] This may explain Twentieth Century–Fox's alleged violation of the Paramount decree in 1978 by forcing theaters to exhibit the unsuccessful film The Other Side of Midnight in

likely only if some unanticipated contingency occurs, not easily avoided contractually. If the potential cheating is anticipated, actors and investors would negotiate for an allocation device.[96] The Loew's case involved movies made in the 1930s and 1940s, when the possibility of future television sales must have seemed quite remote. Therefore explicit contractual protection against this form of opportunism must have been rare.

Although this explanation is appealing, it is not consistent with the facts of *Loew's*. The pre-1948 films in question were made under the "studio system." The actors, writers, and directors were on long term exclusive employment contracts and were paid a flat weekly salary.[97] Executive compensation for some of the producers and others employed by the studio was based in part on total studio profit and an agreement was reached by the distributors and the guild not to claim royalties on these television sales. All the evidence indicates that the distributors had, or acquired, full and exclusive rights to the films licensed for television use.[98]

C. *Price Discrimination*

The most commonly accepted theoretical explanation for block booking is that it is a subtle form of price discrimination, where distributors use a block to set prices on films that unpredictably vary in relative value across geographical markets. This theory is intuitively appealing. Stigler found that first-run theatrical grosses of several different movies released during 1946–47 varied significantly across different U.S. cities. He hypothesized that the aggregate value of a group of films was more predictable and related to general factors of the particular market.[99] In fact, block-sale prices in *Loew's* appear to be fairly predictable across markets.

---

order to rent the highly successful film Star Wars, in which George Lucas had a 40 percent share of net revenues.

[96] An example of a contractual solution to an anticipated cheating opportunity can be found in United States v. Columbia Pictures Corp. 189 F. Supp. 153 (S.D.N.Y. 1960). The government challenged an agreement between Universal Pictures and Screen Gems, a wholly owned subsidiary of Columbia Pictures, in which Universal granted to Screen Gems a fourteen-year exclusive license to distribute for television exhibition approximately six hundred pre-1948 Universal feature films. Since Screen Gems also distributed for television substantially all of Columbia's pre-1948 films, the agreement further required that films in the two libraries would be classified before distribution into categories of comparable quality and that the Universal films would not be sublicensed to TV stations by Screen Gems for less than the Columbia films of comparable quality. The court recognized that without such an agreement it would have been possible for Screen Gems to shift profit from Universal to Columbia by offering TV stations Universal films at lower prices if they also rented Columbia films at correspondingly higher prices. See Robert H. Bork, The Rule of Reason and the Per Se Concept: Price Fixing and Market Division, 75 Yale L. J. 373, 461–64 (1966).

[97] See Balio, *supra* note 70, at 376–77.

[98] For example, Oliver A. Unger testified that both Loew's and Columbia owned their negatives fully. Court Record at 5840, Loew's, 371 U.S. 38.

[99] See Stigler, *supra* note 7, app.

534   THE JOURNAL OF LAW AND ECONOMICS

The variation in prices paid for a single package of eighty-five films sold by National Telefilm Associates across seventy-six different television markets between July 1, 1946, and April 23, 1960, can be explained largely on the basis of a few economic factors.[100]

Once prices for a block are determined in a few markets—that is, quality is estimated—prices in other markets can be predicted and set accurately by such factors as income and population. If Stigler is correct, individual film prices cannot be set accurately across markets on the basis of such similar limited information, since each market area is characterized by people whose tastes differ significantly from those of people in other market areas. Therefore, although the total demand for a group of films may be highly predictable across markets, the relative values of the individual films in the block vary unpredictably between markets. However, as we noted in the introduction, there is no reason for a distributor selling films in a multiple television station market on an exclusive exhibition basis not to let the competitive market operate to reveal buyers' demand prices. Since there is no need for distributors to set prices, there is no need for blocks as a means for distributors to ameliorate the informational advantage assumed to be possessed by buyers.[101]

Stigler's price discrimination explanation makes some sense only in

---

[100] Oliver A. Unger of National Telefilm Associates, when asked at trial about the factors influencing price replied: "Well, the rate card of the station is a factor as to how much time costs in that area. The competitive situation is another important factor to establish value. The set circulation is an important factor, the number of television sets in the area, and of course the quality of the merchandise that is being offered at that time is also a big factor." Court Record at 5856, Loew's, 371 U.S. 38. Our estimated equation is

$$\log (\text{price}) = -7.0 + \underset{(6.4)}{.58} \log (\text{circulation}) + \underset{(9.7)}{2.1} \log (\text{income}) + \underset{(3.8)}{.83} (\text{number}),$$

$R^2 = .82$. The price of the block is taken from Court Record, National Telefilm Associates Exhibit 11, Exhibits at 778, 803–06, Loew's, 371 U.S. 38. Circulation is taken from Broadcast Information Bureau, TV Factbook no. 33, Metropolitan Markets, 249–289 (1962) and is a measure of potential audience. Income is the per family median income by SMSA for 1960, Country and City Data Book, item 28 (where data by SMSA were unavailable, county data were used) and is a measure of the value of advertising messages per viewer reached. Number of stations refers to the number of commercial stations within a fifty-mile radius in each market area, from TV Factbook no. 33. The positive significance of number on price may reflect demand variables unaccounted for by circulation and income or the net positive theoretical effect of number of buyers on price within a Nash equilibrium framework.

[101] If the relative demand for individual films varied significantly and unpredictably among television stations within a market, it would generally pay for a distributor to break the block and sell the individual films separately in a competitive bidding manner. As in all discontinuous markets the distributor would only receive the value of the second highest valuing station. However, the within-market interstation variation is unlikely to be very important because viewers can switch stations to watch a particular movie on whatever station it appears.

BLOCK BOOKING   535

TABLE 1
LOEW'S TELEVISION LICENSING CONTRACTS, JUNE 1956–MARCH 1960

	Loew's Selected Block Sales	Customer Selected Nonblock Sales	Total
One-station markets	a) 21	b) 31	52
	(29)	(23)	
Multiple-station markets	c) 92	d) 59	151
	(84)	(67)	
Total	113	90	203

SOURCE.—Data from Court Record, Exhibits 626, Loew's exhibit 21, Civil Action No. 119-24, Loew's, 371 U.S.; and Quigley Publications, International Television Almanac (1960).

one-station markets. In such a situation, which obtained in many regional markets in the late 1950s, distributors face monopsonistic buyers of their films. Therefore they obviously cannot leave it to competition to determine the final price of their films. The distributors must bargain, and superior knowledge of the value of a block of films compared with the value of each individual film separately may produce a relative bargaining advantage for them.[102]

The evidence from the *Loew's* record indicates that the exact opposite occurred. Distributors were less likely to break preselected blocks in multiple-station markets, where interstation competition could be used to reveal valuations, than in single-station markets, where the supposed increased predictability in the valuation of the block was necessary for the distributor to counteract the superior information possessed by the monopsonistic buyer on the valuations of individual films.

Table 1 presents a two-way classification of each of the 203 Loew's contracts, reflecting whether the transaction involved a Loew's-selected

---

[102] This assumes that buyers have better information than sellers about the relative appeal of individual movies. Otherwise buyers will also want to depend on their knowledge of the value of the block in striking a bargain. The existence of such asymmetrical information seems unlikely. Monopsonistic buyers in one-station markets may appear to be able to bargain price down to the seller's marginal cost, which in this case of previously produced films with essentially no alternative use is essentially zero. However, the seller can be assumed to make a firm commitment not to sell unless he receives his asking price, which he sets equal to the market-clearing price given by the estimated equation in note 100 *supra*. Such a commitment will be credible because the various regional markets are tied together by the exchange of price information and therefore an individual transaction is not isolated. As opposed to the standard bilateral bargaining problem, a seller who cuts the price below his commitment price in one single-station market loses revenues in other single-station markets as other monopsonistic buyers adjust their estimates of the seller's ability to keep his commitment. This potential loss in revenues in other markets serves as an incentive for the seller to maintain his commitment in any one market. The single station observation residuals in our estimated equation are not generally negative or very large.

block or a customer-selected film or group of films and whether the transaction was with a television station in a multiple station or single station
market. Our restatement of Stigler's price discrimination theory predicts
that cell *a* (Loew's "block" sales, one-station markets) and cell *d* (customer selected sales, multiple-station markets) would show more than the
chance number of contracts. The chance numbers (in parentheses) are
calculated on the assumption that there is no relation between the number
of stations in a market and Loew's behavior. Since 56 percent of all
Loew's transactions were block sales (113/203), we would naively expect
56 percent, or 29 of the 52 sales in one-station markets and 84 of the 151
sales in multiple-station markets also to be blocks. If the Stigler price
discrimination hypothesis were correct, we would expect more than 56
percent of sales in one-station markets and fewer than 56 percent of sales
in multiple-station markets to be blocks. Instead, only 40 percent of the
sales in one-station markets (21/52) and 61 percent of the sales in multiple-
station markets were blocks. The evidence indicates a significantly nonrandom distribution of transactions in the *opposite* direction one would
expect from the price discrimination hypothesis.[103]

D. Product Standardization

The films licensed to television stations in *Loew's* generally were of
relatively low individual value. Although Justice Goldberg used *Gone
with the Wind* in his decision as the hypothetical example of a desirable
film with monopoly power to which sellers would tie less desirable
films,[104] such exceptional films were not part of these agreements. The
average three-year rental price for films in the National Telefilm Associates block discussed above was less than $200 and in some markets it
was less than $20.[105] The films were generally "time fillers," randomly
used by the stations at the end of the program day in, for example, the
11:30 P.M. time slot.

These films were of highly uncertain individual value. Potential purchasers could not merely check the original theatrical gross in the particular market of the individual film in question (reported in trade magazines
such as *Variety*) and hope to obtain with some simple conversion formula
an accurate estimate of the film's current TV license value. Very dramatic
demographic changes had occurred in particular markets over the years

---

[103] Using a χ^2 test, the null hypothesis that there is no relation between single or multiple
stations in a market and the presence of block sales can be rejected at a .05 level of
significance ($\chi^2 = 5.807$).

[104] Loew's, 371 U.S. at 52.

[105] Court Record at 803–06, Exhibits 778, Loew's, 371 U.S. 38.

since original release and the values of the films had depreciated at widely different rates.[106] In addition, they could not rent the films on an ex post contingency basis, such as for a share of advertising revenue, because audience flows and the need to standardize for the presence of competitive programming made quality measurements difficult.

However, individual film values were not economically important. The station owners often programmed by choosing individual films randomly from the block, and advertisers purchased blocks of time without knowing during which film their ads would appear. As opposed to the De Beers case—where seller search for individual product quality information was duplicative because buyers would eventually have to determine value accurately when cutting the stone—in this case neither the distributor nor the station owner requires the information for any allocative purpose. All quality search, by both buyers and sellers, would be wasteful.

Information regarding the average value of films is economically relevant in determining price, and blocking can be expected to reduce these information costs. If Director's and Stigler's insight is correct, films' values are individually highly uncertain but are predictable in the aggregate. Distributors packaged films in a manner similar to De Beers's random selection of stones for sights, attempting to give buyers an average representation of the quality of the distributor's library. For example, Associated Artists Productions divided its entire library of 754 pre-1948 Warner Brothers films into thirteen groups of fifty-eight films each, with each group intended to be of the same overall quality and to be "balanced" to contain a similar mix of musicals, comedies, dramas, and westerns.[107] As a result, any buyer with an estimate of the overall quality of the Warner Brothers library also had an estimate of the "value" of each of the thirteen groups.

As opposed to the De Beers and Paramount situations, there may not appear to be a seller brand-name repeat-sale mechanism present to assure buyers that the films in the block are selected randomly. Some of the distribution companies in this case were formed solely for the one-time sale of the old film libraries to television stations. However, because we are dealing with a standardized product and therefore information collected from one transaction can be transmitted cheaply across markets, a

---

[106] George Hartford, vice president and general manager of Station WTOP testified that some older films, particularly musicals, were badly dated and would no longer be well received by the audience, Court Record at 391, Loew's, 371, U.S. 38. However, many of these musicals were later edited, spliced together and rereleased theatrically by MGM with great success as "That's Entertainment."

[107] See the testimony of Eliot Hyman, president of Associated Artists Production, Court Record at 5581, Loew's, 371 U.S. 38.

repeat-sale mechanism is present. If a nonrandom selection of films were made by the distributor, such information could be expected to be discovered after the first few sales and to be reflected in prices paid for the same block in other markets over time.[108]

Films within these distributor-created packages were average priced. If buyers searched through these randomly created blocks and purchased individual films selectively, a negative externality would be created on the buyers of the remaining films in the block. In addition to knowing about the average value of a distributor's quality, buyers are familiar with the transaction price of the block in other markets and hence have information about the particular block's value. Given the predictability of block values across markets, we are dealing with a product that is standardized intermarket. Attempts by individual buyers to find exceptional values within the average-priced block destroy the standardization and create increased uncertainty about the value of the remaining films in the block.

Because Loew's had a fixed supply of films available for license and the marginal cost of licensing a film to an additional station was low, the license fee was almost a pure rent. Buyers' inspection costs would be borne almost entirely by the seller, who would have the incentive to choose selling practices that reduced search costs. Since breaking a block destroys valuable information and could be expected to induce increased buyer search, distributors would resist buyers' offers to purchase a part of a prepackaged block.

This information-cost theory of block booking is consistent with the evidence presented in Table 1. We would expect significantly more blocks to be broken in one-station markets than in multiple-station markets, because when a block is broken other buyers in the same market area can no longer use the knowledge of the average quality of the distributor's library and the price information generated on sales of the particular standardized package in other markets. Buyers in single-station markets, on the other hand, do not impose such externalities.

V. Conclusion

Although it is generally the case that there are many different economic reasons for the existence of any particular marketing practice, the essen-

---

[108] There is some indication that buyers in the various markets were in contact with one another. For example, Oliver A. Unger (of National Telefilm Associates, Inc.) testified that "[t]his is a business of so few people that you [as a film distributor] can do something in New York at 8 o'clock in the morning and you will hear about it in Seattle at 3 that afternoon. This is the fastest underground there ever was." Trial Record at 5870, Loew's, 371 U.S. 38. Since the stations in each of the 240 regional TV markets were not in competition with each other, they may have shared information with one another. In addition, transactions for the various standardized blocks and transaction prices were regularly reported in trade journals such as Variety.

BLOCK BOOKING 539

tial rationale for block booking is the same in all three of the cases we have examined. Blocking serves to prevent buyers from rejecting parts of a package of products that has been average-priced. In the De Beers case, if stones in each sight were individually priced and buyers were permitted to search through and select the particular stones they wished, the probability of rejection would increase and De Beers would be able to sell the remaining stones in each quality category group only at a lower price. Similarly, in the Paramount case buyers cannot be permitted, after the initial exhibition results become available, to pick through the group of films originally contracted for at a particular average price per film and select the subset they wish. And similarly, in the Loew's case buyers must be discouraged from searching for exceptional individual film values within randomly selected groups of films that are priced on the basis of a fairly well-known average value.

The extent of average pricing required in these cases is substantial because of the degree of the underlying quality variance. The goods we have examined are unique in that the quality of the particular good is not easily known or cheaply controlled by the supplier. A precise estimate of the value of individual rough diamonds would require costly, duplicative examination costs. Similarly, the values of films are notoriously variable and not related very predictably to production costs, and accurate presale measures of individual product quality are costly and wasteful.

Average pricing could be eliminated, in principle, by the use of an ex post contractual mechanism such that the value of the good and hence its price would be determined only after final sale of the product to consumers. Even in the presence of substantial ex ante uncertainty regarding values of individual goods, there would presumably be no uncertainty ex post. However, all ex post contracts entail measurement costs in separating out the effects on final value of cooperating inputs in the production process. These costs of accurate ex post pricing are prohibitive in De Beers and *Loew's* and entail substantial incentive problems in *Paramount*.

Finally, in our cases, buyers must rely on the brand name of the supplier. This is not unusual in itself; for almost any good it is prohibitively costly to know before purchase or to specify in an enforceable way every element of quality. However, in the usual case it is generally assumed that sellers know the quality of the goods they are selling and their brand name assures the buyers that this quality will not be less than anticipated.[109] In our cases, sellers do not know very accurately individual product quality before sale, and their brand names assure performance in the sense that buyers have confidence that they have selected a random sample of goods

[109] See Klein & Leffler, *supra* note 34.

from the underlying quality distribution on which the average price is based. Seller brand names then prevent buyers from taking advantage of the informational asymmetries present within such average-pricing schemes.

The particular contractual arrangements chosen by the parties in the various cases are designed in part to minimize these brand name costs. To economize on brand-name capital De Beers has chosen to share their marketing cost savings with buyers, the distributors in *Paramount* have chosen an ex post pricing mechanism, and the distributors in *Loew's* have standardized their products. Sellers are optimizing so as to minimize transaction costs, recognizing that performance called for in every transaction is partially guaranteed by costly private brand-name capital mechanisms and partially guaranteed by costly government-enforced contractual mechanisms.[110] The results of our analysis demonstrate that difficult-to-explain contractual terms can be analyzed rigorously rather than merely labeled as "noncompetitive." Although the contractual arrangements examined are incompatible with the perfectly competitive model, they provide us with an opportunity to improve our understanding of the competitive economy.

---

[110] See Klein, *supra* note 47; and Oliver E. Williamson, Transaction Cost Economics: The Governance of Contractual Relations, 22 J. Law & Econ. 233 (1979).

[4]

Advertising as Information

Phillip Nelson

State University of New York at Binghamton and the University of Chicago

> This haughty youth, He speaks the truth
> Whenever he finds it pays;—
> And in this case, it all took place
> Exactly as he says!
> Exactly, exactly, exactly, exactly as he says!
> [GILBERT AND SULLIVAN, *The Mikado*]

This paper tries to show how the major features of the behavior of advertising can be explained by advertising's information function. For search qualities advertising provides direct information about the characteristics of a brand. For experience qualities the most important information conveyed by advertising is simply that the brand advertises. This contrast in advertising by these qualities leads to significant differences in its behavior.

How does advertising provide information to the consumer? The producer in his advertising is not interested directly in providing information for consumers. He is interested in selling more of his product. Subject to a few constraints, the advertising message says anything the seller of a brand wishes. A mechanism is required to make the selling job of advertising generate information to the consumer.

The first section of this paper shows how such a mechanism exists and how its operation varies by types of market. The middle three sections of the paper try to put the ideas of the first section to the test. The first of these empirical sections uses the model to predict the way in which adver-

Helpful criticisms of an earlier draft of this article were received from Jerome Komisar, Lester Telser, Robert Van Handel, and the participants of a seminar at the University of Rochester and the Conference on the Economics of Information at the University of Chicago. Financial assistance was received from the Research Foundation of the State University of New York.

730   JOURNAL OF POLITICAL ECONOMY

tising/sales ratios will differ by industry. The second section predicts how media choice will vary by industry; the third explores the impact of alternative sources of information on advertising volume. The last section of this paper examines the consequences of relaxing two assumptions made in the rest of my analysis: that consumers use optimal decision rules and that there are no legal constraints on advertising.

Information is generated by advertising because of consumer power in the product market. The nature of that power will vary significantly by the nature of the product being advertised. In "Information and Consumer Behavior" (Nelson 1970), I make a fundamental distinction between qualities of a brand that the consumer can determine by inspection prior to purchase of the brand—"search qualities"—and qualities that are not determined prior to purchase—"experience qualities." An example of a search quality is the style of a dress; an example of an experience quality is the taste of a brand of canned tuna fish. The impact of the market power of consumers on advertising will operate quite differently for search and experience qualities.

If the advertised properties of the product differ from the actual properties, the consumer will know about that difference prior to purchase in the case of search qualities. This reduces considerably—but not entirely—incentives for misleading advertising. Misleading advertising will still exist. First, consumers pay transportation costs before they spot any disparity between actual and advertised search qualities. By exaggerating the utility of the actual search good by any amount up to the transportation costs of consumers, advertising can result in greater sales to the firm than a less exaggerated advertisement. Second, there can be some search quality of a brand which cannot be successfully conveyed by advertising, for example, the "charm" of an apartment. Under these circumstances it might pay the advertiser to exaggerate some characteristic that can be specified by the advertisement. But there are costs to the advertiser of misleading advertising: he suffers a decline in his credibility for future advertisements and pays the costs of processing nonbuying customers. Because of these costs and the relative unimportance of the sources of misleading advertising, consumers can have some confidence that the advertising of search qualities bears a close relation to the truth. The advertising of search qualities provides information to the consumer, even though he attaches a probability less than one to the truthfulness of these advertisements.

In the case of experience qualities the consumer's power over advertising is much less potent than his power over search qualities. The major control that consumers have over the market for experience qualities is whether they repeat the purchase of a brand or not (Nelson 1970). This power is sufficient to authenticate any statement that has either of the

following characteristics: (1) consumers' belief in the truth of that state
ment does not increase the profit from initial sales (as opposed to repeat
sales either directly or indirectly through the recommendations of relatives
and friends) or (2) it is possible for the producer at no cost to himself to
make the advertised statement true rather than false. If either (1) or (2)
holds, the advertiser maximizes his profits by telling the truth if the consumer believes he is doing so.[1]

One of these two requirements will be satisfied by virtually all statements that specify the function of a brand, for example, "Pepto-Bismol is a
remedy for upset stomachs." This statement turns customers with athlete's
foot away as well as attracting customers with bellyaches. Of course, it
is conceivable that there are more of the latter (relative to the available
number of brands) than the former, so that there is a net gain of initial
sales from this statement. But this is where condition (2) comes into play.
If this were the case, it would pay the manufacturer of Pepto-Bismal to
produce at the same costs something that resembled a stomach remedy
rather than something that could be used for athlete's foot. It is conceivable that at that cost the firm could only produce a second-rate stomach
remedy and could produce a first-rate foot balm. But if everybody is
buying Pepto-Bismol for upset stomachs rather than for athlete's foot, any
virtues of Pepto-Bismol for athlete's foot would be irrelevant in determining Pepto-Bismol sales.

Even when the advertisement of an experience quality correctly relates
brand to function—by far the typical case—the consumer has quite incomplete information. He would like to be able to rank stomach remedies
by their utility to him. Advertising provides no direct information that
will help him do that job. (By direct information I mean information
contained in the advertising statement.) After Pepto-Bismol has been
correctly identified as a stomach remedy, the statement that Pepto-

---

[1] This proposition can be seen most clearly in the case of constant average production
costs (AC). In that case, profit can be written

$$Pf = (P - AC)I + (P - AC)R - A, \qquad (10)$$

where Pf = profits, P = price, I = initial sales, R = repeat sales, A = advertising
costs, and $P(R)$ = probability of a repeat purchase given an initial purchase. Advertising
costs are assumed constant, since they should be invariant with respect to the truth or
falsity of the advertising message. Then false advertising will not increase Pf.

$$Pf = (P - AC)I + (P - AC)I\,P(R) - A. \qquad (11)$$

If $(P - AC)I$ is constant, profits increase with the probability of a repeat purchase,
and this probability increases with the truthfulness of an advertisement. $(P - AC)I$ will
be a constant over the relevant decision variable whenever either condition (1) or (2)
holds. If condition (1) holds, $(P - AC)I$ is a constant varying the truthfulness of the
statement but holding the character of the product constant. If condition (2) holds,
$(P - AC)I$ is a constant holding the statement constant but varying the character of the
product.

Bismol is most soothing is without information content. Its producers have an incentive to say so even if it were the least soothing of stomach remedies.

The miniscule amount of direct information from advertising for experience qualities gives the consumer an incentive to extract any conceivable indirect information that would help. Such indirect information is available from advertising. The consumer can learn that the brand advertises. I contend that this is the useful information that the consumer absorbs from the endorsements of announcers, actors, and others who are paid for their encomiums. These and other advertisements for experience goods have no informational content. Their total informational role—beyond the relation of brand to function—is simply contained in their existence. The consumer believes that the more a brand advertises, the more likely it is to be a better buy. In consequence, the more advertisements of a brand the consumer encounters, the more likely he is to try the brand.

Why are advertised brands better buys? The answer to that question is not self-evident. If advertising were distributed at random among brands for a product, it would indeed be newsworthy that a brand advertised; but that news would decrease the probability of a consumer's trying the advertised brand. Advertised brands would cost more by the cost of the advertising and hence would be worse buys.

It is my contention, however, that advertising is not distributed at random among brands of a product. Heavily advertised brands are likely to provide a lower $P*$ (price per unit of utility of the brand)[2] to the average consumer than less heavily advertised brands of the same product. (To give unambiguous meaning to that measure, I assume that consumers all have the same income and utility functions.)

First of all, firms vary in their efficiency in producing the utility that consumers seek. Some firms produce brands that yield more utility to the consumer for a dollar of production cost than do other brands. In general a firm that has lower costs relative to the utility of its brand than other firms will find that it pays to expand its output by both increasing advertising expenditures and decreasing $P*$. This behavior of firms by efficiency generates a negative association between advertising and $P*$ by brands.

Two crucial propositions are contained in the previous paragraph. The proposition—that to sell more the firm will offer a lower $P*$— obviously holds for the usual demand curve, which is negatively sloped. More critically, this proposition also holds for the relationship between demand and price when advertising expenditures adjust optimally to

---

[2] This definition of $P*$ is an attempt to obtain a utility adjusted price. For simple additive utility functions, $P*$ does the job. For other utility functions, different definitions of $P*$ might be required. For purposes of my analysis this variation in the definition of $P*$ is not important as long as a utility adjustment of price is possible.

price. Even though this demand curve can have a positively sloped portion (Demsetz 1959), Schmalensee's (1972) analysis implies that even this demand curve will be declining where it counts—in the neighborhood of equilibrium.[3] The proposition that there is a reverse association between quantity produced and $P*$ can be put to the test. If this proposition were true, it would pay a brand to advertise its rank in its product class more, the higher that rank. Do leading firms advertise their significance more than nonleading firms advertise their lack of leadership? To answer that question, I looked at three issues of *Life* magazine for March 1972 (*Life* 1972). I found six brands claiming that they were at largest brands for their respective product classes. I found none advertising a lower rank. There are far fewer brands that are first in their product class than are not first (even confining ourselves to the sample of brands that advertise in three issues of *Life*). If brands advertised their rank in their product class independently of what that rank happened to be, the probability of an advertisement which advertised rank advertising that the rank is first would be far less than .5. In consequence the probability of our observed results occurring by chance is less than one sixty-fourth.[4]

The second proposition—that the firm that wishes to sell more will advertise more—also has a strong a priori defense. Advertising and $-\Delta P*$ are the two inputs yielding higher quantity demanded. From production theory one anticipates that if the "price" of the two inputs were constant, an increase in the output is usually most profitably achieved by an increase in both inputs. But in this case the "price" of the inputs does not remain constant as one increases quantity. Quantity is the "price" of $-\Delta P*$, that is, the loss to the firm in lowering price to increase quantity demanded is proportional to that quantity. In consequence, one would expect adver-

---

[3] Using Demsetz's (1959) terminology, the average revenue curve allowing advertising to adjust optimally to a change in price is the *mutatis mutandis* average revenue curve (MAR). For MAR to be rising or constant $MMR \geq MAR$, where MMR = marginal *mutatis mutandis* revenue curve. For firms to have positive or zero profits $MAR \geq AC$, where AC = average production and advertising costs and MC = marginal production and advertising costs; but $MMR = MC$. Hence, $MC \geq AC$, which implies that AC is rising or constant. But Schmallensee (1972) has shown that in equilibrium AC must be decreasing. Hence, MAR must be decreasing in equilibrium.

[4] This test would be biased if brands that were not number one advertised themselves as major producers more than those brands which are number one. But this bias is produced by the very proposition I am testing, a proposition that would explain why number one brands choose more explicit rank advertising than others. A more serious problem with this approach is that the data do not support another implication of rational consumer behavior: that firms that advertise the most would advertise that fact. I think the primary reason that the quantity of advertisement is not advertised is that advertising has been so frequently attacked that it is in disrepute. These attacks make it difficult for consumers to understand the ultimate rationalization of their own behavior. (This problem is discussed in more detail in the "Deceptive Advertising" section of this paper.) In consequence, brands do not advertise their advertising rank, though they do advertise that they have advertised, e.g., "As Advertised in *Life*."

tising expenditures to increase because both output increases and the price of the other factor of production increases. The evidence is overwhelming that advertising increases as sales increase.

There are other reasons for a consumer to respond positively to advertising. What is a high-utility brand for some consumers will be a low-utility brand for others. Advertising has the seemingly magical property that those whose tastes are best served by a given brand are those most likely to see an advertisement for that brand. Advertisers choose the media in which they advertise in part to maximize the repeat-purchase probability for their brand. In consequence the producer distributes his advertisements among media so that his message is seen by those who are most likely to repeat purchase his brand. An esoteric, high-price soup gets advertised in the *New Yorker*, while Campbell's soup displays its wares in *Good Housekeeping*.

A third factor operates to increase the reputability of advertised brands. The full analysis of this factor is consigned to the Appendix, but the essence of the argument is simple enough. Advertising increases the probability of a consumer's remembering the name of a brand. Those brands with the highest probability of repeat purchase have the greatest payoff to improved consumer memory. In consequence, brands which provide the highest utility have the greatest incentive to advertise.

A feature of the previous discussion must be emphasized. Nowhere in that analysis was it necessary to assume that consumers respond positively to advertising because the brands that advertised the more heavily were better buys. The self-interest of consumers to respond to advertising only if it increased their utility produces an additional guarantee that highly advertised products will provide higher utility to the consumer. Suppose there were some products for which firm self-interest dictated a negative relationship between advertising and utility per dollar. Consumer self-interest would make the consumers respond negatively to advertising for these products. In consequence, firms would not advertise such products.

In this analysis of the indirect information contained in advertising, the focus has been on experience qualities. The same analysis can be used to show that advertising increases the reputability of brands which are dominantly search goods. However, reputability will play a much smaller role in the advertising for search qualities, because the consumer can obtain so much direct information about these qualities from advertisements and direct inspection. The possession of this direct information reduces the payoff to both consumers and advertisers of advertisements' increasing the reputability of a brand. In my subsequent analysis I shall assume that this difference between the character of advertising for search and experience qualities is so large that the advertising for experience qualities is dominantly indirect information and the advertising for search qualities is dominantly direct information.

Marginal Revenue of Advertising to the Producer

To maximize profits a producer will advertise to the point where his marginal revenue of advertising is equal to his marginal cost of advertising. One expects differences in the behavior of this marginal revenue for search and experience qualities. This difference in turn will produce a differential effect on the quantity of advertising purchased by producers of search and experience qualities.

To demonstrate this effect one needs a theory to generate the marginal revenue of advertising. For search qualities, advertising will increase sales when and only when it gives the consumer information that he did not have before. I will assume that all the information that advertising conveys about a search brand is contained in any given message. The revenue (R) generated by advertising will, therefore, equal:

$$R = QPNG_1; \tag{1}$$

where N = the number of potential customers, that is, those who would buy the brand if confronted with the appropriate signal (in this case, one or more advertising messages), Q = average quantity purchased per customer, P = price, and G_1 = the proportion of potential customers with one or more advertising messages. Of the four components of R only G_1 varies by advertising intensity. The behavior of G_1 has been examined by Stigler (1961) and Gould (1970), but there is a problem with their analysis that makes reexamination necessary.

As Stigler recognizes, there are three relevant processes at work. Consumers acquire advertising information; they leave and enter the market, that is, they are mobile; they forget advertising information. Stigler asserts that the latter two processes produce identical results in the advertising market, except for possible differences in their intensities. I think he is wrong. In the mobility case, the most reasonable simple assumption is that the probability of leaving the market is independent of the number of advertising messages a consumer knows. In the forgetting case, however, the simplest reasonable assumption is that the number of messages forgotten about a brand is directly proportional to the number of messages known about a brand.

I expect, then, mobility and forgetting to be quite different probability processes. Optimally, one should combine the two processes in the same model. Such a model is easy to construct, but I have not been able to solve the equations that the model generates. Instead I have developed two different models. In one there is mobility, but no forgetting; in the others there is forgetting, but no mobility. Because it is simpler and probably more important, I concentrate on the forgetting model. This is simply a matter of economizing on space. My results do not change when I use the mobility model.[5]

[5] My analysis of the mobility model is available upon request.

In my forgetting model I assume that the rate at which consumers confront an advertising message (c) is a constant for all consumers. I also assume that the forgetting rate is directly proportional to the number of advertising messages a person knows. The differential matrix of this stochastic process is

$$F = \begin{bmatrix} -c & c & & & \\ a & -(c+a) & c & & \\ & 2a & -(c+2a) & c & \\ & & 3a & -(c+3a) & c \end{bmatrix}, \qquad (2)$$

where the state space is $(0, 1, \ldots, n)$ advertising messages about a brand and a is the forgetting rate when one knows one advertising message.

I shall try to abstract out of this stochastic process the relationship between the present value of revenue and advertising intensity. This present value of revenue will change over time as the process unfolds. Of these present values both the simplest and the most useful is the one calculated after the stochastic process has settled down to a steady state. Then the present value will merely be the present value of a constant stream of returns. It is this steady-state condition that I will examine.

As is well known (e.g., Karlin 1966), the steady-state distribution (λ) can be obtained by solving

$$\lambda F = 0. \qquad (3)$$

In words, the net movement into any steady state must be zero or it is not a steady state. The solution:

$$\lambda_i = \frac{d^i}{i!} e^{-d} \qquad i = (0, 1, \ldots, n), \qquad (4)$$

where $d = c/a$. In particular the probability of having one or more advertising messages is

$$1 - \lambda_0 = 1 - e^{-d}. \qquad (5)$$

Equation (5) is G_1 in equation (1) and hence is relevant in determining the revenue from advertising in the case of search.

However, G_1 will not be relevant in determining the revenue from advertising for experience qualities. I have assumed that the information the consumer obtains from advertising for experience qualities is that the brand is advertised and is, hence, more likely to be a better buy. In the face of experience qualities, a consumer's optimal strategy is to try a fixed number of brands, say r, and then continue to use the best of the set (Nelson 1970). A consumer to whom advertising for experience qualities provides favorable information will limit his sampling to those brands for which he has received the most advertising messages. Say he has currently received m messages for the rth most advertised brand in his own sample of messages. Assume further that in case of a tie in the number of advertising messages the consumer receives, the consumer prefers the brand whose advertising messages he has most recently received.[6] Then a consumer will try a brand if he receives m messages about the brand, and any messages beyond m are redundant.

For experience qualities one needs a more general form of equation (1). The revenue generated by advertising is

$$R = Q P N G_m \qquad (6)$$

where G_m = the proportion of potential customers with m or more advertising messages, where m is the critical number of advertising messages required for a consumer to sample a brand. (To put the revenue in present-value terms, all one need do is multiply the right side of eq. [6] by $1/w$—where w equals the discount rate.) For the forgetting model, G_m is

$$1 - \sum_{i=0}^{m-1} \lambda_i = 1 - \sum_{i=0}^{m-1} \frac{d^i}{i!} e^{-d}. \qquad (7)$$

The amount of advertising can be measured by the rate at which customers acquire advertising information—or c. The marginal revenue to the producer of advertising is, therefore

$$MR_A = Q P N \frac{\partial G_m}{\partial c}. \qquad (8)$$

Assume that $Q P N$ are the same for advertising for search and experience qualities.[7] The MR_A will differ between search and experience qualities because $\partial G_m/\partial c$ differs by m. (I will assume, for simplicity, that all consumers are faced with the same m in the advertising for any given brand, though this assumption is contrary to fact.)

$$\frac{\partial G_m}{\partial c} = \frac{d^{m-1}}{a(m-1)!} e^{-d}. \qquad (9)$$

---

[6] A more realistic assumption would be that in a case of a tie at m messages, the probability of the consumer's sampling the brand is the inverse of the number of tied brands. But this more realistic assumption increases considerably the complexity of the presentation without adding any new insight into the process.

[7] This assumption is contrary to fact, but its conflict with reality should not produce serious problems in this particular case. In Nelson (1970) I showed that there should be more monopoly power in the market for experience goods than in the market for search goods. Assume the same total market size—and there is no reason to assume that this varies systematically between search and experience goods. Then average firm size should be larger for experience goods than for search goods and there should be fewer firms. If marginal production and advertising costs were constant with respect to size, these two differences should cancel one another out, i.e., total advertising expenditures for the industry would not vary through variation in the size of firms within the industry.

For search qualities $m = 1$; for experience qualities $m \geq 1$. It can be easily shown that

$$\frac{\partial G_m}{\partial c} > \frac{\partial G_1}{\partial c},$$

where $m > 1$ and $G_m'' < 0$.[8] In other words, over the declining portion of $\partial G_m/\partial c$, $\partial G_m/\partial c$ is always greater for experience qualities than for search qualities (or equal when $m = 1$). Since only the declining portion of the marginal revenue curve is relevant for firm decision making when marginal costs are constant or increasing, firms advertising experience qualities will advertise more than firms advertising search qualities when they both advertise.

Can the marginal cost of production and advertising always be above the marginal revenue curve of advertising for experience qualities? This is possible for any given brand of a product (which will then not advertise); it is impossible for the market in general. If for all brands, the marginal cost curve is higher than the marginal revenue curve for an m as low as two, then the market will make the minimum m one. The marginal revenue curve for search and experience will then be the same only in this polar case. Of course the industry's total advertising expenditure are independent of the number of firms as long as marginal costs of production and advertising are constant.

How does one test the proposition that there will be more advertising of experience than of search goods? In "Information and Consumer Behavior" (Nelson 1970), it is shown that goods could be classified successfully by whether the quality variation was ascertained predominantly by search or by experience, and the respective goods were called "search goods" and "experience goods." To take account of some ambiguity in the classification procedure in Nelson (1970), two alternative classifications were used. They are again used here, together with a third classification (Classification II with cameras moved from the search to the experience category). This third classification is motivated by the discussion in Nelson (1970, p. 320 n.). The commodities in these classifications are presented in table 1. The following mean advertising ratios were

[8] $G_m'' = \frac{1}{a^2} d^{m-2} \frac{1}{(m-2)!} e^{-d} \left(1 - \frac{d}{m-1}\right).$

Since $d > 0$, $m \geq 2$, then $G_m'' < 0$ implies $\dfrac{d}{m-1} > 1$, so

$$G_m' - G_1' = \frac{1}{a} e^{-d} \left[\frac{d^{m-1}}{(m-1)!} - 1\right].$$

But $\dfrac{d}{m-i} > \dfrac{d}{m-1}$ for $m-1 > i > 1$. Hence, $\dfrac{d}{m-1} > 1$ implies that $\dfrac{d^{m-1}}{(m-1)!} > 1$.

Hence, $G_m' > G^i$ when $G_m'' < 0$.

TABLE 1

ADVERTISING/SALES RATIOS IN CONSUMER CATEGORY BY INFORMATION CATEGORY*

Good and Infor- mation Category	Advertising/Sales Ratio, 1957	Good and Infor- mation Category	Advertising/Sales Ratio, 1957
Experience durable:		**Experience nondurable:**	
Books	2.702	Beer	6.872
Paints†	1.450	Wine	4.395
Tires	1.385	Liquor	2.408
Appliances	3.296	Dairy products	1.885
Motorcycles and bicycles	1.078	Grain mill products	1.695
Motor vehicles	0.907	Cereals	4.845
Motor vehicle parts		Bakery	2.803
and accessories	0.700	Sugar	0.280
Professional and scientific		Confectionery	3.543
instruments‡	2.086	Miscellaneous foods	4.073
Clocks and watches	5.629	Cigars	2.370
Communications equipment	2.034	Other tobacco	5.429
Average	2.177	Drugs	10.280
Average total experience	3.427	Soaps	7.938
		Perfume	14.723
Search goods:		Petroleum refining	0.507
Knit goods	1.075	Meats	0.610
Carpets	2.052	Periodicals	0.304
Hats	2.124	Average	4.085
Millinery	0.326		
Men's clothing	0.928		
Women's clothing	1.263		
Miscellaneous apparel	1.269		
Furniture	1.451		
Footwear	1.326		
Leather goods	1.204		
Jewelry§	2.202		
Costume jewelry§	2.498		
Average	1.395		

*Goods classified by Classification III data from Telser.(1964).
†Search good in Classification I.
‡Search good in Classifications I and II.
§Experience good in Classification I.

obtained:

Classification I: $X_e = .0347$, $X_s = .0123$, $D = .0234$, $t = 3.67$;

Classification II: $X_e = .0348$, $X_s = .0137$, $D = .0137$, $t = 3.16$;

Classification III: $X_e = .0343$, $X_s = .0132$, $D = .0211$, $t = 3.40$;

where X = mean advertising sales ratio; e = experience goods; s = search goods; D = difference of the means; t = test result of the hypothesis that $D = 0$. For all these classification procedures the differences are large, and hence are economically as well as statistically significant.

The chief problem with this test and subsequent tests to be made is the possible ambiguity in the classification of goods into the two information categories: search and experience. Alternative classification procedures do not appear to have a large effect. Of course, random errors in classification bias result toward zero observed differences in the means, so they do not vitiate the procedure. The big problem in classification is an unconscious (or conscious!) tendency for the classifier to produce the results he is seeking. Hopefully, the present classification, which was developed prior to the present tests, will be found to be valid.[9]

In consequence our results support the hypothesis that producers of experience goods advertise more than producers of search goods. This result is important because it in turn supports our fundamental behavioral proposition: that advertising of experience qualities increases sales through increasing the reputability of the seller, while advertising of search qualities increase sales by providing the consumer with "hard" information about the seller's products.

There is another important feature of these results. They are precisely the opposite of what would be anticipated given an obvious alternative theory of the way in which advertising for experience qualities operates. As I discussed in the first section, there is, indeed, some "hard" information conveyed by advertising for experience goods. A consumer is able to relate brand to function. For search goods advertisements can provide far more information than the relation of brand to function.

If advertising were solely concerned with distribution "hard" information, there should be more advertising measured in dollar terms for search goods than experience goods, simply because there is more "hard" information that can be conveyed about search qualities. Think, for example, of an advertisement saying simply, "Bayer is an aspirin." Then think of an advertisement saying, "Jonathan Logan is a dress," and showing a picture of a Jonathan Logan dress. The latter advertisement takes up more space and, hence, is more expensive. As we have seen, however, the data produce results precisely contrary to this prediction. This strongly suggests that the information content of advertising for experience goods goes far beyond the relation of brand to function—another reason for believing that advertising for experience goods provides information about the reputability of brands.

---

[9] Obviously, the simple test used in the text makes no attempt to control for other variables. Instead I have tried to present as many simple tests as I can in the belief that the many biases to which any one test is subjected (of which excluded variables is only one example) will not operate consistently in all my tests. One example of a possible bias is the close relationship between search goods and style goods. (This relationship is not accidental but engendered by the search—in contrast to the experience—process). It would appear, however, that the bias induced by the association of search and style runs against the test results reported in the text. The evidence we have (e.g., Telser 1964) suggests a positive association between advertising in an industry and the number of new brands in the industry. The same logic which generates that association would make style changes—a characteristic of style goods—generate additional advertising. That search goods tend to be style goods could hardly explain the low levels of advertising in search goods.

This last paragraph does not imply that the relation of brand to function is a nonexistent activity of advertising for experience goods. The implication is only that the effects of this activity are swamped by the effects of advertising to increase the reputability of experience brands. Why? Simply because most advertising of experience goods occurs with such intensity that most people already know the relation of brand to function.

This explanation is itself open to test. The smaller the advertising intensity of an experience good, the more likely that the advertising conveys new information to the consumer of the relation of brand to function. We have just seen that when advertising for experience goods is providing that kind of information the optimal page size of an advertisement ought to be smaller than the optimal page size for search goods, since the latter advertisements have more information to convey.

When, however, advertising for experience goods is designed primarily to increase the reputability of a brand, two forces will tend to increase the page size of advertisements for experience goods relative to this page size for search goods. First, even with the same amount of "hard information" and even when the consumer sees both, a larger advertisement should increase sales for experience goods more than a smaller advertisement. The larger advertisement enhances the reputation of the advertiser more than does the smaller advertisement. (When consumers select brands by volume of advertising, they will choose in terms of the dollar volume of advertising they see rather than simply the number of advertising messages.) Under these same conditions, the smaller and the larger advertisement for search goods would produce the same increase in sales.

Second, the probability of a consumer seeing an advertisement varies more with page size for experience goods than search goods. As we shall see in the next section, the marginal return to the consumer is small for advertisements whose sole additional information is increases in the reputability of a brand. In consequence, such advertisements must depend much more on catching a disinterested consumer's eye than advertisements that consumers seek out. Large page size tends to accomplish that objective (by way of contrast, classified advertisements have both large marginal returns to the consumer and exceedingly small page sizes).

One can, therefore, predict that as the volume of advertising increases by brand, the difference between the average page size of advertisements for experience and search goods increases. I tested this proposition by examining the national brand advertisements in the *New Yorker* for all of 1965. (This magazine was chosen because it is one of the few that has a lot of advertisements of both search and experience goods.) I measured the volume of advertising by the total pages purchased in the *New Yorker* by brand. I then divided this volume of advertising into four categories. As table 2 shows, there is a perfect rank correlation between the differences in page size of experience and search goods and the volume of

TABLE 2

AVERAGE PAGE SIZE OF ADVERTISEMENTS IN THE *New Yorker* IN 1965 BY BRAND, BY VOLUME OF ADVERTISING, AND BY INFORMATION CATEGORY

	VOLUME*							
	< 2		2 < 5		5 < 10		≥ 10	
	No. Brands	Average Page Size	No. Brands	Average Page Size	No. Brands	Average Page Size	No. Brands	Average Page Size
1. Search	138	.553	123	.786	75	.895	28	.789
2. Experience minus books†	122	.466	141	.730	127	.888	73	1.008
3. Experience...........	411	.253	146	.752	128	.883	74	1.036
Differences:								
(1) − (2)		.087		.056		.007		− .219
(1) − (3)		.300		.034		.012		− .247

*Total pages of advertisements in the *New Yorker* for a brand.
†Books omitted in (3) included in (2) because the behavior of books dominates the < 2 volume category.

advertising. The probability of this perfect ordering being produced by chance is one twenty-fourth. In consequence these results are significant at the 5 percent level.[10]

These data yield other striking results. The average page size for the smaller volume advertisers is smaller for experience goods than for search goods, and this result is reversed for large-volume advertisers. In the class of brands that advertised two pages or less in the *New Yorker* in 1965, the difference in average page size between search goods and experience goods was .087. The standard deviation of that difference was .037. Hence this difference is significant at the 5 percent level.[11] For big-volume advertisers (10 or more pages in the *New Yorker* in 1965), the difference in average page size between search and experience goods was − .218; the standard deviation of that difference was .059. This difference is significant at the .01 percent level.

These results explain a phenomenon inexplicable with the simple information models previously used in the analysis of advertising. It is traditional in advertising to have a particular brand sponsor a network television show. This results in three or more commercials during that period for the same brand. Often the information content of these commercials does not differ. Since the audience is quite stable over the course of the program, this advertising behavior makes no sense if the goal of the firm is to maximize the number of people who have one or more bits of information about the brand. Obviously a random distribution of the brand's commercial does a better job than this bunching procedure. But this bunching makes sense in terms of the goal of most television advertising: to increase the reputability of a brand of an experience good.

Marginal Revenue of Advertising to the Consumer

In the usual analysis of advertising, the consumer plays a rather passive role. Our analysis, on the contrary, visualizes consumer decision in the quest for information as a central determinant of the behavior of advertising. One crucial variable governing consumer decisions is the marginal revenue to the consumer in confronting an advertisement. This marginal revenue has to be greater than the time cost to the consumer in order for him to examine an advertisement. This places a constraint on both the amount and type of advertisement a brand will use.

Our model suggest that there should be a systematic difference between

---

[10] I ran this test both including and excluding advertisements for books. The reason for this strategy was that book advertisements dominate the small-volume advertisement category for experience goods. The perfect rank correlation was produced by both procedures.

[11] If books are included in experience goods, the difference is .247 and its standard error .028. The results are significant at the .01 percent level.

the marginal revenue to the consumer for experience goods and the marginal revenue for search goods. The marginal revenue of information to the consumer for a good is the expected improvement in his utility as a result of using this information in his sampling of brands of this good. This expected improvement can be analyzed as the product (in the mathematical sense) of two components: (1) the standard deviation of the utility distribution of brands (i.e., the distribution of $P*$) for that good; (2) the expected improvement in standard deviation units of utility that can be obtained by using that information. The first factor depends on the nature of the market for the good. The second factor depends on the nature of the information available about the good. Since the focus is on information in this analysis, it is not surprising that the second factor is the agent of the expected difference between the marginal revenue of advertising to the consumer for search and experience goods, respectively.

But the first factor cannot be ignored. The nature of the market is also a function of the nature of the information (Nelson 1970). Indeed, the standard deviation of the utility distribution of experience and search goods might well be systematically different. However, the nature of that difference is not at all clear. Two forces operate in opposite directions on the relative magnitude of this standard deviation of search and experience goods. On the one hand, competitive pressure reduces the standard deviation of utilities about which consumers agree more for search goods than for experience goods (Nelson 1970). On the other hand, the greater sample size that consumers use for search goods will increase the standard deviation in utility of characteristics about which consumers disagree for search goods relative to experience goods.[12]

It is impossible to say, a priori, which of the two forces analyzed will dominate in determining the relative variance of the utility of search and experience goods for a given consumer. It would be surprising, however, if this mixed effect could outweigh the impact of the difference in the information characteristics of search and experience goods. In analyzing this difference I will assume that the payoff to the same information would be the same for search and experience goods, that is, the utility distribu-

---

[12] A brand that specializes in satisfying an extreme taste will become the most-preferred brand of those with that taste at the expense of becoming one of the least-preferred brands of those with average taste and tastes at other extremes. The smaller the sample size of brands (assuming that it is greater than one), the smaller the payoff to such specialization. Sample sizes as small as two screen out least-preferred alternatives quite effectively, but do not effectively discriminate between most-preferred brands and brands nearby on a consumer's utility scale. Any increase in sample sizes beyond two increases the payoff to being the most-preferred brands for some people considerably, and only changes the cost of being the least-preferred brand for other people mildly. Hence, greater sample sizes of brands encourage greater variance among brands in the characteristics about which consumers disagree. In a simple model of this process, a sample size of two produces a brand distribution concentrated at the median of the distribution of consumers by their most-preferred quality; an infinite sample size produces a brand distribution that corresponds exactly with that distribution of consumers. (An analysis of this model is available upon request.)

tions by brand for a given customer are the same for search and experience goods.

The big difference in the character of the advertisements of search and experience goods is that advertisements for experience goods are dominantly "soft" or indirect information. Consumers use "soft" information for experience goods because they have no option. The primary information content of advertisements for experience goods is the information that the brand advertises. For search goods, on the other hand, the consumer does have the option of using "hard" or "soft" information. But one of the basic assumptions of our model is that consumers respond to the direct information contained in the advertising message—"hard" information—for search goods. This implies that for search goods this "hard" information has a greater value to the consumer than "soft" information. I predict, therefore, that the marginal revenue of advertisements to the consumer will be greater for search goods than for experience goods.

To test this proposition I look at the distribution by media of advertising for experience and search goods. Consumers will be willing to look at advertisements as long as the marginal revenue to them of so doing is greater than their marginal cost. The marginal cost to the consumer is dominantly a time cost. This time cost will vary by the alternatives use of the time used in watching the advertisement.

Many advertising media take advantage of severe restrictions on the alternative time uses of the consumer. Television and radio intersperse advertisements with programs the consumer wants to hear. By listening to the commercials the consumer sacrifices only those activities he can do during the short time period of the commerical. The cost to the consumer of looking at billboards and transit posters are only the activities he can do while confined to a moving vehicle. Only advertisements in newspapers and magazines demand of the consumer the sacrifice of the best of his possible alternative time uses. For newspapers and magazines he can arrange the time saving from not looking at the advertisements any way he chooses.

Newspapers and magazines have the added property that the consumer can look at the advertisements as many times as he wishes. We would expect some positive relationship between the marginal revenue to the consumer of an advertisement and the number of times he will want to look at that advertisement. Hence, we would expect advertisements with a high marginal revenue to the consumer to concentrate in newspapers and magazines relative to the other advertising media; we would expect just the contrary behavior for advertisements with low marginal revenue to the consumer. We, therefore, predict that there will be more advertisements for search goods in newspapers and magazines relative to the other advertising media compared to the same behavior for experience goods.

I test this proposition by comparing the distribution of advertising for

TABLE 3

RATIO OF TELEVISION NETWORK TO MAGAZINE ADVERTISING
BY GOODS, 1966

Goods	Ratio*
Experience:	
Automobiles	1.93
Foods	2.35
Toiletries	2.46
Tobacco	2.61
Drugs	2.58
Search:	
Apparel	1.59
Household furniture	0.84

*Includes only those goods tabulated for both. Alcohol not included because of prohibition on network advertising of hard liquor (U.S. Bureau of the Census 1967).

TABLE 4

RATIO OF LOCAL TO NATIONAL ADVERTISING BY LOCAL MEDIA, 1966

Media	Ratio*
Newspapers	4.1
Radio spot	2.2
Television spot	0.5
Outdoor	0.6
Transit	1.0

*U.S. Bureau of the Census (1967).

magazines against television network advertising for different kinds of consumer goods. The results overwhelmingly support the hypothesis. Look at the ratio of advertising expenditures for television to these expenditures for magazines for 1966 as reported in table 3. Every one of the experience goods has a higher ratio than the search goods. The geometric mean of this ratio for experience goods is 2.45, while for search goods the geometric mean is 1.16. This difference is statistically significant at the 1 percent level, $t = 4.2$.

We can have more than usual confidence in this test, because we can test the test. Using quite different—but highly persuasive—evidence, Ferguson (1963) has established that local advertisements have a higher marginal revenue to the consumer than national advertisements. (Ferguson's result is predicted by our theory. Local advertising provides for the most part information that can be checked prior to purchase: price and where to find things.) If our tests were indeed a test for variation in the marginal revenue to the consumer, we should find the ratio of local to national advertisements higher for newspapers than for all other local media. Look at table 4 for the ratio of local to national advertising by local media. While there are too few observations to hope for statistical significance, the differences in the order of magnitude involved are huge. This evidence is highly suggestive.

Alternative Sources of Information

Thus far our analysis has concentrated on consumer behavior when faced with two alternatives: to sample (whether by experience or search) at random or with the aid of advertising. Advertising is not the only aid to sampling that the consumer can employ. The most obvious source of assistance that consumers have is the recommendation of relatives and friends and consumer magazines. It seems reasonable to suppose that for experience goods consumers believe these recommendations constitute better information than advertising.[13] Certainly these recommendations must sometimes provide better information or they would never be used. The consumer is surrounded by a sea of advertising whose information is obtained by the consumer at virtually no cost to himself. The consumer, then, always has the alternative of using advertising as his guide. Instead he sometimes uses the guidance of relatives and friends. Hence, that information must sometimes be better information. The more consumers use relatives and friends, the less they respond to advertising.

I showed in "Information and Consumer Behavior" that guidance was used more for goods for which there is a low frequency of purchase than goods for which there is a high frequency of purchase both for experience and search goods. (For simplicity I will henceforth call low frequency of purchase goods "durables" and high frequency of purchase goods "non-durables," though the essence of their behavioral difference is contained in the frequency of purchase). This leads to the reverse prediction for advertising: greater advertising for nondurables than for durables for both experience and search.[14]

However, this relationship should be far stronger for experience goods than for search goods. First, the level of guidance is far less for search goods than for experience goods. In consequence, guidance should have less impact on the demand for advertising for search goods. Second, advertis-

---

[13] For search goods the case is not clear at all. A consumer might well regard a picture of a dress contained in an advertisement as better information than a friend telling her that the dress is pretty.

[14] Durables and nondurables will differ by another important characteristic as well. The value of advertising information to the consumer for a given number of advertising messages will be greater for durables than nondurables. However, this consequence will produce ambiguous effects on advertising expenditures. The lower value of advertising information to the consumer for nondurables will reduce the number of advertising messages that consumers receive for nondurables; but the low value of advertising information to the consumer will also increase the expenses to the producer for every message that the consumer does receive.

748   JOURNAL OF POLITICAL ECONOMY

ing information is better for search goods than it is for experience goods, whereas the information of relatives and friends is worse for search goods than it is for experience goods.[15] Hence, advertising information will compete more effectively with the information of guides in the case of search goods.

I find a significantly higher average advertising sales ratio for nondurable than durable experience goods no matter which of the alternative classification procedures I use for experience goods:

$$\text{Classification I:} \quad \bar{X}_{DE} = 2.293, \quad \bar{X}_{NE} = 4.085, \quad t = 1.92;$$

$$\text{Classification II:} \quad \bar{X}_{DE} = 2.187, \quad \bar{X}_{NE} = 4.085, \quad t = 1.97;$$

$$\text{Classification III:} \quad \bar{X}_{DE} = 2.177, \quad \bar{X}_{NE} = 4.085, \quad t = 2.028,$$

where $\bar{X}_{DE}$ = arithmetic mean advertising/sales ratio for durable experience goods; $\bar{X}_{NE}$ = arithmetic mean advertising/sales ratio for nondurable experience goods; t-values are computed for tests of the difference between two means and are significant at the 5 percent level with a one-tail test procedure. For search goods the sample size is too small for any significance test, but the cursory evidence points to the reverse relationship: higher advertising/sales ratio for durables than for nondurables.

With British data, Doyle (1968) also finds an inverse relationship between durability and advertising/sales ratios. But since Doyle did not make any distinction between search and experience goods, he did not observe that that relationship was confined to experience goods.

Doyle (1968) observes one more relationship that can be explained by advertising's role as information. He finds a significantly negative relationship between advertising/sales ratios by product and the unit price of that product, where the unit is defined roughly as the quantity that is ordinarily purcased at one time, for example, one car, one pound of coffee, etc. A low unit price will mean some combination of the following: high frequency of purchase or low total expenditure on the commodity.

I have already shown why there should be a close relationship between high frequency of purchase and advertising expenditures. Because the classification is so broad, however, the durability measure does not catch all of the effect of frequency of purchase on advertising. So even when durability is explicitly considered in the multiple regression, part of the relationship between unit price and advertising will be attributable to the relationship between price and frequency of purchase.

The relationship between unit price and total expenditures on a product will also yield a negative association between unit price and advertising. The greater the total expenditures of consumers for a product, the greater

---

[15] It can be demonstrated that the correlation of consumer preferences is lower for search goods than for experience goods.

the anticipated variance of utility to consumers of brands of that product. In consequence, when consumers spend a lot for a commodity they will tend to use better—but more expensive—information than advertising: to wit, the guidance of relatives and friends or consumer magazines. Doyle's evidence, then, provides additional support for my explanation of the impact of durability on the advertising/sales ratio. Of course, this is hardly conclusive evidence. Only the cumulative impact of additional studies can produce evidence that could be even remotely so characterized.

Deceptive Advertising

In the preceding pages I have given scant attention to deceptive advertising, though, obviously, deceptive advertising exists. We have seen that some deception will occur even in the case of search qualities, where the consumer has the most market power over the content of advertisements. But the amount of deceptiveness in advertising can be easily exaggerated if one simply looks at the incentives of advertisers to deceive without considering the incentives of consumers not to be deceived. The circumstances under which advertisers have the greatest incentives to deceive if consumers believed them are precisely the circumstances under which consumers would be least inclined to believe advertising. Deception requires not only a misleading or untrue statement, but somebody ready to be misled by that statement.

One possible source of deceptive advertising is consumer confusion. As long as consumers followed the decision rule: believe an advertisement for experience qualities when it tells about the functions of a brand; do not believe the advertisement when it tells how well a brand performs that function—the consumer will be rarely deceived. But there is no guarantee, of course, that consumers will always use that decision rule.

There is another important source of deceptive advertising: the law. Whenever a law on advertising practices is moderately enforced, deceptive advertising is sure to occur. Take, for example, the law prohibiting the mislabeling of the fabric content of clothing. If that law is sufficiently enforced, consumers will believe that a clothing label is usually correct. This will provide an incentive for some manufacturer to mislabel—unless the law is enforced so vigorously that nobody gains from breaking it— a nonoptimal level of law enforcement (Becker 1968; Stigler 1970). In the absence of the law no one could trust any clothing label that it was not in the self-interest of the producer to specify correctly. Hence these clothing labels, though incorrect, would not deceive many people.

The law increases deceptive advertising in another way. Consumers are unlikely to be legal experts. Some, therefore, are likely to believe that certain forms of deceptive advertising are prevented by law when, in fact, they are not. It is not clear that broadening the definition of fraudulent advertising would solve this problem. The more the law protects against fraud, the more people think the law protects against fraud. Misinterpretation of the law's domain will exist, no matter how extensive that domain.

Why, then, would the police power of the state ever be invoked against "deceptive" advertising, since it is quite possible that these laws increase rather than decrease deception in advertising? These laws can accomplish something. They can—at a cost—make more information available to the consumer. Consumer market power reduces deception by consumer distrust of any statement about which it is in the self-interest of producers to deceive. As we have seen, for experience qualities this narrows considerably the information available to consumers from advertising. Some people might deem it important that other information be made available from advertising, that consumers, for example, be able to determine the fabric content of their clothing. Laws can achieve this objective at the price of both enforcement costs and costs to the consumer of the elimination of possible memorable sources of indirect information.

These laws will be relevant almost exclusively to the advertising of experience qualities, since, even without laws, advertising for search qualities provides fairly complete information about the properties of the brand being advertised. Deceptive advertising will be concentrated where the laws are concentrated—almost exclusively in the advertising of experience qualities. There is evidence that supports this contention. Though I find it unsatisfactory, let us use for the moment the Federal Trade Commission's criterion of what constitutes deceptive advertising. Whatever its shortcomings, it has developed independently of the desire to generate data that would either support or reject hypotheses of economists. For the first 6 months of 1965 the Federal Trade Commission found 58 advertisements deceptive about the quality of the product (as distinguished from its price). [16] All were advertisements about experience qualities (U.S. Federal Trade Commission 1970).

Clearly, then, there is some deceptive advertising. The only empirical

---

[16] The Federal Trade Commission did find a number of deceptive advertisements related to price. Ordinarily the price of an article is known prior to purchase. In all cases of deceptive advertising about price, however, the deceptive advertising was about price characteristics that would not be discovered prior to purchase. When payment is postponed, the consumer need not know the price before the purchase. This offers a firm an opportunity to place terms in the contract about which a large proportion of consumers would not be aware prior to purchase. The Federal Trade Commission judged three of these cases in 1965 (U.S. Federal Trade Commission 1970). The other category of deceptive price advertising found by the Federal Trade Commission was the advertisement of a deceptively high regular price (six of these cases in the first 6 months of 1965). In purchasing the good, the consumer usually knows the purchase price but not the regular price. In consequence this deception is not something that would be revealed to the consumer prior to purchase. (The basis for the deception is that consumers often use regular price quotations to economize on search.)

question is one of the magnitude of this phenomenon. My analysis up to now has given little weight to deception in advertising. What changes in this analysis are required if deception is an important rather than an unimportant part of advertising?

Surprisingly, this phenomenon would have little impact on the major conclusion of my analysis. Look again at my demonstration that brands with the lowest P^*s (price/utility) have the greatest incentives to advertise. It does not require intelligent consumer response to advertising—though it provides a basis for such intelligent response. Consumers who actually believe paid-for endorsements are the victims of the most benign form of deception. They are deceived into doing what they should do anyway. In consequence there should not be much difference between the behavior of those who respond to advertising because they are intelligent, and the behavior of the deceived. Under these circumstances it is both exceedingly difficult and not very important to put the deception hypothesis to the test.

This discussion of the deception hypothesis helps explain why economists have been so long deceived about the character of advertising. It does not pay consumers to make very thoughtful decisions about advertising. They can respond to advertising for the most ridiculous explicit reasons and still do what they would have done if they made the most careful judgments about their behavior.

Whatever their explicit reasons, the consumers' ultimate reason for responding to advertising is their self-interest in so doing. That is, it is no mere coincidence that thoughtful and unthoughtful judgments lead to the same behavior. If it were not in consumer self-interest to respond to advertising, then consumers' sloppy thinking about advertising would cost enough that they would reform their ways.

The learning required of consumers in this case is not very complicated. Advertised endorsements have been used for a long time. During this period the consumer, his parents, and his grandparents have consumed countless quantities of advertised and nonadvertised brands. If consumers were losing out by trying advertised products, they would have had an enormous number of opportunities to discover this fact.

Many economists have felt that other consumers think quite imprecisely about advertising—and well they might. But this superficial observation had led economists, but not consumers, astray. Economists have failed to see that consumers' response to advertising persists because of the underlying information role of advertising.

Summary and Conclusion

This paper has attempted to show the way in which advertising as information operates. I have contended that there is a basic difference in the character of the information conveyed by advertising for search and experience goods. For search goods advertising's information is direct. For experience goods the information conveyed is dominantly indirect—simply that the brand advertised. I have shown that this difference in the character of information leads to greater advertising expenditures for experience goods than search goods and greater marginal revenues to the consumer for search goods than experience goods. These implications were found satisfied by the data.

This analysis has not examined the totality of advertising's operation. I have not looked at the relationship between advertising and frequency of purchase of the advertised good—in contrast to brand. For example, food advertisements often contain recipes which provide information for the use of the good in question. Though this may be an important part of advertising's activity, it is irrelevant with respect to the set of implications examined in this article.

There is another possible function of advertising which I have not analyzed because I do not know how: advertising's impact on a consumer's utility function, holding information constant. The change-in-taste idea cannot be effectively tested because no real theory about taste changes has been developed. Fortunately, one does not need such an idea to explain the major features of advertising behavior.

It should be perfectly obvious to anyone who has read this article that an enormous amount of work on advertising still remains to be done. On the theoretical side I have not provided a general equilibrium solution for the amount of advertising expenditures (in particular I have not solved for m in eq. [7]); on the empirical side I have not explained a substantial portion of the variance of advertising/sales ratios by industry. The focus of this paper has been neither to develop a complete theory of advertising nor to present a complete multiple regression analysis of advertising's empirical behavior. Rather, the emphasis in this paper has been to develop a theory of advertising that is both reasonable and productive. The productivity of this theory does not depend upon its completeness (as partial equilibrium analysis in general attests.) A theory is productive if it can generate implications that are consistent with real-world behavior. The theory developed in this article satisfies that requirement. That this theory makes sense out of a wide range of empirical phenomena suggests that it has caught the essence of advertising behavior, that further theoretical (or empirical) work would not vitiate our results.[17]

[17] For example, it has been suggested that the equilibrium that I envision cannot be stable, that all consumers would tend to shift to the better-advertised brand until that brand had all the customers. This contrary-to-fact result can easily be prevented by allowing consumer tastes and income to vary. Nonadvertised brands, then, would specialize in minority consumer taste. (While my analysis has for the most part assumed homogeneous consumers for simplicity, its conclusions do not depend upon this assumption.)

Appendix

Producers of equal efficiency have a choice of making a low-utility brand at high unit profits or a high-utility brand at lower unit profits. It is reasonable to assume that the sales from customers who have no information about the brands' utilities will be the same for the two brands. But consumers will tend to repeat the purchase of higher-utility brands. In consequence, the expected sales of the high-utility brands will be greater. In equilibrium, the total profits of equally efficient firms will be the same whether they make a high- or a low-utility product if firms of this level of efficiency continue to produce both. This implies that the profit generated from the average individual making a purchase without information will be the same for both the high- and low-utility brands. (Since both profits and number of customers with no information are assumed to be the same for both brands, the ratio of the two must be the same.)

Assume, for the moment, that advertising merely increased the probability of a person's making an initial purchase of a brand without any impact on the conditional probability of a repeat purchase given an initial purchase. Then high- and low-utility brands would have equal incentives to advertise, for the marginal probability of a repeat purchase would increase in the same proportion as the probability of an initial purchase.

$$P(R) = P(I)\, P(R/I), \tag{A1}$$

where I = initial purchase, R = repeat purchase. With $P(R/I)$ constant, $P(R)$ increases proportionately with $P(I)$. This implies that the average new customer generated by advertising would yield the same revenue to the firm as did the average old customer with zero information for both high- and low-utility brands. Unless costs behaved in a very peculiar manner, this would imply that the profits generated by advertising were the same for the two brands, since the average old customer with zero information produces equal profits for the two brands.

Why should this not be the state of affairs if advertising were simply informational? After purchasing (and using) a brand, the consumer does not require advertising as a clue to the hidden qualities of a good. He can assess these hidden qualities directly. Why, then, should advertising have any impact on the conditional probability of a repeat purchase?

A simple mechanism that produces this impact is the process of consumer memory. The average consumer uses a lot of different products. It costs him something to remember the brands of these products that he tries. The cost is smaller the more familiar the name of the brand. Advertising makes brand names familiar. We would expect, therefore, the consumer to remember a higher proportion of advertised brands that he has tried than unadvertised brands. Indeed, there is evidence that this phenomenon does, in fact, operate. The ratio of the recalled sales of advertised brands to recalled total sales of a product is higher than their actual market share (Sudman 1962).

This process should have an impact on the conditional probability of a repeat purchase. A necessary condition for a repeat purchase made deliberately is that the consumer remember the name of the brand of which he wishes to make a repeat purchase. But if he remembers the name of the brand, he will not repeat his purchase by mistake. For sufficiently low-utility brands, a consumer who remembers the name of the brand will have a lower conditional probability of a repeat purchase than if he did not remember the name of the brand. For sufficiently high-utility brands, the reverse will be the case.

For a high-utility brand, advertising will produce a greater percentage increase in the marginal probability of a repeat purchase than its impact on the probability of initial purchase, since both terms on the right in equation (A1) increase. Since we assume the impact of an equivalent dose of advertising on the probability of initial purchase to be the same for low- and high-utility brands, it follows that the producers of high-utility brands have a greater incentive to advertise than the producers of low-utility brands.

References

Becker, Gary. "Crime and Punishment: An Economic Approach." *J.P.E.* 76, no. 2 (March 1968): 169–217.

Demsetz, Harold. "The Nature of Equilibrium in Monopolistic Competition." *J.P.E.* 67, no. 1 (February 1959): 22–30.

Dorfman, Robert, and Steiner, Peter. "Optimal Advertising and Optimal Quality." *A.E.R.* 44, no. 5 (December 1954): 826–36.

Doyle, P. "Advertising Expenditure and Consumer Demand." *Oxford Econ. Papers*, n.s. 20, no. 3 (November 1968): 394–414.

Ferguson, James. *The Advertising Rate Structure in the Daily Newspaper Industry.* Engelwood Cliffs, N.J.: Prentice-Hall, 1963.

Gould, John. "Diffusion Process and Optimal Advertising Policy." In *Microeconomic Foundations of Employment and Inflation Theory*, edited by E. Phelps et al. New York: Norton, 1970.

Karlin, Samuel. *A First Course in Stochastic Processes.* New York: Academic Press, 1966.

Life, vol. 72 (1972).

Nelson, Phillip. "Information and Consumer Behavior." *J.P.E.* 78, no. 2 (March/April 1970): 311–29.

Schmalensee, Richard. "A Note on Monopolistic Competition and Excess Capacity." *J.P.E.* 80, no. 3, pt. 1 (May/June 1972): 586–91.

Stigler, George. "The Economics of Information," *J.P.E.* 69, no. 3 (June 1961): 213–25.

——→. "The Optimal Enforcement of Laws," *J.P.E.* 78, no. 3 (May 1970): 526–36.

Sudman, Seymour. "On the Accuracy of Recording of Consumer Panels." Unpublished Ph.D. dissertation, Graduate School Bus., Univ. Chicago, 1962.

Telser, Lester, "Advertising and Competition." *J.P.E.* 72, no. 6 (December 1964): 537–62.

U.S., Bureau of the Census. *Statistical Abstract of the United States, 1967.* Washington: Government Printing Office, 1967.

U.S., Federal Trade Commission. *Decisions Jan. 1, 1965–June 30, 1965.* Washington, Government Printing Office, 1970.

[5]

A Status-based Model of Market Competition[1]

Joel M. Podolny
Stanford University

This article explores the significance of status processes for generating and reproducing hierarchy among producers in a market. It develops a conception of a market as a status order in which each producer's status position circumscribes the producer's actions by providing a unique cost and revenue profile for manufacturing a good of a given level of quality. An examination of pricing behavior among investment banks in the underwriting of corporate securities provides empirical support for this status-based model of market competition. Extensions are discussed.

INTRODUCTION

That there exists a distinction between an actor and an actor's position in the social structure and that rewards are largely a function of position is one of the fundamental insights of the sociological perspective (Simmel 1950). The distinction between actor and position has been applied with much success in the field of stratification research (White 1970; Sørensen 1983). It often figures prominently in sociological critiques of economists' claims that a wide range of economic, social, and political phenomena result from the aggregation of individual preferences (Baron and Hannan 1991), and it underlies the skepticism of the psychologists' claim that behavior can be explained with reference to an actor's personality or disposition (Davis-Blake and Pfeffer 1989).

This article attempts to extend the scope of this insight by applying a particular variant of the distinction between actor and position to market producers. As sociologists have expanded their arena of inquiry to include

[1] I am indebted to Steve Andrews, Bill Barnett, Jeffrey Bradach, Carolyn Boyes-Watson, Cynthia Cook, Karl Eschbach, Meyer Kestnbaum, Peter Marsden, Debra Minkoff, Paul Myers, Jeffrey Pfeffer, Aage Sørensen, and several anonymous *AJS* reviewers for helpful comments on earlier versions of this paper. I am also grateful to Paul DiMaggio for relaying comments from Yale University's Complex Organizations Workshop and to Robert Eccles and William Goode for insights related to the central themes of this work. Correspondence may be directed to Joel Podolny, Graduate School of Business, Stanford University, Stanford, California 94305-5015.

American Journal of Sociology

economic institutions, the market has received increased attention, and some steps have been taken to specify the mechanisms through which the market is shaped by noneconomic factors (Burt 1983; Baker 1984, 1990; Granovetter 1985). More specifically, the idea that market producers occupy socially defined positions in the context of the market was introduced by White (1981*a*, 1981*b*), whose primary concern was to elaborate a typology of markets as role structures. The importance of roles in market contexts has recently been extended by Baker and Faulkner (1991).

Like White, I conceptualize the market as a structure that is socially constructed and defined in terms of the perceptions of market participants, but my focus is not so much on roles as it is on status positions. Winship and Mandel's (1983) distinction between roles as classifications across social structures and positions as locations within social structures helps distinguish my endeavor from earlier work. I do not explore how dynamics differ across markets; I examine how a producer's position in the market affects the relative opportunities open to that producer in comparison to those available to its competitors.

My first objective is to elaborate a general framework that makes explicit the connection between status and economic variables such as cost, revenue, and price. In doing so, I proceed from the micro to the macro level. I begin with a definition of status and, from the definition, build a conception of an isolated status position. From there, I move to the conception of a status order and then discuss how the economic constraints and opportunities that confront a producer are very much contingent upon the producer's position in the status order. Having laid out the framework, I then illustrate its utility by applying it to a particular case: pricing dynamics in the primary securities markets.

WHAT IS STATUS?

I define a producer's status in the market as the perceived quality of that producer's products in relation to the perceived quality of that producer's competitors' products.[2] There are two lenses through which status may be viewed. On the one hand, a producer's status, or more accurately, the association with that status, can be considered something that nonproducing market participants (i.e., consumers, investors, and brokers

---

[2] When colloquially used with reference to markets, the word *status* is applied primarily to luxury goods. Here, I wish to avoid this implicit association. Words like *prestige* seem particularly awkward when applied to products, and the phrase *perceived quality* fails to convey the sense of an implicit hierarchy or ranking which is central to my understanding of markets.

Status-based Model

of exchange) generally value in its own right. Whether considered an end in itself (Frank 1985) or a means toward enhanced power over other individuals (Weber 1978; Veblen 1953), greater status increases the utility derived from the association with or consumption of a good.[3] While this view of status is not inconsistent with the framework I will develop, the assumption that nonproducing market participants value status is not necessary either.

More critical is a second view of market status as a *signal* of the underlying quality of a firm's products. If an actor is uncertain of the actual quality of the goods that confront her in the market, or if she is unwilling or unable to bear the search costs of investigating all the different products in the market, then the regard that other market participants have for a given producer is a fairly strong indicator of the quality of that producer's output.

This conception of status is compatible with the formal economic understanding of signals. According to Spence (1974), a signal is any observable indicator, of a quality or qualities, that meets two criteria: (1) the indicator must be at least partially manipulable by the actor and (2) the marginal cost or difficulty of obtaining the indicator must be nonzero and inversely correlated with the actor's level of quality. A college diploma is a signal of productivity because its attainment is at least partially within an individual's control and because it is more difficult for those who lack organizational skills (or other such attributes that help constitute productivity) to obtain a college degree. A warranty is a signal because its terms are at the discretion of the producer and because the cost of a given warranty is inversely related to quality; the lower-quality producer, almost by definition, will have to make good on the promise specified in the warranty with greater frequency.

Similarly, status meets the two criteria for signals. Even though a producer's status depends largely on the expressed opinions and actions of others, the producer nonetheless exercises at least some control over its status since its own past actions are important determinants of how it is perceived. Moreover, the difficulty of acquiring a reputation for superior quality is inversely associated with the general quality level of the producer.

Economic models of signaling activity are primarily concerned with equilibrium behavior or comparative static analyses of different equilib-

---

[3] Note the proposition that nonproducing market participants value status does not imply that a desire for status is an overarching motive for producers as an alternative to profit maximization. Throughout, I assume that producers are interested in profit maximization, but that they realize that the means for realizing profits is contingent upon the status position occupied in the market.

American Journal of Sociology

rium conditions. A formal condition of equilibrium in signaling models is that the actual distribution of a producer's quality must be equal to the distribution of quality that constituents expect on the basis of the signal. In assuming an equality between what exists and what is expected, these economic models necessarily give less attention to those factors that may undercut this equality and engender only a *loose linkage* between a signal and that which it is supposed to represent.

For the relationship between status and actual quality, this loose linkage originates primarily from four sources: (1) the necessary time lag between changes in the quality of a product and changes in consumer perceptions, (2) the stochastic nature of the link itself, (3) the nature, content, and extent of a producer's relations with others in the market, and (4) the second-order nature of status. Of these four factors, the time lag contributes least to complicating the relationship between actual and perceived quality. Were the time lag the only relevant factor, then the relationship between quality and perceptions could be easily established; the quality at some time t would perfectly determine perceptions at some time $t + 1$.

A second and more significant source of the decoupling is the fact that information diffusion is necessarily a stochastic process. Not every shift in quality of a given level will be detected, not every detected shift will be communicated to the same number of potential future users, and not every communication between users will occur at the same rate.

These first two factors, of course, are not unique to the relationship between status and quality, but are endemic to the link between nearly any signal and that which the signal is supposed to represent. Indeed, they are implied by the signaling framework in which quality must be unobservable for signals to be relevant to market actors' decisions. What at least partially distinguishes the signal of status is that the loose linkage between status and quality is mediated by a producer's ties to others in the market.

A producer's network of relations mediates the link between quality and status in two ways. First, the embeddedness of action in social relations prevents contact between a producer and consumer that could potentially change the latter's opinion of the former. If a low-status producer's good is not even considered a reasonable substitute for those perceived to be of high quality, purchasers of high-quality goods will most likely remain unaware of any changes in the good because of a lack of contact. Conversely, loyal purchasers of a high-status producer's product may not discern a relative decline in the quality of their preferred product if they do not compare it with the array of choices that confront them in the market. Such dynamics have been at work in the automobile industry. In the late 1960s and early 1970s, Japanese automobiles under-

Status-based Model

went considerable improvements in quality, but most Americans did not consider these foreign cars as an option because they did not regard the imports to be of comparable quality to domestic automobiles. Only the exogenous shock of the oil embargo broke the inertia underlying the pattern of exchange relations in the market (Halberstam 1986). Throughout the late 1980s and early 1990s buying patterns have crystallized in a different way, with many Americans not even considering a domestic car as a credible alternative to Japanese imports.[4] Thus, one way that social relations or social networks contribute to the linkage between status and quality is by serving as access constraints, inhibiting contacts which could potentially alter perceptions by bringing them into conformance with changes in the underlying quality of products.

Social relations also mediate between status and quality because status flows through the "interlinkages" between individuals and groups (Goode 1978; Blau [1964] 1989). Ties to higher-status actors enhance the prestige with which one is viewed, while ties to lower-status actors detract from it (Faulkner 1983). Accordingly, the formation and dissolution of social relations necessarily influence how the producer is perceived. In product markets, there are several types of ties that affect perceptions of a producer's status: exchange relations with consumers, ties to third parties associated with the market, and affiliations with other producers.

To the extent that buyers observe not only the products and actions of other buyers, the formation and dissolution of exchange relations with prominent customers has a strong "spillover" effect for a producer. Network-based studies of innovation adoption provide good examples of how a producer's relations with prominent buyers affect other buyers' perceptions of a product. Coleman, Katz, and Menzel (1957) and Burt (1987) have shown that an individual's propensity to adopt an innovation is influenced by whether or not prominent others in that individual's network have done the same.

Ties to third parties are relevant especially when producers and consumers do not meet directly in the market. In such markets, the distribution channels used by a producer can have a powerful effect on the perceived quality of the producer's product (Bonoma and Kosnik 1990).

Examples of interproducer ties relevant to status are joint ventures, individuals who depart from one firm to work for another, or common membership in trade associations (Benjamin 1992). In all three of these cases, status flows through the linkages between market actors in the manner described by Goode (1978). The transfer of individuals between firms is a particularly common conduit of status. By drawing a major

[4] See "The Japanese Borrow Detroit's Favorite Ploy: Rebates," *Business Week* (June 17, 1991).

American Journal of Sociology

figure away from a highly respected competitor, a firm can improve its status. These status-enhancing effects represent an additional contribution to the acquiring firm beyond the human capital that it may gain from the transfer. A familiar example is the mobility of academics between institutions; drawing a prominent member from a highly respected department is a rather typical means for augmenting a department's status.

Thus, there are three types of ties that serve as intermediate signals of quality: ties to prominent buyers, ties to third parties, and ties to other producers. Although this relational component to status is not necessarily inconsistent with economic conceptions of reputation (e.g., Kreps and Wilson 1982), it is equally true that this relational component has not received explicit attention in such work.[5] Of course, to the extent that the recipients of the producer's ties are concerned with their own status, the producer's ability to maintain ties to a particular actor will be inversely correlated with the producer's own quality. Accordingly, these ties to high-status actors are not components of product quality, but are to some degree signals within the larger signal of status. The existence of such ties thus does not eradicate the link between actual quality and status; rather, such ties simply serve to further blur or loosen the relation.

This discussion of ties as intermediate signals can be generalized to suggest a fourth and final reason for the loose linkage between quality and status. Because status is defined in terms of perceptions and because quality is, by definition, unobservable before the transaction, the perceptions through which status is constructed can only be indirectly based upon quality and are directly based upon other signals, of which a producer's network of relations may be only one. In an examination of status among *Fortune 500* corporations, Fombrun and Shanley (1990) observe several factors that seem to affect a corporation's status, including profits, total assets, charitable donations, and market share. Though their work is concerned more with status at the level of the interorganizational field than at the market level, it does nonetheless highlight the fact that status derives from other observables, which can themselves be interpreted as signals. Status, thus, may ultimately be a more multifaceted and encompassing signal than an attribute such as education or a product warranty insofar as it denotes a producer's position relative to its competitors; yet, at the same time, the linkage between status and quality is probably looser than that between quality and other signals.

Because of the loose linkage between status and quality, it becomes possible to draw a distinction between a producer and a producer's position in the market in much the same way that the distinction can be

---

[5] The closest parallel in the economic literature seems to be the work of Montgomery (1991) on job search.

Status-based Model

drawn in organizational contexts (Simmel 1950; White 1970; Sørensen 1983). If quality shifts were recognized immediately, then the status position would be inseparable from the present actions of the producer and, therefore, would not be analytically useful. However, the greater the decoupling, the more the status position insulates and circumscribes the producer's action and the more the producer's reputation becomes external to itself. In short, due to the loose linkage of quality and status, a niche emerges as a given constraint that the producer must confront in trying to decide upon an optimal course of action.

FROM STATUS POSITION TO STATUS ORDER

I listed above a variety of factors that can contribute to the loose linkage between status and quality. But not all of these need be present in a given context for the loose linkage to exist and thus for a producer's status position to manifest itself as a constraint. Like the assertion that consumers value status as an end in itself, certain claims and assumptions may be and perhaps even ought to be included in this discussion because they provide a more accurate characterization of status dynamics in particular markets; these claims, however, are not necessary elements of the status-based model. To be clear, the only assumptions regarding producer quality and the relationship between producer quality and market status that are to be regarded as essential to the model are:

ASSUMPTION 1.—Producer quality is an unobservable prior to the consummation of a transaction.

ASSUMPTION 2.—Market status is a signal of quality on which consumers can and do rely for their decisions.

ASSUMPTION 3.—A producer's relations with others in the market mediates the relationship between status and quality by creating inertial tendencies in the formation of exchange relations and by biasing evaluation in the direction of the status of those to whom the producer is tied.

It will soon be apparent that, when coupled with the implicit behavioral assumption that producers are (boundedly rational) profit maximizers, these three assumptions form the core of the status-based model. Indeed, it should soon be clear that these assumptions are sufficient to derive the loose linkage between status and quality and, accordingly, the conception of the isolated status position.

One can analytically shift from the microlevel conception of isolated status positions to the macrolevel view of the market as a tangible status order if one then makes the additional assumption that market producers can be ordinally ranked along just one dimension. Such an assumption is not as restrictive as it may first appear. The validity of the assumption

American Journal of Sociology

is supported by the fact that buyers are in fact able to discriminate between producers. In order to choose between the various products in the market, buyers must implicitly assign cardinal weights to the various characteristics of products. If they were unable to combine separate characteristics into an assessment of each product's overall quality, then it is not clear how they could rationally select one product over another. Granted, different buyers may express different preferences, but these preferences can be combined such that they confront producers as one aggregate buyer with a set of weights that is simply the sum of individual consumer preferences (White 1981a; see also Berger and Fişek [1974] on the aggregation of status characteristics).

Moreover, this recognition of a status ordering is not incompatible with the fact that producers often divide the buyer side of the market into distinct geographical or demographic segments in which each segment has a different criterion for discrimination. The acknowledgment of a status ordering simply requires a redefinition of the market to reflect divisions on the demand side. If the market is divided, each segment can be treated as its own market and, within each segment, the significance of status can be examined. For example, Coser, Kadushin, and Powell (1982) observe that the publishing industry is divided into several distinct segments, such as trade publications, college texts, and scholarly works; in a more detailed analysis of the latter of these three segments, however, Powell (1985) notes a rather well-defined status order that is largely unique to that segment. If preferences systematically differ across segments, then a producer's status position with respect to one sector need not be the same as its position with respect to another. While the boundary questions raised by the acknowledgment of market segments may make the empirical analysis of a market more difficult, the existence of market segments does not raise any conceptual obstacles to the vision of a status order as defining the market.[6]

---

[6] The model would only be inapplicable to multimarket firms if the existence of firm attributes, which either transcend individual markets or which derive from behavior in a market other than the one of interest, violate the second assumption that a producer's market status is a signal of (and accordingly correlated with) market quality. In other words, if a firm could ignore quality and relational concerns within the focal market and build and maintain status solely on the basis of activities or attributes that stand outside that market, then there would no longer be a loose linkage between market status and market quality but in fact a complete break. Ultimately, it is an empirical question as to whether or not this break exists for multimarket firms, making it especially important to study status processes in markets where such firms exist. Accordingly, the empirical analysis of this article will focus on one market—the investment grade debt market—in which the actors of interest—investment banks—have a presence in multiple markets. Yet, even before such an analysis, it is noteworthy that one can point to examples such as the publishing industry, where firms may

Status-based Model

The loose linkage between actual quality and perceptions of individual producers means that the status order exists as a structural entity. In the extreme, positions persist even in the absence of an occupant. The saying "They don't make things like they used to" underscores the fact that consumers frequently evaluate goods not just with reference to the actual goods in the market, but with reference to their perceptions of past goods. Consumers remain aware of upper-end status positions that have been vacated because of the decline in the quality level of one or more producers.

A second consequence of the loose linkage between status and quality is that access to certain rewards in the market becomes entirely mediated by the position one occupies in the status order. Just as access to the highest salary in a firm is contingent upon occupying a position at the top of the organizational hierarchy, so access to the highest quality manuscripts in the academic book market, for example, is contingent upon occupying a position high in the status order.

THE SIGNIFICANCE OF STATUS

Having elaborated the basic definition of market status, I now turn to a discussion of how the constraints and opportunities presented by a status position affect the producer's gross revenue and costs. *For a producer of a given level of quality,* additional status is most likely to translate into increased revenue, either in the form of higher prices or greater market share. This claim follows from the view of status as something valued in itself and, more important, that status is a signal of quality (see assumption 2). As Veblen (1953) makes clear in his discussion of conspicuous consumption, higher status increases what people are willing to pay because of the power that a good provides in the social sphere. At the same time, to the extent that status serves as a signal that implicitly lowers the risk that the good is below a given quality threshold, individuals are also willing to pay more for the higher-status good.

The probable impact of status on costs is obscured by the fact that higher-status producers are generally of higher quality and higher-quality goods are often more costly to produce. Therefore, the zero-order relationship between status and costs is often positive. However, *if one controls for the quality of the good,* it follows from the view of status as a signal of quality that the effect of status on costs is negative. If consumers

---

occupy a high-status position in one market and a low-status position in another. Such different identities across markets seems to suggest that a multimarket presence does not give rise to an identity that completely transcends individual markets and thus does not eradicate the loose linkage between status and quality within a given market.

American Journal of Sociology

and relevant third parties to a transaction perceive status to be a signal of unobservable quality, then they will be more reluctant to enter into a transaction with a low-status producer than they would be with a high-status producer even if both claim to manufacture the same quality good and sell it for the same price. Empirically, this greater reluctance to accept the quality claims of lower-status producers manifests itself in several cost advantages for the higher-status producers.

First, for the higher-status producer, advertising costs for attracting a given volume of business are lower. More customers simply flow to the producer without the producer actively seeking them out, and often the higher-status producer receives "free advertising" that the lower-status producer is unable to obtain. Examples of this free advertising abound. Publications from highly regarded academic presses are more likely to receive reviews in academic journals than publications from less highly regarded presses (Powell 1985). Business journalists are more prone to ask the employees of prominent firms within a market to offer insights into market trends than they are to ask employees of a less prominent firm (e.g., Kadlec 1986).

More important, if the risk-averse consumer or relevant third parties—such as retailers—require "proof" that the product confronting them is of a given level of quality, status lowers the transaction costs associated with the exchange between buyer and seller. Implicit and explicit promises of a higher-status producer regarding product quality are more likely to be accepted; therefore, the higher-status producer need not devote as much time or expense to convincing the buyer or relevant third parties of the validity of its claims.[7]

A particularly clear example of this inverse relationship between status and transaction costs was provided in an interview with the head of a middle-sized investment banking firm about procedures for underwriting. In primary securities markets, investment banks underwrite the security issues of corporations and political entities that desire to raise capital. In other words, banks assume the risk of buying new security issues from companies or governmental agencies and publicly or privately

---

[7] Recently, Williamson (1991) has attempted to incorporate status-related concerns into the transaction cost framework by conceptualizing reputation as a shift parameter that lowers the transaction costs associated with conducting market exchanges. Williamson argues that in markets where actors are not anonymous, the concern with reputation will bolster actors' ex post commitments to ex ante promises. While Williamson's conception of reputation as something that is more or less present in certain markets is different from my conception of status as a property differentially distributed across producers within a market, it is noteworthy that the inverse relationship between reputation and transaction costs is similar to the inverse relationship between status and transaction costs laid out here.

Status-based Model

reselling them to investors. Despite intense competition among investment banks for the opportunity to lead a security offering, often an investment bank does not place the entire offering itself. Rather, it forms and leads a syndicate of banks.

When asked about the advantages of status, the executive replied:

> Typically, if you hear that Goldman Sachs or Salomon or whatever is doing an underwriting, they usually have pretty stringent requirements, and it is usually a plus for the company that they are doing work for that Goldman Sachs wants to be their investment banker or underwriter or whatever, [that is] a plus with reference to the market place. Half the time, if Goldman Sachs calls or Solomon calls us and says [they] are going to be an underwriter for Ford Motor or whatever and asks, "Do you want to be part of the underwriting group?" we almost don't have to do any diligence; you just say yes. On the other hand, if a smaller firm which just doesn't have the credentials calls us, we will probably do more diligence and will probably be less likely to follow suit.[8]

A third type of costs lowered by status are financial costs. Fombrun and Shanley (1990) note how status enhances a firm's ability to obtain capital from either commercial banks or from issuing securities in the financial markets. The terms for acquiring credit significantly favor the higher-status firms.

These advantages in advertising, transaction costs, and financial cost, which accrue from status, all derive solely from the view of status as a signal that reduces the reluctance of market participants to enter into an exchange relationship with a particular producer. However, if one is willing to draw on Frank (1985) and make the additional and arguably very realistic assumption that employees are willing to accept lower monetary compensation in exchange for higher status, then one can specify a fourth source of lower costs. If an employee does indeed value the status of her workplace, she should be willing to accept a lower wage or salary to work for a higher-status firm than for a lower-status one. Of course, a higher-status firm may actually offer higher salaries than lower-status competitors because it wishes to have employees (perceived to be) of higher quality. However, controlling for the (perceived) quality of the

[8] Despite the competition among investment banks to lead an offering, the bank frequently does not underwrite the offering itself. Rather, it forms and leads a syndicate to distribute some of the risk. In forming the syndicate, the lead manager, along with the issuer, may participate in what could be quite a number of "due-diligence" meetings, where syndicate members "kick the tires" of the corporation to assess the viability of the offering. They hold these meetings as a way of maintaining financial responsibility to investors.

American Journal of Sociology

potential employee, the higher-status firm should be able to acquire the individual at a lower cost.[9]

In short, the consideration of these four factors suggests the following: given two producers at a particular point in time, the costs for a given quality output will be lower for the higher-status producer than the lower-status producer as long as the second core assumption—that status is indeed a signal of quality—is valid.

The inverse relationship between status and costs is in some sense the economic flip side of the argument that social networks represent access restraints that inhibit shifts in opinion. Were the demand for high-status goods completely inelastic, then the low-status producer could do nothing to overcome the access restriction. There is no amount of advertising or no size of warranty that the producer could offer to break the established buying patterns and establish the contact that would be necessary to alter perceptions. The cost difference for manufacturing and distributing a given quality good would for all practical purposes be infinite. However, except in the extreme case of complete inelasticity, the differential access of producers to purchasers of high-quality goods means simply that it will be more costly to manufacture and distribute a given volume of the same quality good.

Though status strongly influences both revenue and costs, most of my discussion has focused on its cost-related benefits. The reason for this focus is not only that the cost-related benefits are less intuitive than those pertaining to revenue, but that the cost-related benefits can actually be of greater significance to the high-status producer. These cost-related benefits afford the producer insulation from the competitive pressure of lower-status producers even in the context of intense price competition, as is perhaps best demonstrated by Stevens's (1991) account of competition among the "Big Six" accounting firms for the audits of major for-profit and nonprofit corporations. While price competition among the six highest-status accounting firms often drove competing bids for the business of the most significant clients to the range of costs and thus effectively eliminated most if not all positive rents from status, the lower-status firms were still unable to compete for the audit opportunities in the high-status niche. In one instance, Stevens details how SBO Seidman, a sec-

---

[9] While highlighting Frank's (1985) observation that individuals are willing to exchange money for status, I wish to distinguish my view from Frank's analysis of intrafirm differences in compensation. Frank argues that, because individuals value status, those in a higher position in the firm are willing to accept less than their marginal productivity. Conversely, those in the lower-status position demand a salary or wage in excess of their marginal productivity. In contrast to Frank, I perceive the individual's "pond" not as a single firm, but as either all firms or a subset of firms within the market.

Status-based Model

ond-tier accounting firm beneath the so-called Big-Six, attempted to compete for the audit of a major charitable organization. Even though SBO Seidman was fully capable of performing the audit, its request to present a bid to the corporation was denied. Only the Big Six were invited. As Stevens comments, "The charity's selection committee limited its competition to the Big Six not because the Big Six stand for superior professional standards . . . , but because the world has stamped a 'Good Housekeeping Seal of Approval' on their audits" (1991, p. 237). In effect, SBO Seidman could not pay transaction costs high enough to compensate for the status differential between it and the highest-status firms.

THE MATTHEW EFFECT AND THE CONSTRAINTS OF STATUS

This observation that status lowers the cost of producing and selling a good of a given quality has several implications. First, it rearranges the relationship between costs, signals, and quality initially posited by Spence (1974). Recall that, according to Spence, the marginal cost of a signal is by definition inversely associated with quality. However, at least for status, it is the marginal cost of quality that is inversely associated with the existence of the signal. The greater one's status, the more profitable it is to produce a good of a given quality. More simply put, whereas the economic view of signals begins with differences in quality between producers and then derives as signals those attributes for which the marginal cost of the signal is greater for the low-quality producer than the high-quality producer, the sociological view takes as its point of departure the reality of the signal and then derives the differences in quality on the basis of who possesses the signal and who does not. Both components are obviously important, but the substantive implication of the sociological view is that not only does actual quality determine perceived quality, but the latter has a reciprocal effect on the former. Because the costs and returns for investment in quality are differentially distributed across producers, the firms in a market have dissimilar incentives to make this investment.

A second implication of the status-cost relationship is the operation in markets of what Merton (1968) termed the Matthew effect. This phrase derives from the first book of the New Testament, which contains the line: "For unto everyone that hath shall be given, and he shall have abundance; but from him that hath not shall be taken away even what he hath." Merton applied the expression to the considerable discrepancy in esteem accorded high- and low-status scientists for similar accomplishments. For example, the likelihood that an article will be widely read and cited is positively correlated with the author's status. More generally, however, the Matthew effect refers to the fact that higher-status actors

American Journal of Sociology

TABLE 1

INTERYEAR CORRELATIONS IN THE DEBT MARKETS, 1982–87

Correlations	Investment Grade Debt	Non-Investment-Grade ("Junk") Debt
Coefficients	.91*	.87*
N	191	393

SOURCE—Securities Corporation Data Base.
* $P = .0001$.

obtain greater recognition and rewards for performing a given task and lower-status actors receive correspondingly less. The term has been applied to a diverse set of social phenomena, such as education (Walberg and Tsai 1983), intraorganizational power (Kanter 1977), and the life course (Dannefer 1987).

The cost and revenue implications of status reveal that the phenomenon is equally applicable to markets. Just as the likelihood that an article will be read and cited is positively correlated with its author's status, so the recognition and rewards that accrue to a higher-status producer for manufacturing a good of a given level of quality is greater. The nonproducing market participants expect that the high-status good is of superior quality and that the low-status good is the opposite. These differing expectations create dissimilar returns on investment for manufacturing a given product that greatly favor the higher-status producer.[10]

The apparent applicability of the Matthew effect raises the important question of why one or a subset of the highest-status producers do not dominate the market. For example, we have noted that, in the primary securities markets, the higher-status banks have lower transaction costs for issuing a security of a given quality. However, despite the fact they have lower transaction costs, the higher-status banks do not dominate the market. Table 1, which is based on data from the Securities Data Corporation (SDC) data base, lists the correlation of market share between year t and $t - 1$ for the years 1982–87 in two of the primary securities markets: the market for investment grade debt and the market for non-investment-grade debt. In the former market, the correlation is .91; the correlation in the later is .88. Figure 1 shows the macrolevel consequences by depicting the Herfindahl indices for these two markets

---

[10] One consequence of this fact is that a high-status producer's position is invariably its own to lose. A change in the status order depends at least as much on poor performance from those at the top as the exceptional performance of those on the bottom; this has been most convincingly demonstrated by the shift in positions occupied by automobile manufacturers in the 1970s (Halberstam 1986).

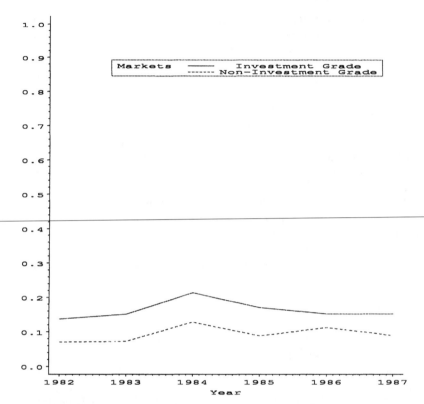

FIG. 1.—Herfindahl indices for debt markets

over this period. The measure approaches zero as the market nears a perfectly competitive situation with an infinite number of producers possessing an infinitely small market share. The measure approaches one as the market becomes a perfect monopoly. Except for a rise in concentration in 1984, the index reveals no consistent trend toward increasing concentration in either market.

Price theory offers only one possible theoretical reason why the higher-status firms would not corner the market if they could command a higher revenue and lower costs across all levels of quality. If the higher-status firms exhibit long-run diseconomies of scale as they expand into the market such that price per unit rises above the market value of the good, then there may be constraints on the expansion of the high-status producer. Possible sources of long-run diseconomies of scale are inherent

American Journal of Sociology

limitations on a factor of production or loss of managerial control. However, one of the earliest results of the industrial organizations literature
was the lack of evidence for long-run diseconomies of scale with respect
to production costs (Bain 1956; Johnston 1960). Therefore, at least within
the production ranges of these studies, there is no empirical grounding
for the assertion that limitations on the high-status producers emerge
from diseconomies of scale.[11]

As a result, it is difficult to explain in light of price theory why the
second half of the quote from Matthew cannot be taken more literally,
why "from him that hath not shall be taken away even what he hath."
If a higher-status producer can manufacture a given quality good at a
lower cost and even command a potentially higher price, what prevents
the higher-status producer from completely dominating the market either
through underbidding the lower-status producers at all quality ranges or
taking over the lower-status producer's operation and attaching its name
to the operation? To resolve the apparent anomaly, it is necessary to
reconsider the third core assumption of the status-based model, which
specifies the relational bases of status.

Since the relationship between actual and perceived quality is mediated
by the producer's ties to others in the market, the producer invariably
changes how it is perceived if it broadens relations with others in the
market. Even relations that may be only indirectly connected to the
actual quality of the product have a similar effect. As noted earlier, ties
to buyers, third parties, and even other producers all affect how one
is perceived, and status necessarily implies a certain exclusivity in the
formation of exchange relations (Goode 1978). Even if there is no differentiation in the perceived quality of the actors to which producers have
ties, the same dynamics apply. The only difference is that status will
depend more on the number than on the identity of these other actors.
As White (1981a) observes, a producer's volume affects how common its
product is perceived to be in comparison to others.

If the reputation of the highest-status actor declines to the point where
its status is just equal or below that of its nearest competitor, its niche
in the status order becomes vacant, opening the opportunity for this
previously lower-ranked actor to display more selective standards and
thus fill the vacated niche. The lower-ranked producer no longer faces a

---

[11] It is important to distinguish diseconomies of scale from growth within a particular
market from diseconomies of scope, which might accrue from growth through mergers
across markets. The dismantling of corporations in the 1980s has been taken by some
as evidence that there are managerial inefficiencies that result from combining firms
producing in separate markets. However, this trend does not call into question the
basic conclusion from Bain (1956) and Johnston (1960) that within a particular market,
there is no evidence for diseconomies of scale.

relative disadvantage in competing for business in the higher-status niche. Rather than being driven from the market, it has the opportunity to occupy the now-vacant position of what was the higher-status producer. Or, if the lower-ranked producer does not attempt to move into the niche, the opportunity is available for an entrepreneur in the wings to do the same. To the extent that a higher-status producer attempts to expand into the position of a lower-status competitor, it changes its reputation and thus alters the cost-and-revenue profile that provided it with the initial advantage. As a result, just as status processes help reproduce inequality by constraining those at the bottom of the status hierarchy, so status processes also place limits on the higher-status producer's expansion into the lower end of the market.

Recognition of this fact leads producers to construct different identities to the extent that they wish to compete in different ends of the market. For example, Hart, Schaffner, and Marx, the nation's leading manufacturer of branded men's tailored clothing in 1980, sold suits under three different labels, each confined to a specific price range (Tedlow 1982). In constructing separate identities, a producer forgoes any short-run advantage in costs or revenue that would accrue to the lower-status product from its association with the higher-status product. The producer realizes that ultimately such an association tarnishes the image of the high-status product as much as it might improve the image of the low-status product. This lower status in turn leads to less net revenue and hinders the degree to which the firm can profitably invest in high quality. Expansion, therefore, requires that the firm enter the market as two distinct actors. It should be noted, however, that this type of expansion does not represent a "solution" to the constraint imposed on the high-status actor since this actor does not derive any competitive advantages from status in the low-quality end of the market. It faces basically the same cost-and-revenue profile as the other low-status actors when manufacturing the low-quality product, since its low-end product is perceived to be identical to the rest; it perhaps derives cost advantages in the low end of the market from improved economies of scale, but not from status.

It is, of course, possible that the producer may be able to quietly alter its quality without strongly influencing market perceptions. Implicit in the idea of loose linkage is the fact that the causal connections between actual quality, market relations, and perceived quality are not completely determinate. However, the recognition that reputation may not diminish is in fact indicative of the general problem faced by the producer seeking to alter its niche. To change positions is to immerse one's production decisions in the vagaries surrounding the relationship between actual and perceived quality. Instead of optimizing within a given cost-and-revenue profile of which one is fairly cognizant, one instead opens oneself up to

American Journal of Sociology

high uncertainty about these profiles because one cannot predict how perceptions on the demand side and actions on the producer side will be affected by a shift in quality.

By cultivating a distinct position or identity in the status order, the producer reduces the unpredictability that confronts the nonproducing market participants' selections of goods. While quality will always remain an unobservable before the consummation of a transaction, a distinct reputation nonetheless constitutes a tangible signal by which consumers can compare producers. At the same time, the occupancy of a distinct status position reduces the unpredictability confronting the producer. An awareness of its own position in the market allows the producer to minimize mistaken production decisions. Even lower-status producers have an incentive to reproduce the status order to the extent that it allows for a minimization of such mistakes.

As Leifer and White (1987) observe, rational producers are aware that their success in a market is a function of their distinct identity, and the reproduction of this identity is a fundamental principle guiding market behavior. Status, thus, becomes an important explanatory variable in understanding the stable inequality of markets in light of the Matthew effect. Status, or, more accurately, the loose linkage between status and actual quality, constrains the profitability of invading either a lower or higher niche.

In emphasizing the features of the market that are conducive to reproducibility, the model developed here is structural, as the term has been classically applied in both sociology and anthropology. Yet, such structural analyses are necessarily incomplete. I ignore such questions as the provocative one raised by White (1981b): "Where do markets come from?" It seems clear that the same stress on reproducibility cannot apply prior to the existence of a tangible structure. I also ignore the dynamics of mobility that occur even after the market structure is established. Even though most markets are stable in the sense that a producer's position in the market one year is invariably a good predictor of its position in the next, mobility clearly occurs. Though all producers benefit from the existence of the status order, all do not benefit equally. Hence, there is reason to believe that lower-status producers may either attempt to enhance their mobility within the status order or change the status order entirely, even if doing so exposes them to vagaries and uncertainties that they would not otherwise have to face. The model is far from a complete account as it does not directly address such dynamic issues. However, even as it stands, the model can be defended on the grounds that it provides a relatively well defined sociological lens with which to view market phenomena.

Status-based Model

At a general level, the theoretical framework provides insights into many features of real-world markets that are either unexamined by or in tension with neoclassical theory. The sustained inequality of positions in markets in light of the fact that higher-status producers can make a given quality good at a lower cost is probably the most important, but there are others. For example, Ijiri and Simon (1977) observe that most producers halt production volume at a point before marginal costs begin to rise beyond price. Such an observation is clearly in tension with the central predictions of neoclassical theory, but it is quite compatible with the notion that status positions provide severe constraints on production decisions. Recognizing that profitability is bound to identity, producers halt production before it reaches a level that threatens that identity.

Another important observation in apparent tension with conventional economic theory is one made by Buzzell and Gale (1987). In a comparative study of firms across markets, they find that returns on investment are positively associated with perceived quality. Such an observation violates neoclassical economic theory's prediction that profits should be driven to zero over the long run. If profits are higher in the higher-quality ranges, then more producers should enter those quality ranges until profits become identical across the full quality spectrum.

In contrast, such a relationship is not only consistent with the status-based model, it is a characteristic of markets that the status-based model predicts *must be present* in a stable market if one assumes (as I do) that producers are indeed profit maximizers. Otherwise, the higher-status producers would constantly be tempted to "cash in" their status and seek to cultivate a lower-status niche.[12]

Nevertheless, in order to develop more substantial support for this particular alternative to the neoclassical view, I move from the general to the particular: an examination of pricing dynamics in the primary securities markets. While it is of course difficult to generalize on the basis of any one case, it is worth noting that there are several features of the investment banking context that would seem to minimize the significance of status processes. Hence, if the relevance of status can be demonstrated in this context, we may presume that it should be relevant in other contexts as well.

---

[12] This observation leads to the hypothesis that markets in which status is positively correlated with profits will be more stable than markets in which status is inversely correlated with profits. For the purposes of testing such a hypothesis, stability can be defined in terms of factors such as shifting market share, changes in relative product quality, or differences in buying patterns.

American Journal of Sociology

INVESTMENT BANKING

As underwriters of securities in primary securities markets, banks enter into relations with three sets of exchange partners—issuers, investors, and competing banks. Here, I will focus primarily on the exchange relationship between issuer and bank, though it is not possible to consider this relation in complete isolation from the others. The service that the bank sells to the issuer is the ability to effectively price and place the security at terms as favorable as possible to the issuer and to "make a market" for a given issue.[13] Placement ability is contingent upon the extent of its connections to investors and often to other banks, which are willing and able to join a syndicate to distribute the security. With strong and varied connections to these two groups, the bank is better able to gauge supply and demand and thus price and place the offering more effectively. In short, what the bank "produces" as underwriter is a mobilized syndicate of banks and an array of investors willing to purchase the security.

The "price" that an investment bank charges a corporation for underwriting a security is called the gross spread. The gross spread is the difference between the dollar value that a corporation pays an investment bank for the offering and the dollar value at which the bank resells the offering to the market.

There are two broad classes of securities that banks underwrite in the primary securities markets: equity and debt. Equity, which is alternatively referred to as stock, represents an ownership stake in the corporation. Debt, of which the most common type is a bond, constitutes a legally binding obligation of the issuer to pay the holder of the debt a sum of money at clearly demarcated points in time.

Relying on divisions that are frequently made in the trade publications (e.g., *Investment Dealers' Digest* [*IDD*]), it is possible to further divide these broad categories of securities into different markets. For example, one special type of equity market is the market for initial public offerings. An initial public offering, or IPO, is a company's first distribution of stock to the public. There are two major corporate debt markets: the market for investment grade debt and the market for non-investment-grade debt. What distinguishes investment grade from non-investment-grade debt is the financial history and soundness of the issuing firm.

The analysis here will focus on the market for investment grade debt. Unlike equity issues, debt issues are evaluated by major ratings agencies, and the ratings provide a strong guideline for the price at which the bond

[13] To "make a market" is to announce a bid price at which it will buy the security and an ask price at which it will sell the security.

Status-based Model

is offered to investors. Moreover, corporate bonds are almost exclusively purchased by institutional investors and are accordingly less frequently traded in secondary markets than equity issues. Because of the pricing guidelines and the comparatively small need for making a market on a given issue, there is comparatively little room for banks to distinguish themselves in issuing debt.

In comparison to non-investment-grade debt, the underwriting of investment grade debt would seem to be especially insulated from status concerns because of the low probability of default that defines investment grade issuers. This type of security is colloquially referred to as "vanilla debt," a label that reflects the lack of complications involved in underwriting the issue. One ex-Shearson broker commented to me that he personally could successfully execute a typical investment grade issue even after he had left the firm. All such an issue would require would be a few phone calls to major institutional investors.

One should not take this somewhat facetious comment to mean that there is *no difficulty* involved in the placement of investment grade debt. Particularly as issues get larger, the challenge of placement becomes greater and requires a more extensive knowledge of and connections to the demand side of the market. Two bankers associated with a much smaller firm than Shearson noted the size of an issue as a reason why their firm would be neither willing nor able to underwrite a given issue. Nevertheless, apart from the factor of size, which is relevant in any of the primary securities markets, the comment is illustrative of the low level of difficulty that bankers attribute to underwriting in this particular market.

Finally, the importance of price in an issuer's selection of an investment bank, especially in the market for investment grade debt, can probably not be overstated. Eccles and Crane (1988) note that the phrase "Loyalty is a basis point" was particularly common among investment bankers in the mid-1980s. A basis point is .01% of the value of the offering. Though the phrase was probably an exaggeration, it reflected the bankers' strong belief that price (i.e., spread) was an extremely important factor in the exchange relationship between issuer and underwriter. An issuer would switch investment banks if it could find a slightly lower price in the market. Such a strong preoccupation with price would seem to imply that status exerts a minimal effect upon the market decisions of issuers and thereby provides some justification for the primary securities markets as a difficult test case for the status-based model.

To frame this assessment in terms of the three assumptions critical to the status-based model of market competition, this context is a challenging one because it is at best only weakly consistent with the assumption that quality is an unobservable; it is implicit, therefore, that the context

American Journal of Sociology

is only weakly consistent with the assumption that consumers (in this case, the issuers) should use status as a signal of quality. To balance the assessment, it is also a market in which interpersonal and interorganizational networks are critical to doing business (Eccles and Crane 1988; Baker 1990). This network nature of investment banking has two consequences. First, it means that the third assumption—that social relations mediate between status and quality—is more easily met in investment banking than in markets where social relations are less critical. Second, the significant role of interpersonal and interorganizational networks in conducting transactions opens the possibility for transaction costs to play a larger role in outcomes than they otherwise would, and to the extent that the advantages of status are contingent upon reductions in transaction costs, status can play a larger role in this market than one in which there are effectively no transaction costs. Thus, there are clearly aspects of the case that are conducive to the importance of status processes, though, on balance, there seem to be a sufficient number of countervailing factors to make this a challenging case for the basic model.

DATA

Data for an examination of the investment grade debt market are drawn from the SDC data base between 1982 and 1987.[14] These data contain extensive information on all of the corporate security offerings underwritten by investment banks over that period. In particular, for each issue, data are available on the type of offering, type of registration, spread, volume, bond rating, and the lead manager and comanagers. The primary purchasers of the SDC data are the investment banks themselves, who use the data mostly to assess their share of the market and their penetration into particular industrial sectors.

THE DYNAMICS OF THE PRICING MECHANISM

The status-based model draws our attention first and foremost to the role of costs and price in sustaining the hierarchical pattern of exchange relations in the market. Because the higher-status producer can manufacture a good of a given quality at a lower cost, it can effectively underbid the lower-status producer seeking to enter the higher-quality niche.

As has been repeatedly emphasized, price is very important in the issuer's selection of an investment bank in the investment grade market. Intense price competition necessarily implies no revenue advantages (i.e.,

[14] These data were graciously made available to me by Robert Eccles and Dwight Crane.

Status-based Model

positive rents) from high status on a given transaction. If issuers are choosing primarily on the basis of price, then the banks should not be able to command a premium for status. Even if issuers would prefer an extremely high-status firm to a comparatively low-status firm, they may be indifferent between those five or six banks at the top of the hierarchy, leading these top banks to compete among themselves on the basis of price in much the same way that the highest-status accounting firms competed with one another in an earlier example.

However, the lack of benefits on the revenue side does not preclude benefits on the cost side. As previously noted, higher status leads to lower transaction costs in forming syndicate and investor relations. The reputation for having stringent requirements means that it is less difficult and less costly for a bank to lead a given offering, and there is some limited qualitative evidence from the industry, such as that regarding Merrill Lynch (e.g., Kadlec 1986), that a higher-status firm can retain an employee of a given level of quality at a more favorable compensation arrangement for the firm. The Matthew effect, therefore, manifests itself in the investment grade market primarily in the form of low transaction costs and perhaps in the form of lower salaries as well, while having little or no effect on revenue.

Given the minimal impact of status on revenue but the advantages on cost, I hypothesize that the price that an investment bank receives for underwriting a given issue should be inversely related to status. In the bidding context in which banks confront issuers, the higher-status banks should take advantage of their lower cost to underbid their competitors for the bonds that they wish to underwrite.

To clarify this hypothesis, it is helpful to refer to a hypothetical scenario. Assume that there are only four investment banks in the industry that compete with one another for every issue. Assume further that the banks are aware of each others' costs (though we will drop this assumption momentarily). Figure 2 depicts such a situation. The vertical axis denotes increasing status; the horizontal axis indicates dollar values expressed in some arbitrary unit. The horizontal line for each bank represents its costs. If a bank successfully bids a dollar amount that falls to the right of the point where the horizontal line ends, then it earns a profit. Thus, if bank 4 makes a bid at D, it earns a profit; an expected bid at C, however, would result in losses. In a situation where all four banks desire the deal, bank 1 can practically guarantee that it will win the deal by issuing a bid at point A, just below bank 2's costs. Another firm will be able to win the deal only if it takes a loss.

Assume now the four banks are considering a second deal. Bank 1 decides that it is not worth the investment, but the other three banks desire the deal. In this case, bank 2 bids at point B and wins the deal to

American Journal of Sociology

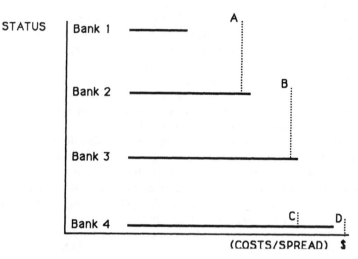

FIG. 2.—Hypothetical scenario of four banks

the extent that other firms are not willing to take a loss. If we make the reasonable assumption that firms cannot consistently take losses on their offerings, then this competitive situation in the context of a different cost structure results in the observed negative relationship between status and spread.

Dropping the assumption that producers are aware of each other's costs does not affect the expected relationship between quality and price. The only consequence of uncertainty about competitors' costs is that producers will make bids closer to their own costs and anticipated risk. Since they cannot be certain about the degree to which they are able to undercut their competitors' bids, they are forced, if they truly want the offering, to lower their bids to compensate for this uncertainty.

If bank 1 tries to corner the market by taking advantage of its lower costs, it will cease to have the reputation for "stringent requirements." Its costs will necessarily increase since it will have greater difficulty obtaining investors and syndicate members for a given quality of security. If these costs rise to the point that bank 1's costs are higher than bank 2's, bank 1 essentially loses the highest-status position in the market and its ability to outbid 2 for future business.

Despite the fact that the actual industry is more complicated than this model, the same dynamics should apply. One major conceptual difference between the imaginary four-bank market and the actual market is that there are probably several groups of banks that are of roughly equivalent status and therefore have essentially identical cost profiles. The five

Status-based Model

or six highest-status firms presumably all face similar costs for performing a given issue. However, the only consequence of this similarity is to drive the banks of equal status to bid as closely as possible to costs when competing against one another. The negative relationship between status and price remains. Another difference is that not every bank is asked to bid on a given issue. But, again, this should not change the fact that of those bidding, the highest-status bank should be able to win the deal by just underbidding the competitor closest in status.

It should be underscored that the status-based model does not predict that price will be negatively associated with status in all markets. Rather, it predicts only that the costs for producing a given quality product are negatively associated with status. The reason that we expect the negative relationship between price and status in the investment grade market is that the advantages of status are primarily on the cost side. However, this situation is simply a special case of a more general relationship that can be easily represented with minimal formalism. If p_h and p_l are the prices charged by a high-status producer and a low-status producer, s_h and s_l are the status of the two producers, and Θ is the premium that a buyer is willing to pay for each unit increment in status, then the pricing mechanism reproduces the hierarchical ordering in the market to the extent that

$$p_h < p_l + \Theta(s_h - s_l). \tag{1}$$

If advantages are strictly on the cost side, then Θ equals zero, and the inequality reduces to $p_h < p_l$.

ANALYSIS

For the purposes of this analysis, I use percentage spread as the dependent variable to denote the price charged by an investment bank. The percentage spread is the gross spread divided by the dollar amount of the offering. Use of percentage spread rather than gross spread allows for greater comparability across issues. Of the 3,541 investment grade offerings listed in the SDC data base between 1982 and 1987, information is available on percentage spread for 2,782 of the issues. Careful inspection of the data suggests that the pattern of missing information is not random; the likelihood that data are missing is frequently correlated with the size of the issue and the revenue of the issuer. Because of this significant missing data on the dependent variable, selectivity bias is a potential danger in the analysis. Following Berk (1983), I correct for selectivity bias via a two-stage procedure. Using a dichotomous logistic model, I construct a "selection equation," which estimates the probability that an

American Journal of Sociology

observation has information on spread. Then I incorporate the predicted probability (PREDPROB) as a regressor in the main equation.

The independent variable of greatest theoretical significance is, of course, status. My measure of status derives from what are called "tombstone advertisements." Tombstone ads are the announcements in major financial papers and trade journals that list the issuer, content, and syndicate members of a given security offering. Figure 3 depicts an example of a tombstone ad drawn from the February 19, 1985, issue of *IDD*. At the top of the advertisement is the name of the issuer and the information about the issue. The lead manager of the issue is always the first bank to be listed, followed by one or several comanagers. In figure 3, the lead manager is Salomon Brothers, Inc. The comanager is Merrill Lynch Capital Markets. The rest of the banks are syndicate members.

Tombstone ads have been in existence since before the turn of the century. Before the emergence of an electronically integrated market, these ads presumably did serve a conventional advertising purpose of informing investors of the existence of the security. However, they no longer serve any such function. They most often appear in publications one or two days after a security has been issued on the market, while the vast majority of institutional investors have been aware of the offering since minutes after it was released for issue.

While the lead management and comanagement positions are highly coveted because they are the highest-status positions on a tombstone, occupancy of these positions does not necessarily mean that a bank is of higher status than all those that appear below. Higher-status banks may agree to join a syndicate that is managed or comanaged by an equal or lower-status bank.

However, in agreeing to be part of the syndicate, banks are extremely conscious of the status ordering within that syndicte. Syndicate banks are arranged hierarchically into what are called brackets; the higher brackets are more prestigious. Like the number of banks, the number of brackets will vary from offering to offering; the quantity can be as small as 1 and not infrequently as large as 9 or 10. Within each bracket, banks are listed alphabetically; there are, therefore, no status distinctions within brackets, only across brackets. In figure 3, the first bracket begins with the First Boston Corporation and concludes with Morgan Stanley; the second bracket begins with ABD Securities and concludes with Dean Witter Reynolds.

Notably, if the lead manager places the bank in a lower bracket than the bank believes is appropriate, the bank will withdraw from the syndicate. Conversely, if the bank is placed higher than is considered proper, members of the syndicate who have been improperly placed below the bank will withdraw from the offering. A particularly prominent example

This announcement is neither an offer to sell nor a solicitation of an offer to buy these securities. The offer is made only by the Prospectus Supplement and the related Prospectus.

New Issue / February 13, 1985

$100,000,000

CHRYSLER FINANCIAL CORPORATION

12⅛% Subordinated Notes due February 15, 1990

Price 100% and accrued interest from February 15, 1985

Copies of the Prospectus Supplement and the related Prospectus may be obtained in any State in which this announcement is circulated only from such of the undersigned as may legally offer these securities in such State.

Salomon Brothers Inc

Merrill Lynch Capital Markets

The First Boston Corporation

Goldman, Sachs & Co.

Lehman Brothers
Shearson Lehman / American Express Inc.

Morgan Stanley & Co.
Incorporated

ABD Securities Corporation

Bear, Stearns & Co.

Alex. Brown & Sons
Incorporated

Deutsche Bank Capital
Corporation

Dillon, Read & Co. Inc.

Donaldson, Lufkin & Jenrette
Securities Corporation

Drexel Burnham Lambert
Incorporated

EuroPartners Securities Corporation

E. F. Hutton & Company Inc.

Kidder, Peabody & Co.
Incorporated

Lazard Frères & Co.

PaineWebber
Incorporated

Prudential-Bache
Securities

L. F. Rothschild, Unterberg, Towbin

Smith Barney, Harris Upham & Co.
Incorporated

Swiss Bank Corporation International
Securities Inc.

UBS Securities Inc.

Wertheim & Co., Inc.

Dean Witter Reynolds Inc.

American Securities Corporation

Daiwa Securities America Inc.

A. G. Edwards & Sons, Inc.   **Interstate Securities Corporation**   **McDonald & Company**
Securities, Inc.

Moseley, Hallgarten, Estabrook & Weeden Inc.

The Nikko Securities Co.
International, Inc.

Nomura Securities International, Inc.

Thomson McKinnon Securities Inc.

Tucker, Anthony & R. L. Day, Inc.

Yamaichi International (America), Inc.

FIG. 3.—Example of a tombstone advertisement

American Journal of Sociology

of the latter occurred in 1987 on a $2.4 billion bond offering by the Farmers Home Administration; 10 banks withdrew from the offering when 13 regional and small minority-owned firms were listed before them on the tombstone (Eccles and Crane 1988).

Major shifts in bracket position are rare events. One is not likely to observe more than one or two shifts in the higher-bracket positions over any given five-year period. Informal observation of the tombstones over the 1980s seems consistent with this claim.

Because syndicate position is such a close reflection of a bank's status in the industry, it has been used as a measure of status in other scholarly work (e.g., Carter and Manaster 1990) and is an appropriate measure for the purposes of this paper. The status scores for selected banks in the investment grade market are listed in table 2. Details of how the status scores for the banks were derived from the tombstone ads and further justification of their use are presented in the Appendix.[15]

To assess the effects of status on percentage spread, it is necessary to include several control variables in addition to PREDPROB, the predicted probability of inclusion in the sample derived from the selection equation. One of these is the size of the offering, AMT, which is measured in terms of logged dollars. Though it is more difficult to underwrite a large offering than a small offering, the marginal difficulty of underwriting each additional dollar increment decreases with the size of the offering. As a result, it seems reasonable to expect that the size of the offering should have a negative effect on the percentage spread. In the investment grade debt market, the rating of the bond is also an important determinant of spreads. A higher rating implies lower risk, which results in a lower spread. *Standard and Poors'* ratings for investment grade debt range from AAA to BBB. Rating information is available for all offerings between 1982 and 1986. For these years, dummy variables are constructed for all ratings above BBB +, with BBB + and below forming a residual category; an additional dummy variable, SPRATMIS, was coded "1" for all offerings in 1987 and "0" for offerings in the other years.

I also control for the recent joint transaction history of the bank and company in all product markets. It seems reasonable to expect that prior or concurrent transactions with a bank will lower the spread due to "client-specific economies." Superior information about an issuer due to prior transactions should allow the bank to underwrite an offering at a lower cost. Two dummy variables, LSIMUL and LHIST1, account for

---

[15] A full listing of the status scores for all the banks is available from the author upon request.

Status-based Model

TABLE 2

<small>SELECTED STATUS SCORES IN THE INVESTMENT GRADE DEBT MARKET</small>

Bank	Status	Rank
Morgan Stanley	3.30879	1
First Boston Corporation	3.03206	2
Goldman Sachs	2.87465	3
Merrill Lynch	2.84215	4
Salomon Brothers	2.82667	5
Lehman Brothers Kuhn Loeb	2.19846	6
Paine Webber	2.10382	7
Prudential Bache Securities	2.09874	8
Dean Witter Reynolds	2.04583	9
Warburg Paribus Becker	2.02556	10
Smith Barney Harris	2.01689	11
Dillon Read	2.01074	12
Bear, Sterns	2.00232	13
Kidder Peabody	1.99902	14
Shearson	1.99621	15
E. F. Hutton	1.99388	16
Donaldson Lufkin & Jenrette	1.98863	17
Lazard Freres	1.98856	18
Wertheim Securities	1.98685	19
L. F. Rothschild, Unterberg	1.98629	20
Drexel Burnham Lambert	1.98431	21
UBS Securities	1.86799	22
M. A. Schapiro and Co.	1.68572	23
Bell Gouinlock	1.57457	24
Atlantic Capital	1.23710	25
Burns-Fry and Timmins	.85649	50
Robert W. Baird and Co.	.66863	75
Sanford C. Bernstein and Co.	.44116	100
Folger Nolan Fleming Douglas	.21968	125
Anderson & Strudwick	.07925	150

this transaction history. In particular, LSIMUL captures whether or not the bank and issuer are involved in another transaction at the time of the deal. I selected a 120-day window around the date of the offering; if the bank leads an offering for the corporation in any of the primary markets or gives merger/acquisition (M&A) advice to the issuer during this period, then LSIMUL is coded "1," if not, LSIMUL is coded "0." Discussions with bankers revealed that the process of deciding on a particular issue and bringing the offer to market can often take about this length of time. Accordingly, if a bank managed two offerings for the same firm over this time period, I regarded the issues as "simultaneous." If the bank managed an offering or assisted in M&A more than 120 days

American Journal of Sociology

but less than 1 year prior to the offering, LHIST1 is coded "1," otherwise LHIST1 is coded "0."

Also relevant to the spread is whether the offering is negotiated or competitive. In the latter, competing banks submit sealed bids to the issuer, and the lowest bid wins the offering. Though this type of offering is not particularly common for corporate securities, many public utilities are required by law to solicit bids in this form. In negotiated offerings, the firm selects a bank on the basis of discussions with one or several investment banks. Price is still an important factor underlying the exchange between corporation and client, though it need not be the only factor which affects the corporation's decision to choose a particular bank. Due to the fact that competitive offerings are awarded strictly on the basis of price, it follows that sealed bids typically have lower spreads. A dummy variable, COMPET, is coded "1" if the offering is competitive and "0" if it is negotiated. Note that even in a sealed bid competitive offering, status can be relevant to market processes to the extent that it leads to a reduction in costs.

Finally, it is important to control for whether or not the security is what is called convertible. Some corporations issue bonds that they are willing to convert into stock at a predetermined conversion rate. This feature reduces the risk of holding the bond and presumably, therefore, also decreases the spread. If the bond offering is convertible, CONVERT = 1; CONVERT = 0 otherwise.

Column A of table 3 presents the results. In discussing these results, I will focus almost exclusively on the effect of status on spread since nearly all the control variables are of little sociological interest. The one possible exception to this rule are the effects of LHIST1 and LSIMUL, which measure client-specific economies. Both variables have a negative effect on spread, though the effect of LSIMUL is not statistically significant. The negative effect is consistent with the view that a firm can derive economic benefits from seeking to embed exchange exchanges in ongoing relations.

Focusing on the variable of main interest, we observe that STATUS has a statistically significant and negative impact on price at the .01 level. A unit change in STATUS leads to a reduction in spread of .080. While the substantive significance of this coefficient may not seem considerable, it is important to evaluate it in light of the phrase that "Loyalty is one basis point" and in light of the difference in status scores across the banks. If we refer back to table 3, we see that the difference in status between, for example, second-ranked First Boston and fourteenth-ranked Kidder Peabody is 1.03 . The difference between these two banks translates into an ability or willingness of the former to underbid the latter by eight basis points.

TABLE 3

EFFECT OF INTERACTION BETWEEN SIZE AND STATUS ON PERCENTAGE SPREAD IN THE INVESTMENT GRADE MARKET

Variable	A	B	C	D
INTERCEPT	1.244 (.153)	1.221 (.152)	8.608 (.750)	14.298 (2.239)
STATUS	−.080 (.013)	−.062 (.013)	−2.813 (.274)	−2.271 (.287)
STATUS * log(AMT)			.151 (.015)	.121 (.016)
Log(VOLHIST)		−.006 (.0008)	−.006 (.0008)	−.126 (.162)
Log(VOLHIST) * log(AMT)				.007 (.001)
Log(AMT)	−.0116(.008)*	−.007 (.008)*	−.413 (.412)	−.451 (.041)
CONVERT	.679 (.0275)	.679 (.027)	.665 (.026)	.658 (.027)
AAA	.004 (.025)*	−.012 (.025)*	−.018 (.025)*	−.021 (.025)*
AA+	−.101 (.027)	−.105 (.027)	−.124 (.027)	−.134 (.027)
AA	−.086 (.024)	−.093 (.023)	−.090 (.023)	−.096 (.023)
AA−	−.084 (.025)	−.079 (.024)	−.080 (.023)	−.087 (.024)
A+	−.053 (.025)	−.055 (.025)	−.054 (.024)	−.062 (.024)
A	−.086 (.023)	−.090 (.023)	−.089 (.022)	−.093 (.022)
A−	−.045 (.026)	−.044 (.025)*	−.040 (.024)*	−.052 (.025)
SPRATMIS	−.111 (.021)	−.091 (.021)	−.088 (.020)	−.096 (.020)
LHIST1	−.008 (.003)	−.007 (.003)	−.008 (.002)	−.008 (.002)
LSIMUL	−.001 (.003)*	$-9*10^{-4}$ (.003)*	−.002 (.003)*	−.002 (.003)*
COMPET	−.186 (.018)	−.178 (.0173)	−.172 (.0170)	−.173 (.0169)
PREDPROB	−.492 (.105)	−.444 (.105)	−.459 (.103)	−.492 (.102)
R^2	.27	.29	.31	.32

NOTE.—$N = 2,787$. Numbers in parentheses are SEs.
*Not significant at the .05 level.

American Journal of Sociology

COMPETING SIGNAL: VOLUME

Higher-status banks are able to underbid lower-status banks because status is a signal of quality. The more that the issuer, potential syndicate members, and investors can be assured of the quality that the underwriter will exhibit in managing the offering, the less difficult and less costly it is for the underwriter to put the deal together. However, as noted earlier, status is a second-order signal, and, while more encompassing and multi-faceted than other signals, the linkage between status and quality is perhaps looser than the linkage between quality and first-order signals. If the lack of status is to represent a real constraint, then lower-status banks must not be able to compensate for their inferior position in the status order by the cultivation of first-order signals.

The primary first-order signal is the recent volume history of the bank. The link between short-term volume history and underwriting quality is quite tight since a bank's quality with respect to both issuers and investors is contingent upon its insight into the market, which in turn depends on the extent to which it is in the deal stream between a relatively large number of issuers and investors. Insofar as underwriting volume is a quantitative indication of the degree to which a bank is in this deal stream, such volume is clearly a determinant of quality. Volume is also a signal of quality properly defined; the marginal difficulty and cost of underwriting a given issue at a given point in time is inversely associated with recent underwriting volume, since lower volume implies less knowl-edge. A bank with less knowledge of the market exposes itself to greater risk in seeking to make competitive bids for a given issue.

There are several institutional manifestations of recent volume as a signal. Perhaps the most important are the league tables, which provide annual or quarterly rankings of the banks according to their volume of underwriting activity in the various primary markets. They are published at quarterly intervals in the major trade journals. The ex-Shearson banker quoted earlier commented that the banks are so obsessed with their position in the tables that they call the SDC and *IDD* information service to insure that the services have not forgotten to include a deal that they have managed. While the banker interviewed believed that the ascribed importance to ranks was unjustified, he also pointed out that many bankers perceived that such an omission could lead to a decline in their rank in the league tables and thereby undercut their standing in the eyes of market participants.

Significantly, Hayes (1971) has observed that volume—at least as an indication of the bank's relational position—is also a critical underpin-ning of status; however, a major difference between volume as a first-order signal and status as a second-order signal is that the latter is rela-

Status-based Model

tively insulated from short-term fluctuations in the former. There are at least two reasons for this fact. First, volume, in and of itself, does not affect status; rather, it is the volume that is underwritten well that influences status. Increased volume will cease to have a positive impact on status if it is achieved either through the underwriting of issues that offer less than expected returns on their investment or through the poor execution of offerings. Repeated exceptionally weak returns on investment will cause the bank's status with investors to decline (e.g., Miller 1986). To the extent that a bank's status with investors declines, it is likely that its status with issuers will decline as well, since the lower status on the investor side will mean that the bank will find it more difficult and therefore more costly to effectively place a security.

A second, more important reason for the difference between volume and status is that volume is not the only factor that underlies status. Another, for example, is a reputation for honesty. When one of Morgan Stanley's associates became involved in an insider trading scandal in 1978, the status of the firm suffered even though few at Morgan Stanley were involved (Chernow 1990, pp. 634–35). When E. F. Hutton was convicted for involvement in a large-scale trading scandal in the late 1980s, its status declined precipitously until it was absorbed by Shearson Lehman American Express in a merger to form Shearson Lehman Hutton. Though there is no highly visible, institutionalized ranking of firms in terms of honesty to parallel that which exists for volume, violations of codes of SEC regulations are noticed by market participants and can have an impact on perceptions of a firm.

Given that the status order and volume rankings are two informational orders in which decisions are potentially embedded, the constraining effects of status ultimately depend on the degree to which the status order exerts an independent effect on market outcomes beyond that exerted by short-term fluctuations in volume. In effect, the issue is one of whether the second-order signal of status has an effect on price when the first-order effect of volume is controlled.

There are some compelling reasons to believe that this status effect should be minimal and that the short-term informational order should be most relevant in primary securities markets. We noted earlier that in the debt markets, especially investment grade debt, there is a rather high degree of information to distinguish the abilities of banks and the qualities of securities. However, to the extent that information is differentially distributed across banks, we would expect recent information to be of almost exclusive importance. Rapidly changing, unpredictable conditions endemic to financial markets would at least seem to suggest that it is only recent knowledge that is of any considerable utility to market participants.

American Journal of Sociology

If informational decisions are based more on the yearly fluctuations in volume and less on the status ordering in the tombstones, then the time lag between shifts in quality and shifts in perception will necessarily be shorter, and the significance of the Matthew effect for the primary securities markets will be minimal. Recall that it is the lag between shifts in quality and shifts in perceptions that insulates a given producer from the competition of those of lower status. If a low-quality bank can come to be regarded as identical to a high-quality bank simply by increasing its volume over a short time frame, then it faces essentially the same cost and revenue profile as that of the high-quality bank. It may have to absorb some short-term costs to expand at a rapid rate, but ultimately there is no persistent constraint on its ability to invade the high-quality niche. In this case, status would simply be a by-product of underlying economic processes. It is only when the lower-quality bank must confront a relatively disadvantageous cost-and-revenue profile over an extended time frame that the status ordering and Matthew effect can be considered relevant.

More specifically, to the extent that the status ordering is indeed irrelevant to market decisions and behavior, then inclusion of a variable for the more recent volume history should eliminate the direct effect of status upon either the terms of trade of particular exchanges or the observed pattern of relations. I, therefore, repeat the prior regressions including a variable for short-term volume history, VOLHIST. This variable is the volume of offerings for which a bank was lead manager in the 12 months prior to the month in which the deal was issued. Volume history thus is a moving one-year window, which I have updated monthly. Obviously, any particular choice of volume history is at some level arbitrary; I selected one year because the league tables rarely summarize more than a year of information. Due to a positive skew in the distribution of the variable, the variable is converted into logged dollars.

Though volume history is included as the primary signal of the short-term informational order, it is important to note that interpretation of a coefficient for volume history cannot be unambiguous. To the extent that economies of scale are relevant, the volume history measure summarizes such effects; moreover, insofar as the volume measure necessarily implies greater knowledge of the supply and demand conditions at the moment of the offering, these knowledge effects are also bound up in this variable. However, we are not so much interested in clearly interpreting the effect of volume as in determining whether the inclusion of the variable eliminates the effect of status upon the terms of trade.

Column B of table 3 presents the results. The most noteworthy finding is that the effect of status remains significant even after the inclusion of the variable for volume, though the apparent status effect does drop from

Status-based Model

$-.080$ to $-.062$. The volume coefficient is negative and statistically significant at the .05 level. The relative magnitudes of the volume and status coefficients provide insight into how much a lower-status bank would have to exceed a higher-status bank in annual volume in order to bid the same as the higher-status actor. The status coefficient is 10 times that of the coefficient for volume history, implying that a given bank would theoretically have to underwrite $\exp(10) = 22026.5$ times the volume of a bank one unit higher in status in order to compensate for the preexisting status differential. When considered in these terms, the .6 unit difference in status between fifth-ranked Salomon Brothers and sixth-ranked Lehman Kuhn Loeb clearly seems impenetrable to a strategy of "eating" deals to signal quality. Even a .005 unit difference in status, such as that between seventh-ranked Paine Webber and eighth-ranked Prudential Bache Securities, seems difficult to overcome simply by increasing volume.

To be clear, volume is a signal of quality that apparently reduces costs and thereby facilitates the bank's bidding ability; however, the effect of this signal is insufficient to overwhelm even minor differences in the status order. The effect of status, even after the inclusion of the volume variable, means that a lower-status bank cannot simply buy its way into a high-status niche by increasing its volume over the short term.

In addition to allowing us to distinguish the relative importance of the two informational orders (status and volume) confronting market participants, these results, especially the negative relationship between price and status, provide a unique opportunity to compare conventional economic models and the status-based model. Economic models invariably predict that if there is a superior good in the market at a lower price than an inferior good, then the inferior good will be driven from the market. In effect, the results in table 3 suggest that the superior good is less expensive than the inferior good; the higher-status producers underwrite a given offering at a lower price than the lower-status producers, but, as we observed earlier in table 1 and figure 1, there is considerable stability in the investment grade market. There is no trend toward increasing concentration, as we would expect if the higher-status banks were monopolizing the market. Such stability is completely consistent with the status-based model. The higher-status banks realize that their reputation with investors, position in the market, and hence cost structure is contingent on their ability to preserve their ties with high-quality clients. Thus, whereas conventional price theory predicts that the negative relationship between price and status should lead to a domination on the part of the highest-status actor(s), the status-based model anticipates the stability of the market that is actually observed.

Moreover, the status-based model also helps make sense of a similar, prior finding that emerged in an analysis of innovation in the primary securities markets. In an examination of 58 product innovations in the investment banking industry between 1974 and 1986, Tufano (1989) found that pioneers of an innovation charge underwriting spreads that are 18–25 basis points lower than imitators charge; he concluded that such a finding is anomalous from the point of view of economic theories of differential pricing. He suggested that perhaps innovators may be trying to "buy market share" by charging a lower price (p. 94). Even if true, such a conclusion does not explain why there are limits on the process. Why is the innovator not able to "buy" the whole market? Since boundaries around financial products are always somewhat arbitrary, it is clearly possible to conceive of these product innovations as defining their own markets. As such, the conclusions of the foregoing analysis can be applied to product innovations.

THE RELATIONSHIP BETWEEN OFFERING SIZE AND UNDERWRITING SPREAD

So far, the results show that, on average, higher-status banks underbid lower-status banks for a given deal in the investment grade market. Such a result is consistent with the claim that issuers are primarily concerned with price in their selection of an underwriter, whereas potential syndicate members and investors are more concerned with status. These groups have reason to be more concerned with status than the issuer. They are creditors, while the issuer is the debtor. As creditors, they have comparatively more to lose if the issue falls in value because of the poor performance of the bank. The issuer, on the other hand, will make the same interest payments regardless of how the security is placed.

Nevertheless, the issuer still faces some risk. If investors or syndicate members lose money on a particular offering, they will almost undoubtedly be less likely to purchase a security from the same issuer in the future. As a result, a poor performance by the underwriter will make it more costly for the issuer to raise money in the financial markets; the issuer will have to compensate the purchasers of its security for what they perceive to be additional risk.

Consequently, there might be some reason to expect positive return on status, especially for the larger offerings. As previously noted, not all issues are considered to be of the same difficulty; in particular, the larger an issue, the more challenge is involved in its placement and the more questions that there would be about a given bank's ability to successfully accomplish the task. For the RJR Nabisco junk bond offering, Kohlberg Kravis Roberts and Co. (KKR) doubted very much if even Salomon Brothers, a special bracket firm and the bank with the second largest

Status-based Model

underwriting volume in the junk bond market, could effectively lead the
offering (Burrough and Helyar 1990). While the RJR offering was indeed
an exceptionally large offering, it does raise the issue of whether or not
there are positive returns to status for increasingly large issues. The fact
that large issuers underbid the lower-status issuers on average does not
preclude the fact that higher-status banks may be able to derive a premium from underwriting the larger, more difficult issues. In terms of the
formalization in (1), it is reasonable to expect that as the issue becomes
larger, Θ should move away from zero, and p_h should become greater
than p_l.

   This reasoning suggests a hypothesis: there should be a positive interaction between the size of the issue and the status of the underwriter in
terms of the regressions on percentage spread. The larger the issue, the
greater the returns to status ought to be. More specifically, given the
earlier regressions, we would expect a positive interaction between
log(AMT) and STATUS.

   Column C of table 3 reproduces the regression in column B with the
inclusion of an interaction term for STATUS and log(AMT). Column D is
the same as C except that it adds an additional interaction term between
log(VOLHIST) and log(AMT). In both regressions, the interaction between STATUS and log(AMT) is positive and highly significant. In column D, the effect of status in the investment grade market is

$$-2.27 + .121 * \log(\text{AMT}).$$

Through algebraic manipulation of terms, it can easily be shown that the
effect of status becomes positive when the offering is greater than $140
million. This value is clearly within the range of observed values; the
median offering size across all banks is $100 million. At $200 million, or
the seventy-fifth percentile in terms of offering size, a one-unit difference
in status, such as that which existed between First Boston and Kidder
Peabody, translates into a four-basis-point benefit for the former over the
latter.

   Considered in conjunction with the results from columns A and B in
table 3, we observe that higher-status banks on average underbid the
lower-status banks; however, for the larger issues, the latter must underbid the former, and, as the qualitative evidence suggests, they must do so
from a relatively disadvantageous cost structure. The result is significant
because it illustrates the fact that for the larger, more difficult issues,
status is relevant not only to the investor and potential syndicate members but to the issuer's decision as well.

   This result points to at least one factor that may be relevant in establishing scope conditions for the applicability of status to a producer's
relations with a particular set of exchange partners, be they consumers

American Journal of Sociology

or some other set of actors associated with the market, and in so doing it helps specify when producers will derive positive rents from status and when they will only derive cost advantages. As a constituency's risk from entering into an exchange relationship with a particular producer increases, we would expect that status should become more relevant to their decision. If the risk is almost entirely borne by third parties to the transaction, such as syndicate members or retailers, then the advantages will strictly be on the cost side. However, to the extent that the risk is borne by consumers, producers will also be able to obtain positive rents as well.[16]

Of course, we would need to be careful about drawing any strong inferences about scope conditions on the basis of one case. As articulated at the outset, the applicability of the status-based model is contingent on the validity of three key assumptions: (1) that quality is unobservable, (2) that status is regarded as a signal of quality, and (3) that perceptions of a producer's status are contingent upon the identity of those to whom the producer is tied. The investment grade market is a compelling case because the first key assumption is minimally met, and there are many features of the market which would lead us to believe that the second assumption would be minimally met as well. Nevertheless, the salience of interpersonal and interorganizational networks in investment banking means that assumption 3 has more prima facie validity than it might have, for example, in mass consumer markets, where individual buyers are largely anonymous with respect to one another. Of course, this third assumption could apply in such markets. The status that consumers ascribe to a particular car manufacturer may indeed be contingent upon the identity of those who drive that manufacturer's cars, but we must nonetheless be careful about generalizing on the basis of this one analysis.

CONCLUSION

I have sketched out a conception of the market in which the constructed and maintained reputations of producers provide a tangible basis for decisions. I have attempted to provide a theoretical and empirical justification for removing price theory from the abstract Walrasian auction or even game-theoretic scenarios and situating it in the tangible status order that underlies and circumscribes the actions of producers. In doing so, I have tried to provide a basis for the convergence of economic and sociological work on markets. As economists look increasingly to processes of

[16] It is difficult to imagine a circumstance in which the producer could derive no cost benefits but positive rents since risk on the consumer side would generate both rents and lower transaction costs for the higher-status producer.

retrospection in decision making (e.g., Kreps 1990), they can potentially gain from how social structure enters into the decision-making process. As the examination of the investment banking industry has been intended to indicate, a concern with status is not incompatible with a recognition of the importance of price theory. A "bidding war" exists among the banks, but the bidding war is embedded in a socially defined context. Only by taking this context into account can we understand the stability of markets when a higher-status producer can offer a good of a given quality at a lower cost than can a lower-status competitor. Status is, therefore, not simply an epiphenomenal reflection of quality. Rather, status exerts a strong influence on market outcomes by providing producers with different incentives to invest in quality and placing constraints on their ability to expand outside their niche in the market. Thus, just as status has been shown to affect behavior in interorganizational fields (Galaskiewicz 1985), so we have seen how status can inform our understanding of the market.

Yet, beyond providing insight into the paradox raised by the applicability of the Matthew effect to markets, this conception of market competition represents a point of departure for further sociological work on markets. One question of interest concerns mobility. The fact that preservation of identity is a constraining force does not mean that firms are unable to shift their position in the market. Mobility and a stable structure are no less compatible in a product market than in a labor-market context. Moreover, it is only once the underlying structure is made clear that the actual determinants of mobility can be accurately examined. Therefore, far from being in tension with a concern for mobility, this framework helps make such an examination possible.

A second issue of interest is to more explicitly incorporate the firm into the analysis of the market. As noted earlier, many firms are actively involved not just in one market, but across multiple markets. I hope the examination of the investment banks has indicated that a multimarket identity is not inconsistent with the dynamics posited by the status-based model. Nevertheless, an interesting question for additional analysis is how the status acquired in one market can be transferred to another market, as when IBM entered the personal computer market after being the dominant actor in the mainframe computer market. It seems reasonable to expect, particularly in young markets, where firms have had little opportunity to establish a reputation in that arena, that "imported" status could be particularly relevant to understanding organizational outcomes. More generally, such an examination could help pave the way for a more systematic understanding of change in markets.

A third issue of interest, which is also related to the issue of change, is the complex role of innovation in status-based competition. If investment

American Journal of Sociology

banking is representative of other markets, innovation is not only consistent with but partially responsible for the reproduction of the status order. The highest-status banks are the ones that are most able to successfully introduce innovations into the market, and the innovator role contributes to the perception of superior quality. Nevertheless, to the degree that a lower-status bank is able to successfully introduce an innovation into the market, the innovator role is a powerful means of mobility, as revealed most dramatically by the rise of Drexel Burnham Lambert in the 1980s. In extreme cases, innovation may lead to a change in the status order itself.

The incorporation of status processes into the understanding of market competition thus seems to provide considerable ground for the development and extension of a sociological approach to markets. Despite some important insights into market processes, current sociological work on markets has so far lacked any unifying concepts or themes beyond the pronouncements that social relations matter and that actors are not as atomized as specified in the neoclassical model. At a minimum, the theoretical conclusions and empirical findings of this article allude to the importance of status and perceptions as one such theme.

APPENDIX

Measurement of Status

For the purpose of this analysis, I collected the tombstone ads which appeared in the *Wall Street Journal* in 1981, the year before the six-year span covered by the SDC data base. During this period, there were 180 tombstones for investment grade debt issues. Having established the status of banks in this initial period, we can explore how the flow of issuers becomes distributed across the status positions in the following years.

One might argue that to assess the effects of status in the later years of our sample, we should collect not just the 1981 data, but also data from the following years. However, there are two reasons not to do so, one practical and the other theoretical. Practically, collection of such additional data imposes considerable cost and time demands, and there are good reasons to suspect that the returns from such additional data collection would be small. The fact that major shifts in status position are relatively rare events means that changes in any given bank's status over this period are likely to be minor. Moreover, we would expect that any bias resulting from the failure to collect the additional years of data would be in the direction of minimizing the observed effect of status. Hence, to the extent that the 1981 data have a significant impact on

Status-based Model

economic outcomes in the later years, it would seem reasonable to infer that the effects of status would be no less significant if the later years were taken into account.

Even if the data were easily obtainable, a reliance upon the 1981 status scores is preferable to contemporaneous status scores. Status is relevant to market outcomes because it is decoupled from quality shifts. If status shifts perfectly mirrored quality shifts, then status would, for all practical purposes, be little more than an artifact of economic processes. In this particular case, the status order is relevant only to the degree that it helps to insulate perceptions of banks from shifts in determinants of underlying true quality. So, in the 1980s, the status order is a significant market structure only to the extent to which a bank's initial status insulates it from the beneficial or adverse effects of market changes. To assess how economic changes affect changes in status, we would of course need longitudinal data on the latter; however, if we wish to examine status not as a dependent but as an independent variable, the need for such longitudinal data is questionable.

One might argue that a drawback of this data is that the derived status scores are based more on the banks' perceptions of each other than on the perceptions of the issuers. However, two factors reduce the potential significance of this problem. First, since status manifests itself in the investment banking context in large part by lowering the transaction costs associated with the formation of banking syndicates, the perceptions of the banks themselves are highly relevant. Second, the assumption that perceptions of the competitors are highly correlated with perception of clients seems fairly plausible; but if the assumption does not hold, we should once again expect that poor measurement would weaken rather than strengthen the results.

Banks that made less than three appearances in the tombstones over the year observed were excluded from the analysis; 170 banks appeared in more than three syndicates. Invariably the excluded banks were relatively minor foreign banks that appeared in syndicate offerings because the issuer was based in their country.

If a strong principle of transitivity applied to the status ordering, we could simply rank the banks by those appearing above and below them. However, the facts that (1) the number of brackets varies from tombstone to tombstone and (2) there are minor fluctuations when a bank obtains an unusually small or large share on a given offering means that this simple procedure will not work for data obtained in 1981 even if it may have worked in an earlier period, such as that studied by Carter and Manaster (1990).

In making use of the tombstone data, I apply one of the standard

American Journal of Sociology

status measures for relational data on status, Bonacich's (1987) $c(\alpha, \beta)$ measure. Formally, the measure is defined as follows:

$$c(\alpha, \beta) = \alpha \sum_{k=0}^{\infty} \beta^k R^{k+1} \mathbf{1}, \tag{1}$$

where α is a scaling factor, β is a weighting factor, R is a relational matrix, which is 0 along the main diagonal and in which cell r_{ij} summarizes the relative superiority (or inferiority) of i with respect to j, and $\mathbf{1}$ is a column vector of ones.[17] For the purposes of this analysis, a given cell r_{ij} is the proportion of times that a bank i appears above bank j in the tombstone ads in which they jointly appear.[18] Thus β was set at three-quarters of the reciprocal of the largest eigenvalue, though alternative positive values were examined and yielded no considerable substantive difference in the status scores. The parameter α is standardized such that

$$\sum_{i=1}^{n} c_i(\alpha, \beta)^2 = n,$$

where n is the number of actors in the social system. Both the construction of the matrices and the calculation of status scores were programmed in FORTRAN, with certain IMSL routines being used.

REFERENCES

Bain, J. S. 1956. *Barriers to New Competition*. Cambridge, Mass.: Harvard University Press.
Baker, Wayne E. 1984. "The Social Structure of a National Securities Market." *American Journal of Sociology* 89:775–811.
———. 1990. "Market Networks and Corporate Behavior." *American Journal of Sociology* 96:589–625.
Baker, Wayne E., and Robert R. Faulkner. 1991. "Role as Resource in the Hollywood Film Industry." *American Journal of Sociology* 97:279–309.
Baron, James N., and Michael T. Hannan. 1991. "The Impact of Economics on Contemporary Sociology." Working paper. Stanford University, Graduate School of Business, Stanford, Calif.

[17] Bonacich's $c(\alpha, \beta)$ measure can alternatively be one of centrality or status. Bonacich (1987) notes that the interpretation of the measure is contingent upon the nature of the ties. If the ties are symmetrical, the measure is more appropriately one of centrality; if the ties are asymmetrical, the measure is more appropriately interpreted as one of status.

[18] If two banks did not appear together, an imputation procedure was used that is discussed more fully in Podolny (1991).

Status-based Model

Benjamin, Beth. 1992. "Collective Status in the Wine Industry." Working paper. Stanford University, Graduate School of Business, Stanford, Calif.

Berger, Joseph T., and M. H. Fişek. 1974. "A Generalization of the Status Characteristics and Expectation States Theory." In *Expectation States Theory: A Theoretical Research Program*, edited by J. Berger, T. L. Conner, and M. H. Fişek. Cambridge, Mass.: Winthrop.

Berk, Richard A. 1983. "An Introduction to Sample Selection Bias in Sociological Data." *American Sociological Review* 48:386–98.

Blau, Peter M. (1964) 1989. *Exchange and Power in Social Life,* 2d ed. New Brunswick, N.J.: Transaction.

Bonacich, Philip. 1987. "Power and Centrality: A Family of Measures." *American Journal of Sociology* 92:1170–83.

Bonoma, Thomas V., and Thomas J. Kosnik. 1990. *Marketing Management: Text and Cases*. Homewood, Ill.: Irwin.

Burrough, Bryan, and John Helyar. 1990. *Barbarians at the Gate: The Fall of RJR Nabisco*. New York: Harper & Row.

Burt, Ronald S. 1983. *Corporate Profits and Cooptation*. New York: Academic Press.

———. 1987. "Social Contagion and Innovation: Cohesion versus Structural Equivalence." *American Journal of Sociology* 92:1287–1335.

Buzzell, Robert D., and Bradley T. Gale. 1987. *The PIMS Principles: Linking Strategy to Performance*. New York: Free Press.

Carter, Richard, and Steven Manaster. 1990. "Initial Public Offerings and Underwriter Reputation." *Journal of Finance* 45 (4): 1045–68.

Chernow, Ron. 1990. *The House of Morgan: An American Banking Dynasty and the Rise of Modern Finance*. New York: Touchstone.

Coleman, James S., Elihu Katz, and Herbert Menzel. 1957. "The Diffusion of a New Drug among Physicians." *Sociometry* 20:253–70.

Coser, Lewis A., Charles Kadushin, and Walter Powell. 1982. *Books: The Culture and Commerce of Printing*. New York: Basic Books.

Dannefer, Dale. 1987. "Aging as Intracohort Differentiation: Accentuation, the Matthew Effect, and the Life Course." *Sociological Forum* 2:211–36.

Davis-Blake, Alison, and Jeffrey Pfeffer. 1989. "Just a Mirage: The Search for Dispositional Effects in Organizational Research." *Academy of Management Review* 14:385–400.

Eccles, Robert, and Dwight Crane. 1988. *Doing Deals: Investment Banks at Work*. Boston: Harvard Business School Press.

Faulkner, Robert E. 1983. *Music on Demand: Composers and Careers in the Hollywood Film Industry*. London: Transaction.

Fombrun, Charles, and Mark Shanley. 1990. "What's in a Name? Reputation Building and Corporate Strategy." *Academy of Management Journal* 33:233–58.

Frank, Robert H. 1985. *Choosing the Right Pond: Human Behavior and the Quest for Status*. Oxford: Oxford University Press.

Galaskiewicz, Joseph. 1985. *Social Organization of an Urban Grants Economy: A Study of Business Philanthropy and Nonprofit Organizations*. New York: Academic Press.

Goode, William J. 1978. *The Celebration of Heroes: Prestige as a Social Control System*. Berkeley: University of California Press.

Granovetter, Mark S. 1985. "Economic Action and Social Structure: The Problem of Embeddedness." *American Journal of Sociology* 91:481–510.

Halberstam, David. 1986. *The Reckoning*. New York: Avon.

Hayes, Samuel L. 1971. "Investment Banking: Power Structure in Flux." *Harvard Business Review* 49, no. 2 (March–April): 136–52.

Ijiri, Yuji, and Herbert A. Simon. 1977. *Skew Distributions and the Sizes of Business Firms*. Amsterdam: North-Holland.

American Journal of Sociology

Johnston, J. 1960. *Statistical Cost Analysis*. New York: McGraw-Hill.
Kadlec, David J. 1986. "Will the Sun Ever Shine on Merrill's Investment Bankers?" *Investment Dealer's Digest* 52, no. 16 (April 21).
Kanter, Rosabeth M. 1977. *Men and Women of the Corporation*. New York: Basic Books.
Kreps, David M. 1990. *Game Theory and Economic Modeling*. Oxford: Oxford University Press.
Kreps, David M., and Robert Wilson. 1982. "Reputation and Imperfect Information." *Journal of Economic Theory* 27:253–79.
Leifer, Eric M., and Harrison C. White. 1987. "A Structural Approach to Markets." In *Intercorporate Relations: The Structural Analysis of Business*, edited by Mark S. Mizruchi and Michael Schwartz. Cambridge: Cambridge University Press.
Merton, Robert K. 1968. "The Matthew Effect in Science." *Science* 159:56–63.
Miller, Gregory. 1986. "Hambrecht & Quist Goes Back to the Basics." *Institutional Investor* 20, no. 2 (February): 72–76.
Montgomery, James D. 1991. "Social Networks and Labor-Market Outcomes: Toward an Economic Analysis." *American Economic Review* 81:1408–81.
Podolny, Joel. 1991. "Status, Status Processes, and Market Competition." Ph.D. dissertation. Harvard University, Department of Sociology.
Powell, Walter W. 1985. *Getting into Print: The Decision-Making Process in Scholarly Publishing*. Chicago: University of Chicago Press.
Simmel, Georg. 1950. "Superordination and Subordination." In *The Sociology of Georg Simmel*, translated by Kurt H. Wolf. Glencoe, Ill.: Free Press.
Spence, A. Michael. 1974. *Market Signaling: Informational Transfer in Hiring and Related Processes*. Cambridge, Mass.: Harvard University Press.
Sørensen, Aage B. 1983. "Processes of Allocation to Open and Closed Positions in Social Structure." *Zeitschrift fuer Soziologie* 12:203–24.
Stevens, Mark. 1991. *The Big Six: The Selling Out of America's Top Accounting Firms*. New York: Simon & Schuster.
Tedlow, Richard S. 1982. "Hart Schaffner & Marx: The Market for Separately Ticketed Suits." Harvard Business School Case 9-582-134.
Tufano, Peter. 1989. "Three Essays on Financial Innovation." Ph.D. dissertation. Harvard University.
Veblen, Thorstein. 1953. *The Theory of the Leisure Class*. New York: New American Library.
Walberg, Herbert, and Shiow-Ling Tsai. 1983. "Matthew Effects in Education." *American Research Journal* 20:359–73.
Weber, Max. 1978. *Economy and Society*, edited by Guenther Roth and Claus Wittich. Berkeley: University of California Press.
White, Harrison C. 1970. *Chains of Opportunity: System Models of Mobility in Organizations*. Cambridge, Mass.: Harvard University Press.
———. 1981a. "Production Markets as Induced Role Structures." *Sociological Methodology*, edited by Samuel Leinhardt. San Francisco: Jossey-Bass.
———. 1981b. "Where Do Markets Come From?" *American Journal of Sociology* 87:517–47.
Williamson, Oliver E. 1991. "Comparative Economic Organization: The Analysis of Discrete Structural Alternatives." *Administrative Science Quarterly* 36:269–96.
Winship, Christopher, and Michael Mandel. 1983. "Roles and Positions: A Critique and Extension of the Blockmodeling Approach." *Sociological Methodology*, edited by Samuel Leinhardt. San Francisco: Jossey-Bass.

[6]

NEITHER MARKET NOR HIERARCHY:

NETWORK FORMS OF ORGANIZATION

Walter W. Powell

Network forms of organization—typified by reciprocal patterns of communication and exchange—represent a viable pattern of economic organization. Networks are contrasted with market and hierarchical governance structures, and the distinctive features of networks are highlighted. Illustrative examples of network arrangements—in craft and high-technology industries, in regional economies, and in formerly vertically integrated fields—are presented. The paper concludes with a discussion of the conditions that give rise to network forms.

Research in Organizational Behavior, Vol. 12, pages 295–336.
Copyright © 1990 by JAI Press Inc.
All rights of reproduction in any form reserved.
ISBN: 1-55938-029-2

In recent years, there has been a considerable amount of research on organizational practices and arrangements that are network-like in form. This diverse literature shares a common focus on lateral or horizontal patterns of exchange, interdependent flows of resources, and reciprocal lines of communication. Yet this rich vein of work has had much impact on students of organizational behavior. This is not particularly surprising, given the many divergent strands of this work. One would need to have followed the fields of international business, technology strategy, industrial relations, organizational sociology, and the new institutional economies, as well as interdisciplinary work on such themes as cooperation, the embeddedness of economic life in social structure, and the proliferation of small business units to have kept abreast. The purpose of this chapter is to render this literature more accessible to scholars in the organizational behavior field. I do so by arguing that relational or network forms of organization are a clearly identifiable and viable form of economic exchange under certain specifiable circumstances.

I begin by discussing why the familiar market-hierarchy continuum does not do justice to the notion of network forms of organization. I then contrast three modes of organization—market, hierarchy, and network—and stress the salient features of each. The logic of network forms is explored systematically in order to demonstrate how networks differ from other forms. I cull the literature in a number of social science and management fields and provide examples of a wide range of organizational arrangements that can be characterized as networks. This review affords considerable insight into the etiology of network forms, and allows me to develop a number of empirically disconfirmable arguments about the circumstances that give rise to networks and allow them to proliferate. I close with some thoughts on the research agenda that follows from these arguments.

MARKETS AND FIRMS

In his classical article on the nature of the firm, the economist Ronald Coase (1937) conceived of the firm as a governance structure, breaking with orthodox accounts of the firm as a "black box" production function. Coase's key insight was that firms and markets were alternative means for organizing similar kinds of transactions. This provocative paper, however, lay fallow, so to speak, for nearly four decades, until it was picked up by Williamson and other proponents of transaction costs economics in the 1970s. This work took seriously the notion that organizational form matters a great deal, and in so doing moved the economics of organization much closer to the fields of law, organization theory, and business history.

The core of Williamson's (1975; 1985) argument is that transactions that involve uncertainty about their outcome, that recur frequently and require substantial "transaction-specific investments"—of money, time or energy that cannot

be easily transferred—are more likely to take place within hierarchically organized firms. Exchanges that are straightforward, non-repetitive and require no
transaction-specific investments will take place across a market interface. Hence,
transactions are moved out of markets into hierarchies as knowledge specific to
the transaction (asset specificity) builds up. When this occurs, the inefficiencies
of bureaucratic organization will be preferred to the relatively greater costs of
market transactions. There are two reasons for this: (1) bounded rationality—the
inability of economic actors to write contracts that cover all possible contingencies; when transactions are internalized, there is little need to anticipate such
contingencies since they can be handled within the firm's "governance
structure"; and (2) "opportunism"—the rational pursuit by economic actors of
their own advantage, with every means at their disposal, including guile and
deceit; opportunism is mitigated by authority relations and by the stronger identification that parties presumably have when they are joined under a common
roof.

   This dichotomous view of markets and hierarchies (Williamson, 1975) sees
firms as separate from markets or more broadly, the larger societal context. Outside boundaries of firms are competitors, while inside managers exercise
authority and curb opportunistic behavior. This notion of sharp firm boundaries
was not just an academic view. A good deal of management practice as well as
antitrust law shared the belief that, in Richardson's (1972) colorful language,
firms are "islands of planned co-ordination in a sea of market relations."

   But just as many economists have come to view firms as governance structures, and are providing new insights into the organization of the employment relationship and the multidivisional firm (to cite only two examples), firms appear
to be changing in significant ways and forms of relational contracting appear to
have assumed much greater importance. Firms are blurring their established
boundaries and engaging in forms of collaboration that resemble neither the
familiar alternative of arms' length market contracting nor the former ideal of
vertical integration.

   Some scholars respond to these changes by arguing that economic changes
can be arrayed in a continuum-like fashion with discrete market transactions located at one end and the highly centralized firm at the other. In between these
poles, we find various intermediate or hybrid forms of organization.[1] Moving
from the market pole, where prices capture all the relevant information necessary
for exchange, we find putting-out systems, various kinds of repeated trading,
quasi-firms, and subcontracting arrangements; toward the hierarchy pole,
franchising, joint ventures, decentralized profit centers, and matrix management
are located.

   Is this continuum view satisfactory? Can transaction costs logic meet the task
of explaining this rich array of alternative forms? Williamson clearly thinks that
it can. Shifting gears somewhat, he remarks that he is "now persuaded that transactions in the middle range are much more common" then he previously recog-

nized (Williamson, 1985, p. 83).[2] But, he avers, the distribution of transactions are such that the tails of this continuum from market to hierarchy are "thick."

I do not share the belief that the bulk of economic exchange fits comfortably at either of the poles of the market—hierarchy continuum. The legal theorist Ian Macneil (1985, p. 485) also disputes this view, arguing that, "discrete exchange can play only a very limited and specialized function in any economy."[3] Moreover, although I was earlier of the view that nonmarket, nonhierarchical forms represented hybrid modes (Powell, 1987), I now find that this mixed mode or intermediate notion is not particularly helpful. It is historically inaccurate, overly static, and it detracts from our ability to explain many forms of collaboration that are viable means of exchange.[4]

The view that transactions are distributed at points along a continuum implies that markets are the starting point, the elemental form of exchange out of which other methods evolve. Such a view is, obviously, a distortion of historical and anthropological evidence. As Moses Finley (1973) tells us so well, there was no market in the modern sense of the term in the classical world, only money in the nature of free booty and treasure trove. Nor did markets spring full blown with the Industrial Revolution. Economic units emerged from the dense webs of political, religious and social affiliations that had enveloped economic activity for centuries. Agnew (1986) documents that the word market first enters the English language during the twelfth century to refer to specific locations where provisions and livestock were sold. The markets of medieval England had a highly personal, symbolic, and hierarchical flavor. E.P. Thompson (1971) used the term "the moral economy" to characterize the intricate pattern of symbolic and statutory expectations that surrounded the eighteenth century marketplace. It was not until the latter part of the eighteenth century that among the British educated classes the term market became separated from a physical and social space and came to imply a boundless and timeless phenomenon of buying and selling (Agnew, 1986).[5]

By the same token, hierarchies do not represent an evolutionary end-point of economic development. A long view of business history would suggest that firms with strictly defined boundaries and highly centralized operations are quite atypical.[6] The history of modern commerce, whether told by Braudel, Polanyi, Pollard, or Wallerstein, is a story of family businesses, guilds, cartels, and extended trading companies—all enterprises with loose and highly permeable boundaries.

Recent work on the growth of small firms also casts doubt on the utility of a continuum view of economic exchange. Larson (1988) and Lorenzoni and Ornati (1988) draw similar portraits from very different settings—high tech start-ups in the United States and craft-based firms in Northern Italy—which do not follow the standard model of small firms developing internally through an incremental and linear process. Instead, they suggest an entirely different model of externally-driven growth in which preexisting networks of relationships enable small firms to gain an established foothold almost overnight. These networks serve as conduits to provide small firms with the capacity to meet resource and functional needs.[7]

The idea that economic exchanges can be usefully arrayed along a continuum is thus too quiescent and mechanical. It fails to capture the complex realities of exchange.[8] The continuum view also misconstrues patterns of economic development and blinds us to the role played by reciprocity and collaboration as alternative governance mechanisms. By sticking to the twin pillars of markets and hierarchies, our attention is deflected from a diversity of organizational designs that are neither fish nor fowl, nor some mongrel hybrid, but a distinctly different form.

To be sure, there are a number of social scientists who question whether the distinction between market and hierarchy is particularly useful in the first place.[9] They contend that no sharp demarcation exists and that the argument is more a matter of academic pigeon-holing than of substantive operational differences. These analysts are united, however, more by their dislike of stylized models of economic exchange than by any shared alternative perspective.

One group of critics emphasizes the embeddedness of economics in social and cultural forces. Markets, in this view, are structured by a complex of local, ethnic, and trading cultures, and by varying regimes of state regulation (Gordon, 1985). Historians and sociologists contend that the market is not an amoral self-subsistent institution, but a cultural and social construction (Agnew, 1986; Reddy, 1984; Zelizer, 1988).[10] Others maintain that markets cannot be insulated from social structure because differential social access results in information asymmetries, as well as bottlenecks, thus providing some parties with considerable benefits and leaving others disadvantaged (Granovetter, 1985; White, 1981).

Another chorus of skeptics point to the intermingling of various forms of exchange. (See Bradach & Eccles, 1989, for a good review of this literature.) Stinchcombe (1985) shows that there are strong elements of hierarchy and domination in written contracts. Goldberg (1980, p. 338) notes that many market exchanges have been replaced by interorganizational collaborations. He contends that much economic activity "takes place within long-term, complex, multiparty contractual (or contract-like) relationships; behavior is in various degrees sheltered from market forces." Similarly, much of the observed behavior in hierarchical firms seems unrelated to either top management directives or the logic of vertical integration. For example, a firm's relationships with its law, consulting, accounting, and banking firms may be much more enduring and personal than its employment relationship with even its most senior employees.[11] The introduction of market processes into the firm also appears to be widespread. Eccles (1985) observes that large firms commonly rely on such market-like methods as transfer pricing and performance-based compensation schemes, while Eccles and Crane

300 WALTER W. POWELL

(1987) report that dual reporting relationships, internal competition, and compensation based on services provided to clients are the current norm in investment banking.

MARKETS, HIERARCHIES, AND NETWORKS

I have a good deal of sympathy regarding the view that economic exchange is embedded in a particular social structural context. Yet it is also the case that certain forms of exchange are more social—that is, more dependent on relationships, mutual interests, and reputation—as well as less guided by a formal structure of authority. My aim is to identify a coherent set of factors that make it

Table 1. Stylized Comparison of Forms of Economic Organization.

	Forms		
Key Features	*Market*	*Hierarchy*	*Network*
Normative Basis	Contract—Property Rights	Employment Relationship	Complementary Strengths
Means of Communication	Prices	Routines	Relational
Methods of Conflict Resolution	Haggling—resort to courts for enforcement	Administrative fiat—Supervision	Norm of reciprocity—Reputational concerns
Degree of Flexibility	High	Low	Medium
Amount of Commitment Among the Parties	Low	Medium to High	Medium to High
Tone or Climate	Precision and/or Suspicion	Formal, bureaucratic	Open-ended, mutual benefits
Actor Preferences or Choices	Independent	Dependent	Interdependent
Mixing of Forms	Repeat transactions (Geertz, 1978)	Informal organization (Dalton, 1957)	Status Hierarchies
	Contracts as hierarchical documents (Stinchcombe, 1985)	Market-like features: profit centers, transfer pricing (Eccles, 1985)	Multiple Partners Formal rules

meaningful to talk about networks as a distinctive form of coordinating economic activity. We can then employ these ideas to generate arguments about the frequency, durability, and limitations of networks.

When the items exchanged between buyers and sellers possess qualities that are not easily measured, and the relations are so long-term and recurrent that it is difficult to speak of the parties as separate entities, can we still regard this as a market exchange? When the entangling of obligation and reputation reaches a point that the actions of the parties are interdependent, but there is no common ownership or legal framework, do we not need a new conceptual tool kit to describe and analyze this relationship? Surely this patterned exchange looks more like a marriage than a one-night stand, but there is no marriage license, no common household, no pooling of assets. In the language I employ below, such an arrangement is neither a market transaction nor a hierarchical governance structure, but a separate, different mode of exchange, one with its own logic, a network.

Many firms are no longer structured like medieval kingdoms, walled off and protected from hostile outside forces. Instead, we find companies involved in an intricate latticework of collaborative ventures with other firms, most of whom are ostensibly competitors. The dense ties that bind the auto and biotechnology industries, discussed below, cannot be easily explained by saying that these firms are engaged in market transactions for some factors of production, or by suggesting that the biotechnology business is embedded in the international community of science. At what point is it more accurate to characterize these alliances as networks rather than as joint ventures among hierarchical firms?

We need fresh insights into these kinds of arrangements. Whether they are new forms of exchange that have recently emerged of age-old practices that have gained new prominence (more on the etiology of networks below), they are not satisfactorily explained by existing approaches. Markets, hierarchies, and networks are pieces of a larger puzzle that is the economy. The properties of the parts of this system are defined by the kinds of interaction that takes place among them. The behaviors and interests of individual actors are shaped by these patterns of interaction. Stylized models of markets, hierarchies, and networks are not perfectly descriptive of economic reality, but they enable us to make progress in understanding the extraordinary diversity of economic arrangements found in the industrial world today.

Table 1 represents a first cut at summarizing some of the key differences among markets, hierarchies, and networks. In market transactions the benefits to be exchanged are clearly specified, no trust is required, and agreements are bolstered by the power of legal sanction. Network forms of exchange, however, entail indefinite, sequential transactions within the context of a general pattern of interaction. Sanctions are typically normative rather than legal. The value of the goods to be exchanged in markets are much more important than the relationship itself; when relations do matter, they are frequently defined as if they were commodities. In hierarchies, communication occurs in the context of the employment contract. Relationships matter and previous interactions shape current ones, but the patterns and context of intraorganizational exchange are most strongly shaped by one's position within the formal hierarchical structure of authority.

The philosophy that undergirds exchange also contrasts sharply across forms. In markets the standard strategy is to drive the hardest possible bargain in the immediate exchange. In networks, the preferred option is often one of creating indebtedness and reliance over the long haul. Each approach thus devalues the other: prosperous market traders would be viewed as petty and untrustworthy shysters in networks, while successful participants in networks who carried those practices into competitive markets would be viewed as naive and foolish. Within hierarchies, communication and exchange is shaped by concerns with career mobility—in this sense, exchange is bound up with considerations of personal advancement. At the same time, intraorganizational communication takes place among parties who generally know one another, have a history of previous interactions, and possess a good deal of firm-specific knowledge, thus there is considerable interdependence among the parties. In a market context, it is clear to everyone concerned when a debt has been discharged, but such matters are not nearly as obvious in networks or hierarchies.

Markets, as described by economic theory, are a spontaneous coordination mechanism that imparts rationality and consistency to the self-interested actions of individuals and firms. One need not go as far as Polanyi (1957) did, when he argued that market transactions are characterized by an "attitude involving a distinctive antagonistic relationship between the partners," but it is clear that market exchanges typically entail limited personal involvement. "A contract connects two people only at the edges of their personalities" (Walzer, 1983, p. 83). The market is open to all comers, but while it brings people together, it does not establish strong bonds of altruistic attachments. The participants in a market transaction are free of any future commitments. The stereotypical competitive market is the paradigm of individually self-interested, noncooperative, unconstrained social interaction. As such, markets have powerful incentive effects for they are the arena which each party can fulfill its own internally defined needs and goals.

Markets offer choice, flexibility, and opportunity. They are a remarkable device for fast, simple communication. No one need rely on someone else for direction, prices alone determine production and exchange. Because individual behavior is not dictated by a supervising agent, no organ of systemwide governance or control is necessary. Markets are a form of noncoercive organization, they have coordinating but not integrative effects. As Hayek (1945) suggested, market coordination is the result of human actions but not of human design.

Prices are a simplifying mechanism, consequently they are unsuccessful at capturing the intricacies of idiosyncratic, complex, and dynamic exchange. As a result, markets are a poor device for learning and the transfer of technological know-how. In a stylized perfect market, information is freely available, alternative buyers or sellers are easy to come by, and there are no carry-over effects from one transaction to another. But as exchanges become more frequent and complex, the costs of conducting and monitoring them increase, giving rise to the need for other methods of structuring exchange.

Organization, or hierarchy, arises when the boundaries of a firm expand to internalize transactions and resource flows that were previously conducted in the marketplace. The visible hand of management supplants the invisible hand of the market in coordinating supply and demand. Within a hierarchy, individual employees operate under a regime of administrative procedures and work roles defined by higher level supervisors. Management divides up tasks and positions and establishes an authoritative system of order. Because tasks are often quite specialized, work activities are highly interdependent. The large vertically-integrated firm is thus an eminently social institution, with its own routines, expectations, and detailed knowledge.

A hierarchical structure—clear departmental boundaries, clean lines of authority, detailed reporting mechanisms, and formal decision making procedures—is particularly well-suited for mass production and distribution. The requirements of high volume, high speed operations demand the constant attention of a managerial team. The strength of hierarchical organization, then, is its reliability—its capacity for producing large numbers of goods or services of a given quality repeatedly—and its accountability—its ability to document how resources have been used (DiMaggio & Powell, 1983; Hannan & Freeman, 1984). But when hierarchical forms are confronted by sharp fluctuations in demand and unanticipated changes, their liabilities are exposed.

Networks are "lighter on their feet" then hierarchies. In network modes of resource allocation, transactions occur neither through discrete exchanges nor by administrative fiat, but through networks of individuals engaged in reciprocal, preferential, mutually supportive actions. Networks can be complex: they involve neither the explicit criteria of the market, nor the familiar paternalism of the hierarchy. basic assumption of network relationships is that one party is dependent on resources controlled by another, and that there are gains to be had by the pooling of resources.[12] In essence, the parties to a network agree to forego the right to pursue their own interests at the expense of others.

In network forms of resource allocation, individual units exist not by themselves, but in relation to other units. These relationships take considerable effort to establish and sustain, thus they constrain both partners ability to adapt to changing circumstances. As networks evolve, it becomes more economically sensible to exercise voice rather than exit. Benefits and burdens come to be shared. Expectations are not frozen, but change as circumstance dictate. A mutual orientation—knowledge which the parties assume each has about the other and upon which they draw in communication and problem solving—is established. In short, complementarity and accommodation are the cornerstones of successful production networks. As Macneil (1985) has suggested, the "entangling strings" of reputation, friendship, interdependence, and altruism become integral parts of the relationship.

Networks are particularly apt for circumstances in which there is a need for efficient, reliable information. The most useful information is rarely that which flows down the formal chain of command in an organization, or that which can be inferred from shifting price signals. Rather, it is that which is obtained from someone whom you have dealt with in the past and found to be reliable. You trust best information that comes from someone you know well. Kaneko and Imai (1987) suggest that information passed through networks is "thicker" than information obtained in the market, and "freer" than communicated in a hierarchy. Networks, then, are especially useful for the exchange of commodities whose value is not easily measured. Such qualitative matters as know-how, technological capability, a particular approach or style of production, a spirit of innovation or experimentation, or a philosophy of zero defects are very hard to place a price tag on. They are not easily traded in markets nor communicated through a corporate hierarchy. The open-ended, relational features of networks, with their relative absence of explicit quid pro quo behavior, greatly enhance the ability to transmit and learn new knowledge and skills.

Reciprocity is central to discussions of network forms of organization. Unfortunately it is a rather ambiguous concept, used in different ways by various social science disciplines. One key point of contention concerns whether reciprocity entails exchanges of roughly equivalent value in a strictly delimited sequence of weather it involves a much less precise definition of equivalence, one that emphasizes indebtedness and obligation. Game theoretic treatments of reciprocity by scholars in political science and economics tend to emphasize equivalence. Axelrod (1984) stresses that reciprocal action implies returning ill for ill as well as good for good. As Keohane (1986) notes, the literature in international relations "emphatically" associates reciprocity with equivalence of benefits.[13] As a result, these scholars take a view of reciprocity that is entirely consistent with the pursuit of self-interest.

Sociological and anthropological analyses of reciprocity are commonly couched in the language of indebtedness. In this view, a measure of imbalance sustains the partnership, compelling another meeting (Sahlins, 1972). Obligation is a means through which parties remain connected to one another. Calling attention to the need for equivalence might well undermine and devalue the relationship.[14] To be sure, sociologists have long emphasized that reciprocity implies conditional action (Gouldner, 1960). The question is whether there is a relatively immediate assessment or whether "the books are kept open, " in the interests of continuing satisfactory results. This perspective also takes a different tack on the issue of self-interest. In his classic work *The Gift*, Marcel Mauss (1967 [1925]), attempted to show that the obligations to give, to receive, and to return were not to be understood simply with respect to rational calculations, but fundamentally in terms of underlying cultural tenets that provide objects with their meaning and significance, and provide a basis for understanding the implications of their passage from one person to another. Anthropological and sociological approaches, then, tend to focus more on the normative standards that sustain exchange; game theoretic treatments emphasize how individual interests are enhanced through cooperation.

Social scientists do agree, however, that reciprocity is enhanced by taking a long-term perspective. Security and stability encourage the search for new ways of accomplishing tasks, promote learning and the exchange of information, and engender trust. Axelrod's (1984) notion of "the shadow of the future"—the more the immediate payoff facing players is shaped by future expectations— points to a broadened conception of self-interest. Cooperation thus emerges out of mutual interests and behavior is based on standards that no one individual can determine alone. Trust is thereby generated. Trust is, as Arrow (1974) has noted, a remarkably efficient lubricant to economic exchange. In trusting another party, one treats as certain those aspects of life which modernity rendered uncertain (Luhmann, 1979). Trust reduces complex realities far more quickly and economically than prediction, authority, or bargaining.

It is inaccurate, however, to characterize networks solely in terms of collaboration and concord. Each point of contact in a network can be a source of conflict as well as harmony. Recall that the term alliance comes from the literature of international relations where it describes relations among nation states in an anarchic world. Keohane (1986) has stressed that processes of reciprocity or cooperation in no way "insulate practitioners from considerations of power." Networks also commonly involve aspects of dependency and particularism.[15] By establishing enduring patterns of repeat trading, networks restrict access. Opportunities are thus foreclosed to newcomers, either intentionally or more subtly through such barriers as unwritten rules or informal codes of conduct. In practice, subcontracting networks and research partnerships influence who competes with whom, thereby dictating the adoption of a particular technology and making it much harder for unaffiliated parties to join the fray. As a result of these inherent complications, most potential partners approach the idea of participating in a network with trepidation. In the various examples presented below, all of the parties to network forms of exchange have lost some of their ability to dictate their own future and are increasingly dependent on the activities of others.

ILLUSTRATIVE CASES OF NETWORK FORMS

It is time to add some flesh to these stylized models. Substantive details enable us to see how these abstractions operate in economic life. I provide examples of networks from a diversity of industries, ranging from highly traditional sectors to the most technologically advanced ones. These disparate examples share some important commonalities. They all involve intricate, multifaceted, durable relationships in which horizontal forms of exchange are paramount. My argument is based on the Simmelian notion that similar patterns of exchange are likely to entail similar behavioral consequences, no matter what the substantive context.

I begin this section with craft industries, a setting where network forms have long been dominant. I turn next to a discussion of industrial districts, where network forms have made a resurgence. I then move to high technology fields; here, networks are a much more novel phenomenon. They are being established for strategic purposes because neither market nor hierarchical forms have delivered the goods. Networks, in this case, are very much associated with the early stages of product life cycles. I conclude with the case of vertical disaggregation, where networks represent an effort to introduce collaboration into well-established contexts in which trust and cooperation have long been absent. The logic is to move from arenas in which networks are common and easy to form to settings where they are developed almost as a last resort.

Networks in Craft Industries

The distinction between craft-based work and formal organization revolves around not only the dissimilar way in which work in organized in the two settings, but also on a different set of expectations about where authority is located. Craft work tends to be project-based, while in bureaucratic organizations a product moves through a series of functional departments where different activities are performed. In craft work each product is relatively unique, search procedures are non-routine, and the work process depends to a considerable degree on intuition and experimentation (Perrow, 1967). The examples presented below represent well-researched cases that highlight the many network features associated with craft production.

Construction. Robert Eccles (1981), in his research on the construction industry, found that in many countries the relations between a general contractor and his subcontractors are stable and continuous over long time periods, and only rarely established through competitive bidding. This type of quasi-integration results in what Eccles calls the "quasi-firm." Although most contracts are set under fixed price terms, no hierarchical organization arises, even though there are clear "incentive for shirking performance requirements." Instead, long-term and fairly exclusive association obviates the need for costly organizational monitoring. In an empirical study of residential construction in Massachusetts, Eccles found that it was unusual for a general contractor to employ more than two or three subcontractors in a given trade. This relationship obtained even when a large number of projects were done in the same year, and despite the fact that a number of alternative subcontractors were available.

Publishing. The book industry is, to a considerable extent, based on network relationships (Coser, Kadushin & Powell, 1982). One effort to recognize and profit from these linkages is the establishment of personal imprint lines within large trade publishing houses. Under these arrangements, successful editors enjoy freedom from corporate constraints, and authors enjoy the intimacy and closeness associated with a small company. These extended networks allow an editor to rely on his or her own judgment and not have to appeal for higher level approval. The large firm is able to keep top-flight editors content and, at the same time, give them a greater financial stake in the books they bring in. Personal imprint editors are on their own as far as acquiring and nurturing authors, yet retain corporate clout for financing, sales, and distribution. Other publishers, in a related effort to hold on to key personnel, have "spun off" subsidiaries that operate in an autonomous fashion within the loose boundaries of the larger company. These "boutique" operations permit, in the words of the head of one such company, "the intimacy of a small operation with no committee meetings and no bureaucracy" (Coser et al, 1982, p. 53).

But these developments are merely reflections of a general phenomenon that is characteristic of certain sectors of the book trade. In trade and scholarly publishing, much of the time editors behave as if they are optimizing not their organization's welfare, but the welfare of the social networks to which they belong. In scholarly publishing, editorial research and evaluation relies extensively on personal networks, which are based on loyalty and friendship, cemented over time. Bonds of allegiance shape the processes of access and discovery. These personal relationships are also vital to economic success. While competition among firms does, to some extent, influence the success or failure of particular publishing houses, these selection pressures are dampened by the dense associational ties and personal relations that support all publishing transactions. The fortunes of a scholarly publishing house often depend more on the rise and fall of various academic paradigms than on the efficiency of a firm's internal operations. In a sense, companies do not so much compete with one another as hitch their fate to the success or failure of different academic networks and intellectual fashions.

Both the spinoff arrangements and the quasi-organizations based on personal networks reflect the fact that editors are located in structurally ambivalent positions: loyalty to their authors and their craft often outweighs allegiance to the firm that employs them. From the employer's perspective, the only means of responding to circumstances in which the most valued assets of the organization—the editor and his or her contacts—are highly mobile is to either allow the editor to set up shop on their own within the corporate boundaries or to try to influence editorial behavior in an unobtrusive manner (Powell, 1985, pp. 144–157).

Film and Recording Industries. Sociologists who study popular culture have long known that the music and movie businesses were external economy industries in which there was heavy reliance on subcontracting and freelance talent. But recent research has shed new light on this particular method of matching investment capital and human capital. These industries thrive on short-term contracts, minimization of fixed overhead, mutual monitoring of buyers and sellers, and a constant weaving and interweaving of credits, relationships, and successes or failures. But the ostensibly open competition that one might expect to pervade these markets is minimal (Peterson & White, 1981). Instead, recurrent small-numbers contracting appears to be the norm.

Cultural industries are characterized by high variance and great unpredictability; conditions which breed high rates of social reconstruction or reproduction (Faulkner & Anderson, 1987). These "project markets" are complex, dynamic, and uncertain. The participants in the firm industry—producers, directors, cinematographers, actors, and musicians—appear at first glance to be highly mobile. They move from studio to studio, from one project to another, with few stable ties to any formal organization. But as Faulkner and Anderson (1987) show, in their analysis of participation in 2,430 films over a fifteen year period (1965–1980), considerable stability and recurrent contracting among the participants is the norm. It is the networks of participants, however, that are stable and enduring, not the film studios, where employees come and go and ownership changes frequently.

Not surprisingly, the key players in the film industry trust others with whom they have worked in the past and found to be reliable. What is striking about Faulkner's and Anderson's analysis is how dramatic the patterns of inclusion and exclusion are. Reproduction persists within film genres and between big money and small money films. They observe (p. 907) that "distinct networks crystallize out of a persistent pattern of contracting when particular buyers of expertise and talent (film producers), with given schedules of resources and alternatives, settle into self-reproducing business transactions with distinct (and small) sets of sellers (directors, cinematographers, and fashionable actors and actresses)." Commercial results feedback and then historically shape the next round of contracting.

These network patterns are interesting in their own right; but Peterson and White (1981) point out that even though they are powerful and long-lasting, they tend to be invisible to most observers. Instead of long-term rates of reproduction most participants observe individual acts of ranking, favors, and contacts.

These craft-based examples are not particularly unique. Network forms of social organization are found in many cultural industries, in research and knowledge production, and in various industrial districts—such as the diamond trade (Ben-Porath, 1980), the garment and fashion business in Milan and New York, the Lyonese silk industry (Piore & Sable, 1984), or the "Third Italy," discussed below. And many of the professions exhibit some network-like features. Architecture is a prime example; but so apparently is engineering where, to judge from one recent study (Von Hippel, 1987), the informal trading of proprietary know-how among technical professionals in competing firms is extensive.[16] What these different activities share in common is a particular kind of skilled labor force, one with hands-on experience with production and the strategic ability to generate new products to keep pace with changing market demands. The people who perform the work have a kind of knowledge that is fungible, that is, not limited to an individual task but applicable to a wide range of activities. The organizations that complement these human capital inputs are highly porous—with boundaries that are ill-defined, where work roles are vague and responsibilities overlapping, and where work ties both across teams and to members of other organizations are strong.

Regional Economies and Industrial Districts

Recent economic changes have created, or perhaps recreated is a more apt description, new forms of collaboration among for-profit firms. In the previous century, a number of regions and industries were closely identified because both the social life and the economic health of such areas as Lyon and Sheffield were closely linked to the fate of the silk and cutlery trades, respectively (see Piore & Sabel, 1984; Sabel, 1989). This rediscovery or reinvigoration of the 19th century industrial districts points to the advantages of agglomeration, in which firms choose to locate in an area not because of the presence of an untapped market, but because of the existence of a dense, overlapping cluster of firms, skilled laborers, and an institutional infrastructure (for a good discussion of the economies of agglomeration, see Arthur, 1987).

German textiles. Charles Sabel and his colleagues (1987) describe the German textile industry, centered in the prosperous state of Baden-Wurttemberg in southwestern Germany, as an "association of specialists, each with unmatched expertise and flexibility in a particular phase or type of production." This flourishing traditional craft industry employs a highly refined system of production that links small and medium-size firms with a wide range of institutional arrangements that further the well-being of the industry as a whole. These support services include industry research institutes, vocational training centers, consulting firms, and marketing agencies. Most textile producers are highly specialized; and, as Sabel et al. (1987) argue, the more distinctive each firm is, the more it depends on the success of the other firms' products that complement its own. This production system depends on an extensive subcontracting system in which key technologies are developed in a collaborative manner. The subcontractors are also connected to overlapping inter-industry supplier networks. These linkages allow textile makers to benefit from the subcontractors' experiences with customers in other industries, and the suppliers are, in turn, buffered from downturns in any one industry. All of these arrangements serve to strengthen the social structure in which textile firms are embedded and to encourage cooperative relations that attenuate the destructive aspects of competition.

The Emilian Model.   Perhaps nowhere have socially integrated, decentralized production units had more of an impact than in Italy, where the economy has outgrown Britain's and is catching up to France's.[17] Modena, the microcosm of Latin Europe's renaissance, is the center of Emilia-Romagna, in north central Italy, and it is here that Italy's economic performance has been most exceptional. Behind this success is both a set of unusual, to an American eye, political and social institutions, and a size distribution of firms that seem more suited to the nineteenth century than the late twentieth.[18]

Firms employing fewer than 50 employees engaged 49 percent of the Italian labor force, and the average manufacturing firm has only 9.19 employees (Lazerson, 1988, p. 330). The proportion of the labor force grouped in smaller units of employment is greater in Emilia than in Italy as a whole (Brusco, 1982). The success of these small enterprises rests on a different logic of production than found in a typical vertically-integrated firm.

These small firms are frequently grouped in specific zones according to their product, and give rise to industrial districts in which all firms have a very low degree of vertical integration (Brusco, 1982). Production is conducted through extensive, collaborative subcontracting agreements. Only a portion of the firms market final products, the others execute operations commissioned by the group of firms that initiate production. The owners of small firms typically prefer subcontracting to expansion or integration (Lazerson, 1988). The use of satellite firms allows them to remain small and preserve their legal and organizational structure as a small company. Often satellite firms outgrow the spawning firms. Though closely related and highly cooperative, the firms remain strictly independent entities.

These industrial districts embrace a wide range of consumer goods and engineering components and machines: knitwear in Modena, clothes and ceramic tiles in Modena and Reggio, cycles, motorcycles and shoes in Bologna, food processing machinery in Parma, and woodworking machine tools in Capri, to name but a few (see Brusco, 1982, pp. 169–170).

Why is production so widely decentralized and so spatially concentrated? The answer appears to be rather idiosyncratic to the Italian case. It is partly a response to labor union power in large firms, where union influence has proved to be a disincentive to job expansion. The small firms exhibit high wage dispersion, with highly skilled workers who have registered as artisans in order to make more than is standard in large-firm industrial relations agreements, and unskilled, temporary employees—students, the elderly, immigrants, who work off the books for much less than they would receive in a large factory, if they could find employment. The districts are also a response to changing tastes and technology, in particular the emerging popularity of custom rather than the standardized goods and the availability of high quality, flexible technologies that are compatible with the needs and budgets of small firms.

These decentralized organizational arrangements depend on a unique set of political and social institutions, most notably the fact that almost all local political authorities are controlled by the Communist party (Brusco, 1982; Lazerson, 1988). A combination of familiar, legislative, ideological, and historical factors buttress Emilia-Romagna's economic progress. The continued existence of the extended family provides for economic relations based on cooperation and trust, and facilitates the search for new employees through family and friendship networks (Lazerson, 1988). The CNA, a national organization with close ties to the Italian Communist party, represents some 300,000 artisanal firms and provides them with a rich array of administrative services. These artisanal associations prepare pay slips, keep the books, and pay the taxes, as well as establish consulting, marketing, and financial services (Brusco, 1982). By coordinating these various administrative activities, the associations establish on a cooperative basis the conditions for achieving economies of scale.

Brusco (1982) and Sabel (1989) make a persuasive case that the Emilian models fosters the skills and initiative of artisanal entrepreneurs. The number of entrepreneurs previously employed by large firms, particularly as foremen, is very high. By tapping both initiative and detailed production knowledge, the small firms are able to offer a vast array of new products. And these small firms, through their multitude of collaborative networks, are able to give shape to new ideas with a speed unimaginable in larger enterprises.

Extended Trading Groups. The kind of collaboration that obtains in the industrial districts of southwestern Germany or north central Italy is based in part on a set of local circumstances, but the principles of mutual organization on which the districts are based are more widely applicable. Interfirm cooperation is often found in economic activities based in a particular region, such as in Japan or Scandinavia, or in locales where firms from similar industries are spatially concentrated, such as Silicon Valley or Route 128 in the United States. The extended trading relationships that develop under these circumstances of physical proximity may vary considerably in their details, but their underlying logic is constant.

Ronald Dore (1983) argues that networks of preferential, stable trading relationships are a viable alternative to vertical integration. His work on the regionally concentrated Japanese textile industry, particularly its weaving segment, aptly illustrates this point. The industry was dominated in the 1950s by large mills, most of which were vertically integrated enterprises with cotton-importing, spinning and finishing operations. By 1980 the larger mills had closed and the integrated firms had divested and returned to their original base in spinning. This "devolution" has led to a series of stable relationships among firms of different sizes. The key to this system is mutual assistance. Dore (1983) gives the example of a finisher who re-equips with a more efficient process, which gives him a cost advantage. This finisher, however, does not win much new business by offering a lower price. The more common consequence is that merchants go to their own finishers and say: "Look how X has got his price down. We hope you can do the same because we really would have to reconsider our position if the price difference goes on for months. If you need bank financing to get the new type of vat we can probably help by guaranteeing the loan." This type of relationship is, of course, not limited to the Japanese textile industry; similar patterns of reciprocal ties are found in many other sectors of the Japanese economy.[19]

What are the performance consequences of these kinds of trading relationships? Dore suggests that the security of the relationship encourages investment by suppliers, as the spread of robotics among Japan's engineering subcontractors amply attests. Trust and mutual dependency result in a more rapid flow of information. In textiles, changes in consumer markets are passed quickly upstream to weavers, and technical changes in production also flow downstream rapidly. There is, Dore asserts, a general emphasis on quality. One would not terminate a relationship when a party cannot deliver the lowest price, but it is perfectly proper to terminate a relationship when someone is not maintaining quality standards.

More recently, Dore (1987) has maintained that Japanese economic relations in general do not have the properties (i.e., opportunism, short-term profit-maximization, and distrust) that we commonly associate with capitalist enterprise and on which we build our theories of economic organization (in particular, transaction cost economics). He contends that the costs of doing business in Japan are lower than in Britain or the United States because of concerns for reputation and goodwill and considerations of trust and obligation. Moreover, he argues, this embedding of business relations in moral and social concerns does not reduce economic vitality, it sustains it and provides Japan with a considerable edge (for further discussion on this point, see the chapter by Lincoln).

But is Japan all that unique? Perhaps it is true, as Dore (1987) suggests, that as a nation, Japanese industry is organized more along the principles of an extended network (see also, Imai & Itami, 1984), but it does not appear to have a monopoly on these practices. Hagg and Johanson (1983), in an analysis of the industrial markets which comprise the core of the Swedish economy, describe a series of long term, stable relationships among industrial producers who share R&D resources and personnel. They suggest that the companies are actually investing in their connections with other companies, and in the process, losing their own identity to some extent. Instead of a competitive environment, there is a sharing of risks and resources and a pooling of information. Haag and Johanson argue that these arrangements eliminate costly safeguards and defensive measures and are better adapted to uncertainty. Competition in intermediate producer markets is not eliminated, rather coalitions of firms compete with other coalitions, not on the basis of price, but in terms of product development and knowledge accumulation.

Swedish researchers have chronicled numerous such collaborative projects, principally among large manufacturing companies (Hakansson, 1987; Johanson & Mattson, 1987). Most of the ventures involve at least one firm with a home base in Sweden, but the researchers do not speculate whether Swedish industry has a particular proclivity for coordinating product development activities with suppliers, consumers, and producers of complementary products. These "network forms of interorganizational relations" tend to be long-term, costly, project-based efforts at product development or technological innovation (Hakansson, 1987). They differ, however, in a number of respects from some of the examples discussed above. They usually involve very large firms, such as Volvo, Saab-Scandis, Ericsson, and Fairchild, and are typically heavy manufacturing projects in fields such as aerospace, metallurgy, mining, and marine engines. Unlike many of the subcontracting relationships, in which one firm serves as a principal and various satellite firms as agents, these production ventures bring companies together as co-contractors. In the language of agency theory, they are both principles and agents: risk-takers who allocate tasks and share in the gains or losses and contributors to the final product.

It was not all that long ago that notions of industrial districts and spatially concentrated production were largely ignored—both intellectually and geographically.[20] Now, every municipality seems busy at work trying to create their own Route 128 or Modena.[21] The success of these forms of extended trading networks has several key ramifications:

1. One of the main consequences has been to blur the boundaries of the firm—boundaries are being expanded to encompass a larger community of actors and interests that would previously have either been fully separate entities or absorbed through merger;

2. A new constellation of forces is being recognized as crucial to economic success: whether in the Third Italy of Silicon Valley, spatially concentrated production involves the cooperation of local government, proximity to centers of higher education, a highly skilled labor pool, extensive ties to research institutes and trade associations, and cooperation among firms with specialized skills and overlapping interests;

3. The spread of technologically advanced, smaller units of enterprise—a growth that comes at the expense of larger companies and is not explained solely by the shift from manufacturing to services (Loveman,

Piore & Sengenberger, 1987), and occurs without notable direct investment or significant employment increase, but rather as a result of expansion through various cooperative interorganizational relationships
(Lorenzoni & Ornati, 1988).

Strategic Alliances and Partnerships

In many respects, partnerships and joint ventures are not new developments.
They have been common among firms involved in oil extraction and petroleum
refining as a means of spreading risks. Chemical and pharmaceutical firms have
long conducted basic research jointly with university scientists. And some of the
most complex partnerships have taken place in the commercial aircraft industry.
Three major global players—Boeing, McDonnell Douglas, and Airbus Industrie—construct their planes via complex joint ventures among firms from
many nations (Mowery, 1987). Boeing and Rolls Royce teamed up to produce
the Boeing 757, and much of the construction of the Boeing 767 is done, through
joint ventures, in Japan and Italy. Airbus Industrie is a four nation European
aircraft consortium, supported in part through loans (or subsidies, if you take the
competition's view) from European governments.[22]

There is widespread evidence, however, that experimentation with various
new kinds of interfirm agreements, collaborations, and partnerships have mush-
roomed in an unprecedented fashion (Friar & Hoewitch, 1985; Teece, 1986;
Zagnoli, 1987; Hergert & Morris, 1988; Mowery, 1988). Firms are seeking to
combine their strengths and overcome weaknesses in a collaboration that is
much broader and deeper than the typical marketing joint ventures and technology licensing that were used previously. These new ventures may take the form
of novel cooperative relationships with suppliers, or collaboration among several
small firms to facilitate research and new product development. More generally,
internally-generated-and-financed research is giving way to new forms of external R&D collaboration among previously unaffiliated enterprises. Indeed, in
some industries, there appears to be a wholesale stampede into various alliance-
type combinations that link large generalist firms and specialized entrepreneurial
start-ups. Nor are these simply new means to pursue research and development;
the new arrangements also extend to production, marketing, and distribution.
And, in some circumstances, large firms are joining together to create "global
strategic partnerships" (Perlmutter & Heenan, 1986) that shift the very basis of
competition to a new level—from firm vs. firm to rival transnational groupings
of collaborators.[23]

In the past, the most common way in which large companies gained expertise
or products that they were unable to develop on their own was to acquire another
company with the needed capability. Mergers and acquisitions in high technology fields have not disappeared, but their track record is generally poor (Doz,
1988). Partnerships are more frequent now because of growing awareness that

other options have serious drawbacks. Recent efforts at various kinds of more limited involvement represent an important alternative to outright takeover. Equity arrangements—deals that combine direct project financing and varying degrees of ownership—are an example. A larger firm invests, rather than purchases, primarily for reasons of speed and creativity. The movement in large companies away from in-house development to partial ownership reflects an awareness that small firms are much faster at, and more capable of, innovation and product development. General Motors explained its 11 percent investment in Teknowledge, a maker of diagnostic systems that use a type of artificial intelligence, by noting that ''if we purchased the company outright, we would kill the goose that laid the golden egg.'' Equity arrangements can be quite complex. Some small companies have several equity partners, and large companies find themselves in the novel position of negotiating product development contracts and licensing arrangements with companies that they partly own. Equity investments are typically "complemented by various agreements, such as research contracts from the larger firm to the smaller one, exclusive licensing agreements to the larger firm, and often loan and other financial agreements provided by the larger firm to the smaller one" (Doz, 1988, p. 32).

These developments, not surprisingly, are particularly common in technology-intensive industries (Mariti & Smiley, 1983; Zagnoli, 1987; Contractor & Lorange, 1988). Both the motivations for collaboration and the organizational forms that result are quite varied. Firms pursue cooperative agreements in order to gain fast access to new technologies or new markets, to benefit from economies of scale in joint research and/or production, to tap into sources of know-how located outside the boundaries of the firm, and to share the risks for activities that are beyond the scope or capability of a single organization. The ensuing organizational arrangements include joint ventures, strategic alliances, equity partnerships, collaborative research pacts of large scale research consortia, reciprocity deals, and satellite organizations. There is no clear cut relationship between the legal form of cooperative relationships and the purposes they are intended to achieve. The form of the agreement appears to be individually tailored to the needs of the respective parties, and to tax and regulatory considerations. The basic thrust, however, is quite obvious: to pursue new strategies of innovation through collaboration without abrogating the separate identity and personality of the cooperating partners.

In these process-oriented fields, knowing how to make a product and how to make it work is absolutely critical to success. In recent years, as product life cycles shorten and competition intensifies, timing considerations and access to know-how have become paramount concerns. Teece and Pisano (1987) suggest that, increasingly, the most qualified centers of excellence in the relevant know-how are located outside the boundaries of the large corporation. Fusfeld and Haklisch (1985) argue that corporations are becoming less self-sufficient in their ability to generate the science and technology necessary to fuel growth. The larger and more technology-intensive the firm, the greater the amount of technical expertise it requires to maintain its position. Whether it is the case that one firm's technological competence has outdistanced the others, or that innovations would be hard to replicate internally, as suggested by the growing reliance on external sources of research and development (see Friar & Horwitch, 1985; Graham, 1985; & Hamilton, 1985), network forms of organization represent a fast means of gaining access to know-how that cannot be produced internally. The network-like configurations that have evolved in high technology can process information in multiple directions. They create complex webs of communication and mutual obligation. By enhancing the spread of information, they sustain the conditions for further innovation by bringing together different logics and novel combinations of information.

Collaborative agreements involve a wide variety of organizations. While the joining together of small firms that possess entrepreneurial commitment and expertise in technology innovation with large scale corporate organizations that have marketing and distribution power represents the prototypical example, these arrangements are certainly not the only option. Many large firms are linking up with other large companies, particularly in international joint ventures.[24] These partnerships are unusual in that they involve the creation of dependencies and linkages among very large firms, such as Toyota and General Motors.

Porter and Fuller (1986) suggest that such coalitions seem well suited to the process of industry and firm globalization, as evidenced by AT&T's alliances with Olivetti, Phillips, NTT, Toshiba and Ricoh. Large telecommunications companies have been very active participants in collaborative international research efforts. Siemens and ICL both have links with Fujitsu, while ICL, Siemens, and Machines Bull have formed a joint research institute in Munich to pool their basic research. Machines Bull is also a partner in a joint venture with Honeywell and N.E.C. Indeed, firms often have stakes in several projects with different partners (and potential competitors) and are engaged in ventures involving several technologies of different stages of development, creating a "loose network of sometimes interlocking companies" (Contractor & Lorange, 1988, p. 24).

Traditionally, international joint ventures were not regarded favorably by multinational firms, especially those based in the United States. International manufacture and marketing occurred through either direct foreign investment or export, and occasionally international licensing was utilized when a firm wished to exploit a process technology. Joint ventures were sometimes resorted to when political exigencies or protectionist policies prevented operating fully owned subsidiaries. This was the standard reason for joint ventures in Japan, certain third world nations, and socialist countries.

Recent collaborations differ substantially from previous strategies. In these new global partnerships, all of the participants contribute technological and managerial expertise, as well as capital. The relationships are multidimensional and long-term, rather than one-shot transfers of technologies. What has happened to cause firms to prefer cooperation to full ownership, or a "go-it-along" approach?

There are numerous factors both pushing and pulling U.S. multinationals into global alliances. On the push side are technological constraints. Much sophisticated technological knowledge is tacit in character (Nelson & Winter, 1982) and cannot easily be transferred by licensing. Indeed, it is the unwritten, intangible character of much firm-specific knowledge that has led U.S. firms, particularly the automakers, to form joint ventures with Japanese manufacturers in an effort to better understand their production processes. Similarly, Japanese companies have been attracted to joint projects with U.S. high tech firms because technological innovation cannot be simply purchased, it requires cumulative knowledge of the linkages among design, production, and sales.

On the pull side are financial concerns and the advantages of risk reduction. In joining a coalition with another firm, both partners may enjoy options that otherwise would not be available to them, ranging from better access to markets, pooling or exchanging technologies, and enjoying economies of scale and scope. Risk-sharing is very attractive in industries where each successive generation of products is expensive to develop, and product life cycles are short.

In some instances, international joint ventures do appear to represent an intermediate position between contracting among independent firms and vertical integration of the entire production chain. This is most common when the venture involves securing complementary inputs representing successive stages of production, or contracting for specific services or distribution arrangements. But this intermediate stage does not appear to be a temporary or unstable arrangement. Indeed, firms in such situations are ceding a good deal of their autonomy and facing considerable interorganizational dependence. Moreover, alliances that involve the pooling of know-how, the ceding of proprietary information, and the sharing of common assets are not intermediate in either an analytical or a developmental sense. They represent a very different form of interorganizational exchange, one in which ongoing vitality rests on continuing mutual dependence.

While U.S. firms have been recently active in international business alliances, collective industrial research is considerably less advanced here than in Japan or Western Europe,[25] where research consortia have proven to be valuable in eliminating costly, duplicative R&D, in achieving economies of scale in research, and in diversifying the search for solutions to technical problems. But it was not until 1984 that Congress passed the National Cooperative Research Act, easing antitrust laws and permitting collaborative research among competing firms. Since then, more than 100 R&D consortiums have been founded, involving more than 500 companies in such fields as biotechnology, telecommunications, automobiles, energy, and steel. Collective industrial research is, nevertheless, still viewed by many in the U.S. industry and government as a form of collusion and as a seedbed for anticompetitive practices.[26]

Despite a growing consensus that the changing nature of technology development encourages collective R&D, firms have been reluctant to share their best
scientists and most attractive projects.[27] It may well be the perceived threat of
Japan, with its extensive government-sponsored networks of collective research,
that is the greatest spur to collaboration among large U.S. firms. Cries of
economic nationalism were motivating forces in the establishment of research
consortia such as Sematech. This consortium of semiconductor firms may signal
a new awareness of the need for collective research. Both IBM and AT&T are,
for the first time, surrendering proprietary designs and processes to competitors
in hopes of aiding the consortium's efforts at trying to revive the domestic semiconductor industry.

Cooperative arrangements are not necessarily easy to sustain, nor do they always entail success.[28] They can create a host of management problems and they
also raise serious questions about effective industrial policy. On the organizational front, Doz (1988) has cautioned that convergence of purpose is often difficult to achieve, consistency of effort can be undermined by parochial subunit
goals, and middle managers and technical specialities may not share top
management's enthusiasm for cooperation. Similarly, Borys and Jemison (1989)
suggest that because partners have not previously worked together, they may
misperceive one another's actions. They observe that collaborations often begin
with considerable resources, heavy obligations, and lofty expectations. Thus, the
pressures to perform successfully may be considerable.

Collaboration can be fraught with other risks. Parties may bring hidden agen-
das to the venture. There is an ever-present threat that one party will capture the
lion's share of the benefits, or defect with the other party's knowledge and expertise.[29] Some analysts worry that U.S. partners to global alliances may provide
"mundane" services such as assembly, distribution, and marketing, which add
little value to the product.[30] The key development work and the higher-paying,
value-added jobs are taken overseas, and the U.S. firm merely completes the
final stages. These issues are far from being resolved, but they point out the complex ways in which collaborative networks may or may not contribute to a
country's stock of organizational talents.

Vertical Disaggregation

Evidence is accumulating that many firms are choosing to shrink their operations in response to the liabilities of large-scale organization. For example,
Mariotti and Cainarca (1986) describe a "downsizing" pattern in the Italian textile industry, where there has been a decline in the number of vertically-integrated firms and growth in "intermediate governance structures." They
attribute this development to three failures that plague vertically-integrated
firms: an inability to respond quickly to competitive changes in international
markets; resistance to process innovations that alter the relationship between dif-

ferent stages of the production process; and systematic resistance to the introduction of new products.[31] Interestingly, in an earlier era, firms actively pursued a strategy of vertical integration in an effort to reap the benefits of administrative coordination, economies of scale, and risk reduction (Chandler, 1977). Today, these "strengths" have results in various weaknesses: structural inertia, slow response times, and decreased employee satisfaction.

Large organizations are designed to do certain things well over and over again. The more that behaviors are repeated, the more predictable they become; thus, the greater likelihood that these actions will become formalized. Child (1972) found that large organizations tend to be more rule-bound and to require greater documentation of their efforts. For certain kinds of activities, such practices are useful, but for others it can result in informational logjams and a serious mismatch between organizational outcomes and the demands of clients and customers in a changing environment. Thus, the very factors that make a large organization efficient and reliable at some tasks render it cumbersome and resistant to change when it comes to other actions (Nelson & Winter, 1982; Hannan & Freeman, 1984).

The information costs in large organizations are further compounded by motivational difficulties as well. One point that Alchian and Demsetz (1972) and Williamson (1975) implicitly demonstrate is that much of the internal structure of large organizations is designed to prevent collective action by employees. This basic attitude of suspicion may explain the finding by social psychologists that job satisfaction (as measured by turnover, absenteeism, and morale) declines with increases in organizational size and/or centralization (Porter & Lawler, 1965; Berger & Cummings, 1979). The design of organizations can affect the behavior of their members in a number of powerful ways.[32] In large hierarchical organizations, promotions up the career ladder are a key part of the reward structure. You have, then, little incentive to disagree with the operating decisions made by people above you in rank because they are the people who must decide on your promotion. Research suggests that hierarchical design dampens employee motivation because individuals are likely to be more committed when they have participated in a decision, and much less enthusiastic when they have been ordered by superiors to undertake a particular task (Hackman & Oldham, 1980).

When the pace of technological change was relatively slow, production processes were well understood and standardized, and production runs turned out large numbers of similar products, vertical integration was a highly successful strategy. But the disadvantages of large-scale vertical integration can become acute when the pace of technological change quickens, product life cycles shorten, and markets become more specialized. Firms are trying to cope with these new pressures in a variety of ways: by explicitly limiting the size of work units, by contracting work out, or through more collaborative ventures with suppliers and distributors. One route leads firms to a rediscovery of the market, to the hostile world of arms-length relationships. Associated with a greater reliance on external contracts are strong efforts at cost-cutting, and greater managerial freedom in the deployment of resources and personnel. Another route leads firms to try to reorganize production, not so much through eliminating jobs, but by searching for new methods of collaboration among formerly antagonistic and/or competitive parties (Walton, 1985; Weitzman, 1984). Both responses entail some form of vertical disaggregation, or the shrinking of large corporate hierarchies.

The U.S. auto industry provides a good example of the crossroads many firms are at as they encounter the limits of vertical integration. The auto industry has undergone a profound shake-up, but the ultimate consequences of these changes have yet to be determined (see Dyer et al., 1987; Quinn, 1987). Prior to the mid-1970s, the big three automakers operated in a comfortable environment with little competitive pressure and scant customer demands for gas-efficient, high quality cars. The auto companies pursued a strategy of tight integration of production, which provided a means to guarantee supplies during periods of peak demand, as well as to protect the secrecy of annual styling changes. Vertical integration also kept down the prices of the independent parts suppliers with whom the companies traded. There was neither any give and take nor trust between the automakers and the subcontractors. Contracts were lost because a supplier bid .01 cents per item higher than a competitor (Porter, 1983). Automakers rigorously inspected supplier facilities, quality control procedures, stability of raw material sources, cost data, and management quality and depth (Porter, 1983, p. 278). They were reluctant to permit a supplier to manufacture a complete system. Instead, automakers preferred a competitive situation in which several firms supplied various components and the final assembly was done in-house.

Today this old system has crumbled in the face of international competition and fallen prey to the contradictions and short-term logic of the regime of competitive supplier relations. Heightened competition exposed a number of serious defects in this system. Abernathy (1978) has argued that vertical ingetration in the auto industry led to inflexibility. One consequence of tight technological interdependence is that change in any one part means the entire process must be altered. Pursuit of a cost-minimization strategy also reduced the automakers' ability to innovate. Susan Helper (1987), in an excellent analysis of supplier relations in the auto industry, observes that the old methods prevented suppliers from developing expertise, thereby reducing the skill requirements of their employees. This made it hard for them to develop any nonautomotive contracts and kept them dependent on the auto companies. It also had a chilling effect on innovation. There was neither any incentive nor capability for the suppliers to update equipment, suggest technological changes, or make long-range plans.

Because of their declining market share and lower profits, automakers are experimenting with an enormous variety of new approaches. A complex web of ties has developed among U.S. automakers, their Japanese rivals, American labor, and auto parts suppliers. These changes are transforming the way the U.S.

auto industry operates, changing the nature of competition worldwide, and sharply blurring the distinction between domestic and imported cars. Joint venture activity is extensive: between Ford and Mazda, General Motors and Toyota, GM and Volvo, and Chrysler and Mitsubishi. Ownership is also held in tandem: Ford owns 25 percent of Mazda, GM 42 percent of Isuzu and 5 percent of Suzuki, Chrysler 12 percent of Mitsubishi Motors. These relationships involve close collaboration and joint production on some projects, and secrecy and exclusiveness on other models.

Equally extensive tinkering is underway with respect to subcontracting arrangements (Helper, 1987). The length of contracts have been expanded, from one year to three to five. More joint design work is being undertaken and sole-sourcing agreements are becoming more common. These new, more collaborative arrangements involve less monitoring and costly inspections, yet defect rates are much reduced. The automakers are becoming more dependent on the technological expertise of the suppliers, whose long-run health is now a factor in the automakers' profits.

At the same time, however, the automakers are pursuing a second strategy: outsourcing to low wage areas. They are simultaneously deciding which suppliers are worth investing in a long-term relationship with and determining which components can be obtained on the basis of price rather than quality. In these cases, there is little concern for collaboration or supplier design work; instead, the effort is aimed at finding third-world suppliers that can provide parts at the lowest possible price.

These disparate options graphically illustrate how practices such as subcontracting have a double edge to them: they may represent a move toward relational contracting (Macneil, 1978), with greater emphasis on security and quality; or they could be a return to earlier times, a part of a campaign to slash labor costs, reduce employment levels, and limit the power of unions even further. Hence, many of the current downsizing efforts seem, at the first glance, to be illogical. Some firms are seeking new collaborative alliances with parts suppliers while at the same time they are trying to stimulate competition among various corporate divisions and between corporate units and outside suppliers. Firms are proposing new cooperative relationships with labor unions and in the same motion reducing jobs and outsourcing them to foreign producers.

Are companies really as confused as it seems? Are these various actions merely the faulty experimentation of poor and indecisive managements? Not necessarily. Though many of the efforts at vertical disaggregation appear to work at cross purposes, there does appear to be an underlying theme. Strong competitive pressures within an industry reduce the number of levels of hierarchy within firms and push companies to redefine the boundaries of their organizations. Firms are externalizing the production of highly standardized components, and searching for new collaborative methods to produce components that require highly skilled, innovative efforts. These collaborations may entail new relationships with labor, close relationships with "outsiders" who are no longer viewed merely as providers of a component but rather as sources of technological creativity that large firms cannot duplicate internally, and new cooperative ventures with competitors to pool risks and to provide access to markets.

THE ETIOLOGY OF NETWORK FORMS

Examples, as the old adage goes, are never proof. Qualitative data are always vulnerable to charges of being selectively presented. But qualitative materials are very useful for theory generation. The cases presented above are, in my view, much more than anecdotes, because taken together they represent a number of highly competitive and/or resurgent industries, and more importantly, they tell a consistent story that enables us to understand the circumstances under which network forms arise. These examples suggest that non-market, non-hierarchical modes of exchange represent a particular form of collective action, one in which:

- cooperation can be sustained over the long run as an effective arrangement;
- networks create incentives for learning and the dissemination of information, thus allowing ideas to be translated into action quickly;
- the open-ended quality of networks is most useful when resources are variable and the environment uncertain;
- networks offer a highly feasible means of utilizing and enhancing such intangible assets as tacit knowledge and technological innovation.

The examples presented above suggest that the conditions that give rise to network forms are quite diverse. The immediate causes, to the extent that they can be discerned, reveal a wide variety of reasons for the proliferation of network-like arrangements. In only a minority of instances is it sensible to maintain that the genesis of network forms is driven by a concern for minimizing transaction costs. Strategic considerations—such as efforts to guarantee access to critical resources, to obtain crucial skills that cannot be produced internally, to pacify the concerns of professional communities or national governments, or even, as in the case of global partnerships, to remake the very nature of international competition—certainly seem to outweigh a simple concern with cost minimization.

The origins and development of network forms seldom reveal a simple chain of events. The loose informal ties that sustain the Japanese keiretsu—the powerful trading companies such as Mitsui, Mitsubishi, and Sumitomo—developed because in the years immediately following the Second World War the U.S. Occupation Authority dissolved the tightly centralized prewar zaibatsu (Gerlach, 1990). In Italy, the extended trading groups of small firms in the north central region emerged as a consequence of restricted job opportunities available to educated young people, due in part to labor union power and large firm rigidities (Sabel, 1989). Thus in some cases, the formation of networks anticipates the need for this particular form of exchange; in other situations, there is a slow pattern of development which ultimately justifies the form; and in still other circumstances, networks are a response to the demand for a mode of exchange that resolves exigencies that other forms are ill-equipped to handle. the network story, then, is a complex one of contingent development, tempered by an adjustment to the social and economic conditions of the time.

The absence of a clear developmental pattern and the recognition that network forms have multiple causes and varied historical trajectories suggest that no simple explanation ties all the cases together. Economizing is obviously a relevant concern in many instances, especially in infant industries where competitive preserves are strong. But it alone is not a particularly robust story, it is but one among a number of theoretically possible motives for action—all of which are consonant with a broad view of self-interest. Clearly many of the arrangements discussed above actually increase transaction costs, but in return they provide concrete benefits or intangible assets that are far more valuable. The reduction of uncertainty, fast access to information, reliability, and responsiveness are among the paramount concerns that motivate the participants in exchange networks.

My claims about network forms of organization obviously have broader ramifications. To the extent that these arguments are persuasive, they suggest that some of the basic tenets of other approaches to economic organization are problematic. For example, an exclusive focus on the transaction—rather than the relationship—as the primary unit of analysis is misplaced. Similarly, approaches that neglect the role of the state in shaping the context in which exchange is conducted are too narrow. The degree to which economic actors rely on the marketplace, private enterprise, or network forms of relational contracting is determined, to a considerable extent, by state policies. From a sociologist's perspective, it makes little sense to separate organizational behavior from its social, political, and historical context. To make serious progress in understanding the diversity of organizational forms, we need arguments that are much more historically contingent and context dependent.

RATIONALE FOR NETWORK FORMS

Does the diversity of network arrangements imply that their pattern of development is largely idiosyncratic? Or do the cases have sufficient generality that we can point to specific enabling conditions that foster the formation and proliferation of networks? If we are able to identify these conditions, then it would be possible to make refutable arguments about the circumstances that promote and sustain network forms. My own modest contribution to the theory of network forms highlights three factors—know-how, the demand for speed, and trust—which are critical components of networks.

Know-how. There are a number of jobs that are based, in large measure, on either intellectual capital or craft-based skills, both of which have been honed through years of education, training, and experience. Many of these kinds of knowledge-intensive activities, such as cultural production, scientific research, design work, mathematical analysis, computer programming or software development, and some professional services, require little in the way of costly physical resources. They are based on know-how and detailed knowledge of the abilities of others who possess similar or complementary skills. Know-how typically involves a kind of tacit knowledge that is difficult to codify (Nelson & Winter, 1982; Teece & Pisano, 1987). These assets are both largely intangible and highly mobile. They exist in the minds of talented people whose expertise cannot be easily purchased or appropriated and who commonly prefer to ply their trade in a work setting that is not imposed on them "from above" or dictated to them by an outside authority. Indeed, markets or hierarchical governance structures may hinder the development of these capabilities because the most critical assets—the individuals themselves—may choose to walk away.

Network forms of organization, with their emphasis on lateral forms of communication and mutual obligation, are particularly well-suited for such a highly skilled labor force, where participants possess fungible knowledge that is not limited to a specific task but applicable to a wide range of activities. Thus, networks are most likely to arise and proliferate in fields in which knowledge and/or skills do not lend themselves to either monopoly control or expropriation by the wealthiest bidder.

Exchange relations vary both in terms of how they are organized, as well with respect to the object of exchange. Transactions can take place in a variety of contexts; but, as Williamson and others have alerted us, certain kinds of goods and services lend themselves more readily to particular forms of exchange. The more general, and more substitutable are resources, the more likely they will be secured through short-term market transactions. Similarly, some kinds of exchanges fit more comfortably under the rubric of networks. Take the case of joint ventures, either domestic or international, which are organized for the purposes of exchanging skills or services between two or more firms. What kind of ventures are more likely to promote long-term collaboration and shared responsibility? Agreements that are based on contracting for the performance of particular services, such as sales or distribution, are not likely to promote cooperation. Indeed, joint ventures of this kind are often discontinued when one party's capabilities "catch up" with those of the other. In contrast, when partners are involved in ongoing, complementary activities—such as pooling of research staffs or joint production arrangements—the relationship is more likely to lead to the sharing of critical information and the development of some measure of trust in one another. The sharing of information, as Buckley and Casson (1988) suggest, often leads to the emergence of common values. This cooperation is particularly likely to develop either in circumstances that require operational integration or under conditions of uncertainty about how to obtain desired outcomes. In both cases, there is a strong motive for parties to share information with one another (Buckley & Casson, 1988).

Thus, the exchange of distinctive competencies—be they knowledge or skills—is more likely to occur in networks. The transfer of resources—tangible items, such as equipment, services, patents, and the like—more commonly occurs through a market transaction or among organizational units, depending on the frequency and the distinctiveness of the items that are exchanged.

The *demand for speed* is based on a compelling economic logic. A regime of intense technological competition robs incumbents of their clout and brings upstarts to the fore. Firms join forces with other companies and/or with university scientists to reduce the risks and to share the expense of developing costly products that have very short life spans. Porter and Fuller (1986) argue that partnerships and coalitions are a more rapid means of repositioning than internal development and are less costly, less irreversible, and more successful than mergers. This view suggests that the business environment has changed in such a manner that it now rewards many of the key strengths of network forms of organization: fast access to information, flexibility, and responsiveness to changing tastes. Networks, then, possess some degree of comparative advantage in coping with an environment that places a premium on innovation and customized products.

What is it about networks that makes them more adaptive and well-suited to coping with change? One of the key advantages of network arrangements is their ability to disseminate and interpret new information. Networks are based on complex communication channels. Kaneko and Imai (1987) emphasize this dynamic property of networks, noting that they are particularly adept at generating new interpretations; as a result of these new accounts, novel linkages are often formed. This advantage is seen most clearly when networks are contrasted with markets and hierarchies. Passing information up or down a corporate hierarchy or purchasing information in the marketplace is merely a way of processing information or acquiring a commodity. In either case the flow of information is controlled. No new meanings or interpretations are generated. In contrast, networks provide a context for learning by doing. As information passes through a network, it is both freer and richer; new connections and new meanings are generated, debated, and evaluated.

Thus, to the extent that competition is based on such factors as the ability to innovate and translate ideas into products quickly, network forms of organization are more likely to proliferate. When competition occurs on the basis of price or manufacturing intensity, networks are likely to be less in evidence.

Trust. Several of the examples, particularly the cases of craft-based networks and industrial districts, suggest that certain social contexts encourage cooperation and solidarity, or a sense of generalized reciprocity. In these situations, exchange relations have been long-term and continuous, hence there is scant need to formalize them. What are the specific attributes that create circumstances in which collaboration is so easily accomplished? Axelrod (1984) has demonstrated the powerful consequences of repeated interaction among individuals. When there is a high probability of future association, persons are not only more likely to cooperate with others, they are also increasingly willing to punish those who do not cooperate. When repeat trading occurs, quality becomes more important than quantity. The reputation of a participant is the most visible signal of their reliability. Reputation bulks large in importance in many network-like work settings because there is little separation of formal business statuses and personal social roles. One's standing in one arena often determines one's place in the other. As a result, there is limited need for hierarchical oversight because the desire for continued participation successfully discourages opportunism. Monitoring is generally easier and more effective when done by peers than when done by superiors. Consensual ideologies substitute for formal rules and compliance procedures.

Networks should be most common in work settings in which participants have some kind of common background—be it ethnic, geographic, ideological, or professional. The more homogeneous the group, the greater the trust, hence the easier it is to sustain network-like arrangements. When the diversity of participants increases, trust recedes, and so does the willingness to enter into long-term collaborations. Calculative attitudes replace cooperative ones, and formal agreements—either contractual or bureaucratic—supplant informal understandings.

It also stands to reason that certain kinds of institutional contexts, that is, particular combinations of legal, political, and economic factors, are especially conducive to network arrangements as well as interorganizational collaborations. Yet we know very little about what kinds of political and economic conditions support network forms. As a result, I hold this discussion for the next section on unresolved issues. It is, however, worth noting that networks appear to involve a distinctive combination of factors—skilled labor, some degree of employment security, salaries rather than piece rates, some externally-provided mechanisms for job training, relative equity among the participants, a legal system with relaxed antitrust standards, and national policies that promote research and development and encourage linkages between centers of higher learning and industry—which seldom exist in sufficient measure without a political and legal infrastructure to sustain them.

A RESEARCH AGENDA

The discussion thus far points to a number of key issues that require more sustained attention, as well as suggests several new topics for the research agenda. We need to know a good deal more about the factors that explain the ecology of network forms. Why is there such considerable cross-national variation in the frequency of network forms? Why are network arrangements so common in some nations and some sectors and not others? The evidence that I have presented suggests that state policies make a difference in the ease with which collaborative arrangements are formed and are sustained, but we have only begun to investigate the relationship between governance structures and state policies. Similarly, network forms are found in a diverse set of industries—craft-based occupations and professions, high technology sectors, and even mature ones such as auto. Can we make sense of this diversity? Do rates of formation vary across industries? Some early research (Friar & Horwitch, 1985; Hamilton, 1985; Hergert & Morris, 1988; Mariti & Smiley, 1983; Zagnoli, 1987) suggests that alliances are much more common in high technology fields, but we do not yet know whether this is a function of a youthful stage in an industry's life cycle or of basic structural features of activities that are highly dependent on the creation of new forms of knowledge.

A good deal more research is needed on the durability of networks. I have suggested above that the distinction between very specific resources and intangible assets might account for divergent patterns. The need to acquire resources may lead to network arrangements that are an interim step, either a half way point between market procurement and outright merger or a transitional move until internal capability is built up. Tacit knowledge, however, is inherently difficult to exchange; it may well lead to repeated, reciprocal interactions, transforming what was initially a relationship approached with some caution and fear into one that is institutionalized and enduring. In these circumstances, collaboration would be expected to shift from a means to an end in itself. Careful comparative research along these lines would be highly useful.

We know very little about the phenomenology of work under different governance structures. Do participants "experience" networks as qualitatively different from market transactions or careers in hierarchical firms? If the argument that markets, hierarchies, and networks are distinctive forms, with their own logic and procedures, is correct, then we should find important behavioral differences among them. Do members of networks exhibit greater loyalty or commitment? Do participants in network arrangements face novel problems of control?

How do people cope with relationships that are both collaborative and competitive, with circumstances in which control is not direct and immediate, and conformity to well-established administrative routines not guaranteed?

What are the performance liabilities of networks? There are, in all likelihood, certain tasks for which networks are poorly suited. When do networks create new levels of complexity that are incommensurate with their intended benefits? Are the gains from network relationships appropriated asymmetrically due to differences in the learning capacity of the participants? Some researchers (Cole, 1985; Pucik, 1988) suggest that much of the imbalance between Western and Japanese partners to joint ventures can be attributed to disparities in learning. Many Japanese firms have in place systematic methods that encourage the transfer of information and know-how from a joint venture throughout their organization (Imai, Nonaka, & Takeuchi, 1985). More work is needed to understand how information is processed through networks and how learning is sustained.

Does participation in a network arrangement alter one's orientation toward future collaboration? Do the partners to a successful network relationship change their calculus and decide to act in different ways because of this experience? Does a reputation for being a fair-minded and successful exchange partner translate into clear economic benefits? These are fundamental questions and they suggest that much work remains to be done. This is not a daunting prospect, however. Indeed, one of my goals in this paper has been to suggest that students of organizational behavior are particularly well-equipped to study and explain the circumstances under which cooperation and collaboration proceed with only limited reliance on contracts and the legal system on the one hand, and on administrative fiat and bureaucratic routines on the other.

ACKNOWLEDGMENTS

This paper has had a long gestation period. It began as a talk to the Industrial Relations Workshop at MIT's Sloan School of Management. The comments and encouragement of Mel Howitch and Mike Piore are greatly appreciated. A second iteration was presented at the Law, Economics, and Organization Workshop at Yale Law School and at the 1986 meetings of The American Sociological Association. The suggestions of Mitch Abolafia, Wayne Baker, Dick Nelson, Oliver Williamson, and Sid Winter were most helpful. An earlier draft of the paper was prepared while I was a fellow at the Center for Advanced Study in the Behavioral Sciences. The writing of the final draft was supported by funds from the Karl Eller Center for the Study of the Private Market Economy at the University of Arizona. I have benefited from comments by a great many people. Space limitations preclude me from thanking everyone properly, but several people who provided yeoman's help should be singled out: Michael Gerlach, Dave Jemison, Bob Keohane, Andrea Larson, Claus Offe and Charles Perrow. I also profited from comments by members of the audience at seminars at the Berkeley, Stanford, and UCLA business schools and the sociology departments at Arizona, Chicago, and Santa Barbara. Of course, I remain responsible for any errors or omissions.

NOTES

1. See Koenig and Thietart (1988) on intermediate forms in the aerospace industry, Thorelli (1986) on industrial marketing networks, Eccles and White (1986) on transfer pricing, and Powell (1987) on hybrid forms in craft and high technology industries.

2. This recognition of intermediate forms has not, however, been accompanied by much in the way of concerted analysis. *The Economic Institutions of Capitalism* may include relational contracting in its subtitle, but the index lists a scant four pages of references to the topic. Similarly, Riordan and Williamson (1985) emphasize polar firm and market choices throughout their analysis, and then acknowledge in their last paragraph that "hybrid modes of organization are much more important than had hitherto been realized."

3. Transaction costs reasoning borrows freely from legal scholars, such as Macaulay and Macneil, who are noted for the development of ideas regarding relational contracting. Gordon (1985), however, questions whether this assimilation is satisfactory, noting that the price of success by economists is the "exclusion of the very elements of contract relations to which Macneil and Macaulay have given most prominence: culture, politics, and power" (p. 575).

4. Transaction cost logic involves the comparison of discrete structural alternatives, typically the comparison that is made is that between market and hierarchy. The problem I have with this analysis is that in many cases where transaction cost reasoning predicts internalization; we find other kinds of governance structures, particularly networks. But one can read Williamson (1985) in a different manner, ignoring the argument about the predominance of markets and hierarchies, and focus instead on the highly important role of credible commitments. The book discusses a marvelous array of mechanisms for creating mutually reliant and self-enforcing agreements. If one conceives of production as a chain of activities in which value is added (Porter, 1985), the question is thus posed: which activities does a firm chose to perform internally and which activities are either downplayed or "farmed out" to members of a network who presumably can carry them out more effectively, due to benefits of specialization, focus, or size (see Jarillo, 1988 for an extended discussion of this network value chain). When production is viewed in this manner, Williamson's arguments about credible commitments are quite useful in assessing what kinds of network agreements are likely to prove durable.

5. This does not mean that market forces were of little consequences before the eighteenth century. Braudel (1982) argues that economic history is the story of slowly-evolving mixtures of institutional forms. He suggests that we can speak of a market economy when the prices in a given area appear to fluctuate in unison, a phenomenon that has occurred since ancient times. But this does not imply that transactions between individuals were of a discrete, impersonal nature.

6. I owe this observation to comments made by Jim Robins.

7. What is remarkable about the firms in these two studies is how explicitly the entrepreneurs follow a "network" strategy, intentionally eschewing internalization for such crucial and recurrent activities as manufacturing, sales, and research and development.

8. On this point, Macneil (1985, p. 496) suggests that "the transaction costs approach is far too unrelational a starting point in analyzing" relational forms of exchange. Richardson (1972, p. 884) provides an apt example of these densely connected forms of exchange: "Firm A, ... is a joint subsidiary of firms B and C, has technical agreements with D and E, subcontracts work to F, is in marketing association with G—and so on. So complex and ramified are these arrangements, indeed, that the skills of a genealogist rather than an economist might often seem appropriate for their disentanglement."

9. Bob Eccles and Mark Granovetter have repeatedly made this point to me in personal communications, insisting that all forms of exchange contain elements of networks, markets, and hierarchies. Since they are smarter than me, I should listen to them. Nevertheless, I hope to show that there is merit in thinking of networks as an empirically identifiable governance structure.

10. This line of work is both novel and promising, but it has yet to demonstrate how social ties and cultural patterns transform economic exchange in a systematic fashion; nor do we as yet have any clear cut notions about how cultural or historical factors create or introduce comparative variations in economic life. The focus, thus far, has been more on the intriguing question of how are economic motives culturally constructed.

11. Some economists (Alchian and Demsetz, 1972; Klein, 1983) go so far as to regard the firm as merely a set of explicit and implicit contracts among owners of different factors of production.

12. Many other scholars have their own definitions. Jarillo (1988, p. 32) defines strategic networks as "long-term, purposeful arrangements among distinct but related for-profit organizations that allow those firms in them to gain or sustain competitive advantage vis-à-vis their competitors outside the network." Kaneko and Imai (1987) conceive of networks as a particular form of multi-faceted, inter-organizational relationships through which new information is generated. Johanson and Mattsson (1987) regard networks as a method of dividing labor such that firms are highly dependent upon one another. Coordination is not achieved through hierarchy or markets, but through the interaction and mutual obligation of the firms in the network. Gerlach (1990) suggests that alliances among Japanese firms are an important institutional alternative that links Japanese firms to one another in ways that are fundamentally different from U.S. business practices. Alliances, in his view, are coherent networks of rule-ordered exchange, based on the mutual return of obligations among parties bound in durable relationships.

I find these various definitions very helpful, but also limited. They all describe networks as a form of dense interorganizational relationships. But networks can also evolve out of personal ties, or market relationships among various parties. Many of the arrangements discussed below, commonly found in the publishing, fashion, computer software, construction, and entertainment businesses are among individuals, independent production teams, or very small business units. Thus, my conception of networks is closer to Macneil's (1978; 1985) ideas about relational contracts than to the above views.

13. In an illuminating essay, Keohane (1986, p. 8) defines reciprocity as exchanges of roughly equivalent values in which the actions of each party are contingent on the prior actions of the others in such a way that good is returned for good, and bad for bad.

14. For example, successful reciprocal ties in scholarly book publishing—between authors and editors or between editors in competing houses—were highly implicit, of long-standing duration, and not strictly balanced (Powell, 1985). It was widely believed that the open-ended quality of the relationship meant that the goods being exchanged—advice, recommendations, or manuscripts—were more valuable and reliable.

15. Parties are, of course, free to exit from a network. But the difficulty of abandoning a relationship around which a unit or a company has structured its operations and expectations can keep a party locked into a relationship that it experiences as unsatisfactory. This problem of domination in networks obviously lends itself to transaction costs discussions of credible commitments.

16. In his study of the U.S. steel minimill industry, Von Hippel (1987) found the sharing of know-how to be based on professional networks, which develop among engineers with common research interests. When a request for technical assistance is made, the person being asked typically makes two calculations: (1) is the information being requested vital to the health of the firm or just useful, but not crucial? and (2) how likely is the requester to reciprocate at a later date? Even though no explicit accounting is made, assistance is commonly offered. Von Hippel argues that this "economically feasible and novel form of cooperative R&D" is probably found in many other industries as well.

17. For useful reports on Italy's economy, see "Europe's sun belt also rises," *U.S. News and World Report*, 7/18/88, pp. 27–29; and "The Italian Economy: A Special Survey," *The Economist*, 2/27/88, pp. 3–34. Both surveys point to the remarkable transformation of Italian industry, led by vast battalions of small firms, but caution that huge government budget deficits, inefficient public services, and an antiquated financial system could hold back further progress.

18. While the organizational structure of Italian firms may not seem modern, they are decidedly successful and high-tech in their operations. Benetton, the fashionable clothing company, is an oft-cited example. With some 2,000 employees, the company orchestrates relations backward with more than 350 subcontractors throughout western Europe and forward with some 100 selling agents and over 4,000 retail stores worldwide. The company's spectacular growth from small family business to far-flung empire has not been built on internalization or economies of scale, but on external relations for manufacturing, design, distribution and sales. These extended networks have both advantages in terms of speed and flexibility and liabilities with regard to maintaining quality standards. See Jarillo and Martinez (1987) and Belussi (1986) for detailed case studies of the company.

19. For more discussion of the interfirm networks that pervade the Japanese economy, see Okumura (1982), Shimokawa (1985), and Gerlach (1990).

20. For a thoughtful analysis of regional economies and changes in the scale of production, see Sabel (1989).

21. Such efforts, alas, will be hard pressed to succeed. See Dorfman (1983) on the largely idiosyncratic, hard-to-duplicate origins of Route 128 technology corridor.

22. The commercial aircraft industry is unusual with respect to the very active role played by governments in insuring that their countries maintain a major presence in the industry. In this case, coalitions and joint ventures are driven as much by political factors and pressures for economic nationalism as by organizational and economic logic. See several of the chapters in Porter (1986) for a discussion of the political aspects of international alliances.

23. Competition over the marketing of tissue plasminogen activator (TPA), an enzyme may expect to be a major drug in treating heart attacks, is the most severe and complicated in biotechnology today. This competitive struggle illustrates how rival transnational alliances race for global market share. The U.S. firm Genentech is allied with Mitsubishi Chemical and Kyowa Hakko in Japan, while another American firm, Biogen, is collaborating with Fujisawa. Numerous other Japanese and European pharmaceutical alliances, ignoring Genentech's claims for patent priority for TPA, are busy with their own TPA research. This contest shows the intensity of transnational alliance competition, but at the same time that Genentech and Fujisawa are at odds over TPA, they are collaborating in the marketing of another biotech drug, tumor necrosis factor (TNF). Yoshikawa (1988) offers a good road map to the complex, crosscutting terrain of biotechnology strategic alliances.

24. The label "joint venture" implies the creation of a separate organization, but this need not be the case. Rather than form a new entity, partners can agree to a co-production arrangement. This is common in manufacturing, particularly aerospace, where each partner produces a section of the final product. Or firms may agree to a research partnership in which scientists and laboratories are shared. Similarly, exploration consortia in extractive industries need not create a new firm, but rather pool the costs and risks of existing activities.

25. The founding chairman of Sematech (a research consortium of 14 semiconductor firms), Charles Sporck, bemoaned that, "We are trailing a pack of nations that are far ahead of us in forming consortiums. We're especially trailing the Japanese." Quoted in Peter Lewis, "Are U.S. Companies Learning to Share?" *New York Times*, 2/7/88, Week in Review, p. 5.

26. Ouchi and Bolton (1988) provide a good summary of the factors that account for the present stage of mixed support in the U.S. for collective industrial research.

27. For a detailed discussion of the origins, development, and initial problems of one large cooperative R&D venture, the Microelectronics and Computer Technology Corporation (MCC) in Austin, Texas, see Peck (1986).

28. Ed Zajac has emphasized to me that the termination of a relationship does not necessarily imply failure. Collaboration is often intended as a means for the transfer of knowledge. Once this process is realized, termination may well be a sign of success.

29. Analysts have cautioned against alliances that involve a relative power imbalance, in which either one partner receives undue benefits or where one partner becomes so dependent on another that they may have no option other than to continue a relationship in which their share is increasingly inferior (see Teece, 1986). This fear, along with the worry that the partner will not perform according to expectations, explains why most potential partners approach an agreement with trepidation. These are typical and well-founded misgivings about any asymmetric exchange relationship.

30. Many commentators have voiced particular concerns about global partnerships, issues that are contested in the current "manufacturing matters" debate (see Cohen & Zysman, 1987). Reich and Mankin (1986) warn that friendly colleagues often revert to hostile competitors. In the Pentax-Honeywell and Canon-Bell & Howell alliances, Japanese partners took advantage of valuable U.S. technology and know-how only to later discard their American partners. *Business Week*, in its well-known March 3, 1986 issue, cautioned against the growth of "hollow corporations," that is, firms that have disaggregated so radically that they are left without any core expertise.

31. Wilkinson (1983) details related developments in Britain, where retailing, clothing, shoemaking, printing, and foodstuffs have undergone vertical disintegration, with the subsequent rise of small firms and numerous subcontracting relationships.

32. Top-down controls create distance between supervisors and subordinates, between powerful executives and less powerful employees. A vertical chain of command, and its accompanying layers of administration, undercuts management's ability to see its directives implemented and creates an environment in which employees see their work as but a tiny cog in a large impersonal machine. The diffuse control structure in large firms both dampens management's ability to move quickly and labor's sense of commitment to the enterprise.

REFERENCES

Abernathy, W. (1978). *The productivity dilemma*. Baltimore: Johns Hopkins University Press.

Agnew, J. (1986). *Worlds Apart: The market and the theater in anglo-American thought, 1550–1750*. New York: Cambridge University Press.

Alchian, A., & Demsetz, H. (1972). Production, information costs, and economic organization. *American Economic Review, 62, 5, 777–795*.

Arrow, K. (1974). *The limits of organization*. New York: Norton.

Arthur, B. (1987). Urban systems and historical path-dependence. To appear in *Urban systems and infrastructure*, R. Herman and J. Ansubel (Eds.). NAS/NAE, forthcoming.

Axelrod, R. (1984). *The evolution of cooperation*. New York: Basic Books.

Belussi, F. (1986). New technologies in a traditional sector: The benetton case. Berkeley Roundtable on the International Economy working paper #19.

Ben-Porath, Y. (1980). The F-connection: Families, friends, and firms in the organization of exchange. *Population and Development Review, 6*, 1–30.

Berger, C., & Cummings, L.L. (1979). Organizational structure, attitudes and behavior." In Barry Staw (Ed.), *Research in Organizational Behavior* (Vol. 1, pp. 169–208).

Borys, B., & Jemison, D.B. (1989). Hybrid organizations as strategic alliances: Theoretical issues in organizational combinations. *Academy of Management Review, 14*(2), 234–249.

Bradach, J.L., & Eccles, R.G. (1989). Markets versus hierarchies: From ideal types to plural forms. *Annual Review of Sociology, 15*, 97–118.

Braudel, F. (1982). *The wheels of commerce*. New York: Harper and Row.

Brusco, S. (1982). The Emilian model: Productive decentralization and social integration. *Cambridge Journal of Economics, 6,* 167–184.

Buckley, P.J., & Casson, M. (1988). A theory of cooperation in international business. Pp. 31–53 in F. Contractor & P. Lorange (Eds.), *Cooperative strategies in international business,* Lexington, MA: Lexington Books.

Chandler, A.D. (1977). *The visible hand.* Cambridge: Harvard University Press.

Child, J. (1972). Organizational structure and strategies of control: A replication of the Aston Study. *Administrative Science Quarterly, 18,* 168–185.

Coase, R. (1937). The nature of the firm. *Economica, 4,* 386–405.

Cohen, S., & Zysman, J. (1987). *Manufacturing matters.* New York: Basic Books.

Cole, R. (1985). The macropolitics of organizational change: A comparative analysis of the spread of small-group activities. *Administrative Science Quarterly, 30,* 560–585.

Contractor, F.J. & Lorange, P. (1988). *Cooperative strategies in international business.* Lexington, MA: Lexington Books.

Coser, L., Kadushin C., & Powell, W.W. (1982). *Books: The culture and commerce of publishing.* New York: Basic Books.

Dalton, M. (1957). *Men who manage.* New York: Wiley.

DiMaggio, P., & Powell, W.W. (1983). The iron cage revisited: Institutional isomorphism and collective rationality in organizational fields. *American Sociological Review, 48,* 147–160.

Dore, R. (1983). Goodwill and the spirit of market capitalism." *British Journal of Sociology, 34(4),* 459–482.

Dore, R. (1987). *Taking Japan seriously.* Stanford, CA: Stanford University Press.

Dorfman, N. (1983). Route 128: The development of a regional high-tech economy. *Research Policy, 12,* 299–316.

Doz, Y. (1988). Technology partnerships between larger and smaller firms: Some critical issues. *International Studies of Management and Organization, 17(4),* 31–57.

Dyer, Davis, M.S., & Webber, A. (1987). *Changing alliances.* Boston: Harvard Business School Press.

Eccles, R. (1981). The quasifirm in the construction industry. *Journal of Economic Behavior and Organization, 2,* 335–357.

Eccles, R. (1985). *The transfer pricing problem: A theory for practice.* Lexington, MA: Lexington Books.

Eccles, R.G., & Crane, D. (1987). Managing through networks in investment banking. *California Management Review, 30(1),* 176–195.

Eccles, Robert G., & Harrison C. White. 1986. "Firm and market interfaces of profit center control." Pp. 203–220 in *Approaches to social theory,* ed. by S. Lindenberg, J.S. Coleman, and S. Novak. New York: Russell Sage.

Faulkner, R.R., & Anderson, A. (1987). Short-term projects and emergent careers: Evidence from Hollywood. *American Journal of Sociology, 92(4),* 879–909.

Finley, M. (1973). *The ancient economy.* Berkeley: University of California Press.

Friar, J., & Horwitch, M. 1985. "The emergence of technology strategy: A new dimension of strategic management." *Technology in Society 7(2/3),* pp. 143–178.

Fusfeld, H., & Haklisch, C. (1985). Cooperative R&D for competitors. *Harvard Business Review, 85(6),* 60–76.

Geertz, C. (1978). The bazaar economy: Information and search in peasant marketing. *American Economic Review, 68(2),* 28–32.

Gerlach, M.L. (1990). *Alliances and the social organization of Japanese business.* Berkeley: University of California Press.

Goldberg, V.P. (1980). Relational exchange: Economics and complex contracts. *American Behavioral Scientist, 23(3),* 337–352.

Gordon, R.W. (1985). Macaulay, Macneil, and the discovery of solidarity and power in contract law. *Wisconsin Law Review, 3,* 565–580.

Gouldner, A. (1960). The norm of reciprocity: A preliminary statement. *American Sociological Review, 25,* pp. 161–178.

Graham, M. (1985). Corporate research and development: The latest transformation. *Technology in Society, 7*(2/3), 179–196.

Granovetter, M. (1985). Economic action and social structure: A theory of embeddedness. *American Journal of Sociology, 91*(3), 481–510.

Hackman, R., & Oldham, G. (1980). *Work redesign.* Reading, MA: Addison-Wesley.

Hagg, I., & Johanson, J. (1983). *Firms in networks: A new view of competitive power.* Business and Social Research Institute, Stockholm.

Hackansson, H. (Ed.), (1987). *Industrial technological development: A network approach.* London: Croom Helm.

Hamilton, W.F. (1985). Corporate strategies for managing emerging technologies. *Technology in Society, 7*(2/3), 197–212.

Hannan, M., & Freeman, J.H. (1984). Structural inertia and organizational change. *American Sociological Review, 49,* 149–164.

Hayek, F. (1945). The use of knowledge in society. *American Economic Review, 35,* 519–530.

Helper, S. (1987). *Supplier relations and technical change.* Ph.D. dissertation, Dept. of Economics, Harvard University.

Hergert, M., & Morris, D. (1988). "Trends in international collaborative agreements." Pp. 99–109 in F. Contractor & P. Lorange (Eds.), *Cooperative strategies in international business.* Lexington, MA: Lexington Books.

Imai, K. & Itami, H. (1984). Interpenetration of organization and market. *International Journal of Industrial Organization, 2,* 285–310.

Imai, K., Nonaka, I. & Takeuchi, H. (1985). Managing the new product development process: How Japanese companies learn and unlearn. Pp. 337–375 in *The uneasy alliance.* Kim B. Clark et al. (Eds.), Boston: Harvard Business School Press.

Jarillo, J.-C. (1988). On strategic networks. *Strategic Management Journal, 9,* 31–41.

Jarillo, J.-C., & Martinez, J.I. (1987). Benetton S.p.A.: A case study. Working paper, IESE, Barcelona, Spain.

Johanson, J., & Mattson, L.-G. (1987). Interorganizational relations in industrial systems: A network approach compared with the transaction-cost approach. *International Studies of Management and Organization, 18*(1), 34–48.

Kaneko, I., & Imai, K. (1987). A network view of the firm. Paper presented at 1st Hitotsubashi—Stanford conference.

Keohane, R. (1986). Reciprocity in international relations. *International Organization, 40*(1), 1–27.

Klein, B. (1983). Contracting costs and residual claims: The separation of ownership and control. *Journal of Law and Economics, 26,* 367–374.

Koenig, C., & Thietart, R.A. (1988). Managers, engineers and government. *Technology in Society, 10,* 45–69.

Larson, A. (1988). Cooperative alliances: A study of entrepreneurship. Ph.D. dissertation, Harvard Business School.

Lazerson, M. (1988). Organizational growth of small firms: An outcome of markets and hierarchies? *American Sociological Review, 53*(3), 330–342.

Lorenzoni, G., & Ornati, O. (1988). Constellations of firms and new ventures. *Journal of Business Venturing, 3,* 41–57.

Loveman, G., Piore, M., & Sengenberger, W. (1987). The evolving role of small business in industrial economies. Paper presented at conference on New Developments in Labor Market and Human Resource Policies, Sloan School, M.I.T.

Luhmann, N. 1979. *Trust and power.* New York: Wiley.

Macneil, I. (1978). Contracts: Adjustment of long-term economic relations under classical, neoclassical, and relational contract law. *Northwestern University Law Review, 72*(6), 854–905.

Macneil, I. (1985). Relational contract: What we do and do not know. *Wisconsin Law Review, 3*, 483–526.

Mariotti, S., & Cainarca, G.C. 1986. The evolution of transaction governance in the textile-clothing industry. *Journal of Economic Behavior and Organization, 7*, 351–374.

Mariti, P., & Smiley, R.H. (1983). Co-operative agreements and the organization of industry. *Journal of Industrial Economics, 31*(4), 437–451.

Mauss, M. (1967, 1925). *The gift.* New York: Norton.

Mowery, D.C. (1987). *Alliance politics and economics.* Cambridge, MA: Ballinger.

Mowery, D.C. (Ed.), (1988). *International collaborative ventures in U.S. manufacturing.* Cambridge, MA: Ballinger.

Nelson, R., & Winter, S. (1982). *An evolutionary theory of economic change.* Cambridge: Harvard University Press.

Okumura, H. (1982). Interfirm relations in an enterprise group: The case of Mitsubishi. *Japanese Economic Studies, 10*(4), 53–82.

Ouchi, W.G., & Bolton, M.K. (1988). The logic of joint research and development. *California Management Review, 30*(3), 9–33.

Peck, M.J. (1986). Joint R&D: The case of microelectronics and computer technology corporation. *Research Policy, 15*, 219–231.

Perlmutter, H., & Heenan, D. (1986). Cooperate to compete globally. *Harvard Business Review, 86*(2), 136–152.

Perrow, C. (1967). A framework for the comparative analysis of organizations. *American Sociological Review, 32*, 194–208.

Peterson, R.A., & White, H. (1981). Elements of simplex structure. *Urgan Life, 10*(1), 3–24.

Piore, M.J., & Sabel, C.F. 1984. *The second industrial divide.* New York: Basic Books.

Polanyi, K. 1957. *The great transformation.* Boston: Beacon.

Porter, L., & Lawler, E. (1965). Properties of organization structure in relation to job attitudes and job behavior. *Psychological Bulletin, 64*(1), 23–51.

Porter, M. (1983). *Cases in competitive strategy.* New York: Free Press.

Porter, M. (1985). *Competitive advantage.* New York: Free Press.

Porter, M. (1986). *Competition in global industries.* Boston: Harvard Business School Press.

Porter, M., & Fuller, M.B. (1986). Coalitions and global strategy. Pp. 315–344 in M. Porter (Ed.), *Competition in global industries.* Boston: HBS Press.

Powell, W.W. (1985). *Getting into print: The decision making process in scholarly publishing.* Chicago: University of Chicago Press.

Powell, W.W. (1987). Hybrid organizational arrangements: New form or transitional development? *California Management Review, 30*(1), 67–87.

Pucik, V. (1988). Strategic alliances with the Japanese: Implications for human resource management. Pp. 487–498 in F. Contractor & P. Lorange (Eds.), *Cooperative strategies in international business.* Lexington, MA: Lexington Books.

Quinn, D.P. (1987). Dynamic markets and mutating firms: The changing organization of production in automotive firms. Working paper presented at APSA meetings, Chicago.

Reddy, W.M. (1984). *The rise of market culture.* New York: Cambridge University Press.

Reich, R.B., & Mankin, E. (1986). "Joint ventures with Japan give away our future." *Harvard Business Review 86*, 2: 78–86.

Richardson, G.B. (1972). The organization of industry. *Economic Journal, 82*, 883–896.

Riordan, M.H., & Williamson, O.E. (1985). Asset specificity and economic organization. *International Journal of Industrial Organization, 3*, 365–378.

Sabel, C.F. (1989). Flexible specialization and the re-emergence of regional economies. Pp. 17–70 in P. Hirst and J. Zeitlin (Eds.), *Reversing Industrial Decline?* Oxford, UK: Berg.

Sabel, C., G. Herrigel, R. Kazis, & Deeg, R. 1987. How to keep mature industries innovative. *Technology Review 90*(3), 26–35.

Sahlins, M. (1972). *Stone age economics.* Chicago: Aldine.

Shimokawa, K. (1985). Japan's keiretsu system: The case of the automobile industry. *Japanese Economic Studies, 13*, 4: 3–31.

Stinchcombe, A. (1985). Contracts as hierarchical documents. Pp. 121–171 in A. Stinchcombe & C. Heimer, *Organization theory and project management.* Oslo: Norwegian University Press.

Teece, D. (1986). Profiting from technological innovation: Implications for integration, collaboration, licensing and public policy. *Research Policy, 15*(6), 785–305.

Teece, D., & Pisano, G. (1987). Collaborative arrangements and technology strategy. Paper presented at conference on New Technology and New Intermediaries, Center for European Studies, Stanford.

Thompson, E.P. (1971). The moral economy of the English crowd in the eighteenth century. *Past and Present, 50,* 78–98.

Thorelli, H.B. (1986). Networks: Between markets and hierarchies. *Strategic Management Journal, 7,* 37–51.

Von Hippel, E. (1987). Cooperation between rivals: Informal know-how trading. *Research Policy, 16,* 291–302.

Walton, R. (1985). From control to commitment in the workplace. *Harvard Business Review 85,* 2: 76–84.

Walzer, M. (1983). *Spheres of justice.* New York: Basic Books.

Weitzman, M. (1984). *The share economy.* Cambridge: Harvard University Press.

White, H.C. (1981). Where do markets come from? *American Journal of Sociology, 87,* 517–547.

Wilkinson, F. (1983). Productive systems. *Cambridge Journal of Economics, 7,* 413–429.

Williamson, O.E. (1975). *Markets and hierarchies: Analysis and antitrust implications.* New York: Free Press.

Williamson, O.E. (1985). *The economic institutions of capitalism.* New York; Free Press.

Yoshikawa, A. (1988). Japanese biotechnology: New drugs, industrial organization, innovation, and strategic alliances. BRIE Working Paper #33.

Zagnoli, P. (1987). Interfirm agreements as bilateral transactions? Paper presented at conference on New Technology and New Intermediaries, Center for European Studies, Stanford.

Zelizer, V. (1988). Beyond the polemics of the market: Establishing a theoretical and empirical agenda. Paper presented at conference on Economy and Society, University of California—Santa Barbara.

Part II
Contracting:
Price and Contract Formation

[7]

The Rigidity of Prices

By Dennis W. Carlton[*]

For many transactions, prices remain rigid for periods exceeding one year. Price rigidity is positively correlated with industry concentration. For several products, the correlation of price changes across buyers is low. The paper also investigates the relationship between price rigidity, price change, and the length of time a buyer and seller have been doing business. The evidence emphasizes the importance of nonprice rationing and the inadequacy of models in which price movements alone clear markets.

Economists focus on price as a mechanism to allocate resources efficiently. It is well recognized that inefficient resource allocation could occur if prices are not free to adjust. Much of macroeconomics relies on some, usually unexplained, source of price rigidity to generate inefficient unemployment. And in industrial organization there is a large literature on "administered" prices which fail to respond to the forces of supply and demand. Recently, there have been several attempts to explain price rigidity (see, for example, Arthur Okun (1981) and Oliver Williamson (1975)) and to develop a theory to explain why efficient resource allocation requires price to be unchanging or "rigid" (see, for example, my forthcoming paper and Robert Hall, 1984). Whether or not price rigidity is efficient, one common conclusion emerging from models with price rigidity is that markets with rigid prices behave very differently than markets with flexible prices. Therefore, an important unanswered question is, just how rigid are prices? Despite the great interest in this question, there have been virtually no attempts to answer it with data on individual transaction prices.

The purpose of this paper is to present evidence on the amount of price rigidity that exists in individual transaction prices. Previous studies of price rigidity have relied almost exclusively on an examination of aggregate price indices collected by the Bureau of Labor Statistics (BLS).[1] The use of BLS data has been strongly criticized on the grounds that the BLS data are inaccurate measures of transaction prices. George Stigler and James Kindahl sought to remedy this deficiency by collecting price data on actual transactions. Stigler and Kindahl then showed that price indices of average transaction prices were more flexible than the BLS price indices.

The difficulty with using indices is that they can mask the behavior of individual transaction prices. For example, suppose that two people buy varying amounts of commodity A monthly for many years. Suppose that each buyer pays a constant price on each transaction for a period of several years, that when the price to one buyer changes, the price to the other buyer is unaffected and that the price rigidity that exists is more pronounced for a downward price movement. All of these facts could be perfectly consistent with a flexible aggregate price in-

*Graduate School of Business, University of Chicago, 1101 East 58th Street, Chicago, IL 60637 and National Bureau of Economic Research. I thank the NSF and the Law and Economics Program at the University of Chicago for support. I thank Frederic Miller, Virginia France, Larry Harris, Deborah Lucas, and Steven Oi for research assistance. I also thank Claire Friedland and George Stigler for making these data available to me and for assisting me in their use. I thank Edward Lazear, Sam Peltzman, George Stigler, two anonymous referees, and participants at seminars at the NBER, Stanford, the universities of Chicago, Montreal, Pennsylvania, and Virginia for helpful comments.

[1] Research on prices includes the early and important work of Frederick Mills (1926), Gardiner Means (1935), and more recently, George Stigler and James Kindahl (1970).

dex as long as the amount purchased by each buyer varies from month to month. Yet the implication that many draw from a flexible price index, namely that price is allocating resources efficiently, could be completely inappropriate. Moreover, there are several interesting questions that cannot be answered by examining aggregate price indices. For example, how long do prices to a buyer remain unchanged, what is the relationship between contract length and price rigidity, and how closely together do the prices to different buyers move?

Using the Stigler-Kindahl data, I have examined the behavior of individual buyers' prices for certain products used in manufacturing. My main conclusions are:

1) The degree of price rigidity in many industries is significant. It is not unusual in some industries for prices to individual buyers to remain unchanged for several years.

2) Even for what appear to be homogeneous commodities, the correlation of price changes across buyers is very low.

3) There is a (weak) negative correlation between price rigidity and length of buyer-seller association. The more rigid are prices, the shorter the length of association.

4) There is a positive correlation between price rigidity and average absolute price change. The more rigid are prices, the greater is the price change when prices do change.

5) There is a negative correlation between length of buyer-seller association and average absolute price change. The longer a buyer and seller deal with each other, the smaller is the average price change when prices do change.

6) There is no evidence that there is an asymmetry in price rigidity. In particular, prices are not rigid downward.

7) The fixed costs of changing price at least to some buyers may be small. There are plenty of instances where small price changes occur. It appears that, for any particular product, the fixed cost of changing price varies across firms and buyers.

8) There is at best very weak evidence that buyers have systematic preferences across products for unchanging prices.

9) The level of industry concentration is strongly correlated with rigid prices. The more concentrated the industry, the longer is the average spell of price rigidity.

The most startling finding to me is that for many products, the correlation of price changes across buyers is low. Some of the theories referred to earlier explain why this is likely to occur, especially for specialized goods. The fact that it occurs for what most economists (though not necessarily businessmen) would regard as a homogeneous product emphasizes how erroneous it is to focus attention on price as the exclusive mechanism to allocate resources. Nonprice rationing is not a fiction, it is a reality of business and may be the efficient response to economic uncertainty and the cost of using the price system. (See my forthcoming paper.)

Two general caveats deserve mention. First, a rigid price, by itself, does not necessarily imply an inefficiency. If supply and demand are unchanging, prices will be rigid. Moreover, even in a changing market, a fixed-price contract for a fixed quantity creates no economic inefficiency in the standard competitive model. If prices change subsequent to the signing of the contract, the buyer incurs a capital gain or loss, but his marginal price remains the same as every other buyer as long as the product can be readily bought and sold. However, if either the buyer cannot readily resell his product, or if the buyer does not have a fixed quantity contract, then a fixed price may well lead to buyers facing different marginal prices. My understanding of the data I use is that the contracts typically leave the quantity unspecified, so that different buyers paying different prices do indeed face different marginal prices. Although this is inefficient in the standard competitive model, it need not be under more realistic assumptions that recognize the cost of making a market. (See my forthcoming paper. See also my 1978, 1979, 1982, 1983 papers for analyses reconciling observed price behavior with market equilibrium.) But the finding of different prices and price movements to different buyers does emphasize the inadequacy of the simple market-clearing model.

VOL. 76 NO. 4 CARLTON: RIGIDITY OF PRICES 639

Second, the time period I examine is one with relatively low levels of inflation and therefore I have made no adjustment for it. However, even if inflation were rampant and all prices indexed so that no (nominal) price rigidity existed, the main conclusion of the paper would stand as long as some of the other empirical findings (such as the low correlation of price movements across buyers) continue to hold. The conclusion is that price alone is not allocating goods and that new theories are required to justify what looks like non-market-clearing behavior.

This paper is organized as follows. Section I describes the Stigler-Kindahl data and discusses measures of price rigidity. Section II analyzes the characteristics of price rigidity found in several general product groupings. Section III investigates the relationship between price rigidity, price change, and length of buyer-seller associations. Section IV examines whether buyers have systematic preferences for price stability across different products. One criticism of using broadly defined product groups as the unit of analysis is that there is so much heterogeneity of products within a single product grouping that results can be biased. Therefore, in Section V, I redo the analysis for a select group of narrowly defined products. Section VI shows how to measure whether the prices to different buyers move in concert and classifies the various products according to how similar are price changes to different buyers. Section VII examines some specific implications the results have for the prediction of price behavior. Section VIII examines whether there is any relationship of the various characteristics of price movements to the industry's structural characteristics.

I. The Stigler-Kindahl Data

Stigler and Kindahl collected data mainly from buyers on actual transaction prices paid for a variety of products. They tried to correct for any explicit or implicit discounting and for any changes in the specifications of the product. Although there is undoubtedly some misreporting of prices, and some unrecorded product changes (for example, physical characteristics, point of delivery, time of

delivery), it is the most accurate and comprehensive data I know of on individual transaction prices.

The buyers who report prices are typically firms in the *Fortune* 500. The identity of the seller is not known.[2] Typically, there is only scant information on quantity purchased, though it is believed that during the course of the reporting buyers were using the product regularly. Ideally, actual transaction prices are reported monthly. However, in several instances, prices are reported less frequently. A decision on how (or whether) to interpolate prices had to be made.

If the price is unchanged between reportings, I assume that the intervening price is also unchanged. If the price is not the same, then I create two different series. One method assumes a change in each unobserved month. The other assumes only one change over the entire period. For example, suppose that for January, the price is $10, and for April, it is $20 with missing reports for February and March. The first interpolation approach assumes that the price was $13.33 in February and $16.67 in March (i.e., linear interpolation), while the second interpolation approach assumes that the price changed to $20 in either February, March, or April. (It turns out that the results on length of rigidity are unaffected by which particular month is assumed for the price change in this second approach.)

The period of observation is January 1, 1957 through December 31, 1966. Few associations between buyers and seller last for

---

[2] The form in which the data exist do not allow conclusive determination that the buyer is dealing with only one seller. However, it is believed that only one seller is involved when the buyer is reporting prices pursuant to a contract. Furthermore, when prices remain unchanged or when the specification of the good remains unchanged from observation to observation, the buyer is also likely to be dealing with only one seller. I thank Claire Friedland, who helped collect the original data, for helpful discussions on this matter. For expositional ease, I will regard each price series as arising from a transaction between one buyer and one seller. I will point out when this assumption would substantially alter the interpretation of the results.

the entire ten-year period, a point which I analyze later on. Transactions often take place under "contract" and the length of the contract (for example, semiannual, annual) is indicated. The Appendix provides additional information on each type of transaction. Many contracts specify neither a price nor quantity. They seem not to be binding legal documents, but rather more like agreements to agree.

The commodities chosen for study were preselected by Stigler and Kindahl to contain many that others had claimed were characterized by inflexible prices. The commodities are intermediate products used in manufacturing. Within broad commodity classes, finer product distinctions are made. So, for example, one can examine the general category of steel or a specific product category like carbon steel pipe less than 3 inches in diameter. Even within fine product specifications, the individual transactions will probably not involve perfectly homogeneous goods. Therefore, I never compare absolute price levels across products, but instead look only at percentage changes in price and compare movements in percentage changes in price across buyers.

There are a few instances where price series are believed to be list prices, and those prices have been excluded from the analysis. Also excluded are price series that contain inconsistent information. For example, a series is excluded if the reporter claims to produce prices through 1965, but instead prices only through 1960 appear. For several transactions, the product undergoes a specification change. When this occurs, I treat the prices under the new specification change as a new transaction.

II. Analysis of Product Groups

Table 1 describes the price rigidity present in the individual transaction prices by product group. The first column in Table 1 lists the type of product purchased. Column 2 lists the number of buyer-seller pairings that are observed for goods of unchanged specification. (One pairing could last anywhere from 1 month to 10 years.) Column 3 lists the average duration of price rigidity. This

last figure is computed as the average length of spell for which price remains unchanged. For example, if the observations on monthly price were \$5, \$5, \$5, \$6, \$6, \$7, \$7, \$7, \$7, the average rigidity would be three months. The procedure for calculating an average rigidity actually involves an underestimate since the price before the period of observation may have been \$5 and the price after the period of observation may have been \$7. Calculations including and excluding the beginning and ending spells were done with no material change in the substantive interpretation of the results. The calculations in Table 1 are based on the second method of interpolation of prices (only one price change between missing observations—see Section I) and include the beginning and the end of each price series. Column 4 reports the standard deviation in the rigidity of prices. Column 5 reports the same estimate of price rigidity as in column 3, except that only "monthly" contract series are used. These series have fewer missing observations than the other types of transactions, hence much less interpolation is needed. (In fact, the results on rigidity for monthly contracts are similar for the two methods of interpolation.) If the implication of the numbers in column 3 across commodities differ greatly from those in column 5, one might be suspicious of the interpolation used in column 3. I expect price flexibility of monthly contracts to exceed that of all other contract types, so column 5 really puts a lower bound on column 3.

To avoid misinterpretation of the results, it may be helpful to review a standard issue in duration analysis. Imagine that there are two observed transactions, each lasting for a one-year period and each involving the same size of monthly purchase. The first transaction involves a different price each month, while the second involves the same price each month. There are 13 spells of rigidity, 12 of which last one month and one of which lasts twelve months. Based on spells, the average rigidity is $24 \div 13$ or 1.8 months with 92 percent of the spells lasting one month and 8 percent lasting twelve months. Conditional on a price change just having occurred, the average time to the next price

VOL. 76 NO. 4   CARLTON: RIGIDITY OF PRICES   641

TABLE 1—PRICE RIGIDITY BY PRODUCT GROUP

Product Group (1)	Number of Buyer-Seller Pairings[a] (2)	Average Duration of Price Rigidity (Spells) (Months) (3)	Standard Deviation of Duration (Spells) (Months) (4)	Average Duration of Price Rigidity Monthly Contracts (Spells) (Months) (5)	Average Duration of Price Rigidity (Transactions) (Months) (6)
Steel	348	13.0	18.3	9.4	17.9
Nonferrous Metals	209	4.3	6.1	2.8	7.5
Petroleum	245	5.9	5.3	2.5	8.3
Rubber Tires	123	8.1	12.0	7.8	11.5
Paper	128	8.7	14.0	8.8	11.8
Chemicals	658	12.8	10.7	9.6	19.2
Cement	40	13.2	14.7	5.6	17.2
Glass	22	10.2	12.1	8.5	13.3
Truck Motors	59	5.4	6.3	3.7	8.3
Plywood	46	4.7	7.7	1.2	7.5
Household Appliances	14	3.6	3.6	2.5	5.9

[a]A "pairing" means a transaction over time for a good of constant specification.

change is 1.8 months. Yet, one-half of all goods sold involve a rigid price over the entire period. In other words, holding monthly purchases constant, the analysis based on spells underestimates the fraction of goods sold with rigid prices. The results in columns 3 and 5 utilize spells data. Therefore, even though I have no quantity information, I expect that these results underestimate the fraction of goods sold at rigid prices.

In column 6, I calculate price rigidity using a transaction as the unit of analysis, not a "spell." For each transaction, I calculate the average price rigidity, and then take an average (with each transaction weighted according to its length) over all transactions. Return to the earlier example of two transactions, each lasting one year, but one involving 12 price changes and the other no price changes. An analysis based on *transactions* (not spells) would calculate average rigidity to be $(1+12)/2$ or 6.5 months. It is that type of calculation that is reported in column 6.

Several interesting facts emerge from Table 1. In several industries, prices are on average unchanged over periods exceeding one year. The degree of price inflexibility varies enormously across products groups. Steel, chemicals, and cement have average rigidities exceeding one year while household

appliances, plywood, and nonferrous metals have average price rigidities of less than five months. For any one product group the standard deviation of rigidity is quite high. In fact, the standard deviation tends to rise as the average duration of rigidity rises. The simple correlation and the Spearman Rank Correlation between the standard deviation and the average duration (cols. 3 and 4) are both above .80. This suggests (though does not prove) either that each product group presented in Table 1 contains heterogeneous products which differ widely in their price flexibility or that for even a homogeneous product a great heterogeneity in price flexibility is present.[3]

Column 5 shows that using monthly contracts rather than all contracts does not change the basic implications of column 3 regarding price rigidity across groups. Column 6 shows that, as expected, the average of price rigidity rises when the unit of analysis is a transaction. Indeed, the results of

[3]An alternative explanation is that price movements for the same product are similar across different transactions at any one instant but not across time. As we will see in Section VI, this explanation will turn out to be incorrect.

TABLE 2—FREQUENCY OF DURATION OF PRICE RIGIDITY FOR VARIOUS TYPES OF
TRANSACTIONS BASED ON SPELLS OF PRICE RIGIDITY[a]

Product	Type of Transaction	Percent of all Trans-actions	Number of Pair-ings[b]	0–3 Months	4 Mo.– 1 Year	1–2 Years	2–4 Years	Over 4 Years
Steel	Annual	3	11	.11	.41	.24	.22	.03
	Quarterly	53	185	.34	.26	.18	.12	.09
	Monthly	32	111	.48	.27	.15	.07	.04
Nonferrous Metals	Annual	4	8	.16	.69	.12	.03	0
	Quarterly	19	40	.61	.29	.08	.02	.02
	Monthly	42	87	.78	.20	.02	.01	0
Petroleum	Annual	27	66	.20	.69	.07	.04	0
	Quarterly	15	37	.74	.23	.02	.00	–
	Monthly	7	16	.83	.15	.02	0	–
Rubber Tires	Annual	26	32	.19	.72	.07	.01	.01
	Quarterly	37	45	.34	.48	.11	.04	.04
	Monthly	20	24	.44	.44	.07	.01	.06
Paper	Annual	17	22	.04	.69	.18	.08	.01
	Quarterly	2	3	.17	.42	.29	.08	.04
	Monthly	28	36	.46	.36	.12	.04	.02
Chemicals	Annual	43	286	.11	.58	.17	.09	.06
	Quarterly	11	72	.37	.30	.12	.16	.04
	Monthly	20	134	.53	.27	.09	.06	.04
Cement	Annual	20	8	.04	.78	.13	.04	0
	Quarterly	50	20	.19	.27	.23	.14	.05
	Monthly	10	4	.64	.29	.02	.04	.02
Glass	Annual	36	8	0	.87	.10	.03	0
	Quarterly	9	2	.25	.50	.19	0	.06
	Monthly	41	9	.51	.22	.18	.09	0
Truck Motors	Annual	14	8	.05	.86	.09	0	0
	Quarterly	2	1	.21	.57	.21	0	0
	Monthly	58	34	.69	.26	.04	.01	0
Plywood	Annual	0	0	0	0	0	0	0
	Quarterly	96	44	.64	.29	.04	.02	.01
	Monthly	4	2	.99	.02	0	0	0
Household Appliances	Annual	21	3	0	.82	.18	0	0
	Quarterly	0	0	0	0	0	0	0
	Monthly	57	8	.78	.22	0	0	0

[a] The numbers in the rows of the table may not add to one because of rounding.

[b] The "Number of Pairings" is not the number of spells of price rigidity in all contracts. See the discussion preceding Table 1, and the footnote to Table 1.

column 6 are striking in that they show that every product group has an average rigidity in excess of roughly six months, and that 6 of the 11 product groups have average rigidities of roughly one year or more.

In Table 2, more detailed evidence is provided on the time pattern of price rigidity by product group for three types of transactions. The three transaction types are monthly, in which case the transaction occurred monthly (with no necessary future commitment), quarterly monthly in which case the transaction was monthly but was observed quarterly, and annual in which case the transaction was pursuant to an annual contract. For most product groups, these three types of transactions account for well over 60 percent of all transactions. (See the Appendix for a description of the various types of transactions that comprise the sample.) One important point to note about these transactions is that an annual "contract" rarely means a price change every twelve months, nor does a monthly contract mean a

VOL. 76 NO. 4 *CARLTON: RIGIDITY OF PRICES* 643

price change every month. Although annual contracts do involve more rigidity than monthly ones, it is incorrect to think of contracts as inflexible price rules set at specified intervals. A more appropriate view is that they are flexible agreements that can be renegotiated when and if the need arises.

The results in Table 2 show that, as one would expect from Table 1, the pattern of rigidity across product groups is highly varied. As a general rule, all product groups for each of the three transaction types in Table 2 are characterized by spells of price rigidity that in the majority of cases last less than one year. Some commodities like nonferrous metals and plywood are characterized by very flexible prices with over 60 percent of all spells in the monthly and quarterly monthly category lasting less than three months. On the other hand, there are definitely a substantial number of transactions involving very inflexible prices. For example, in steel, over 39 percent of the spells of rigid prices in the annual and quarterly monthly category (which comprises over half of all the transactions in steel) last more than one year. Other commodities with important transaction types showing fairly inflexible prices include paper, chemicals, cement and glass. In fact, a histogram analysis based on transactions (not spells) shows that 50 percent or more of all transactions involving steel, cement, chemicals, or glass, have average rigidities of one year or more for frequently used contract types.

As one would expect, the annual category involves less price flexibility than the quarterly category which itself exhibits less flexibility than the monthly category. It is also interesting to note that even within a particular product group and transaction type, there is a high degree of heterogeneity in price flexibility. For example, for chemicals monthly, over 50 percent of spells of rigidity are less than three months, but still a significant fraction (10 percent) involve spells of rigidity in excess of two years. This suggests that within any one product grouping, either the products sold are different, or the buyer-seller pairings have different properties, or the method chosen to allocate (i.e., price vs.

nonprice) across different pairings of buyers and sellers is simply different.[4]

One issue frequently raised in discussions of price flexibility is the cost of making a price change (see, for example, Robert Barro, 1972). There are many types of costs associated with a price change. New price sheets have to be constructed, price information must be conveyed to buyers, buyers may find planning more difficult, buyers may distrust sellers if prices change often, search costs are higher if prices change often, and so on. The real question is how important are these costs. One way to address this question is to see how important small price changes are. Table 3 reports the percent of all price changes that are less than 1/4, 1/2, 1, and 2 percent, in absolute value for the same product groups and transaction types reported in Table 2.

Table 3 makes two points. First, very small price changes occur more often in monthly than in quarterly monthly or in annual transaction types. Second, and most important, there are a significant number of price changes that one would consider small (i.e., less than 1 percent) for most commodities and transaction types. This finding presents a bit of a puzzle if buyers are homogeneous. Either the cost of changing price is small or the costs of being at the "wrong" price—even one off by 1 percent—are very high.[5] Yet these explanations have difficulty explaining how it can be that some transactions seem to involve prices that do not change over long periods. Another explanation is that perhaps price does not need to

---

[4]Alternatively, the heterogeneity in spells could arise because supply and demand are changing over time. This last explanation turns out not to provide the full answer, as we shall see in Section VI. Moreover, a table analogous to Table 2, based on transactions, not spells, confirms the heterogeneity across transactions.

[5]Even if the fixed cost of changing price is small, one cannot necessarily rule out large welfare effects caused by this fixed cost. In a model with distortions, even small fixed costs can lead to large welfare losses. See, for example, N. Gregory Mankiw (1985) and George Akerlof and Janet Yellen (1985). Furthermore, the presence of even small fixed costs might affect the time-series properties of economic variables. See, for example, Julio Rotemberg (1982) and Olivier Blanchard (1982).

TABLE 3—FREQUENCY OF SMALL PRICE CHANGES BY PRODUCT GROUP
BY CONTRACT TYPE

Product	Percent of Price Changes less than				Average Absolute Price Change (Percent)
	1/4 Percent	1/2 Percent	1 Percent	2 Percent	
Steel:					
Annual	4	8	11	27	3.3
Quarterly	5	11	17	24	4.2
Monthly	9	20	36	52	2.5
Nonferrous Metals:					
Annual	2	5	9	27	7.0
Quarterly	2	5	12	25	5.0
Monthly	8	15	28	49	2.9
Petroleum:					
Annual	0	0	8	24	5.3
Quarterly	0	0	2	17	5.4
Monthly	1	5	19	47	2.9
Rubber Tires:					
Annual	12	21	30	44	3.0
Quarterly	7	11	18	34	4.5
Monthly	13	23	38	63	2.3
Paper:					
Annual	4	9	8	27	6.3
Quarterly	0	19	24	33	3.6
Monthly	13	23	43	62	2.0
Chemicals:					
Annual	4	8	13	24	7.7
Quarterly	0	5	11	24	7.3
Monthly	5	14	30	42	5.0
Cement:					
Annual	14	22	32	46	3.3
Quarterly	0	0	1	19	4.1
Monthly	71	75	85	94	5.0
Glass:					
Annual	0	0	7	19	6.5
Quarterly	0	0	20	40	6.2
Monthly	3	20	45	67	2.1
Trucks, Motors:					
Annual	3	3	12	20	3.9
Quarterly	0	0	0	8	7.2
Monthly	12	27	50	75	1.7
Plywood:					
Annual	–	–	–	–	–
Quarterly	1	2	6	19	6.1
Monthly	19	38	54	72	1.9
Household Appliances:					
Annual	0	0	0	25	4.3
Quarterly	–	–	–	–	–
Monthly	22	44	70	95	.8

change in those transactions for which prices are unchanging (i.e., neither supply nor demand curves are shifting). This explanation runs into the problem that, as is suggested from Table 2 (and as will be confirmed later on), within the same product grouping there are likely to be changing prices for one transaction at the same time that there are constant prices for another. The only possible explanations consistent with efficiency seem to be either that firms differ in their allocation ability with some firms relying on

VOL. 76 NO. 4 *CARLTON: RIGIDITY OF PRICES* 645

price more than others, or, alternatively, that every firm must rely more on price when dealing with certain buyers than with others.[6]

The foregoing analysis can also shed light on the question of whether there is an asymmetry in price movements. For example, are prices rigid downward? If prices are rigid downward, then one can think of the fixed cost of changing price as being higher for price declines than price increases. If so, the minimum positive price change should be less than the minimum negative price change. In fact, an analysis of minimum positive and negative price changes reveals no such pattern.

III. Relationship Between Price Rigidity, Price Change, and Length of Buyer-Seller Association

If within a particular product group, there is a wide degree of heterogeneity in price rigidity across buyers, are there any predictable correlations that emerge between price rigidity, price change, and length of buyer-seller association?[7] There are several different theories of price rigidity and the theories often have different implications for these correlations. I now investigate three questions.

First, is there a positive correlation between length of association and price rigidity across transactions for the same product?[8]

[6] I recognize the possibility that nonefficiency explanations may help explain some pricing behavior (for example, Akerlof-Yellen and Daniel Kahneman, Jack Knetsch, and Richard Thaler, 1986), but feel that the efficiency explanations have not yet been fully explored (see my forthcoming paper).

[7] Length of association is measured as the total time the buyer and seller have engaged in a transaction for a product whose specifications may change over the time of the association. This measure is a noisy one, because the buyer and seller may be engaged in other transactions which affect their knowledge of each other, and may have been dealing with each other prior to the beginning of the data set. Moreover, to the extent that a buyer reported prices from several suppliers, rather than one, for each reported price series, the measure of length of association is flawed. (See fn. 2.)

[8] See Table A1 for data by product group on average length of association and average price change. Table 1 reports average duration of price rigidity. Correlation of these three variables across product groups is not as

That is, if buyer A has been dealing with his seller for ten years, while buyer B is beginning a new relationship, are buyer A's prices more rigid? One rationale for this relationship would be that if buyers and sellers deal with each other over long time periods, they set one average price and thereby save on the transaction cost of changing price constantly. However, it is quite possible to justify the reverse relationship. The impediment to changing price may be that the buyer or seller may feel the other side is taking advantage of him (see, for example, Williamson). If buyers and sellers have been dealing with each other for a long period of time, it will be in their interest not to take advantage of the other in the short run for fear of damaging the ongoing relationship (see, for example, Lester Telser, 1980). If buyers and sellers know each other well, because of their long-standing relationship, this fear of being taken advantage of in the short run will be reduced. In such a case, flexible prices may emerge.

Second, is there an inverse correlation between the size of price change and duration of price rigidity across transactions within the same product group? That is, if buyer A purchases steel on a contract in which price changes frequently, while buyer B has a contract in which price changes infrequently, are the price changes (when they occur) of buyer A larger (in absolute value) than those of buyer B? This relationship would make sense if prices are rigid on some transactions because there is a cost to changing price. If so, one would expect that those transactions with the most rigid prices (those to buyer B) have the highest costs of changing price and therefore only large price changes will be observed on those contracts. An alternative prediction would be that some prices are rigid because buyers (or sellers) want price stability for insurance-type reasons. In such a case, price changes on the more rigid con-

good a way of uncovering systematic relationships among these three variables as is correlation of the three variables across transactions for the same product, because many factors differ between product groups.

tract could well be smaller than on the flexible price contract since the function of insurance is to smooth out price fluctuations.

The third question is whether there is a negative association between length of association and the size of price change. If buyers' and sellers' distrust of or lack of knowledge about each other explains rigid prices, then the longer the association, the lower the cost of changing price, and hence the more flexible should be price and the smaller the observed price changes. The opposite prediction could emerge from a theory in which buyers and sellers who deal with each other over long periods care about getting only the average price right. In such a case, one would expect to see rigid prices that infrequently change. When they do change, they will change by larger amounts than prices in less rigid contracts.[9]

Table 4 reports the correlations between length of association, price change (absolute value), and rigidity for each product group, and indicates when the correlations are statistically significant at the 10 percent level, 5 percent level, and 1 percent level.[10] A strong positive association between length of association and rigidity exists only for chemicals, while a strong negative association exists for petroleum, household appliances, and truck motors. To the extent any general relationship exists between length of association and rigidity, it is a *negative* one. The second column of Table 4 indicates that there is a *positive* association between price change and rigidity. All but one correlation is positive, and all seven statistically significant correlations are positive. The third column suggests that there is a *negative* correlation between length of association and price change. All but two correlations are negative, and all five statistically significant correlations are negative.

TABLE 4—CORRELATIONS OF
CONTRACT CHARACTERISTICS

	Correlation Between:		
Product	Length of Association and Rigidity	Rigidity and Average Absolute Percent Price Change	Length of Association and Average Absolute Percent Price Change
Cement	.28	.17	.24
Chemicals	.16[c]	.10[a]	−.12[b]
Glass	−.11	.69[c]	−.24
Household Appliances[d]	−.87[c]	.71[b]	−.66[b]
Nonferrous Metals	.12	.12	−.15[b]
Paper	.03	.20	−.25[a]
Petroleum	−.25[c]	−.06	−.09
Plywood	.10	.54[c]	−.11
Rubber Tires	−.08	.43[c]	−.27[b]
Steel	.03	.14[b]	.01
Trucks, Motors	−.56[c]	.60[a]	−.23

[a]Statistical significance at the 10 percent level.
[b]Statistical significance at the 5 percent level.
[c]Statistical significance at the 1 percent level.
[d]Based on only 11 observations.

In short, the evidence in Table 4 is *consistent* with the following explanation. Buyers and sellers who do not have long associations are more likely to use fixed price contracts because they don't trust or know each other. The "cost" of changing price on such a contract is to risk creation of mutual distrust. Prices change on these contracts only for substantial price movements. Buyers and sellers who have long associations aren't as worried about mutual distrust. Hence, price changes are more frequent (i.e., less rigid prices) and on average smaller.[11]

One common explanation for price (or wage) rigidity has to do with insurance. I have not incorporated that explanation into the one just given for several reasons. First, recent work (Sherwin Rosen, 1985) casts doubt on the theoretical underpinnings of an

---

[9]This assumes that price changes are motivated by changes in the permanent price component whose changes are assumed larger than the transitory component. The reverse relation between permanent and transitory would flip the prediction.

[10]My 1986 working paper reports data on average rigidity, average price change, and average length of association by product by type of contract.

[11]A model that would generate such results would be one where costs are undergoing a random walk, production is constant returns to scale, and the cost of changing price is negatively related to length of association.

insurance explanation. Second, large firms should be able to diversify such risks, and hence not need insurance.[12] Third, as we will see in the next section, the insurance explanation does not seem supported by the data.

IV. Relationship Among Types of Transactions

Do some buyers seek out stable pricing arrangements in which the price changes infrequently? If so, one would expect to see a correlation in the rigidity of pricing across transactions of different commodities. For example, if the transactions of a particular buyer who purchased steel involved price changing much less frequently than the industry average, will it also be the case that the buyer's transactions involving paper have prices that change less frequently than the industry average?

For the product categories of Table 1, I have calculated for each buyer a vector of the average price rigidity for each of the commodities he purchases. I then examine pairs of products to see if there is a correlation across firms in these rigidities, (i.e., does a firm buying steel with overly rigid prices buy paper with overly rigid prices?) There are 227 buyer firms in my sample. There are many fewer (around 60) who purchase any two commodities. The pairwise correlations were primarily positive, but in most cases the correlations were not statistically significant, and were often sensitive to the interpolation method used to calculate price rigidity. The most stable and statistically significant results were the (positive) correlations between price rigidity for contracts in steel and rubber, metals and plywood, and rubber and cement.[13] Because of the instability of the results, these results should be regarded as at best weak support that buyers may have certain preferences across transaction types for different products.

V. Analysis of Specific Products

One drawback to the analysis of the previous sections is that the product groups may be so broad that a heterogeneity appears in the results which is caused only by the heterogeneous nature of the products in any one commodity group. To remedy this problem, I analyzed 32 specific products. These 32 products were chosen primarily because there were numerous data on them. The products analyzed are listed in Table 5 along with information similar to that presented in Table 1.

The results are similar to those of Table 1 in several respects. As in Table 1, there is wide variation across products in the rigidity of price. Even within a single detailed product specification, there still exists a great deal of heterogeneity in durations of spells of rigidity. The standard deviation of duration rises with the average duration.[14] One is struck by the rigidity of some prices. Even for monthly contracts, there are many products (for example, chlorine liquid, steel plate) where the average length of a spell of price rigidity is well over one year. And, column 6 indicates that, using transactions as the unit of analysis, most commodities have average durations of price in excess of eight months.

In Table 6, I present the histograms of spells of price rigidity by commodity for a frequently used contract specification. The pattern that emerges is similar to that in Table 2. Even within detailed product specification for a particular contract type, there is considerable heterogeneity in length of spells of price rigidity. This suggests that the price of a good is changing for some transactions but not for others.[15] Table 6 reveals that although most prices do not remain in effect for over one year, for many products (for example, steel plate, hot rolled bars and rods, oxygen) a significant number of spells (over 20 percent) of rigid prices remain in effect for over two years.

---

[12] This must be qualified by agency theories of monitoring.
[13] One curious finding is that price rigidity is negatively correlated at a statistically significant level for truck and steel contracts.

[14] The simple and rank correlations of average duration and the standard deviation of duration exceed .9.
[15] Histograms like Table 6 based on a transaction (not spell) as the unit of analysis confirm this.

TABLE 5—PRICE RIGIDITY FOR DETAILED PRODUCT SPECIFICATIONS[a]

Product (1)	Number of Buyer-Seller Pairings (2)	Average Duration Price Rigidity (Spells) (Months) (3)	Standard Deviation of Duration (Spells) (Months) (4)	Aver. Duration of Price Rigidity Monthly Contracts (Spells) (Months) (5)	Average Duration of Price Rigidity (Transactions) (Months) (6)
Steel plates	28	18.5	19.4	21.6	20.3
Hot rolled bars and rods	33	15.1	17.6	10.6	˙ ˙
Steel pipe and tubing (3″ or less in diameter)	33	12.1	16.4	12.7	1ɔ.
Copper wire and cable (bare)	26	3.8	5.4	2.6	4.1
Gasoline (regular)	66	6.2	5.7	2.7	8.9
Diesel oil #2	75	4.7	4.3	1.4	6.9
Fuel oil #2	41	7.3	4.9	4.6	8.3
Residual fuel oil #6	59	6.5	6.4	2.9	9.2
Container board, fiberboard	28	11.6	8.0	11.5	12.6
Caustic soda (liquid)	33	16.2	22.9	27.6	21.3
Chlorine liquid	28	19.9	18.7	60.0	27.1
Oxygen, cylinders	30	16.8	14.6	36.3	21.5
Acetylene	22	16.0	16.2	26.4	21.9
Portland cement (sack)	28	16.4	16.8	–	19.0
Steel sheet and strip, hot rolled	25	18.6	18.5	–	19.1
New rail (RR)	20	22.1	31.4	17.1	23.2
Tie plates (RR)	18	21.9	33.0	20.0	23.0
Steel wheels "one wear" (RR)	25	21.4	22.6	24.0	24.9
Track bolts (RR)	18	14.5	17.4	4.4	17.2
Zinc slab ingots	9	5.1	5.4	4.4	5.6
Coal (RR)	20	6.8	12.2	1.4	15.9
Kraft wrapping paper	12	7.5	6.0	5.7	9.2
Paper bags	16	9.4	5.3	20.0	10.3
Sulfuric acid, bulk	15	14.1	18.7	22.3	20.9
Sulfuric acid	19	11.0	17.1	5.1	19.5
Methyl alcohol	18	12.3	12.9	17.4	17.8
Phthalic anhydride	10	7.2	6.1	6.8	8.3
Succinate antibiotic	16	34.4	52.1	57.0	25.4
Kapseals antibiotic	16	56.1	66.7	40.0	44.0
Meprobanate tablets	16	13.8	12.0	18.7	15.5
Librium	13	19.1	23.1	56.0	20.9
Plywood	25	3.7	4.8	1.1	6.2

[a]See Table 1. The dashes in col. 5 indicate no data available.

In Table 7, I present the fraction of price changes that are less than 1/4, 1/2, 1, and 2 percent in absolute value in order to assess the importance of the fixed costs of changing price. Table 7 corroborates the message of Table 3. For most products, there are numerous (over 10 percent) instances of small price changes (below 1 percent). This fact reinforces my earlier conclusion that theories that postulate rigid prices solely because of a common high fixed cost of changing price to each buyer are not supported by the evidence. (See the discussion of the results of Table 3.) The most reasonable explanation is that firms and buyers must differ in their need to rely on the price system to achieve

TABLE 6—HISTOGRAMS OF DURATIONS OF RIGIDITY BY DETAILED
PRODUCT SPECIFICATION BASED ON SPELLS OF RIGIDITY

Product	0–3 Mo.	3 Mo.– 1 Yr	1–2 Yrs	2–4 Yrs	Over 4 Yrs
Steel plate	.24	.24	.23	.18	.11
Hot rolled bars and rods	.36	.21	.21	.16	.07
Steel pipe and tubing (less than 3″ diameter)	.39	.31	.16	.10	.05
Copper wire and cable (bare)	.67	.30	.02	0	.01
Gasoline (regular)(A)	.33	.59	.05	.03	0
Diesel oil #2	.79	.22	0	0	0
Fuel oil #2 (A)	.03	.88	.08	.02	0
Residual fuel oil #6 (A)	.22	.64	.07	.06	0
Container board, fiberboard (A)	0	.73	.19	.06	0
Caustic soda (liquid)(A)	.10	.64	.14	.06	.06
Chlorine liquid (A)	0	.69	.14	.10	.06
Oxygen, cylinders	.32	.27	.14	.26	.01
Acetylene	.37	.24	.15	.21	.01
Portland cement (bag or sack)	.19	.32	.24	.14	.05
Steel sheet and strip, hot rolled	.25	.27	.19	.21	.08
New rail	.53	.07	.16	.06	.18
Tie plates	.53	.08	.17	.06	.16
Steel wheels "one wear"	.13	.35	.22	.22	.09
Track bolts	.27	.34	.23	.06	.11
Zinc slab ingots	.44	.44	.09	.03	0
Coal, for RR	.60	.23	.11	.03	.03
Kraft wrapping paper	0	.40	.40	.20	0
Paper bags	.17	0	.67	.17	0
Sulfuric acid, bulk	.68	.18	.08	0	.05
Sulfuric acid (A)	.13	.56	.20	.05	.05
Methyl alcohol (A)	.38	.38	.15	.07	.01
Phthalic anhydride	.47	.41	.09	.03	0
Succinate antibiotic	0	.30	0	.50	.20
Kapseals antibiotic	0	.08	.08	.31	.54
Meprobanate tablets (A)	.14	.67	.11	.06	.03
Librium (A)	.13	.39	.22	.17	.09
Plywood	.73	.23	.03	.01	.01

Note: All contracts are monthly or quarterly monthly, unless followed by (A) which
indicates annual. The numbers in rows may not add to one because of rounding.

allocative efficiency and that the fixed costs of changing price varies across buyers and across firms.

An analysis of the minimum positive and negative price changes reveals no tendency for one to exceed the other. Just as in the earlier analysis, there appears to be no evidence to support asymmetric price changes.

In Table 8, I present information, comparable to Table 4, on the relationship between price rigidity, length of association, and average price change for transactions in the same product.[16] (Table A2 in the Appendix presents information by product on average absolute price change and average length of association.) The results mirror those of Table 4. There may be a weak negative correlation between rigidity and length of association. Of the 18 correlations,

[16] Most correlations involve between 20 to 30 observations, with 15 being the minimum number of observations required in order to be reported.

TABLE 7—FREQUENCY OF SMALL PRICE CHANGES BY
DETAILED PRODUCT SPECIFICATION

Product	Percent of Price Changes less than			
	1/4 Percent	1/2 Percent	1 Percent	2 Percent
Steel plate	0	1	11	16
Hot rolled bars and rods	1	8	13	28
Steel pipe and tubing (less than 3″ diameter)	4	6	14	27
Copper wire and cable (bare)	3	5	8	19
Gasoline (regular)(A)	0	1	13	27
Diesel oil #2	0	0	2	19
Fuel oil #2 (A)	0	0	7	22
Residual fuel oil #6 (A)	0	0	2	25
Container board, fiberboard (A)	4	4	4	12
Caustic soda (liquid)(A)	2	5	11	15
Chlorine liquid (A)	6	13	17	31
Oxygen, cylinders	0	0	3	14
Acetylene	0	10	18	23
Portland cement (bag or sack)	0	0	1	19
Steel sheet and strip, hot rolled	0	2	7	13
New rail	1	3	6	10
Tie plates	3	5	5	9
Steel wheels "one wear"	4	4	10	16
Track bolts	1	3	14	16
Zinc slab ingots	6	6	11	20
Coal (RR)	3	8	18	37
Kraft wrapping paper	3	8	20	53
Paper bags	0	20	20	60
Sulfuric acid, bulk	3	12	34	54
Sulfuric acid	1	1	57	76
Methyl alcohol (A)	0	15	24	32
Phthalic anhydride	0	0	0	0
Succinate antibiotic	0	0	0	0
Kapseals antibiotic (A)	0	0	0	50
Meprobanate tablets (A)	0	0	0	27
Librium (A)	0	0	0	14
Plywood	1	3	7	18

Note: See Table 6.

only 4 were statistically significant. Two negative correlations were significant at the 1 percent level, while the positive correlations were significant at the 5 and 10 percent levels. (However, the number of positive correlations exceeded the number of negative ones.) The evidence on the correlation between price change and rigidity is clearer. Of the 9 significant correlations, 8 were positive. The number of positive correlations exceeded the number of negative ones. The evidence on the correlation between price change and length of association suggests a negative correlation. Of the 5 significant coefficients, all were negative. (However, the number of negative correlations equalled the number of positives.)

VI. The Heterogeneity of Price Movements Across Buyers

The previous evidence reveals that price movements across different transaction types for the same commodity may be very differ-

VOL. 76 NO. 4   CARLTON: RIGIDITY OF PRICES   651

TABLE 8—CORRELATIONS OF CONTRACT
CHARACTERISTICS

Product	Correlation Between:		
	Length of Association and Rigidity	Rigidity and Average Absolute Percent Price Change	Length of Association and Average Absolute Percent Price Change
Steel sheet and strip, hot rolled	–	– .40[a]	–
Steel plate	.07	– .11	.27
Hot rolled bars and rods	– .00	.32[a]	.26
Steel pipe and tubing (3″ or less in diameter)	– .21	.19	– .32[a]
Plywood	.10	.04	– .34[a]
New rail	.14	.41[a]	– .64[b]
Tie plates	–	.47[b]	–
Steel wheels "One wear"	.07	– .33	– .14
Track bolts	–	.54[b]	–
Copper wire and cable, bare	– .06	.76[c]	– .20
Coal, for RR	–	– .14	–
Gasoline	.02	.08	– .02
Diesel oil #2	– .74[c]	– .22	.27
Fuel oil #6	– .12	– .02	– .14
Sulfuric acid, bulk	.51[b]	– .06	– .45[b]
Sulfuric acid	– .52[c]	.15	.10
Caustic soda, liquid	.35	.58[c]	.22
Chlorine, liquid	.40[a]	– .00	– .56[b]
Oxygen cylinders	.10	– .17	.07
Acetylene	.04	.50[b]	.12
Methyl alcohol	.21	.53[c]	.02
Portland cement, in bag or sack	.34	.19	.33

[a]Significance at the 10 percent level.
[b]Significance at the 5 percent level.
[c]Significance at the 1 percent level.

ent. In this section, I investigate in more detail the heterogeneity of price movements for the same commodity. By limiting the analysis to transactions of the same type, I have automatically screened out considerable heterogeneity. Despite this, I still find a startling amount of heterogeneity. I limit the analysis to annual contracts or quarterly monthly and monthly contracts, depending on the available data. I group price movements from quarterly monthly and monthly together on the grounds that they both represent price series whose prices are not necessarily expected to remain in force for more than one month.

I use two methods to describe how heterogeneous price movements are. The first method measures the difference in the stochastic structure of each price change series while the second attempts to measure correlation in price movements across different transactions.

The first method computes for each individual price series the variance in the percent changes in price (actually the first difference of the log of the price series). A variance σ is computed for each transaction price series. If all the price series have the same stochastic structure, this variance should be the same across different price series for the same commodity. For each of 30 commodities, I present the mean variance (i.e., the mean of σ^2), the variance of σ^2 (i.e., a measure of how σ^2 varies across transactions), and the coefficient of variation (square root of variance of σ^2 divided by the mean).[17]

Table 9 shows that, in general, the individual price series within any one commodity and transaction type seems to be quite different from one another. The commodities that seem to have the least homogeneous transactions are steel pipe, oxygen, sheet steel, steel railway wheels, and coal.

Another method of characterizing the degree of heterogeneity among price series is to look at the correlation of contemporaneous price changes. A slight extension of this method is to examine the correlation of filtered price series. An example will illustrate.

Suppose two monthly price series are

| | 10 | 10 | 10 | 10 | 5 | 5 | 5 | 5 | 7.5 | 7.5 | 7.5 | 7.5, |
| and | 10 | 10 | 10 | 5 | 5 | 5 | 5 | 7.5 | 7.5 | 7.5 | 7.5 | |

One might be especially interested in seeing how closely the percent changes in the price series are correlated. The two derived series of percent price changes are

| – | 0 | 0 | 0 | – 50% | 0 | 0 | 0 | 50% | 0 | 0 | 0 |
| – | 0 | 0 | – 50% | 0 | 0 | 0 | 50% | 0 | 0 | 0 | |

[17]Some products from Table 5 were dropped because of data incompleteness.

TABLE 9—MEASURES OF HETEROGENEITY AMONG PRICE SERIES

Product	Mean Variance of Individual Price Change	Variances of Individual Price Change	Coefficient of Variation
Steel plate	1.33 (10–6)	1.56 (10–9)	29.7
Hot rolled bars and rods	1.73 (10–6)	3.64 (10–9)	34.9
Steel pipe and tubing (3″ or less in diameter)	3.31 (10–6)	2.27 (10–8)	45.5
Copper wire and cable, bare	1.45 (10–5)	4.36 (10–8)	14.4
Gasoline	6.22 (10–5)	1.03 (10–6)	16.3
Diesel #2	1.59 (10–5)	6.50 (10–8)	16.0
Fuel oil #2 (A)	2.93 (10–5)	1.02 (10–7)	10.9
Fuel oil #6	2.57 (10–5)	4.54 (10–7)	26.2
Container board, fiberboard	2.94 (10–5)	5.62 (10–9)	2.5
Caustic soda, liquid	5.26 (10–5)	4.89 (10–8)	4.2
Liquid chlorine (A)	8.48 (10–6)	6.57 (10–8)	30.2
Oxygen, cylinders	3.07 (10–5)	2.49 (10–6)	51.4
Acetylene	6.66 (10–6)	4.63 (10–8)	32.3
Portland cement	1.97 (10–6)	4.79 (10–9)	35.1
Sheet steel and strip (hot rolled)	4.64 (10–6)	1.63 (10–7)	87.0
New rails	9.95 (10–7)	1.44 (10–10)	12.1
Tie plates	1.55 (10–6)	1.43 (10–10)	7.7
Steel railway wheels	9.51 (10–7)	8.08 (10–9)	94.5
Railroad track bolts	2.87 (10–6)	4.93 (10–9)	24.5
Zinc slab, ingot	6.21 (10–5)	7.09 (10–8)	4.3
Coal (RR)	9.15 (10–6)	1.60 (10–7)	43.7
Sulfuric acid, bulk (A)	5.92 (10–5)	1.91 (10–6)	23.3
Sulfuric acid (A)	5.54 (10–5)	9.05 (10–7)	17.2
Methyl alcohol (A)	7.24 (10–5)	1.55 (10–7)	5.4
Phthalic anhydride	2.78 (10–4)	1.52 (10–6)	4.4
Succinate (A)	5.42 (10–6)	3.13 (10–8)	32.6
Kapseals (A)	2.52 (10–6)	2.77 (10–9)	20.9
Meprobanate tablets (A)	2.59 (10–4)	3.83 (10–6)	7.6
Librium (A)	6.39 (10–5)	5.40 (10–7)	11.5
Plywood	2.08 (10–5)	1.43 (10–7)	18.2

Note: See Table 6.

It appears that the two series have no correlation in percent changes. But that conclusion is misleading. Both series change within one month of each other. Suppose that one constructs a new series that takes the arithmetic average of the last two monthly percent changes in prices. Then one obtains two series that look like

```
- - 0    0  -25% -25% 0 0  25% 25% 0 0
- - 0 -25%  -25%    0 0 25% 25%   0 0 0
```

The correlation between the two new series will be positive and will equal .5. If one uses a three-month filter (i.e., average over the last three monthly percent changes in price), the correlation rises to .67. In general, one initially expects correlation to rise as the period of averaging increases.

Before presenting tabulations of correlations by product for different filter sizes, it will be helpful first to decide what is a "high" or "low" correlation. In other words, we must develop some underlying standard as to how closely two very related series should move. Suppose we adopt the position that two price series that change by identical amounts within, say, three months of each other are "highly" correlated. Let $\rho(F)$ be the contemporaneous correlation of the two price series when averaging over F periods is performed. Suppose that the two series representing percent price changes are identical, are displaced from each other by three months, and that price changes are independent of the preceding price change. Then, it is easy to show that

$$\rho(1) = \rho(2) = 0$$

$$\rho(F) = 1 - 3/F \qquad F > 3.$$

This means that for a filter of size 6, the correlation between our two series is .5, and rises to .75 for filters of one year. In general, one should expect that very high correlations (above .7) will probably be unusual for filters below twelve months, even for "well-behaved" price series.

Each of 30 products was analyzed separately. For each product, and for each contract type an average correlation for a particular filter size was computed. For example, suppose that there are 10 individual contract transactions for steel plates, each lasting ten years. The monthly percent change in price (differences in log of price) was calculated for each series for each month. The simple correlation was computed for every combination of contracts (i.e., 45 pairs) and an average correlation over the 45 pairs was then computed. If the average correlation is high, it says that on average the price series move together. If the average correlation is low, it suggests that price movements for the same good are only very loosely related to each other. If the low correlation persists as the filter increases to say two years, it says that knowing how person A's price has changed over a two-year period doesn't help much in predicting how person B's price will change (averaged over the two-year period).

In Table 10, I present measures of average correlation for filters of one month and twelve months for each of the 30 commodities for selected contract types.[18] As ex-

TABLE 10—HETEROGENEITY MEASURES:
CORRELATIONS AMONG PRICE SERIES

Product[a]	$\rho(1)$[b]	$\rho(12)$[b]
Steel plate (M)	.42	.61
Hot rolled bars and rods (M)	.42	.60
Steel pipe and tubing (M)		
(3" or less in diameter)	.16	.25
Copper wire and cable (M)	.53	.78
Gasoline (A)	.02	.07
(M)	.04	.30
Diesel fuel #2 (A)	.00	.06
(M)	.53	.69
Fuel oil #2 (A)	.01	−.03
Fuel oil #6 (A)	.02	.11
(M)	.26	.49
Container board,		
fiberboard (A)	.14	−.03
(M)	.06	.16
Caustic soda, liquid (A)	.07	.07
(M)	.04	.36
Liquid chlorine (A)	.05	.08
Oxygen, cylinders (A)	.03	.17
(M)	.28	.40
Acetylene (M)	.30	.54
Portland cement (M)	.15	.21
Steel sheet and strip, (M)		
hot rolled	.40	.44
Rails (M)	.81	.94
Tie plates (M)	.78	.88
Steel railway wheels	.37	.54
Railroad track bolts	.47	.62
Zinc slab ingots (M)	.52	.90
Coal (RR) (M)	.14	.17
Phthalic anhydride (M)	.27	.68
Sulfuric acid, bulk (A)	.13	.32
Sulfuric acid (A)	.10	.07
Methyl alcohol (A)	.22	.46
Succinate (A)	0.0^c	0.0^c
Kapseals (A)	0.0^c	0.0^c
Meprobanate tablets (A)	.03	−.07
Librium (A)	−.02	−.06
Plywood (M)	.16	.21

[a] Contracts are either quarterly monthly or monthly (indicated by M) or annual (indicated by A).
[b] $\rho(i)$: Correlations of price changes averaged over i months.
[c] No price movement in most contracts.

pected, $\rho(12)$ usually exceeds $\rho(1)$. If we use the criterion that correlations on the order of .5 and above represent price series that move pretty closely together, we see that for several

the timing of price changes (i.e., 0 or ±1 indicating whether or not a price change occurred and its direction) and the same low correlations persisted.

[18] Filters of 2 years produced results similar to those for filters of 1 year. Correlations were also calculated on

products, there is a homogeneity of price movements. On the other hand, there are several products like cement, container board, plywood, and several chemical products that have very low (sometimes even negative) correlations even for twelve-month averaging. In fact, it is startling to find so many products where it is clear that some mechanism other than only price is allocating resources.[19] It is noteworthy that container board exhibits low correlations of price, since I understand that quantity rationing is sometimes used in the paper industry in place of price rationing.[20]

It is interesting to see whether there is any agreement between the two methods of characterizing heterogeneity in Tables 9 and 10. In fact, there is a low degree of agreement. The simple correlation between the measures of heterogeneity in Tables 9 and 10 is below .1 and is not statistically significant. On the other hand, there is a high degree of statistically significant (negative) correlation between $\rho(1)$ (or $\rho(12)$) and other measures of heterogeneity such as the coefficients of variation for rigidity, price change, and length of association.[21] This may imply that the measure in Table 9 is capturing an aspect of price different from the other measures or, alternatively, that the measure in Table 9 is not a useful one.

VII. Implications for Price Behavior

Tables 1 through 10 can form the foundation for several predictions. For example, one could predict the following:

1) The products with high correlations for $\rho(12)$ in Table 10 should tend to have more serial correlation in their *WPI* component than products with low correlations;

2) Industrywide price adjustment for products with high values for $\rho(1)$ in Table 10 should tend to be swift;

3) Price controls on products with long spells of rigid prices (Table 1) are less likely to have harmful efficiency effects than controls on products with short spells of rigidity because nonprice methods are probably already used for products with very rigid prices to allocate resources.

I have not systematically investigated these three claims for each of the products listed in Table 10. However, I have done some work to corroborate at least some of the claims for some products. For example, from Table 10 copper wire and cable has a $\rho(12)$ of .78 while gasoline (monthly) has a $\rho(12)$ of only .30. The correlation between the monthly *WPI* and the monthly *WPI* lagged once (1957–66) for copper wire and cable is .99 which, as expected, exceeds that same measure (.88) for gasoline.[22]

Michael Bordo (1980) has estimated adjustment lags in prices for some of the commodity groups well represented in Table 10, such as metals and metal products, chemicals, and fuel. Based on the size of $\rho(1)$ in Table 10, I would predict the speed of adjustment to be fastest in metals and metal products, and the speed of adjustment in fuels and chemicals to be much slower and roughly equal to each other. In fact, Bordo (p. 1105) finds the mean lag of price adjustment for metals and metal products to 3.66 months, while the lag for fuels and chemicals are 6.64 and 6.20 months, respectively.

Finally, the only evidence I could find on the difficulty of price controls is John Kenneth Galbraith's *A Theory of Price Control* (1952) which is an account of his experience in controlling prices during World War II when he headed the Office of Price Administration (OPA). Although he does not deal explicitly with all the products in Tables 1–10, he does talk about steel products, which from Table 1 have a high degree of price rigidity. Galbraith states: "The Office of Price Administration controlled the price of all steel mill products with far less manpower and trouble than was required for

[19] My 1979 article presents a theory on buyer heterogeneity, which shows how prices to different buyers can exhibit low (or negative) correlations.

[20] Based on personal discussions with industry members.

[21] Table A3 in the Appendix reports these correlations.

[22] The source for *WPI* data was Stigler and Kindahl (Appendix C).

a far smaller volume of steel scrap...it is relatively easy to fix prices that are already fixed" (p. 17).

Although bits of evidence corroborate the predictions for some types of commodities, they obviously are far from conclusive. They do, however, show the value of evidence like that in Tables 1 through 10.

VIII. Structural Determinants of Price Behavior

Is there any correlation between industry characteristics and any of the measures of heterogeneity such as those in Tables 9 and 10? Using 30 products, I correlated the measures of heterogeneity in price movements of Tables 9 and 10 with the following variables: 1) mean absolute growth and variability of price (the higher is this number the higher the expected correlation of price movements); 2) measures of competitiveness (a) four-firm concentration ratio and (b) fraction of shipments beyond 500 miles; 3) growth and variability of total industry shipments; 4) length of buyer-seller association.

Simple correlations never emerged statistically significant (with the exception of the variance of the growth rate in price), though the correlations were generally in the positive direction. However, since no more than 30 observations were available, it would be premature to conclude that these structural characteristics do not influence price heterogeneity in the industry.

Is there any correlation between concentration and duration of price rigidity or length of association or average price change? The only significant correlation was between concentration (four firms) and duration of price rigidity. That correlation was statistically significant at the 5 percent level. The correlation implies that for every 10 point increase in the four-firm concentration ratio, prices remain rigid for an extra 1.6 months.[23] This finding is particularly interesting because it suggests that allocations are performed differently in concentrated and unconcentrated markets. I believe it is premature to draw the conclusions, implicit in the work of Means, Arthur Burns (1936), Galbraith, and others, that the markets have stopped working when they become concentrated. Instead, an alternative interpretation is that as firms become large they supplant the market's exclusive reliance on price as an allocation device and resort to other methods. In a world filled with transaction costs, exclusive reliance on a market-generated price to allocate goods could well be inferior to other nonprice allocation methods. It is the case, however, that markets that use nonprice allocation will respond to market shocks much differently than markets that exclusively use price to allocate. See my forthcoming paper for a fuller development of this theory.

IX. Conclusions

Since this paper began with a summary of the empirical results, I will not repeat them here. The main conclusion is that several of the empirical results are sufficiently startling that we should reexamine the central, often exclusive, role assigned to the price mechanism in theories of efficient resource allocation. It is not necessarily that the price mechanism has failed, but rather that alternative allocation mechanisms are used in addition to the price mechanism to achieve efficiency.

---

[23] The *OLS* equation is (standard errors in parentheses)

$$Av.\ Duration = 4.97 + 16.12\ CR\ 4 \quad R^2 = .22$$
$$\qquad\qquad (3.12) \quad (6.08) \qquad SEE = 4.9$$

where *Av. Duration* is the average length of a spell of price rigidity and *CR 4* is the four-firm concentration ratio. This equation is based on 27 observations. The *CR 4* variable is the 1963 four-firm concentration ratio for the 5-digit SIC code that seems to correspond to the product. This correspondence is not exact and, for that reason together with the small number of observations, the results should be regarded with some caution. Another interesting finding involving concentration is that concentrated industries have a greater frequency of small price changes.

The New Institutional Economics of Markets

TABLE A1—CHARACTERISTICS OF CONTRACTS BY PRODUCT

Product	Average Length of Association Between Buyer and Seller (Months)	Average Size of Absolute Value of Percent Price Change	Product	Average Length of Association Between Buyer and Seller (Months)	Average Size of Absolute Value of Percent Price Change
Steel	105	3.5	Cement	103	3.0
Nonferrous Metals	86	4.0	Glass	91	4.2
Petroleum	87	4.4	Truck Motors	82	2.7
Rubber Tires	98	3.9	Plywood	114	5.0
Paper	91	3.4	Household		
Chemicals	81	7.0	Appliances	75	1.0

TABLE A2—CHARACTERISTICS OF CONTRACTS BY PRODUCT

Product	Average Length of Association Between Buyer/Seller (Months)	Average Size of Absolute Value of Percent Price Change	Product	Average Length of Association Between Buyer/Seller (Months)	Average Size of Absolute Value of Percent Price Change
Steel plates	108	3.8	New rail (RR)	116	3.9
Hot rolled bars and rods	109	3.7	Tiel plates (RR)	119	4.5
Steel pipe and tubing			Steel wheels "one wear"		
(3″ or less in diameter)	114	4.6	(RR)	119	3.8
Copper wire and cable			Track bolts (RR)	119	4.2
(bare)	68	4.4	Zinc slab ingots	104	4.8
Gasoline (regular)	91	3.3	Coal (RR)	119	3.7
Diesel oil #2	94	4.3	Kraft wrapping paper	94	4.3
Fuel oil #2	89	4.6	Paper bags	88	4.8
Residual fuel oil #6	73	5.8	Sulfuric acid, bulk	96	4.8
Container board,			Sulfuric acid	103	3.5
fiberboard	78	5.2	Methyl alcohol	91	7.1
Caustic soda (liquid)	84	7.8	Phthalic anhydride	93	11.7
Chlorine liquid	89	5.0	Succinate antibiotic	58	8.3
Oxygen, cylinders	109	11.5	Kapseals antibiotic	70	14.9
Acetylene	116	6.9	Meprobanate tablets	64	12.1
Portland cement			Librium	48	8.6
(by sack)	104	3.7	Plywood	110	5.2
Steel sheet and strip,					
hot rolled	120	5.9			

TABLE A3—CORRELATIONS AMONG MEASURES OF HETEROGENEITY

	CV DUR	CV DP	CV ASSOC	CV VAR	$\rho(1)$	$\rho(12)$
CV DUR	1	.88[a]	.41[a]	−.03	−.63[a]	−.60[a]
CV DP		1	.35[a]	.39[a]	−.57[a]	−.66[a]
CV ASSOC.			1	−.58[a]	−.47[a]	−.30
CV VAR				1	.08	−.01
$\rho(1)$					1	.91[a]
$\rho(12)$						1

Notes: CV DUR = coefficient of variation of duration; *CV DP =* coefficient of variation of the absolute value of price change (log difference); *CV ASSOC =* coefficient of variation of the length of association; *CV VAR =* coefficient of variation of the actual price changes counting no change as zero change; $\rho(1), \rho(12)$ = correlations of price changes averaged over i months.
[a]Significant at 5 percent level.

APPENDIX

Transactions were classified into one of ten categories by Stigler and Kindahl. The most important classifications include:

Annual contract: contract in force for one year.

Annual average: average of transaction prices during the year.

Annual monthly: annual observations of a transaction that occurs monthly.

Semiannual contract: contract in force for six months.

Semiannual average: average of transaction prices during six months.

Quarterly contract: contract in force for three months.

Quarterly average: average of transaction prices during the quarter.

Quarterly monthly: quarterly observation of a transaction that occurs monthly.

Irregular: irregular.

Monthly: monthly observations of a transaction that occurs monthly.

Tables 1A and 2A of my 1986 working paper report the importance of each classification by product group and for individual products.

REFERENCES

Akerlof, George A. and Yellen, Janet L., "Can Small Deviations from Rationality Make Significant Differences to Economic Equilibrium?," *American Economic Review*, September 1985, *75*, 708–20.

Barro, Robert, "A Theory of Monopolistic Price Adjustment," *Review of Economic Studies*, January 1972, *39*, 17–26.

Blanchard, Olivier J., "Price Desynchronization and Price Level Inertia," NBER Working Paper 900, 1982.

Bordo, Michael, "The Effects of Monetary Change on Relative Commodity Prices and the Role of Long-Term Contracts," *Journal of Political Economy*, December 1980, *88*, 1088–109.

Burns, Arthur, *The Decline of Competition*, New York: McGraw-Hill, 1936.

Carlton, Dennis W., The Rigidity of Prices, NBER Working Paper 1813, 1986.

_____, "The Theory and The Facts of How Markets Clear: Is Industrial Organization Valuable for Understanding Macroeconomics?," in R. Schmalensee and R. Willig, eds., *Handbook of Industrial Organization*, Amsterdam: North-Holland, forthcoming.

_____, "Equilibrium Fluctuations When Price and Delivery Lags Clear the Market," *Bell Journal of Economics*, Autumn 1983, *14*, 562–72.

_____, "The Disruptive Effect of Inflation on the Organization of Markets," in R. E. Hall, ed., *Inflation*, Chicago: University of Chicago Press, 1982.

_____, "Contracts, Price Rigidity, and Market Equilibrium," *Journal of Political Economy*, October 1979, *87*, 1034–62.

_____, "Market Behavior with Demand Uncertainty and Price Inflexibility," *American Economic Review*, September 1978, *68*, 571–87.

Galbraith, J. K., *A Theory of Price Control*, Cambridge: Harvard University Press, 1952.

Hall, Robert E., "The Apparent Rigidity of Prices," NBER Working Paper 1347, 1984.

Kahneman, Daniel, Knetch, Jack L. and Thaler, Richard, "Fairness as a Constraint on Profit Seeking: Entitlements in the Market," *American Economic Review*, September 1986, *76*, 728–41.

Mankiw, N. Gregory, "Small Menu Costs and Large Business Cycles: A Macroeconomic Model of Monopoly," *Quarterly Journal of Economics*, May 1985, *100*, 529–38.

Means, Gardiner C., "Industrial Prices and Their Relative Inflexibility," U.S. Senate Document 13, 74th Congress, 1st Session, Washington 1935.

Mills, Frederick C., *The Behavior of Prices*, NBER General Series, No. 11, New York: Arno Press, 1927.

Okun, Arthur, *Prices and Quantities: A Macroeconomic Analysis*, Washington: The Brookings Institution, 1981.

Rosen, Sherwin, "Implicit Contracts: A Survey," *Journal of Economic Literature*, September 1985, *23*, 1144–75.

Rotemberg, Julio "Monopolistic Price Adjustment and Aggregate Output," *Review of Economic Studies*, October 1982, *49*, 517–31.

Stigler, George and Kindahl, James, *The Behavior of Industrial Prices*, NBER General Series, No. 90, New York: Columbia University Press, 1970.

Telser, Lester, "A Theory of Self-Enforcing Agreements," *Journal of Business*, January 1980, *53*, 27–44.

Williamson, Oliver, *Markets & Hierarchies Analysis and Antitrust Implications: A Study in the Economies of Internal Organization*, New York: Free Press, 1975.

[8]

INFORMATION AND EFFICIENCY: ANOTHER VIEWPOINT*

HAROLD DEMSETZ
University of Chicago

T HE importance of bringing economic analysis to bear on the problems of efficient economic organization hardly requires comment, but there is a need to review the manner in which the notion of efficiency is used in these problems. The concept of efficiency has been abused frequently because of the particular approach used by many analysts. My aim is to examine the mistakes and the vagueness associated with this approach. I shall focus attention on the problem of efficiently allocating resources to the production of information because in this case the issues stand out clearly. Since Kenneth J. Arrow's paper "Economic Welfare and the Allocation of Resources for Invention"[1] has been most influential in establishing the dominant viewpoint about this subject, my commentary necessarily is a critique of Arrow's analysis.

The view that now pervades much public policy economics implicitly presents the relevant choice as between an ideal norm and an existing "imperfect" institutional arrangement. This *nirvana* approach differs considerably from a *comparative institution* approach in which the relevant choice is between alternative real institutional arrangements. In practice, those who adopt the nirvana viewpoint seek to discover discrepancies between the ideal and the real and if discrepancies are found, they deduce that the real is inefficient. Users of the comparative institution approach attempt to assess which alternative real institutional arrangement seems best able to cope with the economic problem; practitioners of this approach may use an ideal norm to provide standards from which divergences are assessed for all practical alternatives of interest and select as efficient that alternative which seems most likely to minimize the divergence.[2]

* The author wishes to thank the Lilly Endowment for financial aid received through a grant to the University of California at Los Angeles for the study of property rights.

1 Kenneth J. Arrow, Economic Welfare and the Allocation of Resources for Invention, in The Rate and Direction of Inventive Activity, 609-25 (1962).

2 A practitioner of the nirvana approach sometimes discusses and compares alternative institutional arrangements. But if all are found wanting in comparison with the ideal, all are judged to be inefficient.

1

The nirvana approach is much more susceptible than is the comparative institution approach to committing three logical fallacies—*the grass is always greener fallacy, the fallacy of the free lunch,* and *the people could be different fallacy.* The first two fallacies are illustrated in a general context in part I of what follows; in part II, they and the third fallacy arise in contexts more specific to the economics of knowledge. Part III is a discussion of Arrow's conclusion about the role of monopoly in the production of knowledge, and part IV offers a general criticism of the nirvana approach.

I

The grass is always greener fallacy can be illustrated by the following two quotations from Arrow's paper.

To sum up, we expect a free enterprise economy to underinvest in invention and research (as compared with an ideal) because it is risky, because the product can be appropriated only to a limited extent, and because of increasing returns in use. This underinvestment will be greater for more basic research. Further, to the extent that a firm succeeds in engrossing the economic value of its inventive activity, there will be an under-utilization of that information as compared with an ideal allocation.[3]

. . . .

The previous discussion leads to the conclusion that for optimal allocation to invention it would be necessary for the government or some other agency not governed by profit-and-loss criteria to finance research and invention.[4]

An examination of the correctness of the premise is the main task of this paper, but for present purposes the premise contained in the first quotation can be assumed to be correct. It is clear from both quotations and from the text in which these quotations are imbedded that Arrow is claiming that free enterprise does not result in an ideal allocation of resources to the production of knowledge. From this premise he draws the general conclusion, given in the second quotation, that optimal allocation requires that the government or other nonprofit agency should finance research and invention.

Whether the free enterprise solution can be improved upon by the substitution of the government or other nonprofit institutions in the financing of research cannot be ascertained solely by examining the free enterprise solution. The political or nonprofit forces that are substituted for free enterprise must be analyzed and the outcome of the workings of these forces must be compared to the market solution before any such conclusions can be drawn.

---

[3] Kenneth J. Arrow, *supra* note 1, at 619.
[4] *Id.* at 623.

INFORMATION AND EFFICIENCY: ANOTHER VIEWPOINT   **3**

Otherwise, words such as "government" and "nonprofit" are without analytical content and their use results in confusion. Since Arrow does not analyze the workings of the empirical counterparts of such words as "government"[5] and "nonprofit," his conclusion can be clarified by restating it as follows: "The previous discussion leads to the conclusion that for optimal allocation to invention it would be necessary to remove the nonoptimalities." The same charge, of course, can be levied against those who derive in a similar way the opposite policy conclusion, one that calls for a reduction in the role played by government.[6]

Given the nirvana view of the problem, a deduced discrepancy between the ideal and the real is sufficient to call forth perfection by incantation, that is, by committing the grass is always greener fallacy. This usually is accomplished by invoking an unexamined alternative. Closely associated in practice with this fallacy is the fallacy of the free lunch. An example of the latter is given in Arrow's discussion of the difficulties posed for the competitive system by uncertainty.

I will first sketch an ideal economy in which the allocation problem can be solved by competition and then indicate some of the devices in the real world which approximate this solution.

Suppose for simplicity that uncertainty occurs only in production relations. Producers have to make a decision on inputs at the present moment, but the outputs are not completely predictable from the inputs. . . . [T]he outputs [are] determined by the inputs and a 'state of nature.' Let us define a 'commodity-option' as a commodity in the ordinary sense labeled with a state of nature. . . .

Suppose—and this is the critical idealization of the economy—we have a market for all commodity-options. What is traded on each market are contracts in which buyers pay an agreed sum and the sellers agree to deliver prescribed quantities of a given commodity *if* a certain state of nature prevails and nothing if that state of nature does not occur. For any given set of inputs, the firm knows its output under each state of nature and sells a corresponding quantity of commodity options; its revenue is then completely determined. It may choose its inputs so as to maximize profits. . . .

---

[5] This is a slight exaggeration. Arrow, in the last few paragraphs of his paper does discuss some problems in substituting the government for the market. The important point, however, is that Arrow is not led to reconsider his allegation of inefficiency in the market place by his short discussion of some of the difficulties of resorting to government.

[6] But for economists at least, the charge of committing the grass is always greener fallacy must be less severe in this case. The economist who suggests that we resort to the market because of unsatisfactory experience with government at least can claim professional knowledge of how the market can be expected to allocate resources. See pt. IV, pp. 19-20 *infra*.

4   THE JOURNAL OF LAW AND ECONOMICS

An equilibrium is reached on all commodity-option markets, and this equilibrium has precisely the same Pareto-optimality properties as competitive equilibrium under uncertainty.

In particular, the markets for commodity-options in this ideal model serve the function of achieving an optimal allocation of risk-bearing among the members of the economy. . . .

But the real economic system does not possess markets for commodity-options.[7]

Here I must raise an objection, for there is nothing in principle that prohibits the sale of commodity options. The real economic system does, in fact, allow exchange of commodity-options.[8] Arrow continues:

[If commodity options are unavailable] the firm and its owners cannot relieve themselves of risk-bearing in this model. Hence any unwillingness or inability to bear risks will give rise to a nonoptimal allocation of resources, in that there will be discrimination against risky enterprises as compared with the optimum.[9]

Arrow here has slipped into the fallacy of the free lunch. The word "nonoptimal" is misleading and ambiguous. Does it mean that free enterprise can be improved upon? Let me suppose that the cost of marketing commodity options exceeds the gain from the adjustment to risk. This would account for their presumed absence. Can it then be said that free enterprise results in a nonoptimal adjustment to risk? To make this assertion is to deny that scarcity is relevant to optimality, a strange position for an economist. In suggesting that free enterprise generates incomplete adjustments to risk, the nirvana approach, by comparing these adjustments with the ideal, is led further to equate incomplete to nonoptimal. This would be correct only if commodity-options or other ways of adjusting to risk are free. In this way, the nirvana approach relies on an implicit assumption of nonscarcity, but since risk shifting or risk reduction cannot generally be accomplished freely the demonstration of nonoptimality is false.

---

[7] Kenneth J. Arrow, *supra* note 1, at 610-11.

[8] A labor contract with an adjustment for changes in the Consumer Price Index is a commodity-option. Such a contract specifies one wage rate if nature reveals one price level and another wage rate conditional upon the appearance of a different price level. Insurance premiums often contain deduction provisions if nature helps the driver avoid an accident. Firms often will sell products to other firms with the price conditional on delivery date, product quality, and prices that are being paid by other firms at the time of delivery. The American housewife is persistently offered a money back guarantee conditional on quality and sometimes independent of quality. Numerous other examples of commodity-options can be cited, such as limit orders to buy or sell that specify reservation prices, but there is no need here for a survey of the great variety of contractual relationships that exist.

[9] Kenneth J. Arrow, *supra* note 1, at 611-12.

II

Arrow calls attention to three problem areas in the production of knowledge and invention, risk-aversion, indivisibilities, and inappropriability. These are discussed in this section. In his analysis of risk-aversion, Arrow recognizes three major substitutes for commodity-option contracts: insurance, common stock, and cost-plus contracts. He finds that each of these fails to completely eliminate the discrepancy between optimal allocation in his ideal norm and allocation in a free enterprise system:

(1) the economic system has devices for shifting risks, but they are limited and imperfect; hence, one would expect an underinvestment in risky activities; (2) it is undoubtedly worthwhile to enlarge the variety of such devices, but the moral factor creates a limit to their potential.[10]

The route by which he reaches these conclusions is revealed by his discussion of the adjustment to risk provided by insurance.

Suppose that each firm and individual in the economy could forecast perfectly what prices would be under each state of nature. Suppose further there were a lottery on the state of nature, so that before the state of nature is known any individual or firm may place bets. Then it can be seen that the effect . . . is the same as if there were markets for commodity-options of all types. . . .

References to lotteries and bets may smack of frivolity, but we need only think of insurance to appreciate that the shifting of risks through what are in effect bets on the state of nature is a highly significant phenomenon. If insurance were available against any conceivable event, it follows . . . that optimal allocation would be achieved. . . .

Unfortunately, it is only too clear that the shifting of risks in the real world is incomplete. There are a number of reasons why this should be so, but I will confine myself to one, of special significance with regard to invention. In insurance practice, reference is made to the moral factor as a limit to the possibilities of insurance. . . . The insurance policy changes the incentive of the insured [in the case of fire insurance], creating an incentive for arson or at the very least for carelessness. . . . As a result, any insurance policy and in general any device for shifting risks can have the effect of dulling incentives. . . .

The moral factor [is] of special relevance in regard to highly risky business activities, including invention. . . . [S]uch activities should be undertaken if the expected return exceeds the market rate of return, no matter what the variance is. The existence of common stocks would seem to solve the allocation problem; any individual stockholder can reduce his risk by buying only a small part of the stock and diversifying his portfolio to achieve his own preferred risk level. But then again the actual managers no longer receive the full reward of their decisions; the

[10] *Id.* at 614.

6 THE JOURNAL OF LAW AND ECONOMICS

shifting of risks is again accompanied by a weakening of incentives to efficiency. Substitute motivations whether pecuniary . . . or nonpecuniary . . . may be found, but the dilemma of the moral factor can never be completely resolved.[11]

My dissatisfaction with Arrow's approach can be explained by first referring to one sentence in the above quotation. "[S]uch activities should be undertaken if the expected return exceeds the market rate of return, no matter what the variance is."[12] This statement would certainly be false for a Robinson Crusoe economy. Suppose that the expected rate of return on one project equals the expected rate of return on a second project. If the variances of the expected returns differ, and if Crusoe is risk averse, there is good economic reason for Crusoe to prefer the less risky project. Reduction of risk is by hypothesis an economic good for Crusoe and he should be willing to pay a positive price, such as a lower expected return, in order to acquire this good. It is clear in this simple case that the economist has no more reason for saying that Crusoe should be indifferent between these projects than he has for saying that Crusoe should be risk neutral.

Once it is admitted that risk reduction is stipulated to be an economic good, the relevant question for society is what real institutional arrangements will be best suited to produce risk reduction or risk shifting. We no longer delude ourselves into thinking that the world would be a more efficient place if only people were not risk averse; the taste for risk reduction must be incorporated into the concept of efficiency.

Given the fact of scarcity, risk reduction is not achievable at zero cost, so that the risk averse efficient economy, as we have already noted, does *not* produce "complete" shifting of risk but, instead, it reduces or shifts risk only when the economic gain exceeds the cost. Once we seek to compare different institutional arrangements for accomplishing this, it is difficult to keep scarcity from entering our calculations so that it becomes obviously misleading and incorrect to assert that an economy, free enterprise or otherwise, is inefficient if it fails to economize on risk as it would if it were costless to shift or reduce risk.

Two types of adjustment to risk seem possible: pooling independent activities so that the variance in expected return is reduced and facilitating the assumption of risk by those who are less risk averse. The market is an institutional arrangement that encourages both types of adjustment by rewarding

---

[11] *Id.* at 612-14.

[12] In the original text, Arrow places a footnote here—"The validity of this statement depends on some unstated assumptions, but the point to be made is unaffected by minor qualifications." The reader perhaps may be able to guess what is meant here and how it would affect my criticism.

those who successfully reduce or shift risk. Thus, future contracts provide a method whereby much risk is shifted to speculators.[13] Conditional contracts of the commodity-option type already discussed also can be purchased for a premium. And even with risk pooling, some risk remains to be borne by sellers of insurance, so that a payment for risk bearing is in order.

Moral hazard is identified by Arrow as a unique and irremedial cause of incomplete coverage of all risky activities by insurance. But in truth there is nothing at all unique about moral hazard and economizing on moral hazard provides no special problems not encountered elsewhere. Moral hazard is a relevant cost of producing insurance; it is not different from the cost that arises from the tendency of men to shirk when their employer is not watching them. And, just as man's preference for shirking and leisure are costs of production that must be economized, so moral hazard must be economized in shifting and reducing risk. A price can be and is attached to the sale of all insurance that includes the moral hazard cost imposed by the insured on insurance companies. And this price is individualized to the extent that other costs, mainly cost of contracting, allow. The moral hazard cost is present, although in differing amounts, no matter what percentage of the value of the good is insured.

The moral hazard problem is no different than the problem posed by any cost. Some iron ore is left unearthed because it is too costly to bring to the surface. But we do not claim ore mining is inefficient merely because mining is not "complete." Some risks are left uninsured because the cost of moral hazard is too great and this may mean that self-insurance is economic. There is no special dilemma associated with moral hazard, but Arrow's concentration on the divergence between risk shifting through insurance and risk shifting in the ideal norm, in which moral hazard presumably is absent, makes it appear as a special dilemma. While it may cost nothing to insure risky enterprises in the world of the ideal norm, it does in this world, if for no other reason than the proclivity of some to commit moral hazards. Arrow's approach to efficiency problems has led him directly to "the people could be different" fallacy.

Payment through insurance premiums for the moral hazard cost imposed on insurance sellers brings into play the usual price mechanism for economizing. The fact that not everything is insured is irrelevant to the question of efficiency. The absence of insurance, especially when moral hazard is important, merely is evidence of the unwillingness to shift all risk to others at

[13] It is not yet clear from available empirical studies whether speculators are in fact compensated, and it has been argued either that they are not risk-averse or that they enjoy the sport so much that they are willing to bear risk without pay.

premium levels that cover the cost imposed on sellers of insurance by these moral hazards.[14]

Clearly, efficiency requires that moral hazards be economized. Otherwise, we implicitly assert that the loss of assets that accompanies the realization of a moral hazard imposes no cost on society. One way of economizing on moral hazards is to allow self-insurance. If the size of the premium that is required to get others to accept moral hazard cost is higher than people wish to pay, it is appropriate to reduce the loss of assets that would accompany moral hazard by allowing prospective buyers of such insurance to self-insure.

Do we shift risk or reduce moral hazards efficiently through the market place? This question cannot be answered solely by observing that insurance is incomplete in coverage. Is there an alternative institutional arrangement that seems to offer superior economizing? There may well be such an arrangement, but Arrow has not demonstrated it and, therefore, his allegation of inefficiency may well be wrong and certainly is premature.

Turning now to the possibility of reducing risk through the device of pooling, we find that Arrow takes the following position.

> The central economic fact about the processes of invention and research is that they are devoted to the production of information. By the very definition of information, invention must be a risky process. . . . Since it is a risky process, there is bound to be some discrimination against investment in inventive and research activities. . . . The only way, within the private enterprise system, to minimize this [moral factor] problem is the conduct of research by large corporations with many projects going on, each small in scale compared with the net revenue of the corporation. Then the corporation acts as its own insurance company. But clearly this is only an imperfect solution.[15]

---

[14] Arrow employs the moral hazard argument in his paper, Uncertainty and the Welfare Economics of Medical Care, 53 Am. Econ. Rev. 941-73 (1963). Mark V. Pauly criticized this use of the moral hazard argument and Arrow replied to the criticism 58 Am. Econ. Rev. 531-38 (1968). My criticism of Arrow's argument is much the same as Pauly's. Two parts of Arrow's reply to Pauly should be noted. First, Arrow concedes "that the optimality of complete insurance is no longer valid when the method of insurance influences the demand for the services provided by the insurance policy." So far so good. However, secondly, Arrow states that "If the amount of insurance payment is in any way dependent on a decision of the insured as well as on a state of nature, then optimality will not be achieved either by the competitive system or by an attempt by the government to simulate a perfectly competitive system." The supporting argument given by Arrow in defense of this second statement leaves much to be desired since it assumes that contracts between the insurer and insured that ration the insurance service are somehow outside the competitive system, that the decision to consume more of the service is somehow a "bad" even though the price of the insurance covers the full cost of the service, and, implicitly, that adherence to contractual agreements is not an important feature of the competitive system.

[15] Kenneth J. Arrow, *supra* note 1 at 616.

INFORMATION AND EFFICIENCY: ANOTHER VIEWPOINT 9

The centralization of research does provide a more diversified portfolio of investment projects that allows owners to reduce the variance of the outcome of their inventive efforts. To some extent firms do centralize research efforts. But a real social cost is borne if this procedure is pushed too far. The more centralized is the production or financing of invention, the smaller is the degree to which the advantages of specialization can be enjoyed and the less keen is the stimulus offered by competition. These costs must be taken into account in identifying the efficient institutional arrangement, and I suppose that these costs do play a major role in limiting the voluntary centralization of research by industry. The efficient arrangement generally will be one that falls between complete centralization and complete specialization.

It may be that government production or financing of invention is a superior arrangement, in which case extensive use of market arrangements can be criticized. Government *can* take a risk neutral attitude (although I doubt that this is a desirable attitude in the nuclear age). But I do not know what attitude actually will be taken toward risk by government. Government is a group of people, each of whom in the absence of compensation to do otherwise, presumably is risk averse. The psychological propensity to be risk averse, if it is present, is found in employees of government as well as in employees of private enterprise, and a government probably is averse to political risks.

I suspect that the government will be less risk averse in some of its activity. The attempt to place a man on the moon by 1970 probably never will be subjected to careful market measures of risk and rate of return, but if it were, it is unlikely that it would appear worthwhile even if it is successful in the technological sense. In some cases, a technological success carries great weight in achieving political success and here government will be less risk averse.

In other governmental activities, however, the government is likely to behave toward risk in a much more risk-averse fashion than is private enterprise. For example, inventing and innovating a superior postal service, although it has some risk associated with it, seems to be technologically possible and economically promising. But the adverse political developments that could follow from the laying off of many postal employees leads the government to hold back. It is very averse to the risk of being voted out of office.

Arrow's analysis of risk merely states that the market copes with risk differently than it would if risk could be shifted or reduced costlessly, or than it would if people were neither risk averse nor susceptible to moral hazard. But a relevant notion of efficiency must refer to scarcity and people as they are, not as they could be.

In his discussion of the inappropriability of new knowledge, Arrow recognizes that if information is to be produced privately, its producers must be able to realize revenues from the use or sale of information. For this to be possible, information must be appropriable, and Arrow is not optimistic about the ease with which the value of information can be captured by its discoverer. Some part of Arrow's pessimism, I believe, is attributable to his tendency to see special and unique problems in establishing property rights to information when the problems are neither special nor unique.

Appropriability is largely a matter of legal arrangements and the enforcement of these arrangements by private or public means. The degree to which knowledge is privately appropriable can be increased by raising the penalties for patent violations and by increasing resources for policing patent violations.

It is true that all "theft" of information cannot be eliminated at reasonable cost. But knowledge is not unique in this respect, since the same can be said of any valuable asset. The equilibrium price that is paid to producers of automobiles will in part reflect the fact that there is a positive probability that the purchaser will have his automobile stolen. The problem of theft is as pervasive as the problem of moral hazard, and although there may be differences in the cost of reducing the theft of different types of assets there is no difference in principle. It may be argued, as Arrow does, that the ease of theft of knowledge is heightened by the fact that knowledge once used becomes easily known by others. But the theft of an automobile also is made easier when it is removed from the home garage.

One characteristic of knowledge that increases the cost of enforcing private rights is the possibility of stealing information without thereby depriving its owner of the "ability" to use the information, although, of course, the profitability to the owner of using the information may be reduced if the thief uses it. Compared with more tangible assets the detection of the theft of knowledge may need to rely to a greater extent on discovering its subsequent use by others. But if Arrow is correct in asserting that "[t]he very use of information in any productive way is bound to reveal it, at least in part,"[16] then detecting its subsequent use by nonowners may be relatively easy. In any case, the reduction in theft of knowledge can be accomplished, without increasing the probability of detection, by raising the penalties to the thief if he is apprehended. A harsher schedule of penalties always can be used to enhance the appropriability of knowledge.[17]

The truth of the matter is that I, at least, have no more than casual notions

---

[16] *Id.* at 615. Arrow states this to support his notion that theft of knowledge is easy.

[17] For a definitive analysis of the role of penalties in crime prevention (and of other aspects of the economics of crime), see Gary S. Becker, Crime and Punishment: An Economic Approach, 76 J. Pol. Econ. 169-217 (1968).

about the cost, per dollar value of knowledge, of establishing property rights in information. Given the appropriate legal apparatus and schedule of penalties it may be no more difficult to police property rights in many kinds of knowledge than it is to prevent the theft of automobiles and cash. And even if some kinds of information are more difficult to protect, I am not sure which institutions yield the better solution to the problem or what public policy deduction should be made.

We now turn to what Arrow identifies as the problems of indivisibility (or, in more current terminology, the problem of public goods).

The cost of transmitting a given body of information is frequently very low. If it were zero, then optimal allocation would obviously call for unlimited distribution of the information without cost. In fact, a given piece of information is by definition an indivisible commodity, and the classical problems of allocation in the presence of indivisibilities appear here. . . .[18]

As we have seen, information is a commodity with peculiar attributes, particularly embarrassing for the achievement of optimal allocation. . . . [A]ny information obtained . . . should, from the welfare point of view, be available free of charge (apart from the cost of transmitting information). This insures optimal utilization of the information but of course provides no incentive for investment in research. In an ideal socialist economy, the reward for invention would be completely separated from any charge to the users of information. In a free enterprise economy, inventive activity is supported by using the invention to create property rights; precisely to the extent that it is successful, there is an underutilization of the information.[19]

The partitioning of economic activity into the act of producing knowledge and the act of disseminating already produced knowledge is bound to cause confusion when the attempt is made to judge efficiency. It is hardly useful to say that there is "underutilization" of information if the method recommended to avoid "underutilization" discourages the research required to produce the information. These two activities simply cannot be judged independently. Since one of the main functions of paying a positive price is to encourage others to invest the resources needed to sustain a continuing flow of production, the efficiency with which the existing stock of goods or information is used cannot be judged without examining the effects on production.

If, somehow, we knew how much and what types of information it would be desirable to produce, then we could administer production independently of the distribution of any given stock of information. But we do not know these things. Arrow's assertion that "[i]n an ideal socialist economy, the reward for invention would be completely separated from any charge to the users

---

[18] Kenneth J. Arrow, *supra* note 1, at 614-15.
[19] *Id.* at 616-17.

of information" begs this whole problem. How would such a system produce information on the desired directions of investment and on the quantities of resources that should be committed to invention? There are ways, of course. Surveys of scientists and managers could be taken and a weighting scheme could be applied to the opinions received; no doubt there are many other ways of making such decisions. But the practice of creating property rights in information and allowing its sale is not clearly inefficient in comparison with these real alternatives.

Arrow does acknowledge the adverse incentive effects that would obtain in a private enterprise economy if information were made freely available, but this does not deter him from asserting that the capitalistic method is inefficient in its distribution of information. This ambiguity and looseness in Arrow's analysis is attributable directly to his viewpoint and approach. If he were to compare a real socialist system with a real capitalistic system the advantages and disadvantages of each would stand out, and it would be possible to make some overall judgment as to which of the two is better. But Arrow compares the workings of a capitalistic system with a Pareto norm that lends itself to static analysis of allocation but, nonetheless, that is poorly designed for analyzing dynamic problems of production. He finds the capitalistic system defective. The socialist ideal, however, resolves static allocation problems rather neatly. But this is only because all the dynamic problems of production are ignored. The comparison of a real capitalistic system with an ideal socialist system that ignores important problems is not a promising way to shed light on how to design institutional arrangements for the production and distribution of knowledge.

Indivisibilities in the use of knowledge become important only when the costs of contracting are relatively large. This point generally has been ignored. If everyone is allowed the right to use already available knowledge because one person's use of existing knowledge does not reduce its availability to others, there will tend to be underinvestment in the production of knowledge because the discoverer of knowledge will not enjoy property rights in the knowledge. But this underinvestment works to the disadvantage of others who would have the output of any additional investment made available to them at no cost. If the cost of contracting were zero, these prospective "freeloaders" would be willing to pay researchers to increase the investment being made. Research activity would be purchased just as any other good.

The relevance of contracting cost is most clearly seen by supposing that there are two prospective freeloaders and one inventor. If the freeloaders are allowed to use successful research without paying the inventor, he will reduce his research efforts. But then the two freeloaders will find it in their interest to buy additional research effort from the researcher. The only implication of indivisibilities in the use of information is that it will pay for the freeloaders to join forces in buying this additional research, for by doing so they can share the required payment. If the cost of arriving at such an agreement is negligible, the resources devoted to experimentation will be the same as if the freeloaders were *required* to pay a fee to the inventor for the use of his successful experiments.

The objective of bargaining between those who produce knowledge and those who use it, whether the researcher has rights to the knowledge he produces or whether this knowledge is freely made available to all, is the production of knowledge at efficient rates. For if knowledge is produced at efficient rates, the social value of the research effort will be maximized. The bargaining between the interested parties will determine how this value is shared. If the cost of contracting, broadly interpreted, is zero, it will be in everyone's interest to reach an agreement that maximizes the value of the research effort because all will have a larger pie to share.

If the cost of contracting is positive, the kind of property rights system that is established may change the allocation of resources in the production of knowledge. If freeloading is allowed, that is, if users of knowledge are given the right to knowledge without paying for it, some prospective users will be inclined to stay out of any cooperative agreement between users. There will be an incentive to users jointly to pay researchers to increase the resources being committed to research, but if some users can remain outside this cooperative effort, they stand to benefit from research paid for by other users. This may lead to an underinvestment (underpurchase?) in research.

It might seem that the tendency for a user to remain outside any cooperative purchasing effort is independent of contracting costs. But this is not so. Broadly interpreted, such costs will include not only the cost of striking a bargain but also the cost of enforcing any bargain that is made. The property rights system that makes produced information freely available to all increases the cost of enforcing agreements. Let the user's purchasing organization attempt to acquire members. What does it have to offer prospective members? It cannot guarantee that those who join will have exclusive rights to the research output purchased, for the law says that anyone can use knowledge. The cost of enforcing a contract that promises exclusivity in the use of whatever knowledge is purchased is raised inordinately by this public policy, and that is why there will be a strong inclination to remain outside the buyer's cooperative effort.

If the legal system is changed so that producers of research have property rights in their research output, they will be able to transfer legal title to purchasers who can then exclude nonpurchasers from the use of the research. The incentive to remain a nonpurchaser is diminished with private appropriation of knowledge precisely because the cost of enforcing exclusive contracts is reduced.

The last assertion in the above quotation from Arrow's paper, "In a free enterprise economy, inventive activity is supported by using the invention to create property rights; precisely to the extent that it is successful, there is an underutilization of the information," does not constitute an argument against the creation of property rights. The indivisibility problem may very well be handled best by a private property system that reduces the cost of contracting and raises the cost of free-loading while, at the same time, it provides incentives and guidance for investment in producing information.

III

The problem discussed in this section is qualitatively different from those discussed above. Here our attention is directed to the structure of the industry in which the knowledge is used.[20] Arrow discusses the relevance of industry structure in that section of his paper subtitled Competition, Monopoly, and the Incentive to Innovate. The objectives and conclusions are stated by Arrow as follows:

I will examine here the incentives to invent for monopolistic and competitive markets, that is, I will compare the potential profits from an invention with the costs. The difficulty of appropriating the information will be ignored; the remaining problem is that of indivisibility in use, an inherent property of information. A competitive situation here will mean one in which the industry produces under competitive conditions, while the inventor can set an arbitrary royalty for the use of his invention. In the monopolistic situation, it will be assumed that only the monopoly itself can invent. Thus a monopoly is understood here to mean barriers to entry; a situation of temporary monopoly, due perhaps to a previous innovation, which does not prevent the entrance of new firms with innovations of their own, is to be regarded as more nearly competitive than monopolistic for the purpose of this analysis. It will be argued that the incentive to invent is less under monopolistic than under competitive conditions but even in the latter case it will be less than is socially desirable.[21]

Arrow arrives at these conclusions under the two varieties of circumstances that are implied by the way in which the problem is set up.

We will assume constant costs both before and after the invention, the unit costs being c before the invention and $c' < c$ afterward. The competitive price before invention will therefore be c. Let the corresponding demand be x_c. If r is the level of unit royalties, the competitive price after the invention will be $c' + r$, but this

[20] I am indebted to Professor Aaron Director for sharing with me his revealing insights into the problem discussed in this section, and, in particular, for suggesting that the results of Arrow's analysis are affected significantly by the difference in scale between the competitive industry and monopoly industry that is implicit in his approach. I would also like to thank Professor George J. Stigler for his critical review of an earlier draft.

[21] Kenneth J. Arrow, *supra* note 1, at 619.

cannot of course be higher than c, since firms are always free to produce with the old methods.[22]

The basic point at issue can be brought forward best by discussing the circumstance in which $c' + r$ is less than c if the royalty is set at its profit maximizing level.

Arrow's argument can be put into geometric form with the aid of Figure I. Let c and c', respectively, be the per unit cost of production before and

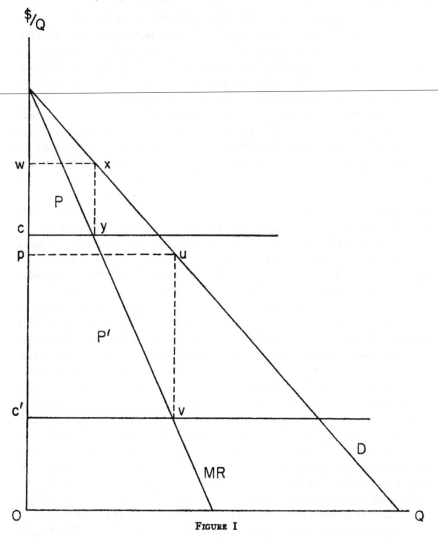

FIGURE I

[22] *Id.* at 620.

after the invention. The inventor selling to a competitive industry sets the per unit royalty, r, so as to maximize the size of the rectangle c'puv; that is, the inventor sets the royalty so that the quantity demand is where marginal revenue, MR, is equal to c'. This results in a price for the competitive industry's product equal to p. Following Arrow's terminology, let P' = c'puv. An inventor selling to the competitive industry illustrated in Figure I would be willing to invest in inventing so long as the cost of the invention to him is less than P'.

Arrow, in posing the alternative situation in which the industry is a monopoly owned by the inventor reasons that before the invention the inventor, acting as would any monopolist, has set price at w to hold the quantity demanded to that rate of output for which c = MR. His profit, P, equals rectangle cwxy. After his invention, his cost per unit will be lowered from c to c'. Maximizing profits with his new cost he will set price at p. This yields a new profit rectangle equal to P'. The basic conclusion reached by Arrow, that "the incentive to invest is less under monopolistic than under competitive conditions," is now clear. The inventor selling to a competitive industry would be willing to invent if his cost is less than P' but the inventor who is a monopolist in the product market would be willing to invent only if the cost of inventing is less than P' — P, for this precisely measures to him the increase in profits attributable to the invention. Since P' — P always is less than P', Arrow concludes that the incentive to invent is less under monopoly.

Arrow's conclusion, however, does not lend itself to a clear interpretation since he has allowed two extraneous issues to influence his analysis. (1) Arrow's inventor not only produces an invention but, in addition, he possesses the monopoly power to discriminate in the royalty charges he sets for the two industries. (2) Arrow neglects to take account of the normal monopoly incentives in the monopoly purchasing the invention; monopoly models generally deduce that a monopolist will use less of all inputs, including an invention, because he produces less output; the demonstration of any *special* effect of monopoly on the incentive to invention requires that adjustments be made for this normally restrictive monopoly behavior. When proper account is taken of these two matters we find that Arrow's conclusions are false.

Let us suppose that competitive inventions or regulations restrict the inventor to charging all users of the invention identical unit royalties, and let p — c' in Figure I measure that royalty. In this case, both the competitive industry and the monopolist accept p — c' as the price of an input. The competitive industry would then pay a total royalty equal to P' to the inventor while the monopoly would pay half this amount since the monopoly's output would increase only to the intersection of pu with MR. The monopoly does offer to pay less total royalty because it produces at a smaller output rate than does the competitive industry. This comes as no surprise. One of the better known deductions in economics is that a nondiscriminating monopolist will sell fewer units of output and use fewer units of input than would be used in the same industry if it were competitively organized.

To remove from the analysis the normal restrictive effect of monopoly on output, let us define MR in Figure I to be the demand curve facing the competitive industry. For any given unit cost, both the monopoly and the competitive industry will produce the same output rate. At a royalty per unit equal to $p - c'$ both industries will produce where pu intersects MR and both will pay the same total royalty to the inventor.

By eliminating the inventor's monopoly power to charge different royalties and simultaneously by adjusting the demand curve facing the competitive industry to eliminate the normal restrictive effect of monopoly on input use, we arrive at the conclusion that a competitive industry will offer no greater incentive to invention than a monopoly. There is no special adverse effect of monopoly on the incentive to invention.

Let us now consider the case where rivalry between inventors, or where regulation fails to equalize the royalties. What will be the incentive to invention offered by the two industries after adjusting their sizes to remove the normal restrictive effects of a prior monopoly? We shall see that in this case the incentive to invention is just the reverse of what Arrow concluded; for industries that would operate at the same levels of output in the absence of the invention, the development of a monopoly invention with price discriminating power will receive greater rewards from a buying industry that is a monopoly.

In Figure II let D_m and MR_m be the demand and marginal revenue facing the monopolist and let D_c and MR_c characterize the industry demand facing the competitive industry. Assume that $MR_m = D_c$ so that for any given constant unit cost both industries will produce the same output rates. At cost $= c$ the competitive industry produces output cu, since demand must equal marginal cost under competition, while for monopoly the output rate cu will be selected because marginal cost must equal marginal revenue. Hence, the size of the two industries will be the same for any given constant unit cost. The effect of monopoly on the size of output has been removed.

At cost c, the monopoly receives profit $P = cptu$, whereas with the cost reducing invention the monopoly profit is $P'' = c'p'yx$. The incentive to monopoly invention given by the monopoly industry is $P'' - P$. The best that the inventor can do if he sells his monopoly invention to an *equal sized* competitive industry is to ask a per unit royalty equal to $p' - c'$ for this will cause the competitive industry to produce an output rate p'v that maximizes the inventor's total royalty c'p'vw. We wish to ascertain whether the incen-

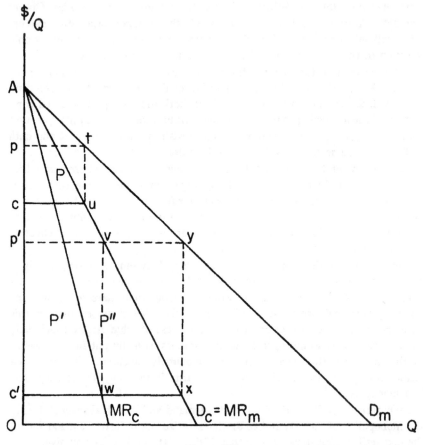

FIGURE II

tive to invention offered by the competitive industry, $c'p'vw = P'$ is larger or smaller than $P'' - P$. Figure II indicates that the incentive to invention offered by the competitive industry is smaller since $P'' - P$ clearly is greater than P. However, to make sure that this is no geometrical illusion, the reader will find an algebraic proof for the linear case in the Appendix. The Appendix also presents a counter example to Arrow's conclusion for a case where both industries start at the same output rate and confront the same demand curve.

The traditional belief that monopoly restricts output may suggest that some measure of antitrust is desirable. If Arrow's analysis is taken to suggest, as I think it must, that there are special adverse effects of monopoly on the incentive to invention, a framer of public policy would deduce that antitrust should be pursued more diligently than is dictated by considerations of output restrictions only. But he would be wrong. If it is thought desirable to encourage invention by granting monopoly power through the patent or through secrecy, the above analysis suggests that antitrust should be pursued less diligently than is dictated by considerations of output restrictions only, for, at least in the linear model of two industries of equal output size, the more monopolistic will give the greatest encouragement to invention.

IV

The problem of efficiency and the possibilities of achieving efficiency through reform were associated historically with the grant of monopoly and tariff privileges by governments. In their historical settings, criticisms of inefficiency took on the characteristic of the comparative institution and not the nirvana approach. Critics of governmental policies who asked for reform were seeking to substitute an institutional arrangement that was both real and fairly well understood. They were confident of the beneficial results and of the practicality of allowing market enterprise to allocate resources. And, although the operation of political forces had not been subjected to the same careful study, the critics did know what they expected if governmentally created protection from those market forces were removed.

A process of refining the analytical concept of competition then set in, culminating in the currently accepted necessary conditions for perfect competition. These conditions, of course, can be only approximated by real institutions. On top of these are placed additional conditions on the nature of production, commodities, and preferences that are necessary if the equivalence of perfect competition and Pareto efficiency is to be established.

While the application of these conceptual refinements is an aid to solving some economic problems, especially in positive economics, their application to normative problems has led to serious errors. If an economy has no serious indivisibilities, if information is complete, etc., then the modern analysis can describe the characteristics of an efficient long-run equilibrium; this description is the main result of modern welfare analysis. But modern analysis has yet to describe efficiency in a world where indivisibilities are present and knowledge is costly to produce. To say that private enterprise is inefficient because indivisibilities and imperfect knowledge are part of life, or because people are susceptible to the human weaknesses subsumed in the term moral hazards, or because marketing commodity-options is not costless, or because persons are risk-averse, is to say little more than that the competitive equilibrium would be different if these were not the facts of life. But, if they are the facts of life, if, that is, they cannot be erased from life at zero cost, then truly efficient institutions will yield different long-run equilibrium conditions than those now used to describe the ideal norm.

It is one thing to suggest that wealth will increase with the removal of legal monopoly. It is quite another to suggest that indivisibilities and moral hazards should be handled through nonmarket arrangements. The first suggestion is based on two credible assumptions, that the monopoly can be eliminated and that the practical institutional arrangement for accomplishing this, market competition, operates in fairly predictable ways. The second assertion cannot claim to have eliminated indivisibilities, risk-averse psychology, moral hazard, or costly negotiations, nor can it yet claim to predict the behavior of the governmental institutions that are suggested as replacements for the market.

I have stated elsewhere what I believe to be the basic problem facing public and private policy: the design of institutional arrangements that provide incentives to encourage experimentation (including the development of new products, new knowledge, new reputations, and new ways of organizing activities) without overly insulating these experiments from the ultimate test of survival. In the context of the problems discussed in Arrow's paper, these institutional arrangements must strive to balance three objectives. A wide variety of experimentation should be encouraged, investment should be channeled into promising varieties of experimentation and away from unpromising varieties, and the new knowledge that is acquired should be employed extensively. No known institutional arrangement can simultaneously maximize the degree to which each of these objectives is achieved. A difficult-to-achieve balance is sought between the returns that can be earned by additional experimentation, by giving directional guidance to investment in experimentation, and by reducing the cost of producing goods through the use of existing knowledge. The concepts of perfect competition and Pareto optimality simply are unable at present to give much help in achieving this balance.

APPENDIX

All notation is consistent with Figure II of the text. In this part of the Appendix we allow the inventor to produce a monopoly invention that he markets to a monopoly and a competitive industry. The industries are defined so that at any given marginal cost the rates of output will be the same.

(1) $P = A - Bq$ be monopoly demand, then total revenue is

(2) $TR = Aq - Bq^2$ and marginal revenue is

(3) $MR_m = A - 2Bq$.

At unit cost c, the monopoly maximizes profits where

(4) $c = MR_m = A - 2Bq$, which allows us to calculate monopoly output as

(5) $q = \dfrac{A - c}{2B}$.

Monopoly profit at c cost is

(6) $P = TR - cq = \dfrac{(A - c)^2}{4B}$ and the incentive to invention with mono-

poly is

(7) $P'' - P = \dfrac{(A - c')^2 - (A - c)^2}{4B}$ where c' is the new lower unit cost.

Under competition, the inventor calculates the marginal revenue associated with the industry demand curve

(8) $D_c = MR_m = A - 2Bq$, so that

(9) $MR_c = A - 4Bq$.

The inventor then selects that per unit royalty such that the resulting output rate is ~~where $c' = MR_c$. That is, where~~

(10) $c' = A - 4Bq$. The competitive industry's output rate will then be

(11) $q = \dfrac{A - c'}{4B}$ and the incentive to invention is

(12) $P' = (A - c')q - 2Bq^2 = \dfrac{(A - c')^2}{8B}$.

Comparing $P'' - P$, from (7), to P', we find that P' must always be less in the case under consideration since

$$(P'' - P) - P' = (A - c') - 2(A - c)$$

and

$$(A - c') > 2(A - c) \text{ if } p' < c.$$

The Arrow proposition is incorrect even if less acceptable but more lenient restrictions are considered. Again, let us assume that the inventor has a monopoly, but let both the competitive industry and the monopoly face the same demand curve. However, assume that the initial per unit cost, k, in the competitive industry is sufficiently above the monopoly's initial cost, c, to yield the same preinvention output rates. Then, let the cost in each industry be reduced by the same amount as a result of the invention. In this way, we pose a situation in which initial output levels are the same but one in which the invention moves both industries along identical demand curves. An arithmetic counterexample of Arrow's proposition follows.

Let the demand curve facing both industries be

(1) $p = 100 - q$

Marginal revenue then is

(2) $MR = 100 - 2q$

Let $c = \$90$ and $c' = 10$; and in each instance equate marginal revenue to marginal cost to derive the monopoly profit maximizing q's:

(3)
$$90 = 100 - 2q$$
$$q = 5$$

(3')
$$10 = 100 - 2q$$
$$q = 45$$

Profit P at $q = 5$ and P'' at $q + 45$ are

(4) $p = 100 - 5 = \$95$ (4') $p' = 100 - 45 = \$55$

(5) $P = (\$95 - 90) \, 5 = \$25$ (5') $P'' = (\$55 - 10) \, 45 = \$2025$

The amount that the monopolist would be willing to pay for this cost reducing invention is $P'' - P = \$2000$.

We now wish to compare this with the rate of return to invention for a competitively organized industry of the same initial scale as the monopoly. To accomplish this while using the same market demand curve, $p = 100 - q$, let us set the competitive industry's preinvention per unit and marginal cost, k, at a high enough level to generate an output rate equal to the initial monopoly output rate of $q = 5$. Since the competitive industry will produce that output rate where $p = mc$, k must be \$95. Now let the invention reduce this cost by the same absolute magnitude as $c - c' = \$80$. For the competitive industry, then, the post invention marginal cost, k', will be $\$95 - \$80 = \$15$.

The inventor now will pick a per unit royalty such that the competitive industry will produce where $k' = MR$ for this will result in the largest possible total royalty payment. Using equation (2), we find this output rate to be

(6) $15 = 100 - 2q; \quad q = 42.50$

The inventor's royalty per unit will be the difference between price and $k' = 15$. From equation (1), we find that $p = \$57.50$ (at $q = 42.50$), so that the inventor's total royalty in the competitive case, P', will be

(7) $P' = (57.50 - \$15) \, 42.50 = \$1806.25$

and we find that this is \$193.75 *less* than the inventor could have earned if he sold the invention to a monopoly of the same initial size.[1]

---

[1] If this problem is repeated for the same percentage reductions in cost for the monopoly and the competitive industry, we would find that the incentives to invention would be equally great.

[9]

Reflections on the Theory of the Firm

by

Armen A. Alchian and Susan Woodward

1. Introduction

Gains from trade arise in markets where diverse agents specialize in productive activities at which they have a comparative advantage. Market prices direct their efforts.

But there are also gains from trade which arise as a result of cooperation not directed by market prices but by "management". Some of this cooperation undoubtedly involves specialization (the same source of gain as in markets), but much of it derives instead from a feature called "teamwork" (ALCHIAN and DEMSETZ [1972]). The chief distinction between economic activity outside the firm (i.e., across markets) vs. inside the firm (i.e., by teams) is that team participants do not make decisions regarding their activities on the basis of market prices, but rather give or seek and receive direction as to what to do (COASE [1952]). Why this difference?

The answer, "high transaction costs", is merely the name for whatever it is that leads to the "firm". What are these "transaction costs"? Simply put, they are the costs of determining quality and negotiating price.

Determining quality is very cheap for some items. The value of a head of lettuce may be fairly certain after only casual observation. It could be potentially much more costly to ascertain the value of a drug or an automobile. The more expensive it is to determine quality before purchase, the more expensive it is for the market to work.

Negotiating price is also easy for some items. Generally speaking, the thicker the market, the fewer the possible values for price and the less room for negotiating. But when markets are thin and a gap arises between the lowest price the seller will take and the highest price the buyer will pay, opportunities arise for buyer and seller to expend scarce resources negotiating price.

At some level of cost of either sort, simple spot exchanges will be abandoned and replaced by longer-lived arrangements which restrain the behavior of the transactors to assure each of getting and paying what was expected. Some of these agreements will be aspects of the constitutions and contracts that comprise what we call the firm, and others will be constraints on the operations of markets. The understanding of these arrangements requires explicit consideration of information costs. The notion of market-directed gains from production via comparative advantage (i.e., production by lower cost producers) offers no insight into long-term contracts among the transactors.

Although the nature of teamwork and its relation to what we call a firm has been explored and found illuminating, (ALCHIAN and DEMSETZ [1972]) teamwork is not the essence of the firm (ALCHIAN [1984], and WILLIAMSON [1985]). Rather, the essence is the nexus of contracts restraining the behavior of the transactors. (See ALCHIAN [1984], and WILLIAMSON [1985]). But we have trouble imagining economic activity organized as "teamwork" that does not have the special relations among people and physical assets that we will argue give rise to the firm. We observe that in most cooperative production, people show up for work at the same place every day. In this paper we are more interested in why they show up at the same place every day (and related issues) than in why some workers are managers and some are managed. But the issues are not unrelated.

Consider that there are cooperative production efforts in which the relation between employer and employee is very short-lived. In most cities there are areas in which day laborers can be found and hired just for the day, usually for activities such as gardening and unskilled construction. Though these workers typically work for a given employer only for a day, many issues of firm organization are present. Are the tools used in the job owned by the employer or by the employees? Or possibly by a third party who rents them? Are they financed with any debt? Is the manager an employee of yet a larger firm or the owner and residual claimant of the activity? The economic forces that determine the answers to these questions are essentially the same as for firms with very long-lived teams.

Teamwork arises where information is costly. Restraining contracts and departures from continuous auction markets arise where information is costly. Teamwork seldom appears without a nexus of contracts, and a nexus of contracts seldom appears in the absence of teamwork. The aspect of teamwork that connects it to the nexus of contracts that we want to call the firm is that so much of the information involved in teamwork is long-lived.

Team production does not necessarily involve managers and managees. Some teams consist of a group of individuals who work together effectively, but without a "leader", such as a law firm. Knowledge of one another's personal talents make working together more productive than working with less well known associates. If the team members are not equally good at discerning one another's productivity, the team will have a manager and employees who follow the manager's instructions. Again, knowledge of one another makes them more productive. Within the team, there is specialization in information about the team, which may consist simply of the team members knowing one another better than outsiders know them, or of specialization on the part of a manager in assessing the talents and guiding the activities of the team members. In either case, because the information is durable, team members all have something to lose if any one is separated from the team.

Most team efforts involve the use of physical assets. Again, the people inside the team are likely to know more about these inanimate team members – the team's physical assets – than do outsiders. They are likely to know how well an asset had been treated and maintained, and how much it has been worked. The differential cost of knowing about these assets – inside vs. outside the firm – will affect whether the firm owns, rents, or debt finances the physical assets it uses. We will explore the qualities that resources have that effect these cost differentials. In particular, we will address the following issues:

1) How and to what extent do the kinds and intended uses of certain combinations of resources determine the contractual arrangements for their use?

2) With which resources (if not owned by the users) does the user have long-term contracts and with which short-term contracts?

3) What protective arrangements have evolved – within firms and across markets – to restrain the resources from exploiting one another?

4) Which activities and related types of resources will motivate organizations that are large and have publicly traded equity claims and which will be small and privately held?

5) What characteristics of the jointly used resources determine the extent of debt rather than equity financing of the activity?

Within the firm, three basic problems must be solved. First, the firm must organize – determine the resources it will use, which tasks it will perform, and apportion the resulting value among the resources used. Second, the firm must monitor the performance of team resources to assure that each resource is delivering promised productivity. Third, the firm must control the potential for team members to renege on the original agreements for apportioning value by demanding a larger share of the firm's income. Economic activities using resources with different levels of monitoring costs and vulnerability to reneging by others will solve these problems in different ways. What we will focus on here is how these two features – monitoring costs and their resulting vulnerability to moral hazard, and vulnerability to hold-up due to the presence of quasi-rents, together make assets "firm-specific" and determine ownership, organization, financing, and some other features of firms and other institutions.

2. Preliminary Concepts: Firm; Composite Quasi-rent; Dependence and Holdup; Moral Hazard and Plasticity

2.1 Firm

The classic, paradigmatic, private property firm we will initially characterize arbitrarily as an organization with (a) continuity of specialized mutual knowledge among several separately owned inputs; and (b) contracts among inputs for continuing services of resources used by the team. The owners of the "firm" will be the owners of the resources whose value depends on the performance of the team that makes up the firm. The owners, or equity holders, will (a) be common to all contracts with input owners; (b) possess the right to sell their contractual status; and (c) hold the claim to the residual value of the team.

2.2 Composite Quasi-rent

We first acknowledge the forgotten precedence of Alfred Marshall, who in his *Principles* [1890] identified "composite quasi-rent". First, a quasi-rent is the excess above the return necessary to maintain a resource's current service flow. It is a recovery of sunk costs. Composite quasi-rent is that portion of the quasi-rent which depends on continued association with some other specific resources, and consequently is vulnerable to expropriation. Marshall's compelling example of such vulnerability was a steel mill that locates near a public utility and makes investments which depend on being able to buy power at some given price. Once the steel mill's investment is complete and the sunk costs are sunk, the utility can raise the price of power and the steel mill will continue to operate because marginal cost, even with the higher cost of power, still exceeds marginal revenue, even though the sunk costs are not being recovered.

Quasi-rent and profit are not the same. If a resource is profitable it will be getting a return that more than recovers sunk costs. However, neither a profit nor a recovery of sunk cost is necessary to induce the continuing services of an existing resource. Should quasi-rent be defined to include not only sunk costs but profits as well? We argue no, as the presence of quasi-rent (as we define it) and the presence of profit effect contractual arrangements differently. We concentrate, but not exclusively, on the protection of the recovery of sunk costs, though as will be obvious, the protective features may protect profits also.

Marshall recognized the danger of parties with sunk costs relying on those in a position to expropriate their quasi-rents. But Marshall assumed the threat was resolved by "doing what is right" or by "haggling". So far as we can ascertain he did not develop its importance for understanding the organization of the firm.

2.3 Dependence and Holdup

A resource is "dependent" when it would lose value if separated from the team (firm). A resource is "unique" when the other resources of the firm are dependent upon it, i.e., the remaining resources of the firm (members of the team) would lose value if it left. Dependence can take on two different aspects.

First, a resource may have made an investment useful only to the current team (i.e., specific to the team) upon joining the team, and is now counting on the team to compensate it for both current effort and for sunk costs. If it leaves the team, it abandons its investment, and does not recoup its sunk costs. But once the investment is made, the temptation is for the rest of the team to expropriate the quasi-rent – to refuse to pay the resource more than its highest value elsewhere – to "holdup" the dependent resource. In the legal literature, investments whose profitability depend on the behavior and continued use of resources of another are called "reliance" investments.

Second, a resource may be both dependent and depended upon. If a set of resources have all made non-recoverable or only partially recoverable investments in order to do the work they do together, they are mutually dependent. In the above example, departure of the resource that had made its investment may require the team to find another similar resource and induce it to make the same investment made by the first. If the team could lose by the departure of the resource either because the search is costly and/or it must agree to compensate the new resource for the investment. If so, the resource and the remainder of the team are mutually dependent. Only if for some reason the firm has been able to find a similar resource for which the investment is not necessary could the first resource be dependent but not unique. Mutual dependence does not require an investment made by any of the resources, only that they are more productive in this assembly than in any other use. Usually, dependence is reciprocal, which implies that dependent resources are unique, and vice versa, and that most specific capital is inter-specific capital.

Inside a firm, value is created by the collection of resources, and there is no market to clearly dictate what each should be paid. The "market" values – the opportunity costs or next best alternatives – of the resources sum to less than the value of their joint product. Hence the firm itself, not the market, must solve the problem of how to apportion the value created by the firm. This may require continuing and costly negotiation; one task of the firm is to minimize these costs.

It is usually true that after a team is formed, separation of the team members results in the loss of composite quasi-rent. Some sunk cost seems inevitable, because the information that makes the intra-firm relations valuable is durable. If a team fails, team-specific resource owners will lose. Their value depends heavily on the decisions of the adminstrative managers. It should be clear as daylight that the resources dependent on the team's fortunes and dependent on some of the other resources within the team would be very wary of vulnerability to expropriation by holdup.

The dependence we have in mind involves a continuous balancing of obligations among members. It is not like a series of short-term exchanges with deferred payment. Dependence in the sense of a creditor dependent on the firm to pay it does not characterize a firm. Such relations generally prevail outside the span of firms, and in fact we argue can only prevail when moral hazard and holdup potential are small. The critical feature is not creditor-type dependence, but instead the productive service flow dependence among inter-specific resources.

In most teams, some resources will be more vulnerable than others to holdup, depending on the degree to which they can threaten to alter the flow of services. For example, a landowner renting land as a site for a skyscraper is an owner of a resource that is "unique" to an immovable building. Though the land is unique to the building, the landowner cannot cheaply alter the services of the land as a means of extracting some of the quasi-rent of the building from the building owner. This unique resource is impotent. But the owner of the building could refuse to pay all of the promised rent, while nevertheless being secure in the knowledge that the landowner has no feasible alternative use of the land. The landowner's remedies by law limit the expropriation the building could extract, but the expense of the remedies limits the protection afforded the landowner through such remedies.

In this land/building example, the resources are mutually dependent (and mutually unique), but only one, the building owner, has a realistic opportunity to exploit the composite quasi-rent. The landowner appears to have more to fear from a holdup under a long-term lease than does the building owner. This is because the building owner can stop its service flow (payment of the rent) but the landowner cannot stop the service flow of the land. An owner of a unique resource will be more tempted to exploit the situation the larger the composite quasi-rent and the more it can control its own flow of services (fail to pay the rent or to show up for work). The more this temptation is likely and can be foreseen, the more will precautionary contractual terms be sought.

2.4 Plasticity and Moral Hazard

The notion of moral hazard can illuminate several aspects of the theory of the firm (MARSHALL [1975]). First, employee/employer relations (ALCHIAN and DEMSETZ [1972]), second, debtor/creditor relations (JENSEN and MECKLING [1976]), and third, the general problem of how owners and non-owners manage assets.

When the quality of an item is costly to detect, it will often pay to manufacture it in a firm rather than buy it in a market. Quality is controlled by supervising employees. But this gives rise to a different problem, the monitoring of employees. The tradeoff is between quality assurance in a market and quality and output control within a firm. When it is costly to monitor the effort of team members, a single member can gain (relaxation, less exertion) by shirking in his performance. The individual who shirks reaps the entire benefit of the shirking himself, but the cost, which is undetectably all due to him, is borne by the entire team because average output, and consequently wages, are lower. The outcome with costly monitoring is inferior to what could be achieved if everyone's effort could be costlessly measured, no one shirked, and average product and wage were commensurately higher.

8*

Another aspect of moral hazard arises when a firm is financed partially with debt, because the equity holders do not bear the full consequences of the decisions they make. Equity holders reap the benefits of good outcomes, but debtholders bear some of the costs of bad outcomes. Equity holders thus have an incentive to increase the riskiness of the firm's assets once they have borrowed. Debtholders know this, of course, and charge for the risk they anticipate bearing. Creditors are compensated for the risk they bear, but a moral hazard loss results. If it were possible for a contract to specify the behavior of equity holders, the equity holders would behave no differently with vs. without debt, and there would be no moral hazard loss.

When a team consists of both human and nonhuman assets, people can manage the assets with different degrees of care. It may be less trouble to manage the assets with less care. When will assets be managed in a profit maximizing fashion? When either it is easy to detect how the asset has been managed (monitoring costs are low), or when the asset managers are also owners and consequently bear the full cost and benefits of managing. Of course we may have different levels of monitoring costs from an assortment of different arrangements, e.g., from literally having owner and manager be the same party, from a party managing an asset owned by the firm for which the manager works, or from a party managing an asset rented from another firm. Since different costs are associated with different ownership arrangements due to the difficulty of controlling moral hazard, these costs will influence ownership of the asset.

The term "moral hazard" has been maligned for its moralistic connotations. Although we are not prepared to argue that shirking and ex post risk augmentation are immoral, we believe that the term correctly suggests that trustworthiness, reputation, and integrity are important an intra-firm and interfirm relations, and that the cultivation of these "virtues" probably has social value. If everyone would simply agree to undertake a given standard of effort and abide by the promise, a more efficient outcome would result. The term "moral hazard" suggests that people cannot be counted on to do what they say they are going to do, and their failure to do so manifests itself in market organization. It also suggests that among the devices used to control such behavior are moralistic agression and social opprobrium. But contracts and litigation may be cheaper.

The presence of moral hazard does not mean that transactions are regretted. Even though many markets bear moral hazard losses, all parties are better off making the transactions than they would have been without them. Workers produce and are paid their marginal products. Borrowers pay an interest rate which compensates the lender for risk. The moral hazard loss simply measures what could be gained if either the cost of monitoring behavior by the insurer/ employer were zero, or if people could be counted on to do as they promise.

Some resources are susceptible to a wider range of morally hazardous uses than are others. Furthermore, in some cases it is more difficult for an observer/

monitor to reliably and objectively establish the degree to which an agent's selections are biased towards the agent's interest. We call resources or invest- ments "plastic" to indicate there is a wide range of legitimate decisions within which the user may choose, or that an observer can less reliably monitor the choice. An administrator of more plastic resources is more able to covertly bias the expected outcomes toward the administrator's interest.

By plastic we do not simply mean risky. We argue, for example, that oil which has only to be pumped and sold is a highly implastic asset. The optimal rate at which to pump the oil depends only on the pattern of prices over time, and there is very little in the way of possibilities for exploiting an oil well either by increasing the riskiness of outcomes for its value or by changing its product into consumption. But an oil well is a risky asset in a world where the price of oil fluctuates.

We can illustrate the idea by a presumption that drug research company managers control decisions about resources that are relatively plastic: the initial options are wider and more difficult to "second guess" than for the resources used in say, a steel mill. We conjecture as further illustrations that enterprises with "intellectual research and capital" e.g. fashion designers, professional service firms such as engineering, law and architecture, computer software creation, are especially plastic and susceptible to moral hazard. In contrast, industries with less plastic resources are railroads, utility services, airlines, petroleum refining (but not exploration), and other activities involving much in the way of "hard" resources.

The quality of being plastic does not directly translate into the asset being subject to moral hazard. Cash, for example, is an asset of extreme plasticity, as it can be exchanged for almost anything, in particular both consumption and financial assets that are much more risky than cash, almost instantaneously. The implication is that managers, as agents of owners, handling large cash balances will be subjected to greater controls and review by principles. On the other hand, it is easy to record what happens to cash, and consequently the plasticity does not preclude the management of such an asset by an agent rather than a principle. The combination of plasticity plus high monitoring costs results in potential morally hazardous exploitation. An implastic asset simply does not need much monitoring.

The presence of teamwork in any economic activity indicates the costliness of information necessary to execute that activity. The information collected in undertaking the enterprise is very often durable. The durability and costliness of the information about the economic activity give rise to the possibility for moral hazard and for holdup, since the resources in the team have an interest in their relations being long-lived, yet what each resource is doing is not precisely known and exactly how much each ought to be paid is not objectively signaled by a market. These two problems give rise to the set of contractual relations we call the firm. We analyze them in the remainder of this paper.

3. Corporate Constitutions

3.1 Ownership Integration

Any resource that will become and remain dependent on the service of other members of a team will seek protection against expropriation. One form of protection is common ownership of the dependent and unique resources as one bundle, i.e., ownership integration (KLEIN, CRAWFORD and ALCHIAN [1978]). Assets owned all together present nothing in the way of holdup because their owners – residual claimants – collect the quasi-rent and profit from the entire set, and are not concerned with allocating the produced value among the resources. Moreover, since the residual claimants are the owners, problems with moral hazard in the case of plastic assets are also solved by ownership integration. Thus, either vulnerability to holdup or plasticity and high monitoring costs, which results in vulnerability to moral hazard, will result in an asset used by a firm being owned by a firm (Holdup vs. plasticity have very different implications for financing decisions, as we shall see later.)

Another form of protection retains separate ownership but gives each of the interdependent resource owners some control and influence and also gives them a prespecified share of the team's residual value, net of non-contingent amounts (e.g., wages or rents) to the independent resources. Although sharing control and residual value is not equivalent to common ownership (since any could leave without permission of the other sharing members), it can with adequate side restrictions concerning hostages (WILLIAMSON [1983]) in the event of a departure of a unique resource, accommodate contractual sharing of net income among the interdependent resources.

3.2 Long-Term Contracts

Long-term, or what the law calls relational, contracts are essential to continuity of teamwork with dependent resources. A long lasting series of spot exchanges, whether or not continuously balancing, differs from a long-term contract. The contract restrains future options and is not responsive to all possible later developments. One of the fixed or restrained terms is price, for if price were allowed to change or be renegotiated whenever either party proposed, no effective commitment would be present. Commitments to a price according to a prespecified arrangement that have met the agreement of both parties constrain the options and restrict future renegotiability, which is precisely the meaning of a long-term contract. Restrictive, long-term contracts protect long-lived dependent resources, which rely on continuing service of a unique resource at a prespecified price. Without dependent and unique resources, there is no point to a constraining long-term contract (GOLDBERG [1976]).

3.3 Firm Ownership

Owners of resources more heavily dependent on the team's product value will value the control of the direction and administration of the team more highly than will those whose alternatives are unaffected by the success or failure of the team. Those resource values most dependent on the performance of the team are called the "equity". It follows that the "equity" holders of the team will also be the directors, administrators and managers (or their principals) of the team's activities, and by convention, are called the "owners of the firm" .

Owners of independent, non-firm-specific resources will not value the right of control as highly because their wealth is not affected by the firm's fortunes. Competition in forming teams and choosing contractual arrangements will result in "firm-specific", dependent resources being the parties who place the highest value on the right to administer, while the "general" resources will, at the revealed costs of initially purchasing administration rights from firm-specific resource owners, choose instead non-administrative rights and prespecified rewards. The party with the right to administer, i.e., ownership of the firm-specific resources and equity holder, will have contracts with all of the general inputs. The contract will include the right to renegotiate with any resource independently of the others, and as well the right to sell the administration rights, i.e., the equity interest, the ownership of firm-specific, firm-dependent resources. This results in the existence of a category of resources called "employees" (the owners of the general resources), whose services are sold to the owners of the firm-dependent resources though in fact no one owns the "firm" as an entity. The firm is an assemblage of resources under a contractual nexus, not all owned in common. We note in passing that employers are not employers because they are less risk averse than employees. The degree of interest (dependency) in the firm's fortunes dictates who does what.

It follows that the members of the Board of Directors will be the agents of the more team-specific resource owners, who primarily (but not exclusively) are the stockholders. All owners of resources who have agreed to make investments that are heavily firm-dependent will value and acquire some representation on the Board. Advocates of representation on corporate Boards of Directors by public, disinterested or firm-independent resource owners are, possibly unwittingly, undermining the viability of efficient forms of production by making it easier for owners of independent resources to expropriate the composite quasi-rent of firm dependent assets, and by reducing initial willingness to invest in such assets.

In some firms, some "labor" may be highly dependent on the firm, while what is ordinarily thought of as "capital" (equipment, inventory, etc.) may be virtually general. A law firm or a medical clinic may be a well-matched team with strong interdependence among "separately owned" people, while all the equipment and premises are very cheaply transferable to other teams or uses.

In that case one would expect the doctors or lawyers to be the manager-director-owner-residual claimants, with the general resource owners renting services to the group. It is in principle not a distinction between people and physical equipment (sometimes erroneously called "labor" and "capital") that is pertinent; rather it is the degree of dependence on the specific other resources and on the firm's product value. In fact, those who are typically called employees may in many cases have made investments highly specific to the firm. They too will seek some representation on the Board. In general, whoever has a value that has become firm specific will seek some form of control over the firm, as will be discussed in a subsequent section on labor unions.

Although a relatively clean separation has been made among (a) stockholders (as residual claimants), (b) creditors (as claimants prior to stockholders to specified dollar amounts), and (c) employees (the name for all those whose values are not dependent on, or specific to, the firm) in fact the participants in the firm do not fall purely in just one of these classes. Some employees may have made firm-specific investments. They may have developed skills or knowledge of more value here than in other firms; they may have purchased homes whose values depend on the firm's success; they may have accumulated rights to subsequent benefits, like pensions, or they may be receiving salaries that are compensation for underpayments in the past designed to elicit a long-term association with the firm. Also they may have high transfer or mobility costs to the next best work. Persons with such human or non-human types of firm-specific resources will demand some means of enforcing their contractual arrangements. They may seek representation on the Board of Directors, or at least some control with respect to certain decisions affecting the probability of the fulfillment of their implicit or explicit contractual, or "customary" arrangements.

The name "equity holder", which suggests someone who invested in firm-specific resources and has rights to any resulting values only if they exceed commitments to other parties, is inappropriate for those whose rights are like those described in the preceding paragraph. They have claims prior to those of residual claimants; they are "creditors" of the firm. The upshot is that resources with values that are firm-specific can be both those that are residual claimants and those that have prior explicit, non-residual claims. All will be willing to pay a price for (i.e., demand) some measure of control over some kinds of decisions about the firm's activity, depending on the degree of firm dependent value. Whether that influence over decisions is made by having directors as agents or by other procedures, such as unions, insurers, bondholder committees initiating private suits, appeals to political authority, or by regulation, will depend on the relative cost of each device.

Not to be forgotten are customers of the firm. A consumer who buys a product, the future performance of which depends on the firm's continued activity, will have purchased a firm-specific resource – much like Marshall's steel mill or a buyer of a computer or automobile for which future spare parts are valuable. An unusual example of customer reliance, social and country clubs, is analyzed later.

3.4 The Corporation

When firm-specific resources are long-lasting and are large in total value, they tend to be owned in common by many stockholders in a corporation, the dominant form of shared ownership. These organizations often have a) persons in managerial positions who are not firm owners, b) firm owners who play no managerial role, and c) some debt financing. As a result of these features, possible conflicts of interest arise among the shareholders, between shareholders and managers, and between shareholders and creditors.

3.4.1 Tension Among Shareholders

The transferable share, limited liability corporation accommodates long-lived dependent teamwork, but also gives firm owners flexibility. The advantage of transferable shares is evident: differences in individual desires for consumption over time can be indulged, and changes in individual preferences, wealth, and beliefs can be accommodated by revisions of individual portfolios without disturbing the productive decisions of the firm itself. Obviously, without transferable shares the potential for shareholder conflicts over investment and dividend policy could kill the corporation.

The advantage of limited liability is not so obvious: alienability of the firm's shares depends on the presence of limited liability (WOODWARD [1985]). Imagine the contrary. If each shareholder had extended liability, the liability of each shareholder and the terms on which credit is extended to the firm will depend on the wealth of each shareholder. Shareholders and creditors both would want information about the shareholder's ability to meet firm commitments. All would want to restrict transferability in order to protect their own position. Limiting liability transfers risks to the creditors (who are of course compensated for bearing it) and makes the identity of the individual shareholders irrelevant. It also eliminates any desire for less than fully transferable shares.

Because limiting liability transfers some risk from equity holders to creditors, and this risk is less effectively controlled by creditors than stockholders, there are some costs associated with limited liability, essentially the same in nature as the costs associated with dept, generally speaking, when the assets of shareholders are finite. But for the multi-shareholder firm, the costs are more than outweighed by the flexibility and fungibility that they buy. Although markets are not the prevailing institution for allocating the individual assets that comprise the firm, the pool of assets and their associated value do exploit "market" economies of scale (the more identical (fungible) the claims, the cheaper the market operates) by being financed with transferable shares.

Another source of tension among shareholders has to do with who is minding the store. Diffusion of stock ownership is often thought to debilitate the corporation because individual stockholders have little incentive to monitor corporate activity. This reasoning confounds relative shares with absolute amounts of wealth. The absolute amount, not the percentage share is pertinent in motivation. Whether a million dollar investment is 100% of an enterprise or is only 5%, it is still a million dollars at stake. If any problem arises as a result of each shareholder having a small relative stake, it is likely the higher costs of influencing a decision to be made by many shareholders. But even in the largest companies the Board of Directors is no larger than for much smaller companies. We see no logical implication from diffusing itself to reduced effectiveness of the Board of Director's monitoring of the activities of the corporation.

3.4.2 Tension Between Managers and Stockholders

Larger enterprises typically require extensive administrative organization. This potentially increases the principal-agent, moral hazard problem. One way to help maintain a congruence of interests is to correlate the agent's (manager's) wealth with that of stockholders. Aside from the standard competitive process that adjusts managers' wages, managers can be granted options for future purchases of stock, or they can be, and often are, major stockholders in the firm (DEMSETZ and LEHN [1985]).

Another way managers can be compensated is by trading the firm's stock on inside information. If a corporation allows insiders to trade on any and all information, outsiders, aware that insiders are trading, and that when they buy or sell they may be buying from or selling to a better informed party, would adjust accordingly what they were willing to pay for the stock, still earning a rate of return commensurate with the risk. Even if this is an inefficient way to compensate managers, the outside shareholders are not the losers. Instead the initial promoters would lose at the time of the initial offering because they get less for the stock. Even if they remain insiders, they have not gained, as their inside trading gains are reflected in the lower price they get for the initial offering. Beyond this consideration, subsequent insider-managers would be getting explicit salaries that are lower than the salaries of non-trading insiders by the amount of the inside-manager's anticipated gains from trading on inside information.

If insiders gain by trading on inside information, they gain at the expense of outsiders. But we argued above that the outsiders earn competitive returns. There is no inconsistency. The outsiders who pay the managers for their services in firms with insider trading are those who choose the inopportune moment to sell when insiders are buying, or to buy when insiders are selling. In firms with no insider trading, managers get salaries directly out of revenues. If managers who trade on inside information get smaller salaries, this leaves a higher profit stream for stockholders, which on average offsets the losses to the outsiders who traded at the wrong moment. All this amounts to a method of payment of part of the salary of managers by a sort of random tax on the market value of the stock, levied on a randomly selected group of the stockholders – those who happened to be trading.

Another implication of the presence of trading insiders and competitive markets is that stockholders who rarely sell, but instead buy and hold, will get a higher than average yield on their holdings, but only in return for less liquidity. It predicts that in firms where there is a larger than average amount of insider trading, there should be a smaller than average amount of outsider trading, which appears to be the case (SEYHUN [1986]). It also suggests that in firms where insider trading is significant, the gross returns to the stock (insiders plus outsiders) will appear to be "too high" for the risk level. In fact, the outsiders are earning competitive returns and the insiders superior returns, and the average exceeds that we would predict simply on the basis of risk. If small corporations have more insider trading, as appears to be true, their stocks should appear to have abnormally high returns, which also appears to be true. We believe that the "small firm" effect, identified in the literature on the asset pricing model as an anomaly, is the "insider trading" effect (WOODWARD [1986]), arising because of the predominance of concentrated ownership, and consequently trading by insiders, in smaller firms.

This argument that shareholders are on average not exploited by insider trading does not answer the question as to whether the best use of a manager's time is managing the firm's assets or his own portfolio. But we see no reason why market forces would not provide an efficient outcome if firms were left to decide for themselves whether or not managers should be allowed to trade on inside information.

A recent event which focused attention on a different kind of inequality among shareholders is a Delaware Chancery court decision in Unocal vs. Mesa permitting Unocal directors to redistribute the firm's wealth among stockholders in a non-pro-rata per share fashion. Mesa had made a tender offer for Unocal, and acquired a sizeable fraction of Unocal's stock. The tender offer was vigorously contested by Unocal. Unocal's Board of Directors in the end fought off the tender offer by an unusual means. Unocal made a tender offer for its own stock at an above market price, but only to the shareholders *other than* Mesa. Mesa sued Unocal and lost.

Obviously, conflicts of interest arise within a Board of Directors whenever the members do not all represent anonymously alienable, fungible interests of principals, as for example stockholders who have no interest in the corporation other than their shared stock value. Even salaried managers have interests based on more than just the common stock value. This conflict among stockholders, who otherwise would have fungible, alienable interests in the firm-specific resources, creates difficulties. This is sensitively heeded in closely held corporations where managers and others whose interests in the corporation depend on more than just the stock value.

The Delaware Court did not merely refuse to second-guess a Board's "rational business judgement"; instead it permitted the Board to unilaterally alter the contract among the corporate Board's principals (the stockholders). The Court failed to heed the distinction between (a) the wealth redistribution or contract alteration among agents' principals, performed by the agent, not the principals, and (b) the right to choose among alternative actions intended to enhance the corporate wealth in which all the stockholders share (or thought they shared). The Unocal–Mesa issue was not one of a challenge to the wisdom or business judgment of the agents. Rather it was whether altering the contractual relationship among the principals and redistributing the corporate wealth among stockholders in ways other than permitted in the corporate charter fell within the conception of a "rational business purpose" and within the powers of the agents.

Since the initial draft of this paper, the United States Securities and Exchange Comission has ruled that discriminatory tender offers of the sort Unocal made are illegal. We believe that this is likely an efficient ruling, and had it not been made, the evolution of the firm would have gone in the direction of corporate charters that would have protected minority shareholders such as Mesa.

3.4.3 Tension Between Creditors and Stockholders

Corporations do not finance their entire operations solely with equity. Current liabilities for wages, purchase orders, and taxes are common forms of debt financing. Firms borrow from banks and issue bonds. Are potential shareholders less optimistic than current shareholders, who instead of paying for expensive equity from pessimistic shareholders offer creditors guarantees for debt financing? If so, the explanation for differing debt/equity ratios across firm should look to factors influencing the level of disagreement among shareholders. We have found little that is illuminating in the optimism/pessimism theory of corporate debt.

Another possibility is that the convention of treating interest paid on debt as a deductible expense of the corporation provides a powerful incentive to move income outside the firm in the form of interest to avoid paying corporate income tax on it. Against this force is the cost of creditor-equity holder conflicts and equity malincentives. Once indebted, the equity holders do not bear the full costs of losses on projects. Their incentive is to take bigger risks, because the bond holders bear part of the downside cost, but the equity holders get all of the upside gains. Bond holders are fully aware of this incentive, and design contracts between themselves and equity holders to control it. But the contracts are not perfect. Bond holders charge equity for the uncontrollable losses imposed on them. So in choosing debt financing, equity holders are trading off the moral hazard costs of debt against the tax advantages.

This view of debt would lead us to look to the degree of plasticity and monitoring costs of a firm's assets for an explanation of the debt-equity ratio.

Compare the opportunities for debt financing a drug company vs. a public utility. Bond holders, in making their debt agreements, seek protection from ex post contractual exploitation (SMITH and WARNER [1979]). Company has a much wider range of legitimate initial choices of research direction and choice than does the public utility. The drug company's activities are more difficult to monitor. This implies that it will be difficult for the debt holders to write a contract with the equity holders to keep the equity holders from exploiting the bond holders. The drug company will find debt expensive. But with the public utility, the assets are cheaper to monitor and assess, and consequently the public will find debt inexpensive.

We emphasize that it is not the riskiness of the assets that are debt financed that matters, but their plasticity – the degree to which the equity holders can exploit the bond holders ex post by altering the asset outcomes. We predict that firms with more plastic assets will have lower debt ratios than will firms with less plastic assets. Our earlier example, the oil well, serves well the point that the issue is not risk. The oil well is very implastic but very risky; but we predict that oil recovery will be a highly debt financed business because it is implastic and easy to monitor.

Another theory of debt is that it serves as a device to allay stockholder/ manager conflicts – monitoring done by bond holders aids equity holders in evaluation the decisions of managers. This argument implies that firms with more plastic assets, i.e., those more difficult to monitor, will issue bonds in order to enlist the bond holders to help monitor management. The "enlist the bond holders" theory thus stands in direct contrast to the "plasticity" theory of firm indebtedness. Unless there is an important difference between assets that are vulnerable to shareholder/manager conflicts of interest vs. those vulnerable to shareholder/creditor conflicts of interest, and we are not convinced there is, we strongly doubt that the monitoring of managers provided by debt holders is a powerful force on the debt/equity ratio.

Yet another possibility is that debt serves as a device to constrain managers from doing anything with the firm's income but pay it to security holders (JENSEN [1986]). For example, in a firm with exceptionally large cash flows of quasi-rents or profits managers could invest the proceeds toward self-aggrandizing but not profitable investments. If instead the firm is committed to large interest and debt repayments, these cash flows would have to be channeled to outsiders and to the rest of the market.

The "commit the quasi-rent" view combines the issues of moral hazard and vulnerability to holdup. A firm with quasi-rents is vulnerable to holdup. We would imagine also that in industries with large sunk costs, and consequently quasi-rents, the assets are also often fairly implastic, as in heavy manufacturing. The "commit the quasi-rent" view argues that quasi-rents call for some kind of mechanism to commit the firm to disburse its rents, but does not specify to whom. The plasticity view argues that implastic assets are cheap to finance with debt. Then the question becomes: who is the likely suspect for the holdup?

IPPOLITO [1985] argues that the presence of unions in heavy manufacturing is explained by the quasi-rents that arise in any economic endeavor with significant sunk costs, and the unions are simply trying to expropriate the quasi-rent. Firms retaliate not with just debt financing, but also by making the union the debt holder by underfunding pension plans.

But the union expropriating the quasi-rent and the managers expropriating the quasi-rent are very different matters. It is not because the assets are difficult to monitor that unions are able to raise wages. They are simply exercising market power through a cartel. But when managers expropriate a quasi-rent by making self-aggrandizing investments, the implication is that the shareholders are unable to judge whether the investments made by the managers are ex ante profitable or not. So if the problem is that shareholders are unable to judge managers' productivity, why try to solve the problem by adding more security holders and their monitoring problems, rather than make the managers stockholders to induce them to act like stockholders? The presence of higher monitoring costs on which this argument seems to depend appears inconsistent with a debt-financing solution given the monitoring problems created by debt financing.

Plasticity of resources also influences whether assets used by the firm will be rented (or leased) vs. owned. Renting an asset and debt financing an asset have important similarities. The renter or borrower obtains an upside value residual, while the creditor bears the downside prospects. Exogenous risks not affected by the behavior of the rentor/debtor are compensable through the rent as they are through debt. But the difficulty of detecting wear and tear, and diversion of use, constrain the degree of both renting and debt financing. These are simply aspects of plasticity. Whenever resources tend to be plastic, and moral hazard is severe, users will tend to be owners, not renters, and tend to finance with equity, not debt.

We acknowledge that we have no good measure of plasticity. "Firm specific risk" (the residual variance left after market and industry correlated variance is eliminated) has been used and shown to be related to debt financing and also to concentrated holdings of stock by managers. It may well be related to plasticity, but since we argue that risk itself is not the issue, we are sure it is not a perfect measure. Nonetheless, some indications of which circumstances will lead to high debt ratios and which to low emerge. In a professional service firm, like law, architecture, medicine, engineering, or economic consulting, members may be so specific to certain customers that if they left the firm, remaining members and shareholders would hold an empty shell. To finance professional firms by outside equity would make the equity holder dependent on the unique insider members. But financing might be secured by the wealth of the "unique" resources. For the same reason, members will be faced with the problem of preventing some unique members from leaving and starting new firms after acquiring customer contacts and reputation while working as a member. One precautionary device is to defer compensation to members until substantially later, even until retirement. But professional firms remain "black boxes" in that their internal contractual and control systems are yet to be analyzed and understood.

4. Contractual Arrangements and Market Conventions

Preceding sections have emphasized internal arrangements germane to corporate charters. But the potential for holdup and morally hazardous exploitation also has resulted in the evolution of some contractual and conventional arrangements of a more general, informal scope. These arrangements facilitate the advantages of intra- and inter-firm specificity.

4.1 Explicitly Rigid and Posted Prices

Posted prices, announced publicly and maintained until publicly revised, are prices at which the posting party will transact any amount. All parties obtain the same price; the price to a particular party could not be changed while all others were getting better prices. The posting and stability of the price indicates reliability as a non-opportunistic buyer (seller) to all dependent sellers (buyers). An implication is that posted prices that are stable should be more commonly present where there is "dependency", i.e., reliance investments.

An example is the oil gathering pipelines in California, where the pipeline gathering system is unique to several oil well owners relying on the pipeline to transport oil to the refiners. The pipelines could opportunistically drop price under the guise of a temporarily reduced market demand, except that assurance against such behavior is provided by the stable posted price to all oil producers. Posted prices are present also in tuna and salmon fishing, where the fishing boats are reliant on a unique buyer-processor. Similarly, they, or a fixed price guarantee, occur in many agricultural products where farmers plant crops relying on a unique buyer-processor.

Note all these situations arise where the classical economies of scale in processing (and pipelines) are large and where the costs of alternative suppliers of the same services are also large. Competition "for the market" rather than "in the market" determines the level of price, and the device which assures the multiple customers that they are not being monopolistically exploited in the posted price. Evidently, they are better able to determine whether the posted price is competitive than they would be to determine the competitiveness of varying prices.

"Most favored nation" clauses differ from posted prices in that the terms include more than prices. They are commitments made by a unique party to dependent parties and should be observed where such dependence exists. Where the dependent parties' products are not homogeneous, price protection alone would not be sufficient to protect from quality alterations. An "advance notice" clause notifies the buyer of future price changes. This, too shields the buyer from opportunistic price changes. The buyer is given time to seek new sources requiring less costly adjustment.

"Take or pay" clauses commit a buyer to taking a specified amount in the future. This protects a seller from a unique buyer who might strategically reduce the amount taken, for which the seller has geared the facilities, in order to force a lower price to expropriate composite quasi-rents of the seller. This provision is found in gas and oil pipeline contracts as a commitment by the buyer to a seller-producer, who is dependent on a unique buyer's transport facilities.

4.2 Implicitly Rigid Prices

Opportunistic price changes (intended to effect a holdup) are not clearly or cheaply distinguishable from price changes to which the parties would have agreed had the demand and supply environment been mutually foreseen. Variations in amount demanded are sometimes temporary and sometimes permanent. Should price be revised instantly to make the amount demanded equal the monetary amount supplied, i.e., instantaneously and continuously clear the market? Variations in such prices would tend to be dampened if there were buyers and sellers who believed that some of the variations were transient values from a stable underlying distribution, and they had sufficiently low storage or waiting costs to exploit the variation and stabilize the price.

However, the notion of a quickly equilibrating market price is baffling save in a very few markets. Imagine an employer and employee. Will they renegotiate price every hour, or with every perceived change in circumstances? If the employee were a waiter in a restaurant, would the waiter's wage be renegotiated with every new customer? Would it be renegotiated to virtually zero when no customers were present, and then back to a high level that would extract the entire customer value when a queue appeared? Obviously, prices and wages do not vary at every moment at which there is a change in the monetary demand or supply, as with the unimaginable waiter. But what is the right interval for renegotiation or change of price? The usual answer, "as soon as demand or supply changes", is uninformative.

A reason for wage and price "inflexibility" is protection of the expropriable composite quasi-rent of dependent resources. As stated earlier, to induce the coalition-dependent investment in the first place, the investor demands protection against the unique resource's subsequent attempts to expropriate that dependent quasi-rent. However, the investor is prepared – indeed desires – to have future revisions that both parties would have agreed to before the investment could they have foreseen that future change, or to which they would have subsequently agreed if the true state of demand and supply were readily known. But it is very difficult to later agree about what really is the current situation, because at the later time a false allegation could be made by the unique party as a subterfuge to capture some expropriable composite quasi-rent.

One protective device is to hold price or terms of trade constant until both parties agree that the new price is one they would have agreed upon if they could have foreseen the new demand and supply conditions prior to their investments. This underlies what the law calls "unconscionable" or "unfair" prices. The parties forestall costly expropriative behavior. The waiter/restaurant case is identical to that of laborers who could refuse to pick a tomato crop at the last minute unless the farmer paid them the entire value of the crop. (This is a reason why farmers resist labor unions and opt for "family" labor instead.) If people were to renegotiate continuously and revise prices at every moment, the holdup possibilities would be severe in many, but not all, situations. If there were many alternative suppliers or buyers instantly available without sacrifice of composite quasi-rents, then quick price changes would be likely, as in markets like the stock market. But between an employee and an employer, momentary or even daily or weekly renegotiation would be susceptible to the disease of "holdups", "expropriation of composite quasi-rents", "unconscionability", "opportunism", etc.

Typically, prices are not varied in real emergency situations to exploit victims for the same reason prices are not continuously renegotiated in routine employment and rental situations. It helps forestall expropriative action and avoids expensive precautionary actions. The principle has wide applicability. For example, imagine a remote highway repair shop which might charge full dependent value (or full consumer surplus) for repairs to a stranded motorist. If that dependent value were to be expropriated in the event of a breakdown, travellers would take precautionary action to reduce breakdown prospects. These precautionary actions can be expensive and might even forestall travel through that region. A sense of "moral outrage" at people who charge an extractive, "exorbitant" price serves the social and economic function of deterring such behavior and thereby reduces dependence on more expensive means of avoiding breakdowns, or choosing not to travel at all. The equilibrium is a delicate one, however, and once such social capital is destroyed by a series of cheats it is not easily replaced (GOLDBERG [1986]). The degree to which "moral outrage" is an efficient device for controlling socially costly behavior merits study.

Similarly, when a disaster isolates a community, the local grocer may deplete remaining inventory at the usual "competitive" price, despite the sudden increased demand. And the customers will tend to share resources. This price stability and sharing avoids the precautionary (costly) holding of larger than optimal inventories (hoarding) solely to avoid such interpersonal wealth transfers. Assurance against dependent value extraction is desired, i.e., people want prevailing prices be those that would have been negotiated in advance earlier had a binding contract been feasible.

4.3 Layoffs and Unemployment Spells

Holdup threats are not effective against an independent, non-reliant resource. So the offers and prices to general resources should respond more readily to momentary transient observed market demands. Homogeneous and independent resource services will have prices that change more quickly and in smaller amounts in response to observed fluctuations, because neither party faces potential expropriative holdups. However, the more firm-dependent resources are exposed to this threat. They seek assurance that the unique resource owners will not alter their behavior under a guise of a falsely alleged decline in the equilibrium price. As a result, price will not respond to every perceived momentary change, and more importantly, will not respond even at the moment of a change in the underlying demand or supply conditions, because those changes are initially undetectable from the background noise. It takes more reliable information to persuade both parties to adjust.

The more firm-dependent resources will face more rigid prices and more spells of unemployment, where rigidity is used as a means of reducing holdups. The unemployment is a side effect of the purpose of price rigidity – the prevention of holdups hidden under the allegation of a change in equilibrium conditions, and is the price paid when mutually dependent resources protect themselves from exploitation. Long-term contracts or conventions, which restrain future behavior and terms of trade, are as essential and characteristic of the "firm" as is teamwork. The price rigidity does not imply market power on either side, as once both parties agree that market conditions have changed, price will change.

An explanation for "layoffs" has been that it is a device to allay the threat of holdup (HALL and LILIEN [1983]). To convince employees that an employer's proposal to reduce the work force is a response to decreased demand, rather than being an attempt at a holdup, the employer suspends operations, which is more costly if demand has not fallen. If demand has really decreased, a shutdown is more economical than a wage cut, because the implied required wage to justify continued operations would be lower than options believed available to employees elsewhere. The temptation to suggest that unemployment cannot be understood until an adequate theory of the firm has been worked out is too powerful to resist. Without an explanation of why and how firms' constituents contract with one another, it seems unlikely that unemployment, layoffs, and wage and price behavior can be explained.

4.4 Labor Unions

Labor unions, whether company or industry, can, by collective action, protect employees' firm-dependent values. Employees who have made their own investments in firm-specific skills in response to employer promises, or who have earned rights to future insurance and retirement benefits, want to monitor the employer's performance and restrain the employer from expropriating those firm specific rewards. This is a major defense of unions, and if this were their only function, firms would not object to them. After all, an employer who borrows from a bank does not oppose monitoring by the bank, as the monitoring makes the loan cheaper. Despite this beneficial effect of organized employees, firms fear the reverse risk of employees expropriating employers quasi-rents (IPPOLITO [1985]).

4.5 First Refusals

A right of first refusal prevents a threat to sell a unique, relied-upon resource to some other user, a threat made solely to extract some of the composite quasi-rent. If the optioned resource really had a new, higher value alternative, then it could move for reasons unrelated to any threat of expropriative behavior. But it might threaten to leave, without really having a higher valued alternative. The right of refusal permits matching a bona-fide offer, and therefore, a threat to sell or remove services unless paid more to match a false outside alternative would not be effective. First refusal does not prevent a unique resource from simply terminating services, even without selling to someone else. Therefore, the optioned item should be one from which the service flow to the current user is not easily controllable by its owner. Nor is the option a device to transfer the risk of market value changes. Instead, the possibility of expropriative action by the unique resource is suppressed by a first refusal option.

5. The Variety of the Firm

5.1 Franchises

Some products are retailed under a common trade name by franchises, each of which is owned by a different party. Franchises exploit the informational economies of scale from the use of a national brand name, but do not exploit the market economies of scale that could result from common ownership with publicly traded shares. McDonald's, for example, has equity traded on the New York Stock Exchange, and presumably could finance all of its hamburger stands with capital raised there, giving financiers the benefits of liquidity and diversification. But it chooses instead to place the risk for each individual unit on the residual claimant/managers of each unit. Evidently the productive outcomes from this arrangement are sufficiently superior to overcome the benefits of more marketable claims.

The behavior of each franchisee determines the quality of its product and therefore affects not only its own revenue, but also the revenue of the fellow franchisees because of the shared brand name. A retailer-franchisee could, by providing inferior service, reduce its costs for a short-lived gain, but harm the reputation and reduce demand for the product sold under the common trade name. Because of the interdependence, common ownership of the franchisor and franchisee would help protect interdependent value.

9*

But the employer-employee relationship does not always provide the most appropriate incentives, especially where operations are not well standardized and rely on discretion. We would expect, for example, that gourmet restaurants (slow food, in contrast to fast food) would not be organized as national chains, because the discretion necessary is not easily monitored and standardized into repetitive management activities. Franchised operations are intermediate between the individual gourmet restaurant and the national chain of restaurants jointly owned. Apparently the franchises are sufficiently monitorable for the parent company to be able to make decisions whether the franchise should continue or be terminated on an intermittent basis, but not sufficiently monitorable to hire a manager to operate the unit.

5.2 Resale Price Maintenance

Some manufacturers depend on a network of retailers to provide services to create and maintain the value of the manufacturer's product and shared reputation for reliability of a known quality. When the provision of these services is difficult to monitor, producers can elicit the provision of the services anyway by locking in a differential between wholesale and retail price by setting wholesale price and also "maintaining" (setting) retail price. Retailers will compete away any rent in the differential by providing the services consumers and the producer desire. If retailers who cheat (sell at prices lower than the maintained resale price – a behavior easier to detect than service provision) are penalized by termination, cheating is deterred, services are provided, and the producer and consumers are better off than if resale prices were not maintained. Without resale price maintenance, retailers would cheat on service provision to the point where no services were provided, and lower prices to the point where no services were paid for, but both customers and the producer would be worse off.

5.3 Joint Ventures

Joint ventures are formed where two usually pre-existing "firms" share in investments on which both will be interreliant. The rationale for joint venture is the interreliance of a unique resource or end product. The resource or product is likely research, invention, information, or anything that has both 1) significant economies of scale (like research or a pipeline) and 2) services on which both parties will rely. A joint venture is an efficient organizational device because it avoids duplication of effort (same pipeline built twice, or same research done twice) and avoids the opportunity for expropriation which would result if only one party owned the resource and sold its services to the other.

5.4 Mutually Owned Teams

A "mutual" organization is one in which the equity holders and the customers are the same individuals. Mutual organization is common in banks, (some are organized with depositors as owners, and some with borrowers as owners) insurance companies, nursing homes, country clubs, and some other social clubs. Mutuality enables the members to (a) prevent outside equity holders from expropriating value by lowering the quality of service, and (b) preserve for incumbents any gains from admitting new members. Mutuals do not permit anonymous alienability of members' ownership interest. A "mutual" member can sell ownership only be ceasing to be a consumer of the group's services, and in some organizations, such as country clubs, can transfer rights to membership only with the permission of the other members.

As Adam Smith so persuasively argued, in most productive activity the profit motive successfully aligns the interests of producers and consumers. In what kinds of economic activity is the additional inducement for this alignment provided by making the consumers explicitly also owners called for? Calling upon our developing theme, it is called for in those cases where information is expensive, expropriation is possible, and long-term relations between producers and consumers prevail, in particular in those cases where the fellow consumers influence the quality of what is produced.

For banks and insurance companies, mutuality removes the incentives for equity holders to take risks which would impair without compensation the security of an insurance fund or deposit, and qualifications for membership influence the quality of the product purchased. For example, one of the earliest (1690s) mutual insurance companies sold life insurance only for wives of clergymen, assuring that all members of the pool would have similar lifestyles (although they surely did not use this term). Alternative mechanisms for solving this same problem are a) reputation acquisition, and b) regulation. The force opposing mutuality in banks and insurance companies is that mutuality constraints the opportunities for diversification of risk by requiring the customers to be equity holders. In organizations such as the US Farm Credit System, a mutual credit organization, it seems unlikely that in the absence of the government umbrella, farmers would want to bear the regional, and in principle diversifiable, components of agricultural lending risk.

For social organizations, such as nursing homes and country clubs, the forces for mutuality are even more powerful. The mutual members themselves are the interdependent resources who interact and create the mutual's service and value. Increasing the number of members can affect each incumbent's realized social satisfaction and the level of congestion. The difference here is that the members are inputs to, not just buyers of, a product. The membership acting in consortium will maximize the average net yield per member. New members will often be charged more than their pro rata share of the club's capital facilities, and thereby incumbents will capture the value of admitting new members, and incumbents will admit new members to the point where they benefit despite increased congestion.

Social clubs are owned by members because the "social value quasi-rent" would be vulnerable to expropriation if it were owned by outsiders. An independent owner could admit new members without compensating existing members for the reduction in average quality. Quality is not just a matter of congestion. If it were, competition among clubs would result in the optimal level of congestion. This would imply that members could switch clubs at no cost. But the members create and obtain interpersonal social services; they themselves produce what the club is providing. Replacement of one club member with another not known to the rest of the group will result in lower quality to the remaining members. The members have "specific capital" in one another, and that specific capital could be expropriated by an independent owner. Mutual ownership tends to preserve the interspecific value for members.

This view of country club ownership bears on the general question of social relations. If people could be costlessly interchanged in social relationships, no expropriable social value would exist, just as in firms where employees have perfect substitutes. But neither firms nor social groups are costlessly created and altered. Social associates, such as marriage partners, result in high specific interpersonal dependence. Why people are more attentive to social associates than to those who simply eat in the same restaurants or worship in the same churches is not easy to explain. We leave unanswered the question of why friendships are more costly and long-lived than relations with mere fellow consumers and acolytes. What is there about "friendships" that requires interpersonal dependence and hence, results in expropriable composite quasi-rents?

6. Conclusion

The variety of contracts used to organize cooperative activity involving dependency reveals that the standard conception of the firm is too narrow. Teamwork is widespread and spans more than ordinary production; it extends, for example, to marriage, engagements, "live-ins", social clubs, churches, and to athletic leagues and associations. Questions like "Is the National Football League a firm or is it 24 separate firms?" and "Is McDonald's one large firm or hundreds of firms?" and "Is the National Collegiate Athletic Association a firm, a cartel, a collusion, a coalition or a cabal?" are not useful questions. Instead, the useful questions are why the various types of contractual arrangements are made among coalitions of owners of resources, and what are the consequences.

Many economists, lawyers, and judges, despite the dictum that "substance, not form" counts, nevertheless answer a question regarding how an organization ought to be allowed to operate by deciding whether or not the organization "is" a "firm". In litigation involving the national Football League a judge declared the league to be 24 different firms, and therefore they were colluding. If, however, the league were declared a joint venture, or a single firm with franchises, the applicable legal rules would have been very different. In that proceeding at no time was it ever made evident what was the criterion for identifying or defining "a firm", let alone on what criteria the arrangement, whatever it be called, should be treated this way or that way.

The criterion surely must recognize the nature of and reason for the restraints of long-term contract – the existence of investments by parties mutually dependent on one another's continued association. Because such dependency and contractual arrangements occur in a great variety of forms, it is of little value to try to define the firm as any particular one of them. More important is an examination of each form of group activity to understand the reasons for and consequences of organizational form, whether it be in social clubs, sporting groups, marriages, or production of goods and services for sale.

References

ALCHIAN, A. A. [1950], "Uncertainty, Evolution and Economic Theory", *Journal of Political Economy*, 58, 211–221.
– – [1984], "Specificity, Specialization, and Coalitions", *Zeitschrift für die gesamte Staatswissenschaft/Journal of Institutional and Theoretical Economics*, 140, 34–39.
– – and DEMSETZ, H. [1972], "Production, Information Costs, and Economic Organization", *American Economic Review*, 62, 777–795.
COASE, R. H. [1937], "The Nature of the Firm", *Economica N.S.*, 4, 386–405.
DEMSETZ, H. and LEHN, K. [1985], The Structure of Corporate Ownership: Causes and Consequences", *Journal of Political Economy*, 93, 1155–1177.
GOLDBERG, V. [1976], "Toward an Expanded Economic Theory of Contracts" *Journal of Economic Issues*, 10, 45–61.
– – [1986], "Fishing and Selling", *Journal of Legal Studies*, 15, 173–180.
HALL, R. E. and LILIEN, D. M. [1979], "Efficient Wage Bargains Under Uncertain Demand and Supply", *American Economic Review*, 69, 868–879.
IPPOLITO, R. A. [1985], "The Economic Function of Underfunded Pension Plans", *Journal of Law and Economics*, 28, 611–652.
JENSEN, M. and MECKLING, W. [1976], "Theory of the Firm: Managerial Behavior, Agency Costs, and Ownership Structure", *Journal of Financial Economics*, 3, 305–360
JENSEN, M. [1986] "The Takeover Controversy: Analysis and Evidence", Working Paper No. MERC 86-01.
KLEIN, B., CRAWFORD, R. A., and ALCHIAN, A. A. [1978], "Vertical Integration, Appropriable Rents, and the Competitive Contracting Process", *Journal of Law and Economics*, 21, 297–326.
MARSHALL, A. [1948], *Principles of Economics*, (8th ed.), New York.
SEYHUN, N. [1986], "Insiders Profits, Costs of Trading, and Market Efficiency", *Journal of Financial Economics*, forthcoming.
SMITH, C. and WARNER, J. [1979], "On Financial Contracting: An Analysis of Bond Covenants", *Journal of Financial Economics*, 7, 111–161.
WILLIAMSON, O. [1983], "Credible Commitments: Using Hostages to Support Exchange", *American Economic Review*, 73, 519–540.
– – [1985] *The Economic Institutions of Capitalism*, New York.

WOODWARD, S. [1985], "The Economics of Limited Liability", *Zeitschrift für die gesamte Staatswissenschaft/Journal of Institutional and Theoretical Economics*, 141, 601–611.
–– [1986], "Insider Trading and the Small Firm Effect, Working paper.

Armen A. Alchian
Professor of Economics
UCLA
Los Angeles, CA 90024
U.S.A.

Susan Woodward
Council of Economic Advisers
Washington, DC 20500
U.S.A.

[10]

SOME ECONOMICS OF PROPERTY RIGHTS

by Armen A. Alchian (*)

1. *Scarcity, Competition and Property.*

In *every* society, conficts of interest among the members of that society must be resolved. The process by which that resolution (not elimination!) occurs is known as *competition*. Since, by definition, there is no way to eliminate competition, the relevant question is what kind of competition shall be used in the resolution of the conflicts of interest. In more dramatic words designed to arouse emotional interest, « What forms of discrimination among the members of that society shall be employed in deciding to what extent each person is able to achieve various levels of his goals »? Discrimination, competition, and scarcity are three inseparable concepts.

2. *Constraints.*

That list of concepts can be expanded—scarcity, competition, discrimination, constraints, property. In other words, constraints exist that prevent our individually achieving a level of want-fulfilment beyond which none of us wants more. In still other words, these constraints, even though imposed by nature, include also the constraints imposed by other people who because they achieve certain levels of want fulfilment leave other people with lower levels. (I do not mean that *all* activities that enable one person to have a greater level of goal fulfilment will also necessarily mean less for someone else; we know that some forms of exchange permit joint increases. But we also know that cooperative action is possible, and also that competitive action is also present). If we concentrate attention on constraints and classes of permissible action we find ourselves studying the *property* aspect of behavior.

Economists are, I think, too prone to examine exchange as a cooperative act whereby the buyer and seller each act in an effort to reach a more desired position. Yet I find it more interesting (now that I understand the cooperative aspect of exchange) to examine the competitive, or property aspect of exhange. The act of exchange is a means whereby the buyer is able to compete against other claimants for the goods being obtained from the seller. The kinds of offers, forms of competition and behavior that the members of society can employ in an endeavour to get more of the goods that would otherwise go to other people, is brought more into the focus of attention. More directly, the forms and kinds of property rights sanctioned in a society define or

(*) Department of Economics, University of California.

identify the kinds of competition, discrimination or behavior characteristic of that society.

Yet if we look at the « fields » of economics, say as presented by the American Economic Association's classification of areas of interest or specialization, we find no mention of the word « property ». Either we can infer that the profession is so obviously aware of the pervasiveness of the effects of various forms of property rights that property rights can not sensibly be regarded as merely a subfield; or else we can infer that economists have forgotten about the possibility of subjective rigorous systematic coherent analysis of the various forms of property rights. My conviction is that the latter inference is the more valid one. As evidence I cite that the only systematic analysis of choice among « goods » postulates utility maximization subject to a budget or *wealth* constraint, wherein the constraint is almost invariably a *private* property type of wealth constraint.

3. *Property Rights.*

If, in what follows, I talk as if the property rights were enforced by formal state police power, let me here emphasize that such an interpretation, regardless of what I may later say, is gross error. It seems to be a fact that individuals will not stand by idly while some other person's property is stolen. It seems to be a fact that *private* property rights are rights not merely because the state formally makes them so but because individuals want such rights to be enforced, at least for a vast, overwhelming majority of people. And yet if I recognize the number of socialist states, I must admit to some confusion (I appeal for edification).

The rights of individuals to the use of resources (i.e., property rights) in any society are to be construed as supported by the force of etiquette, social custom, ostracism, and formal legally enacted laws supported by the states' power of violence or punishment. Many of the constraints on the use of what we call private property involves the force of etiquette and social ostracism. The level of noise, the kind of clothes we wear, our intrusion on other people's privacy are restricted not merely by laws backed by the police force, but by social acceptance, reciprocity and voluntary social ostracism for violators of accepted codes of conduct. The use of arabic numbers rather than roman, the use of certain types of clothing, or styles of speech and address, of printing from left to right and top to bottom, rather than the reverse, or keeping our garden up with Jones', all are subject to the force of social opprobrium. No laws require such behavior. Yet each of us (or nearly every one of us) will punish in one way or another those who violate theses rules. Surely it is not the important rules that are left to the formal state power of enactment and compulsion. Obviously there is heated dispute as to which forms of behavior should be « enforced » by social voluntary ostracism and which by formal state police action.

By a system of property rights I mean a method of assigning to particular individuals the « authority » to select, for specific goods, any use from a non-prohibited class of uses. As suggested in the preceding remarks the concepts of « authority » and of « non-prohibited » relies on some concept of enforcement or inducement to respect the assignment and scope of prohibited choice. A property right for me means some protection against other people's choosing against my will one of the uses of resources, said to be « mine ».

Often the idea or scope or *private* property rights is expressed as an assignment of exclusive authority to some individual to choose any use of the goods deemed to be his private property. In other words the « owners », who are assigned the right to make the choice, have an unrestricted right to the choice of use of specified goods. Notice, that we did not add— « so long as the rights of other people are similarly respected ». That clause is redundant in strict logic. Private property owners can use their goods in any way they choose. If some of these chosen uses involve the use or destruction of other people's private property, it follows that the private property system is being violated, for this use has denied to other people the control of use over the goods classed as private property. To say I have private property rights is to say that no one else has the right to make the choice of use of that good (contained in the class of private property). This means that if I select a use for the goods said to be my private property, the selection must not affect the physical attributes of your goods. If I own some iron, I can make window frames or fence post out of it, but if I shove a piece of iron through « your » glass window I shall be denying you the right of choice of the physical attributes of your private property. However, if I convert the iron to a special kind of good that other people are willing to buy instead of buying what you are selling, you may find that the reduced exchange value of your goods imposes a greater loss of exchange power (wealth) than if I had simply broken your window.

Although private property rights protect private property from physical changes chosen by other people, no immunity is implied for the exchange value of one's property. Nor does it imply that my use of my goods, which may not in any way affect your goods, can not be a use that you find objectionable on moral or emotional grounds. If I use my resources to make lewd pictures for my own use or for exchange with other people, you may find your « utility » much affected. You may be more upset, annoyed, distressed, or hurt by my action than if I had broken your window or stolen some of your wealth.

Private property, as I understand it, does *not* imply that a person may use his property in any may he sees fit so long as no one else is « hurt ». Instead, it seems to mean the right to use goods (or to transfer that right) in any way the owner wishes so long as the physical attributes or uses of all other people's private property is unaffected. And that leaves plenty of room for disturbance and alienation of affections of other people. If I open a restaurant near yours and win away business by my superior service, you are as hurt as if I had burned part of your building. If I open a restaurant and pour smells and smoke over your neighboring land then I have changed the physical attributes of your property; I have violated your private property rights—incidentally a form of violation very common in most societies.

But if the right for me to open a business were denied, this could, if it also were part of a system in which your rights to enter into various businesses were similarly restricted, be considered by you to be an undesirable restriction and one that did you more harm than would be encountered by you in a less restrictive environment.

In sum, it is only the choice over physical attributes that are constrained to owners, not the value-in-exchange effects nor the psychological, emotional effects that you may suffer in the knowledge that I am behaving in what you consider improper ways (short of changing the physical attributes of your property).

4. *Partitioning of Property Rights.*

Whether or not the preceding suggested definition is useful, we examine another issue. What are the effects of various partitionings of use rights? By this I refer to the fact that at the same time several people may each possess some portion of the rights to use the land. « A » may possess the right to grow wheat on it. « B » may possess the right to walk across it. « C » may possess the right to dump ashes and smoke on it. « D » may possess the right to fly an airplane over it. « E » may have the right to subject it to vibrations consequent to the use of some neighboring equipment. And each of these rights may be transferable. In sum, private property rights to various partitioned uses of the land are « owned » by different persons (1).

A lease or rental agreement partitions the rights so that the renter gets the right to make decisions about particular uses of the item by the « owner ». Normally the rights of the renter to decide where the furniture will be placed or when it will be sat on, etc., are not thought of as ownership rights, because they are so frequently allocated to the renter, and because the ultimate value consequence rests on the « owner ». However, our main point here is that the rights can be partitioned, divided and reallocated on a temporary—or even on a permanent basis, so that the « ownership » rights are partitioned among two or more persons. This kind of division is not necessarily a cross-sectional division with each owner now having equal parts of all the ownership rights. Instead it is a selective partitioning with all of some of the subrights staying with the « owner » and all of some other rights

---

(1) A different form of inter-personal sharing of rights is that in which all rights are possessed in common and jointly by the group, but the decision as to any use must be reached by the group. Rights to each different kind of use are not separated and possessed by different people. Instead the rights are commonly owned ; and the problem is in devising or specifying some choice process which will « declare » the decision of the « group » of joint owners.

being transferred temporarily at least to the « renter ». Even though this is called a rental or leasing agreement, it does contain transfers of some of the rights that are included in ownership. The fact that these partitionings of owner are temporary makes it easy to decide who is the « owner » in the conventional sense.

The partitioning of various types of rights to use, has been explored by Ronald Coase (2). He notes that what are commonly called nuisances and torts apply to just such situations in which rights are partitioned and the exercise of one owner's rights involves distress or nuisance for the owners of other rights. For example if a railroad spreads sparks and ignites fires in wheat field near the tracks, the wheat grower can pay the railroad to not spread sparks (if the law gives the railroad the right to spread such sparks). On the other hand if the right to decide about such land use is reserved to the farmer, the railroad could pay him for the right to drop sparks on the land (and save costs of spark screens, etc.). If there were no costs of *negotiating* such exchanges of rights and policing them, the initial partitioning of rights would not affect the way resources are used. (Of course, wealth would be redistributed in accord with the initial assignment of the partitioned rights).

But when we recognize that transaction costs do exist, it seems clear that the partitioned rights will be reaggregated into more convenients clusters of rights. If so, there should be an evolutionary force toward survival of larger clusters of certain types of rights in the sanctioned concept of property rights. But I am at a loss to formulate this more precisely, meaningfully and fruitfully. Except for rare studies like those of Glanvil Williams on the development of the laws of trespass and the two-volume work of Maitland and Pollack on the development of law (and property rights) in the 12th through 14th Centuries, I suspect our main alternative is to initiate studies of our own (3). For example, a study of the property rights in Ireland during the past three hundred years and of water law in the United States may (and I believe, will) enable us to discover more rigorous formulation of the laws of development of property law.

5. *Sharing Property Rights.*

At this point there is a temptation to start classifying various partitioning of property rights, e.g., private, public, bailments, easements, leases, licences, franchises, inheritances, etc. This temptation is easy to avoid, because the task is so difficult. Another temptation is to list the various ways in which property rights of owners—owership rights, as they are called hereafter—whatever they may be, can be shared among people as joint owners or as a partnership. Or cor-

---

(2) « The Problem of Social Costs », *Journal of Law and Economics*, 1960, pp. 1-5.
(3) FREDERICK POLLOCK and FREDERIC MAITLAND, *The History of English Law before the Time of Edward I*, 2nd ed. (Cambridge, 1952); GLANVILLE WILLIAMS, *Liability for Animals*, (Cambridge University Press, Cambridge, 1939).

porations can be created as a means of sharing property rights of owners among voluntary sharers. Or public property may amount to every-one having a share—although, as we shall see, I think this is not the crucial difference between public and private ownership.

The ability of individuals to enter into mutually agreable sharing of the rights they possess is evident from the tremendous variety of such arrangements, e.g., corporations, partnerships, non-profit corporations, licenses, bailments, non-voting common stock, trusts, agencies, employee-employer relationships, and marriages.

Should we be surprised that the government refuses to enforce some voluntary proposed sharing of legitimate property rights among owners? Presumably the « undesirable » effects justify the refusal to sanction some of the ownership sharing. For example, at one time, the state refused to enforce corporate ownership—even though all the members of the corporation entered voluntarily. Will it enforce every voluntary sharing and partitioning of ownership rights among individuals?

The variety of joint sharing of property and ownership rights is a testimony to man's ingenuity. But if one asked what the difference was between any two of them, say public and private ownership, he would find the answer not so easy. In one sense it is adequate to say that the public is the owner as contrasted to a private group. But that is not very helpful if one is interested in discovering what difference it makes for behavior and use of resources. Compare a privately owned golf course with a publicly owned course (or auditorium, bus service, water service, garbage collection, airport, school or even spaghetti factory). There are differences in the way they are operated; at least anyone who has ever compared them will think so. Why do these differences occur? Are the objectives different? Is it because the kind of people who operate one are different from those who operate the other? Is it because of the form of ownership?

I believe (on the basis of something more than casual observation) that behavior under each institution is different, not because the objectives sought by organizations under each form are different, but instead because, even with the same explicit organization goals, the costs-rewards system impinging on the employees and the « owners » of the organization are different. And I suspect that these differences are implied by economic theory, if the trouble is taken to apply the theory. Further, preliminary speculation suggests, for example, that the difference between a privately owned corporation with 1,000 owners and a state-owned entity in a democracy with 1,000 citizens is quite significant, because the 1,000 individuals are furthering their own individuals interests in each entity under two different systems of property rights i.e., the rewards-costs schedules differ.

6. *Private and Public Ownership.*

How do private and public ownership rights differ? To sharpen the issue, consider a small town theater owned by 1,000 corporate shareholders (each with one share) and an auditorium owned by the 1,000 residents as public property. This eliminates the difference of sharing and differences in the number of joint « owners ». Every activity conducted at one could, in principle, just as well be held at the other building. Assume also, the city auditorium is operated to make money, not to subsidize some group, and so is the private theater.

The public auditorium and the private theater both serve the public. It is not the case that the former is designed to provide a public service and the latter not. The privately owned theater will survive only if it can provide services that the public wants at the price asked. It is a source of public service, even though its purpose from the owners' point of view is to make money. But what about the publicly owned auditorium? Is its end that of public service or to make money for the public owners? Suppose its end is public service. This does not *require* that its means of action be any different than if its ends were profits to the owners—public or private. Furthermore assume in both cases the managers and employees were induced to take their jobs only because the salary enhances their own wealth or well-being. They take the jobs—not because they want to provide a public service or wealth for the owners; but instead because they want a better living for themselves. We can assume that those resident citizens who « own » the auditorium and voted for it did so because each felt it would make their own situation preferable—not because they wanted to benefit someone else as a charity device.

But there are differences, and we conjecture the proposition that the differences between public and private ownership arises from *the inability of a public owner to sell his share of public ownership* (and the ability to acquire a share without a purchase of the right). But let us be clear about this. We are not yet asserting that there are no other differences, nor that this difference has not been noticed before. Instead we are emphasizing the *unique* importance of this difference in the ownership rights.

We are not begging the issue by assuming away one general difference—the profit incentive or criterion. Both public and private property can seek profits. The desire to avoid or suppress the effects of the profit-making incentive is, however, often the reason society resorts to public ownership. However the objectives sought by public ownership cannot merely be announced to the managers or operators with expectation that exhortation will be either sufficient or necessary to achieve the objective. Since our general postulate is that people, as individuals, seek to increase their utility and that wealth is a source of utility, we cannot expect people to change their goals or desires. Instead, we rely upon changes in the rewards-costs structure to redirect their activities as they seek to increase their utility or level of satisfaction of their desires (4). And we shall try to show that many differences, that do

_____

(4) Friends of Adam Smith will recognize this as the major postulate of his *Wealth of Nations*, a postulate which seems to have served economists well when not forgotten.

exist between behavior in public and privately owned institutions, reflect this ownership difference—viz., the presence or the absence of the right to sell a share of ownership to someone else.

The difference can be put somewhat less euphemistically. Public ownership *must* be borne by all members of the public, and no member can divest himsel of that owneship. Ownership of public property is not voluntary; it is compulsory as long as one is a member of the public. To call something « compulsory » usually is a good start towards condemning it.

A person must move from one town to another to change his ownership in public property. In one sense it is not compulsory because it is not compulsory that one lives in a particular community. But so long as one does live in any community with public property he is a public owner and cannot divest himself of public ownership; but he can sell and shift private property ownership rights without also having to leave the community.

It is tempting to emphasize the possibility, under public ownership, of someone joining the community and thereby acquiring a share of public ownership, without payment to any of the existing owners. This dilution of a person's share of ownership is resumably absent in private ownership. In fact, a community could close off immigration; but public ownership would continue even if this dilution effect were an important problem. Furthemore, many corporations issue new shares without pre-emptive rights to former owners. Presumably this is done only when the receiver of the new shares pays the corporation something of at least equivalent value. And it is a safe assumption that the management deems the *quid pro quo* to have been worthwhile so far as present purposes are concerned. Still, it is sufficient that even if dilution of public ownership were eliminated by restriction of entry, the inability to sell one's share of public ownership remains a potent factor in the costs-reward system impinging on all members of the public and on the employees and administrators of the publicly owned institution.

7. *Some Implications of Transferability.*

To see what difference is made by the right to transfer ownership shares, suppose public ownership could be sold. It would be possible for me to sell to someone else my share in the publicly owned water, or bus or garbage, or parks, or school system. To separate out the fact that public ventures are usually run without the intent of making a profit, let us suppose that the water or bus system had been instructed to be as profitable as it could. Now that its ownership has become saleable, with capitalized profits or losses accruing to the owners, will incentives be any different?

The answer is suggested by two implications of the specialization of « ownership » which is similar to the familiar specialization of other kinds of skills or activities. The two derivative implications are: (1) concentration of rewards and costs *more* directly on each person responsible for them, and (2) comparative advantage effects of specialized applications of (a) knowledge in control and (b) of risk bearing.

7.1 *Degree of Dependency.* — The greater concentration of rewards and costs means simply that each person's wealth is more dependent upon his own activities. This is brought about as follows: the more he concentrates his wealth holding in particular resources, the more will his wealth respond to his own activities in those areas. Consider the following example: Suppose there are 100 people in a community, with 10 separate enterprises. Suppose that each person, by devoting one-tenth of his time to some one enterprise as an owner, could produce a saving or gain of $ 1,000. Since the individual is a 1/100 part owner he will acquire $ 10. Suppose, further, that he does this for each of the ten different enterprises, in each of which he owns 1/100 part. His total wealth gain will be $ 100, with the rest of the product, $ 9,900, going to the other 99 people. If the other 99 people act in the same way, he will get from their activities an increase of wealth of $ 990,000/ /100 = $ 9,900, which gives him a total of $ 10,000. This is exactly equal to his product most of which was spread over the other owners.

However, if everyone each owns 1/10 part of *one* enterprise only (which means that ownership has been reshuffled from pro rata equal shares in all enterprises to a concentration in one enterprise by each person, although with the same total number of enterprises), the individual will now be assumed to devote his whole time during one year to the one enterprise, so he again produces $ 10,000. (We assume that his productivity is proportional to the number of hours of work, and that it is the same for everyone. Other assumptions will change the arithmetic, but will not destroy the main principle being elaborated). Of this he gets $ 1,000. The remainder, $ 9,000 goes to the owners of the other 9/10 share. Like them, he too receives portions of the other owners' products, and if all are assumed to be exactly alike, then he gets from the other 9 joint owners of his enterprise $ 9,000 for a total of $ 10,000—precisely the same as in the preceding example. The difference is that now $ 1,000 of this is dependent upon his own activities whereas formerly only $ 100 was. Or more pertinently, the amount dependent upon the activities of other people is reduced from $ 9,900 to $ 9,000.

If we go to the extreme where the 10 enterprises are divided into 100, with each person as the sole owner of one enterprise, then all $ 10,000 of his year's wealth increase will depend upon his own activities. The first of these three examples corresponds to public ownership, the second to corporate joint private ownership, and the third to sole proprietorship.

If public ownership rights were made saleable, they would in effect become private ownership rights and there would be a movement toward concentration of ownership of the type in the second example, at least. Why? In the second case, the wealth a person can get is more dependent upon his own activities than in the first case. Many people may prefer to let the situation stay as in Example 1, hoping to collect a major portion of their wealth gain from other people's activities. If this were the case, the total wealth gain would decrease since everyone would have less incentive to work. But it suffices that there be at least one person who prefers to make himself less dependent upon other people's activities than in Example 1 and who prefers at least some more wealth to some more leisure. He will then be prepared to buy up some ownership rights and pay a higher price for them than they are worth to some other people. That he values them more highly is precisely another way of saying that he values independence more than they do, or that he prefers more wealth to less wealth—even if it requires some work by him.

7.2 *Comparative Advantage in Ownership: Control.* — The preceding example did not involve interpersonal differences of abilities, knowledge, or attitude toward risk. But if people differ in any of these respects, as they in fact do, it can be shown that specialization in various tasks — including that of owning a business — will increase wealth. This demonstration is simply the logical theorem of gains from comparative advantage, which we shall not explain here.

Usually the illustrations of comparative advantage are based on « labor » productivities with no reference to « ownership » productivities. But people differ in their talents as owners. Owners bear the risk of value changes, make the decisions of how much to produce, how much to invest, and how it shall be produced and who shall be employed as laborers and managers. Ownership ability includes attitude toward risk bearing, knowledge of different people's productive abilities, foresight and, of course, « judgment ». These talents differ among people according to the particular industry, type of product, or productive resource one is considering. The differences in skills of people as owners make pertinent the principle of comparative advantage through specialization in ownership. If ownership rights are transferable, then specialization of ownership will yield gains. People will concentrate their ownership in those areas in which they believe they have a comparative advantage, if they want to increase their wealth. Just as specialization in typing, music, or various types of labor is more productive so is specialization in ownership. Some people specialize in electronics industry knowledge, some in airlines, some in dairies, some in retailing, etc. Private property owners can specialize in knowledge about electronics, devoting much of their effort and study to learning which electronic devices show promise, which are now most efficient in various uses, which should be produced in larger numbers, where investment should take place, what kinds of research and development to finance, etc. But public ownership practically eliminates possibilities of specialization among owners—though not of employees in the publicly owned venture.

A person who is very knowledgeable about woodworking and cabinet or furniture building would have an advantage as an owner of a furniture company. He would, by being a stockholder, not necessarily make the company any better, but instead he would choose the better company — as judged by his knowledge — as one in which to own shares. The relative rise in the price of such companies enables the existing owners to issue new shares, borrow money more readily, and retain control. In this way the differences in knowledge enables people to specialize in the application of that knowledge to the management and operation of the company—albeit sometimes by indirect lines.

7.3 *Comparative Advantage in Ownership: Risk Bearing.* — A second aspect of ownership specialization is risk bearing. People's attitudes toward risk differ. If various ventures or resources represent different prospects of values, then exchange of ownership will enable a reallocation of risks among people, leading to greater utility in the same sense that exchange of goods does. This risk bearing difference reflects not only attitudes toward risk but beliefs about the prospects of future values of the assets whose ownership can be transferred. Differences in « knowledge » can be used not only in an effort to be more productive but also as a means for distinguishing different risk situations. For example, I may be the top administrator of the Carnation Milk Company, but I may choose to hold stocks in some electronic company because I prefer the risk pattern provided by that stock rather than that provided by ownership in Carnation. In this way a person can separate the productivity of knowledge and effort in what he owns from the risk bearing. He can, if he wants, combine them by holding stock in a company in which he is active. This possibility of separating the *control* (effective administration or operation of the company—an activity which rewards comparative superiority in ability and knowledge) from *risk bearing* is, of course, regarded as an advantage by those who act as employed managers or administrators, and by those who choose to act as corporate stock owners without also bothering to exercise their vote or worry about control. Yet, it is often criticized as undesirable.

Not all of the owners have to think of themselves as owners who are going to exercise their voting rights so effectively as to exert an influence on management. Most of the owners may go along simply because they believe the prospects for profits and losses are sufficiently promising relative to other assets they could own. If losses eventuate, their only alternative is to sell out. To whom? To other buyers who, because of the reduced profit prospects, will offer only a lower price. These « non-active » owners perform a very important function in that they provide the willingness to bear some of the value consequences, at least. So long as scarce resources *exist*, value changes will occur. The question left is then which particular members are to bear the reduced value. Someone has to bear them. Those changes cannot be eliminated.

Often it is said that joint ownership in the modern corporation has separated ownership and control. What this means is that risk bearing and management are more separate. This is correct in that each owner does not have the kind of control he would as the sole owner. But it is a long logical leap to decrying this. It can be a good thing. Specialization in risk bearing and in management or decision-making about particular uses of resources is now possible. Complete separation does not exist for every joint owner, for to the extent that some share owners are inactive or indifferent to alternative choices or management problems, other stockholders (joint owners) will be more influential. In effect, the « passive » owners are betting on the decisions of « active » owners. « Betting » in the sense that they are prepared to pay other people for any losses produced by these « activists » and in turn collect the profits, if any. In the absence of any right to buy and sell shared ownership rights voluntarily everyone would have to bet on the activists as a group (the case of public property). The right to sell concentrates this betting on these who are prepared to pay the most (or demand the least) for the right to do so. And it concentrates the control or management with those who believe they are relatively most able at that task—and these beliefs can be tested with the less able being eliminated more surely in private ownership than in public because (1) the evidence of poor management and the opportunity to capture wealth gains by eliminating it is revealed to outsiders by the lower selling price of the ownership rights, (2) the specialization of ownership functions is facilitated, and (3) the possibility of concentrating one's wealth in certain areas permits greater correlation of personal interest and effort in line with wealth holdings.

We conjecture from the preceding discussion the theorem: *Under public ownership the costs of any decision or choice are less fully thrust upon the selector than under private property.* In other words, the cost-benefit incentives system is changed toward lower costs. The converse of this implication is that the gains to any owner resulting from any cost saving action are less fully effective. These do not mean that the true costs are reduced. The looser correlation between the costs borne by any chooser and the costs of the particular choices he makes is what is implied. Similarly, the capturable gains to the owners of their actions are reduced.

They are *less* fully borne than they would be if the same action were taken in a private property institution, with a similar number of owners (5). From this theorem one would expect that public agencies would, in order to offset or counterbalance this reduced cost bearing, impose special extra costs or constraints on public employees or agents. Public agents who are authorized to spend public funds should be more severely constrained with extra restrictions precisely the costs of their actions are less effectively thrust upon them. And of course these extra constraints do exist. Because of these extra constraints — or because of the « costs » of them — the public arrangement becomes a higher cost (in the sense of « less efficient ») than private property agencies.

---

(5) In other words, this difference between public and private ownership does not flow from differences in numbers of owners.

For example, civil service, nepotism restrictions, tenure, single salary structures for public school teachers, sealed bids, and « lineitem » budget controls, to name a few, are some of the costly devices used.

But it is not easy — indeed impossible — in many instances to impose « corrective » costs as offsets. How would one impose full costs upon a city manager who decided to have a garbage collection system (that turned out to be a big money loser) that the city would tolerate? By not reelecting him. But this cost is less than that borne by the private owner who decides (erroneously) to start a garbage collection system. He loses his job *and* the sunk costs. Similarly, how do we make a voter bear the costs of bad judgment in his votes? Are the prospects of costs that may be imposed on a voter equivalent to the cost-prospects that will be laid on a private owner (with share rights) voting in a private corporation? Not according to the theorem derived from our analysis.

I should, I suppose, avow at random intervals that all this is not a condemnation of public ownership any more than certain « deficiencies » of marriage, the human eye, the upright position of the human being, or smoking are to be regarded as condemnations of marriage, eyes, walking on two feet, or smoking. The « lesser » evils in some institutions — and they exist in all — are borne for the greater good in some of them. We are not arguing that private property even in its purest form is perfect in the cost-bearing sense. No standard of perfection is available. All of our statements have been comparative in degrees of cost bearing.

The converse of this « apologia » is that one should not speak of the imperfections of the market place, either. Nor should one assume in those instances where the market place is inferior in certain respects to, say, public ownership or government control, that we ought to switch from the private property market to the government. The presence of one kind of relative deficiency does not justify a switch to another agency—which has other kinds of deficiencies.

8. *We Summarize*:

As we suggested earlier, public and private ownership are used for different purposes, and in some cases *because* of these different behavioral implications. If public ownership in some government activity were converted to private property, the method of achieving the government objectives would be changed. If city and national parks, or golf courses owned by cities were converted to private property, they would no longer be operated as subsidies for certain groups. If the fire and police department rights were converted to private property rights, vast changes would occur in their operation. And the same goes for the postal system, the garbage collection system, the bus lines, streets, the federal mortgage insurance companies, and the Army, the Navy and the Air Force. When « we » do not want (whatever that means) these changes to occur, these activities are conducted via public ownership instead of privately. And if the effects of greater dependence of benefits and costs on one's own actions are not wanted, resort is made to government activity. Which is not to say that government activity is therefore for that reason good or bad. The extent to which « society » reduces risks that must be individually borne and instead has them borne by society at large — thus reducing the correlation between choice of action and consequences for people as individuals — the greater is the extent of public property. How much this depends upon a *choice* to socialize certain risks, and how much reflects the voting and decision-making *process* are questions I can not answer (*).

ARMEN A. ALCHIAN

(*) Preparation of this paper was facilitated by a grant from the Lilly Endowment of Indianopolis, Indiana to the University of California, Los Angeles, for a study of various forms of property rights.

[11]

Printed in U.S.A.
Vol. 72, No. 6

CONTRACTS: ADJUSTMENT OF LONG-TERM ECONOMIC RELATIONS UNDER CLASSICAL, NEOCLASSICAL, AND RELATIONAL CONTRACT LAW

Ian R. Macneil*

INTRODUCTION

This article concerns the constant clash in modern economic structures between the need for stability and the need to respond to change.[1]

* Ingersoll Professor of Law, Cornell Law School; B.A., University of Vermont, 1950; J.D., Harvard University, 1955.

[1] This paper has grown out of prior published work and of working papers prepared for a number of conferences and seminars: Conference of Polish and American Jurists, Lancut,

The range of the conflict is, of course, immense. This article is aimed at but one segment of the problem: that centered around contractual ways of organizing production and distribution of goods and services. It focuses initially on the relation between classical and neoclassical contract law[2] and the organization of production and distribution in flexible patterns that stress discrete transactional characteristics.[3] It then treats the changes in planning and dispute resolution techniques required where the need for flexibility and change exceeds the dispute-resolving capabilities of a system of neoclassical law.

Variations of the following four questions form the core of the article:

1.   How is flexibility planned into economic relations and what is the legal response to such planning?

2.   How is conflict between specific planning and needs to adapt to subsequent change in circumstances treated?

3.   How are contractual relations preserved when conflicts arise?

4.   How are economic activities terminated when they have outlived their usefulness?

The first section focuses on these issues in a system dominated by discrete transactions, the second on a system with substantial infusions of relational patterns. The third section deals with highly relational patterns, where the first three questions tend to merge, and contains a separate discussion of the fourth question.

Poland, 1974; Hungarian-American Conference on Contract Law and Problems of Large-Scale Enterprise, The Parker School of Foreign and Comparative Law, Columbia University, 1975; Legal Theory Workshop, Yale Law School, 1975; Harvard Law School Faculty Seminar, 1977; Organizations Workshop, University of Pennsylvania, 1977. I am indebted to the sponsors of these conferences and seminars for providing opportunities to air these and other ideas and to the many participants for supplying insights, criticism, and encouragement. In order to make the article complete within itself, it has been necessary at a number of points to repeat parts of articles published earlier—a fact noted where it occurs. This article was written in summer 1977, and references have not been updated across-the-board since then.

   2 Classical contract law refers (in American terms) to that developed in the 19th century and brought to its pinnacle by Samuel Williston in THE LAW OF CONTRACTS (1920) and in the RESTATEMENT OF CONTRACTS (1932). Neoclassical contract law refers to a body of contract law founded on that system in overall structure but considerably modified in some, although by no means all, of its detail. The latter is epitomized by the U.C.C. Art. 2, and RESTATEMENT (SECOND) OF CONTRACTS (Tent. Drafts, 1973-78). *See generally* Macneil, *Restatement (Second) of Contracts and Presentation*, 60 VA. L. REV. 589 (1974), [hereinafter cited as *Presentation*], where, however, both classical and neoclassical contract law are denominated "traditional contract law."

   The Uniform Commercial Code is hereinafter cited as U.C.C. or Code. All citations are to the 1972 official text unless otherwise indicated.

   3 *See* note 9 and accompanying text *infra*.

NORTHWESTERN UNIVERSITY LAW REVIEW

DISCRETE TRANSACTIONS: CLASSICAL CONTRACT LAW

The Nature of Discrete Transactions

A *truly* discrete exchange transaction would be entirely separate not only from all other present relations but from all past and future relations as well. In short, it could occur, if at all, only between total strangers, brought together by chance (not by any common social structure, since that link constitutes at least the rudiments of a relation outside the transaction). Moreover, each party would have to be completely sure of never again seeing or having anything else to do with the other. Such an event could involve only a barter of goods, since even money available to one and acceptable to the other postulates some kind of common social structure. Moreover, everything must happen quickly lest the parties should develop some kind of a relation impacting on the transaction so as to deprive it of discreteness. For example, bargaining about quantities or other aspects of the transaction can erode discreteness, as certainly does any effort to project the transaction into the future through promises.

The characteristics of entirely discrete transactions, if they could occur at all,[4] deprive them of any utility as social tools of production and distribution of scarce goods and services. That fact by no means, however, renders the construct useless as a tool of economic or legal analysis, because some discreteness is present in all exchange transactions and relations. One must simply not forget that great modification is required before the model can represent a reasonably accurate picture of actual economic life. (Unfortunately, this kind of forgetfulness is an endemic problem in both economics and law.) When so modified, the construct will no longer represent an entirely discrete transaction, but will retain substantial discreteness while nevertheless remaining relatively realistic.

We do find in real life many quite discrete transactions: little personal involvement of the parties, communications largely or entirely linguistic[5] and limited to the subject matter of transaction, the subjects of exchange consisting of an easily monetized commodity and money,[6] little

---

[4] The transactions of the theoretical perfectly competitive market defined in old-fashioned terms come very close, but only because the relational effects of social structures such as acceptable money are stripped out in the model: *e.g.*, money is treated like coconuts in the sense that it is assumed to have some value to the seller, but has zero impact in creating any extra-transactional relation between the participants in the market. *See* notes 5, 6, 10 *infra*.

[5] The existence of a common language itself erodes discreteness since it postulates a common social structure.

[6] The availability of money presupposes a strong, existing socioeconomic relation between the parties; nevertheless the "cash nexus" relationship is such an impersonal one as to have little effect in reducing many of the characteristics of discreteness in the transaction.

Adjustment of Relations

or no social[7] or secondary exchange,[8] and no significant past relations nor likely future relations.[9] For example, a cash purchase of gasoline at a station on the New Jersey Turnpike by someone rarely traveling the road is such a quite discrete transaction.[10] Such quite discrete transactions[11] are no rarity in modern technological societies. They have been and continue to be an extremely productive economic technique both to achieve distribution of goods[12] and to encourage their production.

Thus far we have dealt only with present exchanges of existing goods.[13] Such exchanges can, however, play but a limited role in advanced economies. Advanced economies require greater specialization of effort and more planning than can be efficiently achieved by present exchanges through discrete transactions; they require the projection of exchange into the future through planning of various kinds, that is, planning permitting and fostering the necessary degree of specialization of effort. The introduction of this key factor of futurity gives rise to the question: what happens to discreteness when exchanges are projected into the future?

---

[7] *See generally* P. BLAU, EXCHANGE AND POWER IN SOCIAL LIFE (1964).

[8] *See* T. PARSONS & N. SMELSER, ECONOMY AND SOCIETY 109 (1956).

[9] The column headed "Extreme Transactional Pole" in the chart from Macneil, *The Many Futures of Contracts*, 47 S. CAL. L. REV. 691, 738-40 (1974) [hereinafter cited as *Many Futures*], set out in the Appendix, *infra*, gives the characteristics of discrete transactions in more detail.

[10] In real life, even the most apparently discrete transaction is deeply embedded in social relations. Thus, the gasoline purchase is embedded in a great system of property and social relations: money, a social construct, is accepted in payment; the buyer will pay instead of simply taking the gasoline because of his acquiescence in various property rights; the social structure permits the customer to approach the service station attendant, and vice versa, on the assumption that most strangers in such circumstances are not physically dangerous; communication is possible through a common language; the product, simply by being delivered through a certain pump, is not merely gasoline, but gasoline of a certain type, *e.g.*, 89 octane and free of lead, etc. For many practical purposes of analysis, whether of behavior, norms, law, or what have you, these relational aspects can be and are ignored and the transaction sensibly viewed as very discrete. But such analysis invariably must be of limited scope, and when pushed beyond a certain point is defective if the relational elements continue to be excluded from consideration. For example, an analysis of the application of caveat emptor to this "discrete" sale would be highly defective if the brand relationship were omitted from consideration.

[11] From here forward, unless the context indicates otherwise, the terms *discrete transaction, discrete*, and *transaction* will be used to describe near-discreteness, not theoretical pure discreteness. I recognize that the words *transaction* and *transactional* are often used to describe circumstances far from discreteness, but here they are always used in that more limited manner.

[12] Some services could also be included (*e.g.*, haircuts), but services tend generally to involve less discreteness than transactions in goods, unless the goods have service-like qualities, which is true, for example, of durables.

[13] While money itself projects exchanges into the future, inasmuch as it is simply a promise to pay, in a money-saturated economy such as ours we treat it as present wealth, *i.e.*, like an existing good. Our treatment of money is the ultimate in presentiation. *See* note 25 *infra*.

NORTHWESTERN UNIVERSITY LAW REVIEW

The answer is that a massive erosion of discreteness occurs. This is obvious when projection of exchange into the future occurs within structures such as the family, corporations, collective bargaining, and employment, structures obviously relational in nature. Similarly obvious are various relational ways of organizing and controlling markets, for example, the guilds of the feudal era or the planning described by Professor Galbraith in *The New Industrial State*.[14] But this erosion of discreteness occurs even when the projection is by direct and fairly simple promise and where the subject of exchange, if transferred immediately, would permit high levels of discreteness.[15]

Discreteness is lost even in the simple promise situation, because a basis for trust must exist if the promise is to be of any value. Trust in turn presupposes some kind of a relation between the parties. Whether it is that created by a shared morality, by prior experience, by the availability of legal sanction, or whatever, trust depends upon some kind of mutual relation into which the transaction is integrated. And integration into a relation is the antithesis of discreteness.[16]

In spite of the great leap away from pure discreteness occurring when exchange is projected into the future, promises themselves inherently create or maintain at least a certain minimum of discreteness. A promise presupposes that the promisor's individual will can affect the future at least partially free of the communal will, thus separating the individual from the rest of his society. Such separation is an element of discreteness. Promise also stresses the separateness of the promisor and the promisee, another element of discreteness. Moreover, some specificity and measured reciprocity is essential to an exchange of promises—no one in his right mind promises the world. This, again, results in an irreducible level of discreteness.

The foregoing can be seen in the following definition of contract promise: present communication of a commitment to future engagement in a specified reciprocal measured exchange. Thus, the partially discrete nature of promise permits the retention of a great deal of discreteness in

---

[14] J. GALBRAITH, THE NEW INDUSTRIAL STATE 354-62 (1967). *See* A. CHANDLER, THE VISIBLE HAND: THE MANAGERIAL REVOLUTION IN AMERICAN BUSINESS (1977).

[15] Other projectors of exchange are inherently more relational: command, status, social role, kinship, bureaucratic patterns, religious observation, habit, and other internalizations, to mention some. Even a market, however "free" it appears, is inevitably part of a great intertwining of property, personal, social, economic, and legal relations. (Existence of markets is, of course, one of the most important projectors of exchange into the future.)

[16] *See* Lowry, *Bargain and Contract Theory in Law and Economics*, 10 J. ECON. ISSUES 1 (1976). Unfortunately, after making this point Lowry attributes all benefits derived from the transaction to the relation in which it is embedded and concludes erroneously that bargain is therefore a zero-sum game. *See* I. MACNEIL, CASES & MATERIALS ON CONTRACTS: EXCHANGE TRANSACTIONS AND RELATIONS 1-10 (2d ed. 1978) [hereinafter cited as MACNEIL, CASES 2].

transactions where promise projects exchange into the future.[17] Where no massive relational elements counterbalance this discreteness (as they do, for example, in the case of collective bargaining), sense is served by speaking of the contract as discrete, even though the contract is inevitably less discrete than would be an equivalent present exchange.

The combination of exchange with promise has been one of the most powerful social tools ever developed for the production of goods and services. Moreover, discreteness in transactions so projected has its own special virtues. Just as a system of discrete transactions for exchanging present goods may be an effective way to conduct business free of all sorts of extraneous social baggage, so too may discrete transaction contracts serve this function.[18] With this background we can now turn to the questions set out above as they relate to a system of discrete transactions.

Adjustment and Termination of Economic Relations in a System of Discrete Transactions

An economic and legal system dominated by discrete transactions deals with the conflict between various needs for stability and needs for flexibility in ways described below. (The treatment following deals both with present exchanges of existing goods and with forward contracts where exchange is projected into the future. But the latter are assumed to be of a fairly discrete nature, *e.g.*, a contract for 100 tons of iron at a fixed price, delivery in one month.)

Planning Flexibility into Economic Relations.—Within itself, a discrete transaction is rigid, there being no intention to achieve internal flexibility. Planning for flexibility must, therefore, be achieved outside the confines of the transaction. Consider, for example, a nineteenth century manufacturer of stoves who needs iron to be cast into stove parts but does not know how many stoves he can sell. The required flexibility has to be achieved, in a pattern of discrete transactions, by keeping each iron purchase contract small in amount, thereby permitting adjustments of quantity up or down each time a contract is entered. Thus, the needed flexibility comes from the opportunity to enter or to refrain from entering the market for iron. This market is external to the transaction rather than within it. The epitome of this kind of flexibility is the purchasing of needs for immediate delivery, rather than using any kind of a forward contract

---

17 Indeed, it ensures some measure of discreteness even in highly relational exchange patterns whenever promises so defined are utilized, as they often are, *e.g.*, in corporate indentures and collective bargaining agreements.

18 As is plain upon reflection, to give effect to discreteness is to ignore externalities. Such externalities, however, are not necessarily external to the parties; they are simply external to the transaction. For example, the collateral economic loss or emotional pain suffered by a poor person having to repay a bank loan is external to that relatively discrete transaction but is borne by one of the parties. (Such costs may, of course, also have effect as externalities in the usual economic sense, *e.g.*, if the borrower robs a store in desperation.)

NORTHWESTERN UNIVERSITY LAW REVIEW

for future delivery. Such flexibility is reduced by use of forward contracts; the larger and longer they are, the greater is the reduction.

Dealing with Conflict between Specific Planning and Needs to Adapt to Change Arising Thereafter.—Only rarely in a discrete transaction will the items contracted for become useless before the forward contract is performed or become of such lessened value that the buyer either will not want them or will want them in greatly changed form.[19] To put this another way, only rarely will there be *within* the transaction a serious conflict between specific planning and changed needs. To return to the stove manufacturer as an example, seldom will the demand for iron stoves drop so much that the manufacturer comes to regret that he contracted for as much iron as he did.[20]

The discrete transaction technique does not, however, produce a paradise of stability for economic activity; the conflict between specific planning and the need to adapt to change arising thereafter still remains. In those relatively rare cases of difficulties arising while the contract remains unperformed, the conflict exists but is resolved entirely in favor of the specific planning and against the party desiring flexibility. Moreover, outside the discrete transaction, planning must go on; *e.g.*, the seller earlier built an iron smelter in order to sell in the iron market to organizations like the stove manufacturer. Except to the modest extent that the iron producer can shift the risks to the stove manufacturer and other buyers by forward contracts, the risks of change remain with the iron producer. If the demand for iron decreases greatly, the capital invested in building the iron smelter may be largely or entirely lost. Thus, in an economy built on discrete transactions, the risks of change remain but in large measure are not shifted by the transactions. When they are shifted they are shifted totally; *e.g.*, the stove manufacturer bears all those risks to the extent of the quantity for which he contracted.[21] In effect, the contract system does not provide planning for changes; it leaves that to the internal planning of each firm.

Preserving Relations When Conflicts Arise.—Where the mode of

---

[19] This *has* to be the case or else the system will not work and will be replaced by techniques that do work.

[20] This is a different matter from price fluctuations, which may, of course, cause a buyer regret or euphoria for having entered a contract at a particular price. Only fluctuations seriously and adversely affecting the market in which the manufacturer sells his own finished product will cause him not to want the iron at all.

[21] They may, of course, be widely distributed among the stove manufacturer's stockholders and employees, for example, the stake of each of which may be relatively small compared to the whole enterprise (although not necessarily small for the stockholder or employee relative to his own assets). It will be noted, however, that such distribution occurs not by discrete transactions, but by relational contract, i.e., the web of relationship of stockholders-corporation-employees. *See* the last column in the chart in the Appendix, *infra*.

operation is a series of discrete transactions, no significant relations exist to be preserved when conflicts arise. Inside the discrete transaction all that remains is a dispute. Outside the discrete transaction no relation (other than legal rights arising out of the dispute) exists to be preserved. Thus, all that remains is a dispute to be settled or otherwise resolved. The existence of the market that the discrete transactional system presupposes eliminates the necessity for economic relations between the firms to continue in spite of the disputes. That market, rather than continued relations between these particular parties, will supply their future needs.

Terminating Economic Activities Outliving Their Usefulness.— This economic need is simply a particular aspect of the need for planning flexibility into economic relations, the ultimate example of which is to scrap the specific planning altogether. If sheet steel becomes the only technologically sensible substance with which to make stoves, then the stove manufacturer simply makes no more contracts to buy iron. The iron manufacturer continues to produce iron if remaining markets make it worthwhile, or he shifts his production facilities to their next most valuable use. In extreme cases that may mean selling the facilities for scrap or even their abandonment.

* * *

The foregoing description of the responses of the discrete transaction system to the conflict between needs for stability and needs for flexibility may be summarized as follows. Except interstitially, such a system does not shift the risks of loss resulting from such conflicts. Such losses are left to fall largely on the suppliers of goods and services. To the extent that shifting does occur it is total shifting, not a sharing of risks. Given this format, minimizing of risk through planning comes in the *internal* planning of firms, not in *mutual* planning between them through contract. Thus, the iron manufacturer plans for its concern about a declining demand for iron by building a smaller smelter, repairing rather than replacing on old one, etc. It will try, of course, to shift as much of that risk as possible through forward contracts with buyers like the stove manufacturer, but prevailing patterns of relatively short discrete transactions preclude much shifting by that method. In any event, there will be no planning or dealing with the conflicts or possible conflicts through cooperative risk sharing between the iron manufacturer and stove manufacturer.[22]

---

[22] Professor Oliver E. Williamson pointed out to me that the foregoing description ignores the effect on risk distribution of the possible use of inventory-holding market intermediaries, *e.g.*, warehouses. The use of an inventory-holding market intermediary in a discrete system does not, however, seem to me to affect the analysis in the text. The existence of such risk pooling enterprises will, of course, affect behavior of the markets in which both the iron manufacturer and the stove manufacturer are dealing. But, in the discrete transactional system postulated, risks of loss resulting from conflicts between

NORTHWESTERN UNIVERSITY LAW REVIEW

Classical Contract Law and Discrete Transactions

Any contract law system necessarily must implement certain norms. It must permit and encourage participation in exchange, promote reciprocity, reinforce role patterns appropriate to particular kinds of exchange relations, provide limited freedom for exercise of choice, effectuate planning, and harmonize the internal and external matrixes of particular contracts.[23] A contract law system reinforcing discrete contract transactions, however, must add two further goals: enhancing discreteness and enhancing presentiation.[24]

---

needs for stability and flexibility will continue and not be shifted very much by the contracts. Such risks will continue to fall largely on the suppliers of goods and services; and minimizing of risk through planning will continue to come through the internal planning of firms, not through mutual planning between them with contracts. All that will have happened is the introduction of an additional kind of firm which, because of its expertise and participation in a range of markets, is likely to be particularly efficient at dealing with aspects of the conflict between stability and flexibility. This more efficient handler may make markets work better and also lower costs to both the iron manufacturer and the stove manufacturer, but this will be done, in the system postulated, by intra-firm planning, not by inter-firm contract. It would be stretching the relational contract system too far to be useful to encompass within its scope consequences mediated among firms solely by the competitive market operating through discrete transactions. (As mentioned earlier, organized markets are a different matter and may well come within a useful definition of relational contract.)

[23] These norms are explored in more detail in the postscript to *Many Futures, supra* note 9, at 808-16. I am only slowly beginning their more extensive development.

[24] As already noted in the text, providing limited freedom for exercise of choice is a norm of all contracts, whether discrete or relational. But in a discrete contract the importance of this norm is elevated, perhaps ahead of all other norms. Moreover, the two particularly discrete norms singled out in the text may be viewed in large measure as implementations of this more fundamental norm of freedom of exercise of choice. It might very well have been better to analyze discrete transactions from this standpoint; that is, in terms of enhancing freedom of choice, rather than solely in terms of enhancing discreteness and enhancing presentiation. My reluctance to do so is part of a broader pattern of avoidance of the hard issue of the social impact of the kind of analysis appearing in *Many Futures*, note 9 *supra*, and work following it. Since its writing I have lacked the extended periods for reflection necessary to embark on those fascinating issues. I hope to do so during a sabbatical leave in the near future. Meanwhile, I feel confident in doing no more than hinting at the broad policy issues and largely limiting analysis to a micro level.

Where it is desired to carve out certain parts of relations and treat them as discrete, these will be goals of law pertaining to such carved out "discrete transactions" as well. For example, suppose the legislature or court decides that a claim for pay allegedly due a worker should be decided outside the grievance and arbitration processes of the collective bargaining agreement because back pay is a vested individual right. This in effect treats the claim for pay as a relatively discrete transaction in which the discrete norms will likely play a large role in decision making.

Relational norms also exist: (1) harmonizing conflict within the internal social matrix of the relation, including especially harmonizing the conflict between discrete and presentiated behavior with nondiscrete and nonpresentiated behavior; and (2) preservation of the relation. (These are tentative categorizations.)

Presentation[25] is a way of looking at things in which a person perceives the effect of the future on the present. It is a recognition that the course of the future is so unalterably bound by present conditions that the future has been brought effectively into the present so that it may be dealt with just as if it were in fact the present. Thus, the presentation of a transaction involves restricting its expected future effects to those defined in the present, *i.e.*, at the inception of the transaction.[26] No eternal distinctions prevent treating the contract norm of enhancing presentation as simply an aspect of the norm of enhancing discreteness. It is, however, such an important aspect of the projection of exchange into the future in discrete contracts—to say nothing of microeconomic theory—that separate treatment aids analysis significantly.

A classical contract law system implements these two norms in a number of ways.[27] To implement discreteness, classical law initially treats as irrelevant the identity of the parties to the transaction. Second, it transactionizes or commodifies as much as possible the subject matter of contracts, *e.g.*, it turns employment into a short-term commodity by interpreting employment contracts without express terms of duration as terminable at will.[28] Third, it limits strictly the sources to be considered in establishing the substantive content of the transaction. For example, formal communication (*e.g.*, writings) controls informal communication (*e.g.*, oral statements); linguistic communication controls nonlinguistic communication; and communicated circumstances (to the limited extent that any circumstances outside of "agreements" are taken into account at all) control noncommunicated circumstances (*e.g.*, status). Fourth, only

---

25 *Presentiate* is defined in the Oxford English Dictionary as "[t]o make or render present in place or time; to cause to be perceived or realized as present." 8 OXFORD ENGLISH DICTIONARY 1306 (1933).

26 Rarely do we view future events as completely presentiated, but we often come very close, especially respecting the near term. Discreteness plays an essential role in our doing this. No one even thinks he knows enough to presentiate the future, even for a few seconds, of, say, all of New York City, or even of all of a particular industrial plant. But we might feel considerable confidence in presentiating the soon-to-come purchase of goods in our shopping cart as we wait in line at a supermarket checkout. We can do this because we think of that purchase discretely from all the rest of our own lives, the rest of society (other than the checkout clerk and the rest of the people in the line) and all the physical world more than a few feet away.

27 Details of this implementation are spelled out in I. Macneil, Contracts: The Discrete Transactional Norms (unpublished manuscript). The simplifications appearing in this paragraph inevitably sound a bit like a parody of the classical contract system. Needless to say, the real life system, even as distilled in appellate court opinions, is far richer in complexity and conflicting aims and accomplishment than is suggested here. For example, *see* Childres & Spitz, *Status in the Law of Contract*, 47 N.Y.U.L. REV. 1 (1972). Their treatment of the effect of status on the application of the parol evidence rule is built on modern cases only, and hence pertains only to the neoclassical contract law system. But certainly the real life classical system of 1880-1910, to name one period, was never so pure as to prevent analogous analyses of actual decision-making.

28 *See* Note, *Implied Contract Rights to Job Security*, 26 STAN. L. REV. 335 (1974).

NORTHWESTERN UNIVERSITY LAW REVIEW

limited contract remedies are available, so that should the initial presentiation fail to materialize because of nonperformance, the consequences are relatively predictable from the beginning and are not open-
ended, as they would be, for example, if damages for unforeseeable or
psychic losses were allowed. Fifth, classical contract law draws clear
lines between being in and not being in a transaction; *e.g.*, rigorous and
precise rules of offer and acceptance prevail with no half-way houses
where only some contract interests are protected or where losses are
shared. Finally, the introduction of third parties into the relation is
discouraged since multiple poles of interest tend to create discreteness-
destroying relations.

Since discreteness enhances the possibility and likelihood of presentiation, all of the foregoing implementations of discreteness by the
classical law also tend to enhance presentiation. Other classical law
techniques, however, are even more precisely focused on presentiation.[29]
The first of these is the equation of the legal effect of a transaction with
the promises creating it. This characteristic of classical contract law is
commonly explained in terms of freedom of contract, providing maximum scope to the exercise of choice. Nevertheless, a vital consequence
of the use of the technique is presentiation of the transaction. Closely
related to the first technique is the second: supplying a precise, predictable body of law to deal with all aspects of the transaction not encompassed by the promises.[30] In theory, if not practice, this enables the
parties to know exactly what the future holds, no matter what happens to
disrupt performance. Finally, stress on expectation remedies, whether
specific performance or damages measured by the value of performance,
tends to bring the future into the present, since all risks, including market
risks, are thereby transferred at the time the "deal is made."[31]

---

[29] These could also be analyzed in terms of enhancing discreteness.

[30] *See Presentiation, supra* note 2, at 592-94.

[31] A considerable amount of quizzical writing exists concerning the function and efficacy
of expectation damages, as actually implemented in the law, *e.g.*, Vernon, *Expectancy
Damages for Breach of Contract: A Primer and Critique*, 1976 WASH. U.L.Q. 179, 201-03.
Such analyses commonly overlook the function of rules of law as models of customary (and
by definition "desirable") behavior.

For example, the law of expectation damages says to the lender of money: "You may
treat the promises of the borrower to repay the principal and agreed interest as presentiating
the future, because the law measures your remedy for nonperformance exactly in terms of
those promises." Similarly, it says to buyers and sellers of goods: "As of the time of your
contract, you have shifted the market risks of the goods from seller to buyer and you have
shifted the market risks of the purchase price from the buyer to the seller." These abstract
statements of legal rights may be viewed as simply mirroring the economic effects of what
will happen in the vast majority of contracts which will, of course, be performed as agreed.
Their function, so viewed, is to tell the world of contractors: "Your customary behavior is
in accord with the aims of the law; go to it. To do otherwise is legally wrong." Problems
arise with *this* function of the law not so much when particular parties do not "go to it" and
the limitations of implementing the principles are revealed, but when the legal mirror is an

In summary, classical contract law very closely parallels the discrete transactional patterns described in the preceding section. Such a legal system, superimposed on economic patterns of such a nature, constitutes the stereotype of interfirm (or firm and consumer or firm and employee) contracting of the laissez faire era.

Variations from the Discrete Transaction: Neoclassical Contract Law

The discrete transaction is at one end of a spectrum, at the other end of which are contractual relations.[32] Were we to push far in the direction of contractual relations, we would come to the firm itself, since a firm is, in significant ways, nothing more than a very complex bundle of contractual relations.[33] It is not my intention at this point to push that far, but rather to confine consideration of adjustment and termination of long-term economic relations to those where it is clear that the contractual relations are *between* firms rather than *within* a firm. They are, even in traditional terms, contracts. Again, this section will be organized around variations of the questions appearing in the introduction.

Planning Flexibility into Long-Term Contractual Relations and the Neoclassical Response

Two common characteristics of long-term contracts are the existence of gaps in their planning and the presence of a range of processes and techniques used by contract planners to create flexibility in lieu of either leaving gaps or trying to plan rigidly. Prior to exploring the legal response to such planning, an examination of the major types of planning for flexibility used in modern American contracts is in order.[34]

---

inadequate reflection of customary behavior. Thus, if some level of nonperformance becomes both routine and acceptable, at least to the extent that the injured party does not seek expectation damages, an expectation rule becomes a distorted mirror of actual contractual behavior, and "go to it" falls on deaf ears. Distortion in the mirror of legally assumed custom thwarts one of the goals of contract law: implementing intent.

32 *See* text accompanying note 9 *supra*, and chart in the Appendix, *infra*, under the heading "Extreme Relational Pole."

33 I am indebted to Professor Oliver E. Williamson for alerting me to a potential danger of saying this. The statement *appears* to accept the Alchian and Demsetz view of the firm, since they too refer to "the contractual form, called the firm." Alchian & Demsetz, *Production, Information Costs, and Economic Organization*, 62 Am. Econ. Rev. 777, 778 (1972). He is perfectly correct about the danger of misinterpretation. Anyone who persists in thinking of contract solely in the unrealistic and fallacious manner in which it is typically used in the microeconomic model (as Professor Williamson himself certainly does not) will indeed conclude that the statement is an acceptance of the Alchian and Demsetz theory of the firm. Those who are aware of those fallacies should, however, have little difficulty in understanding that it is not. Two articles by economists fall in the latter category: Goldberg, *Toward an Expanded Economic Theory of Contract*, 10 J. Econ. Issues 45 (1976); Williamson, Wachter & Harris, *Understanding the Employment Relation: The Analysis of Idiosyncratic Exchange*, 6 Bell J. Econ. 250 (1975).

34 They are based on Macneil, *A Primer of Contract Planning*, 48 S. Cal. L. Rev. 627,

NORTHWESTERN UNIVERSITY LAW REVIEW

Standards.—The use of a standard uncontrolled by either of the parties to plan the contractual relation is very common. One important example is the provision in many collective bargaining agreements for adjustments of wages to reflect fluctuations in the Consumer Price Index.[35]

The standard incorporated may sometimes be established by third parties not altogether unrelated to the contractual relation. For example, it is common to find building contracts requiring compliance with regulations, plans, or standards of the Federal Housing Administration or the Veterans' Administration. Both of these agencies insure mortgage loans, and their regulations are promulgated to deal with mortgages they insure. Thus, although the regulations are drafted with no particular contract in mind, they aim at a class of contracts, some of which incorporate them by reference. This kind of planning merges into the technique of using direct third-party determination of performance, the subject of the following section.

Direct Third-Party Determination of Performance.—The role of the architect under form construction contracts of the American Institute of Architects (AIA) provides a good example of direct third-party determination of performance. The architect is responsible for determining many aspects of the performance relation, including everything from "general administration" of the contract and making final decisions "in matters relating to artistic effect" to approving the contractor's selection of a superintendent.[36] The use of an expert relatively independent of the parties to determine contract content is, however, no guarantee of smooth performance; witness the fairly large amount of litigation arising under the AIA contracts with respect to delays, payments, and completion of the work. This occurs in spite of the broad authority given the architect, perhaps because a recurrent problem is the scope of finality to be accorded to his determinations.

A particularly important and increasingly used technique for third-party determination of performance content is arbitration. Arbitration is best known for its utilization in resolving "rights disputes,"[37]—disputes about existing rights, usually growing out of existing contracts[38] and

---

657-63 (1975) [hereinafter cited as *Primer*]. The text is a somewhat barebones treatment of the subject. Readers wishing to examine the subject in richer detail would do well to read Goldberg, *Regulation and Administered Contracts*, 7 BELL J. ECON. 426 (1976), and Williamson, *Franchise Bidding for Natural Monopolies—In General and with Respect to CATV*, 7 BELL J. ECON. 73 (1976).

[35] *See* Hurst, *Drafting Contracts in an Inflationary Era*, 28 U. FLA. L. REV. 879, 889-93 (1976); Rosenn, *Protecting Contracts from Inflation*, 33 BUS. LAW. 729 (1978).

[36] In addition, the architect has important functions respecting trouble and dispute resolution.

[37] This is a term common in industrial relations.

[38] An example of arbitration of a noncontract rights dispute would be the submission to arbitration of claims relating to the collision of two ships.

always substantially defined and narrowed by law at the time the arbitration takes place. Planning for the arbitration of rights disputes is an important aspect of risk planning. But arbitration is also used for filling gaps in performance planning, *e.g.*, in industrial relations where the inability of management and labor to negotiate on their own the performance terms of a collective bargaining agreement is known as an "interest dispute."[39] Collective bargaining agreements are not, however, the only agreements that leave open issues relating to future performance and provide for their arbitration. For example, certain joint ventures among design professionals may leave important aspects open to arbitration to provide necessary flexibility.[40]

Interest disputes and hence their arbitration are inherently more open-ended than rights disputes. In the latter, the very notion of "rights"—whether they are based on contract terms or other legal sources, such as the rules of tort law—circumscribes the scope of poten-

---

[39] *See* NATIONAL ACADEMY OF ARBITRATORS, ARBITRATION OF INTEREST DISPUTES (1974). Although the distinction between a rights dispute and an interest dispute can be easily verbalized, it may be difficult to perceive both in practice and in theory. In an interest dispute the status quo may be as rigid a definer of future rights as would be any express agreement.

> Throughout the history of interest arbitration in the newspaper publishing industry, there has been one principle upon which all of the decisions have been based, regardless of whether the specific issue was wages, hours, or manning. Arbitrators will leave the parties where they found them unless that party which seeks a change in the previous bargain, assuming that it was equitable, demonstrates that sufficient changes have occurred which warrant the alteration of the previous bargain.

Adair, *The Arbitration of Wage and Manning Disputes in the Newspaper Industry*, in *id.*, at 31, 47. The current great growth area of interest arbitration is in public employment collective bargaining. *See* Anderson, MacDonald, & O'Reilly, *Impasse Resolution in Public Sector Collective Bargaining—An Examination of Compulsory Interest Arbitration in New York*, 51 ST. JOHN'S L. REV. 453 (1977).

[40] *See* Aksen, *Legal Considerations in Using Arbitration Clauses to Resolve Future Problems Which May Arise During Long-Term Business Agreements*, 28 BUS. LAW. 595, 599 (1973):

> One or more architects will join with various engineers to provide complete design work and supervision for a large project and generally the intention is to use the strengths of each firm and provide for a maximum of efficiency and profit at the negotiation stage. Before the job has been undertaken, the parties must attempt to ascertain the percentage contribution of each party and division of labor and income. But, in this type of arrangement it is often impossible to predict dependably what each contribution will be in terms of work or time and it may have no relationship to the relative size of the joint ventures. Blueprints and specifications may take considerably longer than anticipated, structural design work may be more intricate than was orginally believed or supervision of the job may turn out to be a much more time consuming element. If the joint venturers have tied themselves to fixed percentages of the contract price, there are gross inequities which can result. A negotiated solution which sets tentative percentages and permits arbitral adjustments in the event of changed circumstances guarantees a means of reallocating income in terms of actual work performed without either endangering the project or creating the possibility of economic oppression for one or more of the parties.

Close corporations constitute another example where such issues may arise, although most such issues are probably more likely to be risk and trouble disputes. *See generally* Note, *Mandatory Arbitration as a Remedy for Intra-Close Corporate Disputes*, 56 VA. L. REV. 271 (1970).

NORTHWESTERN UNIVERSITY LAW REVIEW

tial arbitral resolution. In theory, if not in fact, such limits are far looser or perhaps even nonexistent in interest disputes.[41] This calls for particular care in planning arbitration aimed at filling gaps in performance planning, and consideration must always be given to the need to include substantive limits on arbitrator authority.[42] In any event, the planner should be fully aware that identical general language of broad arbitration clauses applied to interest disputes lacks the situational limits usually present when the same language is applied to rights disputes.[43]

One-Party Control of Terms.—Rather than use external standards or independent third parties, the contract may provide that one of the parties to the contract will define, directly or indirectly, parts of the relation. This may go so far as to allow one party a completely free will to terminate the relation. For example, in an option contract a party may purchase the privilege of either going ahead with a contract or not doing so. One-party control of terms in the form of a "deal no-deal" option is important in certain areas of enterprise such as the financial markets, commercial real estate transactions, some kinds of commercial sales of goods,[44] and certain types of consumer transactions, *e.g.*, insurance.

---

[41] *But see* note 39 *supra*. The lack of "rights" as the basis for resolving interest disputes has in the past led courts to hold such disputes to be nonarbitrable because they raise nonjusticiable questions. *See* M. DOMKE, THE LAW AND PRACTICE OF COMMERCIAL ARBITRATION § 12.02 (1968). This has been a particularly lively area of industrial relations, and one not necessarily settled yet. *See, e.g.*, NLRB v. Sheet Metal Workers, Local 38, [1978] LAB. REL. REP. (BNA) (98 L.R.R.M. 2147) (2d Cir. 1978); NATIONAL ACADEMY OF ARBITRATORS, note 39 *supra*.

[42] For example, in the design contracts described in note 40 *supra*, thought might be given to the inclusion of floors or ceilings on percentages to be allowed the various parties. These may also help in some jurisdictions to make legally arbitrable issues the court might otherwise possibly find nonarbitrable because it finds them nonjusticiable.

[43] While arbitrators are less bound by terms of agreements and legal rules than are courts in the sense that a court may often be unable to overrule arbitrators as readily as it could the decision of a lower court in similar circumstances, arbitrators too are part of a society of contract and law. They too in rights disputes tend to follow both agreement terms and law. Even the more expansive proponents of arbitrator discretion in labor relations are very modest in suggesting departures from those hoary standards. For a good summary of varying views of the arbitrator's role in labor arbitration, see Fuller, *Collective Bargaining and the Arbitrator*, 1963 WIS. L. REV. 3.

[44] One example is blanket orders, used extensively by some manufacturers, particularly automobile manufacturers.

The term "blanket order" is often applied to requirements contracts, particularly those in which the obligation of the buyer to purchase may be quite illusory. This is commonly the case with automobile manufacturers' parts orders reserving broad rights to cancel. Under its terms, such a blanket order becomes a firm obligation of the automobile manufacturer only when it sends the supplier a direction to ship a certain number of parts "contracted for" earlier under the blanket order. Nevertheless, the position of the manufacturer is so strong that even such a one-sided arrangement elicits a great deal of cooperation from the supplier. Professor Stewart Macaulay recorded the following from an interview of a supplier:

When you deal with Ford, you get a release which tells you to ship so many items in January and gives an estimate on February and March. Ford is committed to take or pay for the February estimate even if it cancels. However, it is not bound to take the parts estimated for March if it cancels in February. One fabricates the

72:854 (1978) *Adjustment of Relations*

Whenever a party is not clearly paying for the privilege of retaining a free will not to perform his own contractual "obligations," the contract drafter wanting to give that party such freedom walks a narrow line between rigid planning and the danger that the consideration doctrine will make that party's "rights" unenforceable.[45] To cope with the difficulties created by its own doctrine of consideration, the transactional legal structure has produced a wide range of concepts, provisions, techniques, and other devices limiting the impact of the doctrine.[46] The drafter desiring to achieve workable flexibility must be aware both of the limitations the law imposes on available techniques and the opportunities the law offers.

Cost.—A very common technique for achieving flexibility is to provide that compensation for goods or services shall be the cost to the provider, with or without an additional fee (specified in amount or a percentage of the cost or otherwise determined) and with or without definition of what constitutes cost. This technique in a sense combines all of the preceding three. First, this technique utilizes a standard, namely, those of the markets in which the goods and services are purchased. Second, this technique utilizes an element of direct third-party determination in that, while the prices in those markets may be determined without regard to this particular contract, in many cases subcontractors and suppliers will be fixing their own prices with complete awareness of the contract. Finally, there is an element of one-party control since the supplier of the goods and services inevitably has some control over his own costs and hence over the price term of the contract. In general this important technique raises no problems for neoclassical contract law. It may, of course, raise many problems in applying that law to particular situations, over such issues as the definition of costs, assignment of overhead, and the like.

March parts at his own risk, but Ford tries to encourage its suppliers to take this risk so there will be an inventory to handle sudden increased orders. In the example just given, it would be in Ford's interest to pay some of the cost of the March parts to encourage companies to go ahead. If you are a good supplier, it might give you some consideration, but it doesn't have to.

I. MACNEIL, CASES & MATERIALS ON CONTRACTS: EXCHANGE TRANSACTIONS AND RELATIONSHIPS 70 (1971). The legal enforceability of blanket orders in the absence of a specific order is, however, far from clear; their enforcement mechanism apparently turns largely, if not entirely, on the desire of the supplier to continue doing business with the manufacturer.

[45] To the extent, if any, that the doctrine of mutuality adds to the scope of nonenforceability beyond the scope imposed by simple consideration doctrine, the line may be narrowed even further. *See* J. MURRAY, MURRAY ON CONTRACTS § 90 (2d rev. ed. 1974).

[46] For example, protection of contract interests such as the restitutionary and perhaps reliance interests, even when "contracts" are not fully enforceable; developing good faith limitations of various kinds on exercise of one-party controls; manipulation of consideration doctrines; implied obligations; and judicial interpretations contrary to complete one-sideness. *See generally* Farnsworth, *Good Faith Performance and Commercial Reasonableness Under the Uniform Commercial Code*, 30 U. CHI. L. REV. 666 (1963); Summers, *"Good Faith" in General Contract Law and the Sales Provisions of the Uniform Commercial Code*, 54 VA. L. REV. 195 (1968).

NORTHWESTERN UNIVERSITY LAW REVIEW

Agreement to Agree.—A flexible technique used more often than one might initially expect is an "agreement to agree." Since parties can almost always agree later to fill gaps in their relation, such an express provision seems pointless, particularly since, if taken literally, it is meaningless. But common human behavior patterns are seldom if ever pointless, and this is no exception. In general, parties probably use the technique because they are not yet prepared to agree on details requiring agreement, but they want to emphasize to each other that resolution will be required and to express a willingness to engage in the processes of agreement at the appropriate time. These processes undoubtedly more often than not lead to future agreement; but when and if difficulty later ensues in trying to reach agreement, a gap in the contract is revealed. The law should treat such gaps quite similarly to other gaps. The cases are legion,[47] however, in which courts have said "an agreement to agree is not a contract" or some similar bit of doggerel. Often these cases involve circumstances where the court would have held a contract to exist if the gap had occurred in any other manner than a breakdown of an explicit "agreement to agree."[48] Thus, the enunciation of an agreement to agree can be fatal to later securing judicial gap-filling. The planner may avoid this difficulty either by avoiding the technique entirely or by adding an alternative gap-filling technique to come into operation if the parties are unable to agree. Which of these routes is chosen depends at least in part upon how important it is to alert the parties to the need for further negotiation at the appropriate time.

As some of the legal references in the foregoing paragraphs suggest, flexible planning techniques and gaps in planning inevitably raise difficulties for any legal system implementing contractual relations. They raise particular difficulties for classical contract law systems. As already noted, one of the key goals of such a system is enhancing presentiation, a goal inimical to flexibility in contract planning because the latter precludes complete predictability as of the time of the acceptance of an offer.

The neoclassical contract law system may be seen as an effort to escape partially from such rigorous presentiation, but since its overall structure is essentially the same as the classical system it may often be ill-designed to raise and deal with the issues.[49] Nevertheless, the present neoclassical system permits a great deal of flexibility and gap-filling, as is

---

[47] For a discussion of agreements to agree and citations, see 1 P. BONASSIES, G. GORLA, J. LEYSER, W. LORENZ, I. MACNEIL, K. NEUMAYER, I. SAXENA, R. SCHLESINGER, & W. WAGNER, FORMATION OF CONTRACTS 458-64 (R. Schlesinger ed. 1968).

[48] The courts quite often draw the inference that the parties intended the expression "agreement to agree" or similar language to mean more about the consequences of non-agreement than they would have intended if they had said nothing or dealt with the issue by some other flexible technique which also failed. Such an inference is only rarely correct where extensive agreement has occurred relating to other matters, especially where some or all of the remainder of the agreement has been performed.

[49] This proposition is developed at length in *Presentiation*, note 2 *supra*.

demonstrated by the following extract from Professor Murray's recent contract law text, an extract conveying well a sense of the limits beyond which the American neoclassical contract law system will not go in implementing flexibility.

> **Proposals that are too indefinite to constitute offers.**—It seems self-evident that before a proposal can ripen into a contract, upon the exercise of the power of acceptance by the one to whom it is made, it must be definite enough so that when it is coupled with the acceptance it can be determined, with at least a reasonable degree of certainty, what the nature and extent of the obligation is which the proposer has assumed. Otherwise no basis exists for determining liability. However, it is to be emphasized that the requirement of definiteness cannot be pushed to its extreme limits. The fact is that people seldom express their intentions with complete clarity, so that if we were to take the position that any uncertainty in regard to the intentions of the parties invalidates the offer, few offers could be found. The law must of necessity draw a line short of complete definiteness. If we are to have a workable rule, all that can be safely required is that the proposal be reasonably definite. . . .
>
> . . . .
>
> Certain more or less common types of indefiniteness are uniformly held not to invalidate offers. Thus if one undertakes to perform definite services, or to sell ascertainable goods, or to render some other definite performance without, explicitly or by implication, specifying the price to be paid in return for the same, it is generally held that the proposal is a valid offer and that a reasonable price is the measure of the acceptor's undertaking. At least this is true where the performance offered has a market value, or the equivalent, so that some proper standard exists for determining the extent of the acceptor's liability. The theory back of this holding seems to be that a reasonable price is implicit in the offer. It is submitted that the result thus reached is desirable and that in most cases, if not in all, it agrees with the actual intention of the parties. So also, if an undertaking, that is in other respects definite, leaves indefinite the time of performance, it is uniformly held, in the absence of evidence of a contrary intention, that a reasonable time must have been understood, and the agreement will be upheld on that basis. This holding probably also agrees with the parties' actual intention, or at least with what their intention would have been had they given the matter any consideration. It is to be observed, however, that the foregoing principles are applicable only if the parties have omitted any attempt to express any intention in regard to the matters mentioned. *If they have purported to fix a price, or a time of performance, and their expression is so indefinite that its meaning cannot be determined with at least a reasonable degree of certainty, then it will be held that the agreement does not constitute a contract for want of definiteness. This is so because their very attempt to state the matter, or their understanding that it should be left for future determination through mutual agreement, makes it clear that an objectively determined reasonable price or reasonable time, as the case may be, was not contemplated and might be inconsistent with their intention.*

NORTHWESTERN UNIVERSITY LAW REVIEW

. . . .

It is also to be noted that an agreement which is too indefinite in some material aspect for enforcement at the outset, may later become definite as the result of part performance. If performance is rendered by one party in such a way as to make definite what before was indefinite, and this performance is acquiesced in by the other party, there is no apparent reason why the agreement should not be regarded as obligatory from that time forth. The performance may be regarded as the offer which is accepted by the acquiescence of the other party. This is the result usually reached in the decided cases.[50]

While the foregoing extract expresses well the spirit of the neoclassical contract law system, it fails to focus on what I believe to be the fundamental principle underlying the reluctance in such a system to enforce contractual relations in the face of excessive indefiniteness. This principle is founded on the nature of choice-generated exchange and the underlying assumption that the function of a classical or neoclassical contract law system is to enhance the utilities created by choice-generated exchange but not necessarily those created by other kinds of exchange.

When A and B agree to exchange A's good X in return for B's good Y, we conclude, in the absence of factors other than desires for X and Y causing the agreement to occur, that the exchange will enhance the utility levels of each. Where, however, the parties neglect—to take an absurd example—to define in any way what X and Y are, the operators of a contract law system—judge or jury—can have no assurance whatever that judicial definition of X and Y, and enforcement of the exchange, will enhance the utility levels of either A or B, let alone both. The example is absurd, but it demonstrates the limits beyond which enhancement of individual utility levels cannot serve as an adequate reason for enforcing a sufficiently indefinite agreement. Beyond such a point, if enforcement is to be had, other justifications must be found, *e.g.*, avoiding unjust enrichment. Moreover, as Professor Murray suggests, parties can and do fail to define X and Y sufficiently to provide reasonable assurance to a court that enforcing the "contract" would enhance utilities on both sides as those utilities were originally viewed by the parties.[51] If, as is typical of discrete transactions (especially as treated by a classical or neoclassical contract law system), no other reason exists to enforce the exchange, that is the end of it.[52]

---

[50] J. MURRAY, *supra* note 45, § 27 (footnotes omitted) (emphasis supplied) (reprinted with permission of the author and the publisher, the Bobbs-Merrill Co.).

[51] Of course, by the time the legal system becomes involved in this kind of dispute it is, in relatively discrete transactions, normally no longer possible to raise utilities of both. That is why stress in the text is on the phrase "as these utilities were originally viewed by the parties."

[52] The analysis in the text is consistent with that in R. POSNER, ECONOMIC ANALYSIS OF LAW § 4.2 at 69-70 (2d ed. 1977). Posner, however, does not appear to recognize that the analysis is circumscribed by the assumptions of a discrete transactional system; such a

It will also be noted that one of the goals, mentioned earlier, of a classical contract law system is complete presentiation at the time of agreement. The greater the degree of indefiniteness in an agreement, the more a court must fly in the face of this goal in enforcing the agreement. The increasing laxity of the neoclassical system about definiteness, in contrast to the classical system, reflects relaxation of this goal.

Since the neoclassical contract law system remains structured on the classical model in large measure, it too is limited by the foregoing considerations. On the other hand, the neoclassical system, being significantly more relational in nature,[53] can go much further than the classical system, just so long as it does not break out of the classical structure altogether. What happens when a system pushes beyond the limits even of a neoclassical structure will be discussed later.[54]

Conflict between Specific Planning and Needs for Flexibility: The Neoclassical Response

As a general proposition in American neoclassical contract law, specific planning in contractual relations governs in spite of changes in circumstances making such planning undesirable to one of the parties. The same principle of freedom of contract[55] leading to this result permits the parties, however, to adjust their relations by subsequent agreement. A description of these processes and some of the legal considerations follows.[56]

Adjustments of existing contractual relations occur in numerous ways. Performance itself is a kind of adjustment from original planning. Even meticulous performance of the most explicit planning transforms figments of the imagination, however precise, into a new, and therefore different, reality. A set of blueprints and specifications, however detailed, and a newly built house simply are not the same. Less explicit planning is changed even more by performance. For example, the vaguely articulated duties of a secretary are made concrete by his or her actual performance of a day's work. Perhaps this is merely a way of saying that planning is inherently filled with gaps, and that performance fills the gaps, thereby altering the relations as originally planned.

Events outside the performance of the parties also may effect adjustments in contractual relationships. The five dollars per hour promised an employee for his work in 1977 is not the same when paid in November

---

circumscribed analysis may be and often is singularly inadequate when applied to indefiniteness in ongoing contractual relations.

53 For a discussion of this, see *Presentiation*, note 2 *supra*.

54 *See* text accompanying notes 104-40 *infra*.

55 Freedom of contract here means, of course, power of contract, *e.g.*, the power to bind oneself, by agreement, to further action or consequences to which one otherwise would not have been bound.

56 The following paragraphs are based on *Primer, supra* note 34, at 663-66.

NORTHWESTERN UNIVERSITY LAW REVIEW

1977 as it was when promised at the beginning of the year; inflation and other economic developments have seen to that. More or less drastic changes in outside circumstances constantly effect contractual adjustments, however firmly the parties may appear to be holding to their original course.

Nonperformance by one of the parties without the consent of the other also alters contractual relations, although in a way different from performance. This is true no matter how many powers are available to the other party to redress the situation.

Another kind of adjustment occurring in any contractual relation is that based either on mutual agreement or on unilateral concession by one of the parties of a planned right beneficial to him. These alterations, additions, subtractions, terminations, and other changes from original planning may take place at any time during any contractual relation. This is vividly illustrated by various processes of collective bargaining, including periodic renegotiation of the "whole" contract.

When disputes arise out of contractual relations after adjustment by mutual assent or concession, does the original planning or the adjusted planning govern? Keeping in mind the exchange element basic to contractual relations and the various problems the legal system has in dealing with contractual disputes, the answer might seem to depend in any given situation on answers to the following kinds of questions:

1. How sure is it that the adjustment really was mutually agreed upon or conceded?
2. Did one party take improper advantage of the other in securing the concession or agreement?
3. Was the adjustment mutually beneficial, *e.g.*, was there an exchange element in the adjustment itself, or did only one of the parties benefit?
4. If the adjustment benefited only one party, was its purpose to alleviate some difficulty resulting from lack of prior planning or from unplanned consequences of prior planning?
5. How much had the adjustment become integrated into the relation when disputes concerning it arose, *e.g.*, was there unjust enrichment or reliance, among other things?[57]

No comprehensive doctrinal structure has developed in American neoclassical contract law to answer systematically the foregoing ques-

---

[57] Other possible questions are: To what extent was the adjustment part of an ongoing and still viable relation, and to what extent was it only a settlement of disputes arising from a defunct relation? What is the reason for the attack on the adjustments?

Moreover, other ways of stating the issues are perfectly possible and perhaps more useful to anyone setting out to organize the now disorganized legal thinking in the area. For example, overlapping many of the above questions is the following: Was the adjustment in harmony with the rest of the relation, not just as originally planned, but as it had developed to the time of the adjustment in issue and thereafter?

tions.[58] The closest it comes to providing such a structure is the doctrine of consideration, which pervades much thinking on the subject.[59] Consideration doctrine, however, by no means deals comprehensively with all the questions. For one thing the doctrine normally impedes change if it operates at all, thus implementing discreteness and presentiation as of the "original formation."

Where the parties are unable to agree to adjustments to reflect changes in circumstances, neoclassical contract law provides a limited array of doctrines whereby one party may escape some or all the consequences of the change. Doctrines of impossibility of performance, frustration, and mistake are used with varying degress of frequency to relieve parties.[60] More covert techniques such as interpretation or manipulations of technical doctrines such as offer and acceptance and rules governing conditions are also available. But as a general proposition these doctrines aim not at continuing the contractual relations but at picking up the pieces of broken contracts and allocating them between the parties on some basis deemed equitable.

Generally speaking, doctrines of the kind described in the last paragraph achieve such goals as preventing a party from recovering expectation damages when the other party has not performed or preventing unjust enrichment by allowing a party to recover a down payment (restitution) when its purpose in entering the contract has been frustrated. A slowly growing tendency in American law to go farther than this may be discerned. The following sections of the Restatement (Second) of Contracts are illustrative:

Section 292. RELIEF INCLUDING RESTITUTION; SUPPLY- ING A TERM

(1) In any case governed by the rules stated in this Chapter [Impracticability of Performance and Frustration of Purpose], either party may have a claim for relief including restitution under the rules stated in Section 265. . . .

(2) In any case governed by the rules stated in this Chapter, if those rules . . . will not avoid injustice, the court may, under the

---

[58] This is not to suggest the absence of such structures respecting particular kinds of contractual relations. Certainly labor law is not only replete with doctrines centering on such adjustments, but also institutions such as the National Labor Relations Board (NLRB) produce and are affected by those doctrines. The law relating to the internal workings of corporations is another example of legal doctrines centered on constant adjustments of exchange relations.

[59] The cases and problems in MACNEIL, CASES 2, *supra* note 16, at 890-927, suggest a range of the kinds of legal issues raised. For more traditional treatment see J. CALAMARI & J. PERILLO, THE LAW OF CONTRACTS, chs. 4 & 5 (2d ed. 1977); J. MURRAY, *supra* note 45, §§ 72-90.

[60] *See generally*, J. MURRAY, *supra* note 45, §§ 30, 124-30, 197-205. These doctrines are generally keyed back by presentiation notions into the status quo of the original contract as the base point, *e.g.*, use of the idea of tacit assumptions about the continued existence of property being transferred under the contract.

NORTHWESTERN UNIVERSITY LAW REVIEW

rule stated in Section 230, supply a term which is reasonable in the circumstances.[61]

Section 230. SUPPLYING AN OMITTED ESSENTIAL TERM
When the parties to a bargain sufficiently defined to be a contract have not agreed with respect to a term which is essential to a determination of their rights and duties, a term which is reasonable in the circumstances is supplied by the court.[62]

To the extent that the courts apply these rules in a suit, they will begin to provide a legal framework for continuing contractual relations in spite of major changes in circumstances. More explicit on this score are Uniform Commercial Code sections 2-614, 2-615, and 2-616.

Section 2-614 requires tender and acceptance of commercially reasonable substitute berthing, loading or unloading facilities, type of carrier or manner of delivery where those agreed upon become commercially impracticable without fault of either party. It also permits, in certain circumstances, alternative means of payment from those agreed upon. Section 2-615 requires a seller unable to meet his obligations because of specified changed circumstances to allocate his production among his customers (including, at his option, regular customers not under contract) in any manner fair and reasonable. If he does so and gives proper notice, he has not breached his duty under the contract. Under section 2-616 the buyer may then either terminate the contract (thereby discharging any unexecuted portion) or modify the contract by agreeing to take his available quota in substitution for the originally agreed-upon amount. The process under sections 2-615 and 2-616 is something more than simply a voluntary agreement adjusting the situation, since the seller must make the allocation; and the buyer refuses a proper allocation only at the expense of a discharge of the seller.

In summary, two themes may be seen in the development of neoclassical contract law. One is a gradually increasing willingness to recognize conflict between specific planning and subsequent changes in circumstances and to do something about them. The other is a more truncated recognition of the possibility of doing something when such conflicts occur beyond simply picking up the pieces of a dead contract by awarding monetary judgments to someone or refusing to do so. The latter theme merges into the more general issue of continuing relations in the face of trouble, the subject of the following section.

Planning for Nondisruptive Dispute Settlement: The Neoclassical System and Prevention of Disruption

The common presumption of human institutions is that internal conflict, even quite serious conflict, does not necessarily terminate the

---

[61] RESTATEMENT (SECOND) OF CONTRACTS § 292 (Tent. Draft No. 9, 1974).
[62] RESTATEMENT (SECOND) OF CONTRACTS § 230 (Tent. Draft Nos. 1-7, 1973).

institution; indeed, only the most basic and grievous of conflict, if that, will do so.[63] In this respect, the classical contract, along with the discrete transaction it parallels, is a sport. Generally speaking, a serious conflict, even quite a minor one such as an objection to a harmlessly late tender of the delivery of goods, terminates the discrete contract as a live one and leaves nothing but a conflict over money damages to be settled by a lawsuit. Such a result fits neatly the norms of enhancing discreteness and intensifying and expanding presentiation. These norms never, however, completely dominated classical law and certainly do not completely dominate neoclassical law.[64] Nevertheless, the thrust, even of the neoclassical system, is such that explicit planning is often necessary if the participants in a contractual relation desire to continue in the face of serious conflict or even in the face of some kinds of minor conflict.

In light of the above, it often behooves contract planners to plan for continuing relations in the face of conflict. A major example is the "no strike" clause very common in collective bargaining agreements. Normally a "no lockout" clause binding management parallels the "no strike" clause, and grievance procedures and arbitration for disputes accompany them.[65] Another example is found in United States government procurement contracts. The typical disputes clause in such contracts not only provides a mechanism for dispute resolution,[66] but also provides: "Pending final decision of a dispute hereunder, the Contractor shall proceed diligently with the performance of the contract and in accordance with the Contracting Officer's decision."[67] The widely used construction contract forms of the American Institute of Architects (AIA) contain a similar provision: "Unless otherwise agreed in writing, the Contractor shall carry on the Work and maintain its progress during any arbitration proceedings, and the Owner shall continue to make payments to the Contractor in accordance with the Contract Documents."[68]

---

[63] Witness our surviving our own Civil War or the conflict in the interrelation of church and state in any given area in the Middle Ages.

[64] For example, prevailing rules respecting conditions go a long way to keep the relation going in the face of dispute.

[65] The collective bargaining relation typically would continue even if a strike or lockout occurs; what such clauses preserve is the normal operating relation. For a strong statement of employees' duties to perform as commanded and to grieve later, see Dean Shulman's arbitration decision in Ford Motor Co., 3 LAB. ARB. 779 (1944), *quoted in* A. COX, D. BOK, & R. GORMAN, CASES & MATERIALS ON LABOR LAW 571-72 (8th ed. 1977).

[66] The initial decision is by the Contracting Officer, with a right to appeal to a Board of Contracts Appeals (an administrative court). Further appeal is possible in some circumstances, usually to the Court of Claims. This is an oversimplified statement of an immensely complex procedural structure. *See* S. & E. Contractors, Inc. v. United States, 406 U.S. 1 (1972); 4 Report of the Commission on Government Procurement (1972).

[67] Dispute clause required by Armed Services Procurement Regulations, 32 C.F.R. § 7-103.12 (1976). *See* Vacketta & Wheeler, *A Government Contractor's Right to Abandon Performance*, 65 GEO. L.J. 27 (1976).

[68] AMERICAN INSTITUTE OF ARCHITECTS, GENERAL CONDITIONS OF THE CONTRACT FOR

NORTHWESTERN UNIVERSITY LAW REVIEW

Methods of enforcing provisions such as the foregoing vary. Injunctions are granted against strikes and lockouts carried out in violation of no-strike and no-lockout clauses.[69] Conceivably, the provisions in the federal government contracts and in the AIA forms could be enforced specifically. But the government seldom takes that route. And efforts to enforce the AIA provision specifically would run into the general reluctance of American courts to grant specific performance of complicated construction contracts.[70] While this reluctance seems to be diminishing,[71] it has not disappeared. In principle, provisions of this nature should be enforceable specifically by American courts whenever the other requisites for securing specific performance are met, *e.g.*, inadequacy of damage remedies. Indeed, the reluctance to step into complex situations may be less evident where the court views the relief as merely interim relief granted while the main issue is resolved in another forum, such as arbitration.[72]

Provisions such as those discussed above also can be enforced through damage remedies. Violations of no-strike clauses, for example, give rise to rights to damages.[73] Likewise, failure of a contractor to continue performance in spite of a dispute appears to constitute a default irrespective of the merits of the dispute. Presumably similar remedies would be available for breach of other such clauses. Thus, if a contractor quits over a dispute on a construction contract, the owner should be able to recover damages for losses resulting from the quitting irrespective of the merits of the dispute itself.[74] While damage remedies operate retrospectively and, where actually used, do not keep the relation going, the *threat* of their being used may do so.

Apart from providing explicitly for relations to continue during conflicts, the parties may plan processes or agree to substantive terms tending to have that effect. An example of the latter would be a provision

---

Construction, AIA Document A201, art. 7.9.3 (1976).

[69] The provisions of federal and state labor laws prohibiting the issuance of injunctions in labor disputes do not necessarily apply to injunctions enforcing no-strike clauses. *See* Boys Markets, Inc. v. Retail Clerks Union, Local 770, 398 U.S. 235 (1970). How effective such injunctions are is another matter.

[70] D. Dobbs, Handbook on the Law of Remedies § 12.22 (1973).

[71] *Id*. But some of the cases reflecting this change have involved enforcement of arbitrators' orders to perform specifically, and normally no such order will be available when the owner seeks relief against a contractor under Article 7.9.3 during the pendency of the arbitration proceedings.

[72] If the clause provided for continuation of performance while the parties battled their disputes out in court rather than before an arbitrator this reason would not be pertinent. I have never seen such a contract provision, but some are probably lurking out there somewhere.

[73] *See, e.g.*, Local 174, Teamsters v. Lucas Flour Co., 369 U.S. 95 (1962) (no-strike clause inferred from presence of compulsory binding arbitration provision).

[74] The owner's claim would, under the AIA form contract, be subject to arbitration, just as the original dispute was subject to arbitration.

in a sale and installation of complicated machinery giving the seller ninety days after installation in which to adjust the machinery and cure any problems. Provisions for meeting together to discuss problems, for mediation in event of a dispute, and for arbitration are all examples of planning which tends to keep relations going, even without a statement that the parties will do so.[75] The neoclassical contract system provides its normal enforcement mechanisms for such provisions, including limited availability of specific performance.[76] In the case of arbitration, under modern statutes, the system strongly reinforces the process,[77] although reinforcement of arbitration itself does not necessarily mean that the relation will continue.[78]

Where party planning fails to focus on maintaining the relation in the face of conflict, many factors may nevertheless keep it going while the parties iron out disputes. This is, of course, the common human experience, since self-interest, custom, morality, and many other factors may make it more desirable to do so than to terminate the relation. In addition, the neoclassical contract law system offers a range of assistance. Specific performance is the most obvious means, but in spite of expansion in the availability of specific performance in the past decades, it is hardly the primary neoclassical contract remedy.[79] The existence of any contract law remedy tends to have this effect of maintaining the relation. To whatever extent a party is unsure of the legal correctness of his position in a dispute, he will have some desire to continue performing to avoid liability should he turn out to be wrong.[80] Certainly the importance of this in governing a party's actions will depend upon the effectiveness of the remedy.

Some substantive legal rules focus quite particularly on this subject, for example, the general contract principle that the victim of a contract breach cannot recover damages avoidable "through the exercise of reasonable diligence, and without incurring undue risk, expense, or humiliation."[81] In some circumstances this may prevent recovery of damages

---

[75] *See Primer, supra* note 34, at 681-91.

[76] *See* text accompanying note 79 *infra*.

[77] *See Primer, supra* note 34, at 685-91.

[78] If the arbitrators award specific performance and the court enforces the award effectively, this will, of course continue the relation. *See, e.g., In re* Staklinski and Pyramid Elec. Co., 6 N.Y.2d 159, 160 N.E.2d 78, 188 N.Y.S.2d 541 (1959).

[79] For an expression of hope that it will become so by one of the leading neoclassical contract scholars, see Braucher, *Contracts*, in N.Y.U. SCHOOL OF LAW, AMERICAN LAW: THE THIRD CENTURY—THE LAW BICENTENNIAL VOLUME 121, 127 (B. Schwartz ed. 1976).

[80] This applies to duties from whatever source derived, not just from those agreed upon. For example, an employer who discharges an employee for activity that may be protected by the National Labor Relations Act, 29 U.S.C. §§ 151-169 (1970 & Supp. V 1975), not only must reinstate the employee but also must pay back pay if the discharge is later held to be an unfair labor practice.

[81] J. MURRAY, *supra* note 45, at § 227 (footnote omitted). *See* Hillman, *Keeping the Deal*

avoidable by continuing the relation. Another example, in the Uniform Commercial Code, provides that a seller aggrieved by a buyer's breach respecting unfinished goods may

> in the exercise of reasonable commercial judgment for the purposes of avoiding loss and of effective realization either complete the manufacture and wholly identify the goods to the contract or cease manufacture and resell for scrap or salvage value or proceed in any other reasonable manner.[82]

This section permits the seller unilaterally to maintain the relation in spite of the dispute, since identification of the goods to the contract will, within limits, permit the seller to recover the price of the goods[83] rather than merely damages for the breach. (The latter may be far less in amount and more difficult to prove.)

In summary, both planning by parties and the neoclassical system acting in either a supplementary or independent manner, can provide extensively for the continuance of relations even in the face of serious disputes. When, however, self-interest or other motives of the parties are inadequate to accomplish continuation, the reinforcement of the neoclassical contract law system often proves inadequate to the task. We should not, however, sell short that system as a supporter of customs and habits of behavior internalized in such a way that motives to "keep on with it" will prevail.

Terminating Economic Activities and Allocating Losses from Termination

As noted earlier, planning for the termination of economic relations is simply a particular kind of planning for flexibility. For that reason, all the techniques for planning of flexibility discussed before are available for the purpose of planning terminations as well. In addition, the simple technique of putting a time limit on the duration of the contract is not only available, but fits very well with the concept of the discrete transaction, a fixed duration being fundamental to the concept of discreteness. Since discreteness underlies the concepts of the neoclassical contract law structure, some of the kinds of legal difficulties respecting flexibility discussed earlier will not affect provisions respecting termination. For example, a court that might be very reluctant to effectuate a provision giving a seller complete freedom to fix the price would have little doctrinal trouble with a provision allowing the seller complete freedom to terminate the contract.

The generality of the foregoing comments must be limited in certain respects. First, one-sided powers to terminate the relations give rise to

---

Together after Material Breach—Common Law Mitigation Rules, the UCC, and the Restatement (Second) of Contracts, 47 U. COLO. L. REV. 553 (1976).

[82] U.C.C. § 2-704.
[83] U.C.C. § 2-709.

problems of mutuality and to questions of enforceability. For example, suppose that Seller agrees to supply Buyer with all Buyer's requirements for transistors for a five-year period, and Buyer agrees to buy all its requirements for transistors during a five-year period with an option to terminate the relation at any time after the first year upon sixty days notice. The contract establishing this one-sided arrangement could be drafted clearly enough so that a court would enforce it in spite of the absence of substantial mutuality of obligations after the first year. But careless draftsmanship could easily permit a court to hold the contract divisible into two parts: (1) the first year (and perhaps sixty days) during which there was mutuality of obligation and therefore consideration for seller's promise; and (2) the remainder of the time, during which buyer had promised nothing. Under such an analysis, after the first year (and maybe sixty days), consideration for a seller's promise would be lacking and its promise would not be enforceable.[84]

The doctrine of consideration as applied above may be viewed as a regulatory control discouraging parties from providing for unilateral rights of termination of agreements. Occasionally, in contracts where one party is more powerful than the other, American law has gone farther than simply discouraging provisions for such rights. For example, a federal statute[85] confers upon an automobile dealer rights to sue the manufacturer for "failure . . . to act in good faith in . . . terminating, canceling, or not renewing the franchise with said dealer . . . ."[86] This language supersedes any rights, however carefully planned, the manufacturer would otherwise possess to terminate at will. Specific legislation of this kind is relatively rare,[87] although legislation governing employment may have similar effect. For example, civil servants typically have great protection of tenure in their positions, and unemployment insurance schemes imposed on private employers by statute may inhibit discharging employees. Moreover, since collective bargaining almost invariably leads

---

[84] The technique used results in neither being bound, not in both being bound. It is therefore consistent with notions of discreteness, since it shortens the relation.

[85] Automobile Dealers' Day in Court Act, 15 U.S.C. §§ 1221-1225 (1976). While this statute might be viewed as outside the system of neoclassical law, its approach is so consonant with the structure of that system that it may sensibly be viewed as an internal development respecting a particular kind of contract.

[86] 15 U.S.C. § 1222 (1976). The statute also includes the following language: "*Provided*, That in any such suit the manufacturer shall not be barred from asserting in defense of any such action the failure of the dealer to act in good faith." *Id*. (emphasis in original).

This statute and its relative lack of effectiveness are discussed extensively in Macaulay, *The Standardized Contracts of United States Automobile Manufacturers*, in 7 INTERNATIONAL ENCYCLOPEDIA OF COMPARATIVE LAW, ch. 3, 18 (1974). For a recent dealer victory see Shor-Line Rambler, Inc. v. American Motors Sales Corp., 543 F.2d 601 (7th Cir. 1976); for a recent dealer loss, see Autohaus Brugger, Inc. v. Saab Motors, Inc., 567 F.2d 901 (9th Cir. 1978).

[87] A leading state example is Wisconsin's Fair Dealership Law, WIS. STAT. §§ 135.01-.07 (1975). *See* Boatland, Inc. v. Brunswick Corp., 558 F.2d 818 (6th Cir. 1977).

NORTHWESTERN UNIVERSITY LAW REVIEW

to job security for individual employees, the many statutory reinforcements of collective bargaining may reasonably be viewed as legislation of similar nature.

Moving in similar directions are cases such as *Shell Oil Co. v. Marinello*,[88] requiring good cause for the termination of a service station lease-franchise relation. This particular decision was influenced by a New Jersey statute so providing, although, because of its effective date, inapplicable to the dispute in question.[89] No such statute, however, was involved in a recent federal case applying Missouri law.[90] It held that while a franchise agreement silent as to duration is normally terminable at will, the franchisor cannot terminate for a reasonable time from its formation—a reasonable time being long enough to allow franchisee to recover its initial investment and expenses. The court held that in the circumstances of the case eight or nine years was long enough. Also moving in similar direction are common law cases "interpreting" employment contracts without specified duration as being terminable by the employer only for cause[91] and those cases prohibiting terminations or refusals to renew contractual relations for "improper reasons."[92]

Unlike the consideration and mutuality limitations discussed earlier, the foregoing kinds of legal intervention are anti-discrete, since, where effective, they lengthen rather than shorten enforceable contractual relations. Thus, interstitially and gradually, increasingly tight limits are being

---

[88] 63 N.J. 402, 307 A.2d 598 (1973), *cert. denied*, 415 U.S. 920 (1974).

[89] In William C. Cornitius, Inc. v. Wheeler, 276 Or. 747, 556 P.2d 666 (1976), the Oregon Supreme Court refused to follow the decision in Shell Oil Co. v. Marinello, 63 N.J. 402, 307 A.2d 598 (1973), *cert. denied*, 415 U.S. 920 (1974). The court described *Marinello* as the only case holding that service station lease-franchises must be renewable (except for good cause for refusal) and distinguished cases holding unenforceable reserved rights to terminate service station lease-franchises without good cause, *e.g.*, Ashland Oil, Inc. v. Donahue, 223 S.E.2d 433 (W. Va. 1976). *Cornitius* held that the service station owner could omit renewal terms from its leases, the court stating that it was not considering "enforceability of a one-sided cancellation clause in a contract of adhesion." 556 P.2d at 670-71. Careful drafting should enable franchisors in Oregon to avoid ever having such an issue raised against them; they need simply omit renewal provisions, even though renewal will be the normal procedure.

[90] Lockewill, Inc. v. United States Shoe Corp., 547 F.2d 1024 (8th Cir. 1976), *cert. denied*, 431 U.S. 956 (1977).

[91] Monge v. Beebe Rubber Co., 114 N.H. 130, 316 A.2d 549 (1974); Pstragowski v. Metropolitan Life Ins. Co., 553 F.2d 1 (1st Cir. 1977) (applying New Hampshire law).

[92] *E.g.*, L'Orange v. Medical Protective Co., 394 F.2d 57 (6th Cir. 1968) (refusal to renew medical malpractice policy because policyholder testified for plaintiff in a malpractice case); Dickhut v. Norton, 45 Wis. 2d 389, 173 N.W.2d 297 (1970) (eviction of tenant for making a complaint to authorities about housing violations). The Oregon Supreme Court refused to apply the principle in William C. Cornitius, Inc. v. Wheeler, 276 Or. 747, 556 P.2d 666 (1976), without recognizing that this principle is not limited to residential leases and ignoring the court's own recent decision holding tortious the firing of an employee for requesting jury duty after being told not to do so. Nees v. Hocks, 272 Or. 210, 536 P.2d 512 (1975). See note on improper motivations in MACNEIL, CASES 2, *supra* note 16, at 514-15.

imposed on the general principle that parties may plan for unilateral termination of contractual relations and that the courts will effectuate their planning.

Apart from legislatively imposed requirements, unilateral rights to terminate may be exercised leaving losses to fall where they happen to fall. This is analogous to what happens in a system of very discrete transactions, in which most risks of change have to be borne within the firm rather than being shifted to the other party or somehow shared. The difference lies in the option available to the party enjoying the right to terminate unilaterally; with the longer term relational contract that party has the advantages both of the security of the longer term and of short-term discreteness. Parties are, of course, often fully aware of this and may, rather than having the disadvantaged party charge more to cover the added risk, allocate in advance the costs of termination. Perhaps the most complex provisions of this kind are found in the great administrative structure built around the federal government's right to terminate contracts for its convenience.[93] A very general summary of these provisions is that costs incurred in performance of the contract, including overhead and profit on work performed, are allowed, but profit on the parts of the contract not performed because of the termination is not. Franchise agreements giving the franchisor rights to terminate often provide another example of advance allocation of costs so that not all of the costs of termination otherwise falling on the franchisee remain there.[94]

Thus, in summary, the neoclassical system generally poses few doctrinal hurdles to termination, even unilateral termination, if carefully enough planned. But relational limits on unilateral termination are creeping into the neoclassical system.

Overview of the Limits of a Neoclassical Contract Law System

As noted earlier, the two special norms of a classical contract law system are enhancement of discreteness, and expansion and intensification of presentation. Both of these norms aim toward ideals no social or legal system could ever come close to achieving; pure discreteness is an impossibility, as is pure presentation. Thus even the purest classical contract law system is itself a compromise; its spirit and its conceptual structures may be those of pure discreteness and presentation, but its details and its application never can be.

Even apart from these theoretical limitations of a classical contract law system, the limited extent to which it is possible for people to consent

---

93 Armed Services Procurement Regulations, 32 C.F.R. §§ 8-000 to 8-406, 8-701 to 8-712 (1976). Quite similar rights are reserved by blanket supply contracts automobile manufacturers enter with their suppliers. *See* Macaulay, note 86 *supra*.

94 *See generally* E. McGuire, Franchised Distribution (The Conference Board, publ., 1971).

to all the terms of a transaction, even a relatively simple and very discrete one, soon forces the development of legal fictions expanding the scope of "consent" far beyond anything remotely close to what the parties ever had in mind. The greatest of these in American law is the objective theory of contract. The classical American contract is founded not upon actual consent but upon objective manifestations of intent. Moreover, in classical law manifestations of intent include whole masses of contract content one, or even both, parties did not know in fact. For example, ordinary run-of-the-mill purchasers of insurance are, in classical law, deemed to have consented not only to all the terms in the policy, which they did not read and could not have understood if they had, but also to all the interpretations the law would make of those terms. While in theory this enhances presentation (the law presumably being perfectly clear or at least struggling to be so), and may indeed have done so for the insurer, for the insured it commonly has precisely the opposite effect. Nevertheless, it is necessary to cram such absurdities into "objective consent" in order to avoid recognizing the relational characteristics of the system.

Neoclassical contract law partially, but only partially, frees itself of the foregoing difficulties. The freeing comes in the details, not in the overall structure. As suggested above, for example, the neoclassical system displays a good bit of flexibility in adjusting to change, and by no means always does so in terms of fictions about the original intent of the parties. Perhaps one of the most vivid examples of this is Restatement (Second) of Contracts, sections 266 and 267.[95] These define when a failure to perform is material and when unperformed duties under a contract are discharged by the other party's uncured material failure to perform (or offer to perform).[96] Section 267 lists seven circumstances significant in determining the time when the injured party is discharged:

1.   the extent to which the injured party will be deprived of the benefit which he reasonably expected;
2.   the extent to which the injured party can be adequately compensated for the part of that benefit of which he will be deprived;
3.   the extent to which the party failing to perform or to offer to perform will suffer forfeiture;
4.   the likelihood that the party failing to perform or to offer to perform will cure his failure, taking account of all the circumstances including any reasonable assurances;
5.   the extent to which the behavior of the party failing to perform or to offer to perform comports with standards of good faith and fair dealing;
6.   the extent to which it reasonably appears to the injured party that delay may prevent or hinder him in making reasonable substitute arrangements;
7.   the extent to which the agreement provides for performance without delay, but a material failure to perform or to offer to per-

---

[95] RESTATEMENT (SECOND) OF CONTRACTS §§ 266-67 (Tent. Draft No. 8, 1973).

[96] *Id.* For other examples, see *Presentation, supra* note 2, at 603-06.

form on a stated day does not of itself discharge the other party's remaining duties unless the circumstances, including the language of the agreement, indicate that performance or tender by that day is important.[97]

Of the seven factors, four (3, 4, 5, and 6) clearly focus on circumstances at the time of the difficulties, rather than following the presentation approach and trying to key back to the original agreement. An element of that is also present in the others. In 1 and 2 "the benefit he reasonably expected" appears to permit more consideration of post-agreement circumstances than would, for example, the phrase "what he was promised." And 7 puts a burden on the injured party to show that timely performance was important beyond simply providing initially in the contract that performance be without delay. (That is only one of the circumstances to be considered.) This too is anti-presentation.

The burgeoning concept of good faith, in large measure within the neoclassical framework, is another largely anti-presentiating, and very much anti-discrete, concept.[98]

But neoclassical contract law can free itself only partially from the limitations posed by obeisance to the twin classical goals of discreteness and presentation. This obeisance is imposed by adherence to an overall structure founded on full consent at the time of initial contracting.[99] As long as such adherence continues, *i.e.*, as long as it remains a neoclassical system, there are limits to the ignoring of discreteness and presentation in favor, for example, of such factors as those listed above respecting Restatement (Second) of Contracts § 267.[100] Nevertheless, the constantly increasing role of ongoing contractual relations in the American economy continues to put immense pressure on the legal system to respond in relational ways.

In the past such pressures have led to the spin-off of many subject areas from the classical, and later the neoclassical, contract law system, *e.g.*, much of corporate law and collective bargaining (to say nothing of marriage, which was never really in). They have thus led to a vast shrinkage of the areas of socioeconomic activity to which the neoclassical system applies.[101] As the earlier discussion in this paper indicates, they

---

[97] RESTATEMENT (SECOND) OF CONTRACTS § 267 (Tent. Draft No. 8, 1973). The first five circumstances are from § 266, where they determine materiality of the failure to perform.

[98] *See generally* Summers, *supra* note 46.

[99] This characteristic of the neoclassical system is explored in *Presentiation*, note 2 *supra*.

[100] RESTATEMENT (SECOND) OF CONTRACTS § 267 (Tent. Draft No. 8, 1973).

[101] *See* L. FRIEDMAN, CONTRACT LAW IN AMERICA (1965); Macneil, *Whither Contracts?*, 21 J. LEGAL EDUC. 403 (1969). The mistake is sometimes made of concluding that because a subject area has spun off and is widely considered to be a special area, that all elements underlying the classical or neoclassical system disappear from the area. There are hints, or more, of this in G. GILMORE, THE DEATH OF CONTRACT (1974), and Friedman & Macaulay, *Contract Law and Contract Teaching: Past, Present, and Future*, 1967 WIS. L. REV. 805.

have also led to very significant changes leading to the transformation of the Willistonian classical system to what might be called the Realist neoclassical system. The spin-offs can and will continue.

Equally likely, the neoclassical system will continue to evolve in relational directions, while courts and scholars still strive to keep it within the overall classical structure. (This is especially likely in first-year contracts courses in many American law schools and in the casebooks and texts aimed at first-year contracts students and their teachers.) The spin-offs will, however, render the system, as a total system, of less and less practical interest.[102] At the same time, trying to squeeze increasing relational content into the neoclassical system will encounter the same kinds of strains some of my generation are finding in trying to put on the older parts of their wardrobes. Thus, rewards of expanding the neoclassical system will decrease at the same time that intellectual and perhaps other costs of doing so increase.

Elsewhere, I have suggested the possibility that a more encompassing conceptual structure of contract jurisprudence may emerge from the situation just described.[103] Part of such a structure must focus on the issues raised by this paper, adjustment of long-term contractual relations. The concluding section of this paper will deal with some of the consequences of slipping the bounds of the classical contract system altogether, of reducing discreteness and presentation from dominant roles to roles equal or often subordinate to relational norms such as preserving the relation and harmonization of all aspects of the relation, whether discrete or relational.

CONTRACTUAL RELATIONS: RELATIONAL CONTRACT LAW

The introduction to the preceding section carefully limits that section

---

(Probably the most extreme view I have found along this line is Lowry, *supra* note 16, at 16-17.) Nothing could be farther from the truth. Discreteness and presentation are ever with us in the modern world and will continue to be so; the fact that we now recognize them as integrated into ongoing relations does not eliminate them. Nor does it eliminate the need to respond to them as particular facets of ongoing relations. And such response very often will be to enhance them and give them full effect. In such instances, not just neoclassical contract law, but sometimes good old-fashioned classical contract law, may supply the best solutions. But those solutions will be "best" because the overall relational circumstances so indicate, not because of the general dominance of jurisprudential systems based on enhancing discreteness and presentation.

102 Relatively little of "the action" in contractual transactions and relations lies in that system now, as the examination of any law school curriculum will demonstrate. Not only is the first-year neoclassical course shrinking in semester hours in many schools, but also the major part of the teaching of contracts in law school is to be found in subject-specific courses such as commercial law, corporations, labor law, securities regulation, and creditors' rights.

103 *Many Futures*, note 9 *supra*; *Presentation, supra* note 2, at 608-10. Work such as that of Eisenberg, Goldberg, Williamson, and others reinforces my feeling that surely a structure not only is possible, but that some of its outlines are starting to emerge.

to situations where "it is clear that" the long-term economic relations in question are "*between* firms rather than *within* a firm." The situations treated there were, "even in traditional terms, contracts." Such a limitation is unnecessary in introducing the present section. Interfirm contractual relations follow the kinds of patterns discussed here—*e.g.*, in a long-term consortium—but more typical relations of this nature would include such structures as the internal workings of corporations, including relations among management, employees, and stockholders. Corporate relations with long- and short-term creditors, law firms, accounting firms, and managerial and financial consultants may also acquire many of the characteristics discussed and increasingly seem to do so. Collective bargaining, franchising, condominiums, universities, trade unions themselves, large shopping centers, and retirement villages with common facilities of many kinds are other examples now existent. If present trends continue, undoubtedly we shall see new examples, now perhaps entirely unforeseen.

As noted earlier,[104] discreteness and presentation do not disappear from life or law simply because ongoing contractual relations become the organizational mode dominating economic activity. Because they remain with us and because they drastically affect contractual relations, this section will start with an analysis of their role in ongoing relations.

Presentation and Discreteness in Contractual Relations

However important flexibility for change becomes in economic relations, great need will nevertheless always remain for fixed and reliable planning. Or in the terms emphasized here, presentation will always occur in economic relations, since it tends to follow planning as a matter of course. Nor does a modern technological economy permit the demise of discreteness. Very specialized products and services, the hallmark of such an economy, produce a high degree of discreteness of behavior, even though their production and use are closely integrated into ongoing relations. When, for example, an automobile manufacturer orders from another manufacturer with which it regularly deals, thousands of piston rings of a specified size, no amount of relational softening of discreteness and presentation will obscure the disaster occurring if the wrong size shows up on the auto assembly line. Nor would the disaster be any less if the failure had occurred in an even more relational pattern, *e.g.*, if the rings had been ordered from another division of the auto manufacturer. Both discreteness and presentation must be served in such an economic process, whether it is carried out between firms by discrete separate orders, between firms under long-established blanket contracts, or within the firm.[105]

---

104 *See* note 100 *supra*.

105 It would take the imagination of a good science-fiction writer to dream up a technological economy in which this was not true.

NORTHWESTERN UNIVERSITY LAW REVIEW

Even apart from high demands for reliable planning in a technological society, discreteness is a characteristic inherent in human perception. Moreover, as I have suggested elsewhere, any given "present situation," no matter what its origin, tends to be perceived as highly discrete compared to what lies in the past and what is to come in the future.[106] Thus, the status quo, whatever it is, inevitably has about it a fairly high level of discreteness. This fact, coupled with the human propensity to presentiate on the basis of what is currently in the forefront of the mind, creates strong expectations of the future consistent with the status quo. Such expectations tend to be very strong. It is impossible to overstress this phenomenon—it describes not only the conservatism of the nineteenth century Russian peasant but also the intense commitment to change and growth where patterns of change and growth constitute the status quo, *e.g.*, the tenacity in America to patterns of constantly increasing energy consumption.

Expectations created by the above processes can be, and often are, of a magnitude and tenacity as great or greater than those created by good, old-fashioned discrete transactional contracts. Thus, when the phenomenon occurs in contractual relations, any tolerable contract law system must necessarily pay attention to at least some implementation of this kind of discreteness and presentiation.

In view of the foregoing, the need for a contract law system enhancing discreteness and presentiation will never disappear.[107] Moreover, it is possible, even likely, that a neoclassical contract law system will continue in existence to deal with those genuine needs. Such a system will, however, continue to rub in an unnecessarily abrasive manner against the realities of coexistence with relational needs for flexibility and change. Only when the parts of the contract law system implementing discreteness and presentiation are perceived, intellectually and otherwise, not as an independent system, but only as integral parts of much larger systems, will unnecessary abrasion disappear. By no means will all abrasion disappear, of course, because real conflict exists between the need for reliability of planning and the need for flexibility in economic relations.[108] What will disappear is the abrasion resulting from application of contract law founded on the assumption that all of a contractual relation is encompassed in some original assent to it, where that assumption is manifestly false. The elimination of that assumption not only would eliminate the unnecessary abrasion but also would remove the

---

[106] *Many Futures, supra* note 9, at 754-56.

[107] A formal, sovereign-imposed system conceivably could disappear, if contractual relations develop extensively enough to be able to depend entirely on self-generated internal legal systems. But the internal systems too will need to serve these needs.

[108] A point nicely brought out in the context of particular kinds of contracts by Goldberg, *supra* note 34, at 441-42 (university food service contracts) and Williamson, note 34 *supra*.

Adjustment of Relations

penultimate classical characteristic justifying calling a contract law system neoclassical.[109]

What replaces the neoclassical system when, and if, all that remains of classical contract law are discreteness and presentation-enhancing segments of far larger systems, segments perhaps often playing roles subordinate to countless other goals, including those of achieving flexibility and change? The remainder of this paper is an introduction to possible answers to that question.

Processes for Flexibility and Change in Contractual Relations

Change, whether caused by forces beyond social control or actively sought, appears to be a permanent characteristic of modern technological societies. Willy-nilly, flexibility comes along with the phenomenon, since the only alternative is a breakdown of the society. But there are processes of flexibility beyond simply bending with each wind of change on an ad hoc basis. Indeed, we have already seen many such processes respecting contracts and have explored the response to them of a neoclassical legal system. We shall look at them again here to see the response of a legal system which is more frankly relational and which has cast off conceptual obeisance to discreteness and presentation by some all-encompassing original assent. Although no such system as yet exists in American law, I shall speak in the present tense; this is justified, perhaps, by the existence of specific terms of contract law, such as collective bargaining, coming close to the patterns described.

The most important processes used for maintaining flexibility are those of exchange itself, whether the sharply focused bargaining characteristic of labor contract renewals or the subtle interplays of day-to-day activities, or a host of other forms taken by exchange. These patterns of exchange take place against the power and normative positions in which the parties find themselves.[110] This means that exchange patterns occur, *inter alia*, against the background of the discrete and presentiated aspects of the relations, whether those aspects were created by explicit prior

---

[109] Penultimate, not ultimate. If we think of the classical contract law system as the antithesis of the status contractual relations of primitive societies—as I believe Maine did in his famous statement about the move from status to contract—one vital characteristic of the classical contract system will remain: the great effect given to planning. Rightly or wrongly we do not think of primitive societies as engaging in a great deal of planning beyond that arising from habit, custom, mores, and customary law of the society. However accurate or inaccurate this view of primitive societies may be, it is a completely inaccurate view of modern technological society with its immense, indeed insatiable, demands for planning and performance of planning. Thus, as already noted, a relational, post-neoclassical contract law system will necessarily retain *in context* a large measure of the respect for presentiation and discreteness shown by the classical system.

[110] *See generally* Eisenberg, *Private Ordering through Negotiation: Dispute-Settlement and Rulemaking*, 89 HARV. L. REV. 637 (1976).

NORTHWESTERN UNIVERSITY LAW REVIEW

planning, other existential circumstances, or combinations thereof.[111] This requires harmonization of changes with such a status quo but does not require doctrines such as the doctrine of consideration or the more discrete formulations of concepts like executory accord and accords intended as satisfactions. Instead questions like those raised previously are appropriate.[112] There is, however, a substantial difference. In the neoclassical system, the reference point for those questions about the change tends to be the original agreement. In a truly relational approach the reference point is the entire relation as it had developed to the time of the change in question (and in many instances as it has developed since the change). This may or may not include an "original agreement;" and if it does, may or may not result in great deference being given it.

Since contractual relations, such as the employment relation, commonly involve vertical or command-and-subordinate positions[113] of an ongoing nature, *e.g.*, the vice-president in charge of plant operations and his subordinates, much change is brought about by command. As the commands inevitably relate to exchange, as in an order to an employee to report for overtime work, they are techniques for achieving change through nonhorizontal processes, in contrast to those of agreed-upon, horizontal exchange.[114] Again, a relational contract system implements, modifies, or refuses to implement such commands only in the overall context of the whole relation.

---

[111] *Cf. id.* at 672-80 (exchange patterns in a context of dependence).

[112] *See* text accompanying note 57 *supra*.

The 1978 American Law Institute meeting approved Restatement (Second) of Contracts (Tent. Draft No. 13, 1978), which, consistent with the overall neoclassical pattern of Restatement (Second) deals with changes in contracts in a chapter entitled "Discharge by Assent or Alteration." Its only black-letter doctrinal tool is consideration, although relational notions such as good faith do creep into the comments occasionally, *e.g.*, § 351, Comment d. At one point the old battle about Foakes v. Beer, 9 App. Cas. 605 (1884), the principle of which is approved in § 348, almost led to a motion not only to revise § 348, but also the more basic section dealing with the pre-existing duty rule, § 76A, approved by the Institute over a decade earlier. I had a strong feeling that passage of such a motion might well have led ultimately to the complete unraveling of Restatement (Second), the most current tapestry of American neoclassical contract law. But so, I suspect, did others who would have greeted that occurrence with less enthusiasm, and the dangerous moment passed without the motion being made.

[113] As does, of course, not only the discrete transactional technique of allowing one side to specify terms but also any contract as to the rights conferred thereby. The horizontal nature of the formation of contracts and the fact that both sides have rights, too, often is allowed to obscure their command nature once formed.

[114] I do not adhere to the Coasian view recently espoused by Posner, differentiating contract from the firm, *i.e.*, from the command structure. Coase, *The Nature of the Firm*, 4 ECONOMICA 386, 386 n.5, 390-91 (1937); R. POSNER, *supra* note 52, at § 14.1. The corporate firm is no more and no less, in my view, than an immensely complex bundle of ongoing contractual relations. See note 33 *supra* for an expansion of this view. But as is suggested above, those relations are also command relations.

When the conflict levels in exchange processes, wherever they may lie on the command-horizontal spectrum, exceed the resolution capacity of bargaining and other exchange processes, other techniques of dispute resolution must be utilized. Here we find the most dramatic change from the classical or even neoclassical litigation (or rights arbitration[115]) models. Their function is to put an end to the dispute; and, since resolution of the dispute is all that remains of the discrete transaction, the process is a relatively simple and clean one. This process is rather like the discrete transaction itself: sharp in (by commencing suit) and sharp out (by judgment for defendant or collection of a money judgment by plaintiff).[116] Professor Chayes has recently described this model:

> (1) The lawsuit is *bipolar*. Litigation is organized as a contest between two individuals or at least two unitary interests, diametrically opposed, to be decided on a winner-takes-all basis.
>
> (2) Litigation is *retrospective*. The controversy is about an identified set of completed events: whether they occurred, and if so, with what consequences for the legal relations of the parties.
>
> (3) *Right and remedy are interdependent.* The scope of the relief is derived more or less logically from the substantive violation under the general theory that the plaintiff will get compensation measured by the harm caused by the defendant's breach of duty—in contract by giving plaintiff the money he would have had absent the breach; in tort by paying the value of the damage caused.
>
> (4) The lawsuit is a *self-contained* episode. The impact of the judgment is confined to the parties. If plaintiff prevails there is a simple compensatory transfer, usually of money, but occasionally the return of a thing or the performance of a definite act. If defendant prevails, a loss lies where it has fallen. In either case, entry of judgment ends the court's involvement.
>
> (5) The process is *party-initiated* and *party-controlled*. The case is organized and the issues defined by exchanges between the parties. Responsibility for fact development is theirs. The trial judge is a neutral arbiter of their interactions who decides questions of law only if they are put in issue by an appropriate move of a party.[117]

Naturally, no such model will do when the relation is supposed to continue in spite of the dispute, and where a main goal must always be its successful carrying on after the dispute is resolved or otherwise eliminated or avoided.

Professor Chayes went on to develop a morphology of what he terms

---

115 *See* note 39 and accompanying text *supra*.

116 This is, of course, a parody, especially the very last point. Contrary to the fantasies of the law school classroom, the real beginning of many contract dispute cases won by plaintiffs comes *after* rendering of a judgment. Then the deficiencies of execution, and with it the legal remedial system itself, become apparent.

117 Chayes, *The Role of the Judge in Public Law Litigation*, 89 HARV. L. REV. 1281, 1282-83 (1976) (footnotes omitted) (emphasis in original). For critical comments concerning the developments Chayes describes, see Kirkham, *Complex Civil Litigation: Have Good Intentions Gone Awry?*, 3 LAW & LIBERTY 1 (Winter 1977).

NORTHWESTERN UNIVERSITY LAW REVIEW

"public law litigation."[118] Although he does not direct this morphology at contract disputes, I have found it helpful in organizing my thoughts about the processes of dispute resolution in contractual relations. (So modified it focuses on the processes of change in such relations when bargaining and other exchange processes fail.) The following is his morphology, modified where appropriate for use in contractual relations.

1.   The scope of the dispute is not exogenously given by contract terms but is shaped by both the parties and the resolver of the dispute—*e.g.*, the arbitrator—and by the entire relation as it has developed and is developing.

2.   The party structure is not rigidly bilateral but sprawling and amorphous.

3.   The fact inquiry is not only historical and adjudicative but also predictive and legislative.[119]

4.   Relief is not conceived primarily (or sometimes at all) as compensation for past wrong in a form logically derived from the substantive liability and confined in its impact to the immediate parties; instead, it is in great (or even entire) measure forward-looking, fashioned ad hoc on flexible and broadly remedial lines, often having important consequences for many persons, including absentees.

5.   The remedy is not imposed but negotiated and mediated.

6.   The award does not terminate the dispute-resolver's role in the relation; instead, the award will require continuing administration by this or other similarly situated dispute-resolvers.

7.   The dispute-resolver is not passive, that is, his function is not limited to analysis and statement of governing rules; he is active, with responsibility not only for credible fact evaluation but also for organizing and shaping the dispute processes to ensure a just and viable outcome.

8.   The subject matter of the dispute is not between private individuals about private rights but is a grievance about the operation of policies of the overall contractual relation.[120]

In almost every respect the foregoing approaches contrast sharply with a classical contract law system and with the conceptual assumptions of a neoclassical system. For example, two ways by which a classical

---

118 This is an unfortunately narrow choice of words. His summary appears in Chayes, *supra* note 117, at 1302.

119 Chayes states this one: "The fact inquiry is not historical and adjudicative but predictive and legislative." *Id.* In his context this seems to me an overstatement; I have no doubt it is if applied to contractual relations.

120 Readers who examine the chart in the Appendix *infra* will probably have a sense of déjà vu here, as will those familiar with the long-standing debate about the role of the labor arbitrator, and as will readers with a background in legal anthropology. The latter are likely to recognize a kind of neotribalism in the process described, and the labor law experts will see the statement as a generalizing of views expressed by Dean Shulman.

contract law system implements its goals of enhancing discreteness and presentiation are by limiting strictly the sources considered in establishing the substantive content of the transaction in resolving disputes and by utilizing strictly defined (and narrow) remedies.[121] Both of these methods sharply conflict with the relational approaches outlined above. Similarly, although the neoclassical system can accomplish some of the flexibility of these relational patterns, and utilizes some of them, in toto the patterns go far beyond it. In the neoclassical system the parol evidence rule is hardly dead; the fact inquiry is nowhere nearly as wide-ranging; development of flexible and broad remedies is modest indeed; at the end of the day, remedies are imposed, rather than simply negotiated and mediated until some kind of uneasy (and probably temporary) consensus is reached; more often than not a dispute-resolver does expect to wipe his hands of the matter after the appropriate remedy has been determined; the dispute-resolver, at least when he is a judge, tends to remain passive; and the subject matter of dispute often tends to remain, at least formally and often more substantially, between clear poles of interest and polar rights, rather than overall policies of the contractual relation.

The sharp contrast between the classical (and even neoclassical) limitation of sources of substantive content mentioned above and the broad ranging inquiries of a relational system brings us to a key question concerning the interplay of presentiated and discrete aspects of relations with their nondiscrete, nonpresentiated aspects. The premise of the classical system is that no interplay could occur, because all aspects of the contract are presentiated and discrete. This premise continues to underlie the structure of the neoclassical system, but in actual operation that system shifts to a presumption in favor of limitation, although one subject to considerable erosion. In implementing their premises both classical and neoclassical contract law establish hierarchies for determining content (as noted earlier). Formal communications such as writings control informal communications; linguistic communications control nonlinguistic communications; communicated circumstances control noncommunicated circumstances; and finally utilization of noncommunicated circumstances is always suspect.

Do such hierarchies continue in a relational system? The answer is both yes and no. To the extent that presentiated and discrete aspects of contractual relations are created by written documents, they may reflect very sharp focus of party attention and strong intentions to be governed by them in the future. Certainly the wage and seniority structures in most collective bargaining agreements exemplify this. Thus, such documents may occupy very dominant positions in the priorities of values of the relation. When this is the case, something analogous to the classical notions previously set out may very properly be applied by the dispute-

---

[121] *See* text accompanying note 27 *supra*.

NORTHWESTERN UNIVERSITY LAW REVIEW

resolver. There is, however, one big difference. In a system of relational contract law the simple existence of formal communications does not automatically trigger application of the neoclassical hierarchy of presumptions. Rather, a preliminary question must always be asked: do the formal communications indeed reflect the sharp past focus and strong intentions necessary to put these communications high in the priorities of values created by the contractual relation? This question can be answered only by looking at the whole relation, not in the grudging manner of the neoclassical system, but as the very foundation for proceeding further with the hierarchical assumptions, or without them, or with other hierarchies. (An example of the latter occurs in marital disputes: nonlinguistic conduct and informal communications typically far outweigh in importance for resolving such disputes any formal agreements—except sometimes as to property—the parties may have made.)

I feel some temptation to think of the written parts of contractual relations, especially very formal parts, such as collective bargaining agreements and corporate charters and bylaws, as constitutions establishing legislative and administrative processes for the relation.[122] Indeed, that is what many of them are. Nevertheless, danger lurks in this formulation. The danger lies in reintroducing into the law of contractual relations[123] such things as the hierarchies discussed above—not on an ad hoc basis but as a matter of general principle emanating from the concept of "constitution." If that concept or terminology is used to resurrect "constitutions" long decayed and made obsolete by less formally established patterns of communications and behavior, we are, as a matter of principle, back to a relationally dysfunctional neoclassicism.[124] Moreover, only one party or class of parties may know the content of these "constitutions," and they may suffer from other adhesion characteristics. In such circumstances giving them constitutional weight may be very dubious indeed.

---

[122] This is hardly an original thought. *See, e.g.*, Fuller, *supra* note 43, at 5. *See also* Cox, *Reflections upon Labor Arbitration*, 72 HARV. L. REV. 1482, 1490-93, 1498-1501 (1959); Shulman, *Reason, Contract, and Law in Labor Relations*, 68 HARV. L. REV. 999, 1004-05 (1955).

[123] I mean by this term law not only of the sovereign, but also both internal law of the relation—*e.g.*, that established by agreement or internal bodies such as boards of directors—and external law other than that of the sovereign, such as trade association rules.

[124] The following language from IBM v. Catamore Enterprises, Inc., 548 F.2d 1065, 1073 (1st Cir. 1976), *cert. denied*, 431 U.S. 960 (1977), while appropriate enough to the facts of the case, is the kind that can be sadly misused in the face of long time erosion of "constitutions" of contractual relations:

> The first is the substantive principle that when, in the course of business transactions between people or corporations, free and uncoerced understandings purporting to be comprehensive are solemnized by documents which both parties sign and concede to be their agreement, such documents are not easily bypassed or given restrictive interpretations.

In fact, over time, parties to complex relations do "easily bypass" such agreements and give them "restrictive" (or expansive) interpretations. Courts not recognizing this are likely to reach unsatisfactory results.

This brief treatment of processes of flexibility and change in contractual relations can now serve as a background for consideration of characteristics of substantive change in contractual relations.

The Substance of Change in Contractual Relations

All aspects of contractual relations are subject to the norms characterizing contracts generally, whether they are discrete or relational. As noted earlier[125] these are: (1) permitting and encouraging participation in exchange, (2) promoting reciprocity, (3) reinforcing role patterns appropriate to the various particular kinds of contracts, (4) providing limited freedom for exercise of choice, (5) effectuating planning, and (6) harmonizing the internal and external matrixes of particular contracts. These norms affect change in contractual relations just as they affect all their other aspects.

In addition, I have identified two norms particularly applicable to contractual relations:[126] (1) harmonizing conflict within the internal matrix of the relation, including especially, discrete and presentiated behavior with nondiscrete and nonpresentiated behavior; and (2) preservation of the relation.[127] These norms affect change in contractual relations, just as they affect all their aspects.

A great deal of change in ongoing contractual relations comes about glacially, through small-scale, day-to-day adjustments resulting from an interplay of horizontally arranged exchange—*e.g.*, workers creating new ways of cooperatively defining their work or minor changes in the way in which deliveries are made—and from the flow of day-to-day commands through the vertical patterns of the relation. In addition, within a broad range, change will come about through commands of a more sweeping nature, *e.g.*, to sell the appliance division of the firm or develop a major new line of products. This is, of course, focused change and raises all kinds of problems, not the least of which involve the two relational norms. Moreover, command changes of this magnitude in a modern society almost invariably overlap areas that must be dealt with by horizontal arrangements, *e.g.*, the terms of the collective bargaining agreement governing severance or transfer of old employees and the hiring of new employees. Finally, there are horizontal changes in contractual

---

125 *See* text accompanying note 23 *supra*; *Many Futures*, *supra* note 9, at 808-16. The word norm is used here generally to include the way people actually behave, the "oughts" that their behavior generates vis-à-vis each other, and the "oughts" their behavior generates externally to their relation, *e.g.*, in sovereign contract law. There may, of course, be occasion to differentiate, but commonly this usage is fine enough.

126 *See* note 24 *supra*.

127 The discrete norms—enhancing discreteness and presentation—were not truly separate from the general norms of effectuating planning and exercising choice but were an intensification of these general norms that was so great and opened up so many facets as to justify new labels. This is also true of the relational norms. Both grow out of the last of the general norms and could be treated as part of it.

NORTHWESTERN UNIVERSITY LAW REVIEW

relations themselves partially or wholly horizontal in origin. If, for example, we consider a collective bargaining agreement as an arrangement separate from the firm itself (by my lights, a somewhat artificial thing to do), the shifting of a major part of a wage increase from cash into layoff compensation would constitute a focused horizontal change.[128] Similarly, a consortium of businesses determining whether to go into a new line of activity would be engaged in horizontally focused change.

We have thus far considered change coming about either through gradual accretion, through command operating within acceptable limits of the relation, or through successful negotiation and agreement. While these offer many problems for a relational contract system and its related legal structure, the big *legal* difficulties come when change is pushed that has failed to come about in those ways. What happens when this occurs?

In answering that question it is well to remember that we are dealing with situations where the desire is to continue the relation, not to terminate it. Moreover, my sense is that normally the most important factor is the status quo; that is to say, that the dispute-resolver will be conservative and will not move far from the status quo. This is borne out by the sense of arbitrators experienced in "interest arbitration" that the base point of such arbitration is the presentiated status quo.[129] Anyone interested in change through the dispute-resolution process has a heavy burden of persuasion. Dispute-resolution processes governed by the norm of continuing the relation are, if this view is correct, essentially conservative.

The foregoing conclusion does not lead to the conclusion that change will not result from this kind of interest-dispute-resolution process. Anyone the least familiar with arbitration of public employee interest disputes knows this.[130] The very fact that a party is willing to press this far suggests in most cases a basis for some change, although bargaining being what it is, probably not as much as the aggressive party tries to get. Moreover, status quo in a dynamic society does not mean a static status quo; as noted earlier in another connection, the status quo itself may very well be one in which changes in a certain direction are expected. If they do not come or come less than expected, then the interest-dispute-resolver is faced with a situation where the status quo calls for change, not for simply sticking to patterns now viewed as obsolete.[131]

---

[128] In the growth society of the past 40 years, such patterns have largely dealt with increments to the wage package, and hence their nature as a fundamental change has been somewhat disguised. In a no-growth or slow-growth society, trade-offs may have to be made between existing cash wages and fringe benefits. Such trade-offs will indeed be perceived as changes.

[129] *See* note 39 *supra*.

[130] I confess to overlooking this obvious point until someone at the Harvard Seminar, *see* note 1 *supra*, I think it was Professor Chayes, mentioned it.

[131] "In some cases, such as wages, change over time actually becomes the norm, so that a

Exploration of the other relational norm—harmonizing conflicts within the internal social matrix of the relation—reinforces the foregoing conclusions. Such harmonization is unlikely to come through revolutionary changes[132] that conflicting interests have been unable to accede to through negotiation or mediation. Changes typically can be harmonized with the remainder of the relation only by making them consistent with the status quo, again a conservative notion. But it must be noted that if the status quo is a dynamic one moving over time in certain directions—*e.g.*, increasing levels of real wages—change in accord with those patterns is essential to preserve the status quo itself. This is the kind of harmonization we should expect from a dispute-resolver implementing this norm.

My work on developing general contractual norms and relational norms has progressed slowly since *The Many Futures of Contracts*.[133] Certainly other norms besides the two mentioned will have a bearing on change in a system of relational contract law. Two categories should be mentioned, the first of which will have a ring of familiarity to all students of contracts: the restitution, reliance and expectation interests. In a system of discrete transactions, it is now generally accepted that protection of these three interests constitutes a basic norm of contract law. This does not change as we move from classical to neoclassical contract law and on to relational contract law; such interests remain fundamental.

One important change, however, does occur. In classical contract law it is expectations created solely by defined promises and reliance on defined promises that are protected. Only the restitution interest had a broader foundation, and restitution fitted uneasily in the structure of classical contract law, often being conceptualized as not part of that law at all. In neoclassical contract law the expectation and reliance interests remain based primarily on promise, although exceptions do exist. For example, *Drennan v. Star Paving Co.*[134] can be read as holding that reliance on something (industry patterns or common decency?) created the promise rather than the other way around.[135] Restitution, increasingly recognized in neoclassical contract law as an integral part of the system (again perhaps slightly uneasily), stands out as perhaps the least promise-

---

party who resists an accustomed change may be perceived as himself the proponent of change.'' Eisenberg, *supra* note 110, at 676 n.122.

132 This is to say nothing about the efficacy of revolution for other purposes; soothing conflict within a structure is simply not one of its goals.

133 Note 9 *supra*.

134 51 Cal. 2d 409, 333 P.2d 757 (1958).

135 More recent examples are: Lockewill, Inc. v. United States Shoe Corp., 547 F.2d 1024 (8th Cir. 1976), *cert. denied*, 431 U.S. 956 (1977) (*see* text accompanying note 90 *supra*); Carlson v. Olson, 256 N.W.2d 249 (1977); Reisman & Sons v. Snyder's Potato Chips, 32 Somerset Leg. J. 3 (Pa. C.P. Somerset County 1976) (in spite of a holding that a franchisor had no promissory obligation to continue the franchise, the court held that the franchisee's reliance on the relation precluded termination). *Cf.* Sheridan, *The Floating Trust: Mutual Wills*, 15 ALBERTA L. REV. 211 (1977) (agreements to make mutual wills may impose restrictions on revoking or altering the arrangement).

NORTHWESTERN UNIVERSITY LAW REVIEW

oriented part of the system. In this sense restitution paves the way for treatment of the three contract interests in relational contract law. No longer are those interests bottomed primarily on defined promises, nor are efforts necessary to squeeze them within promissory contexts. In such a system recognition is easily accorded to the creation of such interests arising naturally from *any* behavior patterns within the relation. Substantive changes in relations must therefore take into account the three basic contract interests of restitution, reliance, and expectations, irrespective of their sources.

As illustrative of the foregoing, consider an employee of a small business who has been treated very decently by his employer for thirty years. He quite naturally comes to expect decent treatment throughout the relation including through retirement. Moreover, he relies on that expectation; and if the expectation is not realized, the employer may very well have derived benefits from the reliance by the employee that, in terms of the relation as it existed, are unjustified. We can, and do, infer promises in such situations, but they are far from the defined promises of discrete transactions. Moreover, something besides promise lies behind the social desiderata of seeing that these interests of the employee do not go unprotected. Expectations, as noted earlier, are a form of presentiation however they may be created. When they are reasonable under the circumstances, irrespective of how the circumstances were created, societies tend to be very loath to see them thwarted. An already mentioned example is the reluctance of virtually all of American society to accept even the temporary thwarting of post-World War II expectations of continued economic growth.

The final category of relational norm to be considered here is very open-ended. As contractual relations expand, those relations take on more and more the characteristics of minisocieties and ministates. Indeed, even that is an understatement. In the case of huge bundles of contractual relations, such as a major national or multinational corporation, they take on the characteristics of large societies and large states. But whether small or large, the whole range of social and political norms become pertinent *within* the contractual relations. In ongoing contractual relations we find such broad norms as distributive justice, liberty,[136] human dignity, social equality and inequality, and procedural justice, to mention some of the more vital. Changes in such contractual relations must accord with norms established respecting these matters, just as much as they do the more traditional contract norms. Changes made ignoring this fact may be very disruptive indeed.[137]

---

[136] *See* D. Ewing, Freedom Inside the Organization (1977); Keeffe Bros. v. Teamsters Local Union No. 592, 562 F.2d 298 (4th Cir. 1977).

[137] At this point, just as contractual relations exceed the capacities of the neoclassical contract law system, so too the issues exceed the capacities of neoclassical contract law scholars. They must become something else—anthropologists, sociologists, economists,

Termination of Contractual Relations

Termination of contractual relations is an extremely complex subject, far too complex to do more than touch here.[138] Nevertheless a number of points should be made. One is that, unlike discrete transactions, many contractual relations are, for all practical purposes, expected never to end. IBM, the relation between the United Auto Workers and General Motors, and Harvard University are expected to go on forever. Even in the face of great trouble, relations of this kind often do not end, but continue on in new forms; *e.g.*, Northeast Airlines is merged into Delta, or rail passenger service is transferred to Amtrak, along with physical facilities, the labor force, and much of the management. The realities of such transformations often evoke processes very similar to relational patterns of change already discussed, rather than clean-cut application of clear rights and obligations in the discrete transactional tradition.

Of course, many long-term contractual relations are recognized (by outsiders, if not always by the participants) as vulnerable to traumatic termination. Small businesses, branch plant operations of large businesses, and in part, marriages, clubs, and many franchises, serve as illustrations. Depending in part on the relations themselves and in part on such external factors as their importance to the community and the political heft of various of their participants, their termination may or may not be treated by the legal system in relational ways, procedurally or substantively.[139] To the extent that they are treated relationally, their terminations will be similar to those massive contractual relations that had not been expected to end at all.

On the other hand, many long-term contractual relations are, from the start, expected to terminate. A small partnership expecting not to take in new members, or marriage without progeny are examples. Many business consortiums are of this nature. When such relations terminate

---

political theorists, and philosophers—to do reasonable justice to the issues raised by contractual relations. Exchange and planning, the basic areas of expertise of the contracts scholar, have now become just two of the many factors in a complete social organism.

138 For an earlier discussion of this subject, see *Many Futures, supra* note 9, at 750-53.

139 *E.g.*, McGrath v. Hilding, 41 N.Y.2d 625, 363 N.E.2d 328, 394 N.Y.S.2d 603 (1977). Plaintiff divorced defendant after three months of marriage and remarried her former husband. During the brief marriage plaintiff contributed money to building an addition to defendant's house relying on an oral premarital promise to give her a tenancy by the entirety. The promise was not performed, and plaintiff sought equitable relief based on a constructive trust. The lower courts rejected as collateral defendant's offer to prove marital misconduct by plaintiff. The New York Court of Appeals remanded for a new trial, stating that whether defendant's enrichment was unjust could not be determined by inquiring only about an "isolated transaction." Rather it must be a "realistic determination based on a broad view of the human setting involved." *Id.* at 629, 363 N.E.2d at 331, 394 N.Y.S.2d at 606.

NORTHWESTERN UNIVERSITY LAW REVIEW

traumatically early, their treatment will follow patterns already discussed. When they follow the expected course, the legal system will treat their termination as it does other aspects of the relation. Some discrete aspects may be given effect; *e.g.*, legacies to the widow will be enforced explicitly. Some aspects may instead invoke relational norms; *e.g.*, the widow, even by will or maybe even by mutual agreement, cannot be cut out of the estate entirely or lose her rights in community property.

A final point to be made is the distinction between termination of a contractual relation and termination of an individual's participation in a contractual relation. Sometimes the two coincide, *e.g.*, the death of a spouse in a childless marriage. But contractual relations outside the nuclear family tend in modern society to be multiperson and to survive the departure or death of individual participants. Further, typically it is the ongoing relation rather than the individual that is the more powerful of the two.[140] Where, as in employment, this fact is coupled with a high degree of dependency of the individual on the particular relation, we are likely to find considerable protection of that dependency. Such protection may grow up internally (*e.g.*, through collective bargaining), may perhaps be coerced in considerable measure from outside (*e.g.*, labor laws and tax provisions favoring pensions), or may simply be imposed (*e.g.*, mandatory contributions by both employer and employee to Social Security).

In sum, terminations of long-term contractual relations tend to be like other aspects of relations, messily relational rather than cleanly transactional.

SUMMARY

A system of discrete transactions and its corresponding classical contract law provides for flexibility and change through the market outside the transactions, rather than within them. This enables the system to work while the transactions themselves remain highly discrete and presentiated, characteristics preserved and enhanced by classical contract law.

A system of more relational contract and its corresponding neoclassical contract law remains theoretically structured on the discrete and classical models, but involves significant changes. Such contracts, being more complex and of greater duration than discrete transactions, become dysfunctional if too rigid, thereby preventing the high level of presentiation of the discrete transaction. Thus, flexibility, often a great deal of it, needs to be planned into such contracts, or gaps need to be left in the planning to be added as needed. The neoclassical system responds to this by a range of techniques. These run from some open evasion of its

---

[140] In his later years this appears to have been true even of someone extraordinarily powerful as Howard Hughes.

72:854 (1978)   *Adjustment of Relations*

primary theoretical commitment to complete presentiation through initial consent on to the more common techniques of stretching consent far beyond its actual bounds and by fictions to squeeze later changes within an initial consent framework.

Somewhere along the line of increasing duration and complexity, trying to force changes into a pattern of original consent becomes both too difficult and too unrewarding to justify the effort, and the contractual relation escapes the bounds of the neoclassical system. That system is replaced by very different adjustment processes of an ongoing-administrative kind in which discreteness and presentiation become merely two of the factors of decision, not the theoretical touchstones. Moreover, the substantive relation of change to the status quo has now altered from what happens in some kind of a market external to the contract to what can be achieved through the political and social processes of the relation, internal and external. This includes internal and external dispute-resolution structures. At this point, the relation has become a minisociety with a vast array of norms beyond the norms centered on exchange and its immediate processes.

NORTHWESTERN UNIVERSITY LAW REVIEW

APPENDIX[141]

Transactional and Relational Axes

CONCEPT	EXTREME TRANSAC-TIONAL POLE	EXTREME RELATION-AL POLE
1. Overall relation type	Nonprimary	Primary
A. Personal involvement	Segmental, limited, non-unique, transferable	Whole person, unlimited, unique, non-transferable
B. Types of communication	Limited, linguistic, formal	Extensive, deep, not limited to linguistic, informal in addition to or in lieu of formal
C. Subject matter of satisfactions	Simple, monetizable economic exchange only	In addition to economic, complex personal non-economic satisfactions very important; social exchange; non-exchange
2. Measurability and actual measurement of exchange and other factors	One side of exchange is money; other side is easily monetized; both are actually measured; no other aspects	Both exchanges and other factors are relatively difficult to monetize or otherwise measure, and the parties do not monetize or measure them
3. Basic sources of socio-economic support	Apart from exchange motivations themselves, external to the transaction	Internal to the relation, as well as external
4. Duration	Short agreement process; short time between agreement and performance; short time of performance	Long term; no finite beginning; no end to either relation or performance, except perhaps upon death of parties
5. Commencement and termination	Sharp in by clear agreement; sharp out by clear performance	Commencement and termination, if any, of relation likely to be gradual; individual entry into existing relation often gradual, as may be withdrawal; individual entry may be by birth, and withdrawal by death

---

[141] From *Many Futures, supra* note 9, at 738-40, slightly modified.

902

72:854 (1978)   *Adjustment of Relations*

6. Planning
    A. Primary focus of planning   Substance of exchanges   Structures and processes of relation; planning of substance of exchanges primarily for initial period

    B. Completeness and specificity

        (1) Possible when planning occurs   Can be very complete and specific; only remote contingencies (if those) are beyond reasonable planning capacity   Limited specific planning of substance possible; extensive specific planning of structures and processes may be possible

        (2) Actual planning accomplished   Very complete and specific; only the practically unplanable (of which there is little) left unplanned   Limited specific planning of substance carried out; extensive planning of structures may or may not occur

    C. Sources and forms of mutual planning

        (1) Bargaining and adhesion   Specific consent to price of a good produced unilaterally by seller; short bid-ask bargaining, if any   Adhesion without bargaining unlikely except in case of entry of new members into existing relation; otherwise extended mutual planning merging imperceptibly into ongoing relation being established; a "joint creative effort"

        (2) Tacit assumptions   Inevitably present, but inherently relational and anti-transactional   Recognized aspect of relational planning, without which relations cannot survive

        (3) Sources and forms of post-commencement planning   No post-commencement planning   Operation of relation itself is prime source of further planning, which is likely to be extensive; may or may not be extensive explicit post-commencement planning

    D. Bindingness of planning   Planning is entirely binding   Planning may be binding, but often some or all of it is characterized by some degree of tentativeness

    E. Conflicts of interest in planning   Enterprise planning can be expressed only through partially zero-sum allocative planning, hence all mutual planning is conflict laden.   Enterprise planning may be separable at least in part from allocative planning, and hence relatively low in conflict; merger of non-allocative enterprise plan-

903

NORTHWESTERN UNIVERSITY LAW REVIEW

		ning with allocative planning may occur in ways muting conflict and providing nonnegotiational ways for dealing with it.
7. Future cooperation required in post-commencement planning and actual performance	Almost none required	Success of relation entirely dependent on further cooperation in both performance and further planning
8. Incidence of benefits and burdens	Shifting or other specific assignment of each particular benefit and burden to one party or the other	Undivided sharing of both benefits and burdens
9. Obligations undertaken		
A. Sources of content	Genuinely expressed, communicated and exchanged promises of parties	Relation itself develops obligations which may or may not include genuinely expressed, communicated and exchanged promises of the parties
B. Sources of obligation	External to parties and transaction except for their triggering it by manifestation of consent	Both external and internal to the relation; same as the sources of content of the obligation as to internal element
C. Specificity of obligation and sanction	Specific rules and rights specifically applicable and founded on the promises; monetizable or monetized (whether by mutual party planning i.e. promissory or otherwise i.e. by rule)	Nonspecific; nonmeasurable, whether based on customs, general principles or internalizations all arising from relation or partly from external sources; restorative unless breach results in termination, then may become transactional in nature
10. Transferability	Entirely transferable with the sole exception of an obligor's ultimate liability for nonperformance	Transfer likely to be uneconomic and difficult to achieve even when it is not impossible[142]
11. Number of participants	Two	May be as few as two, but likely to be more than two and often large masses
12. Participant views of transaction or relation		
A. Recognition of exchange	High	Low or perhaps even none

---

[142] I no longer believe this to be accurate; corporations can, for example, be sold and the work force may go right along. *See* MACNEIL, CASES 2, *supra* note 16, at 778.

72:854 (1978)   *Adjustment of Relations*

B.	Altruistic behavior	None expected or occurring	Significant expectations of occurrence
C.	Time-sense	Presentiation of the future	Futurizing of the present, i.e. to the extent past, present and future are viewed as separate, the present is viewed in terms of planning and preparing for a future not yet arrived
D.	Expectations about trouble in performance or among the participants	None expected, except perhaps that planned for; if it occurs expected to be governed by specific rights	Possibility of trouble anticipated as normal part of relation, to be dealt with by cooperation and other restorational techniques

[12]

THE JOURNAL OF
POLITICAL ECONOMY

| *Volume LXX* | APRIL 1962 | *Number 2* |

AN EXPERIMENTAL STUDY OF COMPETITIVE
MARKET BEHAVIOR[1]

VERNON L. SMITH

Purdue University

I. INTRODUCTION

RECENT years have witnessed a growing interest in experimental games such as management decision-making games and games designed to simulate oligopolistic market phenomena. This article reports on a series of experimental games designed to study some of the hypotheses of neoclassical competitive market theory. Since the organized stock, bond, and commodity exchanges would seem to have the best chance of fulfilling the conditions of an operational theory of supply and demand, most of these experiments have

been designed to simulate, on a modest scale, the multilateral auction-trading process characteristic of these organized markets. I would emphasize, however, that they are intended as simulations of certain key features of the organized markets and of competitive markets generally, rather than as direct, exhaustive simulations of any particular organized exchange. The experimental conditions of supply and demand in force in these markets are modeled closely upon the supply and demand curves generated by the limit price orders in the hands of stock and commodity market brokers at the opening of a trading day in any one stock or commodity, though I would consider them to be good general models of received short-run supply and demand theory. A similar experimental supply and demand model was first used by E. H. Chamberlin in an interesting set of experiments that pre-date contemporary interest in experimental games.[2]

[1] The experiments on which this report is based have been performed over a six-year period beginning in 1955. They are part of a continuing study, in which the next phase is to include experimentation with monetary payoffs and more complicated experimental designs to which passing references are made here and there in the present report. I wish to thank Mrs. Marilyn Schweizer for assistance in typing and in the preparation of charts in this paper, R. K. Davidson for performing one of the experiments for me, and G. Horwich, J. Hughes, H. Johnson, and J. Wolfe for reading an earlier version of the paper and enriching me with their comments and encouragement. This work was supported by the Institute for Quantitative Research at Purdue, the Purdue Research Foundation, and in part by National Science Foundation, Grant No. 16114, at Stanford University.

[2] "An Experimental Imperfect Market," *Journal of Political Economy*, LVI (April, 1948), 95–108. For an experimental study of bilateral monopoly, see S. Siegel and L. Fouraker, *Bargaining and Group Decision Making* (New York: McGraw-Hill Book Co., 1960).

Chamberlin's paper was highly suggestive in demonstrating the potentialities of experimental techniques in the study of applied market theory.

Parts II and III of this paper are devoted to a descriptive discussion of the experiments and some of their detailed results. Parts IV and V present an empirical analysis of various equilibrating hypotheses and a rationalization of the hypothesis found to be most successful in these experiments.

Part VI provides a brief summary which the reader may wish to consult before reading the main body of the paper.

II. EXPERIMENTAL PROCEDURE

The experiments discussed in Parts III and IV have followed the same general design pattern. The group of subjects is divided at random into two subgroups, a group of buyers and a group of sellers. Each buyer receives a card containing a number, known only to that buyer, which represents the maximum price he is willing to pay for one unit of the fictitious commodity. It is explained that the buyers are not to buy a unit of the commodity at a price exceeding that appearing on their buyer's card; they would be quite happy to purchase a unit at any price below this number—the lower the better; but, they would be entirely willing to pay just this price for the commodity rather than have their wants go unsatisfied. It is further explained that each buyer should think of himself as making a pure profit equal to the difference between his actual contract price and the maximum reservation price on his card. These reservation prices generate a demand curve such as DD in the diagram on the left in Chart 1. At each price the corresponding quantity represents the maximum amount that could be purchased at that price. Thus, in Chart 1, the highest price buyer is willing to pay as much as $3.25 for one unit. At a price above $3.25 the demand quantity is zero, and at $3.25 it cannot exceed one unit. The next highest price buyer is willing to pay $3.00. Thus, at $3.00 the demand quantity cannot exceed two units. The phrase "cannot exceed" rather than "is" will be seen to be of no small importance. How much is actually taken at any price depends upon such important things as how the market is organized, and various mechanical and bargaining considerations associated with the offer-acceptance process. The demand curve, therefore, defines the set (all points on or to the left of DD) of possible demand quantities at each, strictly hypothetical, ruling price.

Each seller receives a card containing a number, known only to that seller, which represents the minimum price at which he is willing to relinquish one unit of the commodity. It is explained that the sellers should be willing to sell at their minimum supply price rather than fail to make a sale, but they make a pure profit determined by the excess of their contract price over their minimum reservation price. Under no condition should they sell below this minimum. These minimum seller prices generate a supply curve such as SS in Chart 1. At each hypothetical price the corresponding quantity represents the maximum amount that could be sold at that price. The supply curve, therefore, defines the set of possible supply quantities at each hypothetical ruling price.

In experiments 1–8 each buyer and seller is allowed to make a contract for the exchange of only a single unit of the commodity during any one trading or market period. This rule was for the sake of simplicity and was relaxed in subsequent experiments.

Each experiment was conducted over a sequence of trading periods five to ten minutes long depending upon the number of participants in the test group. Since the experiments were conducted within a class period, the number of trading periods was not uniform among

has been closed, and the buyer and seller making the deal drop out of the market in the sense of no longer being permitted to make bids, offers, or contracts for the remainder of that market period.[3] As soon as a bid or offer is accepted, the contract price is recorded together with the minimum supply price of the seller

CHART 1

TEST 1

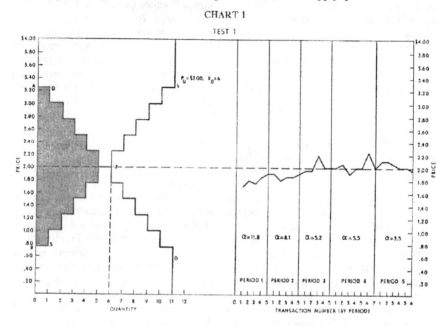

the various experiments. In the typical experiment, the market opens for trading period 1. This means that any buyer (or seller) is free at any time to raise his hand and make a verbal offer to buy (or sell) at any price which does not violate his maximum (or minimum) reservation price. Thus, in Chart 1, the buyer holding the $2.50 card might raise his hand and shout, "Buy at $1.00." The seller with the $1.50 card might then shout, "Sell at $3.60." Any seller (or buyer) is free to accept a bid (or offer), in which case a binding contract

and the maximum demand price of the buyer involved in the transaction. These observations represent the recorded data of the experiment.[4] Within the time limit

[3] All purchases are for final consumption. There are no speculative purchases for resale in the same or later periods. There is nothing, however, to prevent one from designing an experiment in which purchases for resale are permitted if the objective is to study the role of speculation in the equilibrating process. One could, for example, permit the carry-over of stocks from one period to the next.

[4] Owing to limitations of manpower and equipment in experiments 1–8, bids and offers which did not lead to transactions could not be recorded. In subsequent experiments a tape recorder was used for this purpose.

of a trading period, this procedure is continued until bids and offers are no longer leading to contracts. One or two calls are made for final bids or offers and the market is officially closed. This ends period 1. The market is then immediately reopened for the second "day" of trading. All buyers, including those who did and those who did not make contracts in the preceding trading period, now (as explained previously to the subjects) have a renewed urge to buy one unit of the commodity. For each buyer, the same maximum buying price holds in the second period as prevailed in the first period. In this way the experimental demand curve represents a demand per unit time or per trading period. Similarly, each seller, we may imagine, has "overnight" acquired a fresh unit of the commodity which he desires to sell in period 2 under the same minimum price conditions as prevailed in period 1. The experimental supply curve thereby represents a willingness to supply per unit time. Trading period 2 is allowed to run its course, and then period 3, and so on. By this means we construct a prototype market in which there is a flow of a commodity onto and off the market. The stage is thereby set to study price behavior under given conditions of normal supply and demand.[5] Some buyers and sellers, it should be noted, may be unable to make contracts in any trading period, or perhaps only in certain periods. Insofar as these traders are submarginal buyers or sellers, this is to be expected. Indeed, the ability of these experimental markets to ration out submarginal buyers and sellers will be one measure of the effectiveness or competitive performance of the market.

The above design considerations define a rejection set of offers (and bids) for each buyer (and seller), which in turn defines a demand and a supply schedule for the market in question. These schedules do nothing beyond setting extreme limits to the observable price-quantity behavior in that market. All we can say is that the area above the supply curve is a region in which sales are feasible, while the area below the demand curve is a region in which purchases are feasible. Competitive price theory asserts that there will be a tendency for price-quantity equilibrium to occur at the extreme quantity point of the intersection of these two areas. For example, in Chart 1 the shaded triangular area *APB* represents the intersection of these feasible sales and purchase sets, with *P* the extreme point of this set. We have no guarantee that the equilibrium defined by the intersection of these sets will prevail, even approximately, in the experimental market (or any real counterpart of it). The mere fact that, by any definition, supply and demand schedules exist in the background of a market does not guarantee that any meaningful relationship exists

[5] The design of my experiments differs from that of Chamberlin (*op. cit.*) in several ways. In Chamberlin's experiment the buyers and sellers simply circulate and engage in bilateral higgling and bargaining until they make a contract or the trading period ends. As contracts are made the transaction price is recorded on the blackboard. Consequently, there is very little, if any, multilateral bidding. Each trader's attention is directed to the one person with whom he is bargaining, whereas in my experiments each trader's quotation is addressed to the entire trading group one quotation at a time. Also Chamberlin's experiment constitutes a pure exchange market operated for a single trading period. There is, therefore, less opportunity for traders to gain experience and to modify their subsequent behavior in the light of such experience. It is only through some learning mechanism of this kind that I can imagine the possibility of equilibrium being approached in any real market. Finally, in the present experiments I have varied the design from one experiment to another in a conscious attempt to study the effect of different conditions of supply and demand, changes in supply or demand, and changes in the rules of market organization on market-price behavior.

between those schedules and what is observed in the market they are presumed to represent. All the supply and demand schedules can do is set broad limits on the behavior of the market.[6] Thus, in the symmetrical supply and demand diagram of Chart 1, it is conceivable that every buyer and seller could make a contract. The $3.25 buyer could buy from the $3.25 seller, the $3.00 buyer could buy from the $3.00 seller, and so forth, without violating any restrictions on the behavior of buyers and sellers. Indeed, if we separately paired buyers and sellers in this special way, each pair could be expected to make a bilateral contract at the seller's minimum price which would be equal to the buyer's maximum price.

It should be noted that these experiments conform in several important ways to what we know must be true of many kinds of real markets. In a real competitive market such as a commodity or stock exchange, each marketer is likely to be ignorant of the reservation prices at which other buyers and sellers are willing to trade. Furthermore, the only way that a real marketer can obtain knowledge of market conditions is to

observe the offers and bids that are tendered, and whether or not they are accepted. These are the public data of the market. A marketer can only know his own attitude, and, from observation, learn something about the objective behavior of others. This is a major feature of these experimental markets. We deliberately avoid placing at the disposal of our subjects any information which would not be practically attainable in a real market. Each experimental market is forced to provide all of its own "history." These markets are also a replica of real markets in that they are composed of a practical number of marketers, say twenty, thirty, or forty. We do not require an indefinitely large number of marketers, which is usually supposed necessary for the existence of "pure" competition.

One important condition operating in our experimental markets is not likely to prevail in real markets. The experimental conditions of supply and demand are held constant over several successive trading periods in order to give any equilibrating mechanisms an opportunity to establish an equilibrium over time. Real markets are likely to be continually subjected to changing conditions of supply and demand. Marshall was well aware of such problems and defined equilibrium as a condition toward which the market would move *if* the forces of supply and demand were to remain stationary for a sufficiently long time. It is this concept of equilibrium that this particular series of experiments is designed, in part, to test. There is nothing to prevent one from passing out new buyer and/or seller cards, representing changed demand and/or supply conditions, at the end of each trading period if the objective is to study the effect of such constantly changing conditions on market behavior.

[6] In fact, these schedules are modified as trading takes place. Whenever a buyer and a seller make a contract and "drop out" of the market, the demand and supply schedules are shifted to the left in a manner depending upon the buyer's and seller's position on the schedules. Hence, the supply and demand functions continually alter as the trading process occurs. It is difficult to imagine a real market process which does not exhibit this characteristic. This means that the intra-trading-period schedules are not independent of the transactions taking place. However, the *initial* schedules prevailing at the opening of each trading period are independent of the transactions, and it is these schedules that I identify with the "theoretical conditions of supply and demand," which the theorist defines independently of actual market prices and quantities. One of the important objectives in these experiments is to determine whether or not these initial schedules have any power to predict the observed behavior of the market.

In three of the nine experiments, once-for-all changes in demand and/or supply were made for purposes of studying the transient dynamics of a market's response to such stimuli.

III. DESCRIPTION AND DISCUSSION OF EXPERIMENTAL RESULTS

The supply and demand schedule for each experiment is shown in the diagram on the left of Charts 1–10. The price and quantity at which these schedules intersect will be referred to as the predicted or theoretical "equilibrium" price and quantity for the corresponding experimental market, though such an equilibrium will not necessarily be attained or approached in the market. The performance of each experimental market is summarized in the diagram on the right of Charts 1–10, and in Table 1. Each chart shows the sequence of contract or exchange prices in the order in which they occurred in each trading period. Thus, in Chart 1, the first transaction was effected at $1.70, the second at $1.80, and so on, with a total of five transactions occurring in trading period 1. These charts show contract price as a function of transaction number rather than calendar time, the latter of course being quite irrelevant to market dynamics.

The most striking general characteristic of tests 1–3, 5–7, 9, and 10 is the remarkably strong tendency for exchange prices to approach the predicted equilibrium for each of these markets. As the exchange process is repeated through successive trading periods with the same conditions of supply and demand prevailing initially in each period, the variation in exchange prices tends to decline, and to cluster more closely around the equilibrium. In Chart 1, for example, the variation in contract prices over the five

trading periods is from $1.70 to $2.25. The maximum possible variation is from $0.75 to $3.25 as seen in the supply and demand schedules. As a means of measuring the convergence of exchange prices in each market, a "coefficient of convergence," a, has been computed for each trading period in each market. The a for each trading period is the ratio of the standard deviation of exchange prices, σ_0, to the predicted equilibrium price, P_0, the ratio being expressed as a percentage. That is, $a = 100 \ \sigma_0/P_0$ where σ_0 is the standard deviation of exchange prices around the equilibrium price rather than the mean exchange price. Hence, a provides a measure of exchange price variation relative to the predicted equilibrium exchange price. As is seen in Table 1 and the charts for all tests except test 8, a tends to decline from one trading period to the next, with tests 2, 4A, 5, 6A, 7, 9A, and 10 showing monotone convergence.

Turning now to the individual experimental results, it will be observed that the equilibrium price and quantity are approximately the same for the supply and demand curves of tests 2 and 3. The significant difference in the design of these two tests is that the supply and demand schedules for test 2 are relatively flat, while the corresponding schedules for test 3 are much more steeply inclined.

Under the Walrasian hypothesis (the rate of increase in exchange price is an increasing function of the excess demand at that price), one would expect the market in test 2 to converge more rapidly than that in test 3. As is evident from comparing the results in Charts 2 and 3, test 2 shows a more rapid and less erratic tendency toward equilibrium. These results are, of course, consistent with many other hypotheses, including the

TABLE 1

Test	Trading Period	Predicted Exchange Quantity (x_0)	Actual Exchange Quantity (x)	Predicted Exchange Price (P_0)	Average Actual Exchange Price $(\bar{P})$	Coefficient of Convergence $[\alpha = (100\,\sigma_0)/(P_0)]$	No. of Submarginal Buyers Who Could Make Contracts	No. of Submarginal Buyers Who Made Contracts	No. of Submarginal Sellers Who Could Make Contracts	No. of Submarginal Sellers Who Made Contracts
1......	1	6	5	2.00	1.80	11.8	5	0	5	0
	2	6	5	2.00	1.36	8.1	5	0	5	0
	3	6	5	2.00	2.02	5.2	5	0	5	0
	4	6	7	2.00	2.03	5.5	5	1	5	1
	5	6	6	2.00	2.03	3.5	5	0	5	0
2......	1	15	16	3.425	3.47	9.9	4	2	3	1
	2	15	15	3.425	3.43	5.4	4	2	3	1
	3	15	16	3.425	3.42	2.2	4	2	3	0
3......	1	16	17	3.50	3.49	16.5	5	1	6	2
	2	16	15	3.50	3.47	6.6	5	0	6	1
	3	16	15	3.50	3.56	3.7	5	0	6	0
	4	16	15	3.50	3.55	5.7	5	0	6	0
4A....	1	10	9	3.10	3.53	19.1	None	None	None	None
	2	10	9	3.10	3.37	10.4	None	None	None	None
	3	10	9	3.10	3.32	7.8	None	None	None	None
	4	10	9	3.10	3.32	7.6	None	None	None	None
4B.....	1	8	8	3.10	3.25	6.9	None	None	None	None
	2	8	7	3.10	3.30	7.1	None	None	None	None
	3	8	6	3.10	3.29	6.5	None	None	None	None
5A.....	1	10	11	3.125	3.12	2.0	7	0	7	0
	2	10	9	3.125	3.13	0.7	7	1	7	0
	3	10	10	3.125	3.11	0.7	7	1	7	0
	4	10	9	3.125	3.12	0.6	7	0	7	0
5B.....	1	12	12	3.45	3.68	9.4	4	0	3	2
	2	12	12	3.45	3.52	4.3	4	0	3	0
6A.....	1	12	12	10.75	5.29	53.8	5	3	None	None
	2	12	12	10.75	7.17	38.7	5	3	None	None
	3	12	12	10.75	9.06	21.1	5	2	None	None
	4	12	12	10.75	10.90	9.4	5	0	None	None
6B.....	1	12	11	8.75	9.14	11.0	4	1	None	None
	2	12	6	8.75	....	....	4	1	None	None
7......	1	9	8	3.40	2.12	49.1	3	1	None	None
	2	9	9	3.40	2.91	22.2	3	0	None	None
	3	9	9	3.40	3.23	7.1	3	1	None	None
	4	9	8	3.40	3.32	5.4	3	0	None	None
	5	9	9	3.40	3.33	3.0	3	0	None	None
	6	9	9	3.40	3.34	2.7	3	0	None	None
8A.....	1	7	8	2.25	2.50	19.0	5	0	4	0
	2	7	5	2.25	2.20	2.9	5	0	4	0
	3	7	6	2.25	2.12	7.4	5	0	4	0
	4	7	5	2.25	2.12	7.0	5	0	4	0
8B.....	1	7	6	2.25	2.23	7.8	5	0	4	0
	2	7	6	2.25	2.29	6.1	5	0	4	0
9A....	1	18	18	3.40	2.81	21.8	6	3	None	None
	2	18	18	3.40	2.97	15.4	6	2	None	None
	3	18	18	3.40	3.07	13.2	6	2	None	None
9B....	1	20	20	3.80	3.52	10.3	4	3	2	0
10......	1	18	18	3.40	3.17	11.0	4	2	None	None
	2	18	17	3.40	3.36	3.2	4	1	None	None
	3	18	17	3.40	3.38	2.2	4	0	None	None

CHART 2

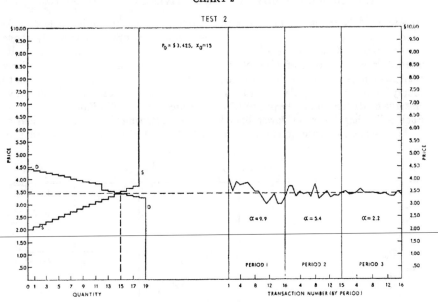

TEST 2

$P_0 = \$3.425$, $x_0 = 15$

CHART 3

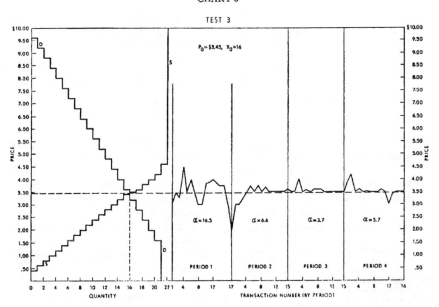

TEST 3

$P_0 = \$3.45$, $x_0 = 16$

excess-rent hypothesis, to be discussed later.[7]

The tests in Chart 4 are of special interest from the point of view of the Walrasian hypothesis. In this case the supply curve is perfectly elastic—all sellers have cards containing the price $3.10. Each seller has the same lower bound on his reservation price acceptance set.

equilibrium since there is a considerable excess supply at prices just barely above the equilibrium price. From the results we see that the market is not particularly slow in converging, but it converges to a fairly stable price about $0.20 above the predicted equilibrium. Furthermore, in test 4B, which was an extension of 4A, the interjection of a decrease in

CHART 4

TEST 4A AND TEST 4B

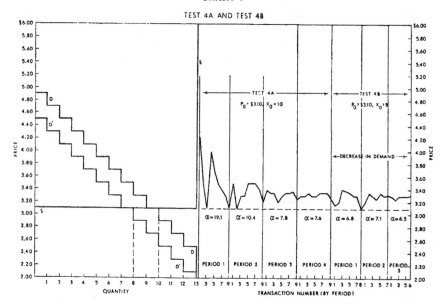

In this sense, there is no divergence of attitude among the sellers, though there might be marked variation in their bargaining propensities. According to the Walrasian hypothesis this market should exhibit rapid convergence toward the

[7] The results are inconsistent with the so-called Marshallian hypothesis (the rate of increase in quantity exchanged is an increasing function of the excess of demand price over supply price), but this hypothesis would seem to be worth considering only in market processes in which some quantity-adjusting decision is made by the marketers. The results of a pilot experiment in "short-run" and "long-run" equilibrium are displayed in the Appendix.

demand from DD to $D'D'$ was ineffective as a means of shocking the market down to its supply and demand equilibrium. This decrease in demand was achieved by passing out new buyer cards corresponding to $D'D'$ at the close of period 4 in test 4A. As expected, the market approaches equilibrium from above, since contracts at prices below equilibrium are impossible.

The sellers in this market presented a solid front against price being lowered to "equilibrium." In the previous markets there was a divergence of seller attitude, so that only a very few marginal and near-marginal sellers might offer serious resistance to price being forced to equilibrium. And this resistance tended to break down when any of the stronger intramarginal sellers accepted contracts below equilibrium.

From these results it is clear that the static competitive market equilibrium may depend not only on the intersection of the supply and demand schedules, but also upon the shapes of the schedules. Specifically, I was led from test 4 to the tentative hypothesis that there may be an upward bias in the equilibrium price of a market, which will be greater the more elastic is the supply schedule relative to demand.[8] For example, let A be the area under the demand schedule and above the theoretical equilibrium. This is Marshall's consumer surplus, but to avoid any welfare connotations of this term, I shall refer to the area as "buyers' rent." Let B be the area above the supply schedule and below the theoretical equilibrium (Marshall's producer surplus) which I shall call "sellers' rent." Now, the tentative hypothesis was that the actual market equilibrium will be above the theoretical equilibrium by an amount which depends upon how large A is relative to B. Similarly, there will be a downward bias if A is small relative to B.

Test 4 is of course an extreme case, since $B = 0$. In test 3, A is larger than B, and the trading periods 3 and 4 exhibit a slight upward bias in the average actual exchange price (see Table 1). This provides some slight evidence in favor of the hypothesis.

As a consequence of these considerations, test 7 was designed specifically to obtain additional information to support or contradict the indicated hypothesis. In this case, as is seen in Chart 7 (see below), buyers' rent is substantially smaller than sellers' rent. From the resulting course of contract prices over six trading periods in this experiment, it is evident that the convergence to equilibrium is very slow. From Table 1, the average exchange prices in the last three trading periods are, respectively, \$3.32, \$3.33, and \$3.34. Average contract prices are still exhibiting a gradual approach to equilibrium. Hence, it is entirely possible that the static equilibrium would eventually have been attained. A still smaller buyers' rent may be required to provide any clear downward bias in the static equilibrium. One thing, however, seems quite unmistakable from Chart 7, the relative magnitude of buyers' and sellers' rent affects the speed with which the actual market equilibrium is approached. One would expect sellers to present a somewhat weaker bargaining front, especially at first, if their rent potential is large relative to that of buyers. Thus, in Chart 7, it is seen that several low reservation price sellers in trading periods 1 and 2 made contracts at low exchange prices, which, no doubt, seemed quite profitable to these sellers. However, in both these trading periods the later exchange prices were much higher, revealing to the low-price sellers that, however profitable their initial sales had been, still greater profits were possible under stiffer bargaining.

A stronger test of the hypotheses that buyer and seller rents affect the speed of adjustment and that they affect the final equilibrium in the market would be obtainable by introducing actual mon-

[8] Note that the Walrasian hypothesis might lead one to expect a downward bias since excess supply is very large at prices above equilibrium if supply is very elastic relative to demand.

etary payoffs in the experiment. Thus, one might offer to pay each seller the difference between his contract price and his reservation price and each buyer the difference between his reservation price and his contract price. In addition, one might pay each trader a small lump sum (say $0.05) just for making a contract in any period. This sum would represent

any such reluctance that is attributable to artificial elements in the present experiments.[9]

The experiment summarized in Chart 5 was designed to study the effect on market behavior of changes in the conditions of demand and supply. As it happened, this experiment was performed on a considerably more mature group

CHART 5

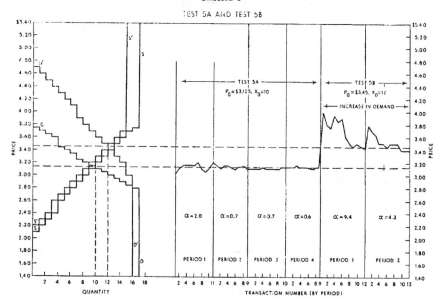

"normal profits," that is, a small return even if the good is sold at its minimum supply price or purchased at its maximum demand price. The present experiments have not seemed to provide any motivation problems. The subjects have shown high motivation to do their best even without monetary payoffs. But our experimental marginal buyers and sellers may be more reluctant to approach their reservation prices than their counterparts in real markets. The use of monetary payoffs, as suggested, should remove

of subjects than any of the other experiments. Most of the experiments were performed on sophomore and junior engineering, economics, and business majors, while test 5 was performed on a

[9] Since this was written, an experiment has been tried using monetary payoffs and the same supply and demand design shown in Chart 4. The result, as conjectured in the text, was to remove the reluctance of sellers to sell at their reservation prices. By the second trading period the market was firmly in equilibrium. In the third period all trades were at $3.10! Apparently $0.05 per period was considered satisfactory normal profit.

graduate class in economic theory. In view of this difference, it is most interesting to find the phenomenally low values for a exhibited by test $5A$. The coefficient of convergence is smaller for the opening and later periods of this market than for any period of any of the other tests. Furthermore, trading periods 2–4 show a's of less than 1 per cent, indicating an inordinately strong and rapid tendency toward equilibrium. In this case, no offers or bids were accepted until the bidding had converged to prices which were very near indeed to the equilibrium. Contract prices ranged from \$3.00 to \$3.20 as compared with a possible range from \$2.10 to \$3.75.

At the close of test $5A$ new cards were distributed corresponding to an increase in demand, from DD to $D'D'$, as shown in Chart 5.[10] The subjects, of course, could guess from the fact that new buyer cards were being distributed that a change in demand was in the wind. But they knew nothing of the direction of change in demand except what might be guessed by the buyers from the alteration of their individual reservation prices. When trading began (period 1, test $5B$), the immediate response was a very considerable upward sweep in exchange prices with several contracts being closed in the first trading period well above the new higher equilibrium price. Indeed, the eagerness to buy was so strong that two sellers who were submarginal both before and after the increase in demand (their reservation prices were

[10] Note also that there was a small (one-unit) decrease in supply from SS to $S'S'$. This was not planned. It was due to the inability of one subject (the seller with the \$2.10 reservation price) in test $5A$ to participate in test $5B$. Therefore, except for the deletion of this one seller from the market, the conditions of supply were not altered, that is, the sellers of test $5B$ retained the same reservation price cards as they had in test $5A$.

\$3.50 and \$3.70) were able to make contracts in this transient phase of the market. Consequently, the trading group showing the strongest equilibrating tendencies exhibited very erratic behavior in the transient phase following the increase in demand. Contract prices greatly overshot the new equilibrium and rationing by the market was less efficient in this transient phase. In the second trading period of test $5B$ no submarginal sellers or buyers made contracts and the market exhibited a narrowed movement toward the new equilibrium.

Test $6A$ was designed to determine whether market equilibrium was affected by a marked imbalance between the number of intramarginal sellers and the number of intramarginal buyers near the predicted equilibrium price. The demand curve, DD, in Chart 6 falls continuously to the right in one-unit steps, while the supply curve, SS, becomes perfectly inelastic at the price \$4.00, well below the equilibrium price \$10.75. The tentative hypothesis was that the large rent (\$6.75) enjoyed by the marginal seller, with still larger rents for the intramarginal sellers, might prevent the theoretical equilibrium from being established. From the results it is seen that the earlier conjecture concerning the effect of a divergence between buyer and seller rent on the approach to equilibrium is confirmed. The approach to equilibrium is from below, and the convergence is relatively slow. However, there is no indication that the lack of marginal sellers near the theoretical equilibrium has prevented the equilibrium from being attained. The average contract price in trading period 4 is \$10.90, only \$0.15 above the predicted equilibrium.

At the close of trading period 4 in test $6A$, the old buyer cards corresponding to DD were replaced by new cards

CHART 6

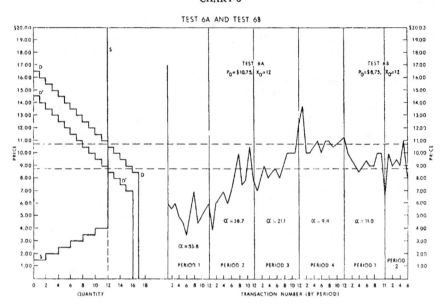

CHART 7

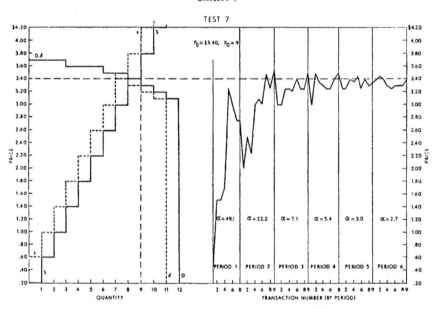

124   VERNON L. SMITH

corresponding to $D'D'$ in Chart 6. Trading was resumed with the new conditions
of decreased demand (test 6B). There
was not sufficient time to permit two
full trading periods of market experience
to be obtained under the new demand
conditions. However, from the results
in Chart 6, it is evident that the market
responded promptly to the decrease in

(test 8A), only sellers were permitted
to enunciate offers. In this market, buyers
played a passive role; they could either
accept or reject the offers of sellers but
were not permitted to make bids. This
market was intended to simulate approximately an ordinary retail market.
In such markets, in the United States,
sellers typically take the initiative in

CHART 8

TEST 8A AND TEST 8B

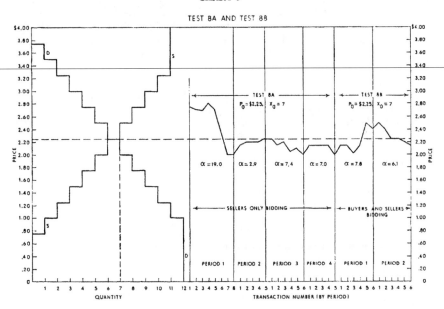

demand by showing apparent convergence to the new equilibrium. Note in
particular that there occurred no significant tendency for market prices to over-
shoot the new equilibrium as was observed in test 5B.

All of the above experiments were conducted under the same general rules of
market organization. Test 8 was performed as an exploratory means of testing the effect of changes in market organization on market price. In the first
four trading periods of this experiment

advertising their offer prices, with buyers
electing to buy or not to buy rather
than taking part in a higgling and bargaining process. Since sellers desire to
sell at the highest prices they can get,
one would expect the offer prices to be
high, and, consequently, one might expect the exchange prices to show a persistent tendency to remain above the
predicted equilibrium. The result was
in accordance with this crude expectation
in the first market period only (test 8A,
Chart 8). Since sellers only were making

offers, the price quotations tended to be very much above equilibrium. Five of these offers were accepted at prices ranging from $2.69 to $2.80 by the five buyers with maximum reservation prices of $2.75 or more. This left only buyers with lower reservation prices. The competition of sellers pushed the offer prices lower and the remaining buyers made contracts at prices ($2.35, $2.00, and $2.00) near or below the equilibrium price. The early buyers in that first market period never quite recovered from having subsequently seen exchange prices fall much below the prices at which they had bought. Having been badly fleeced, through ignorance, in that first trading period, they refrained from accepting any high price offers in the remaining three periods of the test. This action, together with seller offer price competition, kept exchange prices at levels persistently below equilibrium for the remainder of test 8*A*. Furthermore, the coefficient of convergence increased from 2.9 per cent in the second trading period to 7.4 and 7.0 per cent in the last two periods. At the close of the fourth trading period, the market rules were changed to allow buyers to make quotations as well as sellers. Under the new rules (test 8*B*) two trading periods were run. Exchange prices immediately moved toward equilibrium with the closing prices of period 1 and opening prices of period 2 being above the equilibrium for the first time since period 1 of test 8*A*.

It would seem to be of some significance that of the ten experiments reported on, test 8 shows the clearest lack of convergence toward equilibrium. More experiments are necessary to confirm or deny these results, but it would appear that important changes in market organization—such as permitting only sellers to make quotations—have a distinctly disturbing effect on the equilibrating

process. In particular the conclusion is suggested that markets in which only sellers competitively publicize their offers tend to operate to the benefit of buyers at the expense of sellers.

Turning to tests 9*A* and 10 (shown in Charts 9 and 10), it should be noted that the buyers and sellers in these tests received the same cards as their counterparts in test 7. The only difference was that the former entered the market to effect two transactions each, instead of one. Thus the three buyers with $3.70 cards could each buy two units at $3.70 or less in tests 9 and 10. This change in the design of test 7 resulted in a doubling of the maximum demand and supply quantities at each hypothetical price.

By permitting each buyer and seller to make two contracts per period, twice as much market "experience" is potentially to be gained by each trader in a given period. Each trader can experiment more in a given market—correcting his bids or offers in the light of any surprises or disappointments resulting from his first contract. In the previous experiments such corrections or alterations in the bargaining behavior of a trader had to await the next trading period once the trader had made a contract.[11]

[11] This process of correction over time, based upon observed price quotations and the actual contracts that are executed, is the underlying adjustment mechanism operating in all of these experiments. This is in contrast with the Walrasian *tâtonnement* or groping process in which "when a price is cried, and the effective demand and offer corresponding to this price are not equal, another price is cried for which there is another corresponding effective demand and offer" (see Leon Walras, *Elements of Pure Economics*, trans. William Jaffe [Chicago: Richard D. Irwin, Inc., 1954], p. 242). The Walrasian groping process suggests a centralized institutional means of trying different price quotations until the equilibrium is discovered. In our experiments, as in real markets, the groping process is decentralized, with all contracts binding whether they are at equilibrium or non-equilibrium prices.

Comparison of the results of the three trading periods in test 9A with the first three trading periods of test 7 shows that the tendencies toward equilibrium (as measured by a) were greater in test 9A during the first two periods and smaller in the third period. The same comparison between tests 7 and 10 reveals a stronger tendency toward equilibrium in test 10 than in the first three periods

of trade increased to the new equilibrium rate of twenty units per period. Note that the equilibrium tendency in the trading period of test 9B was greater than in any of the perious periods of test 9A. The increase in demand, far from destabilizing the market as was the case in test 5B, tended to strengthen its relatively weak equilibrium tendencies.

CHART 9

TEST 9A AND TEST 9B

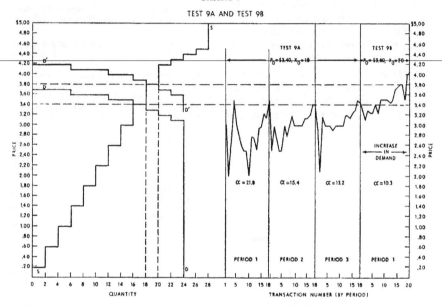

of 7. Hence an increase in volume appears to speed the equilibrating process. Indeed, the three trading periods of test 10 are roughly equivalent to the six trading periods of test 7, so that doubling volume in a given period is comparable to running two trading periods at the same volume.

In test 9B the consequences of an increase in demand were once again tested. Contract prices responded by moving upward immediately, and the volume

IV. EMPIRICAL ANALYSIS OF EXPERIMENTAL DATA: THE "EXCESS-RENT" HYPOTHESIS

The empirical analysis of these ten experiments rests upon the hypothesis that there exists a stochastic difference equation which "best" represents the price convergence tendencies apparent in Charts 1–10. The general hypothesis is that

$$\Delta p_t = p_{t+1} - p_t = f[x_1(p_t),$$
$$x_2(p_t), \ldots] + \epsilon_t, \quad (1)$$

where the arguments $x_1, x_2, \ldots$ reflect characteristics of the experimental supply and demand curves and the bargaining characteristics of individual test groups, and ϵ_t is a random variable with zero mean. For a given experimental test group, under the so-called Walrasian hypothesis $x_1(p_t)$ might be the excess demand prevailing at p_t, with $f = 0$ when $x_1 = 0$.

My first empirical investigation is concerned with the measuremet of the equilibrating tendencies in these markets and the ability of supply and demand theory to predict the equilibrium price in each experiment. To this end note that equation (1) defines a stochastic phase function[12] of the form $p_{t+1} = g(p_t) + \epsilon_t$. An equilibrium price P_0 is attained when $P_0 = g(P_0)$. Rather than estimate the

phase function for each experiment, it was found convenient to make linear estimates of its first difference, that is,

$$\Delta p_t = a_0 + a_1 p_t + \epsilon_t.$$

The corresponding linear phase function has slope $1 + a_1$. The parameters a_0 and a_1 were estimated by linear regression techniques for each of the ten fundamental experiments and are tabulated in column 1 of Table 2.[13] Confidence

[12] See, for example, W. J. Baumol, *Economic Dynamics* (New York: Macmillan Co., 1959), pp. 257–65.

[13] The least squares estimate of a_1 in these experiments can be expected to be biased (see L. Hurwicz, "Least-Squares Bias in Time Series," chap. xv, in T. Koopmans, *Statistical Inference in Dynamic Economic Models* [New York: John Wiley & Sons, 1950]). However, since in all of the basic experiments there are twenty or more observations, the bias will not tend to be large.

CHART 10

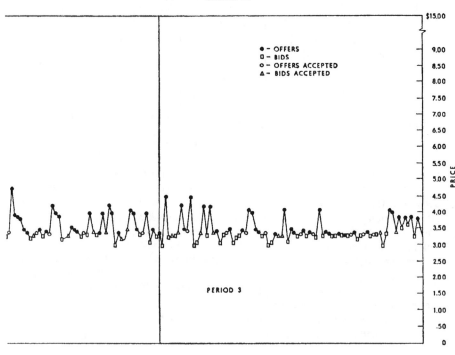

TABLE 2

Experiment	$(\Delta p_t = a_0 + a_1 p_t)$	Walrasian $(\Delta p_t = \beta_{01} + \beta_{11}x_{1t})$	Modified Walrasian $(\Delta p_t = \beta_{01} + \beta_{11}x_{1t} + \beta_{21}x_{2t})$	Excess Rent $(\Delta p_t = \beta_{01} + \beta_{21}x_{2t})$	Modified Excess Rent $(\Delta p_t = \beta_{01} + \beta_{21}x_{2t} + \beta_{31}x_{3t})$
1	$0.933 - 0.474\,p_t$ (±0.329)	$-0.026 + 0.070\,x_{1t}$ (±0.042)	$-0.027 + 0.068\,x_{1t} - 0.0056\,x_{2t}$ (±0.015) (±0.0220)	$-0.028 + 0.486\,x_{2t}$ (±0.322)	$-0.031 + 0.491\,x_{2t} - 0.0054\,x_{3t}$ (±0.104) (±0.0215)
2	$1.904 - 0.560\,p_t$ (±0.250)	$.002 + .035\,x_{1t}$ (± .015)	$-.170 + .042\,x_{1t} - .0693\,x_{2t}$ (± .006) (± .0311)	$.008 + .141\,x_{2t}$ (± .067)	$-.070 + .152\,x_{2t} - .0313\,x_{3t}$ (± .024) (± .0649)
3	$2.275 - 0.647\,p_t$ (±0.292)	$.157 + .107\,x_{1t}$ (± .045)	$.093 + .105\,x_{1t} + .0042\,x_{2t}$ (± .014) (± .0317)	$.071 + .227\,x_{2t}$ (± .097)	$.022 + .225\,x_{2t} + .0064\,x_{3t}$ (± .031) (± .0315)
4A	$2.852 - 0.849\,p_t$ (±0.287)	$.761 + .168\,x_{1t}$ (± .057)	$.794 + .169\,x_{1t} - .0007\,x_{2t}$ (± .018) (± .0564)	$.145 + .129\,x_{2t}$ (± .049)	$.139 + .130\,x_{2t} - .0017\,x_{3t}$ (± .016) (± .0641)
5A	$2.448 - 0.784\,p_t$ (±0.302)	$-.031 + .023\,x_{1t}$ (± .009)	$-.035 + .023\,x_{1t} - .0029\,x_{2t}$ (± .003) (± .0043)	$-.007 + .205\,x_{2t}$ (± .098)	$-.009 + .204\,x_{2t} + .0015\,x_{3t}$ (± .032) (± .0048)
6A	$1.913 - 0.220\,p_t$ (±0.174)	$-.675 + .243\,x_{1t}$ (± .175)	$.010 + .285\,x_{1t} + .0211\,x_{3t}$ (± .057) (± .0847)	$-.309 + .038\,x_{2t}$ (± .037)	$.305 + .034\,x_{2t} + .0146\,x_{3t}$ (± .013) (± .0906)
7	$1.216 - 0.368\,p_t$ (±0.116)	$-.102 + .074\,x_{1t}$ (± .049)	$-.070 + .075\,x_{1t} + .0063\,x_{3t}$ (± .009) (± .0738)	$.007 + .051\,x_{2t}$ (± .021)	$.058 + .053\,x_{2t} + .0096\,x_{3t}$ (± .007) (± .0750)
8A	$0.225 - 0.121\,p_t$ (±0.226)	$-.040 + .020\,x_{1t}$ (± .030)	$-.027 + .025\,x_{1t} - .0462\,x_{2t}$ (± .011) (± .0487)	$-.036 + .051\,x_{2t}$ (± .094)	$.022 + .064\,x_{2t} - .0396\,x_{3t}$ (± .035) (± .0505)
9A	$1.633 - 0.554\,p_t$ (±0.273)	$-.450 + .061\,x_{1t}$ (± .036)	$-.447 + .085\,x_{1t} + .0198\,x_{3t}$ (± .012) (± .0423)	$-.209 + .071\,x_{2t}$ (± .029)	$-.065 + .094\,x_{2t} - .0222\,x_{3t}$ (± .009) (± .0356)
10	$1.188 - 0.356\,p_t$ (±0.233)	$-0.039 + 0.020\,x_{1t}$ (±0.014)	$-0.028 + 0.020\,x_{1t} + 0.0008\,x_{2t}$ (±0.004) (±0.0199)	$-0.022 + 0.055\,x_{2t}$ (±0.032)	$-0.008 + 0.056\,x_{2t} + 0.0011\,x_{3t}$ (±0.014) (±0.0194)

intervals for a 95 per cent fiducial probability level are shown in parentheses under the estimate of a_1 for each experiment. With the exception of experiment $8A$, the 95 per cent confidence interval for each regression coefficient is entirely contained in the interval $-2 < a_1 < 0$, which is required for market stability. Hence, of these ten experiments, $8A$ is the only one whose price movements are sufficiently erratic to prevent us from rejecting the null hypothesis of instability, and of the ten basic experiments this

$$t = \frac{a_0 + a_1 P_0}{S(a_0 + a_1 P_0)}$$

for the sample estimates on the assumption that $\Delta p_t = 0$ when $p_t = P_0$ in the population. These t-values are shown in column 1, Table 3, for the ten primary and the five "B" auxilary experiments. Low absolute values of t imply that, relative to the error in the prediction, the predicted equilibrium is close to the theoretical. The four lowest absolute t-values are for experimental designs with the smallest difference between equilibri-

TABLE 3

EXPERIMENT	$t = (a_0 + a_1 P_0)/[S(a_0 + a_1 P_0)]$ (1)	WALRASIAN			EXCESS RENT			DEGREES OF FREEDOM (8)
		$|\beta_{01}|$ (2)	$S(\beta_{01})$ (3)	$t = \beta_{01}/S(\beta_{01})$ (4)	$|\beta_{01}|$ (5)	$S(\beta_{01})$ (6)	$t = \beta_{01}/S(\beta_{01})$ (7)	
1.........	−0.673	0.026	0.019	−1.36	0.028	0.021	−0.66	21
2.........	0.460	.002	.029	0.08	.008	.030	0.25	42
3.........	1.008	.157	.055	2.88	.071	.046	1.56	57
4A.........	4.170	.761	.137	5.57	.145	.048	3.05	30
4B.........	3.219	.391	.284	1.37	.161	.052	3.08	16
5A.........	−0.333	.031	.008	−3.72	.007	.006	−1.16	33
5B.........	−0.230	.002	.034	0.05	.013	.026	−0.51	20
6A.........	−1.412	.675	.362	−1.87	.309	.311	−0.99	42
6B.........	2.176	.299	.314	0.95	.179	.290	0.62	13
7.........	−0.740	.102	.057	−1.78	.007	.045	0.15	44
8A.........	−1.597	.040	.029	−1.40	.036	.032	−1.13	18
8B.........	−0.140	.010	.042	−0.24	.016	.043	−0.37	8
9A.........	−0.647	.450	.151	−2.99	.209	.065	−3.21	49
9B.........	−0.021	.012	.112	0.11	.016	.071	−0.23	17
10.........	−0.731	0.039	0.033	−1.19	0.022	0.028	−0.80	47

is the one in which the trading rules were altered to permit only sellers to quote prices.[14]

The regressions of column 1, Table 2, and associated computation provide a means of predicting the adjustment pressure on price, Δp_t, for any given p_t. In particular, we can compute

[14] Three of the five auxiliary "B" experiments demonstrated a similar instability (in the fiducial probability sense), but the samples were considerably smaller than their "A" counterparts, they represented considerably fewer trading periods, and they had different and varying objectives. The unstable ones were $4B$, $8B$, and $9B$.

um buyers' and sellers' rent. These results provide some additional evidence in favor of our conjecture in Part III, that the equilibrium is influenced by the relative sizes of the areas A and B. However, from the t-values it would seem that the influence is small except for test 4, where $B = 0$. In this case, the null hypothesis ($\Delta p_t = 0$ when $p_t = P_0$) is rejected even at a significance level below .005.

Four specific forms for the difference equation (1) were studied in detail and tested for their ability to predict the theoretical equilibrium price. These will be referred to as the Walrasian, the excess-rent, the modified Walrasian, and the modified excess-rent hypotheses, respectively. The Walrasian hypothesis is $\Delta p_t = \beta_{01} + \beta_{11} x_{1t}$, where x_{1t} is the excess demand prevailing at the price, p_t, at which the tth transaction occurred. Because of the conjecture that buyers' and sellers' rent might have an effect on individual and market adjustment, an excess-rent hypothesis was introduced. This hypothesis is $\Delta p_t = \beta_{02} + \beta_{22} x_{2t}$, where x_{2t} is the algebraic area

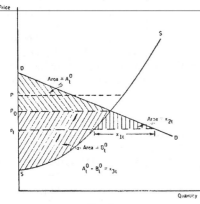

Fig. 1

between the supply and demand curves, and extends from the equilibrium price down to the price of the tth transaction, as shown in Figure 1. The modified Walrasian hypothesis is $\Delta p_t = \beta_{03} + \beta_{13} x_{1t} + \beta_{33} x_{3t}$, where $x_{3t} = A_t^0 - B_t^0$, the algebraic difference between the equilibrium buyers' rent, A_t^0, and the equilibrium sellers' rent, B_t^0. The motivation here was to introduce a term in the adjustment equation which would permit the actual equilibrium price to be biased above or below the theoretical equilibrium, by an amount proportional to the algebraic difference between buyers' and

sellers' rent at the theoretical equilibrium. It was believed that such a general hypothesis might be necessary to account for the obvious price equilibrium bias in experiment 4 and the slight apparent bias in experiments 3, 6A, 7, and 9A. A similar motivation suggested the modified excess-rent hypothesis, $\Delta p_t = \beta_{04} + \beta_{24} x_{2t} + \beta_{34} x_{3t}$.

Since the trading process in these experiments was such that transactions might and generally did take place at non-equilibrium prices, the supply and demand curves shift after each transaction. Hence, in generating observations on x_{1t}, x_{2t}, and x_{3t}, the supply and demand curves were adjusted after each transaction for the effect of the pairing of a buyer and a seller in reducing their effective demand and supply. Thus, in Chart 7, the first transaction was at $0.50 between the seller with reservation price $0.20 and a buyer with reservation price $3.50. Following this trasaction the new effective demand and supply curves become Dd and ss as shown. The next transaction is at $1.50. Our hypothesis is that the increase in price from $0.50 to $1.50 is due to the conditions represented by Dd and ss at the price $0.50. Thus, for the first set of observations $\Delta p_1 = p_1 - p_0 = \$1.50 - \$0.50 = \$1.00$, $x_{11} = 11$, $x_{21} = 20.10$, and $x_{31} = -9.60$ as can be determined from Chart 7. The second transaction paired a $3.70 buyer and a $0.60 seller. The next set of observations is then obtained by removing this buyer and seller from Dd and ss to obtain x_{12}, x_{22}, and x_{32} at $p_2 = 1.50$, with $\Delta p_2 = p_2 - p_1 = 0$, and so on.

Using observations obtained in this manner, regressions for the four different equilibrating hypotheses were computed for the ten fundamental experiments as shown in Table 2, columns 2–5. A 95 per cent confidence interval is shown in parentheses under each regression coefficient. With the exception of experiment 8A, the regression coefficients for every experiment are significant under both the Walrasian and the excess-rent hypotheses. On the other hand, β_{33} in the modified Walrasian hypothesis is significant only in experiment 2. In none of the experiments is β_{34} significant for the modified excess-rent hypothesis. These highly unambiguous results seem to suggest that little significance can be attached to the effect of a difference between equilibrium buyers' and sellers' rent in biasing the price equilibrium tendencies.

On this reasoning, we are left with the closely competing Walrasian and excess-rent hypotheses, showing highly significant adjustment speeds, β_{11} and β_{22}. In discriminating between these two hypotheses we shall compare them on two important counts: (1) their ability to predict zero price change in equilibrium, and (2) the standard errors of said predictions. Since $x_{1t}^0 = x_{2t}^0 = 0$, in equilibrium, this requires a comparison between the absolute values of the intercepts of the Walrasian and the excess-rent regressions, $|\beta_{01}|$ and $|\beta_{02}|$, and between $S(\beta_{01})$ and $S(\beta_{02})$. Under the first comparison we can think of $|\beta_{01}|$, shown in column 2, Table 3, as a "score" for the Walrasian hypothesis, and $|\beta_{02}|$, shown in column 5, as a "score" for the excess-rent hypothesis. A low intercept represents a good score. Thus, for experiment 1, in equilibrium, there is a residual tendency for price to change (in this case fall) at the rate of 2.6 cents per transaction by the Walrasian and 2.8 cents by the excess-rent regressions. A casual comparison of columns 2 and 5 reveals that in most of the experiments $|\beta_{01}| > |\beta_{02}|$, and in those for which the reverse is true the difference is quite small, tend-

ing thereby to support the excess-rent hypothesis. A more exact discrimination can be made by applying the Wilcoxon[15] paired-sample rank test for related samples to the "scores" of columns 2 and 5. This test applies to the differences $|\beta_{01}| - |\beta_{02}|$, and tests the null hypothesis, H_0, that the Walrasian and excess-rent alternatives are equivalent (the distribution of the differences is symmetric about zero). If applied to all the experiments, including the "B's" $(N = 15)$, H_0 is rejected at the $< .02$ significance level. The difference between our paired series of "scores" in favor of the excess-rent hypothesis is therefore significant. It is highly debatable whether all the experiments should be included in such a test, especially 4, which did not tend to the predicted equilibrium, 8, which represented a different organization of the bargaining, and possibly the "B" experiments, where the samples were small. Therefore, the test was run omitting all these experiments $(N = 8)$, giving a rejection of H_0 at the .05 level. Omitting only 4 and 8 $(N = 11)$ allowed H_0 still to be rejected at the $< .02$ level.

If we compare the standard errors $S(\beta_{01})$ and $S(\beta_{02})$ in Table 3, columns 3 and 6, we see that again the excess-rent hypothesis tends to score higher (smaller standard errors). Applying the Wilcoxon test to $S(\beta_{01}) - S(\beta_{02})$ for all the experiments $(N = 15)$, we find that this difference, in favor of the excess-rent hypothesis, is significant at the $<.01$ level. The difference is still significant at the $<.01$ level if we omit 4 and 8 from the test, and it is significant at the .05 level if we also eliminate all the "B" experiments.

The *t*-values for the two hypotheses

[15] See, for example, K. A. Brownlee, *Statistical Theory and Methodology in Science and Engineering* (New York: John Wiley & Sons, 1960), pp. 196–99.

are shown in columns 4 and 7 of Table 3. They tend also to be lower for the excess-rent hypothesis.

Bearing in mind that our analysis is based upon a limited number of experiments, and that revisions may be required in the light of further experiments with different subjects or with monetary payoffs, we conclude the following: Of the four hypotheses tested, the two modified forms show highly insignificant regression coefficients for the added explanatory variable. As between the Walrasian and the excess-rent hypotheses, the evidence is sharply in favor of the latter.

V. RATIONALIZATION OF THE EXCESS-RENT HYPOTHESIS

Having provided a tentative empirical verification of the hypothesis that price in a competitve (auction) market tends to rise or fall in proportion to the excess buyer plus seller rent corresponding to any contract price, it remains to provide some theoretical rationale for such a hypothesis. From the description of the above experiments and their results, the excess-rent hypothesis would seem to have some plausibility from an individual decision-making point of view. Given that a particular contract price has just been executed, it is reasonable to expect each trader to compare that price with his own reservation price, the difference being a "profit" or rent which he considers achievable, and to present a degree of bargaining resistance in the auction process which is greater, the smaller is this rent. Such resistance may tend to give way, even where the rents on one side or the other are very small, if it becomes clear that such rents are unattainable. Thus, if equilibrium buyers' rent exceeds sellers' rent, any early tendency for contract prices to remain above equi-

librium (and balance the rents achieved on both sides) might be expected to break down, as it becomes evident that the "paper" rents at those prices may not be attainable by all of the sellers. By this argument, it is suggested that the propensity of sellers to reduce their offers when price is above equilibrium is related to their attempts to obtain some—even if a "small"—amount of rent rather than to a direct influence of excess supply.

A particularly interesting aspect of the excess-rent hypothesis is that it leads naturally to an interesting optimality interpretation of the static competitive market equilibrium. The principle is this: in static equilibrium a competitive market minimizes the total virtual rent received by buyers and sellers. By "virtual rent" I mean the rent that would be enjoyed if all buyers and sellers could be satisfied at any given disequilibrium price. To see this optimality principle, let $D(p)$ be the demand function and $S(p)$ the supply function. At $p = P$, the sum of buyer and seller virtual rent is

$$R = \int_P^\infty D(p)\,dp + \int_0^P S(p)\,dp$$

and is represented by the area from DD down to P and from SS up to P in Figure 1. R is a minimum for normal supply and demand functions when

$$\frac{dR}{dP} = -D(P) + S(P) = 0,$$

that is, when demand equals supply with $P = P_0$. Note particularly that there is nothing artificial about this conversion of the statement of an ordinary competitive market equilibrium into a corresponding minimum problem. Whether one desires to attach any welfare significance to the concepts of consumer and producer surplus or not, it is completely plausible to require, in the interests of strict market efficiency, that no trader be imputed more rent than is absolutely necessary to perform the exchange mechanics. Hence, at price P in Figure 1, virtual rent exceeds equilibrium rent, and if this price persists, some sellers get more rent than they "should."

It should perhaps be pointed out that the excess-rent and Walrasian hypotheses are close analogues in that both deal with virtual, unattainable quantities. Thus, under the Walrasian hypothesis the "virtual" excess supply at P in Figure 1 is unattainable. Indeed, it is this fact that presumably causes price to fall. Similarly, at P, the excess rent area above S and D is unattainable, and leads to price cutting. Also note that the Walrasian hypothesis bears a gradient relationship, while the excess-rent hypothesis shows a global adjusting relationship, to the rent minimization principle. At $P > P_0$ the Walrasian hypothesis says that price tends to fall at a time rate which is proportional to the marginal rent, dR/dP, at that price. The excess-rent hypothesis states that price tends to fall at a time rate which is proportional to the global difference between total rent at P and at P_0.

Samuelson has shown how one may convert the Cournot-Enke problem of spatial price equilibrium into a maximum problem.[16] The criterion to be maximized in a single market would be what he calls social payoff, defined as the algebraic area under the excess-demand curve. In spatially separated markets the criterion is to maximize net social payoff, defined as the sum of the social payoffs in all regions minus the total transport costs of all interregional ship-

[16] P. A. Samuelson, "Spatial Price Equilibrium and Linear Programming," *American Economic Review,* XLII (June, 1952), 284–92.

ments. But, according to Samuelson, "this magnitude is artificial in the sense that no competitor in the market will be aware of or concerned with it. It is artificial in the sense that after an Invisible Hand has led us to its maximization, we need not necessarily attach any social welfare significance to the result."[17] I think the formulation of competitive market equilibrium as a rent minimization problem makes the "Invisible Hand" distinctly more visible and more teleological.[18] It also has great social (though not necessarily welfare) significance in relation to "frictionless" market efficiency. Rent is an "unearned" increment which literally cries out for minimization in an efficient economic organization. Furthermore, as we have seen with the excess-rent and Walrasian hypotheses, both the abstract teleological goal of the competitive market and the dynamics of its *tâtonnement* process are branches of the same market mechanism.

In view of the electrical circuit analogue so often mentioned in connection with spatially separated markets, a final bonus of the minimum rent formulation is the fact that it represents a more direct analogy with the principle of minimum heat loss in electric circuits.[19] Nature has devised a set of laws to govern the flow of electrical energy, which, it

[17] *Ibid.,* p. 288.

[18] The discovery of the excess-rent hypothesis draws me nearer to the camp of "Invisible Hand" enthusiasts, but only because of the greater visibility of the Hand. I cannot quite carry my market metaphysics as far as does Samuelson. It is well known that any problem in economic equilibrium can be converted into a maximum (or minimum) problem, but I question the value of such a transformation (beyond technical advantages) if it is purely artificial without any meaningful interpretation; and if we work at it, such a meaningful transformation may often be found.

[19] Samuelson, *op. cit.,* p. 285.

can be shown, minimizes the inefficient, wasteful loss of heat energy from electrical systems. Similarly, the market mechanism provides a set of "laws" which minimizes the "wasteful" payment of excessive economic rent.

VI. SUMMARY

It would be premature to assert any broad generalizations based upon the ten experiments we have discussed. Yet conclusions are important for purposes of specifying the exact character of any findings, whether those findings are ultimately verified or not. In this spirit, the following tentative conclusions are offered concerning these experiments:

1. Even where numbers are "small," there are strong tendencies for a supply and demand competitive equilibrium to be attained as long as one is able to prohibit collusion and to maintain absolute publicity of all bids, offers, and transactions. Publicity of quotations and absence of collusion were major characteristics of these experimental markets.

2. Changes in the conditions of supply or demand cause changes in the volume of transactions per period and the general level of contract prices. These latter correspond reasonably well with the predictions of competitive price theory. The response to such changes may, however, produce a transient phase of very erratic contract price behavior.

3. Some slight evidence has been provided to suggest that a prediction of the static equilibrium of a competitive market requires knowledge of the shapes of the supply and demand schedules as well as the intersection of such schedules. The evidence is strongest in the extreme case in which the supply curve is perfectly elastic, with the result that the empirical equilibrium is higher than the theoretical equilibrium.

4. Markets whose institutional organization is such that only sellers make price quotations may exhibit weaker equilibrium tendencies than markets in which both buyers and sellers make price quotations—perhaps even disequilibrium tendencies. Such one-sided markets may operate to the benefit of buyers. A possible explanation is that in the price-formation process buyers reveal a minimum of information concerning their eagerness to buy.

5. The so-called Walrasian hypothesis concerning the mechanism of market adjustment seems not to be confirmed. A more adequate hypothesis is the excess-rent hypothesis which relates the "speed" of contract price adjustment to the algebraic excess of buyer plus seller "virtual" rent over the equilibrium buyer plus seller rent. This new hypothesis becomes particularly intriguing in view of the fact that a competitive market for a single commodity can be interpreted as seeking to minimize total rent.

APPENDIX

In the course of this experimental study and its analysis several additional or peripheral issues were investigated, a discussion of which would not fit clearly into the main body of this report. Three such issues will be discussed briefly in this appendix for the benefit of readers interested in some of the numerous additional lines of inquiry that might be pursued.

I. EVIDENCE OF INTER-TRADING-PERIOD LEARNING

In testing the various equilibrating hypotheses under investigation in this paper, no attempt was made to distinguish the effects of different trading periods. The sample of observations for each experiment embraced all the trading periods of that experiment with transactions running continuously from the first trading period through the last. It would appear, however, that learning occurs as the experiment progresses in such a way as to alter the parameters of each equilibrating hypothesis from one trading period to the next. To obtain some idea of the extent of these alterations, regressions for the excess-rent hypothesis were computed by individual trading period for tests $6A$, $9A$, and 10. These regression equations are summarized in Table 4. It is evident that there is a tendency for the intercepts of these regressions to converge toward zero as the number of trading periods increases. Convergence of the intercepts suggests that the later trading period regressions may be better equilibrating equations (better predictors of zero price change when excess rent is zero) than the earlier period regressions.

II. CONVERGENCE OF BID, OFFER, AND CONTRACT PRICES

In experiments 9 and 10 a tape-recorder was used for the first time to obtain a record of all bid and offer prices as well as the contract prices. No analysis has as yet been attempted with these additional data. However, a graph of the bid, offer, and contract prices in their serial sequence of occurrence is suggestive. Such a sample graph is shown in Chart 11 for experiment 10. Perhaps the most interesting fact revealed in this

TABLE 4

EXCESS-RENT REGRESSIONS $\Delta p_t = \beta_{02} + \beta_{22}x_{2t}$ BY TRADING PERIOD

Trading Period	Experiment 6A	Experiment 9A	Experiment 10
1	$-2.769+0.101\,x_{2t}$	$-0.335+0.078\,x_{2t}$	$-0.160+0.087\,x_{2t}$
2	$-2.876+0.216\,x_{2t}$	$-0.148+0.061\,x_{2t}$	$-0.053+0.408\,x_{2t}$
3	$0.273+0.029\,x_{2t}$	$-0.191+0.093\,x_{2t}$	$0.007+0.349\,x_{2t}$
4	$0.121+0.391\,x_{2t}$		

CHART 11

BIDS, OFFERS, AND TRANSACTIONS ON TEST 10

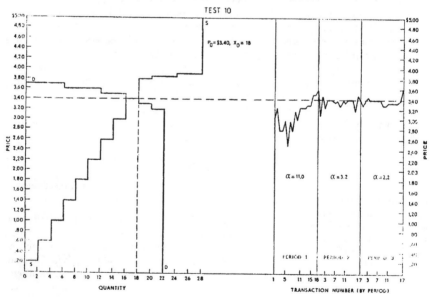

chart is the apparent tendency for the variance of the bids and offers to stabilize early, with the contract prices continuing to converge within this variation in bids and offers. Thus it is at the beginning of period 1, up to about the eighth transaction, that the bids and offers seem to show the most pronounced variation. This variation then remains reasonably steady to the very end of the last trading period. Contract prices

III. A PILOT EXPERIMENT IN "SHORT-RUN" AND "LONG-RUN" EQUILIBRIUM

An important characteristic of the ten experiments discussed in this paper was the absence of any quantity-adjusting decision-making behavior on the part of either buyers or sellers. Such experiments represent the simulation of markets for commodities which do not have to be delivered or

CHART 12

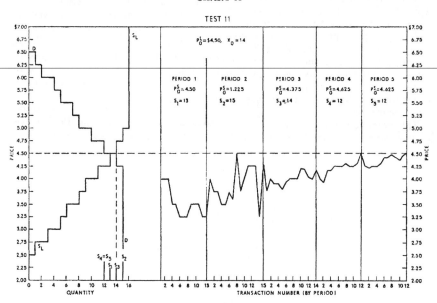

converge, but the traders continue to attempt to get better terms by making repeatedly high offers and low bids. In this connection note that the unaccepted offers are further above the contract prive level than the unaccepted bids are below the contract price level. Similar results were evident in a corresponding chart (not shown) for experiment 9. This, apparently, is the auction market's way of compensating for the fact that, in this particular experiment, sellers were in a "softer" (higher rent) position than buyers.

even produced until after the sale contract is executed. Hence, the possibility of distress sales, leading to losses by sellers, is ruled out by experimental design. In long-run price theory we think of producers entering or leaving an industry in response to the profits or losses they expect to make. The results of one pilot experiment to simulate this process is shown in Chart 12. The significant new element in this experiment was giving all sellers the option at the beginning of each trading period of entering the market or remaining "out of produc-

tion." It was understood that if they entered the market it was at a cost equal to
the price on their card, and this cost was
a net loss to any seller failing to make
a sale. Also in this experiment some sellers
were producers of two units and some of
one unit. Specifically, there were six sellers
with one unit and five with two units.
Similarly, some buyers were two-unit buyers
and some were one-unit buyers. It was not
known to the traders generally how many
or who were traders in one or in two units.
This procedure was employed primarily to
prevent traders from having exact knowledge of short-run supply by simply counting
the number of sellers in the market in any
trading period. Buyers in particular were
thereby faced with some uncertainty to
temper their knowledge that sellers were
under strong selling pressure once they entered the market.

The experiment was conducted over five
trading periods. In period 1 two sellers with
a capacity to produce three units (the \$4.75
and \$3.00 sellers in Chart 12) elected to
remain out of production. They were market
observers only. Therefore the period 1 short-
run theoretical supply was perfectly inelastic
at $S_1 = 13$. In period 2 only the \$4.50
seller, who sold at a loss the first time,
remained out, giving $S_2 = 15$. In period
3 the \$5.00 and \$4.50 sellers remained out
giving $S_3 = 14$, and in periods 4 and 5
production stabilized with the \$5.00, \$4.50,
and \$4.25 producers out of the market,
giving $S_4 = S_5 = 12$.

From the results is it clear that this
market approaches its "long-run" equilibrium price, \$4.50, more slowly than was the
case in the previous experiments. The approach is from below as might be expected
by the "distress sale" characteristic of the
market. The pressure on producers to sell
seems to have had its strongest effect in
period 1, in which market prices tended
to decline from their opening. Prices moved
erratically in period 2, and in the remaining
periods climbed steadily in the direction
of equilibrium.

[13]

TRANSACTION-COST ECONOMICS: THE GOVERNANCE OF CONTRACTUAL RELATIONS*

OLIVER E. WILLIAMSON
University of Pennsylvania

T HE new institutional economics is preoccupied with the origins, incidence, and ramifications of transaction costs. Indeed, if transaction costs are negligible, the organization of economic activity is irrelevant, since any advantages one mode of organization appears to hold over another will simply be eliminated by costless contracting. But despite the growing realization that transaction costs are central to the study of economics,[1] skeptics remain. Stanley Fischer's complaint is typical: "Transaction costs have a well-deserved bad name as a theoretical device . . . [partly] because there is a suspicion that almost anything can be rationalized by invoking suitably specified transaction costs."[2] Put differently, there are too many degrees of freedom; the concept wants for definition.

* This paper has benefited from support from the Center for Advanced Study in the Behavioral Sciences, the Guggenheim Foundation, and the National Science Foundation. Helpful comments by Yoram Ben-Porath, Richard Nelson, Douglass North, Thomas Palay, Joseph Sax, David Teece, and Peter Temin and from the participants at seminars at the Yale Law School and the Institute for Advanced Study at Princeton are gratefully acknowledged. The paper was rewritten to advantage after reading Ben-Porath's discussion paper, the F-Connection: Family, Friends, and Firms and the Organization of Exchange, and Temin's discussion paper, Modes of Economic Behavior: Variations on Themes of J. R. Hicks and Herbert Simon.

[1] Ronald Coase has forcefully argued the importance of transaction costs at twenty-year intervals. See R. H. Coase, The Nature of the Firm, 4 Economica 386 (n.s. 1937), reprinted in Readings in Price Theory 331 (George J. Stigler & Kenneth E. Boulding eds. 1952) and R. H. Coase, The Problem of Social Cost, 3 J. Law & Econ. 1 (1960). Much of my own work has been "preoccupied" with transaction costs during the past decade. See especially Oliver E. Williamson, Markets and Hierarchies: Analysis and Antitrust Implications (1975). Other works in which transaction costs are featured include: Guido Calabresi, Transaction Costs, Resource Allocation, and Liability Rules: A Comment, 11 J. Law & Econ. 67 (1968); Victor P. Goldberg, Regulation and Administered Contracts, 7 Bell J. Econ. 426 (1976); Benjamin Klein, Robert G. Crawford, and Armen A. Alchian, Vertical Integration, Appropriable Rents, and the Competitive Contracting Process, 21 J. Law & Econ. 297 (1978); and Carl J. Dahlman, The Problem of Externality, 22 J. Law & Econ. 141 (1979). For an examination of Pigou in which transaction costs are featured, see Victor P. Goldberg, Pigou on Complex Contracts and Welfare Economics (1979) (unpublished manuscript).

[2] S. Fischer, Long-Term Contracting, Sticky Prices, and Monetary Policy: Comment, 3 J. Monetary Econ. 317, 322 n. 5 (1977).

233

Among the factors on which there appears to be developing a general consensus are: (1) opportunism is a central concept in the study of transaction costs;[3] (2) opportunism is especially important for economic activity that involves transaction-specific investments in human and physical capital;[4] (3) the efficient processing of information is an important and related concept;[5] and (4) the assessment of transaction costs is a comparative institutional undertaking.[6] Beyond these general propositions, a consensus on transaction costs is lacking.

Further progress in the study of transaction costs awaits the identification of the critical dimensions with respect to which transaction costs differ and an examination of the economizing properties of alternative institutional modes for organizing transactions. Only then can the matching of transactions with modes be accomplished with confidence. This paper affirms the proposition that transaction costs are central to the study of economics, identifies the critical dimensions for characterizing transactions, describes the main governance structures of transactions, and indicates how and why transactions can be matched with institutions in a discriminating way.

I am mainly concerned with intermediate-product market transactions. Whereas previously I have emphasized the incentives to remove transactions from the market and organize them internally (vertical integration),[7] the analysis here is symmetrical and deals with market, hierarchical, and intermediate modes of organization alike. The question of why there is so much vertical integration remains interesting, but no more so than the question of why there are so many market- (and quasi-market) mediated transactions. A discriminating analysis will explain which transactions are located where and give the reasons why. The overall object of the exercise essentially comes down to this: for each abstract description of a transaction, identify

[3] Opportunism is a variety of self-interest seeking but extends simple self-interest seeking to include self-interest seeking with guile. It is not necessary that all agents be regarded as opportunistic in identical degree. It suffices that those who are less opportunistic than others are difficult to ascertain ex ante and that, even among the less opportunistic, most have their price. For a more complete discussion of opportunism, see Oliver E. Williamson, *supra* note 1, at 7-10, 26-30. For a recent application see Benjamin Klein, Robert G. Crawford, & Armen A. Alchian, *supra* note 1.

[4] The joining of opportunism with transaction-specific investments (or what Klein, Crawford, and Alchian refer to as "appropriable quasi rents") is a leading factor in explaining decisions to vertically integrate. See Oliver E. Williamson, The Vertical Integration of Production: Market Failure Considerations, 61 Am. Econ. Rev. 112 (Papers & Proceedings, May 1971); Oliver E. Williamson, *supra* note 1, at 16-19, 91-101; and Benjamin Klein, Robert G. Crawford, & Armen A. Alchian, *supra* note 1.

[5] But for the limited ability of human agents to receive, store, retrieve, and process data, interesting economic problems vanish.

[6] See Carl J. Dahlman, *supra* note 1.

[7] See note 4 *supra*.

the most economical governance structure—where by governance structure I refer to the institutional framework within which the integrity of a transaction is decided. Markets and hierarchies are two of the main alternatives.

Some legal background to the study of transactions is briefly reviewed in Section I. Of the three dimensions for describing transactions that I propose, investment attributes are the least well understood and probably the most important. The special relevance of investments is developed in the context of the economics of idiosyncrasy in Section II. A general contracting schema is developed and applied to commercial contracting in Section III. Applications to labor, regulation, family transactions, and capital markets are sketched in Section IV. Major implications are summarized in Section V. Concluding remarks follow.

I.   Some Contracting Background

Although there is widespread agreement that the discrete-transaction paradigm—"sharp in by clear agreement; sharp out by clear performance"[8]—has served both law and economics well, there is increasing awareness that many contractual relations are not of this well-defined kind.[9] A deeper understanding of the nature of contract has emerged as the legal-rule emphasis associated with the study of discrete contracting has given way to a more general concern with the contractual purposes to be served.[10]

---

[8] I. R. Macneil, The Many Futures of Contract, 47 S. Cal. L. Rev. 691, 738 (1974) [hereinafter cited without cross-reference as Macneil, Many Futures of Contract].

[9] With respect to commercial contracts, see Karl N. Llewellyn, What Price Contract?—An Essay in Perspective, 40 Yale L. J. 704 (1931); Harold C. Havighurst, The Nature of Private Contract (1961); Lon L. Fuller, Collective Bargaining and the Arbitrator, 1963 Wis. L. Rev. 3; *id.*, The Morality of Law (1964); Stewart Macaulay, Non-Contractual Relations in Business, 28 Am. Soc. Rev. 55 (1963); Lawrence M. Friedman, Contract Law in America (1965); Arthur Allen Leff, Contract as a Thing, 19 Am. U. L. Rev. 131 (1970); I. R. Macneil, Many Futures of Contracts; *id.*, Contracts: Adjustment of Long-Term Economic Relations under Classical, Neoclassical, and Relational Contract Law, 72 Nw. U. L. Rev. 854 (1978) [hereinafter cited without cross-reference as Macneil, Contracts]; and Victor P. Goldberg, Toward an Expanded Economic Theory of Contract, 10 J. Econ. Issues 45 (1976). Labor lawyers have made similar observations regarding contracts governing the employment relationship. See Archibald Cox, The Legal Nature of Collective Bargaining Agreements, 57 Mich. L. Rev. 1 (1958); Clyde W. Summers, Collective Agreements and the Law of Contracts, 78 Yale L. J. 525 (1969); and David E. Feller, A General Theory of the Collective Bargaining Agreement, 61 Cal. L. Rev. 663 (1973).

[10] The technical versus purposive distinction is made by Clyde Summers, *supra* note 9. He distinguishes between "black letter law," on the one hand (539, 543, 548, 566) and a more circumstantial approach to law, on the other (549-51, 561, 566). "The epitome of abstraction is the *Restatement*, which illustrates its black letter rules by transactions suspended in mid-air, creating the illusion that contract rules can be stated without reference to surrounding circumstances and are therefore generally applicable to all contractual transactions" (566). He observes that such a conception does not and cannot provide a "framework for integrating rules and principles applicable to all contractual transactions" (566) but that this must be sought in a more

Ian Macneil, in a series of thoughtful and wide-ranging essays on contract, usefully distinguishes between discrete and relational transactions.[11] He further supplies twelve different "concepts" with respect to which these differ.[12] Serious problems of recognition and application are posed by such a rich classificatory apparatus. More useful for my purposes is the three-way classification of contracts that Macneil offers in his most recent article, where classical, neoclassical, and relational categories of contract law are recognized.

A. Classical Contract Law

As Macneil observes, any system of contract law has the purpose of facilitating exchange. What is distinctive about classical contract law is that it attempts to do this by enhancing discreteness and intensifying "presentiation,"[13] where presentiation has reference to efforts to "make or render present in place or time; to cause to be perceived or realized at present."[14] The economic counterpart to complete presentiation is contingent-claims contracting—which entails comprehensive contracting whereby all relevant future contingencies pertaining to the supply of a good or service are described and discounted with respect to both likelihood and futurity.[15]

Classical contract law endeavors to implement discreteness and presentiation in several ways. For one thing, the identity of the parties to a transaction is treated as irrelevant. In this respect it corresponds exactly with the "ideal" market transaction in economics.[16] Second, the nature of the agreement is carefully delimited, and the more formal features govern when formal (for example, written) and informal (for example, oral) terms are contested. Third, remedies are narrowly prescribed such that, "should the initial presentiation fail to materialize because of nonperformance, the consequences are relatively predictable from the beginning and are not open-

---

affirmative view of the law in which effective governance relations are emphasized. Contract interpretation and completing contracts are among these affirmative functions.

[11] See especially Macneil, Many Futures of Contract; Macneil, Contracts; and references to related work of his cited therein.

[12] Macneil, Many Futures of Contracts 738-40; Macneil, Contracts 902-05.

[13] Macneil, Contracts 862.

[14] *Id.* at 863 n. 25.

[15] For a discussion of complex contingent-claims contracting and its mechanics, see Kenneth J. Arrow, Essays in the Theory of Risk Bearing 121-34 (1971); J. E. Meade, The Controlled Economy 147-88 (1971); and Oliver E. Williamson, *supra* note 1, at 20-40.

[16] As Lester G. Telser & Harlow N. Higinbotham put it: "In an organized market the participants trade a standardized contract such that each unit of the contract is a perfect substitute for any other unit. The identities of the parties in any mutually agreeable transaction do not affect the terms of exchange. The organized market itself or some other institution deliberately creates a homogeneous good that can be traded anonymously by the participants or their agents." Organized Futures Markets: Costs and Benefits 85 J. Pol. Econ. 969, 997 (1977).

ended."[17] Additionally, third-party participation is discouraged.[18] The emphasis, thus, is on legal rules, formal documents, and self-liquidating transactions.

B. *Neoclassical Contract Law*

Not every transaction fits comfortably into the classical-contracting scheme. In particular, long-term contracts executed under conditions of uncertainty are ones for which complete presentation is apt to be prohibitively costly if not impossible. Problems of several kinds arise. First, not all future contingencies for which adaptations are required can be anticipated at the outset. Second, the appropriate adaptations will not be evident for many contingencies until the circumstances materialize. Third, except as changes in states of the world are unambiguous, hard contracting between autonomous parties may well give rise to veridical disputes when state-contingent claims are made. In a world where (at least some) parties are inclined to be opportunistic, whose representations are to be believed?

Faced with the prospective breakdown of classical contracting in these circumstances, three alternatives are available. One would be to forgo such transactions altogether. A second would be to remove these transactions from the market and organize them internally instead. Adaptive, sequential decision making would then be implemented under common ownership and with the assistance of hierarchical incentive and control systems. Third, a different contracting relation which preserves trading but provides for additional governance structure might be devised. This last brings us to what Macneil refers to as neoclassical contracting.

As Macneil observes, "Two common characteristics of long-term contracts are the existence of gaps in their planning and the presence of a range of processes and techniques used by contract planners to create flexibility in lieu of either leaving gaps or trying to plan rigidly."[19] Third-party assistance in resolving disputes and evaluating performance often has advantages over litigation in serving these functions of flexibility and gap filling. Lon Fuller's remarks on procedural differences between arbitration and litigation are instructive:

. . . there are open to the arbitrator . . . quick methods of education not open to the courts. An arbitrator will frequently interrupt the examination of witnesses with a request that the parties educate him to the point where he can understand the testimony being received. This education can proceed informally, with frequent interruptions by the arbitrator, and by informed persons on either side, when a point

---

[17] Macneil, Contracts 864.

[18] *Id.*

[19] *Id.* at 865.

needs clarification. Sometimes there will be arguments across the table, occasionally even within each of the separate camps. The end result will usually be a clarification that will enable everyone to proceed more intelligently with the case. There is in this informal procedure no infringement whatever of arbitrational due process.[20]

A recognition that the world is complex, that agreements are incomplete, and that some contracts will never be reached unless both parties have confidence in the settlement machinery thus characterizes neoclassical contract law. One important purposive difference in arbitration and litigation that contributes to the procedural differences described by Fuller is that, whereas continuity (at least completion of the contract) is presumed under the arbitration machinery, this presumption is much weaker when litigation is employed.[21]

C. *Relational Contracting*

The pressures to sustain ongoing relations "have led to the spin-off of many subject areas from the classical, and later the neoclassical, contract law system, e.g., much of corporate law and collective bargaining."[22] Thus, progressively increasing the "duration and complexity" of contract has resulted in the displacement of even neoclassical adjustment processes by adjustment processes of a more thoroughly transaction-specific, ongoing-administrative kind.[23] The fiction of discreteness is fully displaced as the relation takes on the properties of "a minisociety with a vast array of norms beyond those centered on the exchange and its immediate processes."[24] By contrast with the neoclassical system, where the reference point for effecting adaptations remains the original agreement, the reference point under a truly relational approach is the "entire relation as it has developed . . . [through] time. This may or may not include an 'original agreement'; and if it does, may or may not result in great deference being given it."[25]

II.   THE ECONOMICS OF IDIOSYNCRASY

Macneil's three-way discussion of contracts discloses that contracts are a good deal more varied and complex than is commonly realized.[26] It further-

[20] Lon L. Fuller, *supra* note 9, at 11-12.

[21] As Lawrence Friedman observes, relationships are effectively fractured if a dispute reaches litigation. *Supra* note 9, at 205.

[22] Macneil, Contracts 885.

[23] *Id.* at 901.

[24] *Id.*

[25] *Id.* at 890.

[26] To be sure, some legal specialists insist that all of this was known all along. There is a difference, however, between awareness of a condition and an understanding. Macneil's treatment heightens awareness and deepens the understanding.

more suggests that governance structures—the institutional matrix within which transactions are negotiated and executed—vary with the nature of the transaction. But the critical dimensions of contract are not expressly identified, and the purposes of governance are not stated. Harmonizing interests that would otherwise give way to antagonistic subgoal pursuits appears to be an important governance function, but this is not explicit in his discussion.

That simple governance structures should be used in conjunction with simple contractual relations and complex governance structures reserved for complex relations seems generally sensible. Use of a complex structure to govern a simple relation is apt to incur unneeded costs, and use of a simple structure for a complex transaction invites strain. But what is simple and complex in contractual respects? Specific attention to the defining attributes of transactions is evidently needed.

As developed in Section III, the three critical dimensions for characterizing transactions are (1) uncertainty, (2) the frequency with which transactions recur, and (3) the degree to which durable transaction-specific investments are incurred. Of these three, uncertainty is widely conceded to be a critical attribute;[27] and that frequency matters is at least plausible.[28] The governance ramifications of neither, however, have been fully developed—nor can they be until joined with the third critical dimension: transaction-specific investments. Inasmuch as a considerable amount of the "action" in the study of governance is attributable to investment differences, some explication is needed.

A. *General*

The crucial investment distinction is this: to what degree are transaction-specific (nonmarketable) expenses incurred. Items that are unspecialized among users pose few hazards, since buyers in these circumstances can easily turn to alternative sources, and suppliers can sell output intended for one order to other buyers without difficulty.[29] Nonmarketability problems arise

---

[27] For a recent study of contractual relations in which uncertainty is featured, see Peter Temin, Modes of Economic Behavior: Variations on Themes of J. R. Hicks and Herbert Simon (March 1979) (Working Paper No. 235, MIT Dep't of Econ.).

[28] Gordon Whinston emphasizes frequency in his "A Note on Perspective Time: Goldberg's Relational Exchange, Repetitiveness, and Free Riders in Time and Space" (October 1978) (unpublished paper).

[29] See Lester A. Telser & Harold N. Higinbotham, *supra* note 16; also Yoram Ben-Porath, The F-Connection: Families, Friends, and Firms and the Organization of Exchange (December 1978) (Report No. 29/78, The Hebrew University of Jerusalem) and Yoram Barzel, Measurement Cost and the Organization of Markets (April 1979) (unpublished paper). Note that Barzel's concern with standardization is mainly in connection with final-product markets, whereas I am more interested in nonstandard investments. The two are not unrelated, but identical quality can often be realized with a variety of inputs. I am concerned with specialized (transaction-specific) inputs.

when the *specific identity* of the parties has important cost-bearing consequences. Transactions of this kind will be referred to as idiosyncratic.

Occasionally the identity of the parties is important from the outset, as when a buyer induces a supplier to invest in specialized physical capital of a transaction-specific kind. Inasmuch as the value of this capital in other uses is, by definition, much smaller than the specialized use for which it has been intended, the supplier is effectively "locked into" the transaction to a significant degree. This is symmetrical, moreover, in that the buyer cannot turn to alternative sources of supply and obtain the item on favorable terms, since the cost of supply from unspecialized capital is presumably great.[30] The buyer is thus committed to the transaction as well.

Ordinarily, however, there is more to idiosyncratic exchange than specialized physical capital. Human-capital investments that are transaction-specific commonly occur as well. Specialized training and learning-by-doing economies in production operations are illustrations. Except when these investments are transferable to alternative suppliers at low cost, which is rare, the benefits of the set-up costs can be realized only so long as the relationship between the buyer and seller of the intermediate product is maintained.

Additional transaction-specific savings can accrue at the interface between supplier and buyer as contracts are successively adapted to unfolding events, and as periodic contract-renewal agreements are reached. Familiarity here permits communication economies to be realized: specialized language develops as experience accumulates and nuances are signaled and received in a sensitive way. Both institutional and personal trust relations evolve. Thus the individuals who are responsible for adapting the interfaces have a personal as well as an organizational stake in what transpires. Where personal integrity is believed to be operative, individuals located at the interfaces may refuse to be a part of opportunistic efforts to take advantage of (rely on) the letter of the contract when the spirit of the exchange is emasculated. Such refusals can serve as a check upon organizational proclivities to behave opportunistically.[31] Other things being equal, idiosyncratic exchange rela-

---

[30] This assumes that it is costly for the incumbent supplier to transfer specialized physical assets to new suppliers. On this, see Oliver E. Williamson, Franchise Bidding for Natural Monopolies—in General and with Respect to CATV, 7 Bell J. Econ. 73 (1976). Klein, Crawford, & Alchian use the term "appropriable quasi rent" to refer to this condition. Use versus user distinctions are relevant in this connection: "The quasi-rent value of the asset is the excess of its value over its salvage value, that is, its value in its next best *use* to another renter. The potentially appropriable specialized portion of the quasi rent is the portion, if any, in excess of its value to the second highest-valuing *user*." Benjamin Klein, Robert G. Crawford, & Armen A. Alchian, *supra* note 1, at 298.

[31] Thorstein Veblen's remarks on the distant relation of the head of a large enterprise to transactions are apposite. He observes that under these impersonal circumstances "The mitigating effect which personal conduct may have in dealings between man and man is . . . in great

tions which feature personal trust will survive greater stress and display greater adaptability.

Idiosyncratic goods and services are thus ones where investments of transaction-specific human and physical capital are made and, contingent upon successful execution, benefits are realized. Such investments can and do occur in conjunction with occasional trades where delivery for a specialized design is stretched out over a long period (for example, certain construction contracts). The transactions that I wish to emphasize here, however, are exchanges of the recurring kind. Although large-numbers competition is frequently feasible at the initial award stage for recurring contracts of all kinds, idiosyncratic transactions are ones for which the relationship between buyer and supplier is quickly thereafter *transformed* into one of bilateral monopoly—on account of the transaction-specific costs referred to above. This transformation has profound contracting consequences.

Thus, whereas recurrent spot contracting is feasible for standardized transactions (because large-numbers competition is continuously self-policing in these circumstances), such contracting has seriously defective investment incentives where idiosyncratic activities are involved. By assumption, cost economies in production will be realized for idiosyncratic activities only if the supplier invests in a special-purpose plant and equipment or if his labor force develops transaction-specific skills in the course of contract execution (or both). The assurance of a continuing relation is needed to encourage investments of both kinds. Although the requisite incentives might be provided if long-term contracts were negotiated, such contracts are necessarily incomplete (by reason of bounded rationality). Appropriate state-contingent adaptations thus go unspecified. Intertemporal efficiency nevertheless requires that adaptations to changing market circumstances be made.

How to effect these adaptations poses a serious contracting dilemma, though it bears repeating that, absent the hazards of opportunism, the difficulties would vanish—since then the gaps in long-term, incomplete contracts could be faultlessly filled in an adaptive, sequential way. A general clause, to which both parties would agree, to the effect that "I will behave responsibly rather than seek individual advantage when an occasion to adapt arises," would, in the absence of opportunism, suffice. Given, however, the unenforceability of general clauses and the proclivity of human agents to make false and misleading (self-disbelieved) statements, the follow-

---

measured eliminated. . . . Business management [then] has a chance to proceed . . . untroubled by sentimental considerations of human kindness or irritation or of honesty." The Theory of Business Enterprise 53 (1927). Veblen evidently assigns slight weight to the possibility that those to whom negotiating responsibilities are assigned will themselves invest the transactions with integrity.

ing hazard must be confronted: joined as they are in an idiosyncratic condition of bilateral monopoly, both buyer and seller are strategically situated to bargain over the disposition of any incremental gain whenever a proposal to adapt is made by the other party. Although both have a long-term interest in effecting adaptations of a joint profit-maximizing kind, each also has an interest in appropriating as much of the gain as he can on each occasion to adapt. Efficient adaptations which would otherwise be made thus result in costly haggling or even go unmentioned, lest the gains be dissipated by costly subgoal pursuit. Governance structures which attenuate opportunism and otherwise infuse confidence are evidently needed.

B. *Examples*

Some illustrations may help to motivate what is involved in idiosyncratic transactions. Specialized physical capital is relatively straightforward. Examples are (1) the purchase of a specialized component from an outside supplier or (2) the location of a specialized plant in a unique, proximate relation to a downstream processing stage to which it supplies vital input.

Thus assume (*a*) that special-purpose equipment is needed to produce the component in question (which is to say that the value of the equipment in its next-best alternative use is much lower), (*b*) that scale economies require that a significant, discrete investment be made, and (*c*) that alternative buyers for such components are few (possibly because of the organization of the industry, possibly because of special-design features). The interests of buyer and seller in a continuing exchange relation are plainly strong under these circumstances.

Plant-proximity benefits are attributable to transportation and related flow-process (inventory, thermal economy, and so on) economies. A specialized plant need not be implied, but long life and a unique location are. Once made, the investment preempts the unique location and is not thereafter moveable (except at prohibitive cost). Buyer and supplier again need to satisfy themselves that they have a workable, adaptable exchange agreement.[32]

Idiosyncratic investments in human capital are in many ways more interesting and less obvious than are those in physical capital. Polanyi's discussion of "personal knowledge" is illuminating:

The attempt to analyze scientifically the established industrial arts has everywhere led to similar results. Indeed even in the modern industries the indefinable knowledge is still an essential part of technology. I have myself watched in Hungary a new, imported machine for blowing electric lamp bulbs, the exact counterpart of which

---

[32] The *Great Lakes Carbon* case is an example of the latter, 1970–1973 Trade Reg. Rep. Transfer Binder ¶ 19,848 (FTC Dkt No. 8805).

was operating successfully in Germany, failing for a whole year to produce a single flawless bulb.[33]

And he goes on to observe with respect to craftsmanship that:

. . . an art which has fallen into disuse for the period of a generation is altogether lost. . . . It is pathetic to watch the endless efforts—equipped with microscopy and chemistry, with mathematics and electronics—to reproduce a single violin of the kind the half-literate Stradivarius turned out as a matter of routine more than 200 years ago.[34]

Polanyi's discussion of language also has a bearing on the argument advanced above that specialized code words or expressions can and do arise in the context of recurring transactions and that these yield economies. As he puts it, "Different vocabularies for the interpretation of things divide men into groups which cannot understand each other's way of seeing things and acting upon them."[35] And subsequently he remarks that:

To know a language is an art, carried on by tacit judgments and the practice of unspecifiable skills. . . . Spoken communication is the successful application by two persons of the linguistic knowledge and skill acquired by such apprenticeship, one person wishing to transmit, the other to receive, information. Relying on what each has learnt, the speaker confidently utters words and the listener confidently interprets them, while they mutually rely on each other's correct use and understanding of these words. A true communication will take place if, and only if, these combined assumptions of authority and trust are in fact justified.[36]

Babbage reports a remarkable example of transaction-specific value in exchange that occurred in the early 1800s. Although he attributes the continuing exchange in the face of adversity to values of "established character" (trust), I believe there were other specialized human and physical investments involved as well. In any event, the circumstance which he describes is the following:

The influence of established character in producing confidence operated in a very remarkable manner at the time of the exclusion of British manufactures from the Continent during the last war. One of our largest establishments had been in the habit of doing extensive business with a house in the centre of Germany; but, on the closing of the continental ports against our manufacturers, heavy penalties were inflicted on all those who contravened the Berlin and Milan decrees. The English manufacturer continued, nevertheless, to receive orders, with directions how to con-

[33] Michael Polanyi, Personal Knowledge: Towards a Post-Critical Philosophy 52 (2d ed. 1962).

[34] *Id.* at 53.

[35] *Id.* at 112.

[36] *Id.* at 206.

sign them, and appointments for the time and mode of payment, in letters, the handwriting of which was known to him, but which were never signed, except by the Christian name of one of the firm, and even in some instances they were without any signature at all. These orders were executed; and in no instance was there the least irregularity in the payments.[37]

While most of these illustrations refer to technical and commercial transactions, other types of transactions also have an idiosyncratic quality. Justice Rhenquist refers to some of these when speaking of the general class of cases where "the litigation of an individual's claim of deprivation of a right would bring parties *who must remain in a continuing relationship* into the adversarial atmosphere of a courtroom"[38]—which atmosphere he plainly regards as detrimental to the quality of the relationship. Examples that he offers include reluctance to have the courts mediate collective bargaining disputes[39] and to allow children to bring suit against parents.[40]

But surely we must ask what is distinctive about these transactions. I submit that transaction-specific human capital is central to each. Why else would it take the Hungarians so long to operate the German light-bulb machine? And what else explains the loss of Stradivarius's craftsmanship? Likewise the understanding and trust which evolve between Babbage's transmitter and receiver are valued human assets which, once developed, will be sacrificed with reluctance. And the disruption of continuing relationships to which Justice Rhenquist refers occasions concern precisely because there are no adequate substitutes for these idiosyncratic relations.[41]

The general argument of this paper is that special governance structures supplant standard market-cum-classical contract exchange when transac-

---

[37] Charles Babbage, On the Economy of Machinery and Manufacturers 220-21 (1832). More recent examples of contracts wherein private parties can and evidently do "ignore" the law, even at some peril, when the law and the interests of the parties are at variance are offered by Stewart Macaulay, The Use and Nonuse of Contracts in the Manufacturing Industry, 9 Practical Lawyer 13, 16 (1963): "Requirements contracts probably are not legally enforceable in Wisconsin and a few other States. Yet, chemicals, containers, and a number of other things are still bought and sold there on the basis of requirements contracts.

"Decisions of the United States Court of Appeals for the Seventh Circuit indicate that a clause calling for a 'seller's price in effect at time and place of delivery' makes a contract unenforceable. The Wisconsin cases are not clear. Yet steel and steel products usually are sold in this way."

[38] Remarks of Mr. Justice Rhenquist, The Adversary Society, Baron di Hirsch Meyer Lecture, University of Miami School of Law, February 2, 1978, at 19 (emphasis added).

[39] *Id.* at 11-13.

[40] *Id.* at 16-19.

[41] As Ben-Porath puts it, "The most important characteristic of the family contract is that it is embedded in the identity of the partners without which it loses its meaning. It is thus specific and non-negotiable or nontransferable." Yoram Ben-Porath, *supra* note 29, at 6.

tion-specific values are great. Idiosyncratic commercial, labor, and family relationships are specific examples.

III. COMMERCIAL CONTRACTING

The discussion of commercial contracting begins with a brief statement on economizing. The proposed schema for characterizing transactions and their governance is then developed, including the relation of the schema with Macneil's three-way classification of contract.

A. *Economizing*

The criterion for organizing commercial transactions is assumed to be the strictly instrumental one of cost economizing. Essentially this takes two parts: economizing on production expense and economizing on transaction costs.[42] To the degree that transaction costs are negligible, buying rather than making will normally be the most cost-effective means of procurement.[43] Not only can static scale economies be more fully exhausted by buying rather than making, but the supplier who aggregates uncorrelated demands can realize collective pooling benefits as well. Since external procurement avoids many of the bureaucratic hazards of internal procurement (which hazards, however, are themselves of a transaction-cost kind),[44] external procurement is evidently warranted.[45]

As indicated, however, the object is to economize on the *sum* of production and transaction costs. To the degree production-cost economies of external procurement are small and/or the transaction costs associated with external procurement are great, alternative supply arrangements deserve serious consideration. Economizing on transaction costs essentially reduces

---

[42] More generally, the economizing problem includes choice between a special-purpose and a general-purpose good or service. A general-purpose item affords all of the advantages of market procurement, but possibly at the sacrifice of valued design or performance characteristics. A special-purpose item has the opposite features: valued differences are realized but market procurement here may pose hazards. For the purposes of this paper, intermediate-product characteristics are mainly taken as given and I focus principally on production and transaction-cost economies. A more general formulation would include product characteristics in the optimization.

[43] This ignores transient conditions, such as temporary excess capacity. (In a zero-transaction-cost world, such excesses vanish as assets can be deployed as effectively by others as they can by the owner.)

[44] On these hazards and their transaction-cost origins, see Oliver E. Williamson, *supra* note 1, at 117-31.

[45] Dennis Carlton shows that economies of "vertical integration" can frequently be realized in a market where, absent integration, buyers and suppliers are randomly paired. As he defines vertical integration, however, this can be accomplished as effectively by long-term contract as it can by in-house production. Dennis W. Carlton, Vertical Integration in Competitive Markets under Uncertainty, 27 J. Indus. Econ. 189 (1979).

to economizing on bounded rationality while simultaneously safeguarding the transactions in question against the hazards of opportunism. Holding the governance structure constant, these two objectives are in tension, since a reduction in one commonly results in an increase in the other.[46]

Governance structures, however, are properly regarded as part of the optimization problem. For some transactions, a shift from one structure to another may permit a simultaneous reduction in both the expense of writing a complex contract (which economizes on bounded rationality) and the expense of executing it effectively in an adaptive, sequential way (by attenuating opportunism). Indeed, this is precisely the attraction of internal procurement for transactions of a recurrent, idiosyncratic kind. Not only are market-aggregation economies negligible for such transactions—since the requisite investments are transaction-specific—but market trading in these circumstances is shot through with appropriable quasi-rent hazards. The issues here have been developed elsewhere.[47] The object of this paper is to integrate them into a larger contractual framework.

Note in this connection that the prospect of recovering the set-up costs associated with specialized governance structures varies with the frequency with which transactions recur. Specialized governance structures are much easier to justify for recurrent transactions than for identical transactions that occur only occasionally.

B. *Characterizing Transactions*

I asserted earlier that the critical dimensions for describing contractual relations are uncertainty, the frequency with which transactions recur, and the degree to which investments are idiosyncratic. To simplify the exposition, I will assume uncertainty exists in some intermediate degree and focus initially on frequency and the degree to which the expenses incurred are transaction-specific. The separate importance of uncertainty will then be developed in Section III.D. Three frequency and three investment categories will be recognized. Frequency can be characterized as one-time, occasional, and recurrent; and investments are classed as nonspecific, mixed, and idiosyncratic. To further simplify the argument, the following assumptions are made: (1) Suppliers intend to be in business on a continuing basis; thus the special hazards posed by fly-by-night firms can be disregarded. (2) Potential suppliers for any given requirement are numerous—which is to say that *ex ante* monopoly in ownership of specialized resources is assumed away. (3)

---

[46] Thus a reduction in monitoring commonly gives rise to an increase in opportunism. Monitoring the employment relation, however, needs to be done with special care. Progressively increasing the intensity of surveillance can elicit resentment and have counterproductive (for example, work-to-rule) results. Such perversities are less likely for interfirm trading.

[47] See note 30 *supra*.

The frequency dimension refers strictly to buyer activity in the market.[48] (4) The investment dimension refers to the characteristics of investments made by suppliers.[49]

Although discrete transactions are intriguing—for example, purchasing local spirits from a shopkeeper in a remote area of a foreign country to which one never again expects to visit nor to refer his friends—few transactions have this totally isolated character. For those that do not, the difference between one-time and occasional transactions is not apparent. Accordingly, only occasional and recurrent frequency distinctions will be maintained. The two-by-three matrix shown in Figure I thus describes the six types of transactions to which governance structures need to be matched. Illustrative transactions appear in the cells.

		Investment Characteristics		
		Nonspecific	Mixed	Idiosyncratic
Frequency	Occasional	Purchasing Standard Equipment	Purchasing Customized Equipment	Constructing a Plant
Frequency	Recurrent	Purchasing Standard Material	Purchasing Customized Material	Site-Specific Transfer of Intermediate Product Across Successive Stages

FIGURE I
ILLUSTRATIVE COMMERCIAL TRANSACTIONS

C. Governance Structures

Three broad types of governance structures will be considered: non-transaction-specific, semi-specific, and highly specific. The market is the classic nonspecific governance structure within which "faceless buyers and sellers . . . meet . . . for an instant to exchange standardized goods at

---

[48] This seems reasonable for most intermediate-product market transactions.

[49] Production aspects are thus emphasized. Investments in governance structure are treated separately.

equilibrium prices."[50] By contrast, highly specific structures are tailored to the special needs of the transaction. Identity here clearly matters. Semi-specific structures, naturally, fall in between. Several propositions are suggested immediately. (1) Highly standardized transactions are not apt to require specialized governance structure. (2) Only recurrent transactions will support a highly specialized governance structure.[51] (3) Although occasional transactions of a nonstandardized kind will not support a transaction-specific governance structure, they require special attention nonetheless. In terms of Macneil's three-way classification of contract, classical contracting presumably applies to all standardized transactions (whatever the frequency), relational contracting develops for transactions of a recurring and nonstandardized kind, and neoclassical contracting is needed for occasional, nonstandardized transactions.

1. *Market Governance: Classical Contracting.* Market governance is the main governance structure for nonspecific transactions of both occasional and recurrent contracting. Markets are especially efficacious when recurrent transactions are contemplated, since both parties need only consult their own experience in deciding to continue a trading relationship or, at little transitional expense, turn elsewhere. Being standardized, alternative purchase and supply arrangements are presumably easy to work out.

Nonspecific but occasional transactions are ones for which buyers (and sellers) are less able to rely on direct experience to safeguard transactions against opportunism. Often, however, rating services or the experience of other buyers of the same good can be consulted. Given that the good or service is of a standardized kind, such experience rating, by formal and informal means, will provide incentives for parties to behave responsibly.

To be sure, such transactions take place within and benefit from a legal framework. But such dependence is not great. As S. Todd Lowry puts it, "the traditional economic analysis of exchange in a market setting properly corresponds to the legal concept of *sale* (rather than contract), since sale presumes arrangements in a market context and requires legal support primarily in enforcing transfers of title."[52] He would thus reserve the concept of contract for exchanges where, in the absence of standardized market

---

[50] Yoram Ben-Porath, *supra* note 29, at 7.

[51] Defense contracting may appear to be a counterexample, since an elaborate governance structure is devised for many of these. This reflects in part, however, the special disabilities of the government as a production instrument. But for this, many of these contracts would be organized in-house. Also, contracts that are very large and of long duration, as many defense contracts are, do have a recurring character.

[52] S. Todd Lowry, Bargain and Contract Theory in Law and Economics, 10 J. Econ. Issues 1, 12 (1976).

alternatives, the parties have designed "patterns of future relations on which they could rely."[53]

The assumptions of the discrete-contracting paradigm are rather well satisfied for transactions where markets serve as a main governance mode. Thus the specific identity of the parties is of negligible importance; substantive content is determined by reference to formal terms of the contract; and legal rules apply. Market alternatives are mainly what protect each party against opportunism by his opposite.[54] Litigation is strictly for settling claims; concentrated efforts to sustain the relation are not made because the relation is not independently valued.[55]

2. *Trilateral Governance: Neoclassical Contracting.* The two types of transactions for whic:ı trilateral governance is needed are occasional transactions of the mixed and highly idiosyncratic kinds. Once the principals to such transactions have entered into a contract, there are strong incentives to see the contract through to completion. Not only have specialized investments been put in place, the opportunity cost of which is much lower in alternative uses, but the transfer of these assets to a successor supplier would pose inordinate difficulties in asset valuation.[56] The interests of the principals in sustaining the relation are especially great for highly idiosyncratic transactions.

Market relief is thus unsatisfactory. Often the setup costs of a transaction-specific governance structure cannot be recovered for occasional transactions. Given the limits of classical contract law for sustaining these transactions, on the one hand, and the prohibitive cost of transaction-specific (bilateral) governance, on the other, an intermediate institutional form is evidently needed.

Neoclassical contract law has many of the sought-after qualities. Thus rather than resorting immediately to strict reliance on litigation—with its

---

[53] *Id.* at 13.

[54] Although recurrent, standard transactions are ones for which an active spot market commonly exists, term contracting may also be employed—especially as planning economies are thereby realized by the parties. See Dennis W. Carlton, Price Rigidity, Forward Contracts, and Market Equilibrium, J. Pol. Econ. (forthcoming). The duration of these contracts will not be long, however, since the assets in question can be employed in other uses and/or in the service of other customers. The result is that changing market circumstances will be reflected relatively quickly in both price and quantity and relatively stringent contracting attitudes may be said to prevail.

[55] "Generally speaking, a serious conflict, even quite a minor one such as an objection to a harmlessly late tender of the delivery of goods, terminates the discrete contract as a live one and leaves nothing but a conflict over money damages to be settled by a lawsuit. Such a result fits neatly the norms of enhancing discreteness and intensifying . . . presentiation." Macneil, Contracts 877.

[56] See the articles cited in note 30 *supra*.

transaction-rupturing features—*third-party assistance* (arbitration) in resolving disputes and evaluating peformance is employed instead. (The use of the architect as a relatively independent expert to determine the content of form construction contracts is an example.)[57] Also, the expansion of the specific-performance remedy in past decades is consistent with continuity purposes—though Macneil declines to characterize specific performance as the "primary neoclassical contract remedy."[58] The section of the Uniform Commercial Code which permits the "seller aggrieved by a buyer's breach . . . unilaterally to maintain the relation"[59] is yet another example.

3. *Transaction-specific Governance: Relational Contracting.* The two types of transactions for which specialized governance structures are commonly devised are recurring transactions of the mixed and highly idiosyncratic kinds. The nonstandardized nature of these transactions makes primary reliance on market governance hazardous, while their recurrent nature permits the cost of the specialized governance structure to be recovered.

Two types of transaction-specific governance structures for intermediate-production market transactions can be distinguished: bilateral structures, where the autonomy of the parties is maintained, and unified structures, where the transaction is removed from the market and organized within the firm subject to an authority relation (vertical integration). Bilateral structures have only recently received the attention they deserve and their operation is least well understood.

(a) *Bilateral Governance: Obligational Contracting.* Highly idiosyncratic transactions are ones where the human and physical assets required for production are extensively specialized, so there are no obvious scale economies to be realized through interfirm trading that the buyer (or seller) is unable to realize himself (through vertical integration). In the case, however, of mixed transactions, the degree of asset specialization is less complete. Accordingly, outside procurement for these components may be favored by scale-economy considerations.

As compared with vertical integration, outside procurement also is good in eliciting cost control for steady-state supply. Problems, however, arise when adaptability and contractual expense are considered. Whereas internal adaptations can be effected by fiat, outside procurement involves effecting adaptations across a market interface. Unless the need for adaptations has been contemplated from the outset and expressly provided for by the contract,

---

[57] Macneil, Contracts 866.

[58] *Id.* at 879.

[59] *Id.* at 880. The rationale for this section of the Code is that "identification of the goods to the contract will, within limits, permit the seller to recover the price of the goods rather than merely damages for the breach. . . , ([where the] latter may be far less in amount and more difficult to prove)." *Id.*

which often is impossible or prohibitively expensive, adaptations across a market interface can be accomplished only by mutual, follow-on agreements. Inasmuch as the interests of the parties will commonly be at variance when adaptation proposals (originated by either party) are made, a dilemma is evidently posed.

On the one hand, both parties have an incentive to sustain the relationship rather than to permit it to unravel, the object being to avoid the sacrifice of valued transaction-specific economies. On the other hand, each party appropriates a separate profit stream and cannot be expected to accede readily to any proposal to adapt the contract. What is needed, evidently, is some way for declaring admissible dimensions for adjustment such that flexibility is provided under terms in which both parties have confidence. This can be accomplished partly by (1) recognizing that the hazards of opportunism vary with the type of adaptation proposed and (2) restricting adjustments to those where the hazards are least. But the spirit within which adaptations are effected is equally important.[60]

Quantity adjustments have much better incentive-compatibility properties than do price adjustments. For one thing, price adjustments have an unfortunate zero-sum quality, whereas proposals to increase, decrease, or delay delivery do not. Also, except as discussed below, price-adjustment proposals involve the risk that one's opposite is contriving to alter the terms within the bilateral monopoly trading gap to his advantage. By contrast, a presumption that exogenous events, rather than strategic purposes, are responsible for quantity adjustments is ordinarily warranted. Given the mixed nature of the exchange, a seller (or buyer) simply has little reason to doubt the representations of his opposite when a quantity change is proposed.

Thus buyers will neither seek supply from other sources nor divert products obtained (at favorable prices) to other uses (or users)—because other sources will incur high setup costs and an idiosyncratic product is nonfungible across uses and users. Likewise, sellers will not withhold supply because better opportunities have arisen, since the assets in question have a specialized character. The result is that quantity representations for idiosyncratic products can ordinarily be taken at face value. Since inability to adapt both quantity and price would render most idiosyncratic exchanges nonviable, quantity adjustments occur routinely.

---

[60] As Stewart Macaulay observes, "Disputes are frequently settled without reference to the contract or to potential or actual legal sanctions. There is a hesitancy to speak of legal right or to threaten to sue in . . . negotiations" where continuing business is valued. Stewart Macaulay, *supra* note 9, at 61.

The material which follows in this subsection was originally developed in connection with the study of inflation. See Michael L. Wachter & Oliver E. Williamson, Obligational Markets and the Mechanics of Inflation, 9 Bell J. Econ. 549 (1978).

Of course, not all price adjustments pose the same degree of hazard. Those which pose few hazards will predictably be implemented. Crude escalator clauses which reflect changes in general economic conditions are one possibility. But since such escalators are not transaction-specific, imperfect adjustments often result when these escalators are applied to local conditions. We should therefore consider whether price adjustments that are more closely related to local circumstances are feasible. The issue here is whether interim price adjustments can be devised for some subset of conditions such that the strategic hazards described above do not arise. What are the preconditions?

Crises facing either of the parties to an idiosyncratic exchange constitute one class of exceptions. Faced with a viability crisis which jeopardizes the relationship, ad hoc price relief may be permitted. More relevant and interesting, however, is whether there are circumstances whereby interim price adjustments are made routinely. The preconditions here are two: first, proposals to adjust prices must relate to exogenous, germane, and easily verifiable events; and second, quantifiable cost consequences must be confidently related thereto. An example may help to illustrate. Consider a component for which a significant share of the cost is accounted for by a basic material (copper, steel). Assume, moreover, that the fractional cost of the component in terms of this basic material is well specified. An exogenous change in prices of materials would under these circumstances pose few hazards if partial but interim price relief were permitted by allowing pass-through according to formula. A more refined adjustment than aggregate escalators would afford thereby obtains.

It bears emphasis, however, that not all costs so qualify. Changes in overhead or other expenses for which validation is difficult and which, even if verified, bear an uncertain relation to the cost of the component will not be passed through in a similar way. Recognizing the hazards, the parties will simply forgo relief of this kind.

(b) *Unified Governance: Internal Organization.* Incentives for trading weaken as transactions become progressively more idiosyncratic. The reason is that, as the specialized human and physical assets become more specialized to a single use, and hence less transferable to other uses, economies of scale can be as fully realized by the buyer as by an outside supplier.[61] The choice of organizing mode then turns on which mode has superior adaptive

---

[61] This assumes that factor prices paid by buyer and outside supplier are identical. Where this is not true, as in some unionized firms, buyers may choose to procure outside because of a differential wage rate. This is a common problem in the automobile industry, which has a very flat and relatively high wage scale.

properties. As discussed elsewhere, vertical integration will invariably appear in these circumstances.[62]

The advantage of vertical integration is that adaptations can be made in a sequential way without the need to consult, complete, or revise interfirm agreements. Where a single ownership entity spans both sides of the transactions, a presumption of joint profit maximization is warranted. Thus price adjustments in vertically integrated enterprises will be more complete than in interfirm trading. And quantity adjustments, of course, will be implemented at whatever frequency serves to maximize the joint gain to the transaction.

Unchanging identity at the interface coupled with extensive adaptability in both price and quantity is thus characteristic of highly idiosyncratic transactions which are vertically integrated. Obligational contracting is supplanted by the more comprehensive adaptive capability afforded by administration.

The match of governance structures with transactions that results from these economizing efforts is shown in Figure II.

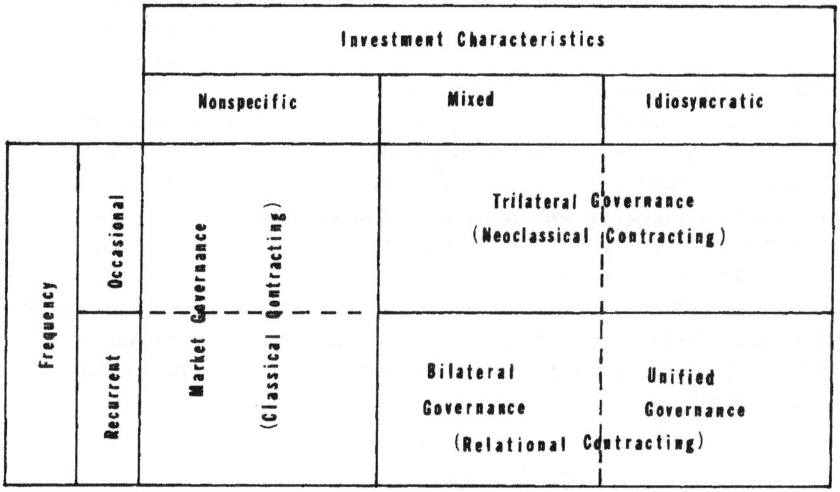

FIGURE II
MATCHING GOVERNANCE STRUCTURES WITH COMMERCIAL TRANSACTIONS

D. *Uncertainty*

Transactions conducted under certainty are relatively uninteresting. Except as they differ in the time required to reach an equilibrium-exchange

[62] See the references cited in note 4 *supra*.

configuration, any governance structure will do. More relevant are transactions where uncertainty is present to an intermediate or high degree. The foregoing has dealt with the first of these. The question here is how the governance of transactions is affected by increasing the degree of uncertainty.

Recall that nonspecific transactions are ones for which continuity has little value, since new trading relations are easily arranged. Increasing the degree of uncertainty does not alter this. Accordingly, market exchange continues and the discrete-contracting paradigm (classical contract law) holds across standardized transactions of all kinds, whatever the degree of uncertainty.

Matters are different with transaction-specific investments. Whenever investments are idiosyncratic in nontrivial degree, increasing the degree of uncertainty makes it more imperative that the parties devise a machinery to "work things out"—since contractual gaps will be larger and the occasions for sequential adaptations will increase in number and importance as the degree of uncertainty increases. This has special relevance for the organization of transactions with mixed investment attributes. Two possibilities exist. One would be to sacrifice valued design features in favor of a more standardized good or service. Market governance would then apply. The second would be to preserve the design but surround the transaction with an elaborated governance apparatus, thereby facilitating more effective adaptive, sequential decision making. Specifically, a more elaborate arbitration apparatus is apt to be devised for occasional, nonstandard transactions. And bilateral governance structures will often give way to unified ones as uncertainty is increased for recurrent transactions.

Reductions in uncertainty, of course, warrant shifting transactions in the opposite direction. To the extent that uncertainty decreases as an industry matures, which is the usual case, the benefits that accrue to integration presumably decline. Accordingly, greater reliance on obligational market contracting is commonly feasible for transactions of recurrent trading in mature industries.

IV. OTHER APPLICATIONS

The three dimensions for describing transactions—frequency, investment idiosyncrasy, and uncertainty—apply to transactions of all kinds. The same general considerations that apply to governance structures for commercial transactions carry over as well. The specific governance structures for organizing commercial transactions do not, however, apply without modification to the governance of other types of transactions. Applications of the framework to the study of labor markets, regulation, family law, and capital markets are briefly sketched here.

A. *Labor*

Occasional labor-market transactions typically take the form of repair or replacement services—the plumber, electrician, and so forth. Especially in older homes or structures, these transactions can take on an idiosyncratic quality. Although such transactions can be interesting, the transactions on which I want to focus are recurrent labor-market transactions of the nonspecific, mixed, and idiosyncratic kinds.

Clyde Summers's examination of collective agreements in relation to the law of contracts disclosed that, while the collective bargain differed greatly from the ordinary bargain of commerce, collective agreements are nonetheless a part of the "mainstream of contract."[63] He suggested that the study of contract proceed on two levels: the search for an underlying framework and, within that framework, an examination of the distinctive institutional attributes that distinguish each type of transaction. With respect to the first of these he conjectured that "the principles common to the whole range of contractual transactions are relatively few and of such generality and competing character that they should not be stated as legal rules at all."[64]

I am persuaded that Summers's two-part strategy for studying contract leads to a deeper understanding of the issues. And I believe that the framework set out in the preceding sections of this paper provides much of the underlying unity called for by Summers. What differs as one moves across various contracting activities is the institutional infrastructure.

(1) *Nonspecific Transactions.* Nonspecific labor-market transactions are ones where employer and employee are largely indifferent to the identity of each. Migrant farm labor is an example. Although an unchanging employment association between firm and worker may be observed to continue over long intervals for some of these employees, each party is essentially meeting bids in the spot market. A valuable ongoing relationship, in which specific training and on-the-job learning yield idiosyncratic benefits, is thus not implied. Both wages and employment are variable and market governance applies to transactions of this kind. Consider, therefore, mixed and idiosyncratic labor-market transactions.

(2) *Mixed Transactions.* Probably the most interesting labor-market transactions are those where large numbers of workers acquire an intermediate degree of firm-specific skill. Note that, inasmuch as the degree of idiosyncrasy is a design variable, firms would presumably redesign jobs to favor more standardized operations if it were impossible to devise governance structures which prevented antagonistic bargaining relations from developing between firms and idiosyncratically skilled employees. Although

[63] Clyde W. Summers, *supra* note 9, at 527.
[64] *Id.* at 568.

least-cost production technologies would be sacrificed in the process, net gains might nevertheless be realized since incumbent workers would realize little strategic advantage over otherwise qualified but inexperienced outsiders.

Justice Rhenquist has observed that "Adjudicatory review of the decisions of certain institutions, while perhaps insuring a 'better' decision in some objective sense, can only disrupt on-going relationships within the institution and thereby hamper the institution's ability to serve its designated societal function."[65] Examples of adjudicatory review with respect to which he counsels caution include collective bargaining agreements.

The reasons for this are that adjudicatory review is not easily apprised of the special needs of the transaction and the prospect of such review impairs the incentive of the parties to devise bilateral governance structure. The *Vaca v. Stipes* holding, which Justice Rhenquist cites, is fully consistent with this interpretation. There the Court held that an individual could not compel his union to take his grievance to arbitration, since if the law were otherwise "the settlement machinery provided by the contract would be substantially undermined, thus . . . [introducing] the vagaries of independent and unsystematic negotiations."[66] Archibald Cox elaborates as follows:[67]

. . . giving the union control over all claims arising under the collective agreement comports so much better with the functional nature of a collective bargaining agreement. . . . Allowing an individual to carry a claim to arbitration whenever he is dissatisfied with the adjustment worked out by the company and the union . . . discourages the kind of day-to-day cooperation between company and union which is normally the mark of sound industrial relations—a relationship in which grievances are treated as problems to be solved and contracts are only guideposts in a dynamic human relationship. When . . . the individual's claim endangers group interests, the union's function is to resolve the competition by reaching an accommodation or striking a balance.

The practice described by Cox of giving the union control over arbitration claims plainly permits group interests—whence the concern for system viability—to supersede individual interests, thereby curbing small-numbers opportunism.

General escalator or predetermined wage adjustments aside, wages are unchanging under collective bargaining agreements.[68] Interim adaptations are nonetheless essential. These take three forms: (1) quantity adjustments,

---

[65] Remarks of Mr. Justice Rhenquist, *supra* note 38, at 4.

[66] 386 U.S. 171, 191 (1967).

[67] Archibald Cox, *supra* note 9, at 24.

[68] The reason, of course, is that it is very costly and apt to be unproductive to reopen wage bargaining during the period covered by a contract. Since to reopen negotiations for one type of job is to invite it for all, and as objective differences among jobs may be difficult to demonstrate, wage bargaining is foreclosed except at contract-renewal intervals.

(2) assignment changes, and (3) refinement of working rules as a result of grievances.

Quantity adjustments are made in response to changing market opportunities. Either the level or the mix of employment is adjusted as economic events unfold. Given that valuable firm-specific training and learning reside in the workers, layoffs with a presumption of reemployment when conditions improve are common. Conformably, the degree to which the machinery governing access to jobs is elaborated ought to vary directly with the degree to which jobs in a firm are idiosyncratic. Thus promotion ladders in firms where a succession of interdependent jobs are highly idiosyncratic should be long and thin, with access mainly restricted to the bottom, whereas promotion ladders in nonidiosyncratic activities should be broadly structured.[69] Likewise, promotion on merit ought to be favored over promotion strictly by seniority in firms where jobs are more idiosyncratic.[70]

(3) *Highly Idiosyncratic Transactions.* Recall that idiosyncratic transactions involve not merely uniqueness but uniqueness of a transaction-specific kind. Also recall that our concern in this section is with recurring transactions. Thus, although there are many uniquely skilled individuals (artists, athletes, researchers, administrators), unique skills are rarely of a transaction-specific kind. On the contrary, most of these individuals could move to another organization without significant productivity losses.

The exceptions are those where the benefits which accrue to experience (inside knowledge) and/or team interaction effects are great. Whereas commercial transactions of a highly idiosyncratic nature are unified under a common ownership, limits on indenture foreclose this option for labor-market transactions. Instead of "merger," complex contracts designed to tie the interests of the individual to the organization on a long-term basis are negotiated. Severe penalties are provided should either party seek unilateral termination. Nonvested, long-term, contingent reward schemes are devised. More generally, transaction-specific infrastructure will be highly individuated for such transactions.

B. *Regulation of Natural Monopoly*

Again the argument is that specialized governance structure is needed to the degree efficient supply necessarily joins buyers and sellers in a bilateral

---

[69] Michael L. Wachter & Oliver E. Williamson, *supra* note 60, at 567.

[70] Thus although both nonidiosyncratic and idiosyncratic jobs may be organized collectively, the way in which the internal labor markets associated with each are organized should reflect objective differences between them. Additionally, the incentive to provide an orderly governance structure varies directly with the degree to which efficiencies are attributable thereto. *Ceteris paribus,* nonidiosyncratic jobs ought to be organized later and the governance structure less fully elaborated than for idiosyncratic jobs. Both propositions are borne out by the evidence.

trading relation of a continuing nature. And again, the object of governance is to (1) protect the interests of the respective parties and (2) adapt the relationship to changing circumstances.

Although differing in details, both Victor Goldberg[71] and I[72] have argued that specialized governance structure is needed for services for which natural monopoly features are great. Such structure presumably has the purpose of providing sellers (investors) and buyers with security of expectations, which is a protective function, while at the same time facilitating adaptive, sequential decision making. Rate-of-return regulation with periodic review has these features. To the extent, however, that such regulation is observed in conjunction with activities where transaction-specific investments are insubstantial (as, for example, in the trucking industry), the case for regulation is not at all apparent—or, if it is to be made, must appeal to arguments very different from those set out here.

C. *Family Law*

The issue here is whether the role of adjudication should be *expanded* to help govern family relationships. Granting that adjudication as ultimate relief can and often does serve a useful role for sustaining family relations, such relations are plainly idiosyncratic to an unusual degree and a specialized governance structure is surely the main mode of governance. As the role of adjudication is expanded, reliance upon internal structure is apt to be reduced. Therefore, except when individual rights are seriously threatened, withholding access to adjudication may be indicated.

Justice Rhenquist's remarks concerning the corrosive effects of adversary hearings on the family are apposite: "Any sort of adversary hearing which pits parent against child is bound to be disruptive, placing stresses and tensions on the intra-familial relationships which in turn weaken the family as an institution."[73] Whether, as this suggests, parent-child family relations are optimized where adjudication is zero or negligible is beyond the scope of this paper. It suffices for my purposes merely to note that valued family relations are recurrent and idiosyncratic and that a specialized, transaction-specific governance structure must be encouraged lest the parties withhold investing heavily in the institution.[74]

---

[71] Victor P. Goldberg, *supra* note 1.

[72] Oliver E. Williamson, *supra* note 30.

[73] Remarks of Mr. Justice Rhenquist, *supra* note 38, at 19.

[74] For a more extensive discussion of family transactions, see Yoram Ben-Porath, *supra* note 29, at 4-7.

D. *Capital Market Transactions*

The ease of verification is critical to the operation of capital markets.[75] Where verification is easy, markets work well and additional governance is unnecessary. Where verification is difficult or very difficult, however, additional governance may be indicated. Occasional transactions are apt to benefit from third-party assistance, while recurring transactions are ones for which bilateral or unified governance will presumably be observed. Assessing capital-market transactions within the proposed framework is thus accomplished by substituting "ease of verification" for "degree of transaction-specific investment." Once this is done, the governance structures appropriate to capital markets are broadly similar to those within which commercial transactions are organized.

V. Implications

Dimensionalizing transactions and examining the costs of executing different transactions in different ways generate a large number of institutional implications. Some of these are summarized here.

A. *General*

1. Nonspecific transactions, either occasional or recurrent, are efficiently organized by markets.

2. Occasional transactions that are nonstandardized stand most to benefit from adjudication.

3. A transaction-specific governance structure is more fully developed where transactions are (1) recurrent, (2) entail idiosyncratic investment, and (3) are executed under greater uncertainty.

B. *Commercial Transactions*

1. Optimization of commercial transactions requires simultaneous attention to (1) production economies, (2) transaction-cost economies, and (3) component design.

2. The reason why Macaulay observes so few litigated cases in business[76] is because markets work well for nonspecific transactions, while recurrent, nonstandard transactions are governed by bilateral or unified structures.

3. As uncertainty increases, the obligational market-contracting mode will not be used for recurrent transactions with mixed investment features. Such transactions will either be standardized, and shifted to the market, or organized internally.

---

[75] This feature was called to my attention by Sanford Grossman.

[76] Stewart Macaulay, *supra* note 9.

4. As generic demand grows and the number of supply sources increases, exchange that was once transaction-specific loses this characteristic and greater reliance on market-mediated governance is feasible. Thus vertical integration may give way to obligational market contracting, which in turn may give way to markets.

5. Where inventory and related flow-process economies are great, site-specific supply and transaction-specific governance (commonly vertical integration) will be observed. Generic demand here has little bearing.

6. The organization of the interface between manufacturing and distribution reflects similar investment considerations: goods and services that can be sold without incurring transaction-specific investment will be distributed through conventional marketing channels while those where such investments are great will be supported by specialized—mainly bilateral (for example, franchising) or unified (forward integration)—governance structures.

7. The governance of technical change poses special difficulties. The frequently noted limits of markets[77] often give way to more complex governance relations, again for the same general reasons and along the same general lines as are set out here.[78]

C. *Other Transactions*

1. The efficiency benefits of collective organization are negligible for nonspecific labor. Accordingly, such labor will be organized late, often only with the assistance of the political process.

2. Internal labor markets become more highly individuated as jobs become more varied and idiosyncratic.

3. Regulation can be interpreted in part as a response to the transactional dilemma posed by natural monopoly.

4. A transaction-cost justification for regulating activities for which transaction-specific investments are lacking (for example, trucking) is not apparent. The possibility that politics is the driving consideration in such industries warrants consideration.

5. Adjudication should proceed with caution in the area of family law lest valued transaction-specific investments be discouraged.

6. Ease of verification is the capital-market counterpart of transaction-specific investments. Upon making this substitution, the organization of capital markets and intermediate-product markets is broadly similar.

---

[77] Kenneth J. Arrow, Economic Welfare and the Allocation of Resources for Invention, in The Rate and Direction of Economic Activity 609 (1962).

[78] Aspects are discussed in Oliver E. Williamson, *supra* note 1, at 203-05.

VI. Concluding Remarks

Transaction-cost economics is an interdisciplinary undertaking that joins economics with aspects of organization theory and overlaps extensively with contract law. It is the modern counterpart of institutional economics and relies heavily on comparative analysis.[79] Frictionless ideals are useful mainly for reference purposes.

Although mathematical economics captures only a fraction of the transaction-cost phenomena of interest,[80] this has not been the only obstacle. Headway with the study of transaction-cost issues has been impeded by lack of verbal definitions. Identifying the critical dimensions with respect to which transactions differ has been a significant omission.

This paper attempts to rectify this deficiency and identifies uncertainty, frequency of exchange, and the degree to which investments are transaction-specific as the principal dimensions for describing transactions. The efficient organization of economic activity entails matching governance structures with these transactional attributes in a discriminating way.

Although the main applications in this paper are to commercial contracting, the proposed approach generalizes easily to the study of labor contracts. It also has ramifications for understanding both public utility regulation and family relations. A unified approach to contract thus emerges.

The fact that the broad features of so many varied transactions fit within the framework is encouraging. The importance of transaction costs to the organization of economic activity is thus confirmed. But the world of contract is enormously complex,[81] and the simple economizing framework proposed here cannot be expected to capture more than main features. Elaborating the framework to deal with microanalytic phenomena, however, should be feasible. And extending it to include additional or substitute dimensions (of which the ease of verification, in the case of capital-market transactions, is an example) may sometimes be necessary.

[79] Reliance on comparative analysis has been repeatedly emphasized by R. H. Coase, *supra* note 1.

[80] See Carl J. Dahlman, *supra* note 1, at 144-47.

[81] Benjamin Klein, Robert C. Crawford, & Armen A. Alchian, *supra* note 1, at 325.

Part III
Postcontractual Activities:
Execution, Control and Enforcement

[14]

Business and Politics, Vol. 4, No. 3, 2002

Carfax Publishing
Taylor & Francis Group

Private Ordering on the Internet: The eBay Community of Traders[1]

DAVID P. BARON
Stanford University

ABSTRACT   *eBay provides an online auction venue for remote and anonymous members of its online community to realize gains from trade. As a venue it never sees the items sold, verifies the item listings, handles settlements, or represents the buyer or seller. Despite the associated market imperfections and incentive problems, over five million auctions are active on an average day. Trading is based on trust among members of the eBay community, and trust is supported by a multilateral reputation mechanism based on member feedback. eBay supplements the reputation mechanism with rules and policies that mitigate incentive problems, reduce transactions costs, and support trust among members and between members and the company. Reputations and the rules and policies provide a private ordering of eBay's community. This paper examines this private ordering in the context of the company's strategy and in the shadow of the public order.*

1. Introduction

Since its founding in 1995 eBay has been one of the true successes of the Internet. eBay hosted person-to-person online auctions for the members of its community. That community was composed of anonymous and remote individuals who were unlikely to have repeat dealings. Trade was impersonal with, for example, a seller knowing only the eBay user name of bidders until the winner of the auction provided a shipping address. Buyers did not have an opportunity to inspect the goods on which they bid, and the winning bidder paid for the item prior to shipment. Moreover, enforcement was costly, so trades were neither supported by contracts nor in most cases by public enforcement of implicit contracts. Unlike an offline auction house eBay never saw the items offered for sale nor certified their authenticity or quality or the accuracy of the descriptions provided by the sellers. Furthermore, eBay did not act as an agent of the seller or the buyer, certify the credit worthiness of buyers, or play a role in settling the transaction. eBay thus faced challenges different from those of historical analogues and required organizational responses to address the risks to traders in the context of its institutional environment. Despite the inherent incentive and

---

1. This paper has benefited from interviews with eBay personnel involved with its community and private ordering. Those interviews and independent research are reflected in the case "eBay: Private Ordering for an Online Community," P-37, Graduate School of Business, Stanford University, written by David Hoyt under the author's supervision. The author would like to thank David Hoyt, John McMillan, Garth Saloner, and two anonymous referees for their helpful comments. This research has been supported by NSF Grant No. SES-0111729.

1369-5258 print/ISSN 1469-3569 online/02/030245-30 © 2002 Taylor & Francis Ltd
DOI: 10.1080/1369525022000047004

David P. Baron

contracting problems that could become more serious as the number of traders increased, trade flourished with over five million auctions active on an average day. Its community of traders represented eBay's principal asset, and its strategic focus was to support and expand the community by creating value for its members. This included providing order for its community.

This private ordering was based on trust. On its website eBay explained, "The key to eBay's success is trust. Trust between the buyers and sellers who make up the eBay community. And trust between the user and eBay, the company." Trust began with the basic honesty of people, that they would not take advantage of others. Yet with remote and anonymous traders opportunism was possible and threatened trust. Trust among the members of the eBay community thus had to be supported, and a multilateral online reputation mechanism based on feedback provided by the transacting parties was the centerpiece of that support. The reputation mechanism not only provided information to traders but also established a target for punishment. The mechanism was supplemented by rules designed by eBay to govern who could be a member, what members could trade, and how they were to conduct themselves on its Web site. The mechanism was also supported by programs designed by eBay to reduce the cost of trust borne by the trading community. The multilateral online reputation mechanism, the rules, and the programs supported the private ordering of eBay's community.

eBay began as a website for trading Pez dispensers, and when people began to offer other items for sale, founder Pierre Omidyar charged a fee in an attempt to stop them. Inundated by checks from the undissuaded, he decided to expand the site to allow more items to be traded. Trade grew spontaneously as it did at other websites.[2] This growth was driven by the considerable gains to trade available to buyers and sellers. Those gains were driven by demand-side increasing returns and may well have been sufficient to sustain online auction markets. eBay's success, however, also depended on supporting its community through the design of its private ordering.

In the early days of eBay, order occurred spontaneously among the members of the community. Members established informal standards, provided feedback on other members' performance, and policed the site. Some traders formed neighborhood watch groups to police their trading areas; i.e., the items in which they traded. One group of six members that called itself "The Posse" monitored activity on the eBay site. Traders who violated implicit standards could quickly have their reputations damaged by The Posse. Spontaneous order was facilitated by the relatively small number of traders and listings (in the thousands) and by the communication they exchanged through email and on bulletin boards.

eBay supported the development of order by establishing its Feedback Forum where members could provide feedback on other members, enabling them to establish an online reputation. The private ordering that developed was supported by a set of norms that continued to guide eBay and which the company hoped would guide its members as well:

---

2. Kollock (1999) discusses the spontaneous development of trade on sites not sponsored by a company.

Private Ordering on the Internet

> eBay is a community where we encourage open and honest communication between all of our members. We believe in the following five basic values.
> We believe people are basically good.
> We believe everyone has something to contribute.
> We believe that an honest, open environment can bring out the best in people.
> We recognize and respect everyone as a unique individual.
> We encourage you to treat others the way that you want to be treated.[3]

As online person-to-person trading caught on, the eBay community grew rapidly. By 2002 eBay operated in 18 countries, and its community included 50 million active members who traded in thousands of product categories with annual transactions of $9 billion. As it grew, its members became more anonymous and distant, and the challenge for eBay was to enable community members to continue to have confidence that their transactions would be completed as anticipated. Opportunism, however, posed a threat to trust. And, even in the absence of fraud, disputes arose among members. Disputes pertained, for example, to the accuracy of the item descriptions provided by the seller, the timeliness of shipping, packaging and damage, payments, and a host of other issues. Moreover, the items themselves could cause problems as in the case of pirated software or banned products. These problems required an elaboration of the rules developed by eBay.

This paper examines the private ordering of eBay's online community of traders as a component of its business strategy.[4] eBay's basic strategy may be characterized in its simplest form as increasing the value of its community to its members and capturing a share of that value. Growing and strengthening that community was thus the focus of its ongoing strategy, and trust was a foundation for that strategy. Trust allowed gains to trade to be realized by anonymous traders, and supporting trust through a reputation mechanism and support activities was at the heart of eBay's strategy.

The asset represented by eBay's community could be leveraged to increase the scope of the trading opportunities available to the community and the return to the company. Many sellers wanted access to a community of 50 million traders, and eBay could provide access in exchange for a share of the additional value created. For example, in early 2002 eBay formed an alliance with Sothebys.com to give its community access to the 13,000 items for sale on that site and subsequently to expand its offerings at the high end of the auction market. eBay also expanded its travel services by providing Priceline.com's airline booking system to its community. eBay also allowed large companies to sell on its site, including, for example, IBM and Sun Microsystems selling leased computers retrieved from failed dotcoms. Adding services created value for the community,

---

3. Emphasis in the original.
4. In the typology of Armstrong and Hagel (1996) eBay has a "community of transaction" focusing on trades and has organized "communities of interest" that focus on particular categories of items.

but adding sellers has an externality to the extent that incumbent sellers incurred increased competition. Many small sellers, for example, complained about large companies selling on the site. The challenge for eBay was to selectively expand services and offerings to increase value just as shopping malls sought the optimal mix of retail outlets.

The next section examines the nature of eBay's auctions, and the following section considers eBay's positioning relative to the public order. The economics of online auction markets are then examined with a focus on economic drivers, market imperfections, and market responses to those imperfections. eBay's situation is then related to historical accounts of private orderings that developed in response to incentive problems arising in trade among remote parties. eBay's private ordering is then considered with a focus on the role of the multilateral online reputation mechanism and the feedback and reputation accounting system in mitigating incentive problems. eBay's support of its private ordering through design is then analyzed. Conclusions are offered in the final section.

2. eBay and Online Auctions

eBay provided a venue for online person-to-person trading that matched buyers and sellers allowing them to realize gains from trade. Its principal market format was an auction in which sellers described the items offered, including photographs, and posted fixed ending dates, an initial minimum bid, and a bid increment.[5] Sellers had the option of setting a secret reserve price that was revealed only by a bid exceeding the reserve. Sellers also provided information on payment methods and shipping and handling charges. Bidders could choose their initial bid and authorize eBay to automatically increase it to a specified limit in response to another bid.[6] If the reserve price were met, the winning bidder was obligated to complete the transaction. The buyer and seller exchanged email messages to arrange for payment and shipping. The seller paid eBay a small fee between $0.30 and $3.30 for each listing and for each completed sale paid a commission that depended on the transaction price. The commission was 5.25 percent for the first $25 of the sale price, 2.75 percent for the amount between $25 and $1,000, and 1.50 percent for the amount above $1,000.[7] In 2001 eBay's revenue reached $749 million, and its net income was $90.4 million. In the first six months of 2002 revenue grew to $511 million and net income to $101.9 million.

eBay's rules were contained in a user agreement all members were required to accept. In addition to providing legal protection to the company and making clear that it provided only a venue for trading, the agreement identified the scope

---

5. Bajari and Hortacsu (2000) provide a theoretical and empirical study of eBay auctions.

6. The auction thus has the feature of a Vickery auction with the winner paying the valuation of the second-highest bidder.

7. The fee on real estate and vehicles was fixed because of government regulations. eBay also collected a small fee for posting a secret reserve price and for various listing options. It also received revenue from advertising and partnering.

Private Ordering on the Internet

of activity on its site and who could conduct it.[8] For example, minors were not allowed to use its site. The agreement described how buying and selling operated and the services eBay provided to assist buyers and sellers. The agreement warned, "Please use caution, common sense, and practice safe trading when using our site."

The warning reflected the possibility of traders not fulfilling their promises and obligations or worse. Trading among remote and anonymous traders who did not have repeated interactions involved a variety of incentive problems. Moreover, it provided opportunity for fraud and other illegal activity. Fraud was difficult to stop because traders not only were anonymous but could cloak and change their online identities. Fraud could take a number of forms. Sellers could list fictitious goods or not ship an item once a buyer had paid for it. A buyer could refuse to pay for an item she had won. The response to fraud was both through the reputation mechanism as well as through policing and punishment activities within both the private ordering and the public order. Sanctions ranged from the suspension of trading rights to criminal prosecution.

The economics of eBay's business centered on the gains from trade available to its community and the costs of supporting that community. Since eBay's revenue was a function of listings and trades, its objective was to expand its community and increase trading. In the short-run its costs were largely fixed, and in the longer-run its costs were associated with support staff and servers to handle the volume of listings and trades, marketing expenses, product development, administration, and community support services. Putting aside the pricing issue, maximizing its profits was nearly the same as maximizing the number of items offered on its site.[9]

The gains from trade depended on buyers' valuations of the items listed, sellers' opportunity costs, trading costs, and the cost of trust. The cost of trust was the loss of value to the community due to concerns about the trustworthiness of trading partners. eBay's role was to provide an efficient venue for trading and to reduce trading costs and the cost of trust. Trading costs included the cost of listing items and executing the transactions. For example, eBay helped reduce trading costs by developing a tool to automate listings for sellers. eBay also reduced trading costs by creating local markets in which information and delivery costs could be reduced. By mid-2001 eBay had local sites for 60 cities in the United States.

To increase the value of its site, eBay provided services to its community. It allowed sellers to link each of their auctions to a page listing their other eBay auctions. eBay took this a step further by allowing sellers to set up virtual storefronts. It did not, however, allow sellers to link to other Web sites, such as

---

8. The user agreement stated that eBay did not participate in any transaction. "As a result, we have no control over the quality, safety, or legality of the items advertised, the truth or accuracy of the listings, the ability of sellers to sell items or the ability of buyers to buy items. We cannot ensure that a buyer or seller will actually complete a transaction."

9. eBay also considered the costs of certain sales in deciding the scope of its venue. It chose not to allow the sale of wine because of the complexity of the tax and regulation systems across the states. Similarly, eBay did not allow listings for tobacco and firearms. eBay's Butterfields offline auction house had held firearms auctions.

their auctions on other sites. eBay worked to prevent sellers from taking transaction offsite, as considered in more detail below.

eBay also provided services to "Power Sellers," members who had minimum monthly sales of $2,000 and 98 percent positive feedback. Power Sellers, for example, were allowed to purchase banner ads on eBay's site. They were also provided with a variety of benefits, including dedicated email, a dedicated account manager, and a hotline. To serve large sellers, eBay initiated a Preferred Provider Program listing auction software providers that could help large sellers administer their businesses. eBay also made health insurance available for large sellers.

Buyers also incurred transaction costs. One such cost was associated with searching for items. An efficient search engine was one means of reducing the costs to buyers, but another was the selection of categories and subcategories of items that allowed a buyer to browse efficiently down an aisle of interest. eBay also allowed members to establish a "My eBay" folder which listed transactions, bids and their status, and tracked auctions selected by the buyer. Trading costs for both buyers and sellers were also reduced by providing a payment system, Billpoint, as an alternative to the independently-provided service PayPal.[10] eBay was also responsive to buyers' and sellers' concerns. For example, it had a policy of answering members' email promptly.

3. Positioning Relative to the Public Order

A central strategic issue in any market is the extent of the participation of the firm in the economic activity. From its inception eBay provided a venue for online trading using an auction format. Positioning itself as a venue meant not participating in the trading or transactions. This positioning had implications for its trading community and its responsibilities with respect to the public order, such as state auction house laws and potential liability for fraud and infringement of intellectual property rights. Its positioning affected its community in two ways. First, it limited the types of support eBay could provide its members. Second, it affected the behavior it required of its community members. Positioning relative to the public order thus impacted the scope of its activities and the relations between the company and its community.

eBay's business model was to serve as a venue for person-to-person auctions rather than as a traditional auction house. eBay differed from traditional auction houses in a number of ways. First, it neither inspected nor saw the items for sale. Second, it did not serve as an agent of any trader. Third, it neither authenticated items nor put its reputation or warranty behind any item. Fourth, it was not involved in the transaction between the buyer and seller. Instead, eBay functioned much like the classified ad pages in a newspaper. These distinctions were important because eBay sought to position itself outside the reach of state auction laws and regulations.

---

10. In 2002 eBay acquired PayPal.

Private Ordering on the Internet

A crucial issue for eBay was whether it could be held liable for the actions of the members of its community, such as the listings provided by sellers or the postings on its bulletin boards. The Communications Decency Act (CDA) of 1996 shielded an Internet service provider from liability for what was said or written on an Internet site, whereas an Internet content provider could be liable for postings. eBay positioned itself as an Internet service provider thus receiving protection under the CDA.

Even though eBay avoided the reach of state auction laws and had positioned itself as an ISP, it was sued under a California law allowing lawsuits against companies that violated state law. Two separate lawsuits alleged that pirated software and fake sports memorabilia, respectively, were sold on its site. In both cases the judges ruled that eBay was protected by the CDA from liability for what sellers offered on its site.[11]

Its positioning limited the assistance that eBay could provide to its community. eBay had to be careful not to provide content, such as commenting on the authenticity of items listed for sale. Instead, eBay provided links to sites where users could obtain opinions, authentication, and grading of items.

eBay also positioned itself relative to violations of the law by the buyers and sellers on its site. A small number of sellers engaged in fraud, others sold items that violated copyrights, and others sold banned items. eBay monitored its site for possible fraud, and the members of its community also monitored for fraud. Reducing fraud supported trust and integrity within its community

Although eBay monitored for possible fraud, it did not monitor for copyright violations. Copyright violations caused little if any harm to community members, but community members had an obligation to the public order. eBay's responsibility to monitor its community's respect for intellectual property rights was unclear, since the CDA did not pertain to intellectual property. A federal Court of Appeals decision in *Fonovisa, Inc. v. Cherry Auctions, Inc.* held that an offline swap meet owner was liable for copyright violations because pirated recordings were sold on its venue.[12] The Court ruled that the owner had the ability to monitor its site for illegal items and failed to do so. eBay had some ability to monitor its site for possible copyright violations, but with nearly one million new listings a day, complete monitoring was virtually impossible.

The Digital Millennium Copyright Act (DCMA) of 1998 clarified the monitoring issue by stating that Web sites were liable if they monitored for intellectual property infringements and failed to find some infringing items. A site, however, had a safe harbor if it did not monitor, provided it removed violating items when notified by a copyright holder. eBay had already implemented such a program, now referred to as VeRO (verified rights owner), and it decided to rely on that program rather than attempt to monitor listings and be exposed to liability for infringing items it missed. Monitoring was thus performed by the copyright holders, who asked eBay to remove infringing items from its site. eBay assisted

---

11. The text of one opinion, which was not officially published, can be found at: http://www.2001law.com/article_429.htm. The other case, *Gentry v. eBay, Inc.*, can be found at: http://legal.web.aol.com/decisions/dldecen/gentry.html
12. For the text of the ruling, see: http://www.law.cornell.edu/copyright/cases/76_F3d_259.htm

the copyright holders by creating a system in which VeRO participants could query on key words and automatically receive by email notification of any listing with those key words.

This did not satisfy the Business Software Alliance (BSA) which developed a model code requiring Internet sites to pre-screen listings for copyright violations. Even though Amazon.com agreed to the code, eBay refused to do so because of the potential liability under the DCMA. As a result of the logic of the two California court rulings, however, eBay began restricted monitoring by examining what was within the "Four Corners" of a seller's listing, dropping listings identified as infringing a copyright. eBay had concluded that the CDA provided protection if it relied only on the content of the listing provided by a seller.

Since its community was its principal asset, eBay sought to protect that asset from intrusion by others. BiddersEdge and other auction aggregators searched eBay's site to provide auction information to their users. BiddersEdge used a robot to copy recursively all of eBay's listings and then searched the copy to provide auction information to its users. Because of a Supreme Court ruling that overturned the "sweat-of-the-brow" doctrine eBay's auction database was not protected by copyright. To prevent BiddersEdge from being a portal to its auctions, eBay filed a lawsuit alleging a number of violations of law. The court concluded that BiddersEdge illegally trespassed on the eBay Web site and occupied 1.5 percent of eBay's server capacity. The court issued a preliminary injunction ending the practice.

By either good fortune or considerable foresight eBay had also positioned itself well with regard to outside attempts to draw on its community. A competitor BidBay entered the online auction market with a logo and cover page that closely resembled eBay's. In addition to the similarity of its name, BidBay's cover page used the same color scheme, location of the company name, and location of the menu bar, search window, and category list as did eBay. In intellectual property law, the most defensible trademarks are those that are "arbitrary and fanciful." An eBay attorney explained, "eBay is a completely coined name. It means nothing."[13] eBay filed a trademark infringement lawsuit against BidBay.

4. The Economics of the Online Auction Market

Economic Drivers

The online auction market had many of the features of information markets. Economies of scale and scope were present on both the demand and supply sides. On the supply side the marginal cost of expanding the venue to accommodate additional traders was likely below average cost. Similarly, broadening the scope of product offerings to include automobiles, real estate, and other items

---

13. *San Jose Mercury News*, 31 July 2001.

Private Ordering on the Internet

lowered the average cost of hosting auctions.[14] Moreover, search costs were low on the Internet, allowing more of the potential gains from trade to be realized through better matching.

The principal economies of scale and scope, however, were not on the supply side but on the demand side. The demand-side economies of scope resulted from the greater benefits to buyers and sellers when a broader array of items were listed. Demand-side increasing returns also resulted from network externalities characteristic of many Internet services.[15] The greater the number of buyers the more attractive was the eBay venue to sellers, and the greater the number of sellers the more attractive the venue was to buyers.

In addition, as its trading grew, users became locked into eBay. A seller might have an interest in switching to Yahoo! Auctions, which was free, but unless buyers also switched the seller would face a thin market. Buyers would not switch because the sellers remained on eBay, and the sellers remained there because the buyers were there. Members who traded in a particular class of items potentially could collectively switch to another online auction site, but they would incur high costs of coordinating their switching.[16] Since other companies including AuctionWatch.com provided services, including account management, to sellers, one recurring threat to eBay's lock-in was that large sellers might be attracted away by such a site. eBay included AuctionWatch.com in its Preferred Provider Program.

eBay also had the opportunity to offer complementary goods, which in its case represented alternative formats for sales as well as an expansion in the scope of item categories. For example, it acquired half.com, where items were sold at fixed prices. Network externalities and the provision of complementary goods both contributed to the demand-side increasing returns.

Working in the opposite direction from these demand-side increasing returns was the potential for deterioration in trust among increasingly remote and anonymous traders as the size of the community grew. As considered in more detail below, the cost of trust was reduced by the reputation mechanism, allowing buyers to ask sellers questions about an item offered for sale, providing protection for buyers, policing the site for illegal items and activity, countering fraud, facilitating dispute resolution among members, and responding to members' concerns.

The demand-side increasing returns generated sufficient positive feedback to outweigh the increased cost of trust, and the U.S. online auction market grew rapidly and tipped in favor of eBay. In addition to the demand-side increasing returns, eBay was the first mover in the U.S. market, and Yahoo! Auctions,

---

14. Some potential economies of scope were illusory. In 1999 eBay acquired Butterfields, a high-end offline auction house, but in 2002 it sold the unit.
15. See Shapiro and Varian (1999) for any analysis of network externalities and other characteristics of information-based markets.
16. See Saloner, Shepard, and Podolny (2001, p. 313).

Amazon.com, and other online auction sites were unable to wrest market share from eBay, even though some did not charge fees for listings or transactions.[17]

Market Imperfections

Market imperfections resulting from remote and anonymous trading had the potential for limiting the realization of the gains from trade in online auction markets. Imperfections were common in markets, however, and market participants had a variety of means of addressing such imperfections. For example, online securities trading firms required the establishment of an identity and an account for completing transactions. eBay's positioning relative to the public order, however, precluded acting either as an agent or a clearinghouse for traders.

Online auction markets also had a number of imperfections that had the potential to limit the development of the markets. In contrast to spot transactions in offline markets, traders were anonymous and remote, buyers could not examine the items before bidding, buyers paid in advance for items they had not inspected, and sellers had little recourse if a winning bidder refused to pay. Mail-order catalog markets dealt with the inability of buyers to examine items by allowing returns and backing product descriptions and quality with their reputation. This reputation was bilateral, since a buyer with repeat purchases could develop experience with a seller. Reputation was also multilateral, since firms could develop reputations enhanced through advertising or word-of-mouth. Moreover, disputes could be taken to the seller, whose identity and location were known. In contrast, on the online auction market repeat purchases were the exception, and seller's identities were masked.

Market imperfections also resulted from the cost of accessing the public order—the law of contracts. Offerings and bids on eBay constituted a legal obligation to complete the transaction.[18] In reality, however, the costs of public enforcement of such contracts relative to the value of the item meant that market participants were unlikely to turn to the courts. In particular, the informational burden of proving a case in court when an item was described only in print and photograph but never physically inspected nor demonstrated was quite high. The high transactions costs of accessing the public order meant that third-party enforcement could not be relied on for the resolution of disputes. This left a role for eBay to enhance the enforceability of contracts and assist in resolving disputes.

The realization of the gains from trade were also potentially limited by the cost of executing transactions. The principal transactions costs were associated with search, payment, and shipping. Since many of the items sold had relatively

---

17. In contrast, Yahoo! Auctions was the first-mover in Japan, and the market tipped in its favor. eBay struggled in its attempt to overturn the tipping and in 2002 withdrew from the Japanese market. Shortly thereafter, Yahoo! Auctions withdrew from most of the European market.

18. eBay auction pages stated, "**Your bid is a contract.** Place a bid only if you're serious about buying the item. If you are the winning bidder, you will enter into a legally binding contract to purchase the item from the seller." (Emphasis in the original.)

Private Ordering on the Internet

low values, reducing the cost of transactions could have a significant impact on the size of the market.

The online auction market also had imperfections characteristic of a number of offline markets. These imperfections were due to asymmetric information, imperfect *ex post* monitoring, and incomplete contract enforcement. Asymmetric information was present because a seller had superior information about the items offered for auction. Buyers had only the description and pictures provided by the seller but were required to pay in advance of shipping. A lemons problem, as identified by Akerlof (1970), was thus possible. If the gains from trade were sufficiently high, however, the lemons problem was likely to be mitigated. The gains from trade could be large, since many sellers had high transactions costs of selling items offline and buyers from around the world had the opportunity to search at low cost. If a lemons problem was present, it could in principle be alleviated by the establishment of a premium for quality supported by reputation as identified by Klein and Leffler (1981) and Shapiro (1982, 1983). Establishing such a reputation, however, required an information and reputation mechanism.

Another incentive problem resulted from the combination of asymmetric information and imperfect monitoring. Since buyers paid for items prior to shipping, they learned the quality of the item only when they received and inspected it. If the good were not of the quality anticipated, the buyer had little recourse. Traders could individually assure their trading partners. For example, a seller could develop a brand that a buyer could damage if unsatisfied with a purchase. A seller might do this either online or by linking an online brand to an offline business. If, however, buyers were not repeat customers, they would have little incentive to inform other buyers about their experience. Sellers, of course, could offer to take the item back, and many sellers on eBay had a returns policy. The costs of shipping and handling, however, stood in the way.[19]

Traders could go beyond a returns policy and post bonds to ensure that they would complete promised transactions. Implementation of a bonding system, however, had high informational requirements, since claims would have to be adjudicated in some manner. The same issues involved in the enforcement of contracts thus were involved.

A moral hazard problem thus was present, since sellers had an opportunity to take advantage of the buyer by exaggerating descriptions of the item, delaying shipping, or not packaging the item carefully for shipping. The burden thus rested primarily with sellers to reassure buyers.[20] This had the characteristic of a one-sided prisoners' dilemma; i.e., the seller had an opportunity to take advantage of the reliance of the buyer. Kreps (1990) showed that this one-sided prisoners' dilemma can be mitigated in the case of seller selling to a series of buyers if buyers could provide information about their experience with the seller. Reputation was a principal means of assuring trading partners that the terms of

---

19. Kollock (1999, p. 110) described a norm of traders on a barter site for playing cards. The person with the fewer "references" (lower reputation) sent his card first, and the other trader sent her card only after receiving and inspecting the other card. Traders with similar reputations sent their cards simultaneously.
20. Buyers also had incentives to establish a reputation to assure sellers that they would not renege on a winning bid. This is considered in more detail below.

David P. Baron

an agreement could be met. If those terms were not met, a buyer, for example, could stop purchasing from a seller. In the absence of repeated transactions, however, a reputation mechanism could be ineffective, so sellers had to develop a multilateral reputation to assure infrequent buyers. For a multilateral reputation mechanism to be effective, a buyer had to have some means of conveying her experiences to other potential buyers. In the absence of such an information mechanism, multilateral reputations could be ineffective. The Internet and the feedback mechanism served this function, but a free-rider problem was potentially present because traders had little incentive to provide the feedback needed to make the reputation mechanism effective.

A less severe moral hazard problem was present on the buyer's side. After winning an item, a buyer could have reservations and decide not to send the payment due. Buyers could change their minds about the item or be dissuaded if the costs of shipping and handling were greater than anticipated. This moral hazard problem could be resolved through *ex post* enforcement of the contract between the buyer and the seller, but enforcement was costly particularly for the low-priced items that constituted many of the trades. Punishment had to come from the refusal of future traders to trade with a member with a poor reputation.

Another imperfection resulting from anonymity was opportunism. A seller could succumb to the moral hazard problem and shade descriptions of items even though she might be unwilling to engage in outright fraud. Another seller might be willing to commit fraud if a calculation of the benefits and the potential cost from being disciplined or prosecuted yielded an expected gain. A seller could, for example, offer items for sale, collect payments from winning bidders, and not ship the items. Moreover, the seller could mask her identity, and reappear with a different identity to repeat the fraud. The opportunities to engage in fraud had the potential to inhibit trade.

Even when reputation was effective for assuring remote and anonymous traders, a reputation could be harvested. For example, a seller of ceramic figurines on eBay developed a top reputation over a five-year period, and in early 2002 offered a large number of items for sale, collected the payments from the winning bidders, and disappeared.[21] Reputation harvesting was a risk in any market, and preventing such fraud required the powers of the public order.

In addition, market participants might trade illegal goods, such as items that violated copyright or items banned by government regulatory agencies. Market participants could also trade items that were offensive to other traders. Such trades had the potential to weaken the trading community and the growth of online auctions.

5. Markets with Remote and Anonymous Traders: Theory and Evidence From Historical Accounts

eBay's challenge was to support trust among traders who were remote and anonymous, would never meet face-to-face, and would not have repeat encoun-

---

21. The case was turned over to the FBI. (*The Wall Street Journal*, 22 February 2002.)

Private Ordering on the Internet

ters. In addition, no institution was available to provide enforcement. McMillan and Woodruff (2000) argued that for a private ordering to resolve the inherent incentive problems in such situations required both organization and coordination of punishments. They wrote (p. 2458):

> In communities where people can hide behind their anonymity, private order, if it is to operate at all, must be organized. Private-order organizations in notably diverse settings, from medieval Europe to present-day Mexico, work in similar ways. An organization such as a market intermediary or a trade association disseminates information about contractual breaches and coordinates the community's response to breaches. The usual sanction is to boycott the offender.

As McMillan and Woodruff indicated, the problem of developing trade among remote traders had analogies in history. In many of these cases institutions were not present, and in other cases institutions arose in response to information and reliance problems. eBay's case was similar in many respects. For example, trade developed spontaneously on its site just as trade emerged among merchants a millennium earlier.

The development of remote trade in the Mediterranean and through fairs in medieval Europe occurred in conjunction with the establishment of offices and organizations for the maintenance of reputations among self-interested traders. The law merchant studied by Milgrom, North, and Weingast (1990) was an office that allowed reputations of traders to be developed and communicated to those with whom they might trade in the future. Merchants would travel long distances to the Champagne and other faires to display their goods and reach agreements on trades to be completed in the future. Such trades relied solely on the word of the merchants, since there was no government to enforce agreements. The office of the law merchant arose to help establish trust among the merchants. The law merchant was a local merchant with expertise in the good in dispute who received information, rendered judgments in the event of a dispute, kept a record of each merchant's reputation, and provided that information to other merchants. This system worked because merchants anticipated future trades even though those trades might be with different merchants; i.e., the reputations were multilateral.

The law merchant and the reputation mechanism mitigated a number of incentive problems arising from the timing of trades, moral hazard associated with the quality of the goods delivered, and asymmetric information about the honesty of traders. eBay's multilateral reputation mechanism had many of the same features with the Internet serving the informational and reputation accounting functions as well as facilitating dispute resolution, as considered below.

Present day trade associations serve some of the same roles as the law merchant. Woodruff (1998) studied the Mexican footwear industry, which was served by two trade associations that supported a multilateral reputation mechanism. The associations collected and aggregated data on whether retailers paid their bills, returned merchandise claiming it was defective, or cancelled orders.

257

David P. Baron

A manufacturer could obtain a report on a retailer before shipping products, so retailers had an incentive to invest in their reputations. The associations also helped resolve disputes and collect delinquent payments. Because retailers feared being cut off from supplies, most of the disputes were settled quickly and without use of the courts. This mechanism was facilitated by the geographic proximity of the manufacturers, their control of three-quarters of the production in Mexico, and a set of captive retailers.[22]

Greif (1989, 1993) analyzed the ethnically-linked Maghribi traders who operated in the Mediterranean in the eleventh century. The traders found it efficient to hire each other as agents to conduct transactions in distant ports. For example, traders shipped goods to their agents in other ports who were responsible for sales and remittance. The Maghribi traders functioned as a coalition and developed an information network in support of a multilateral reputation mechanism that induced agents to honor the terms of implicit contracts and not take advantage of their distant principals. Enforcement was multilateral through the refusal by coalition members to hire a violator as an agent in the future. The implicit contracts were also supported by reliance on the Merchants' Law, which provided mutual understandings about how agents were to deal with circumstances not explicitly covered by the principal's instructions.[23] The result was a horizontal private ordering among approximate equals.

Long-distance trade also flourished in the Mediterranean in the twelfth century because merchant guilds in the Italian city-states facilitated collective action to establish trust and provide sanctions for self-interested merchants. In contrast to the Maghribi traders, the merchants of Genoa dealt with the agency problems inherent in long-distance trade by investing in overseas possessions, "such as posts, houses, customs agreements, legal rights, and so on," (Greif, 1994) that facilitated trade with Africa and Europe.[24] The Genoese overcame a collective action problem among the merchants by consolidating power in a single family that extended its reach through marriage. The merchants then were able to finance investments and establish a military capability to protect their investments and defend against rivals from Pisa and Venice. In the case of Genoa, long-distance trade was facilitated by a vertical private ordering headed by a dominant family.

As in the case of the Maghribi traders the reputation mechanism operative in eBay's community originally developed horizontally. As the community grew, the mechanism was supplemented (vertically) by eBay. In contrast to the Genoa merchants eBay did not act autocratically in supporting the reputation mechanism but instead encouraged the participation of community members. eBay supplemented the mechanism with services intended to reduce trading costs and address imperfections. eBay thus resembled more the community of Maghribi traders than the merchants of Genoa. eBay's role was much like the Merchants'

---

22. When import restrictions were loosened in 1988, imports captured nearly one-third of the Mexican market. Imports gave retailers alternative sources of supplies, and their incentives to maintain reputations with Mexican manufacturers diminished.

23. The incentives that supported adherence to the implicit contracts also served as an entry barrier which provided an incentive to maintain the coalition.

24. See Lopez (1976).

258

Private Ordering on the Internet

Law, which supplemented the reputation mechanism by dealing with the incompleteness of the reputation mechanism.

Clay (1997) studied trade in California during the Mexican era of 1830–46. The nexus of trade was formed by merchants located near ports. The merchants traded with local residents, with ships traveling the California coast, and with ports in Hawaii, Mexico, and Europe. As with the Maghribi traders, the merchants had fixed locations but bought and sold goods in other ports by hiring merchants located in those ports as agents. Merchants thus hired each other as agents. Because the agents were self-interested, remotely located, and credit was extended for a year or more, opportunism was possible. Yet little occurred. This was not the result of law and its enforcement, since local judicial officers did not have enforcement authority. Instead, order and trust were provided privately.

Trust resulted because the merchants anticipated future trades and could be punished in proportion to their opportunism. Punishment consisted of the refusal to do business with the offending merchant for some period of time. The resulting trust was supported by an informal information network in which letters and news were brought by the ships. Thus, a merchant in Monterey could learn of prices, supply, and demand in Los Angeles and make inferences about how his agent there had performed. In the case of eBay, the Internet served as the information network.

Arrangements among the merchants were governed by implicit contracts, the terms of which were adjusted in the event of delivery of goods of less than the anticipated quality. In the case of damaged goods "merchants often arranged for an impartial survey by third parties (p. 241)." Clay noted (p. 243), "merchants attempted to preclude disputes and privately resolve those that arose," generally in an "amicable" manner. eBay's private ordering included both opportunities for third-party opinions and a dispute resolution mechanism to encourage resolution within the community.

A private ordering could be established through face-to-face and repeated interactions that allowed norms to develop and be sustained. Ellickson (1991) studied the norms of ranchers and homeowners in Shasta County, California, and found that they settled disputes based on norms largely without reliance on the law and often in a manner contrary to the law. They were able to rely on norms and punishments, primarily through gossip, because they had repeated interactions and were proximate. That is, repetition and proximity allowed norms to be respected. eBay's community, however, was remote and anonymous.

Except for the remoteness and anonymity of its traders, eBay had some of the characteristics of an organized exchange market. The New York Stock Exchange (NYSE) was formed in 1792 to mitigate a set of incentive problems associated with the trading of securities. Banner (1998) argued that it was formed to establish trading rules to fill a regulatory vacuum resulting from the unenforceability of securities trading contracts. As in the case of eBay the NYSE provided a venue for matching buyers and sellers and reducing search and transactions costs. The NYSE helped enforce contracts through a "miniature legal system" that included suspensions and blacklisting of brokers who broke agreements. The collection of information on traders allowed the establishment of reputations for trustworthiness. The NYSE, however, differed in important aspects from eBay.

259

David P. Baron

In the early years of the exchange the members (brokers) acted as agents of investors, screened potential members, provided information about the credit-worthiness of traders, and screened the securities sold.[25] eBay served none of these functions.

eBay's circumstances also differed from the other historical accounts. First, except for specialized trading neighborhoods there was little likelihood of reciprocity, as in the case of merchants hiring each other as agents. Second, repeated interactions among traders on eBay were a small fraction of the opportunities for trade. Both of these factors hindered the development of bilateral reputations. Moreover, many of the buyers and some of the sellers were infrequent rather than repeat players. The incentives provided by future interactions were typically one-sided in the eBay community, resting with the sellers. As in the case of the merchants in Mexican California, reputations were established multilaterally. Furthermore, information was available at virtually no cost, allowing reputations to be assessed by infrequent as well as frequent traders. Although traders on eBay were remote and would never meet, reputation substituted for face-to-face and repeated interactions.

In an important respect eBay's private ordering challenge was closer to that developed at the Champagne faire and among the merchants of Mexican California. The private orderings of the Maghibi traders, the merchants of Genoa, the Mexican footwear industries, and financial exchanges involved a relatively well-identified set of participants on at least one side of the market and remained relatively closed to entry. Indeed, the information and reputations systems that supported these private orderings might have been put at risk by expanding the set of participants. In contrast, eBay's community was open to all as was the Champagne faire and the markets in Mexican California, and trade flourished.

The private ordering in the historical accounts considered here developed largely in the absence of public order. In medieval Europe and Mexican California either national governments did not exist or enforcement of private agreements was ineffective. The private ordering of eBay's community, however, developed in the context of the public order and involved the positioning of its private ordering relative to the public order.

In contrast to the private ordering that arose among distant traders in medieval Europe and in California, the private ordering of eBay's community was supported by a company. eBay's role in the private ordering was more active than a player in a system of norms or in a coalition or association. eBay provided the infrastructure for, and owned, the venue. eBay explicitly designed its private ordering with the objective of creating value for the members of the community and for the enterprise. With respect to the development of order within its community, eBay's interests were closely aligned with those of the members.[26]

---

25. Some of the differences can be explained by the fact that the NYSE members acted as a cartel and hence had incentives to engage in cartel maintenance and support activities, such as lobbying against onerous regulations.

26. The interests of eBay and its community were opposed on some matters, as in the case of pricing.

The common interest was to have a safe, well-lighted, and efficient venue where members could have trust in each other and in eBay itself.

6. Private Ordering Through Design

The market imperfections inherent in an online auction market with anonymous and remote traders could be addressed only to a limited extent by the actions of the traders themselves. This left an important role for eBay to address the remaining imperfections and to reduce the costs of participating in the auctions it hosted. This section considers in more detail measures taken by eBay to deal with the remaining imperfections. As indicated in the previous sections eBay's community of traders was to some extent ordered by the actions of buyers and sellers in response to market opportunities and imperfections, but eBay sought to enhance that order through design. Its objective can be viewed as reducing the cost of trust by developing mechanisms to allow buyers and sellers to transact safely. Since participation in the community was voluntary, the size and composition of the community itself was a function of its efforts. Reputation was the centerpiece of those efforts.

The establishment, maintenance, and updating of an online reputation required information and communication. Those with the best information were the traders themselves, since they knew whether the quality of the merchandise was as represented, payment had been timely, and the good was delivered as promised. Within the broader eBay community were a number of communities of traders in particular items, primarily collectibles. These communities had repeated transactions among the same traders which allowed bilateral reputations to be established. Most members, however, transacted with many different parties, so bilateral reputation formation was insufficient to establish trust. Resnick and Zeckhauser (2001), for example, studied 138,158 buyer-seller pairs and found few repeat pairs. Moreover, the "vast majority" of the repeat pairs involved transactions conducted in close proximity presumably to save shipping costs.

Although bilateral reputation formation could not be relied on to engender widespread trust, a multilateral reputation mechanism, where a seller's reputation was based on the experiences of all those who traded with her, could generate trust. A multilateral reputation mechanism also provided for uncoordinated, multilateral punishment of a trader who violated the trust of other traders.[27] Punishment involved not bidding on items offered by a seller with a bad reputation or bidding less for those items or in the case of sellers by refusing to sell to a buyer with a bad reputation. This multilateral reputation mechanism generated incentives similar to those in a long-term relationship between a buyer and a seller.

The private ordering established among the members of eBay's community was not formally organized by its members nor was the punishment coordinated as McMillan and Woodroof argued. Instead, the Internet enabled the collection and transmission of dispersed transactions and reputation information that

---

27. See Kandori (1992) for a theory of multilateral or community enforcement of norms.

allowed a private order to function with little organization or coordination. eBay did not participate in the reputation and information systems other than to establish rules, such as whether feedback could be retracted. Punishment was voluntary and uncoordinated and occurred because individuals feared that they would have a bad experience with a member with a bad reputation, as others had had in the past. The effectiveness of this system was reflected by the importance members placed on their online reputations and on the substantial feedback that was generated.

The efficacy of a private ordering can be improved through design. Over time eBay developed a set of rules for its community to reduce the cost of trust and provided a set of services to reduce the costs of trading. In some cases, the rules were a response to incidents that identified weaknesses in the private ordering.

Reputation and Feedback

Reputation allowed both buyers and sellers to assure their trading partners that they would complete the transaction as promised and not make promises they could not keep. Reputations were assets of the traders, and most members carefully guarded them. These assets were non-tradable and could not be transferred to other market sites. Reputation had two kinds of effects for sellers. First, a bidder might be willing to bid more for an item offered by a seller with a strong reputation than for an identically described item offered by a seller with a weak reputation. Second, more bidders might be willing to bid on the item offered by a seller with a stronger reputation. McDonald and Slawson (2000) estimated these two effects using eBay auction data. They found that a stronger reputation, as measured by the feedback accounting system discussed in the following section, resulted in a higher winning bid.[28] They also found a greater number of bids for items offered by sellers with stronger reputations. Lucking-Reiley, Bryan, Prasad, and Reeves (2000) studied auctions of Indian-head pennies and found that the seller's positive feedback rating resulted in a statistically significant positive effect on the sales price, whereas negative feedback had the opposite and much larger effect. Similarly, Melnik and Alm (2000) studied auctions of gold coins and found a small but statistically significant positive effect of reputation on the sale price. Houser and Wooders (2000) found similar results for the auction of Pentium III processors. Resnick and Zeckhauser found that a stronger reputation of a seller increased the probability of a sale, but the effect on the price was indeterminate. Although the empirical evidence is not overwhelming, it suggests that there is a return to the investment in a reputation.

Members who anticipated trading repeatedly had stronger incentives to form and maintain reputations. Many of the sellers on eBay were repeat sellers who used eBay to conduct a business or supplement their incomes. Buyers transacted less frequently than sellers, so there was an asymmetry in the incentives for reputation maintenance. For example, in their sample of trades McDonald and

---

28. As Resnick, Zeckhauser, Friedman, and Kuwabara (2000) argued, this is consistent with a lemons model (Akerlof 1970). It is also consistent with the reputation models of Shapiro and Klein and Leffler.

Private Ordering on the Internet

Slawson found that the average eBay feedback rating of sellers was 53.6, whereas the average reputation of buyers was 23.2. Resnick and Zeckhauser found that the median feedback score of sellers in their sample was 33 and buyers was 8.

Traders had some means of directly addressing the trust issue. Sellers could make private assurances to buyers. For example, one seller stated on each listing: "GUARANTEE: Our merchandise is unconditionally guaranteed as to originality and description. If you are dissatisfied for any reason the item may be returned for a full refund (less shipping) as long as it is returned in the same condition and within a three day inspection period." Sellers could also offer their item as a hostage by accepting payment by credit card. A buyer then would know that if the item was not as described by the seller she could challenge the payment with the credit card company. The buyer would also know that the seller incurred the cost associated with payment by credit card, which could signal the seller's intent to reassure buyers. Such bonding was a poor substitute for reputation, however.

For high-value items eBay established eBay Premier, where auction houses and dealers would put their offline reputations behind the items they offered. Items such as fine art, wine, rare collectibles, and antiques were offered on eBay Premier. Sellers participating in eBay Premier provided a "Premier Guarantee" in which they stood behind the authenticity of their items.[29]

Feedback And Accounting

An online reputation mechanism required a feedback and accounting mechanism as well as communication of reputations to present and future trading partners. The Internet was ideal for these purposes.[30] Feedback could be posted by traders and made available to potential buyers on the seller's auction listings. The marginal cost of establishing and communicating reputations in this manner was low on the Internet. Moreover, feedback was durable, since storage costs were modest.[31]

The multilateral reputation mechanism was based on making feedback public, and members were encouraged but not obligated to do so. eBay stated, "You will probably want to make your Feedback Profile public because that generates trust and increases the likelihood that other eBay members will do business with you. After all, you'd probably want to see another member's Feedback Profile before you bought from them, right?" Virtually all members made their feedback profile available.

A member's feedback profile included the written comments of trading partners and a feedback rating. The written feedback provided important information but was time consuming to access. eBay reduced the access costs by aggregating the feedback. Feedback was classified as negative, neutral, or positive, with positive feedback receiving + 1 points, neutral feedback 0 points,

29. eBay Premier was scheduled to be replaced by a new site in the alliance with Sothebys.com.
30. See Avery, Resnick, and Zeckhauser (1999) for a theory of online evaluations similar to a reputation system.
31. Because of storage costs, however, eBay stored completed auction results only for the past month.

David P. Baron

and negative feedback −1 points. The aggregate score and the number of transactions were reported as the "seller's rating" on an auction listing and the "buyer's rating" when a bid was made.[32] A score that reached certain levels earned a star of one of nine colors.

The multilateral reputation mechanism had imperfections that increased the cost of trust, and eBay attempted to mitigate those imperfections. Feedback and reputation could become stale, or a member with a good reputation could begin to harvest his reputation. Similarly, eBay's aggregation rule masked information, since a member with a rating of 100 could have 100 positive feedbacks, whereas another could have 200 positives and 100 negatives. Since the impact of feedback was asymmetric, i.e., negative feedback was much more influential than positive feedback, members were interested in the disaggregated information. eBay thus summarized in a convenient table the number of positives, neutrals, and negatives for the past week, month, and six months.

A potential imperfection in the feedback mechanism was due to free-riding. After completing a transaction a buyer had little incentive to provide feedback to a seller with whom she was unlikely to trade again. The extent of the free-rider problem was not known, but considerable feedback was clearly provided. Using data from the first half of 1999 Resnick and Zeckhauser found that 52.1 percent of the buyers and 60.6 percent of the sellers provided feedback. One explanation for the substantial provision of feedback was the sense of community, however anonymous and remote it might be, and in the "personal relationship" that temporarily existed when a buyer and seller were making arrangements for payment and shipping. The exchange of email messages between the buyer and seller could establish a temporary bond that motivated traders to provide feedback.

The explanation, however, was more likely found in a norm of reciprocity.[33] A seller had a stronger interest in a good reputation than did a buyer, so the seller had an incentive to induce the buyer to provide feedback. This could be accomplished through courteous email messages and timely shipping, but it could also be sparked by providing positive feedback to the buyer. This encouraged the buyer to reciprocate, thus mitigating the free-rider problem. One seller stated in a note included with an item shipped to his buyers, "Feedback is very important to both buyers and sellers. I always give feedback when I receive payment. It is amazing how many people send me e-mail thanking me for the item I sent them, but neglected to give positive feedback. Please follow through with this transaction, and take a minute to do this. I have done it for you! Thanks!" The stronger the community and the more positive the buyer's experience on eBay the more likely feedback would be provided.

Although reciprocity could induce positive feedback, it could hinder negative feedback. Negative feedback was seldom given. Resnick and Zeckhauser found that 0.6 percent of the feedback provided by buyers was negative with a

---

32. See Kollock (1999, pp. 115–6) for a discussion of feedback and aggregation rules on other online auction sites.

33. Resnick and Zeckhauser refer to this as a "high-courtesy-equilibrium."

somewhat smaller percent for sellers.[34] In Bajari and Hortascu's data the average feedback rating was 203 and the average number of negative feedbacks was 0.43. This could simply reflect the fact that the vast majority of people are honest, but it could also reflect a concern for retaliation. A dissatisfied trader considering giving negative feedback might fear that the other trader would retaliate with negative feedback. Resnick and Zeckhauser, for example, found that "Sellers are far more likely to provide negative feedback after a buyer['s] negative or neutral (19.4 percent) than they are overall (1.2 percent)."[35] Consequently, negative feedback was likely undersupplied. Nevertheless, the prospect of negative feedback was an inducement to traders to fulfill expectations. One seller posted on each listing, "Payment is due within 10 days or you risk losing the item and neg. feedback."

Since negative feedback damaged a reputation, feedback extortion was possible. A member could threaten to provide negative feedback unless some concession were offered. Or, a member could provide negative feedback and offer to retract it if a concession were granted. The extent of the feedback extortion hazard was not known, but eBay took two measures to address it. First, feedback could not be retracted unless, for example, it had been sent to the wrong address, constituted harassment, or had no connection with eBay.[36] Second, the recipient of negative feedback was allowed to provide an explanation of her side of the matter. Resnick and Zeckhauser found that 29 percent of those receiving negative feedback responded.

One issue in the management of a feedback mechanism was who should be permitted to provide feedback. Initially, any eBay member was allowed to provide feedback, so a seller could, for example, provide comments on the goods offered by another seller. Or, a non-bidder could provide feedback on the responsiveness of a seller to answering questions. To avoid possible abuses of the feedback system, eBay restricted feedback to those who participated in a transaction. The reputations established thus were based on actual trades. The feedback system was also restricted to the eBay site, and feedback could not be exported to or imported from other sites. The former was prohibited to increase the cost of developing a reputation on another auction site. The latter was prohibited according to eBay because the company did not have the capability of importing written feedback and "a composite number, without the corresponding feedback does not reflect your true online reputation within our community."

Offsite Transactions And Email Harvesting

One risk to eBay as an enterprise was that members might take their transactions offsite. For example, a seller might contact the winning bidder and offer offsite another of the item at the same price. Or, a seller might contact losing bidders

---

34. Buyers provided more negative or neutral feedback for less experienced sellers than for more experienced sellers.
35. They speculated that much of the negative feedback may be due to botched transactions such as items lost in the mail.
36. Feedback could also be retracted as a result of a court order.

David P. Baron

and offer offsite another of the item at a fixed price. In effect, the seller would be offering the first item on eBay's site as a means of advertising. Some sellers provided a link to their own Web sites on which other items were offered for sale. Offsite transactions were a potential problem for eBay because sellers were allowed to design their own auction listings.

eBay drew a line in the sand against offsite trades and hyperlinks to non-eBay sites where items were listed for sale. To accommodate sellers who wished to link to their other auctions on its site, eBay provided each seller with a "visit seller's other auctions" link to a page listing all their eBay offerings. With five million auctions in progress at any moment, however, it was difficult to monitor the listings to determine if links to non-eBay sites were provided. eBay thus enlisted the community to help it police the site for such links.

eBay's rationale for these practices was two-fold. First, it lost revenue when transactions were made offsite. Second, although links to a seller's home page, for example, might be of interest to buyers, eBay was concerned that offsite transactions did not carry the protections available on its own site. Members who had a bad experience offsite then might blame eBay. For example, a seller sold a Rolex watch, and then contacted the second-highest bidder offering to sell another Rolex. The bidder paid several thousand dollars only to discover that the second Rolex was a fake.

eBay also faced the problem of email harvesting. Some companies sent robots onto its site to collect email addresses that they would then spam with offers. Others collected either by hand or by robot the email addresses of all the bidders on products it had manufactured. They then directly contacted those addresses offering to sell new items. eBay's user agreement prohibited such harvesting, and eBay restricted the availability of email addresses to the participants in an auction to avoid email harvesting and spamming. For legitimate use eBay partnered with other companies or organizations to allow eBay listings for a particular type of item to be accessed through a link that appeared on those companies' sites.

Katkar and Lucking-Reiley (2001) identified another form of email harvesting. A seller specified a high secret reserve price with the intention of not selling the item. When the auction ended, the seller had the email addresses of all the bidders on the item and could contact them offering to sell the item offsite. The researchers sent a survey form to randomly selected high bidders of unsuccessful auctions with secret reserves. Twenty-seven percent of the respondents reported that they had been contacted by the seller offering to sell the item at a specified price.

Private Punishment

The reputation mechanism provided assurance to traders, but occasionally a trader abused the system. This resulted in negative feedback and left the issue of what to do about members with bad reputations. Similarly, some members violated the user agreement, as in the cases of offsite transactions and email harvesting.

Private Ordering on the Internet

In response to such problems, eBay imposed punishments. If a member's feedback rating reached –4, the member was automatically suspended. eBay also suspended members for repeated failure to ship goods sold or for buyers who did not pay for goods for which they were the high bidder. Membership could also be suspended or terminated because of an inability to "verify or authenticate any information you provide" such as a credit card number for a seller. Members could also be suspended or terminated if their actions caused "legal liability for you, our users or us."

Explicit punishment was uncommon, since the reputation mechanism functioned effectively in most cases. An online reputation, however, was masked, since an eBay user name was chosen by the member. Consequently, a member could change his user name to avoid a weak reputation. eBay addressed this problem by placing a "shades" (sunglasses) icon by the user name of anyone who had changed names or joined eBay during the previous 30 days.

The more serious problem was a member intent on committing fraud or other violations of the user agreement. A suspended or banned user could return with a different user name, email address, and credit card. For example, a metals trader accused of fraud by scores of members had purchased the account of a member with a strong reputation. eBay had some ability to monitor sellers, since it required credit card information to bill them for listing and transactions fees. Nevertheless, anonymity gave fraud perpetrators a degree of cover. To address this problem, eBay first required members who were not otherwise identifiable to provide credit card information to establish their identity. eBay also allowed members to have their identity verified by a third party, Equifax Secure, which gave members an ID Verify icon for use in their feedback profiles.

Supporting Participation and Community

eBay's primary asset was its community, but eBay was also an important asset to its community. Many members believed that it was their community as much as it was eBay's. In 1997 the number of listings had increased to the point at which new item categories had to be developed. eBay decided on new categories, revised its front page, and implemented the changes. eBay also changed the way feedback scores were displayed on an auction page. In both cases it was flooded with weeks of angry emails and telephone calls complaining about the changes. It was forced to rescind some of the changes and revise others.

eBay realized that many members viewed the community as theirs. This called for a collaborative approach to its community. The company formed a diverse group of twelve community members, some of whom were nominated by the community, and brought them to its offices for an exchange of information and ideas. eBay discussed changes it was considering and asked for feedback, but much of the time was spent simply listening to the ideas and views of the group. The interchange was very successful, and the process was institutionalized as "Voices." eBay established new Voices groups on a quarterly basis to discuss planned changes and hear the views of members. Voices members continued their discussions with the company through email and telephone conversations. Some matters such as price changes were not discussed, however. Voices not only enabled eBay to serve its members better, but it also helped identify new market opportunities for the company. Participation by the community also helped develop trust between the community and eBay. Although Voices members constituted a tiny fraction of the eBay community, their communication particularly among sellers helped build that trust.

Trust and Community Sentiments

The cost of trust was reduced by the comfort of members with the community. This included not only a member's satisfaction with listings, bidding, and trades but also with what the community encompassed. Some members were uncomfortable with items sold on its site. Items associated with hate groups, Nazi items, and "murderabilia"—items associated with mass murderers—were offensive to many members.[37] Yet, some World War II items, for example, were of interest to museums, scholars, and history buffs. Items associated with the assassination of President Lincoln, for example, were of historical significance. eBay faced the problem of drawing a line between items that were objectionable and those that might be of historical significance, recognizing that any such line would be unsatisfactory to some members. eBay formulated a policy to "judiciously disallow" Nazi, Ku Klux Klan and other hate group materials, as well as items associated with notorious individuals who had committed murderous acts during the past 100 years.[38]

This policy was put to the test when in the wake of the September 11 terrorist attacks. Sellers listed New York newspapers and World Trade Center items for sale. eBay responded by removing items exploiting the tragedy and suspended nine members. eBay also banned until October any items associated with the World Trade Center or the Pentagon.

eBay operated internationally, and countries had different policies regarding the sale of certain items. France, for example, banned the sale of Nazi items. In a case that drew considerable attention France filed a lawsuit against Yahoo! Auctions for the sale of Nazi memorabilia. eBay was careful to design its national auction sites to respect domestic laws and sentiments.

Privacy

An important component of trust between the community and eBay was privacy protection. eBay did not share members' personal information with third parties and allowed members to determine how eBay contacted them. eBay, however, used session cookies to collect information and provided aggregate profiles to advertisers. The company provided a chart that indicated how a member's information could be used by five types of organizations: advertisers, internal

---

37. The victims rights group Justice for All called on eBay to band murderabilia, and the Simon Wiesenthal Center complained of the sale of Nazi items.

38. eBay understood that removing such items from its site would not prevent their sale. Listings on ePier increased by 5,000 in one month when eBay banned war memorabilia with Nazi markings. When eBay banned the sale of firearms, listings on AuctionArms increased from 300 to 6,000 in two days. (AuctionWatch.com, 22 June 2001)

service providers, external service providers, eBay community representatives, and legal requests.[39]

Insurance, Escrow, Authentication, and Third-Party Opinions

Reputation was effective in supporting trade, but trust could be strengthened through institutional arrangements. For example, buyers faced risks when trading with new sellers, sellers with a marginal reputation, or in some cases with a trader with a good reputation. To reduce the risk, eBay offered without charge insurance against fraud for all items up to a value of $200 with a $25 deductible.[40]

For transactions with a value above $500 eBay provided access to an online escrow service Tradenable Inc. The escrow system allowed a buyer to make payment to Tradenable. The seller then shipped the item to the buyer, and if the buyer approved, Tradenable paid the seller.

To provide information, buyers could use escrow and consult with independent third-party experts such as coin dealers and antiques appraisers. eBay could create value for its community by providing information and putting its reputation behind items, but it chose not to do so for two reasons. First, it typically had little expertise in the types of items offered for sale, and developing such expertise would be costly. More importantly, however, as indicated above if eBay were to provide information or authentication, as did an offline auction house, it could fall under the jurisdiction of state auction laws and subject to regulation. Moreover, such activities could make it an Internet content provider rather than an Internet service provider. That would expose it to a host of potential legal liabilities that it preferred not to assume.

Instead, eBay linked members to Internet sites where they could obtain professional opinions on certain items. The sites provided information ranging from a quick opinion to authentication and grading services involving physical inspection of the item. This approach allowed eBay to capture a portion of the rents from the increased trust generated by reducing the informational asymmetry.

Disputes and Their Resolution

Differences of opinion between buyers and sellers could easily result, and some developed into disputes. Most disputes were resolved through the exchange of information to clear up misunderstandings between traders. Some disputes remained, however. eBay was approached by SquareTrade Inc., which offered to provide online dispute resolution and mediation services. Square-Trade's Direct Negotiation online mechanism facilitated settlement, and the company also offered the intervention of a mediator to resolve the remaining disputes. eBay decided to provide the online mechanism to the community

---

39. See the case "eBay: Private Ordering for an Online Community." See also Duh, Jamal, and Sunder (2001) for an analysis of privacy, integrity, and security at eBay.
40. The insurance system was administered by Lloyd's of London.

without charge, and the mediated dispute resolution service was provided for a fee of $15 with eBay paying the rest of the cost. eBay was not involved in the resolution of any disputes, but if members were unable to resolve the dispute, they could access eBay's fraud protection programs, such as insurance.

Sellers could certify that they would rely on the dispute resolution mechanism to resolve problems. This strengthened their reputations and generated trust by providing recourse to buyers. Sellers that pledged to use the online mechanism could display a SquareTrade icon on their listings.

Banned, Recalled, and Regulated Items

Some members used eBay to dispose of items from their attics, basements, or garages. For example, a community member noticed a listing for "jarts," a lawn darts game banned by the Consumer Products Safety Commission (CPSC) because of the danger of injury. eBay faced the problem of how to protect its community from such dangers. It decided to work with the CPSC to identify products with potential problems, including recalled and banned items. eBay established an "About Me" page on its site for the CPSC and provided a link to information on its Web site. More importantly, when a seller listed one of these products, a pop-up screen appeared providing a link to the CPSC Web site where an explanation of the problem could be found. A member who bid on such an item also encountered the pop-up window. Both sellers and buyers thanked eBay for alerting them to the problem. This produced considerable traffic at the CPSC site and resulted in the removal from circulation of a substantial number of dangerous items. eBay established similar programs with a number of other government agencies, including the Department of Fish and Wildlife, Food and Drug Administration, Environmental Protection Agency, and Postal Service, to deal with items that may be against a law or regulation, such as import-export laws or the Endangered Species Act.

Infringing Items

A problem for any Internet venue was to ensure that it was not associated with illegal activities. A particular problem for eBay was the sale of items such as pirated software and recordings that violated intellectual property law. As indicated above, the CDA provided a shield to telephone companies and Internet service providers for what users posted on their systems. Copyright infringement, however, presented a complex challenge.

eBay's VeRO program allowed rights owners to identify violating items, which eBay then removed. Rights owners demanded, however, that eBay pre-screen its listings. Such screening would be complicated, since, for example, eBay would have to determine which edition of a recording, U.S. or European, was being sold, since they might have different protections. eBay refused to pre-screen because it feared it might be held liable under the DCMA, but it instituted the Four Corners policy in response to pressure from the Business Software Alliance. eBay wanted to monitor its site for infringing items and lobbied in Washington for an amendment to the DCMA to provide a safe harbor for responsible monitoring.

Fraud: Policing and Enforcing

A community based on trust was vulnerable to fraud. Data on fraud rates were not available, but fraud was believed to be relatively rare. In 1997 eBay's president stated that 99.99 percent of trades were successfully completed.[41] eBay later reported that the fraud rate was one in 40,000. Although the rate was low, fraud posed a threat to the growth of eBay's trading community. The FBI reported that 43 percent of the fraud complaints it received in 2001 were associated with online auctions.

Fraud often began with the item description, and on each listing page eBay stated, "These items are not verified by eBay; caveat emptor." Policing the venue and punishing violators were necessary, however. Members of the community could effectively participate in the battle against fraud and other illegal activities by forming "neighborhood watch" groups. For example, the traders of a collectible could monitor the activity of those trading in that item and post concerns on the bulletin boards provided by eBay. As another example, a seller offered an "1879c Morgan Hill Silver Dollar." A knowledgeable community member noticed the item and reported to eBay that he believed that no such coin had ever been minted. The trader and eBay then cooperated with the Secret Service leading to the arrest of the seller.

eBay could also do its own monitoring, since the DCMA pertained to copyrights and not fraud. One form of fraud was shill bidding where a seller used aliases or enlisted others to drive up the price of an item.[42] eBay employed shill-hunter software to detect such practices, but it also relied on the community to detect shill-bidding rings. On one bulletin board a user posted a message: "[user name] = Do you know how to spell *S-H-I-L-L*??" If shill bidding was detected, eBay notified the appropriate law enforcement agencies.[43] For example, in 2001 federal indictments were issued for three men accused of shill bidding on 1,100 auctions. eBay and the FBI were alerted to the ring when an auctioned painting reached a price of $135,000.

eBay also dealt with the risk of fraud through its own screening to lessen the problem of sellers giving phony contact information. In addition to requiring sellers to provide credit card information, eBay entered into an agreement with VeriSign to verify the addresses and telephone numbers of new sellers on eBay.[44] The agreement could lead to the collection of additional information on sellers to allow more complete verification.

Individuals who believed that they had been wronged were encouraged to communicate with the other party to the transaction to determine if there was a

---

41. See Kollock, p. 117.
42. Shill bidding was not illegal in some states.
43. Another fraudulent practice was bid shielding where a member submitted a very high bid to shield a lower bid from a conspiring bidder. The member would then withdraw his shielding bid just before the auction ended, allowing the shielded bid to win.
44. This agreement replaced the one with Equifax.

misunderstanding and to use SquareTrade if there remained a problem. If those steps failed and the user believed that she had been defrauded, she could file a fraud report with eBay after a waiting period of 30 days. eBay's fraud protection program covered:

1. Paying for an item and never receiving it or
2. Receiving an item that is less than what is described—such as winning a solid gold necklace but receiving a copper one instead.

The insurance program provided coverage for victims, but fraud complaints remained a concern.

To deal with such complaints, eBay established an Investigations department to investigate complaints filed by community members. Seller offenses included shill bidding, not delivering the item according to terms and conditions stated on the listing, refusing a complete a successful transaction, intercepting a transaction intended for another seller, and avoiding eBay's fees as in the case of offsite transactions. eBay could help detect fraud by aggregating data from dispersed victims. If a member reported an act of fraud, eBay would contact other winning bidders who might have been victims of the same seller to determine if they had had problems. eBay put defrauded members in contact with the appropriate law enforcement office.[45]

7. Conclusions and Strategy Implications

The private ordering of eBay's community of buyers and sellers had a number of antecedents in economic history. In contrast to those private orderings, however, eBay provided only a venue for trading and did not represent or coordinate the actions of the members of its community. It also did not participate in transactions nor serve the other functions of offline auction houses or exchanges. This left a host of market imperfections and potential incentive problems. The Internet, however, allowed an online reputation mechanism to support trust among anonymous traders, most of whom would not have repeated bilateral interactions. The reputation mechanism was multilateral and based on feedback provided by the parties to a transaction. This mechanism was the heart of eBay's strategy of building a community and sharing in the value created for its members.

The feedback mechanism did not eliminate all incentive problems, however, so there was a role for eBay to strengthen its community through design. This included the provision of services, such as insurance, escrow, and dispute resolution. It also relied on participation by the community to identify means of better serving their interests and building trust between the community and eBay.

Caution should be exercised in drawing generalizations based on the experiences of one company, but certain strategy principles can be derived from theory and illustrated by eBay's experience. An online market such as that hosted by eBay creates value by matching buyers and sellers so that gains from trade can

---

45. Snyder (2000) called for online auction sites to authenticate items offered for sale and for the government to impose "swift and severe" penalties against sites where fraudulent items are sold.

be realized. The strategy of a venue is then to maximize those gains and capture a share of the value created. Matching on an online trading venue has many of the characteristics of an information-based market. Demand-side increasing returns are present due to network externalities and opportunities to provide complementary goods. The user base is crucial, and first movers have an advantage in building that base. In eBay's case lock-in resulted from the coordination costs of traders collectively moving to a competing venue. The conditions for positive feedback were thus present and the U.S. online auction market tipped in favor of eBay.

Expanding the online community is a central component of strategy. The larger the community the greater are the potential gains from matching and the better is the price information provided through the market mechanism. As the size of the community increases, however, members become more remote and repeated interactions are a smaller portion of trades. Opportunism could grow and trust erode in such a situation. A principal component of strategy thus is to create mechanisms to mitigate market imperfections and incentive problems. Reputation is the natural response to the problem of trust, and reputation mechanisms quickly and spontaneously emerged in the early days of online markets. Nevertheless, online reputation mechanisms have imperfections, and those imperfections can hinder trade. A central task for management then is to design an efficacious reputation mechanism and to respond to the imperfections identified. This must be done in relation to the public order, and design must be judged relative to potential regulation and liabilities. eBay's strategy illustrates the types of responses that can strengthen a reputation mechanism, reduce the cost of trust, and lower transactions costs.

With mechanisms in place that mitigate market imperfections, the community emerges as the company's principal strategic asset. To the extent that the community is locked-in and the market has tipped, that asset can be leveraged to add further value to the community. The limits of such opportunities are not evident, and eBay appears to have considerable room to expand its offerings, services, and community.

When the opportunity to develop a community is present and the conditions for tipping are present, only a small number of online trading communities would be expected to persist. This means that in the competition to become the winner, strategy is increasingly important, since there may be no second chance. Developing trust and reducing its cost are the centerpieces of this strategy. eBay's experience provides important lessons in how trust can be generated in a large community through feedback and reputation based on the participation of community members and supported by rules, policies, and services designed by the company.

References

Akerlof, George A. 1970. "The Market for 'Lemons': Quality Uncertainty and the Market Mechanism." *Quarterly Journal of Economics* 84: 488–500.

Armstrong, Arthur and John Hagel III. 1996. "The Real Value of Online Communities." *Harvard Business Review* (May–June): 134–141.

David P. Baron

Avery, Christopher, Paul Resnick, and Richard Zeckhauser. "The Market for Evaluations." *The American Economic Review* 89 (June): 564–584.

Bajari, Patrick and Ali Hortacsu. 2000. "Winner's Curse, Reserve Prices and Endogenous Entry: Empirical Insights from eBay Auctions." Working paper, Stanford University.

Banner, Stuart. 1998. "The Origin of the New York Stock Exchange, 1791–1860." *Journal of Legal Studies* 27: 113–140.

Clay, Karen. 1997. "Trade Without Law: Private-Order Institutions in Mexican California." *Journal of Law, Economics and Organization* 13: 202–231.

Duh, Rong-Ruey, Karim Jamal, and Shyam Sunder. 2001. "Control and Assurance in E-Commerce: Privacy, Integrity and Security at eBay." Working paper, Yale University.

Ellickson, Robert C. 1991. *Order Without Law.* Cambridge, MA: Harvard University Press.

Greif, Avner. 1989. "Reputation and Coalitions in Medieval Trade: Evidence on the Maghribi Traders." *Journal of Economic History* 49: 857–882.

Greif, Avner. 1993. "Contract Enforceability and Economic Institutions in Early Trade: The Maghribi Traders' Coalition." *American Economic Review* 83: 525–548.

Greif, Avner. 1994. "On the Political Foundations of the Late Medieval Commercial Revolution: Genoa during the Twelfth and Thirteenth Centuries." *Journal of Economic History* 54: 271–287.

Houser, Daniel and John Wooders. 2000. "Reputation in Auctions: Theory, and Evidence from eBay." Working paper, University of Arizona.

Kandori, Michihiro. 1992. "Social Norms and Community Enforcement." *Review of Economic Studies* 59: 63–80.

Katkar, Rama and David Lucking-Reiley. 2001. "Public Versus Secret Reserve Prices in eBay Auctions: Results from a Pokemen Field Experiment." Working paper, University of Arizona.

Klein, Benjamin and Keith B. Leffler. 1981. "The Role of Market Forces in Assuring Contractual Performance." *Journal of Political Economy* 89: 615–641.

Kollock, Peter. 1999. "The Production of Trust in Online Markets." In *Advances in Group Processes*, Vol. 16, Greenwich, CT: JAI Press, 99–123.

Kreps, David M. 1990. "Corporate culture and economic theory." In Alt, James and Shepsle, Kenneth. eds. *Perspectives on Positive Political Economy*. Cambridge: Cambridge University Press: 90–143.

Lopez, Robert Sabatino. 1976. *The Commercial Revolution of the Middle Ages,* Cambridge: Cambridge University Press: 950–1350.

Lucking-Reiley, David, Doug Bryan, Naghi Prasad, and Daniel Reeves. 2000. "Pennies from eBay: the Determinants of Price in Online Auctions." Working paper, University of Arizona.

McDonald, Cynthia G. and V. Carlos Slawson, Jr. 2000. "Reputation in an Internet Auction Model." Working paper, University of Missouri-Columbia.

McMillan, John and Christopher Woodruff. 2001. "Private Order Under Dysfunctional Public Order." *Michigan Law Review* 98: 2421–2458.

Melnik, Mikhail I. and James Alm. 2001. "Does a Seller's eCommerce Reputation Matter?" Working paper, Georgia State University.

Milgrom, Paul R., Douglass C. North and Barry R. Weingast. 1990. "The Role of Institutions in the Revival of Trade: The Law Merchant, Private Judges, and the Champagne Fairs." *Economics and Politics* 2: 1–23.

Resnick, Paul, Richard Zeckhauser, Eric Friedman, and Ko Kuwabara. 2000. "Reputation Systems." *Communications of the ACM* 43: 45–48.

Resnick, Paul and Richard Zeckhauser. 2001. "Trust Among Strangers in Internet Transactions: Empirical Analysis of eBay's Reputation System." Working paper, University of Michigan.

Saloner, Garth, Andrea Shepard, and Joel Podolny. 2001. *Strategic Management.* New York: Wiley.

Shapiro, Carl. 1982. "Consumer information, product quality, and seller reputation." *Bell Journal of Economics* 13: 20–35.

Shapiro, Carl. 1983. "Premiums for High Quality Products as Returns to Reputations." *Quarterly Journal of Economics* 98: 659–679.

Shapiro, Carl and Hal R. Varian. 1999. *Information Rules.* Boston, MA: Harvard Business School Press.

Snyder, James M. 2000. "Online Auction Fraud: Are the Auction Houses Doing All They Should or Could to Stop Online Fraud." *Federal Communications Law Journal* 52: 453–472.

Woodruff, Christopher. 1998. "Contract Enforcement and Trade Liberalization in Mexico's Footwear Industry." *World Development* 26: 979–991.

[15]

Constitutions as Governance Structures:
The Political Foundations of Secure Markets

Comment

by

PETER BERNHOLZ

1. Introduction

Since it is the task of a discussant to find the weak spots and gaps in a paper, let me stress that I enjoyed reading WEINGAST's [1993] paper. It restates clearly some problems and relationships which have been well-known for a long time and tries to look at them from a fresh perspective.

The references are comprehensive though they overemphasize the contributions by Riker and his students, since they omit much of the other earlier work by Public Choice Theorists and Political Scientists. The result that majority rule has no natural equilibrium or stable policy (WEINGAST [1993, 289]), e. g., is related to logrolling, which can be generalized and interpreted as a substantive interpretation of Arrow's impossibility theorem (BERNHOLZ [1980]). But most of the authors who did original work in that field are not mentioned (MÜLLER [1979, esp. 49–58] and MÜLLER [1989, 82–95]).

2. The Problem

Weingast takes up the old Hobbesian–Lockean problem: A sovereign must exist to prevent anarchy and to protect property rights, but must, at the same time, be constrained so that he does not misuse the monopoly of power needed for this task to limit or abolish freedom or to weaken property rights by new taxes or regulations.

As a first principle for achieving this aim, "a constitution must provide for its own preservation" (WEINGAST [1993, 289]). The second principle, instituting democracy alone is insufficient to protect markets (WEINGAST [1993, 289]), is more an empirically tested result of public choice theory than a principle. The third principle, "institutions that limit majority choices are a necessary component to establishing and maintaining guarantees for economic and political rights" (WEINGAST [1993, 289]), is a postulate which follows from the postulate: preserve private property and well-functioning markets and the result just mentioned. To reach the aims postulated by the first and third "principles," a fourth principle must be fulfilled. It "requires, first, that the authority to regulate markets is not vested in the highest political government in the hierarchy; and second, that the lower governments are prevented from using their regulatory authority to erect trade barriers against the goods and services from other political units" (WEINGAST [1993, 291]). For otherwise the central government could intervene with regulations and thus erode efficient markets, whereas the prevention of domestic trade barriers prevents lower governments from misusing their authority to regulate markets.

Unfortunately Weingast has not mentioned another postulate together with the four principles referred to above, a postulate which plays a critical role later in his arguments. For "Because rules can be disobeyed or ignored, something must be added to police deviations [by the government]. Our approach suggests that the foundation for institutional restriction fundamentally rests in the attitudes of citizens" (WEINGAST [1993, 305]). Thus, market-preserving federalism actually rests on a fifth "principle," namely " a set of shared beliefs among citizens who react against the state when the latter attempts to transgress the boundaries defined by those institutions" (WEINGAST [1993, 305]). Obviously the supposed necessity and sufficiency of this postulate rests on two hypotheses. The first asserts that all constitutional restrictions can be altered or removed. The second states that a sufficient condition to prevent this are positive attitudes and opinions of citizens that these restrictions are a fundamental and necessary component of their society.

Weingast's second "principle" has, of course, been well-known for centuries. As Montesquieu stated it already in 1748: "Democratic ... states are not in their own nature free. Political liberty is to be found only in moderate governments; and even in these it is not always found. It is there only if there is no abuse of power. But constant experience shows us that every man invested with power is apt to abuse it ... To prevent this abuse, it is necessary ... that power should be a check to power" (MONTESQUIEU [1970, 396 sq.]). Similarly, de Tocqueville in 1840 pointed out that "In democratic communities nothing but the central power has any stability in its position or any permanence in its undertakings, ... Now it is in the nature of all governments to seek constantly to enlarge their sphere of action; hence it is almost impossible that such a government should not ultimately succeed, ... There is always a multitude of men engaged [in democratic eras] in difficult or novel undertakings, ... Such persons will admit, as a general principle, that the public authority ought not to interfere in private concerns; but, as an exception to that rule, each of them craves its assistance in the particular concern on which he is engaged and to draw upon the influence of the government for his own benefit, ..." (DE TOCQUEVILLE [1945, vol. 2, 311]).

It might be objected that the authors quoted were concerned with preserving individual liberty and not with a well-functioning economic system. But fortunately for freedom, the two are intimately connected. And it is quite obvious that at least de Tocqueville saw this relationship already in 1835: "It is clear that despotism ruins individuals by preventing them producing wealth much more than by depriving them of what they have already produced; ... Freedom, on the contrary, produces far more goods than it destroys, and the nations who are favored by free institutions invariably find that their resources increase even more rapidly than their taxes" (DE TOCQUEVILLE [1945, vol. 1, 220 sq.]).

The third "principle" has also been prominent in classical political philosophy. To quote Montesquieu: "To prevent this abuse [of power] it is necessary from the very nature of things that power should be a check to power. A government may be so constituted, as no man shall be compelled to do things to which the law does not oblige him, nor forced to abstain from things which the law permits. ... When the legislative and executive powers are united in the same body of magistrates, there can be no liberty; ... Again, there is no liberty, if the judiciary power be not separated from the legislative and executive" (MONTESQUIEU [1970, 397]).

Weingast's first principle that "a constitution must provide for its own preservation" was, I believe, implicitly shared by many classical political thinkers, including de Tocqueville and 'The Federalist.' The problem, of course, is whether and how it can be implemented.

Finally, the first part of the fifth "principle," namely the hypothesis that all constitutional restrictions can be altered or removed, is quite Hobbesian in nature. To quote Hobbes' work of 1651: "The sovereign of a commonwealth, be it an assembly, ... is not subject to the civil laws. For having power to make, and repeal laws, he may when he pleaseth, free himself from that subjection, by repealing those laws that trouble him, and making of new;" (HOBBES [1970, 312 sq.]). Thus only the second part of the fifth "principle" seems to be a new idea, i.e., the hypothesis that, to prevent the erosion of the constitution, positive "attitudes and opinions of citizens" that it is "a fundamental and necessary component of their society" (WEINGAST [1993]) are sufficient. We will return to this hypothesis later.

Weingast bases his second principle, "democracy alone is an insufficient political foundation for the protection of markets," purely on the result that "the absence of a majority rule equilibrium means that no policy is stable" (WEINGAST [1993, 289]). This limitation is unfortunate. I believe that Weingast would certainly agree that rational ignorance and ideological convictions of voters can be exploited by parties, bureaucracies and interest groups to benefit minorities, and that the implied tendencies are probably more important for the growth of government than the instabilities implied by the Arrow Theorem (for an overview see BERNHOLZ [1982], BORCHERDING [1985], LYBECK [1986], MÜLLER [1989]).

3. The Proposed Solution

According to Weingast, the solution to the problems discussed above is federalism, provided that it is "market-preserving." This implies a hierarchy of governments with "a delineated scope of authority" for each. Why there should be, following RIKER's [1964, 11] definition, only *two* levels is not comprehensible. For each level of government the constitution must provide a guarantee of autonomy. And for federalism to be market-preserving it is required that (a) the authority to regulate markets is not vested with the highest political government in the hierarchy and (b) the lower governments are prevented from using their regulatory authority to erect [domestic] trade barriers. Finally, to maintain market-preserving federalism, the support of the constitution by the population as mentioned above must be present.

Apart from the last supposedly sufficient condition for maintaining market-preserving federalism, I can agree with the arguments presented. The latter condition is, however, exogenously given. But we have to ask ourselves how the constitution-supporting attitudes of the population come about and whether it is probable that they can to be maintained. The first question is only answered in a rather limited way when the historical evidence is discussed. The second is not answered at all. I would, however, hypothesize that, with the change of generations, a successful market-preserving constitution loses support in the population. For freedom and economic success are taken for granted as quasi natural events and it is forgotten which institutions are necessary to maintain them. Other ends such as substantive equality and ecological concerns, or new ideologies, gain broad adherence as supreme values. But this consensus tends to support actions damaging a market-preserving constitution, freedom and rule of law. And the supporters of such changes even do not realize these consequences.

There are other problems not covered by Weingast's simple game-theoretic model. He himself points out that "virtually any outcome can be sustained as an equilibrium of the repeated game" (WEINGAST [1993, 299]). Thus the game is not particularly helpful. It also does not catch some important aspects of the general problem. What happens if the "transgression" by the sovereign is such that it benefits not only himself but a certain group of society, e. g., the military, the bureaucracy or interest groups? Will not their support then be sufficient to extend his powers, given the possibility of using force or the rational ignorance of voters?

I agree with Weingast that the problem of policing a sovereign is a problem of coordinating beliefs and that it is possible for a constitution to serve as a coordinating device. But it is also an information problem in a different sense. Citizens must know not only the main contents of the constitution, but also be able to detect the transgressions by the sovereign. To coordinate their actions, they possibly need to know the preferences of the other citizens and their situations. Given all these problems, can it still be assumed that the sovereign loses power without the necessary support among citizens? Or is not merely the support of the military and the bureaucracy or of some well-informed interest groups vis-a-vis rationally uninformed and uncoordinated voters sufficient to maintain the sovereign's rule?

4. Solutions Other Than Federalism

Weingast defines the political system of England after the Glorious Revolution as a federal system, since there existed a central government but also considerable rights and privileges were vested at the local level. Such a definition is certainly new, since nowhere, to my knowledge, has England or Britain been considered to have a federal system. I have looked into several Encyclopaedias and all believe the existence of states, Länder or Cantons to be essential for Federalism (ENCYCLOPAEDIA BRITANNICA [1966 vol. 9, 133–135]). Of course, one can select definitions at one's own discretion if this makes sense within the theory proposed. But it seems that Weingast's approach points to a more substantive problem.

In the section on "Market-Preserving 'Federalism' and the Rule of Law in England" and "Application of the Model to the Glorious Revolution," three factors are mentioned which were relevant in the emerging consensus between Whigs and Tories about the limits of national regulatory authority.

First, "... the Bill of Rights. This document first identified those actions of the previous sovereign that constituted fundamental violations of citizens' rights and second provided a list of activities the sovereign could no longer undertake. ... The new consensus held that the support for the sovereign could be withdrawn if the sovereign violated the Revolution Settlement's terms" (WEINGAST [1993, 302]).

Second, the preservation of local political liberty became important. The consensus thus extended not only to the limits of national regulatory authority but also to the importance of local autonomy.

Third, the rule of law, for "respecting agreed on limits on the state, is clearly a central aspect of the rule of law" (WEINGAST [1993, 305]). But "whether a society is characterized by the rule of law depends upon the attitude and behavior of individuals" (WEINGAST [1993, 305]). Unfortunately Weingast does not mention here the importance of independent courts and the Common Law tradition in implementing the rule of law.

Now only the second of these factors is related to federalism, whereas the others have to do with decentralization and division of power. A division of power was evolving between King, Parliament and Courts, which became operative with the emerging consensus of the two parties represented in Parliament. Also, these developments guaranteed decentralization not only at the level of communities but also by preserving and enlarging the domain of autonomous decision making of private individuals. Thus Weingast is no longer speaking only about market-preserving federalism, but rather more about decentralization and division of government power as market-preserving devices. He is concerning the latter, if one substitutes market preservation for liberty, in full accord with Montesquieu, who states: "When the legislative and executive powers are united in the same person, or in the same body of magistrates, there can be no liberty; ... Again, there is no liberty, if the judiciary power be not separated from the legislative and executive" (MONTESQUIEU [1970, 397]).

Obviously, the Founding Fathers of the American constitution tried skilfully not only to use federalism but also the division of government powers and decentralization to guarantee not only liberty but also free markets and secure individual property. We may also well ask the question whether in Britain during the last decades the ever diminishing role of King or Queen and the House of Lords, which has eroded the division of power between legislative and executive, has nothing to do with the growth of (central) government and the decline of the rights and privileges of communities.

Starting from these remarks, one is inspired to ask whether federalism is a necessary, sufficient or even necessary *and* sufficient condition to preserve free markets with private property and individual liberty. I believe that it is not a necessary condition, as demonstrated by the success of Hong Kong, Japan, France and Taiwan. Whether federalism is a sufficient condition may also be doubted, if it is not combined with a strict division of power, as the example of modern England shows.

5. How can a Political Regime Allowing Free Markets and Strong Private Property Come About?

Weingast rightly stresses the importance of consensus for creating market-preserving regimes. But which and whose consensus is necessary? In China since 1979, decentralization and reforms moving towards free markets have been taken from above by the rulers. The same is true for the successful reforms in Japan after the Meiji restauration and more recently in Taiwan, South Korea, Singapore and Hong Kong.

It seems that the international competition among states has been an important factor for the introduction of free markets and private property, since market economies with strong private property outperform planned or strongly interventionist systems because of their greater economic efficiency and innovative capabilities. For this implies that such systems in time provide an ever stronger base for relative international military and political power of the nations enjoying them. E. g., the concern about their future position as Big Powers seems to have lead Japan in the 1860s, China since 1979 and the former Soviet Union to their reform efforts (BERNHOLZ [1992]). Thus before Gorbatchev became Secretary General of the Politbureau, he had already stressed the necessity for reform in the Soviet Union. According to the NEUE ZÜRCHER

ZEITUNG [1984], which referred to reports in the Soviet Press, "the youngest member of the Politbureau was the main speaker at a (Communist Party) conference on ideology." The article reports that Gorbatchev stated that

"it was inescapable to transform the Soviet economy and to raise its technical and organizational performance to a qualitatively higher level. This course, to increase productivity and to intensify work effort, was made necessary by objective factors, ...; no alternative existed. Only such a modernized economy could meet the necessities of the population, allow a strengthening of the position of the USSR on the international stage and make it possible for her to enter the new millennium as a powerful and flourishing state. ...One could not learn from the presentation, in which way the Soviet economic production should be modernized and which reform ideas Gorbatchev would like to apply."

In Japan, the Meiji Restoration of the 1860s was also a revolution from above, led by sections of the nobility against the weakened power of the shogun and skilfully using the device of restoring factual power to the Tenno. The restoration was decisively shaped or even caused by the realization of the superiority of the powers of Western states after the forced opening of Japanese harbors to Western trade, beginning with Commodore Perry in 1854. Thus the new slogan of the day became "fukoku-kyohei," "rich country, strong arms" (ENCYCLOPAEDIA BRITANNICA [1966, vol. 12, 924]). The reforms took the form of a wholesale adoption of Western constitutional, legal, educational, economic, technical, administrative and military systems, which proved so successful in the longrun.

If we turn to the cases of South Korea and Taiwan it seems also that the foreign policy situation vis-a-vis North Korea and Communist China may have been the most important consideration for the leaders to give capitalism a chance. It would thus be of interest to hear the specialists' opinions on the reasons causing the rulers of South Korea and Taiwan to allow and even to further a capitalist development, limiting their own powers and thus indirectly motivating their populations to ask for more political rights and even for democratic regimes.

Finally "the Rise of the West" also has probably much to do with the international rivalry among states (NORTH and THOMAS [1973], NORTH [1981], JONES [1981]). As WEEDE [1987, 2] puts it, "European *disunity* has been our good luck." After the breakdown of the Roman Empire, feudalism with its many power centers developed and a split opened up between religious and temporal power (Pope and Emperor and Kings). A strong rivalry arose between these powers or emerging states and their rulers to gain, to preserve and to extend their powers. This forced European rulers to become interested in the well-being and loyalty of their subjects and above all in economic development to secure a greater tax base and thus stronger armies. But economic development in its turn depended on the development of adequate property rights and on free markets. As a consequence, competition among states forced on reluctant rulers a limitation of their domestic powers. The development of competing legal systems and the rule of law, of property rights and of due process of law was assisted not only by interstate competition but also by the separation of church and state, the prevention of a theocracy (BERMAN [1984]). Limited government and pluralistic society were thus a predemocratic achievement. They were not planned by anybody, but emerged and proved to be successful. First capitalism and later democracy were their progeny.

On the other hand, whether institutions maintaining capitalism for an indefinite future can be designed is still doubtful. A broad consensus of the population on some supreme values such as substantive equality, ecological, religious or ideological aims may develop and erode the rule of law and individual liberty, free markets and property. Or the self-interested call for state intervention may, in time, lead to a weakening of federalism, the division of power and (or) a reinterpretation of the constitution by courts and parliaments. Thus the Hobbesian problem is still with us, and may be similar to the squaring of the circle. No clear-cut solution may be possible but only an asymptotic approach to a solution by ever better institutional designs in the course of time. Here lies the merit of Weingast's paper.

References

BERMAN, H. J. [1982], *Law and Revolution*, Harvard University Press: Cambridge-London.

BERNHOLZ, P. [1980], "A General Social Dilemma: Profitable Exchange and Intransitive Group Preferences," *Zeitschrift für Nationalökonomie*, 40, 1–23.

–– [1982], "Expanding Welfare States, Democracy and Free Market Economy: Are They Compatible?," *Zeitschrift für die gesamte Staatswissenschaft, JITE*, 138 (3), 583–598.

–– [1992], "On the Political Economy of the Transformation of Political and Economical Regimes," Eighth Annual Lecture in the Virginia Political Economy Lecture Series, Center for Study of Public Choice, Fairfax, Virginia.

BORCHERDING, T. E. [1985], "The Causes of Government Expenditure Growth: A Survey of the U.S. Evidence," *Journal of Public Economics*, 28, 359–382.

CURTIS, M. (ed.) [1970], *The Great Political Theories*, Disus/Avon Books: New York.

ENCYCLOPAEDIA BRITANNICA [1966], published by W. Prenton: London-Chicago-Geneva-Sydney-Toronto.

HOBBES, T. [1970], "Leviathan," partly reprinted pp. 296–322 in: M. Curtis (ed.), *The Great Political Theories*, Disus/Avon Books: New York.

JONES, E. L. [1981], *The European Miracle*, Cambridge University Press: Cambridge.

LYBECK, J. A. [1986], *The Growth of Government in Developed Economies*, Gower: Hants.

MONTESQUIEU [1970], "The Spirit of the Laws," partly reprinted in: M. Curtis (ed.), *The Great Political Theories*, pp. 389–403, Disus/Avon Books: New York.

MÜLLER, D. C. [1979], *Public Choice*, Cambridge University Press: Cambridge-London-New York-Melbourne.

–– [1989], *Public Choice II*, Cambridge University Press: Cambridge-London-New York-Melbourne.

NEUE ZÜRCHER ZEITUNG [1984], December 13.

NORTH, D. C. [1981], *Structure and Change in History*, W. W. Norton: New York.
— and THOMAS, R. [1973], *The Rise of the Western World. A New Economic History*, Cambridge University Press: Cambridge.
RIKER, W. H. [1964], *Federalism: Origin, Operation, and Significance*, Little Brown: Boston.
TOCQUEVILLE, A. DE [1943], *Democracy in America*, Vintage Books/Random House: New York.
WEEDE, E. [1987], "From The Rise of the West to Eurosclerosis: Are There Lessons for the Pacific Region?," *Asian Culture Quarterly*, 15 (1), 1–14.
WEINGAST, B. [1993], "Constitutions as Governance Structures: The Political Foundations of Secure Markets," *Journal of Institutional and Theoretical Economics*, 149 (1), 286–311.

Professor Peter Bernholz
Institut für Volkswirtschaft
Universität Basel
Petersgraben 51
CH-4003 Basel
Switzerland

[16]

Contract Enforceability and Economic Institutions in Early Trade: The Maghribi Traders' Coalition

By Avner Greif[*]

This paper presents an economic institution which enabled 11th-century traders to benefit from employing overseas agents despite the commitment problem inherent in these relations. Agency relations were governed by a coalition — an economic institution in which expectations, implicit contractual relations, and a specific information-transmission mechanism supported the operation of a reputation mechanism. Historical records and a simple game-theoretical model are used to examine this institution. The study highlights the interaction between social and economic institutions, the determinants of business practices, the nature of the merchants' law, and the interrelations between market and nonmarket institutions. (JEL N75, D23, J41)

Without the ability to exchange, the potential for growth is rather limited. Indeed, the historical process of European economic growth is marked by ever-expanding exchange relations. The contribution of an enhanced ability to exchange went beyond its direct economic impacts as, for example, the late-medieval European commercial revolution from the 11th to the 14th centuries led to fundamental social and political changes (see e.g., Robert S. Lopez, 1976; Henri Pirenne, 1939, 1956). Yet not much is

known about the historical institutional developments that enabled exchange relations to expand, even though such knowledge can shed light on the nature and evolution of modern institutions and facilitate the understanding of the institutional transitions that developing economies still face.[1]

Few studies have attempted to examine analytically various aspects of the pre-modern institutional framework that supported exchange. Paul R. Milgrom et al. (1990) have argued that merchant courts at the Champagne fairs of the 12th and 13th centuries can be analyzed as an institution that supported impersonal exchange relations over time. It provided proper incentives for gathering information, honoring agreements, reporting disputes, and adhering to judgments. Moreover, by centralizing certain record-keeping functions and effectively permitting only merchants in good standing to remain at the fairs, this institution also achieved significant economies in transaction costs. The role of the European medieval *merchant guild* in enabling rulers to commit themselves to the security of alien

*Department of Economics, Stanford University, Stanford, CA 94305. This paper is a revised version of Chapter 2 of my dissertation, written under the supervision of J. Mokyr, J. Panzar, and W. Rogerson at Northwestern University. I thank them for their most helpful discussions and encouragement. I benefited from the encouragement, suggestions, and remarks of D. Aron, C. W. Calomiris, P. A. David, D. Klein, P. R. Milgrom, D. C. North, O. E. Williamson, and two anonymous referees. The participants of seminars held at Northwestern University, the University of California at Berkeley, the University of Chicago, the University of Texas at Austin, Stanford University, the Massachusetts Institute of Technology, Yale University, the University of Arizona at Tucson, the University of Michigan at Ann Arbor, and Washington University in St. Louis contributed helpful comments. Esther-Mirjam Sent's editorial assistance contributed to the exposition of the paper. The research was supported by a Sloan dissertation fellowship and NSF grant no. 9009598-01. The usual caveat applies.

[1]In their pathbreaking works Douglass C. North and Robert Paul Thomas (1973) and North (1981) have pointed to the historical relations between institutions and growth.

merchants has been examined in Greif et al. (1992). In the absence of such a commitment, merchants were not likely to frequent trading centers abroad—a costly outcome for both the rulers and the merchants. Bilateral and uncoordinated multilateral reputation mechanisms failed to overcome this commitment problem at the efficient level of trade, since, without supporting organizations, the cost to the ruler of abusing the rights of "marginal traders" was not high enough to deter abuse. The merchant guild increased this cost and enabled trade to expand to its efficient level by coordinating the responses of the merchants to transgression and by ensuring solidarity of incentives among the merchants.

This paper is concerned with an institution that surmounted a commitment problem intrinsic in the relations between merchants and their overseas agents. In pre-Modern trade, a merchant had to organize the supply of the services required for the handling of his goods abroad. He could either travel along with his merchandise between trade centers or hire overseas agents to supply the service. Employing agents was efficient, since it enabled the merchant to save the time and risk of traveling, to diversify his sales across trade centers, and so forth. Without supporting institutions, agency relations are not likely to be established, since the agents can act opportunistically and embezzle the merchant's goods. Anticipating this behavior, a merchant will not hire agents, and efficient cooperation is not initiated. The importance of this organizational problem for pre-Modern trade efficiency is reflected in the fact that the merchant–agent relations are present in all the main forms of business association employed during that time.

This paper examines the institution that enabled 11th-century Mediterranean traders to overcome this commitment problem.[2] An historical source found in Fustat (Old Cairo) known as the *geniza* ("deposit place" in

Hebrew) contains about a thousand contracts, price lists, traders' letters, accounts, and so forth, that reflect 11th-century trade in the Muslim Mediterranean.[3] These documents were written by Jewish traders, known as the Maghribi traders (the Maghrib is the Muslim world's West), who operated mainly, but not exclusively, in the western basin of the Mediterranean. The Maghribi traders had the custom of depositing in the *geniza* of a Fustatian synagogue every document that was written in Hebrew characters (Goitein, 1967a p. 149). Since they conducted their commercial correspondence in Judeo-Arabic (an Arabic dialect written in Hebrew characters) it is reasonable to conjecture that the documents found in the *geniza* contain a representative sample of their commercial correspondence.[4]

The hypothesis advanced in this paper is that agency relations among the Maghribi traders were governed by an institution that might be called a coalition. Expectations, implicit contractual relations, and a specific information-transmission mechanism constituted the constraints that affected an individual trader's choice of action. In particular, these constraints supported the operation of a reputation mechanism that enabled the Maghribis to overcome the commitment problem. In turn, the reputation mechanism reinforced the expectations on which the coalition was based, motivated traders to adhere to the implicit contracts, and led to entry and exit barriers which ensured the sustainability of the coalition. An examination of this coalition casts light on several related issues in this historical episode such as the determinants of business practices, the interactions between social and economic institutions, the nature of the Merchants' Law, and the role of history in institutional evolution.

Historical documents rarely lend themselves to institutional analysis, and the *geniza* is no exception. Furthermore, due to

[2] This paper is a part of an ongoing research project, the results of which are also presented in Greif (1989, 1990, 1992a,b). Greif (1989) is mainly an historical examination of the Maghribi traders' coalition.

[3] For an introduction to the *geniza*, see the introduction in Shelomo Dov Goitein (1967a); for the system of reference to a *geniza* document, see Goitein (1967a), Moshe Gil (1983b), or Greif (1989).

[4] On Judeo-Arabic, see Joshua Blau (1961, 1965).

its nature, the type of institutional analysis conducted here is not likely to generate hypotheses that can be verified statistically. Accordingly, this study employs the historical documents to evaluate the importance and attributes of the agents' commitment problem and then uses this information to construct an explicit game-theoretical model that captures the essence of this problem. Explicit statements from the historical records are utilized to identify the strategies used by the Maghribi traders. Once the equilibrium strategies are recognized, the model is extended to generate predictions about facts other than those assumed in the model that are reflected in the historical records. Confronting these predictions with the historical evidence supports the accuracy of the conjectures about the nature of the coalition and provides additional insights.

The rest of this paper is organized as follows. The first section provides the general background concerning trade and business associations among the Maghribi traders. Section II discusses the commitment problem that curtailed agency relations and the role of the reputation mechanism in circumventing this problem. Section III models the commitment problem and examines the efficiency of the strategies used by the Maghribi traders and whether they constitute an equilibrium. Section IV presents the coalition and employs the model to generate predictions that substantiate the claim that agency relations were governed by the coalition. Various aspects of the coalition are highlighted. Section V discusses the role of the Merchants' Law, and conclusions follow.

I. Commerce, Overseas Agents, and Efficiency

The *geniza* indicates that 11th-century Mediterranean trade was free, private, and competitive, with no official restrictions fettering migration or the transfer of raw materials, finished goods, or money across the Mediterranean (see Archibald R. Lewis, 1951 pp. 189–91; Goitein, 1967a pp. 29–35, 266–72; Gil, 1983b [Vol. 1] pp. 205–30). Within each trade center, commercial transactions were conducted competitively. In

bazaars and storehouses, buyers and sellers negotiated and competed over prices using brokers, open-bid auctions, and direct negotiation (Goitein, 1967a pp. 157, 187, 192–5). However, trade was characterized by uncertainty. Prices, for example, were subject to large variations as a result of the production and communication technologies of the period (see e.g., Dropsie 389, a, ll. 4–5, b, ll, 27–8 [Gil, 1983a pp. 113–25]) (see also Goitein, 1967a pp. 217–29, 301–5; Greif, 1985 p. 92). Commercial relations between different regions also contributed to price fluctuations, since all the countries around the Mediterranean constituted one trade region connected by sea and land caravans. Thus, changes affecting business in one country were felt abroad. However, price fluctuations were not the only factor that contributed to commercial uncertainty. It resulted also from uncertainty with respect to the duration of a ship's voyage, whether the ship would reach its destination, the condition in which the goods would arrive, the cost of storage, and so forth (see Goitein, 1967a pp. 148–61, 200–1, 273–322; Norman A. Stillman, 1970 pp. 70–88; Greif, 1985 pp. 3, 69–78).

Eleventh-century trade is reflected in the *geniza* through documents written by the Maghribi traders. These were the descendants of Jewish traders who left the increasingly politically insecure surroundings of Baghdad and emigrated to North Africa during the 10th century. Each of the several dozen traders mentioned in the documents invested in merchandise worth between several hundred and several thousand dinars —substantial sums considering that the monthly expenses of a middle-class family in Fustat were between two and three dinars (Goitein, 1967a pp. 214–17; Gil, 1983b [Vol. 1] pp. 200–30; Greif, 1985 pp. 73–6).[5] To cope with the uncertainty and complexity of trade, the Maghribi traders operated through *overseas agents*. An overseas agent is anyone who supplies the services required for a commercial venture while the capital,

---

[5]For expenses, see Goitein (1967a p. 46) and Gil (1983a p. 91).

profit, or both are shared with a merchant located in a different trade center. (Henceforth the term "merchant" will be used to denote an individual who receives the residual revenue after the agent receives his compensation. The term "trader" will refer to both agents and merchants.)

Agents provided merchants with many trade-related services, including loading and unloading the ship; paying the customs, bribes, and transportation fees; storing the goods; transferring the goods to the market; and deciding when, how, and to whom to sell the goods and at what price and at which credit terms (Goitein, 1967a p. 166). Agency relations among the Maghribis were extremely flexible, as merchants operated through several agents at the same time and even at the same trade center and seem to have been at ease initiating and canceling agency relations following the needs of their complex and uncertain occupation (see e.g., Stillman, 1980; Greif, 1985).

Agency relations enabled the Maghribi traders to reduce the cost of trade by better allocating risk through diversification, by benefiting from agents' expertise, and by shifting trade activities across trade centers, goods, and time. Agency relations enabled merchants to operate as sedentary traders, thus saving the cost and risk of the sea journey, and enabled traveling merchants to gain from relying on agents to handle the merchants' affairs in their absence (Greif, 1985, 1989; Goitein, 1967a).

The efficiency gain from operating through agents is impossible to assess quantitatively. However, the superiority of pre-Modern trade systems in which cooperation through overseas agents prevailed over those in which it did not has been recognized by many scholars (see Lopez and Irving W. Raymond, 1955 p. 174; Raymond De Roover, 1965 pp. 43, 45–6, 70–4; M. M. Postan, 1973 pp. 66–71). Furthermore, the Maghribi traders themselves perceived that operating through agents was crucial for business success. This is reflected in the extent to which they established agency relations and by traders' statements. For example, one trader wrote to his business associate who served as his overseas agent that "all profit occurring to me comes from

your pocket" (TS 13 J 25, f. 18 [Goitein, 1967a p. 164]), while another mentioned that in trade "people cannot operate without people" (DK 22, b, l. 18 [Gil, 1983a pp. 97–106]).[6]

II. The Commitment Problem and Reputation-Based Community Enforcement Mechanism

Agency relations among the Maghribis were characterized by a commitment problem. Efficiency was enhanced by letting an overseas agent transact business with capital he did not own. When the capital was in his possession, however, he could embezzle it. Without a supporting institution, merchants anticipating opportunistic behavior would not operate through agents; thus mutually beneficial exchanges would not be carried out. To gain from cooperation, there was a need for an institution capable of surmounting this commitment problem, an institution through which an agent could commit himself *ex ante*, before receiving the merchant's capital, to be honest *ex post*.[7]

The historical records implicitly indicate the existence of such an institution among the Maghribis, as agency relations were the rule rather than the exception. Further, agency relations as reflected in the *geniza* were characterized by the prevalence of trust. Despite the many opportunities for agents to cheat, only a handful of documents contain allegations of misconduct (see Goitein, 1973 p. 7).[8] How was the merchant–agent commitment problem resolved?

---

[6] For the extent of agency relations through business associations, see Murad Michael (1965) and Stillman (1970).

[7] Were a merchant to sell the benefits from a particular trade venture, or the "business" as a whole to an overseas agent, he would have to become the agent. Selling it to a local agent meant losing the advantages of an overseas agency.

[8] Misconduct is mentioned in less than 5 percent of the approximately 250 documents examined for this study. This was not the case in Italy, where allegations of misconduct are well reflected in the historical records (e.g., De Roover, 1965 pp. 88–9).

There are situations in which a legal system surmounts a commitment problem. The historical evidence, however, suggests that this was not the case among the Maghribi traders. Many, if not most, of the agency relations in the *geniza* were not based on legal contracts. Only a few documents indicate that commercial disputes between merchants and agents were brought before the court, and the operation of the court in these cases seems to have been time-consuming and expensive (see Bodl. MS Heb., a3 f. 26 [Goitein, 1973 p. 97]). For example, sometime around the turn of the 11th century Hillel ben Isaac served as an agent for Nahum al-Hazan. About half a century later, in 1065, Nahum's two grandsons applied to the court, suing Hillel for what they claimed he still owed their late grandfather. In their letter they mentioned that they had "nominated Rabbi Maşli'ah some time ago" to represent them in court, a nomination that probably took place sometime before 1038 (TS 10 J 4, f. 3 [Greif, 1985 appendix, pp. 5–7]).[9] Furthermore, the court also faced difficulties in tracking down agents who emigrated (Moshe Maimonides, 1951 p. 210; Goitein, 1967a p. 439 [note 39]).

Most likely, the legal system was not used to mitigate the merchant–agent commitment problem, mainly due to the asymmetric information that characterized agency relations. Because of the complexity and uncertainty of long-distance commerce, the outcome of a commercial transaction depended on many realizations that could not be directly observed either by the merchant or by the legal system (Greif, 1989). Further, since the timing of ships' departures depended on weather conditions, a report concerning the results of commercial transaction sent by an agent reached the merchant a few months after the transaction

had taken place. Hence, a merchant who believed that he had been cheated could only sue the agent several months after the transaction had been completed. How could the court, several months later, verify the condition of the goods upon their arrival, the price received for the goods, the amount of the bribe given in the port, the cost of delivery, whether the goods were stolen from the agent's warehouse, and so forth?[10] Furthermore, the Jewish law restricts the ability to sue agents. For example, an agent entrusted to buy certain items cannot be sued for "bringing [to the merchant] an item worth 1 [dinar] for [which he charges the merchant] 100 [dinars]" (Maimonides, 1951 p. 208) (see additional discussion in Greif [1989]). Indeed, in 1095 an agent who received 70 dinars reported that he had lost all but 20 dinars. The furious merchant, although certain that he had been cheated, was unable to sue the agent since his claim did not have any legal base (TS 13 J 2, f. 5 [Goitein, 1967a p. 176]).

The conviction of the furious merchant that the agent had cheated him was, most likely, based on information which enabled him to monitor the agent imperfectly. A Maghribi merchant was associated with many Maghribi traders residing in different trade centers, and it was customary to reciprocate in the supply of trade-related information that was so crucial to business success.[11] Reciprocity, most likely, prevented "free-riding" on these information flows. (see e.g., TS 20.76; TS 13 J 15, f. 9 [Goitein, 1973 pp. 113–19, 320–2]; TS 10 J 11, f. 22, a, ll. 11–12 [Goitein, 1967a pp. 195, 201–9]; Greif, 1985 pp. 95 [note 60], 133). These information flows within the Maghribis traders group, as well as a merchant's experience, circumvented to some extent the

---

[9] For other examples, see Bodl. MS. Heb. f. 42 (S. Poznanski, 1904 pp. 171–2), TS 20.152 and Bodl. MS Heb. a3 f. 9 (Gil, 1983b [Vol. 2] pp. 724–32), and Bodl. MS Heb., a3 f. 26 (Goitein, 1973 p. 97). On Rabbi Maşli'ah and the timing of his nomination, see Greif (1985). For a similar situation in 15th-century Italy, see De Roover (1965 p. 88).

[10] For the dependency of a trade venture's outcome on these factors see, for example, TS 20.122, b. 1. 10; Dropsie 389, a, ll. 21–3 (Gil, 1983a pp. 113–25); TS 10 J 10, f. 30, ll. 11–12 (Gil, 1983b [Vol. 3] p. 193); Bodl. MS Heb. a3, f. 26 (Goitein, 1973 p. 98 [section B]); and note 62 in Greif (1985 p. 96).

[11] For the importance of information flow for commercial success see, for example, Dropsie 389, a, ll. 2–4 [Gil, 1983a pp. 113–25], Michael (1965) and Gil (1983b [Vol. 3] pp. 96–101).

asymmetric information between merchants and agents and enabled the former to monitor the latter (see e.g., DK 22, a, ll. 11, ff. [Gil, 1983 pp. 97–106]; ULC Or 1080 J 42 [Gil, 1983b (Vol. 3) p. 300]; TS Box Misc 28, f. 225 [Gil, 1983b (Vol. 3) pp. 96–101]). The ability to monitor, however, was most likely imperfect in the sense that a merchant could also be mistaken in concluding that his agent was dishonest. For example, around the middle of the century Maymun ben Khalpha of Palermo sent a letter to Naharay ben Nissim of Fustat. Discussing a conflict that Neharay had with one of his agents, Maymun makes clear that in contrast to Naharay he contends that the agent was honest and should not be accused of cheating (DK 22, b [Gil, 1983a]).

The theory of repeated games with imperfect monitoring illuminates how a commitment problem can be surmounted in the absence of an effective legal system. According to the theory of repeated games, by paying an agent a wage "high" enough during each period he is known to be honest, and by making future employment conditional on past conduct, a merchant can insure that the present value of the lifetime expected utility of an honest agent is larger than what the agent can obtain by cheating and facing the prospect of being unemployed. Hence, the best the agent can do, *ex post*, is to be honest. Since this is known, *ex ante*, to the merchant, he can trust his agent, and the agent acquires a reputation for honesty.[12] There are situations, however, in which the maximum punishment imposed by an individual merchant is not sufficient to enable the agent to commit himself, and a collective punishment may be necessary to

support cooperation.[13] When the actions taken by the agents can be only imperfectly monitored, however, there is a positive probability that an agent, although honest, will be considered a cheater. To sustain cooperation it may be optimal to punish the agent for a specific period of time during which he collaborates in his own punishment (see Edward Green and Robert Porter, 1984; Dilip Abreu et al., 1986, 1990; Drew Fudenberg et al., 1989; Abreu et al., 1991) (for an excellent recent survey, see David G. Pearce [1991]).

The *geniza* contains several documents that explicitly reflect the Maghribi traders' responses to suspicions that an agent had cheated a merchant. These documents suggest (i) that a reputation mechanism governed agency relations and, in particular, that merchants conditioned future employment on past conduct, practiced community punishment, and ostracized agents who were considered cheaters until they compensated the injured and (ii) that agents were ready to forgive current gain to sustain their good standing in the merchants' group. Since this evidence has been presented in detail somewhere else (Greif, 1989), a few examples will suffice here.

Around 1055 it became known in Fustat that Abun ben Zedaka, an agent who lived in Jerusalem, embezzled the money of a Maghribi trader. The response of the Maghribi traders was to cease any commercial relations with him. His bitter letter indicates that merchants as far away as Sicily had ostracized him. Only after a compromise was achieved and he had compensated the offended merchant were commercial relations with him resumed (TS 13 J 25, f. 12; TS 12.279; see also TS 8 J 19, f. 23 [Gil, 1983b (Vol. 3) pp. 218–33]. About 50 years earlier, in the first decade of the 11th century, Samhun ben Da'ud, a prominent trader from Tunisia, sent a long letter to his business associate, Joseph ben 'Awkal of Fustat.

[12]Roughly speaking, a player's reputation is a function from past history to a probability distribution over his strategies. See discussion and applications in Philip Nelson (1974), Benjamin Klein and Keith B. Leffler (1981), Paul R. Milgrom and John Roberts (1982), Carl Shapiro (1983), Paul L. Joskow (1984 p. 14), Shapiro and Joseph E. Stiglitz (1984), Oliver E. Williamson (1985 pp. 121, 138), George Akerlof and Janet Yellen (1986), and David M. Kreps (1990a).

[13]For the theory of collective enforcement, see Jonathan Bendor and Dilip Mookherjee (1990), Masahiro Okuno-Fujiwara and Andrew Postlewaite (1990), and Michihiro Kandori (1992).

The letter says that Joseph made his future dealings with Samhun conditional upon his record: "If your handling of my business is correct, then I shall send you goods." It happened, however, that Samhun did not handle Joseph's business to his satisfaction —Joseph believed that Samhun had intentionally not remitted his revenues on time. Joseph's response was to impose economic sanctions against Samhum by ignoring Samhum's request to pay two of Samhun's creditors in Fustat. By the time Samhun found out about it "their letters filled with condemnation had reached everyone." The content of these letters caused Samhun to complain that "my reputation (or honor) is being ruined" (DK 13, a. ll. 26–9 [Stillman, 1970 pp. 267–75]; Goitein, 1973 pp. 26–34).

Around the middle of the century, Khalluf ben Musa described how he had handled the sale of two loads of pepper—one of his own and the other belonging to another merchant. The pepper price was very low, and therefore "[I] held it until the time when the sailing of the ships approached in the hope it would rise. However, the slump got worse. Then I was afraid that suspicion might arise against me and I sold your pepper to Spanish merchants for 133 [quarter dinars].... It was the night before the sailing of the ships—pepper became much in demand...[since] boats [with buyers] arrived...I...[sold] my pepper at 140–142. But brother, I would not like to take the profit for myself. Therefore, I transferred the entire sale to our partnership." To prevent suspicion, the agent preferred to sell the merchant's pepper early and hence received for it much less than he later received for his pepper. To compensate the merchant, he shared the gain and the loss with him. He did not behave this way, however, out of concern for his future relations with that specific merchant. His letter is explicit about his desire not to serve as an agent for this merchant in the future (Bodl. MS Heb., a3 f. 13 [Goitein, 1973 p. 123]).

Finally, the *geniza* indicates that, if an agent who had been accused of cheating were to receive agency services from other Maghribi traders, they could cheat him free from community retaliation. The words of a

Tunisian merchant who was accused in 1041–1042 of cheating exemplify this. That merchant complains that when it became known that he had cheated, "people became agitated and hostile to [me] and whoever owed [me money] conspired to keep it from [me] (Bodl. MS Heb., a2 f. 17, section D [Goitein, 1973 p. 104]; see also Greif, 1989).

Agency relations among the Maghribi traders were characterized by a commitment problem in the presence of asymmetric information regarding agents' conduct. The evidence suggests that information flows among the Maghribis mitigated information asymmetry and enabled merchants to monitor their agents imperfectly. The theory of repeated games with imperfect monitoring indicates that cooperation in agency relations could have been sustained by conditioning future patterns of cooperation on the history of the relations. Indeed, the historical records indicate the operation of an informal community enforcement mechanism that was based on this principle.

Yet, many questions should be addressed: Why was the community punishment self-enforcing? Why was a boycott effective? Why was it not undermined by agents' ability to seek employment by non-Maghribis? Why was the merchants' commitment to future employment of honest agents credible despite the (potential) temptation to hire non-Maghribi agents? What was the mechanism that coordinated punishment? After all, for a collective punishment to be effective, there must be a consensus about which actions constitute "cheating." In short, what was the exact nature of the institution that governed agency relations? The formal model presented in the next section provides the foundation for addressing this issue.

III. Model: The Agent Commitment Problem and Multilateral Punishment Strategy

Constructing a model aimed at facilitating the examination of the actual functioning of a contract-enforcement institution in a specific historical episode presents a methodological problem. Should the assumptions concerning the basics of the model be restricted only to those reflected in the historical records? Or is any assumption about the model which does not conflict with the evidence legitimate? The approach taken in this paper is that the model should be based, to the extent possible, on assumptions justifiable by the historical evidence, and the model that can account for the phenomena under consideration with the fewest additional assumptions should be used.

Thus, the model presented below does not impose the assumption that generates what is arguably the most intuitive explanation for collective punishment; that is, that merchants perceived an agent who cheated to be of a "bad type" who would keep on cheating in the future if hired.[14] There is nothing in the evidence that directly justifies such an assumption or indirectly justifies it by indicating that an agent who had proved himself honest in the past was considered to be more likely to be honest in the future. On the contrary, there is evidence suggesting that merchants were likely to participate in collective punishment even when they believed that the agent was honest. In Maymun's letter, mentioned above, he makes clear that he believes that Naharay's agent was honest and "should not be accused [of cheating]...." Yet, Maymun feared that if the agent would be openly accused it would affect his relations with the agent, presumably since Maymun would have to participate in a collective punishment: "You know that he is our [the Maghribi traders'] representative..., [so the conflict] bothers us all (DK 22, b, ll. 5–17 [Gil, 1983a pp. 97–106]).[15]

Further, a model based on agents' types seems unable to provide a satisfactory explanation for some historical phenomena. For example, as discussed below, the Maghribis did not hold agency relations with

Jewish Italian merchants although, ignoring agency cost, these were perceived by the Maghribis to be very profitable. A model based on agents' types can account for this behavior, but this requires either imposing strategies contingent on social affiliations or else assuming that members of one group could not verify whether a specific member of the other group ever cheated (i.e., that a non-Maghribi could not "free-ride" on the information generated among the Maghribis by observing actions). Neither possibility is appealing. There is no reason to believe that these Jews "discriminated" against each other, and whether a specific individual was serving as an agent could easily be verified since merchants could examine a ship's cargo, its ownership, and its destination (see Goitein, 1967a pp. 336–7).

Whatever the importance of asymmetric information regarding agents' types in accounting for the collective punishment practiced by the Maghribis, an efficiency-wage complete-information model of the agent's commitment problem indicates that there is another mechanism which can support collective punishment and account for other historical phenomena.[16] In this model, the collective punishment is feasible due to the availability of information, and it is self-enforcing due to a link between expectations with respect to future hiring and the stream of rent required to keep an agent honest. To simplify the presentation of the insights generated by this model, it abstracts away from imperfect monitoring.[17]

---

[14]On this mechanism, see, for example, Kreps (1990a) and Milgrom and Roberts (1982).

[15]Similar considerations led to the rejection of a model in which costly participation in collective punishment is supported since nonparticipation provokes retaliation (e.g., David G. Pearce, 1991; Kandori, 1992).

[16]For efficiency wage models, see, for example, Shapiro and Stiglitz (1984) and Akerlof and Yellen (1986).

[17]To capture the asymmetry and imperfectness of information, as well as commercial uncertainty, the model presented here can be extended as follows. The revenue is observed only by the agent and is a random variable x with domain $[a, b]$. The agent reports a revenue realization $y \in [a, b]$. A wage is a contract which is a function of the agent's report, $w:[a, b] \to [a, b]$ $w(y) \le y$ $\forall y$. The merchant observes the actual realization in probability $f(y, x)$ where $1 > f(\cdot) > 0$, $\forall y \ne x$ (information asymmetry), and $f(\cdot) > 0$ when $x = y$ (imperfect monitoring).

Consider a perfect and complete information economy in which there are M merchants and A agents, each of whom lives an infinite number of periods. Further, assume that $M > A$ and that agents have a time discount factor δ. In each period, a merchant can hire an agent from the pool of unemployed agents, and each agent can be hired by only one merchant. A merchant who does not hire an agent receives a payoff of $\kappa > 0$. A merchant who hires an agent offers him a wage W. An employed agent can decide whether to be honest or to cheat. If he is honest, the merchant's payoff is $\gamma - W$, and the agent's payoff is W. (Hence, the gross gain from cooperation is γ.) If the agent cheats, however, his payoff is α and the merchant's payoff is 0. After the allocation of the payoffs, the merchant can decide whether to terminate his relations with that agent or not. There is also the possibility that the merchant is forced to terminate the relation due to some exogenous reason, an event that can occur in each period with probability τ. An agent who is unemployed during some period receives the reservation utility, $\bar{w} \geq 0$. It is assumed that $\gamma > \kappa + \bar{w}$ (cooperation is efficient), $\gamma > \alpha > \bar{w}$ (cheating entails a loss, and an agent prefers cheating over receiving his reservation utility), and $\kappa > \gamma - \alpha$ (a merchant prefers operating by himself if the agent is to cheat him or to receive a wage α).

While the above formulation captures the essence of the agent's commitment problem, some elaboration on its details is in order. A merchant could initiate agency relations, and since an employed agent held the merchant's capital, he was assured of receiving his wage. The need to shift commercial operations over places and goods and the high uncertainty of commerce and life during the 11th century curtailed a merchant's ability to commit himself to future wages or employment. Hence, the model assumes a stationary wage scheme (which was indeed practiced among the Maghribis) and a limited ability to commit to future employment. Like any other economic agents, the Maghribi traders did not enjoy an infinite lifespan. The results obtained from this infinite-horizon model, however,

are equivalent to those obtained from a finite-horizon model with a constant probability of termination. Furthermore, among the Maghribi traders, relatives were considered morally responsible for each other's business dealings, and traders' sons followed their fathers' occupation and were their old-age "insurance policies" (see Goitein, 1973 p. 60).[18] Hence, the value of one's reputation did not diminish with old age.

Consider a *multilateral punishment strategy* (MPS) according to which a merchant offers an agent a wage W^*, rehires the same agent if he has been honest (unless forced separation has occurred), fires the agent if he has cheated, never hires an agent who has ever cheated any merchant, and (randomly) chooses an agent from among the unemployed agents who never have cheated if forced separation has occurred. An agent's strategy calls for being honest if paid W^* and for cheating if paid less than W^*. Is MPS a subgame-perfect equilibrium (SGPE)? Will a merchant retaliate against an agent who has not cheated him?

To address these questions the wage, W^*, that will be offered by the merchants should be determined. For this aim, denote by h_h the probability that an unemployed honest agent (i.e., an agent who was honest when last employed) will be rehired and by h_c the probability that an unemployed cheater (i.e., an agent who cheated when last employed) will be rehired. Proposition 1 presents the relations between the lowest wage for which an agent's best response is to be honest and the above parameters.[19]

PROPOSITION 1: *Assume that $\delta \in (0,1)$, $h_c < 1$, and $h_c \leq h_h$. The optimal wage, the lowest wage for which it is an agent's best*

---

[18]Goitein (1978 pp. 33–4) noted that "both the government and public opinion were prone to hold a father, brother, or even more distant relative responsible for a man's commitments, although strict law, both Islamic and Judaic, did not recognize such a claim."

[19]This specification enables the examination of the optimal wage under both MPS and the bilateral punishment strategy discussed in Section IV.

response to play honest, is $W^* = w(\delta, h_h, h_c, \tau, \overline{w}, \alpha) > \overline{w}$, and w is monotonically decreasing in δ and h_h and monotonically increasing in h_c, τ, $\overline{w}$, and α.[20]

PROOF:

To show that an agent cannot gain from playing cheat one period if offered W^*, denote by V_h the present value of lifetime expected utility of an employed agent who, whenever hired, plays honest. Denote by V_h^u the present value of the lifetime expected utility of an unemployed honest agent. Denote by V_c^u the lifetime expected utility of an unemployed cheater (who will be playing honest in the future if hired). These lifetime expected utilities are

$$V_h = W^* + \delta(1 - \tau)V_h + \tau V_h^u$$

$$V_i^u = \delta h_i V_h + \delta(1 - h_i)(\overline{w} + V_i^u) \quad i = h, c.$$

Cheating once yields $\alpha + V_c^u$, and hence an agent will not cheat if $V_h \geq \alpha + V_c^u$. Substituting and rearranging yields that an agent's best response is playing honest if and only if

$$W \geq (T - \delta\tau H_h)[\alpha/(1 - \delta H_c)$$

$$+ \delta\overline{w}(P_c/(1 - \delta H_c) - \tau P_h)]$$

$$= W^*$$

where

$$T = 1 - \delta(1 - \tau)$$

$$H_i = h_i/[1 - \delta(1 - h_i)] \qquad i = h, c$$

$$P_i = (1 - h_i)/[1 - \delta(1 - h_i)] \qquad i = h, c.$$

The properties of w can be derived directly from this expression.

Under MPS, an agent is motivated to be honest by the carrot of a premium over his reservation utility and the stick of firing. If

[20]More exactly, this monotonicity is weak in some neighborhoods of the extreme values of the parameters.

the induced difference between the present values of the lifetime expected utility of an unemployed and employed agent is higher than the one-period gain from cheating, the best response of an agent is to be honest. Hence, the optimal wage decreases as an honest agent is more likely to receive future wage premiums (higher h_h), can gain less by cheating (lower α), is more likely to remain employed if he is honest (lower τ), has worse opportunities elsewhere (lower $\overline{w}$), and has a smaller chance of being hired if he is a cheater (lower h_c). Further, the optimal wage decreases as an agent values future income more (higher δ), since rewarding for honesty and punishing for cheating is done in the future.

For the MPS to constitute a symmetric SGPE, each merchant should find it optimal to hire agents. On the equilibrium path this condition amounts to a wage low "enough," that is,

$$W^* = w(\cdot, h_c, h_h) \leq \gamma - \kappa$$

where $h_c = 0$, and $h_h = \tau M/[A - (1 - \tau)M]$. Assume that this condition holds. Will a merchant find it optimal to retaliate against an agent who did not cheat him? When switching agents does not impose any cost —as was assumed here—merchants may as well punish a cheater, and hence the MPS is an SGPE. Having the credibility of multilateral punishment rest on a knife-edge result, however, is unsatisfactory. Clearly, Maymun ben Khalpha considered punishing the Sicilian agent to be costly. Therefore, a more relevant question is whether the multilateral punishment strategy motivates a merchant to *strictly* prefer hiring an honest agent rather than a cheater.

As Proposition 2 demonstrates formally, a merchant strictly prefers to hire an honest agent under the MPS, merely since a cheater is not expected to be hired by other merchants. An honest agent is expected to be hired in the future, but an agent who has ever cheated is not. Since the optimal wage decreases in the probability of future hiring, a cheater's optimal wage is higher than an honest agent's wage, and hence each merchant strictly prefers to hire an honest agent.

It is the uncoordinated response of all the merchants and the interrelations between their expected future behavior and an agent's optimal wage as perceived by an individual merchant that insures solidarity of incentives. The possibility of forced separation links the optimal wage that a specific merchant has to pay his agent and the agent's expected future relations with other merchants, and it is this link that increases the optimal cheater's wage above an honest agent's wage, since punishments are independent from the agent's past conduct while rewards are not. Hence, merchants follow the multilateral punishment *despite* the fact that the agent's strategy does not call for cheating any merchant who violated the collective punishment, and *despite* the fact that cheating in the past does not indicate that the agent is a "lemon." Hence, it is reasonable that Maymun was concerned about Naharay's interpretation of his agent's actions because open accusation would have initiated an uncoordinated response that would have affected Maymun's business with that agent.

PROPOSITION 2: *Assume that* $\delta \in (0,1)$ *and* $h_c < 1$. *Under MPS a merchant strictly prefers to hire an honest agent.*

PROOF:

Under MPS the probability that an agent who has ever cheated would be rehired if he cheated or was honest this period and became unemployed is $h_c^c = h_c^h = 0$. The same probabilities for an agent who has never cheated before are $h_c^h = 0$ and $h_h^h = \tau M / [A - (1 - \tau)M] > 0$, respectively. The optimal wage for a cheater is $W_c^* = w(\cdot, h_h^c = 0, h_c^c = 0)$, and the optimal wage for a honest agent is $W_h^* = w(\cdot, h_h^h > 0, h_c^c = 0)$. Hence, since $h_c \leq h_h$ for cheaters and honest agents, Proposition 1 implies that $W_c^* > W_h^*$.[21]

[21]For this proof it is sufficient that players can recognize cheaters and honest agents. On the role of "social labels" in random matching games see Okuno-Fujiwara and Postlewaite (1990) and Kandori (1992).

IV. The Maghribi Traders Coalition: Theory and History

The historical anecdotes presented above indicate that collective punishment of a specific nature facilitated by a network of information transmission was practiced among the Maghribis. Theory indicates the importance of expectations concerning future hiring in making the collective punishment credible. Hence, history and theory lend support to the main hypothesis of this paper, namely, that agency relations among the Maghribis were governed by a *coalition*, which is defined as a group of traders whose member merchants are expected to hire only member agents, and these agency relations are governed by MPS. Furthermore, if an agent who has been caught cheating operates as a merchant, coalition agents who cheat him are not subject to collective retaliation (i.e., they are not considered by other members to have cheated). Finally, an internal informal information-transmission mechanism enables merchants to monitor agents and makes cheating known to all.

The Maghribi traders' letters directly support the above hypothesis by indicating that the Maghribis practiced MPS, that an agent who cheated a cheater was not subject to MPS, and that the Maghribis shared the appropriate information-transmission mechanism. Yet, can the hypothesis be further substantiated? Can a coherent explanation of historical observations be advanced based on the assumption that a coalition governed agency relations? Can predictions based on this assumption be generated and confirmed by the historical records?

Indeed, the historical records are rich in facts that should be explained. The Maghribis were the descendants of merchants who lived in the Abbasid Caliphate centered in Baghdad until the first half of the 10th century, when they emigrated for political reasons mainly to Tunisia (Gil, 1983b [Vol. 1] pp. 215–16; Greif, 1985 pp. 124–7). This area prospered at the time, under the control of the Fatimid caliphate. As time passed, the Maghribi traders extended their trade from Spain to Constantinople. While the agency relations required for this expansion could have been established with non-Maghribi traders (Jewish or Muslim), evidence of such relations is rare. Instead, members of the Maghribi traders' group emigrated abroad and during the 11th century one finds Maghribi traders who emigrated from Tunisia to other trade centers in the Muslim world such as Spain, Sicily, Egypt, and Palestine. Members of these colonies kept agency relations for generations with the descendants of other Maghribi traders (Goitein, 1967a pp. 156–9, 186–92; Gil 1983b [Vol. 1] pp. 200–29; Greif, 1985 pp. 124–7).

Since the Maghribis adopted the customs and language of the Muslim world, emigration outside the Muslim sphere of influence was culturally and materially difficult. Indeed, the Maghribis did not emigrate to the emerging trade centers of Italy despite the Maghribis' perception that trade with the Christian world was most profitable. This perception is reflected, for example, in the words of a merchant from Palermo, Sicily, who complained around 1035 that even the Rums (i.e., in this case, Christians from the Latin world) were not ready to buy the inferior black ginger! (Dropsie 389, b, ll. 6–7 [Goitein, 1967a p. 45]) (see also Bodl. MS Heb. C 28 f. 11, ll. 11–13). Despite the perceived profitability of this trade, Maghribi traders did not establish agency relations with the Italian Jewish traders who were active during this period. The communities within which the Maghribi traders operated held communal ties with the Italian Jewish communities, and there were no political restrictions that could have hindered cooperation between the Maghribis and the Italian Jews. Yet the documents never reflect agency relations between the Maghribis and Jewish traders from the Christian world (e.g., TS 8 Ja I, f. 5 [Goitein, 1973 pp. 44–5]; see also Goitein, 1973 pp. 44, 211; Greif, 1989).

In the trade centers to which the Maghribi traders emigrated, a well-established Jewish community already existed, and Maghribi traders integrated into the existing communal structural. Yet they preserved their separate social identity as long as they were active in long-distance trade. Their separate social identity is reflected in the documents in which they are referred to as "our people, the Maghribis the travelers (traders)" (Goitein, 1967a pp. 30–4, 148–9, 157; Gil, 1971 pp. 12–15, 1983b [Vol. 1] pp. 215, 223; Greif, 1985 p. 153 [note 32]) (see e.g., DK 13, section G, F [Goitein, 1973 p. 32]; TS Box Misc. 25, f. 106, a, l. 9 [Gil, 1983b [Vol. 2] p. 734]; TS 13 J 26, f. 24, b, ll. 3–5; TS Box Misc. 25, f. 106, l. 9 [Gil, 1983b (Vol. 2) pp. 601, 734]). The Maghribis operated in the Mediterranean during the 11th century until the Italian naval and military supremacy drove the traders out from the Muslim world. Then they turned to the Indian Ocean trade until toward the end of the 12th century when they were forced by the Muslim rulers of Egypt to withdraw.[22] At that point they integrated within the Jewish communities and vanished from the stage of history.

The above historical observations raise intriguing questions. Why were seemingly profitable agency relations with non-Maghribis not established? How can the governance of agency relations by a coalition and the possibility of establishing an agency with nonmembers be reconciled? After all, this possibility seems to undermine the foundations of the coalition. It undermines the member merchants' commitment to hire honest member agents in the future, and it undermines the effectiveness of the collective punishment since agents can potentially enter agency relations with nonmember merchants. Why then was the coalition sustainable? To support the hypothesis that a coalition governed agency relations, the issue of relations with non-Maghribis should be explained by or reconciled with the hypothesis. Furthermore, can theoretical insights relate the Maghribis' immigration to Tunisia and the emergence of the coalition and also account for the fact that the Maghribis retained their social identity only as long as they were active in long-distance trade?

---

[22] For their trade in the Indian ocean, see Goitein (1958) and Walter J. Fischel (1958); Goitein's unpublished *India Book* contains further information.

To address these questions there is a need to examine the relations between coalition and efficiency. A coalition enhances efficiency relative to a situation in which agency relations are governed by the *bilateral punishment strategy* (BPS) usually considered in the efficiency-wage literature (e.g., Shapiro and Stiglitz, 1984). This strategy is identical to the MPS except that merchants do not condition their hiring on past conduct (because they do not have information regarding past actions, because they do not expect others to make hiring conditional on that information, or because they do not observe the wage paid to the agent and believe that cheating reflects underpayment). Under BPS, merchants would not hire agents in situations in which they would hire agents under MPS. Consider, for example, the case in which each merchant can commit himself to hire an agent for only one period ($\tau = 1$). Under BPS, for any finite wage, agents will cheat. Hence agents are never hired. Under MPS, however, an agent takes into account the consequences of cheating a particular merchant in terms of future employment with other merchants. Hence, the optimal wage will be finite and may be low enough to support cooperation. Proposition 3 indicates that, in general, MPS supports cooperation when BPS fails due to the limited ability of each merchant to commit himself to rehire an honest agent by decreasing the probability that a cheater will be rehired, h_c.

PROPOSITION 3: *For ease of presentation, suppose that the agents' time discount factor* (δ) *approaches* 1. *Define a to be the ratio of agents to merchants, that is,* $a = A/M$. *Recall that* $\overline{w} < \alpha$ *and* $a > 1$. *Given a, cooperation is feasible for all* $\tau \in [0,1]$, *if and only if* $\gamma - \kappa \geq (a-1)\overline{w} + \alpha + \varepsilon$ $\forall \varepsilon > 0$ *under BPS, but if and only if* $\gamma - \kappa \geq a\overline{w} + \varepsilon$ $\forall \varepsilon > 0$ *under MPS. Given* τ, *cooperation is feasible for all* $a \geq 1$ *if and only if* $\gamma - \kappa \geq \alpha + \varepsilon$ $\forall \varepsilon > 0$ *under BPS, but if and only if* $\gamma - \kappa \geq \overline{w} + \varepsilon$ $\forall \varepsilon > 0$ *under MPS.*

PROOF:

Take the limits of W^* as δ goes to 1 using the fact that $h_c = h_h = \tau M/[A-(1-\tau)M]$ under BPS, and that $h_c = 0$ and $h_h =$ $\tau M/[A-(1-\tau)M]$ under MPS. Finally, use the relations between W^* and the appropriate parameters as specified in Proposition 1 to take the appropriate limits.

MPS enhances efficiency, since it enables cooperation when each merchant's ability to commit to future hiring is rather limited. Furthermore, as long as the ability of a merchant to commit to future hiring is less than perfect, coalition decreases the optimal wage, W^*, relative to the situation in which BPS governs agency relations. This reduction reflects a decrease in the probability that a cheater will be hired, h_c, and an increase in the probability that an honest agent will be hired (h_h), which is due to the restriction of agency relations to a specific subset of the agents' group. This wage reduction further enhances efficiency by making agency relations profitable in situations in which the total gain from cooperation is relatively low (γ is small). While in such cases cooperation is efficient, it will be initiated only if it is profitable to a merchant, that is, only if $W^* \leq \gamma - \kappa$. Since the optimal wage under MPS is lower than under BPS, more cooperation will be initiated. The wage reduction and the enhanced efficiency imply that organizing agency relations in a coalition increases member merchants' profits and may, at the same time, increase the lifetime expected utility of a coalition-member honest agent relative to a situation in which agency relations were governed by BPS.

Efficiency gains generated by a coalition encourage its emergence, while the coalition rewards member merchants and agents in a manner which encourages agency relations among coalition members. Hence, by affecting efficiency and profitability, the sustainability of a coalition can be assured: member merchants are motivated to establish agency relations with member agents, while the latter are better off being employed by member merchants.

Additional factors also contribute to the sustainability of a coalition. Expectations with respect to future hiring, the nature of the networks for information transmission, and strategic considerations discourage members from initiating agency relations with nonmembers and discourage nonmembers from initiating agency relations with members. To illustrate the impact of these factors, consider an economy in which two identical coalitions emerge. By definition, coalition members are not expected to establish intercoalition agency relations. Will these expectations be self-enforcing? A merchant will initiate intercoalition agency relations only if it is expected that the other coalition's merchants will use MPS against a member agent who cheated a nonmember merchant. Otherwise, the merchant strictly prefers to establish intracoalition agency relations, since the optimal wage in intercoalition agency relations is $w(\cdot, h_c = h_h > 0)$, which is, by Proposition 1, strictly higher than the optimal wage in intracoalition agency relations, $w(\cdot, h_c = 0, h_h > 0)$. For this wage differential to exist, it is sufficient that the merchant is uncertain whether MPS will be applied in intercoalition relations.[23]

A merchant is likely to be uncertain whether MPS will be applied in intercoalition relations due to information barriers between coalitions and strategic considerations. Within a coalition, each trader is known to others, and this enables informal information flows that the agent does not control to facilitate monitoring and to inform traders about cheating. In intercoalition agency relations, however, this mechanism does not function. Furthermore, coalition members are strategically motivated to ignore an outsider's accusations concerning the conduct of a coalition member agent. If the coalition members simply

"take the word" of an outsider, an agent is vulnerable to blackmail by nonmembers, which reduces his lifetime expected utility as an honest agent. This reduction comes at the expense of member merchants, since it increases the optimal wage. Hence, coalition members find it optimal to ignore an outsider's accusations. In contrast, insiders' accusations are not likely to be ignored since they can be assessed more accurately and since, when accusing an agent, an insider merchant puts his own reputation on the line. "Had I listened to what people say," wrote Khalluf ben Musa to his partner in response to the accusation that he had retained revenues received for the partner's goods, "I never would have entered into a partnership with you" (Bodl. MS Heb. a 3, f. 13, section B [Goitein, 1973 p. 121]) (see also DK 13, section G; ULC Or 1080 J 48; Bodl. MS Heb. a2 f. 17 [Goitein, 1973 pp. 32, 92–3, 103]; Goitein, 1967a pp. 168, 196; Greif, 1985 p. 143).

As MPS does not apply in intercoalition relations, the wage required to keep an agent honest in intercoalition agency relations is higher than the intracoalition wage. Hence, merchants are discouraged from establishing intercoalition agency relations, and the expectations that intercoalition agency relations will not be initiated are self-enforcing. Note that this result holds even in situations in which these intercoalition relations are more efficient. More precisely, intercoalition agency relations will not be established if the increase in the gains from cooperation does not compensate a merchant for the wage increase. Note that this result does not hold under BPS. When agency relations become possible across two identical traders' groups in which BPS prevails, efficient intergroup agency relations will be initiated.

Expectations with respect to future hiring, the nature of the networks for information transmission, and strategic considerations are the factors that ensure the sustainability of a coalition. These factors encourage member merchants to hire only member agents and discourage member merchants from hiring nonmember agents. Thus, these factors enable member mer-

---

[23] Formally, denote the coalitions by K and J, and denote by M_s and A a merchant and an agent from coalition s, respectively, $s \in \{K, J\}$. Denote by μ the expected probability that the merchants from coalition t will consider an A_t last employed by M_s as a cheater if he cheated M_s. All other things being equal, for any $\mu \in [0, 1)$, no individual merchant finds it optimal to establish intercoalition agency relations.
PROOF:
For any μ, the probability that A_t who cheated M_s will be rehired is $h_c^{t,t}(\mu) = \mu h_c^{t,t} + (1-\mu)h_h^{t,t} > 0$. The probability that A_s who cheated M_s will be rehired is 0. By Proposition 1, this implies that the honesty-inducing wage is higher in intergroup agency relations than in intragroup agency relations.

chants to commit to hire only member agents even if efficient agency relations can be established with nonmembers. At the same time, these factors make the collective punishment effective since it discourages nonmember merchants from hiring member agents, thus enabling member agents to commit themselves not to enter agency relations outside the coalition. By discouraging intercoalition agency relations, these factors make the expectations on which the coalition rests self-enforcing. Hence, once a coalition is formed through some historical process, agency relations will be established only among the traders for whom expectations were initially crystallized.[24]

These theoretical observations suggest that the informal social networks for information transmission, which became available to the Maghribis in the process of their immigration to Tunisia, enabled them to support agency relations based on MPS. Further, this immigration process determined the social identity of the individuals with respect to whom expectations of collective punishment and future hiring were established. Once these expectations were crystallized (i.e., once the Maghribi traders' coalition was formed), only descendants of Maghribis were perceived by others as members, and hence only they could become members. Further, the factors that encouraged intracoalition agency relations and discouraged agency relations with nonmembers made membership a valuable asset. Hence the descendants of a Maghribi trader followed the trade of their fathers and continued to be active in long-distance commerce as members of the Maghribi traders' coalition.

As the Maghribis expanded the geographical scope of their trade, the profitability of intracoalition agency relations was high enough to encourage emigration and the establishment of colonies in other trade centers. Since Maghribi merchants were motivated to employ other coalition members, they were able to commit themselves to future employment of Maghribi agents. This assured the emigrants that they would be compensated for the cost of emigration. Emigration to Italy, however, was more difficult culturally and hence forgone. Nonmember Italian Jews were not employed as agents, despite the common religion and the potential gains from trade with Italy, since the additional gains from establishing agency relations outside the coalition did not compensate for the relatively high agency cost.

The Maghribi traders' social structure provided them with the initial information-transmission mechanism required for the emergence of an economic institution—the Maghribi traders' coalition. At the same time, the coalition provided the interactions required to sustain the social structure, while the Maghribis' social identity provided the means to coordinate expectations required for the functioning of the coalition.[25] When the Maghribis ceased to operate in long-distance trade and their coalition ceased to function, the motivation for social interactions diminished, their social structure lost its vitality, and the Maghribi traders assimilated into the existing Jewish communities.

As long as the Maghribi group survived, it retained social characteristics and trade practices which differed substantially from those of the Italian traders and can be consistently explained as reflecting the governance of agency relations by a coalition. The social structure of the Maghribi traders' group was "horizontal," as traders functioned as agents and merchants at the same time. Each trader served as an agent for several merchants while receiving agency services from them or other traders (see e.g., Stillman, 1970; Greif, 1985). In contrast, among the Italian traders of the late medieval period, merchants and agents constituted two distinct subgroups. Agency relations were organized "vertically," as wealthy merchants who did not function as

---

[24]On the relevant theory of path-dependence, see Paul A. David (1988a,b).

[25]For these types of relationships between economic activity and social structure, see George C. Homans (1950) and Herbert A. Simon (1987 pp. 100–14).

agents employed ambitious young traveling agents who did not function as merchants (Frederic C. Lane, 1944 pp. 178–96; Lopez and Raymond, 1955 pp. 174, 185–6; De Roover, 1965 pp. 51–3). For example, in the cartulary of John the Scribe, which reflects the Genoese trade of the mid-12th century, 180 merchants are mentioned, 12 of whom invested 40.4 percent of the total Genoese investment in trade. About 300 agents are known, but only 36 individuals functioned as both agents and merchants. Eugene H. Byrne (1916 p. 159) concluded that "as a rule" the Genoese agents during the late 12th century were "not men of great wealth or of high position in Genoa" (see also Byrne, 1920 pp. 210–11, 1928 pp. 160–1; Hilmar C. Kruegar, 1957, 1962).

The differences between the Maghribis and the Genoese were not confined to their social structure. These two groups also differed in the choice of forms of business association through which agency relations were established. The common denominator of the forms of business association employed by the Maghribis was that they required both parties (the merchant and the agent) to invest capital in the commercial venture. In sharp contrast, the Genoese traders established agency relations mainly through *commenda* contracts, which required only the merchant to invest.[26]

The Maghribi and the Genoese traders operated mainly in the western basin of the Mediterranean, and their merchandise consisted largely of textiles and luxury goods. Further, the two groups were familiar with similar forms of business association and employed, roughly speaking, the same technology.[27] Yet, despite these similarities the two groups differed in their social structures

and choice of forms of business associations. How does the choice of forms of business association and the social characters of a traders' group relate to the strategy employed in agency relations? Are the forms of business association and the social character of the Maghribi traders consistent with the claim that agency relations were governed by a coalition?

To address these questions, assume that a merchant can hire either an agent (who does not invest in trade) or another merchant (who is able to invest in trade) to provide agency services. Recall that within a coalition a capital premium is generated; that is, the return on the capital of a coalition member merchant is higher than that available to him outside the coalition or if he cheats another coalition merchant while serving as an agent to him. If a merchant has to establish agency relations outside the coalition (or within the coalition after he has cheated) he has to rely on BPS, which implies a lower profit for the reasons discussed above. Receiving this capital premium within a coalition is conditional on past conduct, and hence it provides a coalition member merchant with a commitment device not available to an agent. The value of the future capital premium constitutes a "bond" that insures honesty. Hence, ceteris paribus, it is profitable for each merchant to employ a merchant as his agent.

To demonstrate how the capital premium provides a bond within a coalition, consider the honesty condition for a merchant. This honesty condition should take into account the fact that if he cheats while employed as an agent, a merchant's subsequent relations with his member agents would be governed by BPS. A merchant will be honest if the present value of his lifetime utility obtained from being honest, V_h^a, is not smaller than the gains from one period of cheating, α, plus the present value of his lifetime expected utility as an unemployed cheater agent, $V_c^{u,a}$, minus the reduction in the present value of his lifetime expected utility as a merchant that results from cheating, $V_h^m - (R_c + \delta V_c^m)$. ($R_c$ is the merchant's net profit from employing an agent in the period in which he cheats.) Hence, the hon-

---

[26] For an elaboration on these forms of business associations and the differences between the Jewish and the Genoese, see Lopez and Raymond (1955), Krueger (1962), De Roover (1965), Goitein (1967a, 1973 pp. 11–15), Gil (1983b [Vol. 1] pp. 208–12), and Greif (1989, 1990).

[27] "Familiar" means that either they actually used these forms or that the forms were authorized as legal (see Greif, 1989).

esty condition is

$$V_h^a \geq \alpha + V_c^{u,a} - \left[V_h^m - (R_c + \delta V_c^m) \right].$$

Recall from the proof of Proposition 1 that the honesty condition for an agent (who does not invest in trade) is $V_h^a \geq \alpha + V_c^{u,a}$. Since BPS governs the relations between a merchant who had cheated and his agents, $V_h^m > R_c + \delta V_c^m$. Hence, ceteris paribus, a merchant strictly prefers hiring a merchant over hiring an agent. When the ceteris paribus assumption is relaxed, the analysis implies that hiring only or mostly merchants is an equilibrium within a coalition for a larger set of parameters than under BPS.

On the other hand, it should be noted that, according to Proposition 1 under MPS and BPS, the higher the reservation utility, the higher is the wage required to insure honesty. Hence, ceteris paribus, a merchant would prefer to hire an agent rather than another merchant if the reservation utility of the latter is higher. Furthermore, in reality it may be the case that a merchant's reservation utility is higher than that of an agent since a wealthy merchant is likely to allot some of his capital in non-trade-related investment. Hence, within a coalition the capital a merchant invests in trade enhances his ability to commit, while the capital he invests elsewhere hinders this ability. However, if agency relations are governed by BPS, capital invested in trade does not enhance the ability to commit, while, as before, capital invested elsewhere hinders the ability to commit.[28]

These theoretical considerations offer a coherent explanation of the differences between the Maghribis and the Genoese that is consistent with the hypothesis that agency relations among the Maghribis were governed by a coalition. Among the Maghribis, agency relations were governed by a coalition, and merchants stood to lose their capital premium if they ever cheated. At the same time, the Maghribis were professional traders who, as far as can be judged by their letters, invested most, if not all, their working capital in trade. Hence, their capital did not hinder their ability to commit. The resulting incentives shaped the nature of the Maghribi traders' social structure and choice over forms of business associations. By and large, each of them was a well-to-do merchant with the capital required to enhance his ability to commit.[29] Each Maghribi trader provided agency services to some Maghribi and received agency services from others. Establishing agency relations among merchants enabled the Maghribis to utilize forms of business associations in which both parties invested in trade and which, presumably, enabled them to benefit from diversification while retaining economies of scale and scope.

In Italy, one may conjecture, agency relations were governed by BPS, and thus the capital a merchant invested in trade did not enhance his ability to commit. Furthermore, the Genoese cartularies indicate that Genoese merchants, by and large, invested a significant portion of their capital in non-trade-related ventures. For example, they bought real estate, farmed taxes, and were active in agriculture. These investments, according to the theory, hindered their ability to commit. Hence, merchants were motivated to recruit agents with low reservation utilities. Vertical social structure and *commenda* relations were the result (see discussion in Greif [1990]).

Theoretical considerations also illuminate the rationale behind patterns of employment of agents and bookkeeping among the Maghribi traders. Among the Maghribi traders, agency relations resembled the relations between a modern firm and its workers, in that typically no explicit legal commitment governed the length of the relationship. Where a commitment was made, it was for a short period of time. The duration

---

[28]The above discussion ignores the possibility that a cheater invests the capital he embezzles in trade. Introducing this possibility only strengthens the results.

[29]Although some of the Maghribis were net givers of wage premium and some were net receivers of capital premium.

of agency relations *ex post* varied from a single season to several generations with sons replacing their fathers (Goitein, 1967a pp. 169–70, 178; Greif, 1985 p. 133).[30] Further, the Maghribi traders used a per-trade-venture rather than a multiventure accounting system, in which the income and expenses associated with each trade venture were detailed (Goitein, 1967a pp. 178, 204–9).

These trade practices are consistent with the operation of a reputation mechanism within a coalition. Intuitively, whenever a reputation mechanism is employed, a merchant may prefer short-term contracts, since the shorter the contract, the sooner the merchant can discover deviation, and thus the less he will have to pay to keep the agent honest.[31] In other words, a sequence of short-term contracts was more efficient than a single long-term contract. Further, a per-venture accounting system is more efficient than a multiventure accounting system whenever a reputation mechanism is employed, since it facilitates comparing agents' reports with any relevant information.

V. The Merchants' Law: Coordination and Comprehensive Contracts

The operation of a coalition is based on uncoordinated responses of merchants located at different trade centers. Hence, for the threat of collective punishment to be credible, "cheating" must be defined in a manner that ensures collective response. If some merchants consider specific actions to constitute "cheating" while others hold a different opinion, the effectiveness of the collective threat is undermined.[32] The re-

quired coordination can be achieved by specifying an agent's obligations in an explicit contract—ideally, a comprehensive contract. Given the 11th-century communication technology and the uncertainty and complexity of trade, detailed contracts entailed high negotiation costs. If a merchant and an agent had to agree upon a contract before any goods could be shipped to an agent, the negotiation costs would have made trade through agents impractical.[33]

Indeed, the *geniza* reflects the extensive use of incomplete contracts, usually in the form of letters with instructions that involve no negotiation: "Do whatever your propitious judgment suggests to you," wrote Musa ben Ya'qub from Tyre, Lebanon, to his partner in Fustat sometime in the second half of the 11th century (ULC Or. 1080 J 42 [Goitein, 1973 p. 94]).[34] Merchants often authorized their agents to do whatever they deemed best if none of the prespecified contingencies occurred. Incomplete contracts, however, undermine the operation of a coalition, since which actions should be considered cheating are not defined. Furthermore, when incomplete contracts are used, an agent can act strategically to reach circumstances in which he benefits from the incompleteness of the contract.[35]

Theoretically, hierarchy (authority relations) may be used as a substitute for an *ex ante* comprehensive contract by assigning the merchant with the right to all (*ex post*) decisions (Williamson, 1985). Similarly, culture may substitute for comprehensive contracts by specifying *ex ante* systematic rules

---

[30] In the Italian trade cities, *commenda* relations were also of short duration (see e.g., Lopez, 1952 p. 323).

[31] See Abreu et al. (1990) for differences on this point between models with perfect and imperfect monitoring.

[32] For relevant theory, see Jeffrey S. Banks and Randall L. Calvert (1989).

[33] The inappropriateness of comprehensive contracts in long-distance medieval trade is reflected in the difference between the Maliki and the Hanafi schools of law in Islam (see Abraham L. Udovitch (1970 pp. 208–9). For theoretical considerations of the inability to specify comprehensive contracts, see Williamson (1985), Sanford J. Grossman and Oliver D. Hart (1986), and Hart (1988).

[34] For a similar situation in Europe, see N. S. B. Gras (1939 p. 80).

[35] To some degree, such a situation is reflected in Dropsie 389 [Gil 1983a].

of behavior.[36] These cultural rules indicate what members of the organization should do after an unforeseen state of nature occurs. Hierarchy and culture, however, differ substantially. While culture requires *ex ante* learning of the rules but no *ex post* communication, hierarchy does not require *ex ante* learning but requires *ex post* information-transmission between the parties.

Given the communication and transportation technology of the 11th century, it is not surprising that hierarchy was not used among the Maghribi traders.[37] Instead, they employed a set of cultural rules of behavior —a Merchants' Law—that specified how an agent should act to be considered honest in circumstances not mentioned in the merchant's instructions. The Merchants' Law was shared by all the Maghribi traders and served as a default contract between agents and merchants. When it became known that an agent failed to follow the Merchants' Law, he was considered a cheater.

The importance of the Merchants' Law in determining the expectations and attitudes toward an agent's behavior is reflected, for example, in the letter, mentioned above, which was sent by Maymun ben Khalpha to Naharay ben Nissim. In discussing the conflict between Naharay and his agent, Maymun justified the agent's actions by arguing that he "did something which is imposed by the trade and the communication [system]; [what you asked him to do] contradicts the Merchants' Law" (or "the way of the trade"). In another letter, a "very angry" merchant accused his business associate of taking "actions [that] are not those of a merchant" (DK 22, b, ll. 5–9 [Gil, 1983a pp. 97–106]; TS 12.434, l. 7 [Goitein, 1967a p. 202 (note 50)]) (see also Goitein, 1967a p. 171).

Unfortunately, not much is known about the content of the Merchants' Law, and the most convincing evidence for its existence and the process of its formation is found outside the *geniza*. In the middle of the 12th century, Maimonides, a major Jewish spiritual leader who lived in Fustat, wrote in his legal code, "...if [an agent] enters a partnership with another without specifying any terms, he should not deviate from the custom current in the land in regard to the merchandise they deal with" (Maimonides, 1951 p. 223).[38] Similarly, the early-medieval Islamic legal literature contains numerous instances in which systematic legal reasoning is suspended because of the "custom of the merchants" (Udovitch, 1970 pp. 13, 250–9). Unfortunately, neither the legal literature nor the *geniza* reflects exactly how the Merchants' Law was formulated and changed (but see DK 22, a, margin right [Gil, 1983a pp. 97–106]; Goitein, 1973 pp. 111–12; Greif, 1985 p. 136).

Within the Maghribi traders' coalition, the Merchants' Law promoted efficiency by providing a coordination device necessary for the functioning of the coalition, economizing on negotiating cost and enabling flexibility in establishing agency relations. However, the Merchants' Law also imposed a rigidity on the system, as its process of adjustment was, most likely, impeded by agents' concerns regarding what others would be thinking about their actions rather than what the outcome of their actions would be. This is reflected in the words of Joseph ben Yeshua, who wrote to a merchant that without written instructions he could not do as he was instructed since he did not wish that "people will...say that I did something that I was not ordered" (Bodl. MS Heb. d 66, f. 60, a, margin, ll. 7–9 [Gil, 1983b (Vol. 3) p. 216]).

---

[36]See discussion in Colin Camerer and Ari Vespsalaninen (1987) and Janet T. Landa (1988) (cf. Kreps, 1990b).

[37]See DK 22, a, 9–11 [Gil, 1983a pp. 97–106] as an example of letters that explicitly indicate that it was impractical for an agent to await new instruction when an unspecified contingency occurred.

[38]Note that this may indicate that the Merchants' Law was not specific to the Maghribi traders coalition but was shared by a larger group. In the *geniza* see DK 13, b, 11.7–11 [Stillman, 1970 p. 272], Dropsie 389, b, 11.22–3 [Gil, 1983a pp. 113–25], and TS 20.26, section I [Goitein, 1973 p. 117].

VI. Conclusion

A specific economic institution, the coalition, governed agency relations among the Maghribi traders. The coalition was an institution in the sense that it determined the constraints a trader faced. The information flows, the other traders' strategies, and the Merchants' Law constituted the constraints that affected an individual trader's choice of action. The nature of the coalition and its importance are evident from direct quotations of Maghribi traders and the impact of the coalition on their behavior, social structure, and business practices. The evidence suggests that the coalition was a response to problems of contract enforceability and coordination that arose in complex trade characterized by asymmetric information, slow communication technology, inability to specify comprehensive contracts, and limited legal contract enforceability.

Within the coalition, information flows balanced the asymmetric information, enabled monitoring, and coordinated responses. The multilateral punishment, the value of the information flows for commercial success, and the importance of the Merchants' Law as a substitute for comprehensive contracts generated wage and capital premiums. Receiving these premiums was conditional on past conduct, while intergenerational transfers insured a horizon long enough to support the operation of a reputation mechanism. Since the premiums' present value was larger than what an agent could gain by cheating, agents could credibly commit themselves to be honest. While the Merchants' Law provided a unified interpretation of actions and thus coordinated responses, the operation of the coalition was based on information flows within a well-defined group of traders and expectations concerning future hiring and collective punishment. The credibility of the collective punishment was based on the links generated by the MPS between the optimal wage and expectations concerning future hiring by member merchants. Finally, expectations with respect to future hiring, the nature of the networks for information transmission,

and strategic considerations ensured the sustainability of the coalition.

The emergence of the coalition and its size reflect an institutional path-dependent process. The coalition reflects the relationships between an historical process initiated by political events, the resulting social entity, and the positive reinforcement between economic and social institutions. In particular, networks for transmission of information within a social structure of an immigrants' group determined the coalition's initial size. In the coalition that emerged based on that initial social structure, the original social identity served as a signal that coordinated actions and expectations. The economic institution that governed agency relations, by promoting such relations and information transmission among a specific group of individuals, preserved the initial social structure, which in turn determined the boundaries of the economic institution.

By reducing agency costs and other transaction costs, the coalition promoted efficiency. It enabled operation through agents, even when the cost of establishing agency relations between a specific merchant and an agent in isolation was prohibitively high. In addition, the Merchants' Law economized on negotiation cost, governed the transmission of information and the provision of services, and substituted comprehensive contracts in the relations between a specific agent and merchant. On the other hand, the coalition seems not to have been an optimal institution. The same factors which ensured its sustainability prevented the coalition from expanding in response to welfare-enhancing opportunities. The Merchants' Law potentially introduced another distortion, as its adaptation was probably conducted in a manner that did not ensure optimal changes. Further, within a coalition, agents are more concerned about the interpretations of their actions by other members than about the outcomes of their actions. Hence, their actions, while aiming at maximizing their expected utility, do not necessarily maximize total profit. An introduction of some form of leadership might have mitigated these distortions, perhaps at the cost of introducing others.

The study of nonmarket economic institutions employed in different historical periods is likely to enhance knowledge of the origins, nature, and implications of institutions. The study of the coalition indicates the importance of the interrelations between political, social, and economic factors in giving rise to a specific nonmarket institution (see Greif [1992b] for general discussion). Further, it suggests that, due to the nature of these interrelations, once a specific institution emerges, it may become a part of a self-enforcing stable system which is not prone to change in response to welfare-enhancing opportunities. Hence, economic growth in different economies may be diverse due to distinct institutional frameworks of historical origin. Indeed, the coalition resembles contemporary economic institutions like those described by J. S. Furnivall (1956), Stewart Macaulay (1963), and Janet T. Landa (1978).

Further, following Coase, it is customary in historical and theoretical research to distinguish between the operation of market and nonmarket institutions. The Maghribi traders' coalition was a nonmarket institution which, by governing agency relations, influenced the integration of interregional markets. Hence, the study of this coalition indicates the importance of a nonmarket institution in providing the institutional framework required for the operation of the market. The nature of nonmarket institutions influences the cost, if not the feasibility, of trade and thereby effects the process of market integration. As market integration is commonly believed to be a key to economic growth, historical institutional analysis of nonmarket institutions and their relations to market integration is likely to lead to better understanding of the processes of economic growth.

REFERENCES

Abreu, Dilip, Milgrom, Paul R. and Pearce, David G., "Information and Timing in Repeated Partnerships," *Econometrica*, November 1991, *59*, 1713–33.

_____, Pearce, G., David and Stacchetti, Ennio, "Optimal Cartel Equilibria with Imperfect Monitoring," *Journal of Economic Theory*, June 1986, *39*, 251–69.

_____, _____ and _____, "Toward a Theory of Discounted Repeated Games with Imperfect Monitoring," *Econometrica*, September 1990, *58*, 1041–64.

Akerlof, George A. and Yellen, Janet L., *Efficiency Wage Models of the Labor Market*, Cambridge: Cambridge University Press, 1986.

Banks, Jeffrey S. and Calvert, Randall L., "Communication and Efficiency in Coordination Games," Working Paper No. 196, Department of Political Science, University of Rochester, 1989.

Bendor, Jonathan and Mookherjee, Dilip, "Norms, Third-Party Sanctions, and Cooperation," *Journal of Law, Economics, and Organization*, Spring 1990, *6*, 33–63.

Blau, Joshua, *A Grammar of Medieval Judaeo-Arabic*, Jerusalem: Magnes Press, 1961.

_____, *The Emergence and Linguistic Background of Judaeo-Arabic*, London: Oxford University Press, 1965.

Byrne, Eugene H., "Commercial Contracts of the Genoese in the Syrian Trade of the Twelfth Century," *Quarterly Journal of Economics*, November 1916, *31*, 128–70.

_____, "Genoese Trade with Syria in the Twelfth Century," *American Historical Review*, January 1920, *25*, 191–219.

_____, "The Genoese Colonies in Syria," in L. J. Paetow, ed., *The Crusade and Other Historical Essays*, New York: F. S. Crofts, 1928, pp. 139–82.

Camerer, Colin and Vespsalaninen, Ari, "The Efficiency of Corporate Culture," paper presented in the Colloquium on Strategy Content Research, Northwestern University, 1987.

David, A. Paul, (1988a) "The Future of Path-Dependent Equilibrium Economics," Center for Economic Policy Research Working Paper No. 155, Stanford University, 1988.

_____, (1988b) "Path-Dependence: Putting the Past into the Future of Economics,"

Technical Report No. 533, IMSSS, Stanford University, 1988.

De Roover, Raymond, *The Organization of Trade.* (The Cambridge Economic History of Europe, Vol. 3), Cambridge: Cambridge University Press, 1965.

Fischel, Walter J., "The Spice Trade in Mamluk Egypt," *Journal of Economic and Social History of the Orient,* April 1958, *1,* 157–74.

Fudenberg, Drew, Levine, David K. and Maskin, Eric, "The Folk Theorem with Imperfect Public Information," mimeo, Massachusetts Institute of Technology, 1989.

Furnivall, J. S., *Colonial Policy and Practice: A Comparative Study of Burma and Netherlands India,* New York: New York University Press, 1956.

Gil, Moshe, *The Tustars, The Family and the Sect,* Tel Aviv: Tel Aviv University Press, 1971.

_____, (1983a) "The Jews in Sicily Under the Muslim Rule in the Light of the *Geniza* Documents," unpublished manuscript, Tel Aviv University, 1983; appeared in Italian in *Italia Judaaica,* Rome: Instituto Poligrafico e Zecca dello Stato.

_____, (1983b) *Palestine During the First Muslim Period (634–1099)* (in Hebrew and Arabic), Tel Aviv: Ministry of Defence Press and Tel Aviv University Press, 1983.

Goitein, Shelomo Dov, "New Light on the Beginning of the Karim Merchants," *Journal of Economic and Social History of the Orient,* April 1958, *1,* 175–84.

_____, (1967a) *A Mediterranean Society: Economic Foundations,* Los Angeles: University of California Press, 1967.

_____, (1967b) "Jewish Trade in the Mediterranean in the Beginning of the Eleventh Century" [in Hebrew], *Tarbiz,* July 1967, *36,* 366–95.

_____, *Letters of Medieval Jewish Traders,* Princeton, NJ: Princeton University Press, 1973.

_____, *A Mediterranean Society: The Family,* Los Angeles: University of California Press, 1978.

Gras, N. S. B., *Business and Capitalism: An Introduction to Business History,* New York: F. S. Crofts, 1939.

Green, Edward and Porter, Robert, "Noncooperative Collusion Under Imperfect Price Information," *Econometrica,* January 1984, *52,* 87–100.

Greif, Avner, "Sicilian Jews During the Muslim Period (827–1061)" [in Hebrew and Arabic], Master's thesis, Tel Aviv University, 1985.

_____, "Reputation and Coalitions in Medieval Trade: Evidence on the Maghribi Traders," *Journal of Economic History,* December 1989, *49,* 857–82.

_____, "Reputation and Coalitions in Medieval Trade: Evidence on the Genoese Traders," mimeo, Stanford University, 1990.

_____, (1992a) "Cultural Beliefs and the Organization of Society: Historical and Theoretical Reflection on Collectivist and Individualist Societies," mimeo, Stanford University, 1992.

_____, (1992b) "Institutions and Commitment in International Trade: Lessons from the Commercial Revolution," *American Economic Review,* May 1992 (*Papers and Proceedings*), *82,* 128–33.

_____, **Milgrom, Paul R. and Weingast, Barry R.,** "The Merchant Gild as a Nexus of Contracts," mimeo, Stanford University, 1992.

Grossman, Sanford J. and Hart, Oliver D., "The Cost and Benefits of Ownership: A Theory of Vertical and Lateral Integration," *Journal of Political Economy,* August 1986, *94,* 691–719.

Hart, Oliver, "An Economist's Perspective on the Theory of the Firm," mimeo, Massachusetts Institute of Technology, 1988.

Homans, George C., *The Human Group,* New York: Harcourt, 1950.

Joskow, Paul L., "Vertical Integration and Long-Term Contracts: The Case of Mine-Mouth Coal Plants," paper presented in the Economic and Legal Organization Workshop, Department of Economics, Massachusetts Institute of Technology, 1984.

Kandori, Michihiro, "Social Norms and Community Enforcement," *Review of Economic Studies,* January 1992, *59,* 63–80.

Klein, Benjamin and Leffler, Keith B., "The Role of Market Forces in Assuring Contractual Performance," *Journal of Political Economy*, August 1981, *89*, 615–41.

Kreps, David M., (1991a) *A Course in Microeconomic Theory*, Princeton, NJ: Princeton University Press, 1990.

_____, (1990b) "Corporate Culture and Economic Theory," in James E. Alt and Kenneth A. Shepsle, eds., *Perspectives on Positive Political Economy*, Cambridge: Cambridge University Press, 1990, pp. 90–143.

Krueger, Hilmar C., *Genoese Merchants, Their Partnerships and Investments, 1155 to 1164* (Studi in Onore di Armando Sapori), Milan: Institudo Editoriale Cisalpino, 1957.

_____, *Genoese Merchants, Their Partnerships and Investments, 1155 to 1230*, Studi in Onore di Amintore Fanfani), Milan: Multa Paucis, 1962.

Landa, Janet T., "The Economics of the Ethnically Homogeneous Chinese Middleman Group: A Property Rights–Public Choice Approach," Ph.D. dissertation, Virginia Polytechnic Institute and State University, 1978.

_____, "A Theory of the Ethnically Homogeneous Middleman Group: Beyond Markets and Hierarchies," working paper, Hoover Institution, Stanford University, 1988.

Lane, Frederic C., "Family Partnerships and Joint Ventures in the Venetian Republic," *Journal of Economic History*, November 1944, *4*, 178–96.

Lewis, Archibald R., *Naval Power and Trade in the Mediterranean, A.D. 500–1100*, Princeton, NJ: Princeton University Press, 1951.

Lopez, Robert S., "The Trade of Medieval Europe in the South," in M. M. Postan and E. Miller, eds. *The Cambridge Economic History of Europe, Vol. 2*, New York: Cambridge University Press, 1952, pp. 257–353.

_____, *The Commercial Revolution of the Middle Ages, 950–1350*, New York: Cambridge University Press, 1976.

_____ **and Raymond, Irving W.,** *Medieval Trade in the Mediterranean World*, New York: Columbia University Press, 1955.

Macaulay, Stewart, "Noncontractual Relations in Business: A Preliminary Study," *American Sociological Review*, February 1963, *23*, 55–70.

Maimonides, Moshe, *Mishne Torah*, Vol. 12 [translated by I. Klein], Judaica series, New Haven, CT: Yale University Press, 1951.

Michael, Murad, *The Archives of Naharay ben Nissim, Businessman and Public Figure in Eleventh Century Egypt* (in Hebrew and Arabic), Ph.D. dissertation, Hebrew University, Jerusalem, 1965.

Milgrom, Paul and Roberts, John, "Predation, Reputation, and Entry Deterrence," *Journal of Economic Theory*, August 1982, *27*, 280–312.

_____, **North, Douglass, C. and Weingast, Barry R.,** "The Role of Institutions in the Revival of Trade: The Medieval Law Merchant, Private Judges, and the Champagne Fairs," *Economics and Politics*, March 1990, *1*, 1–23.

Nelson, Philip, "Advertising as Information," *Journal of Political Economy*, July/August 1974, *78*, 729–54.

North, Douglass C., *Structure and Change in Economic History*, New York: Norton, 1981.

_____ **and Thomas, Robert Paul,** *The Rise of the Western World*, Cambridge: Cambridge University Press, 1973.

Okuno-Fujiwara, Masahiro and Postlewaite, Andrew, "Social Norms and Random Matching Games," CARESS Working Paper No. 90-18, University of Pennsylvania, 1990.

Pearce, David G., "Repeated Games: Cooperation and Rationality," Cowles Foundation Discussion Paper No. 983, 1991.

Pirenne, Henri, *Mohamed and Charlemagne*, New York: Norton, 1939.

_____, *A History of Europe*, New York: University Books, 1956.

Postan, M. M., *Medieval Trade and Finance*, Cambridge: Cambridge University Press, 1973.

Poznanski, S., "Ephraim ben Schemria de Fustat" [in French and Hebrew], *Revue des Etudes Juives*, 1904, *48*, 146–75.

Shapiro, Carl, "Premiums for High Quality Products as Return to Reputation," *Quarterly Journal of Economics*, November 1983, *98*, 659–79.

_____ and Stiglitz, Joseph E., "Equilibrium Unemployment as a Worker Discipline Device," *American Economic Review*, June 1984, *74*, 433–44.

Simon, Herbert A., *Models of Man, Social and Rational*, New York: Garland, 1987.

Stillman, Norman A., *East – West Relations in the Islamic Mediterranean in the Early Eleventh Century*, Ph.D. dissertation, University of Pennsylvania, 1970.

Udovitch, Abraham L., *Partnership and Profit in Medieval Islam*, Princeton, NJ: Princeton University Press, 1970.

Williamson, Oliver E., *The Economic Institutions of Capitalism*, New York: Free Press, 1985.

[17]

Coordination, Commitment, and Enforcement: The Case of the Merchant Guild

Avner Greif, Paul Milgrom, and
Barry R. Weingast

Stanford University

We interpret historical evidence in light of a repeated-game model to conclude that *merchant guilds* emerged during the late medieval period to allow rulers of trade centers to commit to the security of alien merchants. The merchant guild developed the theoretically required attributes, secured merchants' property rights, and evolved in response to crises to extend the range of its effectiveness, contributing to the expansion of trade during the late medieval period. We elaborate on the relations between our theory and the monopoly theory of merchant guilds and contrast it with repeated-game theories that provide no role for formal organization.

One of the central questions about the institutional foundations of markets concerns the power of the state. The simplest economic view of the state as an institution that enforces contracts and property rights and provides public goods poses a dilemma: A state with suffi-

This paper was originally prepared for the conference on Economic Policy in Political Equilibrium, June 14–16, 1990. We thank Yoram Barzel, Douglass C. North, Jean-Laurent Rosenthal, Nathan Sussman, and an anonymous referee for helpful comments; Esther-Mirjam Sent and Joshua Gans for editorial assistance; and the National Science Foundation for financial support. The participants at the conference on Markets and Organizations organized by the Center for Economic Research at Tilburg and seminar participants at the University of California at Berkeley, Boston University, Indiana University, the University of Illinois at Urbana-Champaign, Harvard University, the Hebrew University, Stanford University, and Tel-Aviv University contributed helpful comments.

[*Journal of Political Economy*, 1994, vol. 102, no. 4]

cient coercive power to do these things also has the power to withhold protection or confiscate private wealth, undermining the foundations of the market economy. In the particular case of medieval cities, these threats were sometimes realized, discouraging trade by foreign merchants to the mutual disadvantage of the ruler and the merchants. It is our thesis that merchant guilds emerged with the encouragement of the rulers of trading centers to be a countervailing power, enhancing the ruler's ability to commit and laying an important institutional foundation for the growing trade of that period.

European economic growth between the tenth and the fourteenth centuries was facilitated by the "Commercial Revolution of the Middle Ages"—the reemergence of Mediterranean and European long-distance trade after an extended period of decline (e.g., Lopez 1976). For this commercial expansion to be possible, institutions had to be created to mitigate the many kinds of contractual problems associated with long-distance trade. Assessing the significance of these institutions requires a subtle analysis. Indeed, the effectiveness of institutions for punishing contract violations is sometimes best judged like that of peacetime armies: by how little they must be used. Thus, when one reads the historical record to determine whether a major role of merchant institutions was to ensure contract compliance, the number of instances of enforcement is not a useful indicator. Instead, one must ask, What were the things that threatened, and on occasion thwarted, efficient trading? Can the powers and organizational details of merchant institutions be explained as responses to those threats? Did failures of enforcement trigger major changes in these institutions?

A comprehensive analysis of a contract enforcement institution must consider why the institution was needed, what sanctions were to be used to deter undesirable behavior, who was to apply the sanctions, how the sanctioners learned or decided what sanctions to apply, why they did not shirk from their duty, and why the offender did not flee to avoid the sanction. Some analyses meeting these criteria have been developed. One is Greif's (1989, 1993a) analysis of the contractual relations between merchants and their overseas agents in eleventh-century Mediterranean trade. To reap the benefit of employing overseas agents, an institution was required to enable the agents to commit to act on behalf of the merchants. One group of merchants known as the "Maghribi traders" managed their agency relations by forming a coalition whose members ostracized and retaliated against agents who violated their commercial code. Interrelated contractual arrangements motivated merchants to participate in the collective retaliation against agents who had cheated, and close community ties assured that each member had the necessary information to participate in sanctions when necessary.[1] Similarly, Milgrom, North, and Weingast (1990) have argued that the use of merchant courts in the Champagne fairs during the twelfth and the thirteenth centuries can be analyzed as an institution that created proper incentives for gathering information, honoring agreements, reporting disputes, and adhering to the judgments of the merchant courts. Moreover, by centralizing certain record-keeping functions and effectively permitting only merchants in good standing to remain at the fairs, this institution also achieved significant economies in transaction costs relative to other feasible enforcement institutions.

The cited papers provide consistent analyses of institutions used to overcome contractual problems among individual merchants active in long-distance trade. Individual merchants, however, were not the only important parties: the rulers of the trading centers at which the merchants met and brought their goods were an important independent force. Trading centers needed to be organized in ways that secured the person and property of the visiting merchants. Before a trading center became established, its ruler might be inclined to pledge that alien traders would be secure and that their rights would be respected. Once trade was established, however, the medieval ruler faced the temptation to renege on that pledge, failing to provide the promised protection or abusing the merchants' property rights by using his coercive power. In the age prior to the emergence of the nation-state, alien merchants could expect little military or political aid from their countrymen. Without something tangible to secure the ruler's pledge, alien merchants were not likely to frequent that trading center—an outcome that could be costly for both the ruler and the merchants. That rulers recognized the importance of this problem is well reflected in the words of the English king, Edward I, who noticed in 1283 that because alien merchants' property rights were not properly protected, "many merchants are put off from coming to this land with their merchandise to the detriment of merchants and of the whole kingdom" (*English Historical Documents*, 3:420).[2]

On the basis of the theory of repeated games, one might conjecture that since trade relationships between a specific merchant and ruler consist of a potentially long sequence of trading visits, the rulers' commitment problem could be overcome by either a *bilateral reputa-*

---

[1] For an analysis of the institution that governed agency relations in twelfth-century Genoa, see Greif (1993*b*). For game-theoretical and comparative historical analysis of the evolution and functioning of various trading institutions among the twelfth-century Genoese and the eleventh-century Maghribi traders from the Muslim world, see Greif (1994).

[2] The recognition that unprotected alien merchants would not come to England is also expressed in the *Carta Mercatoria* of 1303 (*English Historical Documents*, 3:515).

tion mechanism, in which a merchant whose rights were abused ceased trading, or a *multilateral reputation mechanism,* in which the cheated merchant and his close associates ceased trading. Yet the historical records indicate that, by and large, the ruler-merchant relations were governed by neither bilateral nor informal multilateral arrangements. On the contrary, ruler-merchant relations were governed by administrative bodies rooted outside the territory of the ruler, which held certain regulatory powers over their member merchants in their own territory and supervised the operation of these merchants in foreign lands. What roles could these administrative bodies theoretically play in overcoming the ruler's commitment problem? What roles did they play in fact?

To investigate these questions, we utilize historical records to develop a series of game-theoretic models corresponding to different institutional arrangements. The theoretical analyses indicate that although some trade is possible even without supporting organizations, sustaining the efficient level of trade is more demanding. Without administrative bodies capable of coordinating and sometimes compelling merchants' responses to a ruler's transgressions, trade could not expand to its efficient level. The corresponding historical analysis then suggests that during the late medieval commercial revolution, a specific institution—the *merchant guild*—developed the necessary attributes to enforce agreements with rulers, thus overcoming the commitment problem and enabling trade expansion. Merchant guilds exhibited a range of administrative forms from subdivision of a city administration to an intercity organization. Yet these forms all shared the common function of ensuring the coordination and internal enforcement required to surmount the commitment problem by permitting effective collective action. We emphasize two points at the outset. First, our argument concerns merchant guilds and not craft guilds.[3] Second, we define merchant guilds according to their function rather than their "official," late medieval name. Hence, as we discuss below, our theory applies to a wider range of medieval merchant organizations than those labeled as merchant guilds.

The evaluation of merchant guilds as supporting efficient trade is complementary to the view more common among economic historians that merchant guilds emerged to reduce negotiation costs, to administer trade and taxation, to extract privileges from foreign cities, and to shift rent in their own city (see, e.g., Gross 1890; Thrupp 1965; North and Thomas 1973). While the existence of merchant

---

[3] Economists have long associated the latter with the monopolization of a given craft within a specific town. For a recent economic analysis of craft guilds, see Hickson and Thompson (1991). See also Gustafsson (1987).

guilds could affect the distribution of rents besides enhancing the security of agreements, the unadorned theory of merchant guilds as cartels presents a puzzle: If the purpose of the guilds was to create monopoly power for the merchants and to increase their bargaining power with the rulers, why did *powerful* rulers during the late medieval period cooperate with alien merchants to establish guilds in the first place? What offsetting advantages did the rulers enjoy? The puzzle is resolved if the guild's power enabled trade to expand to the benefit of the merchants and rulers alike.[4]

While this paper emphasizes the function of the merchant guild in facilitating trade between political units during the late medieval period, it also sheds light on the changing nature of guilds over time and the complex nature of guilds at any point in time. Although certain features of the merchant guild enabled it to advance trade during the late medieval period, these same features were, in some cases, utilized during the premodern period to restrict trade. Furthermore, even during the late medieval period, some merchant guilds had quasi-monopoly rights in their own territories. These rights were part of the relations between rulers and local merchants. Since our paper concentrates on the relations between ruler and *alien* merchants, such rights are not considered here. It is interesting to note, however, that our theory suggests that a merchant guild's monopoly rights in its home locality may have been instrumental in advancing trade between different localities. This type of monopoly rights generated a stream of rents that depended on the support of other members and so served as a bond, allowing members to commit themselves to collective action in response to a ruler's transgressions.[5]

The paper proceeds as follows. Section I reports the relevant history. It describes the serious problems trading centers and merchants faced in providing security for merchants and their goods, demonstrates that the guild structure had the features required to resolve the problem, and recounts milestones in the evolution of the guild among German traders and the related expansion of trade. Section II formalizes the analysis. Its game-theoretic model allows us to explore the incentives of traders and cities and explain why a guild organization could sometimes successfully support an efficient level

---

[4] De Roover (1965) asserts that the guild's role "was, of course, to provide collective protection in foreign lands, to secure trade privileges, if possible, and to watch over the strict observance of those already in effect" (p. 111). While his intuition carried him a long way, it did not explain how the guilds could provide protection and assure observance of rights by local rulers in foreign lands in which the ruler had a preponderance of military force.

[5] This is not to argue, however, that this function was necessarily the main reason for these local monopoly rights.

of trading activity when a simple reputation mechanism could not. Section III concludes the paper by considering the subsequent history—the transformation and decline of the merchant guild associated with the rise of the state—and suggests other applications of the theoretical framework.

I. The Commitment Problem and the Role of Merchant Guilds

Institutions and Commitment

Long-distance trade in late medieval Europe was based on the exchange of goods brought from different parts of the world to central cities or fairs located in geographically or politically favorable places. Yet the presence of gains from trade and locations suitable to conduct exchange does not imply that exchange could occur without an institutional environment in which the merchants and their property were secure. The concern that rulers felt to provide security, reflected in the words of Edward I quoted above, should be understood against the background of events such as the following one that occurred in Boston, England, in, or shortly before, 1241. A Flemish merchant accused an English trader of not repaying a commercial loan. This resulted in

> an uproar on all sides and the English merchants assembled to attack the Flemings, who retired to their lodging in the churchyard. . . . The English threw down the pailings, broke the doors and windows and dragged out Peter Balg [the lender] and five others, whom they foully beat and wounded and then set in the stocks. All the other Flemings they beat, ill-treated and robbed, and pierced their cloths with swords and knives. . . . Their silver cups were carried off as they sat at table, their purses cut and the money in them stolen, [and] their chests broken open and money and goods, to an unknown extent, taken away. [Curia Regis, 121, m. 6; published by Salzman (1928)]

Such disorders were not peculiar to England but mark the history of long-distance medieval trade. For example, the commercial relations between Byzantine and Italian city-states were often hindered by insecurity during the twelfth century. The Genoese quarter in Constantinople was attacked by the Pisans in 1162. At least one merchant was killed, and the other Genoese merchants had to escape to their ship leaving all their valuables behind them. In 1171 the Venetians attacked and destroyed the same Genoese quarter. About 10 years later a mob destroyed all the Italian quarters in Constantinople during the "Latin massacre" of 1182 (Day [1988]; for additional examples, see also De Roover [1965, p. 61]; Lane [1973, p. 34]; Kedar [1976, p. 26 ff.]).

In light of the theory of repeated games, one might conjecture that a ruler's commitment problem could be solved by a *bilateral reputation mechanism* in which individual merchants whose person and property were not protected by a local ruler would refuse to return with their goods in the future. The ruler, while perhaps reaping short-run gains from ignoring a merchant's rights, stood to lose the future stream of rents from the cheated merchant's trade.[6] As we demonstrate formally in Section II, this intuition is misleading. At the level of trade that maximizes the total net value of trade—that is, at the *efficient volume of trade*—a bilateral reputation mechanism cannot resolve the commitment problem. In our formal theory, the reason is that, at the efficient volume of trade, the value of the stream of future rents collected by the ruler from an individual marginal merchant is almost zero and is therefore smaller than the value of the goods that can be seized or the cost of the services that can be withheld. The same conclusion would hold even at lesser volumes of trade if the frequency of visits by an individual trader were low. As long as ruler-merchant relations are governed only by a bilateral reputation mechanism, our theory holds that trading volume cannot expand to its efficient level.

The preceding discussion and the formal model below allow only one kind of sanction for cheated merchants: the withdrawal of trade. Military action might seem another important alternative. In the late medieval period, however, defensive technology was superior to offensive technology, and the costs and risks of offensive military action at distant ports limit its credibility as a sanction for trade violations.[7]

A possible means to increase the punishment is a multilateral response by all the merchants to transgressions against any subgroup of merchants. Indeed, the history of the relations between trade centers and alien merchants presents several examples of multilateral retaliations against rulers who had reneged on their contractual obli-

---

[6] Clearly, there was a limit to the security a ruler could provide the merchants. Accordingly, we have detailed above instances in which rights were abused in major cities or trade centers in which the relevant ruler had a relatively high level of ability to secure rights.

[7] Parker (1988, p. 7) comments that "After the proliferation of stone-built castles in western Europe, which began in the eleventh century . . . in the military balance between defence and offense, the former had clearly become predominant." This situation changed only during the so-called Military Revolution of the fifteenth century.

gations. For example, circa 1050 the Muslim ruler of Sicily imposed a 10 percent tariff (instead of the 5 percent tariff specified in the Islamic law) on goods imported to Sicily by Jewish traders. The traders responded by imposing an embargo and sending their goods to the rival trade center, Tunisia. The embargo was effective, and after a year the Sicilian ruler relented and removed the tariff (David Kaufmann Collection, Hungarian Academy of Science, Budapest, document no. 22, pt. a, lines 29–31; pt. b, lines 3–5; Gil [1983, pp. 97–106]; Taylor-Schechter Collection, University Library, Cambridge, document no. 10 J 12, folio 26, p. a, lines 18–20; Michael [1965, 2:85]).

The examples above suggest that a *multilateral reputation mechanism* might be able to surmount the commitment problem without the aid of any formal organization. In each case, merchants imposed a collective punishment on the city that included participation by merchants who had not been directly injured. Several of the cited offenses were offenses *against an entire group of merchants*. In medieval trade, however, a city could also discriminate among merchants, abusing or not protecting them selectively. For example, a city could confiscate the belongings of some traders or withhold legal protection from them without directly harming other alien merchants. Indeed, the Sicilian rulers increased the tariff only to Jewish traders; and during two attacks on the Genoese quarter in Constantinople, other Italian merchants were not harmed. This suggests two interconnected reasons why, without a supporting organization, a multilateral reputation mechanism may be insufficient to surmount the commitment problem at the efficient level of trade. The first involves contract ambiguities and asymmetric information, whereas the second reflects the distinct incentives among different traders generated by a multilateral response.

Long-distance premodern trade took place in a highly complex and uncertain environment. Unanticipated events and multiple interpretations of existing agreements were always possible under these circumstances, implying that the definition of a "contract violation" was often ambiguous. Information asymmetry, slow communication, and different interpretations of facts among merchants imply that without an organization that coordinates responses, it was not likely that all the merchants would respond to the abuse of any group of merchants. As demonstrated formally in Section II, if the fraction of merchants who detect and react to an abuse against any group of merchants is only proportionate to the number abused, then a multilateral reputation mechanism is ineffective at the efficient volume of trade. It is ineffective for the same reason that a bilateral reputation mechanism is ineffective: a threat by a group of marginal traders to withdraw their trade is barely significant once trade has expanded to its efficient level.

To permit an efficient expansion of trade in the medieval environment, there was a need for an organization that would supplement the operation of a multilateral reputation mechanism by *coordinating* the responses of a large fraction of the merchants. Only when a coordinating organization exists can the multilateral reputation mechanism potentially overcome the commitment problem. In our formal model, when a coordinating organization exists there is a Markov perfect equilibrium at which traders come to the city (at the efficient level of trade) as long as a boycott has never been announced; none of them comes to trade if a boycott has been announced. The ruler respects merchants' rights as long as a boycott has never been announced but abuses their rights otherwise. Thus, when a coordinating institution exists, trade may plausibly expand to its efficient level.

Although the behavior described forms a perfect equilibrium, the theory in this form remains unconvincing. According to the equilibrium strategies, when a coordinating institution organizes an embargo, merchants are deterred from disregarding it because they expect the ruler to abuse violators' trading rights. But are these expectations reasonable? Why would a city not *encourage* embargo breakers rather than punish them? As verified in Section II, this encouragement is potentially credible. During an effective embargo, the volume of trade shrinks and the value of the marginal trader increases; it is then possible for bilateral reputation mechanisms to become effective. That is, there may exist mutually profitable terms between the city and the traders that the city will credibly respect. This possibility limits the potential severity of an embargo and, correspondingly, potentially hinders the ability of any coordinating organization to support efficient trade. To support the efficient level of trade, a multilateral reputation mechanism may need to be supplemented by an organization with the ability both to *coordinate* embargo decisions and to *enforce* them by applying sanctions on its own members.

Evidence of the Role of Formal Organizations

The discussion so far has focused on two issues: a demonstration that guaranteeing the security of alien merchants and their goods was problematic in medieval Europe and that both historical evidence and theoretical reasoning suggest that a simple reputation mechanism could not completely resolve the problem. In this subsection, we identify more direct evidence that merchants and rulers recognized the need to provide believable assurances of security for traders and their goods, that they negotiated trading arrangements that often included a role for formal organizations, that these organizations served an important coordination and enforcement role, and that trade expanded in cities that negotiated these agreements. Notice that this pattern of facts is inconsistent with at least the simplest cartel theories of guilds, which predict that guilds would form only after trade relations were already established and would limit entry and price competition, leading to the trading of *smaller* quantities.

That medieval rulers and merchants recognized the need to secure alien merchants' property rights before trade expansion could occur is borne out repeatedly in the historical record. Christians traders, for example, did not dare to trade in the Muslim world unless they received appropriate securities. Similarly, throughout Europe itself, merchants did not trade in locations in which they did not have security agreements. The Italians began traveling to other European cities and to the Champagne fairs, and the Germans began traveling to Flanders, England, and the Slavic East only after negotiating appropriate safety agreements (see, e.g., De Roover 1948, p. 13; De Roover 1965; Dollinger 1970).

Safety agreements allowing the merchants some measure of internal organization appear crucial to trade expansion. The Genoese trade with North Africa provides an instructive illustration. Prior to 1160, the Genoese trade with North Africa never exceeded 500 lire. In 1161, the Genoese legate, Otobonus d'Albericis, and the local ruler of North Africa, Abd alMumin, signed a 15-year agreement securing the property rights of the Genoese. Genoese trade more than doubled to 1,057 lire and remained at this higher level in later years. Moreover, the agreement focused on security issues. Though it specified a 2 percent reduction in the 10 percent custom, it was hardly concerned with the distribution of gains from trade. Given that the expected gains from goods that reached North Africa were, on average, more than 26 percent during this period, it is highly unlikely that the custom reduction accounts for the expansion of trade that followed (Krueger 1932, pp. 81–82; Krueger 1933, pp. 379–80).

Merchants from other trading cities had similar experiences. For example, the Catalan merchants' trade expanded "within only a few months" after they received, in 1286, privileges and the right to have a consul in Sicily (Abulafia 1985, pp. 226–27). The trade of the German merchants in Bruges expanded after they received privileges and the right to have a *Kontor* (establishment or office) (Dollinger 1970, p. 41). The Italians' trade with Flanders flourished only after they were allowed to establish local organizations, called *nations* (De Roover 1948, p. 13).

There also exists indirect evidence that the parties recognized the importance of an *institutionalized commitment* to security rather than mere promises. Muslim rulers provided European traders with *aman*, a religious obligation to secure the merchants' rights. Some cities in England went so far as to elect an alien merchant as mayor. Yet it seems that a specific institution—the *merchant guild*—was the most common successful institution. The core of a merchant guild was an administrative body that supervised the overseas operation of merchant residents of a specific territorial area and held certain regulatory powers within that territorial area. In England, for example, the merchants of a town were granted the right to establish a society of merchants that retained specific commercial privileges in the internal and external trade of the town and usually had representation in the trade centers in which its members traded. On the European continent, many towns were controlled by the mercantile elite who organized a merchant guild to advance their interests. In some Italian and German towns the merchant guilds were virtually identical with the town's government itself, and in some Italian cities the merchants' operations were supervised by the city (Gross 1890; Rashdall 1936, pp. 150–53; Rorig 1967).[8]

Guilds provided merchants with the leadership and the information transmission mechanisms required for coordinated action. In the examples we have studied, it was the guild that decided when to impose a trade embargo and when to cancel it.[9] The trade center usually provided the guild with the right to obtain information about disputes between its members and that center's authorities or between its members and other traders. The guild's regulations facilitated the collection and transmission of information among its members.[10]

Though the term "merchant guild" was not used in Italy, the Italian cities served the same functions on behalf of their resident merchants. The city's role in coordinating embargo decisions is well reflected in the relationships between Genoa and Tabriz, a vital city on the trade route to the Persian Gulf and the Far East. In 1340 Tabriz's ruler confiscated the goods of many Genoese traders. Genoa responded by declaring a *devetum* (a commercial embargo) against Tabriz. In 1344, however, Tabriz's ruler sent ambassadors to Genoa promising an indemnity for everything that had been taken from the Genoese and

[8] For a general discussion of the concept of corporation in medieval English law, see Pollock and Maitland (1968, 1:486 ff.).

[9] An exception is the case of the Maghribi traders. That case, however, seems to reflect the situation in the Muslim world rather than in Europe (see Greif 1994).

[10] Guild members were required to travel together, to live and store their goods throughout their stay in quarters that belonged to the guild, to examine the quality of each other's goods, and to witness each other's sales (see, e.g., Moore 1985, p. 63 ff.). As De Roover (1948, p. 20) noted, the "main purpose of the consular organization [of the Italians in Bruges] was . . . to facilitate the exchange of information."

favorable treatment in the future. As a consequence, the *devetum* was removed and the Genoese traders flocked to Persia. However, the ruler of Tabriz did not keep his promise to protect their rights, and the Genoese traders were robbed and many of them were killed. The material damage reached 200,000 lire, an immense sum. When the ruler later invited the Venetians and Genoese to trade, he "could not give them the guarantees they required. . . . [Hence] the Italian merchants, eager as they were to recover their prosperous trade in Persia and to reopen the routes to India and China, felt it was unsafe to trust a mere promise" (Lopez 1943, pp. 181–84). As discussed below, however, it was the Genoese traders as a whole who could not trust a "mere promise"; an individual Genoese trader might still be able to trust the ruler of Tabriz while the *devetum* was in force.

An incident that occurred during the Genoese embargo of Tabriz confirms the historical importance of enforcement within the merchant group and confirms that merchant guilds assumed this enforcement role. In 1343, during the *devetum* against Tabriz, a Genoese merchant named Tommaso Gentile was on his way from Hormuz to China. Somewhere in the Pamir plateau he became sick and had to entrust his goods with his companions and head back to Genoa the shortest way. That way, however, passed through Tabriz. When knowledge concerning his journey through Tabriz reached Genoa, Tommaso's father had to justify this transgression with the "Eight Wisemen of Navigation and the Major [Black] Sea," that is, the superior colonial board of Genoa. These officers accepted the thesis of an act of God and acquitted Tommaso from every penalty, inasmuch as he had gone through Tabriz without merchandise (Lopez 1943, pp. 181–83).

The merchant guild's strategy of conditioning future trade on adequate past protection, the use of ostracism to achieve security (rather than privileges or low prices), and the relationship between acquiring information, coordination, and the ability to boycott are reflected again in the agreement made in 1261 between the Flemish merchants from Ghent, Ypres, Douai, Cambray, and Dixmude who purchased English wool. "For the good of the trade," they decided that "if it should happen that any cleric or any other merchant anywhere in England who deals with sales of wool deals falsely with any merchant in this alliance . . . , by giving false weight or false dressing of the wool or a false product, . . . and if they do not wish to make amends, we have decided that no present or future member of this alliance will be so bold as to trade with them" (Moore 1985, p. 301). To make this threat of boycott functional, they "decided that there will be in each of these cities one man to view and judge the grievances, and to persuade the wrongdoers to make amends" (p. 301).

The credibility and force of a coordinating organization's threat to embargo depended crucially on the ruler's ability to undermine an embargo by offering special terms to embargo violators. In theory, the marginal gains from additional trade rise during an embargo. Both this theoretical observation and the observation that guilds needed to take special measures to prevent shipments to the embargoed city are confirmed by the historical evidence. For example, in 1284, a German trading ship was attacked and pillaged by the Norwegians. The German towns responded by imposing an embargo on Norway. The export of grain, flour, vegetables, and beer was prohibited. According to the chronicler Detmar, "there broke out a famine so great that [the Norwegians] were forced to make atonement" (Dollinger 1970, p. 49). The temptation for an individual merchant to smuggle food to Norway in this situation is clear. To sustain the embargo, the German towns had to post ships in the Danish Straits.[11] The fact that the success of a trade embargo depended crucially on obtaining the support of virtually all the merchants involved was also clear to the cities on which an embargo was inflicted. When, in 1358, the German towns imposed an embargo on Bruges, the city attempted to defeat the embargo by offering merchants from Cologne extensive trade privileges (pp. 65–66).

Placing ships in a strait and imposing fines are specific ways to overcome the distinct incentives problem. The evidence, however, suggests that the credibility of the threat to carry out an embargo was, in many cases, sustained by a different means. Credibility was established by endowing guilds with the ability to impose commercial sanctions on their member merchants. In England and other regions in Europe a local guild usually had exclusive trade privileges in its own town, typically including monopoly rights over retail trade within the town, exclusive exemption from tolls, and so forth, as well as the right to exclude, under certain circumstances, members from the guild (Gross 1890, pp. 19–20, 38 ff., 65; De Roover 1948, pp. 18–19).[12] These guilds, therefore, were able to provide their members with streams of rents in their hometowns. Receiving these rents, how-

---

[11] See also Dollinger's description of the embargo on Novgorod (p. 48). Anyone who broke the embargo was to suffer the death penalty and the confiscation of his goods.

[12] Exclusive commercial rights for the guild should not be confused with monopoly rights. Entry into the guild was permitted during the period under consideration. The German *Kontore* were established by the merchants who actually traveled abroad to trade. In England, e.g., even individuals who did not live in a specific town could join its merchant guild, and each member had to pay an entry fee (see, e.g., Gross 1890; Dollinger 1970). Note that by creating barriers and consequent rents, such a system also motivates each merchant to adhere to the guild rules, including honoring guild-sponsored embargoes. As shown below, this in turn permits a higher volume of trade than would be possible without the entry restrictions.

ever, could have been made conditional on following the recommendations, rules, and directives of the guild. Hence these rents could serve to tie a member to the guild by making change of residence costly and to ensure solidarity among the guild's members.[13]

The Flemish regulations of 1240 illustrate the role of the stream of rents in providing the appropriate incentives: A merchant who ignored the ban imposed by the guild on another town was expelled, losing his rent stream: "If any man of Ypres or Daouai shall go against those decisions [made by the guild] . . . for the common good, regarding fines or anything else, that man shall be excluded from selling, lodging, eating, or depositing his wool or cloth in ships with the rest of the merchants. . . . And if anyone violates this ostracism, he shall be fined 5s" (Moore 1985, p. 298).

Evolution of Guild Organizations

Perhaps the best example of the guild's contribution to fostering the growth of trade is the evolution and operation of the institution that governed the relations among the German merchants, their towns, and the foreign towns with which they traded. To achieve the coordination and enforcement that was required for the reputation mechanism to operate effectively, a means was needed to influence the behavior of merchants from *different* towns. This fact led to the rise of an interesting form of guild—the German Hansa.[14] Several extensive studies have mined the abundant historical records of the Hansa and enable us to examine its evolution in light of our theoretical analysis.

Our analysis of the evolution of the guild in northern Europe emphasizes episodes in which conflict occurred and trade was affected. In purely theoretical terms, conflict can be explained as an equilibrium phenomenon when information about the behavior of the parties is imperfect,[15] as it surely was in the periods we are studying. Moreover, in the episodes we study, conflict was followed by institutional change, and it seems implausible to model them as equilibrium outcomes. Instead, we shall regard the episodes themselves as disequilibrium outcomes and the resulting changes as adaptations to chang-

---

[13] This is not to claim that this was the chief role of these rents. Our analysis examines the role of the merchant guild in the expansion of trade between political units and not within political units.

[14] Clearly, we do not claim that the efficiency attributes of the Hansa that we discuss below were sufficient for its emergence. For a general discussion of the relationships between social and political institutions, gains from trade, and the emergence of institutions that facilitate trade, see Greif (1992, in press).

[15] For the imperfect monitoring approach, see the pioneering work by Green and Porter (1984). For refinements of this approach, see Abreu, Pearce, and Stacchetti (1986) and Abreu, Milgrom, and Pearce (1991).

ing circumstances or as improvements based on accumulated experience.

Specifically, we focus on the development of the German Hansa. For historical reasons, membership in the basic organizational unit that coordinated the activities of German merchants abroad—the *Kontor*—was not conditional on residency in one particular town. Any German merchant who arrived in a non-German city could join the local *Kontor*. A *Kontor* had the same function as the guild in coordinating the responses of the German merchants in disputes with the town; however, it lacked the ability to punish merchants in the towns in which they resided, weakening its ability to enforce sanctions against its members. If our theory is correct, the difference between the German *Kontore* and other guilds should have made the *Kontore* less effective and should have led to changes in or the dissolution of that form of merchant organization. The history of the contractual relations among the city of Bruges, the local *Kontor*, and the German towns provides a clear illustration of the evolution of merchant organization.

In 1252, a *Kontor* of German merchants obtained extensive trading privileges from Bruges, and a permanent settlement followed (Weiner 1932, p. 218). The *Kontor* was led by six aldermen elected by the German merchants present in the town. Two of the aldermen were from Rhenish towns, two from Westphalian-Wendish towns, and two from Prussian-Baltic towns, reflecting the range of origins of the participating German merchants (De Roover 1965, p. 114; Dollinger 1970, p. 86). The trading privileges given to the alien merchants in Bruges were continually abused, and eventually riots broke out, endangering both people and property. The situation is described in a document dated 1280 reporting that "it is unfortunately only too well known that merchants travelling in Flanders have been the objects of all kinds of maltreatment in the town of Bruges and have not been able to protect themselves from this" (Urkundenbuch der Stadt Lubeck, vol. 1, no. 156, p. 371; translated by Dollinger [1970, p. 383]). Along with most of the other alien traders who operated in Bruges, the German merchants retaliated in 1280 by transferring their trade to Aardenburg. After 2 years of negotiation, a new agreement was reached and the *Kontor* returned to Bruges.

Seemingly successful, the embargo failed to guarantee the property rights of the German merchants, since Bruges simply ignored its agreement with them (Dollinger 1970, pp. 48–51). It should be noted, however, that Bruges did respect the rights of other alien merchants who frequented the city. Our analysis points to the reason for that discrimination. The embargo was not imposed by the German merchants alone but by all alien merchants in Bruges, including the important and well-organized Italian and Spanish *nations*. While the lesson for Bruges from that episode was to respect the rights of those well-organized groups, it became clear to the city that the German merchant organizations were different. The *Kontor* proved incapable of enforcing its decisions on its members. Because the *Kontor* encompassed only the German merchants actually present in Bruges—rather than all the potential German traders who might want to trade during a boycott—its threat of sanctions was not credible. For a time, German merchants had to accept inferior treatment.

Another embargo, from 1307 to 1309, was thus required to force Bruges to respect its contractual agreements with the Germans, and in this embargo, only they participated. What had changed between 1280 and 1307 was the ability of the German traders from different towns to coordinate their responses and enforce their embargo. A milestone occurred in 1284 when the Wendish German towns imposed an embargo on Norway. Merchants from the city of Bremen refused to cooperate in the embargo, and the other German towns excluded Bremen's merchants from all German *Kontore*. The German towns had achieved the coordination needed to expel one of their members. The importance of the achievement is indicated by the fact that the act of expelling a city came to be referred to by a special word, *Verhansung* (Weiner 1932, p. 219; Dollinger 1970, p. 49).

After 1307, the ability of the German merchants to commit themselves to coordinate their actions and to enforce their decisions on individual merchants and towns was rather advanced, thus guaranteeing Bruges's adherence to its contractual obligations. Bruges respected the charters agreed on in 1307 and 1309, and consequently Flanders's trade flourished and expanded for the next 50 years (Dollinger 1970, p. 51). As our theoretical analysis indicates, once the ability of the German *Kontor* to coordinate and enforce its decisions on its members was well developed, the contract enforcement problem could be resolved and trade expanded.

It was not until the middle of the century, when the cost of providing security around Bruges rose drastically, that a new level of cooperation among the German towns was required to force Bruges to provide the security required to support efficient trade. The Hansa relations with Bruges deteriorated around 1350, mainly because Bruges was not ready to compensate the Germans for their damages in Flanders from the war between England and France. The Hansa responded by strengthening its internal organization. In 1356 the German Hansa held its first *diet*. It was decided that the *Kontor* of Bruges should be operated according to the decisions of the diet. Apparently recognizing the need for coordination among towns, the *Kontor* accepted this decision. The prominent historian of the Hansa,

Dollinger, has emphasized the importance of this change: "In law, and not only in fact, the towns, acting through the general diet were establishing their authority over their merchants in foreign ports" (Dollinger 1970, p. 63).

A Hanseatic embargo of Bruges followed in 1358. It was announced that any disobedience, whether by a town or an individual, was to be punished by perpetual exclusion from the Hansa. Bruges attempted to defeat the embargo by offering trade privileges to individual cities, including both non-Hanseatic ones such as Kampen and a Hanseatic one, Cologne. Our theory suggests that by offering these privileges it hoped to undermine the effectiveness of the new leadership. While the non-Hanseatic cities accepted Bruges's terms, Cologne refused to cooperate. The embargo proved a success, and in 1360, Bruges came to terms with the Hansa. This time, reflecting the parties' more complete understanding of the range of circumstances in which the city would have to provide services, the privileges were written "in much detail as to prevent any one-sided interpretations" (Dollinger 1970, p. 66).[16]

The institution of the German Hansa was now crystallized. It was a nexus of contracts among merchants, their towns, and foreign cities that advanced exchange. The Hansa's leadership served to coordinate and enforce cooperation between German merchants and towns—a cooperation that served the interests of all sides. The trade of northern Europe prospered for generations under the supremacy of the Hansa. Although the trade embargo of 1360 was not the last, later trade disputes seemed to center around distributive issues such as the provision of trade privileges. Commitment for security was no longer an issue.

It is illuminating to contrast the development of the Hansa among German towns with the rather different organization among the Italian merchants. The solid internal political and commercial organization of the Italian cities and their prominence in trade enabled them to overcome the coordination and internal enforcement problems. Collective action among the merchants from Italian cities was ensured. And, because none of the cities was a "marginal player" in the ports in which they traded, coordination among the cities was unnecessary.[17] In contrast, the German *Kontor* was a local organization in a trading center that lacked the ability to enforce its decisions on its members, who came from various German towns. As noted,

[16] For further details of this embargo, see Weiner (1932, p. 220) and Dollinger (1970, pp. 63–66).

[17] For the relative size of Italian and German cities, see Bairoch, Batou, and Chèvre (1988). Some intercity cooperation was also practiced among the Italians when smaller cities "affiliated" themselves with larger ones. See the discussion below.

the German towns were small, and before the establishment of the Hansa, most were relatively insignificant in large trading centers such as Bruges.

The historical analysis presented in this section supports our hypothesis that the medieval merchant guild was an institution that overcame the ruler's commitment problem and facilitated trade expansion. Although the merchant guilds exhibited a range of administrative forms—from subdivision of a city administration (such as that of the Italian city-states) to the intercity organization (of the Hansa)—their functions were the same: to ensure the coordination and internal enforcement required to surmount the commitment problem by permitting effective collective action. The actions taken by rulers and traders, their strategies as reflected in their regulations, and the expansion of trade that followed the establishment of guilds all confirm the importance of this role of the guild organization.

II. The Formal Model

The theoretical modeling is kept intentionally simple and is directed to analyzing the potential of various plausible mechanisms for overcoming the ruler's commitment problem. Each of the mechanisms we consider might feasibly permit commitment by the ruler at some levels of trade; we focus on the growing need for more sophisticated mechanisms as the level of trade rises and approaches the efficient level.

We model the basic environment in which trade took place as having two kinds of players: a city and individual merchants. The merchants, identical and large in number, are identified with the points on the interval $[0, \bar{x}]$. The city—a potential trading center—has the following trading technology: If the number of traders passing through the city in a single period is x, the gross value of trade in that period is $f(x)$. In addition, we suppose that there is a cost of $c > 0$ per unit of value traded incurred by the city for the services it provides and a cost $\kappa > 0$ per unit of value incurred by each trader, so that the net value of trade is $f(x)(1 - c - \kappa)$. We assume that trade is profitable, that is, $c + \kappa < 1$. We also assume that f is nonnegative and differentiable, that $f(0) = 0$, and that f achieves a maximum at some unique value $x^* > 0$, which we call the *efficient volume of trade*. In our model, the city funds its services and earns additional revenues by charging a toll or tax of $\tau \geq c$ per unit of value passing through its ports, so that its total tax revenues are $\tau f(x)$. If it provides the services contracted for, then its net revenue for the period is $f(x)(\tau - c)$. If the city breaches its contract by failing to provide services to a fraction ϵ of the traders, it saves costs of $\epsilon c f(x)$, so its payoff for the trading period is $f(x)[\tau - c(1 - \epsilon)]$.[18] Traders who are not cheated each earn profits—net of costs, tolls, and taxes—of $(1 - \tau - \kappa)f(x)/x$. Traders who are cheated pay taxes and incur costs κ but receive no revenues; they each earn $-(\tau + \kappa)f(x)/x$.

All of this is repeated period after period, and the players' payoffs from the whole repeated game are the discounted sum of the periodic payoffs using discount factor δ. Thus the city's payoff when the trading volume is x_t in period t is given by

$$\sum_{t=0}^{\infty} \delta^t f(x_t)[\tau - c(1 - \epsilon_t)], \qquad (1)$$

and the payoffs of the individual traders are determined similarly as the discounted sum of their periodic payoffs.

The specification of the model captures the idea that merchants are substitutes as far as the ruler is concerned and each of them is relatively "small." The historical observation that rulers could discriminate between traders is captured through the specification of the ruler's strategy. We abstract away from the issue of competition among alternative trade centers since an essence of medieval trade was that it was based on exchange of goods brought by traders from several regions to a specific trading place. Thus, by and large, the threat of a group of traders from a specific region to permanently switch to an alternative potential trade center, without the cooperation of traders from other regions, was not credible.

The historical records also indicate, as discussed above, that merchants were most likely to trade abroad when they perceived their rights to be secure. The specification of the merchants' payoffs is based on this observation. The specification of the ruler's payoff reflects the fact that a ruler could gain from abusing rights or from allowing his subjects to do so. While the model equates the gains from abusing rights with the protection costs saved, one can alternatively think of gains from abuse as reflecting gains from the ruler's confiscation of merchants' goods. This specification of the ruler's and the merchants' payoffs also allows us to distinguish between issues of distribution and efficiency. We treat the tax rate as given and hence abstract away from examining the process through which the gains from trade are allocated. Any losses to the merchants above the agreed-on rate of taxation, however, are defined to be an abuse. Analytically, this specification implies that any first-best arrangement is characterized by the level of trade x^* in every period and no cheating

---

[18] Note that this formulation captures the gains to the ruler from either abusing rights directly or neglecting to provide merchants with costly protection.

by the city. Different first-best utility allocations are achieved by setting different tax rates τ. Technically, this conclusion reflects our assumption that some value is being lost when the ruler fails to provide protection, which reflects events such as those that took place in Boston, as described earlier: Failure to provide protection led to a destruction of goods and loss of value. Whatever the merchants were willing to pay the ruler—namely all issues of transfer—is modeled here as part of the tax.

Game 1: Informationally Isolated Traders: Bilateral Reputation Mechanism

Our first model represents the situation of traders who travel alone or in small groups with no social or economic organization, so that they remain unaware of how the city has treated other merchants. Although this model is surely too extreme to be fully descriptive, it highlights the difficulties faced by individual traders negotiating with the city on their own.

In this game, a trader must decide whether to bring his goods to the city in each period, knowing only the history of his own decisions and his own past treatment by the city. A strategy for the trader is a sequence of functions mapping the trader's personal history into decisions about whether to offer his goods for trade in that period. Similarly, the city must decide whom to cheat under various conditions. A strategy for the city is a sequence of functions identifying a (measurable) subset of the current traders for the city to cheat as a function of who shows up to trade currently and the full past history of the game.

Readers familiar with either the economics of reputations or the theory of repeated games will recognize that the repetition of the interactions between the city and the individual traders creates the possibility for reputations to be created that enforce good behavior by the city. The idea is that a trader who is once cheated might refuse to return to the city in future periods, leading to a loss of profits for the city. The effectiveness of this threat depends on both the frequency of trade and the periodic value of the individual merchant's trade to the city. If the frequency of trade is sufficiently high and the volume sufficiently low, so that the value of the repeat business of any individual trader to the city is high, the simple reputation mechanism can be effective for providing incentives to the city to protect individual rights. In our model, however, when the volume of trade rises to the efficient level, the value of repeat business to the city falls to zero, so the usual conclusions of the Folk theorem of repeated games do not apply.

PROPOSITION 1. No Nash equilibrium of game 1 can support honest trade ($\epsilon_t \equiv 0$) at the efficient level ($x_t \equiv x^*$), regardless of the levels of c, τ, κ, or δ.

Proof. Suppose that there was such an equilibrium, and consider the payoff to the city if it deviates from the equilibrium strategy and cheats a fraction ϵ of the first-period traders. In the initial period, its payoff is $f(x^*)[\tau - c(1 - \epsilon)]$. In subsequent periods, the informational assumptions of the model imply that the play of at most ϵ traders is affected. Consequently, at least $1 - \epsilon$ traders come to the city in each future period, and the city's payoff from treating them honestly is, in present value terms, at least $\gamma(\tau - c)f(x(1 - \epsilon))$, where, for convenience, we define $\gamma = \delta/(1 - \delta)$. So the city's total payoff from cheating a fraction ϵ of the traders in the first period and adhering to the purported equilibrium thereafter is at least

$$f(x)[\tau - c(1 - \epsilon)] + \gamma(\tau - c)f(x(1 - \epsilon)), \qquad (2)$$

and this expression coincides exactly with the actual payoff when $\epsilon = 0$, that is, when the city adheres to the purported equilibrium. The derivative of expression (2) with respect to ϵ at $\epsilon = 0$ and $x = x^*$ is

$$cf(x^*) - \gamma(\tau - c)x^*f'(x^*) = cf(x^*) > 0, \qquad (3)$$

because $f'(x^*) = 0$. This establishes that the city has a profitable deviation; that is, the specified behavior is not consistent with Nash equilibrium. Q.E.D.

No mechanism based only on sanctions by those who are cheated can support honest trading at the efficient level, x^*, because when trading is conducted at that level, the marginal trader has zero net value to the city. By cheating a few marginal traders, the city loses nothing in terms of future profits but saves a positive expense in the present period. To support the efficient level of trading, some kind of collective action among merchants is needed.[19]

We have stated the proposition in terms of a Nash equilibrium because it is a negative result and we want to emphasize that, even with the most inclusive of noncooperative equilibrium concepts, there is no way to support the efficient volume of trade. For our later

---

[19] This result is not an artifact of our specification of costs. For example, if we had specified that the costs borne by the city include some fixed costs per trader (possibly in addition to the proportional costs), the city would have an even stronger incentive to reduce the number of traders, because it bears only a fraction τ of the resulting loss of value but saves all the service costs. Making costs proportional to value minimizes the distortion in the city's incentives but still leaves it tempted to seek short-term gains by cutting services at the expense of individual traders when only the bilateral reputation mechanism is at work.

positive results, we shall utilize stronger, more convincing equilibrium concepts.

Game 2: Informationally Isolated Small Groups of Traders: An Uncoordinated Multilateral Reputation Mechanism

While information in medieval times was slow to diffuse by modern standards, it was nevertheless available. In particular, if a specific merchant was ever abused, even in the absence of any organization for information diffusion, some of his peers were likely to learn of it. For example, the traders cheated in Bruges might become known to some others from the same hometown or to their traveling companions. Can this process of limited, uncoordinated information diffusion enable the ruler to commit himself at the efficient level of trade?

To examine this issue, suppose that an incident in which the city cheats a group of traders always becomes known to a larger group of traders. Formally, whenever a set T of traders is cheated, there is a set of traders $\hat{T} \supset T$, each of whom learns of the event. We assume that there is some constant K ($1 \leq K < \infty$) such that if the number of traders cheated is $\mu(T)$, then the number of those who learn about the event, $\mu(\hat{T})$, is no more than $K\mu(T)$: If few traders are cheated, then proportionately few discover that the event has occurred. In game 2, traders make their decisions to bring goods on the basis of what they know of their own past behavior and the city's, including whatever they may know about how the city has cheated others. Potentially, an incident of cheating may then lead to a withdrawal of trade by a group that is many times larger than the group that was cheated. Even if this potentiality could be realized, however, it would not be sufficient to support an efficient volume of trade.

PROPOSITION 2. No Nash equilibrium of game 2 can support honest trade ($\epsilon_t \equiv 0$) at the efficient level ($x_t \equiv x^*$), regardless of the levels of c, τ, κ, or δ.

The proof is essentially the same as for proposition 1, except that the bound on the number who decline to trade in the future is multiplied by K. In particular, (3) is replaced by $cf(x^*) - \gamma K(\tau - c)x^*f'(x^*) = cf(x^*) > 0$.

Violations against a few merchants that are noticed by proportionately few cannot be deterred by a threat of retaliation by just those with firsthand knowledge.

The real situation faced by the traders is considerably more complicated than what we have modeled in games 1 and 2. One important missing element concerns informal and word-of-mouth communication. Although we allowed that some traders were informed when the city cheated another trader, we also assumed that traders knew nothing about who else was currently trading. This assumption was a device to rule out endogenous communication among the traders in the game, by which one trader may infer that another was cheated because someone did not show up to trade. In theory, this kind of communication can be significant (Kandori 1992). No doubt, both word of mouth and some inferences of this kind could take place, but we have built our formal model to disallow them on the assumption that they were of minor importance for enforcing contract compliance. To the extent that informal communications and indirect inferences could provide effective information, the need for organized communication and coordination is reduced.

Game 3: Guild with Coordinating Ability

We have now seen that it is impossible for the city and the traders to sustain an efficient level of trade based only on sanctions applied by small groups. Given the historical evidence of the existence of organizations that governed the relationships between the traders and the city, it is natural to examine whether these relationships could contribute to trade expansion.

There is a serious issue of how the guild ought to be modeled. In our view, a crucial characteristic that separates formal institutions such as guilds from informal codes of behavior is the creation of specialized roles such as those of the guild's aldermen. Determining how the guild selects its aldermen, what private interests those merchants may have, and how the guild manages the principal-agent problem of controlling the aldermen is a serious and complex issue that merits close analysis. Nonetheless, including such a model here would only obscure the main point of this paper. So we set these issues aside for future research and model the guild here as a mere automaton. By assigning different information and behavioral rules to the guild, we can evaluate its contribution to trade expansion.

In this subsection, we examine the role of the guild as an *organization* for communication and coordination. In our formal model, if the city cheats a set of traders, T, then the guild is assumed to discover the event and announce a boycott with probability $\alpha(T) \geq \mu(T)$. This specification entails that the more merchants were abused, the more likely the guild is to conclude that some abuse has occurred. On the other hand, it does not imply that the guild has information superior to that available to the merchants under the uncoordinated reputation mechanism examined in game 2.

In this game, the guild makes boycott announcements mechanically and without any means of enforcement. Traders learn the guild's announcement in each period, but they are not forced to heed it. It simply becomes part of the information that is available to them and to the city. Otherwise, the game is the same as game 1. Despite the guild's lack of enforcement ability, the mere change in information alters the set of equilibria.

PROPOSITION 3. Suppose that $\tau + \kappa \le 1$ and

$$c \le \gamma(\tau - c). \tag{4}$$

Then the following strategies form a Markov perfect equilibrium of game 3:[20] The city does not cheat unless a boycott is announced by the guild leader; after a boycott is announced, it cheats any trader who offers to trade. Traders offer to trade in a given period if and only if no boycott has been announced.

The proposition is formally proved by direct verification. The condition (4) is just the condition that what the city stands to gain by cheating a trader, which is proportional to $cf(x^*)$, be less than the average future profits from each trader, which are $\gamma(\tau - c)f(x^*)$. With group enforcement, it is *average* trading profits rather than marginal profits that determine the city's incentives. It is that fact that accounts for the continued effectiveness of group sanctions even at the efficient level of trade.

As remarked earlier, the equilibrium strategies contain a counterintuitive element: that the city cheats any trader who offers to trade during a boycott. It is the traders' unanimous expectations that the city will behave that way that cause them all to honor the boycott. But why should the city not welcome traders during the boycott rather than cheat them? Since we are looking at a Markov perfect equilibrium, the city can be expected to cheat embargo-breaking traders only if it is actually in the city's interest to do so once the embargo has been announced. Given the specified strategies, if y traders violate the boycott and offer their goods, the city expects a payoff of $(\tau - c)f(y)$ in the current period and zero in future periods, if it acts honestly. If it cheats, it expects $\tau f(y)$ in the current period and zero in the future, so cheating is, indeed, optimal.

Although the strategies described in proposition 3 do constitute an equilibrium, the expectations and behavior that they entail seem implausible. The equilibrium requires, for example, that no matter how desperate the city may be for renewed trade relationships once

---

[20] This is a Nash equilibrium of the game with the properties that (1) the player's strategies at any date depend only on whether a boycott has been announced and (2) each player's strategy at each date maximizes his payoff from that date onward, given the equilibrium strategies of the other players.

a boycott has been announced, the city must nevertheless cheat anyone who ventures to trade with it. In addition, the traders must expect
that behavior. By the equilibrium logic, the city does this because it
expects the boycott to take full hold in the next round anyway, so it
anticipates that any cooperation it may offer would be fruitless.

This equilibrium behavior does not match the historical facts very
well, and it is of doubtful import even as theory, because it supposes
that the city and potential embargo breakers play the equilibrium
with the lowest possible value for themselves. Similar criticisms have
been leveled at the equilibria of other repeated-game models, notably
by Pearce (1987), Bernheim and Ray (1989), Farrell and Maskin
(1989), and Abreu and Pearce (1991). None of the alternative solution
concepts that these authors suggest applies directly to our model, but
all suggest that it is more reasonable to suppose that some cooperation
may be achieved between traders and the city even after a boycott is
announced. As an example, we emphasize the possibility that mutually profitable *bilateral* agreements between the city and individual
traders may be reached even during a boycott. It will be apparent
from the logic of the arguments that any other kind of cooperation
would lead to qualitatively similar conclusions.

Let us therefore suppose that if some traders agree to trade with
the city despite the embargo, they cannot rely on the threat of a
group boycott to enforce their own claims against the city. What,
then, can enforce honest behavior by the city during the boycott? We
consider that it is the threat by a cheated trader to withdraw his own
future trade. Proposition 1 established that the efficient level of trade
x^* could not be supported by such an equilibrium, but it leaves open
the possibility that some inefficiently low level of trade can be supported. We are therefore led to ask, What is the highest level of
exchange, x', that can be supported in this way?

PROPOSITION 4. Assume that f is concave. Consider the strategies
in which the city cooperates in each period with just those traders
that it has never before cheated and each trader offers to trade in
each period if and only if he has not been cheated before. These
strategies constitute a subgame perfect equilibrium of game 1 when
the volume of traders is x and the taxes are τ if and only if, for all y
$\leq x$,

$$0 \geq cf(y) - \gamma(\tau - c)yf'(y). \tag{5}$$

A sufficient condition is that (i) $0 \geq cf(x) - \gamma(\tau - c)xf'(x)$ and (ii) the
elasticity $e(x) = [d \ln f(x)]/[d \ln(x)]$ be a decreasing function of x.

Proof. It is obvious that the traders' strategies are best replies from
any point in the history of the game to the strategy of the city, so we
need consider only the optimality of the city's strategy.

Beginning with x current traders, consider the subgame achieved after $x - y$ traders depart, when there are $y \leq x$ traders remaining. By cheating a fraction ϵ of the y current traders, the city's payoff will be $g(\epsilon; y) = [\tau - (1 - \epsilon)c]f(y) + \gamma f(y(1 - \epsilon))(\tau - c)$. A necessary condition for the optimality of $\epsilon = 0$ is $\partial g(\epsilon; y)/\partial \epsilon \leq 0$ at $\epsilon = 0$. An easy calculation verifies that this is just the same as condition (5), so the latter condition is necessary for all y.

By the optimality principle of dynamic programming, it is sufficient to show that there is no subgame in which the city would do strictly better by setting $\epsilon > 0$ in the initial period and then adhering to its equilibrium strategy thereafter, given the strategies of the others. If f is concave, then, for all y, $g(\epsilon; y)$ is concave in ϵ, so a sufficient condition is that, for all y, $\partial g(\epsilon; y)/\partial \epsilon \leq 0$ at $\epsilon = 0$, which is again equivalent to (5), proving sufficiency.

The elasticity can be rewritten as $e(x) = xf'(x)/f(x)$. The condition (5) is that $e(y) \geq c/[\gamma(\tau - c)]$ for all $y \leq x$, which follows from $e(x) \geq c/[\gamma(\tau - c)]$ and the hypothesis that $e(\cdot)$ is decreasing. Q.E.D.

Let x' be the largest solution of (5). The equilibrium described by proposition 4 suggests an interesting interpretation of the levels of trade x' observed during boycotts and explains why some merchants continued to trade but others did not. According to the theory, additional traders, beyond the number x', would be cheated by the city and would be unable to exact retribution for their losses. Alternatively, if we think of the level of trade $x < x^*$ during the boycott as being determined by factors outside the model (such as existing alliances or other interests), then condition (5) implies that the minimum tax rate necessary to deter cheating is less the lower x is. This confirms the intuition that an embargo breaker may be able to negotiate an unusually attractive deal, both because the value of trade per trader ($f(x)/x$) is higher when x is small and because the minimum tax rate τ necessary to prevent cheating is lower for small x.

Proposition 4 implies that in the absence of a strong guild—one that can enforce the boycott on its members—the guild cannot credibly threaten to reduce the city's income to less than $f(x')$. This threat may or may not be sufficient to support honest trade, depending on the parameters γ, τ, and c. That is, a boycott with leaks may or may not be enough to deter the city from violating its agreement. If this kind of boycott is not enough, then there may be mutual gains to be had by strengthening the guild and enabling it to make a more powerful threat. In particular, a guild with ability to enforce its boycott decision on all the merchants may be able to assure trade expansion.

The force of any potential boycott depends not only on $f(x')$ and $f(x^*)$ but also on the net rate of profit, $\tau - c$, earned by the city. Incentives for honest behavior by the city are stronger when the taxes and tolls are high, because the city then has more to lose from a boycott. A strong guild can make it feasible to offer lower taxes and tolls while still promoting honest behavior by the city, which, in a richer model, could lead to additional advantages in terms of an increased value of trade.

Game 4: The Guild with Coordination and Enforcement Abilities

The final variant is a game in which the guild has the ability to enforce compliance from the individual traders. We offer no formal analysis of this case. It is obvious that the only role of enforcement by the guild against member merchants in our formal model is to prevent trade during boycotts. Accordingly, the results are the same as in proposition 3, but now the traders participate in the boycott because they are required to do so rather than because they expect participation to serve their individual interests.

III. Discussion

All models in economics are stylized to highlight particular points, and ours are no exception. Our game models treat all merchants as small and perfect substitutes for one another; they abstract from the costs of running a guild and the problems of enforcing good behavior on the part of guild leaders; they omit the issues of competition among different trading centers and do not delve into how organized merchants actually enforce sanctions against their own members. Although the models' narrow focus highlights the need for cohesiveness among merchants and gives what we think is a convincing account of many details of the historical record, the omitted features are also important for understanding the history of merchant guilds. Merchant guilds were primarily an urban rather than rural phenomenon. That may be accounted for by the costs of organizing merchants over large geographic areas. Guild membership also extended gradually. In Germany, large cities took the lead in forming intercity guilds. This pattern, too, seems to reflect the costs and other barriers to forming large organizations, and the potential for success for small guilds is surely an important part of the dynamics of guild development.

Although our models treat merchants as homogeneous in their commercial affairs with the city, their geographic diversity was the very basis for the trade. There were exports of timber and Senegalese gold from North Africa; silk, spices, drugs, flax, and wine from the Middle East and Byzantium; luxury furs, cheese, butter, fish, and iron from Scandinavia and Russia; grains from Germany; wine from France and Spain; textiles from Flanders; wool, copper, dried fish, and goat- and sheepskins from England; and so on.

When groups of merchants are close substitutes for one another, competition among them can undermine the joint action needed to enforce rights obtained from rulers of trading centers. The patterns of guild membership along product lines that the theory implies are nearly identical to the patterns implied by a theory of the merchant guild as an instrument of monopoly, so it is important to emphasize how the other predictions of the theories differ.

Our theory predicts that rulers will *encourage* the establishment of merchant guilds with specific rights and an effective organization. Such encouragement would not be expected if the sole purpose of guilds was to shift some of the fixed gains from trade from rulers to merchants unless the encouragement itself reflects the merchants' ability to coerce the rulers to shift rent in merchants' favor. The evidence reveals that, even when merchants could not coerce rulers by the threat of embargo and even when the privileges provided to the merchants did not entail any shift in the rent, rulers did grant merchants various rights,[21] including the rights to organize, to hold courts and assemblies, to elect their own consuls, and to participate on juries when merchants were being tried. Our theory predicts that establishment of these guild rights would lead to trade *expansion*, but a cartel theory of guilds would suggest that guilds would form to reduce trade in goods in order to drive up relative prices. The evidence cited earlier supports the conclusion that, at least during the late medieval period, guilds led to trade expansion. While it is likely that the merchant guilds sought to advance the merchants' interests in many ways, including negotiating for rights to control prices, these rent-seeking activities cannot account for the patterns we have identified.

Of special interest for our theory are the richness and complexity of the guild system. The guild functioned as a nexus of contracts, weaving separate agreements with the individual merchants and the cities in which its members traded into a system whose parts were mutually supporting. Exclusive (but not necessarily monopolistic!) trading arrangements with the city allowed the guild to organize merchants, and other rights helped it to keep informed about disputes and to help the city enforce good behavior by merchants. The guild's

---

[21] In addition to the evidence mentioned above, see Carus-Wilson (1967, p. xviii) and *English Historical Documents*, 3:515–16. The role of the guild in securing rights rather than in achieving privileges in Bruges is suggested by the city policy to provide all *nations* with the same rights (see De Roover 1948, p. 15).

contracts with the merchants were fundamental to allow it to enforce its agreements with the city and with other merchants, including those from towns that tried to smuggle goods past its embargoes. The Hansa, effectively involving intercity contracts, further strengthened the merchants' hands in enforcement.

As centuries passed and trade gave impetus to political integration, larger political units emerged, taking on themselves the functions that the merchant guild previously had performed. The political, commercial, and military relations among rulers enabled each to commit to the safety of the alien merchants frequenting his realm. Illustrative are such acts as those of the English kings, who made agreements and enforced embargoes to provide the English Merchants of the Staple and the Merchant Adventurers with security in their dealings with the Hanseatic league. As the state system evolved, the need for the merchant guilds to secure merchants' rights declined.[22]

Merchant guilds, however, did not necessarily disappear, and some guilds became fiscal instruments that hindered trade expansion in the emerging states. Other guilds consolidated their political power and, after securing their members' rights, turned to limit the rights of their competitors. For example, the German Hansa of the late medieval period was a new political entity aimed at preserving the property rights of German merchants. Although its establishment enabled northern European trade to flourish, once organized, the Hansa's concern was not efficiency but profitability. In its constant efforts to preserve trade rights and supremacy, the Hansa crushed the advance of other traders' groups without consideration of their comparative efficiencies. Thus a merchant guild that had facilitated trade in the late medieval period was transformed into a monopolistic organization that hindered trade expansion during the premodern period.[23]

Up to this point, we have focused exclusively on the role of the merchant guild in a particular time and place, but we believe that the principles that applied then help to explain the emergence of other organizations in other places and times. Our analysis explains why a powerful party might find it advantageous to help weaker powers organize themselves into entities that can exert countervailing power, in order to allow itself to commit to certain mutually beneficial arrangements. For example, prior to the Revolution, the French kings developed an elaborate system to help secure their borrowing and

[22] For the relations between the Hansa and England during this later period, see Colvin (1971) and Postan (1973).

[23] See the discussion above regarding the Hansa embargoes during the late fourteenth century. Regarding the English traders, see Dollinger (1970) and Lloyd (1991). For a general discussion, see Greif (in press).

thereby enhance their ability to borrow (see Bien 1987; Root 1989; Hoffman 1994). The ingredients of this system—using the officer corps both to aggregate loans and to help borrowers coordinate and relying on the *parlements* to authorize the legality of royal edicts—suggest an attempt by the kings to create organizations capable of collective action to enforce the king's fiscal promises. Similarly, part of Britain's financial and military success following the Glorious Revolution in 1688 involved creating the Bank of England. This organization seems to have had the necessary attributes identified by our theory, for instance, the ability to announce the initiation of a credit boycott and to punish lenders who attempted to lend to the government.[24] The theoretical ideas introduced in this paper provide a promising new framework for analyzing these events and institutions.

References

Abreu, Dilip; Milgrom, Paul; and Pearce, David. "Information and Timing in Repeated Partnerships." *Econometrica* 59 (November 1991): 1713–33.
Abreu, Dilip, and Pearce, David. "A Perspective on Renegotiation in Repeated Games." In *Game Equilibrium Models*, vol. 2, *Methods, Morals and Markets*, edited by Reinhard Selten. New York: Springer-Verlag, 1991.
Abreu, Dilip; Pearce, David; and Stacchetti, Ennio. "Optimal Cartel Equilibria with Imperfect Monitoring." *J. Econ. Theory* 39 (June 1986): 251–69.
Abulafia, David. "Catalan Merchants and the Western Mediterranean, 1236–1300: Studies in the Notarial Acts of Barcelona and Sicily." *Viator* 16 (1985): 209–42.
Bairoch, Paul; Batou, Jean; and Chèvre, Pierre, eds. *The Population of European Cities from 800 to 1850: Data Bank and Short Summary of Results.* Geneva: Droz (for Center Internat. Econ. Hist.), 1988.
Bernheim, B. Douglas, and Ray, Debraj. "Collective Dynamic Consistency in Repeated Games." *Games and Econ. Behavior* 1 (December 1989): 295–326.
Bien, David D. "Offices, Corps, and a System of State Credit: The Uses of Privilege under the Ancien Regime." In *The French Revolution and the Creation of Modern Political Culture*, vol. 1, *The Political Culture of the Old Regime*, edited by Keith M. Baker. Oxford: Pergamon, 1987.
Carus-Wilson, Eleanora M. *Medieval Merchant Venturers: Collected Studies.* 2d ed. London: Butler and Tanner, 1967.
Colvin, Ian D. *The Germans in England, 1066–1598.* 1915. Reprint. London: Kennikat, 1971.
Day, Gerald W. *Genoa's Response to Byzantium, 1155–1204: Commercial Expansion and Factionalism in a Medieval City.* Urbana: Univ. Illinois Press, 1988.
De Roover, Raymond. *Money, Banking and Credit in Mediaeval Bruges: Italian Merchant-Bankers, Lombards and Money-Changers.* Cambridge, Mass.: Mediaeval Acad. America, 1948.
———. "The Organization of Trade." In *Cambridge Economic History of Europe*, vol. 3, *Economic Policies in the Middle Ages*, edited by M. Michael Postan, E. E. Rich, and Edward Miller. Cambridge: Cambridge Univ. Press, 1965.

[24] This argument is developed at length in Weingast (1992).

Dollinger, Philippe. *The German Hansa.* Stanford, Calif.: Stanford Univ. Press, 1970.

English Historical Documents. Vol. 3, *1189–1327.* Edited by Harry Rothwell. London: Eyre and Spottiswoode, 1975.

Farrell, Joseph, and Maskin, Eric. "Renegotiation in Repeated Games." *Games and Econ. Behavior* 1 (December 1989): 327–60.

Gil, Moshe. "The Jews in Sicily under the Muslim Rule in the Light of the *Geniza* Documents." Manuscript. Tel Aviv: Tel Aviv Univ., 1983. Also in Italian in *Italia Judaaica.* Rome: Inst. Poligrafico e Zecca dello Stato.

Green, Edward J., and Porter, Robert H. "Noncooperative Collusion under Imperfect Price Information." *Econometrica* 52 (January 1984): 87–100.

Greif, Avner. "Reputation and Coalitions in Medieval Trade: Evidence on the Maghribi Traders." *J. Econ. Hist.* 49 (December 1989): 857–82.

———. "Institutions and International Trade: Lessons from the Commercial Revolution." *A.E.R. Papers and Proc.* 82 (May 1992): 128–33.

———. "Contract Enforceability and Economic Institutions in Early Trade: The Maghribi Traders' Coalition." *A.E.R.* 83 (June 1993): 525–48. (*a*)

———. "On the Nature and Evolution of Political and Economic Institutions: Commitment, Reputation, and Self-Enforcing Institutions in Late Medieval Genoa." Manuscript. Stanford, Calif.: Stanford Univ., Dept. Econ., 1993. (*b*)

———. "Cultural Beliefs and the Organization of Society: A Historical and Theoretical Reflection on Collectivist and Individualist Societies." *J.P.E.* 102 (October 1994), in press.

———. "Trading Institutions and the Commercial Revolution in Medieval Europe." In *Proceedings of the Tenth World Congress of the International Economic Association,* edited by Michael Kaser. London: Macmillan, in press.

Gross, Charles. *The Gild Merchant: A Contribution to British Municipal History.* Oxford: Clarendon, 1890.

Gustafsson, Bo. "The Rise and Economic Behavior of Medieval Craft Guilds: An Economic-Theoretical Interpretation." *Scandinavian Econ. Hist. Rev.* 35, no. 1 (1987): 1–40.

Hickson, Charles R., and Thompson, Earl A. "A New Theory of Guilds and European Economic Development." *Explorations Econ. Hist.* 28 (April 1991): 127–68.

Hoffman, Philip. "Taxes, Fiscal Crises, and Representative Institutions: The Case of Early Modern France." In *Fiscal Crises and the Growth of Representative Institutions,* edited by Philip Hoffman and Kathryn Norberg. Stanford, Calif.: Stanford Univ. Press, 1994.

Kandori, Michihiro. "Social Norms and Community Enforcement." *Rev. Econ. Studies* 59 (January 1992): 63–80.

Kedar, Benjamin Z. *Merchants in Crisis: Genoese and Venetian Men of Affairs and the Fourteenth-Century Depression.* New Haven, Conn.: Yale Univ. Press, 1976.

Krueger, Hilmar C. "The Commercial Relations between Genoa and Northwest Africa in the Twelfth Century." Ph.D. dissertation, Univ. Wisconsin—Madison, 1932.

———. "Genoese Trade with Northwest Africa in the Twelfth Century." *Speculum* 8 (July 1933): 377–95.

Lane, Frederic C. *Venice: A Maritime Republic.* Baltimore: Johns Hopkins Univ. Press, 1973.

Lloyd, Terrence H. *England and the German Hanse, 1157–1611: A Study of*

Their Trade and Commercial Diplomacy. Cambridge: Cambridge Univ. Press, 1991.

Lopez, Robert Sabatino. "European Merchants in the Medieval Indies: The Evidence of Commercial Documents." *J. Econ. Hist.* 3 (November 1943): 164–84.

———. *The Commercial Revolution of the Middle Ages, 950–1350.* New York: Cambridge Univ. Press, 1976.

Michael, M. "The Archives of Naharay ben Nissim, Businessman and Public Figure in Eleventh Century Egypt." Ph.D. dissertation, Hebrew Univ., 1965.

Milgrom, Paul R.; North, Douglass C.; and Weingast, Barry R. "The Role of Institutions in the Revival of Trade: The Medieval Law Merchant, Private Judges, and the Champagne Fairs." *Econ. and Politics* 2 (March 1990): 1–23.

Moore, Ellen Wedemeyer. *The Fairs of Medieval England.* Toronto: Pontifical Inst. Mediaeval Study, 1985.

North, Douglass C., and Thomas, Robert Paul. *The Rise of the Western World: A New Economic History.* Cambridge: Cambridge Univ. Press, 1973.

Parker, Geoffrey. *The Military Revolution: Military Innovation and the Rise of the West, 1500–1800.* Cambridge: Cambridge Univ. Press, 1988.

Pearce, David. "Renegotiation-Proof Equilibria: Collective Rationality and Intertemporal Cooperation." Manuscript. New Haven, Conn.: Yale Univ., Dept. Econ., 1987.

Pollock, Frederick, and Maitland, Frederic William. *The History of English Law before the Time of Edward I.* 2 vols. 2d ed. Cambridge: Cambridge Univ. Press, 1968.

Postan, M. Michael. "The Trade of Medieval Europe: The North." In *Cambridge Economic History of Europe,* vol. 2, *Trade and Industry in the Middle Ages,* edited by M. Michael Postan and Edward Miller. Cambridge: Cambridge Univ. Press, 1965.

———. "The Economic and Political Relations of England and the Hanse from 1400 to 1475." In *Medieval Trade and Finance.* Cambridge: Cambridge Univ. Press, 1973.

Rashdall, Hastings. *The Universities of Europe in the Middle Ages.* Vol. 1, *Salerno, Bologna, Paris.* Edited by F. M. Powicke and A. B. Emden. Oxford: Oxford Univ. Press, 1936.

Root, Hilton L. "Tying the King's Hands: Credible Commitments and Royal Fiscal Policy during the Old Regime." *Rationality and Society* 1 (October 1989): 240–58.

Rorig, Fritz. *The Medieval Town.* Berkeley: Univ. California Press, 1967.

Salzman, L. F. "A Riot at Boston Fair." *Hist. Teachers' Miscellany* 6 (1928): 2–3.

Thrupp, Sylvia L. "The Gilds." In *Cambridge Economic History of Europe,* vol. 3, *Economic Organization and Policies in the Middle Ages,* edited by M. Michael Postan, E. E. Rich, and Edward Miller. Cambridge: Cambridge Univ. Press, 1965.

Weiner, A. "The Hansa." In *The Cambridge Medieval History,* vol. 7, *Decline of Empire and Papacy,* edited by J. R. Tanner, C. W. Previté-Orton, and Z. N. Brooke. Cambridge: Cambridge Univ. Press, 1932.

Weingast, Barry R. "Institutional Foundations of the 'Sinews of Power': British Financial and Military Success Following the Glorious Revolution." Manuscript. Stanford, Calif.: Stanford Univ., Hoover Inst., 1992.

[18]

The Role of Market Forces in Assuring Contractual Performance

Benjamin Klein

University of California, Los Angeles

Keith B. Leffler

University of Washington

The conditions under which transactors can use the market (repeat-purchase) mechanism of contract enforcement are examined. Increased price is shown to be a means of assuring contractual performance. A necessary and sufficient condition for performance is the existence of price sufficiently above salvageable production costs so that the nonperforming firm loses a discounted stream of rents on future sales which is greater than the wealth increase from nonperformance. This will generally imply a market price greater than the perfectly competitive price and rationalize investments in firm-specific assets. Advertising investments thereby become a positive indicator of likely performance.

I. Introduction

An implicit assumption of the economic paradigm of market exchange is the presence of a government to define property rights and

We thank Armen Alchian, Thomas Borcherding, Harold Demsetz, James Ferguson, Jack Hirshleifer, Matt Lindsay, Roy Kenney, John Long, Ian Macneil, Kevin Murphy, Phillip Nelson, Joseph Ostroy, Peter Pashigian, Sam Peltzman, George Priest, John Riley, Jonathan Skinner, George Stigler, Earl Thompson, and participants at seminars at UCLA and the University of Chicago during 1977–78 for helpful suggestions and comments. Jonathan Skinner also provided valuable research assistance. The Foundation for Research in Economics and Education and the University of Chicago Law School Law and Economics Program provided Klein with research support, and the Center for Research in Government Policy and Business, University of Rochester, provided Leffler with research support.

[*Journal of Political Economy*, 1981, vol. 89, no. 4]

enforce contracts. An important element of the legal-philosophical tradition upon which the economic model is built is that without some third-party enforcer to sanction stealing and reneging, market exchange would be impossible.[1] But economists also have long considered "reputations" and brand names to be private devices which provide incentives that assure contract performance in the absence of any third-party enforcer (Hayek 1948, p. 97; Marshall 1949, vol. 4, p. xi). This private-contract enforcement mechanism relies upon the value to the firm of repeat sales to satisfied customers as a means of preventing nonperformance. However, it is possible that economic agents with well-known brand names and reputations for honoring contracts may find it wealth maximizing to break such potentially long-term exchange relationships and obtain a temporary increase in profit. In particular, the determinants of the efficacy of this market method of contract performance and therefore the conditions under which we are likely to observe its use remain unspecified.

This paper examines the nongovernmental repeat-purchase contract-enforcement mechanism. To isolate this force, we assume throughout our analysis that contracts are not enforceable by the government or any other third party. Transactors are assumed to rely solely on the threat of termination of the business relationship for enforcement of contractual promises.[2] This assumption is most realistic for contractual terms concerning difficult-to-measure product characteristics such as the "taste" of a hamburger. However, even when the aspects of a contract are less complicated and subjective and therefore performance more easily measurable by a third party such as a judge, specification, litigation, and other contract-enforcement costs may be substantial. Therefore, explicit guarantees to replace or repair defective goods (warranties) are not costless ways to assure contract performance. Market arrangements such as the value of lost repeat purchases which motivate transactors to honor their promises may be the cheapest method of guaranteeing the guarantee.

While our approach is general in the sense that the value of future exchanges can motivate fulfillment of all types of contractual prom-

---

[1] Hobbes ([1651] 1955, pp. 89–90) maintains that ". . . he that performeth first, has no assurance the other will perform after; because the bonds of words are too weak to bridle men's ambition, avarice, anger, and other Passions, without the fear of some coercive Power; which in the condition of here Nature, where all men are equal, and judges of the justness of their own fears cannot possibly be supposed."

[2] This assumption is consistent with the pioneering work of Macaulay (1963), where reliance on formal contracts and the threat of explicit legal sanctions was found to be an extremely rare element of interfirm relationships. Macaulay provides some sketchy evidence that business firms prevent nonfulfillment of contracts by the use of effective nonlegal sanctions consisting primarily of the loss of future business. This "relational" nature of contracts has been recently emphasized by Macneil (1974), and also by Goldberg (1976) and Williamson (1979).

ises, we focus in this paper on contracts between producers and consumers regarding product quality. In order for a repeat-sale enforcement mechanism to operate, we assume that the identity of firms is known by consumers[3] and that the government enforces property rights to the extent that consumers voluntarily choose whom to deal with and must pay for the goods they receive.[4] In addition, managers of firms are assumed to be wealth maximizing and to place no value on honesty per se.

In Section II, the conditions are outlined under which firms will either honor their commitments to supply a high level of quality or choose to supply a quality lower than promised. In order to emphasize the ability of markets to guarantee quality in the absence of any government enforcement mechanism, a simple model is presented which assumes that consumers costlessly communicate among one another. Therefore, if a firm cheats and supplies to any individual a quality of product less than contracted for, all consumers in the market learn this and all future sales are lost. A major result of our analysis is that even such perfect interconsumer communication conditions are not sufficient to assure high quality supply. Cheating will be prevented and high quality products will be supplied only if firms are earning a continual stream of rental income that will be lost if low quality output is deceptively produced. The present discounted value of this rental stream must be greater than the one-time wealth increase obtained from low quality production.

This condition for the "notorious firm" repeat-purchase mechanism to assure high quality supply is not generally fulfilled by the usual free-entry, perfectly competitive equilibrium conditions of price equal to marginal and average cost. It becomes necessary to distinguish between production costs that are "sunk" firm-specific assets and those production costs that are salvageable (i.e., recoverable) in uses outside the firm. Our analysis implies that firms will not cheat on

---

[3] Nonidentification of firm output leads to quality depreciation via a standard externality argument; i.e., supply by a particular firm of lower than anticipated quality imposes a cost through the loss of future sales not solely on that firm but on all firms in the industry (see Akerlof 1970; Klein 1974).

[4] For simplicity, we assume that "theft," as opposed to nonfulfillment of contract, is not possible. While "fraud," in the sense of one party to the transaction intentionally supplying less than contracted for, is analytically similar to "theft," we draw a distinction along this continuum by assuming that the government only permits "voluntary" transactions in the sense that transactors choose whom to trade with. Therefore, while consumers cannot "steal" goods, they can, in principle, pay for the goods they receive with checks that bounce; and while firms cannot rob consumers, they can, in principle, supply goods of lower than promised quality. Although we recognize the great difficulty in practice of separating the underlying government enforcement mechanisms, e.g., property law, from the private promise-enforcing mechanisms we are attempting to analyze, this distinction between theft and fraud is analytically unambiguous.

promises to sell high quality output only if price is sufficiently above salvageable production costs. While the perfectly competitive price may imply such a margin above salvageable costs, this will not necessarily be the case. The fundamental theoretical result of this paper is that market prices above the competitive price and the presence of nonsalvageable capital are means of enforcing quality promises.[5]

In Section III our theoretical model of quality-guaranteeing price premiums above salvageable costs is extended to examine how the capital value of these price-premium payments can be dissipated in a free-entry equilibrium. The quality-guaranteeing nature of nonsalvageable, firm-specific capital investments is developed. Alternative techniques of minimizing the cost to consumers of obtaining an assured high quality are investigated. We also explore market responses to consumer uncertainty about quality-assuring premium levels. Advertising and other production and distribution investments in "conspicuous" assets are examined as competitive responses to simultaneous quality and production-cost uncertainties. Finally, a summary of the analysis and some concluding remarks are presented in Section IV.

II. Price Premiums and Quality Assurance

Assume initially that consumers costlessly know all market prices and production technologies but not the qualities of goods offered for sale. For simplicity, the good being considered is assumed to be characterized by a single objective quality measure, q, where quality refers to the level of some desirable characteristic contained in the good. Examples are the quietness of appliance motors, the wrinkle-free or colorfast properties of clothing, or the gasoline mileage of an automobile. We also assume that the economy consists of consumers who consider buying a product x each period, where the length of a period is defined by the life (repurchase period) of product x, and who are assumed to costlessly communicate quality information among one another. Therefore, if a particular firm supplies less-

---

[5] The notion that an increased price can serve as a means of assuring high quality supply by giving the firm a rental stream that will be lost if future sales are not made is not new. Adam Smith ([1776] 1937, p. 105) suggested this force more than 200 years ago when he noted that "the wages of labour vary according to the small or great trust which must be reposed in the workman. The wages of goldsmiths and jewellers are everywhere superior to those of many other workmen, not only of equal, but of much superior ingenuity; on account of the precious metals with which they are intrusted. We trust our health to the physician; our fortune and sometimes our life and reputation to the lawyer and attorney. Such confidence could not safely be reposed in people of a very mean or low condition." Similar competitive mechanisms recently have been analyzed by Becker and Stigler (1974) and Klein (1974).

than-contracted-for quality to one consumer, the next period all consumers are assumed to know. In addition, this information is assumed not to depreciate over time.[6]

Identical technology is assumed to be available to all entrepreneurs. Hence, there are many potential firms with identical total cost functions, $C = c(x,q) + F(q)$, where F is fixed (invariant to rate) costs. Higher quality and larger quantities require higher production costs, $F_q > 0$, $c_q > 0$, $c_x > 0$, and marginal cost is assumed to increase with quality, $c_{xq} > 0$. Fixed costs are assumed initially to be expenditures made explicitly each period rather than capital costs allocated to the current period. For example, they may include a payment on a short-term (one-period) rental agreement for a machine but not the current forgone interest on a purchased machine or the current period's payment on a long-term rental agreement—both of which imply long-term and hence capital commitments.

We therefore are explicitly distinguishing between "fixed" costs in the sense employed here of constant (invariant to output) current costs and "sunk" (nonsalvageable) capital costs. The usual textbook proposition that a firm will not shut down production as long as price is greater than average variable cost blurs this distinction and implicitly assumes that all fixed costs are also sunk capital costs. Our assumption of the complete absence of any long-term commitments is analytically equivalent to perfect salvageability of all capital assets. If all long-term production-factor commitments were costlessly reversible, that is, all real and financial assets such as the machine or the long-term machine rental contract could be costlessly resold and hence perfectly salvageable, there also would not be any capital costs. Only the nonsalvageable part of any long-term commitment should be considered a current sunk capital cost.

If buyers are costlessly informed about quality, the competitive price schedule, P_c, for alternative quality levels is given by the minimum average production costs for each level of quality and is designated by $P_c = P_c(q)$. This is represented in figure 1 for two alternative quality levels, q_h and q_{min}, by the prices P_1 and P_0. Suppose, however, that the quality of product x cannot be determined costlessly before purchase. For simplicity, assume prepurchase inspection reveals only whether quality is below some minimum level, q_{min}, and that

---

[6] If we modify the assumptions of our model to make interconsumer communication less than perfect and allow inflows of new ignorant consumers over time and permit individuals to forget, the potential short-run cheating gain by firms would be increased. Therefore, the quality-assuring price premium would be higher than we derive below. In this case increased firm size, by making it more likely that the individuals one is sharing product-quality information with (e.g., family and friends) have purchased from the same firm, lowers the potential short-run cheating gain by essentially reducing the repurchase period.

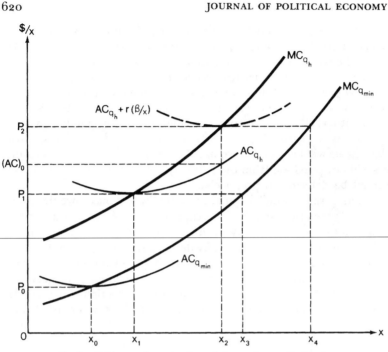

FIG 1.—Pricing and production of alternative quality levels

the costs are prohibitive of determining whether quality is above q_{min} prior to purchase.[7] Obviously, whenever the market price that consumers will pay for asserted high quality exceeds the cost of producing minimum quality output, the firm can increase its initial period profits by producing the minimum quality output and deceptively selling it as a higher quality product.

If producers are to have an incentive to produce high quality products (in the absence of governmentally enforceable contracts), consumers must somehow reward high quality production and punish low quality production. We assume in this competitive framework that consumers will purchase from particular sellers randomly chosen from the group of homogeneous sellers over which consumer information is transmitted. If a consumer receives a product of a quality at least as high as implicitly contracted for, he will continue to purchase randomly from this group of sellers. On the other hand, if quality is less than contracted for, all consumers cease to purchase from the particular sampled "cheating" firm.

[7] The quality of the good beyond the minimum level is therefore what Nelson (1970) has labeled as an "experience" characteristic. Making the minimum quality level endogenous does not substantially change the following analysis.

Consider now an initial "competitive" equilibrium in which a single firm contemplates selling a quality below that expected by customers. Given the competitive market price for some high quality, $P_c(q_h) \equiv P_1$ in figure 1, this particular firm could increase its initial period quasi rents by producing minimum quality and selling it at the high quality price. However, since buyers are assumed to communicate fully with one another, all future customers of high quality output, that is, sales at prices greater than $P_c(q_{min}) \equiv P_0$ in figure 1, are lost. That is, a firm that cheats will become known as a "notorious" cheater, and consumers will not purchase from the firm any product the quality of which cannot be determined prepurchase.[8]

Whether sales of high or minimum quality will maximize the firm's wealth depends on whether the capital value of future quasi rents from continued high quality production exceeds the differential initial period quasi rents from quality depreciation. In terms of figure 1, at the perfectly competitive price for high quality output, P_1, price is equal to the average costs of high quality production. Therefore, the quasi rents from continued high quality production are zero. If, alternatively, the firm were to deceptively produce minimum quality output, as a price taker it would expand its production to x_3 (where $P_1 = MC_{q_{min}}$) and receive a one-period quasi rent, the present value of which is equal to:

$$W_1 = \frac{1}{1+r} \left\{ (P_1 - P_0)x_3 - \int_{x_0}^{x_3} [MC_{q_{min}}(x) - P_0] dx \right\}. \tag{1}$$

Therefore, at the perfectly competitive price for any quality above q_{min} firms will always cheat consumers and supply q_{min}.

Faced with this possibility, consumers would recognize that regardless of producers' promises they will not obtain the higher quality product. Therefore, consumers would be willing to pay only the costless information price of the minimum quality product whose quality they can verify prepurchase, P_0. Because of such rational consumer anticipations, firms will not be able to cheat, but desired high quality output will not be supplied.

There may, however, be a price higher than the perfectly competitive price of high quality output, P_1, that if it were the equilibrium market price would (a) motivate honest production of the high quality good and (b) not completely dissipate the consumers' surplus from purchase of higher quality. Consider a price such as P_2 in figure 1. A

---

[8] A terminated firm cannot begin business in this industry under a new name. However, the highest valued alternative use of the entrepreneurial skills is included in salvageable fixed production costs. The firm considered here is assumed to face the same opportunities elsewhere as the firms that are honest in production of x. Therefore, the cheating firm can elect to enter a new industry.

firm supplying high quality output will now expand its production to x_2. The price premium $\tilde{P}$, defined as the increase in the price above minimum average cost of high quality, provides firms supplying high quality with a perpetual stream of quasi rents the present value of which (assuming unchanging cost and demand conditions over time) is equal to:

$$W_2 = \frac{1}{r} \left\{ \tilde{P}x_2 - \int_{x_1}^{x_2} [MC_h(x) - P_1]dx \right\}. \tag{2}$$

The price premium also increases the gains to a firm from supplying minimum quality at the high price. A firm that chooses to cheat will now expand its output (in terms of fig. 1 to x_4) and earn the extra premium on all units sold.[9] Therefore, the capital value of the quasi rents from supplying quality less than promised is:

$$W_3 = \frac{1}{1+r} \left\{ [\tilde{P} + (P_1 - P_0)]x_4 - \int_{x_0}^{x_4} [MC_{q_{min}}(x) - P_0]dx \right\}. \tag{3}$$

A firm will honor its implicit quality contract as long as the difference between the capital values of the noncheating and cheating strategies, $W_2 - W_3$, is positive. Consider the quasi-rent flow of the cheating and noncheating alternatives, that is, the terms in braces in our expressions (2) and (3). Define QR_2 equal to rW_2 and QR_3 equal to $(1 + r)W_3$. A firm will then elect not to cheat if and only if:

$$\frac{QR_3}{QR_2} \leq \frac{(1+r)}{r}. \tag{4}$$

Therefore, there will be a price premium that motivates firms to honestly produce high quality as long as:

$$\lim_{\tilde{P} \to \infty} \left(\frac{QR_3}{QR_2} \right) \leq \frac{(1+r)}{r}. \tag{5}$$

Using L'Hospital's rule, equation (5) will be satisfied as long as

$$\frac{1}{r} > \frac{(x_4 - x_2)}{x_2} \tag{6}$$

for all $P > P_3$, where P_3 is some finite price. Intuitively, as the price increases it is only the increase in quasi rents on the additional units of minimum quality output that favors the deceptive strategy. Equation (6) insures that price increases beyond some level increase W_2 more than W_3 such that eventually W_2 is greater than W_3.

---

[9] Note that although x_2 may be greater or less than x_3, depending on the price premium chosen, given upward-sloping supply functions and the condition that $MC_{q_h}(q) > MC_{q_{min}}(q)$ for all q, it must be the case that $x_4 > x_2 > x_1$.

The condition specified in equation (6) is quite reasonable. It will be satisfied as long as a cheating firm does not accompany cheating with very large output increases. If, for example, the real interest rate were .05 we require only that the output increase by a cheating firm not be more than 20 times the total output that would be produced if the firm were not cheating. Hence, under very general cost conditions a price premium will exist that motivates competitive firms to honor high quality promises because the value of satisfied customers exceeds the cost savings of cheating them.[10]

While we cannot state broad necessary conditions for the form the cost function must take to imply the existence of a quality-assuring price, "reasonable" sufficient conditions can be stated. In particular, all cases of vertically parallel marginal cost curves, as illustrated in figure 1, where quality is produced by a fixed input not subject to decreasing returns to scale (such as the use of a better motor) and where the second derivative of marginal cost is greater than or equal to zero imply the existence of a quality-assuring price. The Appendix contains simulation results under the more unrealistic assumption of isoelastic marginal cost functions. These simulations indicate the exceptional nature of the conditions when equation (6) is not satisfied. When a quality-assuring price does not exist, the cost functions are generally such that at reasonable premiums cheating output would be expanded by very large factors (often factors of many thousands). Since marginal cost functions for most products can be expected to become quite steep if not vertical at output expansions of much less than these factors, a quality-assuring price premium can generally be expected to exist.

Throughout the remainder of the paper we assume the existence of a quality-assuring price. For given cost and demand conditions, the minimum quality-assuring price will depend upon the level of quality

---

[10] The potential function of price premiums as quality guarantors is also applicable to markets in which firms face downward-sloping demands. In this case, the inability of firms to increase sales without reductions in price limits the gains available from deceptive minimum quality production as price increases. The existence of a price sufficient to guarantee quality now depends on the elasticity of demand in addition to the cost savings from quality reductions at various quantities. In addition, when price-searching firms do not have stable future demands, consumer knowledge of cost and current demand conditions is not sufficient to estimate the quality-assuring price. The anticipated future demand vis-à-vis current demand is also relevant. For example, where consumers expect a growing demand for the output of a firm that continues to produce high quality output, the rate of quasi-rent flow from high quality (or future deceptive minimum quality) production increases over time. As compared to a firm with the same initial but constant demand, the growing firm will receive a larger capital value return at any price from high quality production in the initial period. Firms facing expected demand growth will therefore require smaller quality-assuring price premiums. See Klein, McLaughlin, and Murphy (1980) for an analysis of the less than perfectly elastic firm demand case.

considered and is denoted by $P* = P*(q, q_{min}, r)$. Our analysis implies that the quality-assuring price will increase as quality increases, as minimum quality decreases (for all q greater than q_{min}), and as the interest rate increases. These conditions are consistent with the familiar recognition that, given a particular quality level, quality-cheating problems are less severe the higher the level of quality that can be detected prepurchase and the shorter the period of repurchase.[11]

Intuitively, the quality-assuring price treats the potential value of not producing minimum quality as an explicit opportunity cost to the firm of higher quality production. Hence the quality-assuring price must not only compensate the firm for the increased average production costs incurred when quality above that detectable prior to purchase is produced, but must also yield a normal rate of return on the forgone gains from exploiting consumer ignorance. This price "premium" stream can be thought of as "protection money" paid by consumers to induce contract performance. Although the present discounted value of this stream equals the value of the short-run gain the firm can obtain by cheating, consumers are not indifferent between paying the "premium" over time or permitting the firm to cheat. The price "premium" is a payment for high quality in the face of prepurchase quality-determination costs. The relevant consumer choice is between demanding minimum quality output at a perfectly competitive (costless information) price or paying a competitive price

[11] We can complicate our model by dropping the assumption that nondeceiving firms are anticipated to produce forever. If firms have a finite life, and the last period of production is known by both firms and consumers, there will be no premium sufficient to guarantee quality. No matter how high the premium paid by consumers for a high quality good in the last period, firms will supply "deceptive" minimum quality because there are no future sales to lose. Consumers aware of the last period will therefore demand only the minimum quality in that period. But then the next to the last period becomes the last period in the sense that, independent of the price premium, firm wealth is maximized by supplying minimum quality and going out of business. Consumers will then only pay for minimum quality output in the next to last period, and so on. High quality will never be produced. However, the necessary unraveling of the premium solution to assure high quality requires prior consumer knowledge of a date beyond which the firm will not produce. If consumers merely know that firms have finite lives but cannot with certainty specify a date beyond which a particular firm will not exist, price premiums may assure quality. While consumers are aware that some transactions will be with firms in their last period and hence cheating will occur, the expected gain from purchasing high promised quality can be positive. Our price premium–repeat business quality enforcement mechanism is analytically equivalent in form to the "super-game" solutions to the prisoner's dilemma problem developed in the game-theory literature. A general result of that analysis is that a cooperative solution can exist if one assumes either an infinitely long super game (as we have assumed in our model), or a super game of finite length but with transactors who have sufficient uncertainty regarding the period when the super game will end (see, e.g., Luce and Raiffa [1957], pp. 97–102, or, for a more recent solution to the problem that is similar in emphasis to our approach, Telser [1980]).

"premium," which is both necessary and sufficient, for higher quality output.[12]

There is a possibility that the required quality-guaranteeing price premium may exceed the increased consumer surplus of purchasing higher quality rather than the minimum quality product. If consumers can easily substitute increased quantity of the low quality product for increased quality, then the value of guaranteed high quality will be relatively low. Therefore, although a quality-guaranteeing price exists, a higher than minimum quality product may not be produced. For those goods where the substitution possibilities between quality and quantity are lower (e.g., drugs), consumer demand for confidence will be relatively high and the high quality guarantee worth the price premium. We assume throughout that we are dealing with products where some demand exists for the high quality good in the range of prices considered.

III. Competitive Market Equilibrium: Firm-specific Capital Investments

Our analysis has focused on the case where costless information (perfectly competitive) prices do not imply sufficient firm-specific rents to motivate high quality production. A price premium was therefore necessary to induce high quality supply. Thus, if price assures quality, the firms producing quality greater than q_{min} appear to earn positive economic profits. However, this cannot describe a full market equilibrium. When the price is high enough to assure a particular high level of quality, additional firms have an incentive to enter the industry. But if additional firms enter, the summation of the individual firms' outputs will exceed the quantity demanded at the quality-assuring price. Yet this output surplus cannot result in price reductions since the quality-assuring price is, in effect, a minimum price constraint "enforced" by rational consumers. All price-taking firms supplying a particular promised quality q above the minimum face a horizontal demand curve at $P^* = P^*(q)$, which is of an unusual nature in that prices above or below P^* result in zero sales. Consumers know that any price below P^* for its associated quality results in the

---

[12] As opposed to the Darby and Karni (1973) analysis, this particular model implies an equilibrium quantity of "fraud" equal to zero, where fraud is the difference between anticipated and actual quality. Given the symmetrical information assumptions regarding cost functions, parties to a contract know when and by how much a contract will be broken. An unanticipated broken quality contract is therefore not possible. The implicit economic (as opposed to common usage) concept of "contract" refers to anticipated outcomes and not to verbal promises or written agreements; thus there will be no broken quality "contracts."

supply of q_{min}. They therefore will not purchase from a firm promising that quality at a price lower than P^*.

A. Brand Name Capital Investments

Competition to dissipate the economic profits being earned by existing firms must therefore occur in nonprice dimensions. However, the zero-profit equilibrium is consistent with only a very particular form of profit-absorbing nonprice competition. The competition involves *firm-specific capital* expenditures. This firm-specific capital competition motivates firms to purchase assets with (nonsalvageable) costs equal to the capital value of the premium rental stream earned when high quality is supplied at the quality-assuring price. That is, if $P^*(q)$ is not to increase, the investment leading to zero profits must be highly firm specific and depreciate to zero if the firm cheats and supplies q_{min} rather than the anticipated quality. Such firm-specific capital costs could, for example, take the form of sunk investments in the design of a firm logo or an expensive sign promoting the firm's name. Expenditures on these highly firm-specific assets are then said to represent brand name (or selling) capital investments.

The competitive process also forces the firm-specific capital investments to take the form of assets which provide the greatest direct service value to consumers. The consumers' "effective" price of purchasing a quality-assured good, where the effective price is defined as the purchase price of a product, P^*, less the value of the services yielded by the jointly supplied brand name assets, is thereby minimized. Competition among firms in seeking and making the most highly valued firm-specific brand name capital investments will occur until the expected wealth increase and, therefore, the incentive to enter the industry are eliminated.

If the firm decides to cheat it will experience a capital loss equal to its anticipated future profit stream. Since $P^*(q)$ is derived so that the threat of loss of this future profit stream motivates guaranteed quality, the zero-profit equilibrium "brand-name capital," β, which serves as an explicit hostage to prevent cheating, equals, in terms of figure 1, where $P^*(q_h) = P_2$,

$$\beta = \frac{[P_2 - (AC)_0]x_2}{r}. \tag{7}$$

That is, the market value of the competitive firm's brand name capital is equal to the value of total specific or "sunk" selling costs made by the firm which, in turn, equals the present value of the anticipated premium stream from high quality output. If we continue to assume that there are no capital (and therefore "sunk") costs of production, the zero-profit equilibrium is shown in figure 1 where average "total" cost (which includes average production costs, AC_{q_h}, plus average brand-name capital [i.e., nonsalvageable "selling"] costs, $r[\beta/x]$) just equals price, P_2.

What assures high quality supply is the capital loss due to the loss of future business if low quality is produced. Since the imputed value of the firm's brand name capital is determined by the firm's expected quasi rents on future sales, this capital loss from supplying quality lower than promised is represented by the depreciation of this firm-specific asset. The expenditures on brand name capital assets are therefore similar to collateral that the firm loses if it supplies output of less than anticipated quality and in equilibrium the premium stream provides only a normal rate of return on this collateral asset.

Note that the "effective" price paid by consumers, which equals the quality-assuring price less the value of the consumer services yielded by the brand name capital, may be minimized by the investment in specific selling assets with some positive salvage value. Even though this results in an increased quality-guaranteeing price, assets with positive salvage values may yield differentially large direct consumer service flows. All brand name capital assets must, however, satisfy a necessary condition that the salvage value per unit of output be less than the consumer service value. Firms competing to minimize the effective price will choose specific assets by trading off increased consumer service value with decreased salvage value. This may explain why stores which supply high quality products often have amenities (such as a luxurious carpet cut to fit the particular store) even though only small direct consumer services may be yielded relative to cost.[13]

B. *Nonsalvageable Productive Assets*

The market equilibrium we have developed implies an effective price for high quality output that is higher than what would exist in a zero information cost world. While the costless-information solution is meaningless as an achievable standard of "efficiency," alternative marketing arrangements may be usefully compared to this benchmark. Viable, competitive firms will adopt the arrangements which, considering all transacting and contracting costs, minimize the devia-

---

[13] If the "sunk" asset yields absolutely no consumer services, then the firm will not use it. Even though profits would be eliminated by purchase of such an asset, consumers would be indifferent between a firm that invested in the asset and a firm that did not. In a world where consumers do not possess full knowledge of cost conditions, however, use of obviously specific assets may be employed even if yielding no direct consumer service flow because they may efficiently inform consumers regarding the sunk capital cost to the firm. This is discussed in greater detail in Sec. IIIC.

tions between the costless-information price and the effective price. One potentially efficient alternative or supplement to the pure price-premium method of guaranteeing quality may be the use of nonsalvageable productive assets rather than brand name (selling) assets.

In order to simplify the analysis of price premiums in guaranteeing quality, we have assumed that all production costs, including fixed costs, were noncapital costs and therefore, by definition, salvageable. More realistically, firms can control both the capital intensity of production and the salvage value of any fixed assets employed in the production process. In particular, if the firm uses a production process that has a nonsalvageable capital element, the normal rate of return (quasi-rent stream) on this element of production capital effectively serves as a quality-assuring premium. In terms of our model, the capital value of the quasi-rent stream when a firm cheats (eq. [3]) is now modified so that the net gain from cheating equals W_3 minus this nonsalvageable capital cost. Alternatively, in the zero-profit equilibrium the total level of collateral must still equal the potential gross gains from cheating, but part of the collateral is now provided by the nonsalvageable production assets rather than the brand name capital assets.

For example, if a machine is somewhat illiquid, buying it rather than renting it short term provides some of this collateral and lowers the quality-guaranteeing price. In fact, because of positive selling costs, capital assets generally have a salvage value less than cost. Thus capital inputs, especially those that have a high turnover cost, will have a value in terms of providing quality assurance in addition to their productive value. Even if the asset is not firm specific, if there is any time delay after the firm cheats and is terminated by consumers in selling the asset to another firm, the firm loses the real rate of interest for that time period on the capital. In addition to physical capital, human capital costs, especially entrepreneurial skills, are also often highly nonsalvageable in the face of consumer termination and therefore also provide significant quality assurance.

The general theoretical point is that the presence of positive quality-information costs favors an increase in the capital intensity of production, including the extent of long-term, illiquid contractual arrangements with suppliers of productive inputs. In particular, the minimum-cost production technique is no longer necessarily that which minimizes solely the average cost of production. "Sunk" production capital now accomplishes two functions—the supply of production services and the supply of quality-assuring services. Therefore, increases in average production costs accompanied by larger increases in sunk production assets may minimize the effective consumer product price. Profit maximization requires firms to trade off "inefficient" production technologies and the quality-assurance cost savings implied by the presence of firm-specific (sunk) capital assets in the productive process and hence the reduced necessity for the firm to make sunk selling cost (brand name capital) investments. Although the more capital intensive production technology may increase the perfectly competitive price of high quality output, P_0, it reduces the price premium, $P_2 - P_1$, necessary to assure the supply of that high quality. In fact, even a very slight modification of the minimum production cost technology, such as an alteration in some contractual terms, may imply the existence of large enough nonsalvageable assets so that the need for a quality-guaranteeing price premium is eliminated entirely.[14]

C. Consumer Cost Uncertainty: A Role for Advertising

The discussion to this point has assumed complete consumer knowledge of firms' costs of producing alternative quality outputs and knowledge of the extent to which any capital production costs or brand name capital selling costs are salvageable. This knowledge is necessary and sufficient to accurately calculate both the quality-guaranteeing premium and price. However, consumers are generally uncertain about cost conditions and therefore do not know the minimum quality-guaranteeing price with perfect accuracy. In fact, consumers cannot even make perfect anticipated quality rankings across firms on the basis of price. That one firm has a higher price than another may indicate a larger price premium or, alternatively, more inefficient production. In this section, we examine how the more realistic assumption of consumer cost uncertainty influences market responses to prepurchase quality uncertainty.

We have shown that increases in the price premium over average recoverable cost generally increase the relative returns from production of promised (high) quality rather than deceptive minimum (low) quality. The existence of a high price premium also makes expenditures on brand name capital investments economically feasible. The magnitude of brand name capital investments in turn indicates

---

[14] For example, franchisers can assure quality by requiring franchisee investment in specific production capital. A general arrangement by which this is accomplished is by not permitting the franchisee to own the land upon which its investments (e.g., capital fixtures) are made. Rather, the franchiser owns or leases the land and leases or subleases it to the franchisee, thereby creating for the franchisee a large nonsalvageable asset if he is terminated by the franchiser. This highly franchiser-specific asset can therefore serve as a form of collateral and potentially eliminate any need for a price premium. See Klein (1980) for a more complete discussion of this franchising solution, including the potential reverse cheating problem that is created by such contractual arrangements.

the magnitude of the price premium. When a consumer is uncertain about the cost of producing a particular high quality level of output and therefore the required quality-assuring premium, information about the actual level of the price premium will provide information about the probability of receiving high quality. If consumers are risk averse, this uncertainty about receiving anticipated high or deceptively low quality output will increase the premium that will be paid. The premium will include both a (presumably unbiased) estimate of the quality-assuring premium and an extra payment to reduce the risk of being deceived.

Thus, when consumers do not know the minimum quality-guaranteeing price, the larger is a firm's brand name capital investment relative to sales, the more likely its price premium is sufficient to motivate high quality production. Competitive investment in brand name capital is now no longer constrained to assets which yield direct consumer service flows with a present discounted value greater than the salvage value of the assets. Implicit information about the sufficiency of price as a guarantee can be supplied by "conspicuous" specific asset expenditures. Luxurious storefronts and ornate displays or signs may be supplied by a firm even if yielding no direct consumer service flows. Such firm-specific assets inform consumers of the magnitude of sunk capital costs and thereby supply information about the quasi-rent price-premium stream being earned by the firm and hence the opportunity cost to the firm if it cheats. Both the informational services and the direct utility producing services of assets are now relevant considerations for a firm in deciding upon the most valuable form the brand name capital investment should take.

The value of information about the magnitude of a firm's specific or "sunk" capital cost, and therefore the magnitude of the price premium, is one return from advertising. Indeed, the role of premiums as quality guarantors provides foundation for Nelson's (1974) argument that advertising, by definition, supplies valuable information to consumers—namely, information that the firm is advertising. A sufficient investment in advertising implies that a firm will not engage in short-run quality deception since the advertising indicates a nonsalvageable cost gap between price and production costs, that is, the existence of a price premium. This argument essentially reverses Nelson's logic. It is not that it pays a firm with a "best buy" to advertise more, but rather that advertising implies the supply of "best buys," or more correctly, the supply of promised high quality products. Advertising does not directly "signal" the presence of a "best buy," but "signals" the presence of firm-specific selling costs and therefore the magnitude of the price premium. We would therefore expect, ceteris paribus, a positive correlation not between advertising intensity and

ASSURING CONTRACTUAL PERFORMANCE   631

"best buys," as Nelson claims, but between advertising intensity and the extent of quality that is costly to determine prepurchase.[15]

Conspicuous sunk costs such as advertising are, like all sunk costs, irrelevant in determining future firm behavior regarding output quality. However, consumers know that such sunk costs can be profitable only if the future quasi rents are large. In particular, if the consumer estimate of the initial sunk expenditure made by the firm is greater than the consumer estimate of the firm's possible short-run cheating gain, then a price premium on future sales sufficient to prevent cheating is estimated to exist. Our analysis therefore implies that independent of excludability or collection costs, advertising that guarantees quality will be sold at a zero price and "tied in" with the marked-up product being advertised.[16]

Our theory also suggests why endorsements by celebrities and other seemingly "noninformative" advertising such as elaborate (obviously costly to produce) commercials, sponsorships of telethons, athletic events, and charities are valuable to consumers. In addition to drawing attention to the product, such advertising indicates the presence of a large sunk "selling" cost and the existence of a price premium. And because the crucial variable is the consumers' estimate of the stock of advertising capital (and not the flow), it also explains why firms advertise that they have advertised in the past (e.g., "as seen on 'The Tonight Show'"). Rather than serving a direct certifying function (e.g., as recommended by *Good Housekeeping* magazine), information about past advertising informs consumers about the magnitude of the total brand name capital investment.[17]

Firms may also provide valuable information by publicizing the

---

[15] Nelson's argument is based on an assumption similar to the Spence (1973)-type screening assumption regarding the lower cost to more productive individuals of obtaining education. Nelson's argument, however, is circular since consumers react to advertising only because the best buys advertise more and the best buys advertise more only because consumers buy advertised products. Schmalensee (1978) has shown that the Nelson scenario may imply "fly-by-night" producers who advertise the most and also deceptively produce minimum quality. Like Spence's signaling model, the government could, in principle, tax this investment and thereby save real resources without reducing the effectiveness of this information if consumers were aware of the tax rate. However, advertising serves many purposes. In particular, advertising also can supply valuable consumer information about the particular characteristics and availability of products. For optimality the government would therefore have to determine the appropriate tax rate for each advertising message and consumers would have to be aware of each of these particular tax rates.

[16] Mishan (1970) has argued for legislation which would require advertising to be sold separately at a price which covers advertising costs. This would completely destroy the informational value of advertising we are emphasizing here.

[17] Note, however, that just as firms may deceive consumers about quality to be supplied, they may also attempt to deceive them about the magnitude of the advertising investments made, e.g., purchasing a local spot on "The Tonight Show" and advertising the advertising as if an expenditure on a national spot was made.

large fees paid to celebrities for commercials. Information about large endorsement fees would be closely guarded if the purpose were to simulate an "unsolicited endorsement" of the product's particular quality characteristics rather than to indicate the existence of a price premium. Viewed in this context, it is obviously unnecessary for the celebrity to actually use the particular brand advertised. This is contrary to a recent FTC ruling (see Federal Trade Commission 1980).

This analysis of advertising implies that consumers necessarily receive something when they pay a higher price for an advertised brand. An expensive name brand aspirin, for example, is likely to be better than unadvertised aspirin because it is expensive. The advertising of the name brand product indicates the presence of a current and future price premium. This premium on future sales is the firm's brand name capital which will be lost if the firm supplies lower than anticipated quality. Therefore, firms selling more highly advertised, higher priced products will necessarily take more precautions in production.[18]

We have emphasized the informational value of advertising as a sunk cost. Other marketing activities can serve a similar informational role in indicating the presence of a price premium. For example, free samples, in addition to letting consumers try the product, provide information regarding future premiums and therefore anticipated quality. Such free or low-price samples thus provide information not solely to those consumers that receive the samples but also to anyone aware of the existence and magnitude of the free or low-price sample program. More generally, the supply by a firm of quality greater than anticipated and paid for by consumers is a similar type of brand name capital investment by the firm. By forgoing revenue, the firm provides information to consumers that it has made a nonsalvageable investment of a particular magnitude and that a particular future premium stream is anticipated to cover the initial sunk alternative cost.[19]

[18] The greater is the cost to consumers of obtaining deceptively low quality, the greater will be the demand for quality assurance. The very low market share of "generic" children's aspirin (1 percent) vis-à-vis generic's share of the regular aspirin market (7 percent) is consistent with this implication (see IMS America, Ltd. 1978). Many individuals who claim "all aspirin is alike" apparently pay the extra price for their children where the costs of lower quality are greater and therefore quality assurance is considered more important.

[19] Our analysis of advertising also illuminates the monopolistic competition debate. Chamberlin's (1965) distinction between production costs, defined as what is included in the "package" that passes from seller to buyer, and selling costs (e.g., advertising), which are not part of the package transferred, suggests that selling costs usefully may be considered as a privately supplied collective factor. For example, a firm which holds selling costs, such as expenditures on a store sign, constant as his sales increase does not appear to be decreasing the average "quality" of his product. Demsetz (1959, 1968) made the contrary assumption that average quality does fall as sales increase, holding

Finally, even when consumers systematically underestimate the quality-assuring price because of downward-biased estimates of production or marketing costs or upward-biased estimates of anticipated demand growth, firms in a monopolistically competitive environment may not cheat. Such price-setting firms may possess specific nonsalvageable assets (such as trademarks) upon which they are earning a sufficient quasi-rent premium to induce high quality supply. However, the existence of independent competitive retailers that do not have any ownership stake in this firm-specific asset and yet can significantly influence the quality of the final product supplied to consumers creates a severe quality-cheating problem for the manufacturer. In this context, rational but imperfectly informed consumers will not demand a sufficient premium to prevent retailer cheating. Manufacturers may protect their trademarks by imposing constraints on the retailer competitive process including entry restrictions, exclusive territorial grants, minimum resale price maintenance, and advertising restrictions that will assure quality by creating a sufficiently valuable premium stream for the retailers. If this manufacturer-created premium stream is greater than the potential short-run retailer return from deceptive low quality supply, the magnitude of which is determined in part by the manufacturer by its level of direct policing expenditures, the retailer will not cheat and the consumer will receive anticipated high quality supply.[20]

IV. Conclusion

We have shown that even the existence of perfect communication among buyers so that all future sales are lost to a cheating firm is not sufficient to assure noncheating behavior. We have analyzed the

---

selling costs constant, by merely ignoring Chamberlin's distinction and its possible theoretical significance and identifying quality costs with selling costs (aggregating both into the concept "demand increasing costs"). However, since in a monopolistically competitive environment the price premium that will assure quality depends upon the demand expected in the future, the quality incentive implied by an advertising investment also depends upon consumers' expectations about future demand. In particular, the relevant variable indicating an incentive to produce high quality is the level of advertising capital compared to anticipated future sales. Hence advertising is not a pure public good in a firm's production function as Chamberlin implicitly assumed, and the arbitrary contrary assumption made by Demsetz is possibly justifiable.

[20] See Klein et al. (1980) for a complete analysis of this case applied to the FTC Coors litigation. Coors appears to have employed exclusive territories on the wholesale level and resale price maintenance on the retail level to create a sufficient premium to encourage the necessary refrigeration of their nonpasteurized beer. Implications of this analysis in terms of providing a possible rationale for similar constraints on the competitive process enforced by trade associations and government regulatory agencies are also examined.

generally unrecognized importance of increased market prices and nonsalvageable capital as possible methods of making quality promises credible. We obviously do not want to claim that consumers "know" this theory in the sense that they can verbalize it but only that they behave in such a way as if they recognize the forces at work. They may, for example, know from past experience that when a particular type of investment is present such as advertising they are much less likely to be deceived. Therefore, survivorship of crude decision rules over time may produce consumer behavior very similar to what would be predicted by this model without the existence of explicit "knowledge" of the forces we have examined.

Our analysis implies that consumers can successfully use price as an indicator of quality. We are not referring to the phenomenon of an ignorant consumer free riding on the information contained in the market price paid by other more informed buyers but rather to the fact that consumer knowledge of a gap between firm price and salvageable costs, that is, the knowledge of the existence of a price premium, supplies quality assurance. The former argument, that a naive buyer in a market dominated by knowledgeable buyers can use price as a quality signal because the relative market price of different products reflects differences in production costs and therefore differences in quality, crucially depends upon a "majority" of the buyers in the market being knowledgeable.

As Scitovsky (1945, p. 101) correctly notes, ". . . the situation becomes paradoxical when price is the index by which the average buyer judges quality. In a market where this happens price ceases to be governed by competition and becomes instead an instrument wherewith the seller can influence his customer's opinions of the quality of his wares." However, even when the "average" buyer uses price as an index of quality, we need not fear, as Scitovsky does, the havoc this supposedly wreaks on the economic theory of choice. All consumers in a market may consistently use price, given their estimates of salvageable production costs, as an indicator of the firm's price-premium stream and therefore as an indicator of the anticipated quality of the output to be supplied by the firm. Scitovsky did not consider that price not only influences buyers' expectations but also influences producers' incentives.

We do not wish to suggest that use of implicit (price premium–specific investment) contracts is always the cheapest way to assure quality supply. When quality characteristics can be specified cheaply and measured by a third party, and hence contract enforcement costs are anticipated to be low, explicit contractual solutions with governmentally enforced penalties (including warranties) may be a less

ASSURING CONTRACTUAL PERFORMANCE   635

costly solution. When explicit contract costs are high and the extent of short-run profit from deceptively low quality supply and hence the quality-assuring price premium is also high, governmental specification and enforcement of minimum quality standards may be an alternative method of reducing the costs of assuring the supply of high quality products.[21] And, finally, vertical integration, which in this consumer-product context may consist of home production or consumer cooperatives, may be a possible alternative arrangement (see Klein, Crawford, and Alchian 1978).

The three major methods in which to organize transactions can be usefully considered within this framework as (*a*) explicit contractual or regulatory specification with third-party enforcement, (*b*) direct (two-party) enforcement of implicit contracts, and (*c*) one-party organization or vertical integration. This paper has analyzed the brand name repeat-purchase mechanism represented by the second alternative. More generally, however, all market transactions, including those "within" the firm such as employer-employee agreements, consist of a combination of the two basic forms of contractual arrangements. Some elements of performance will be specified and enforced by third-party sanctions and other elements enforced without invoking the power of some outside party to the transaction but merely by the threat of termination of the transactional relationship.

Our analysis implies that, given a particular level of explicit contract costs, we are more likely to observe an increased reliance on the brand name contract-enforcement mechanism the lower the rate of interest and the lower the level of prepurchase quality-determination costs. The lower the interest rate the greater the capital cost to a firm from the loss of future sales and therefore the lower the equilibrium price premium. Hence we can expect the termination of future exchange method of enforcing contracts to be more effective. More generally, since the interest rate in our model refers to the period of product repurchase, the quality assurance will be less costly for less durable goods that have greater repurchase frequency. Franchising chains, for example, take advantage of this effect by making it possible for

---

[21] Such governmental regulations, however, do not avoid the contractual problems of ex ante explicitly defining in an enforceable manner all major elements of performance. Nor do they necessarily avoid the implicit contractual conditions of a price-premium stream (created by entry restrictions, an initial forfeitable bond, and/or minimum price restraints) to effectively enforce the governmental regulations (see Klein et al. 1980). In addition, by making it illegal to supply less than the regulated quality, individuals that would voluntarily demand lower quality than the regulated standard incur a loss of consumer surplus. Distribution effects are created, since while the regulation may decrease the cost of supplying high quality output it increases the cost of supplying lower quality output.

consumers to pool information from sales of seemingly disparate sellers, thereby decreasing the period of repurchase and the quality-assuring price.

Similarly, purchase from a diversified firm increases the frequency of repeat purchase and lowers the necessary price premium. As long as consumers react to receiving unexpectedly low quality from a diversified firm by reducing purchases of the firm's entire product line, all the firm's nonsalvageable capital serves to assure the quality of each product it produces. This economy of scale in communicating quality-assurance information to consumers may be one motivation for conglomerate mergers. If a firm sells a set of products, each of which is produced by capital with salvage value less than costs, the quality-guaranteeing price premium on each product will be lower than if production were done by separate firms.

Finally, we can expect greater reliance on the non-third-party method of contract enforcement the lower the direct costs to the consumer of determining quality of the product prepurchase. The higher the costs of producing the minimum quality output that cannot be distinguished prepurchase from a given promised high quality output and the faster these minimum quality production costs rise with increased output, the lower the potential short-run cheating gain and therefore the lower the price premium. When the low quality cost function is such that a cheating firm can expand output a substantial amount with little increase in cost, use of the brand name enforcement mechanism is unlikely.

When the low quality cost function becomes so flat that the premium solution does not exist, the implicit contract-enforcement mechanism we have analyzed will not be used. When this condition is combined with an extremely high cost of quality assurance via explicit contractual guarantees, governmental supply may be the cheapest alternative. An obvious example is the good "money," where the marginal cost of production is essentially zero, the short-run cheating potential extremely large, and where the cost of a commodity money or the necessary bullion reserves to assure performance via convertibility is also extremely high. Governmental supply is the generally adopted but far from costless solution (see Klein 1974). Other products where the "hold-up" potential is very large and where explicit contract costs are high (such as police or fire protection services) are also generally supplied by non-profit-maximizing government agencies rather than by unregulated profit-maximizing firms earning large quasi rents on unsalvageable (firm-specific) capital assets. In general, minimization of the cost of assuring performance will imply an optimal combination of governmental regulation and/or supply, explicit contractual enforcement, vertical integration, and the implicit (brand name) contractual enforcement mechanism we have analyzed.

Appendix

Simulation of the Quality-assuring Price

If we assume that output of high and low (minimum) quality is produced by constant-elasticity cost functions of the form:

$$C_h = F_h + \beta_h x_h^\alpha, \tag{A1}$$

$$C_l = F_l + \beta_l x_l^\alpha, \tag{A2}$$

the quality-assuring price premium, $\tilde{P}$, will be given by:[22]

$$\tilde{P} = \left\{ \frac{\left[1 - \dfrac{(F_l/F_h)r}{1+r} \right]}{1 - \dfrac{r}{1+r}\left(\dfrac{\beta_l}{\beta_h}\right)^{1/(\alpha-1)}} \right\}^{(\alpha-1)/\alpha} . \tag{A3}$$

This expression indicates that as the ratio of low to high quality fixed costs, (F_l/F_h), decreases the quality-guaranteeing price-premium increases (because the short-run profit from cheating increases). But, as long as F_l can be assumed to be less than or equal to F_h, fixed costs cannot affect the existence of the quality-guaranteeing price premium. Similarly, as the interest rate, r, increases, the quality-guaranteeing price premium increases but will always exist. It is the marginal cost elasticity, $[1/(\alpha - 1)]$, and the ratio of the marginal cost slopes, (β_l/β_h), that determine the existence of a quality-assuring price premium. An increase in the elasticity of marginal cost or a decrease in the ratio of the low to high quality marginal cost slopes, by increasing the possible expansion of the low quality output at the high quality-guaranteeing price, increases the quality-guaranteeing price premium and the likelihood that it may not exist. Simulation results as a function of these parameters are presented in table A1 below. The ratio of the quality-assuring price to the minimum average cost of high quality production, P_2/P_1 in terms of figure 1, along with the ratio of low quality output at the quality-assuring price relative to the minimum high quality average cost output, x_4/x_1 in terms of figure 1, is presented. When the quality-assuring price does not exist, the ratio of low quality output at a P_2/P_1 ratio of 2 to the output at the minimum average cost of low quality output, x_0, is presented in brackets to indicate the shape of the low quality cost function. The results indicate that these cases of nonexistence generally occur where the low quality cost curve is so flat relative to the high quality cost curve that cheating output can be expanded dramatically relative to the noncheating output. For example, when the marginal cost elasticity is assumed to be 10.0 and the ratio of marginal cost slopes is assumed to be 0.25, it implies that low quality output can be profitably expanded by more than a billion times beyond its minimum average cost rate when the market price is double the perfectly competitive high quality price.

---

[22] The derivation is available to readers upon request.

TABLE A1

SIMULATION OF QUALITY-ASSURING PRICES

Interest Rate r	Ratio of Fixed Costs (F_l/F_h)	Marginal Cost Elasticity $[1/(\alpha-1)]$	Ratio of Marginal Cost Slopes (β_l/β_h)	Price-Premium Ratio (P_2/P_1)	Output Ratio (x_4/x_1)
.03	.5	.5	.25	1.031	2.03
.03	.5	.5	.50	1.018	1.43
.03	.5	.5	.75	1.013	1.16
.03	.5	2.0	.25	1.227	24.07
.03	.5	2.0	.50	1.037	4.30
.03	.5	2.0	.75	1.013	1.82
.03	.5	4.0	.25	Does not exist	$[4.10 \times 10^3]$
.03	.5	4.0	.50	1.130	26.12
.03	.5	4.0	.75	1.017	3.37
.03	.5	10.0	.25	Does not exist	$[1.07 \times 10^9]$
.03	.5	10.0	.50	Does not exist	$[1.05 \times 10^6]$
.03	.5	10.0	.75	1.067	33.97
.03	1.0	.5	.25	1.021	2.02
.03	1.0	.5	.50	1.008	1.42
.03	1.0	.5	.75	1.003	1.16
.03	1.0	2.0	.25	1.221	23.84
.03	1.0	2.0	.50	1.032	4.26
.03	1.0	2.0	.75	1.008	1.81
.03	1.0	4.0	.25	Does not exist	$[4.10 \times 10^3]$
.03	1.0	4.0	.50	1.127	25.81
.03	1.0	4.0	.75	1.013	3.34
.03	1.0	10.0	.25	Does not exist	$[1.07 \times 10^9]$
.03	1.0	10.0	.50	Does not exist	$[1.05 \times 10^6]$
.03	1.0	10.0	.75	1.066	1.82×10^4
.09	.5	.5	.25	1.097	2.09
.09	.5	.5	.50	1.056	1.45
.09	.5	.5	.75	1.039	1.18

(continued overleaf)

.09	.5	2.0	.25	Does not exist	[64.0]
.09	.5	2.0	.50	1.127	5.08
.09	.5	2.0	.75	1.040	1.92
.09	.5	4.0	.25	Does not exist	$[4.10 \times 10^3]$
.09	.5	4.0	.50	Does not exist	$[2.56 \times 10^2]$
.09	.5	4.0	.75	1.053	3.89
.09	.5	10.0	.25	Does not exist	$[1.07 \times 10^9]$
.09	.5	10.0	.50	Does not exist	$[1.05 \times 10^6]$
.09	.5	10.0	.75	Does not exist	$[1.82 \times 10^4]$
.09	1.0	.5	.25	1.065	2.06
.09	1.0	.5	.50	1.026	1.43
.09	1.0	.5	.75	1.009	1.16
.09	1.0	2.0	.25	Does not exist	[64.0]
.09	1.0	2.0	.50	1.111	4.93
.09	1.0	2.0	.75	1.024	1.87
.09	1.0	4.0	.25	Does not exist	$[4.10 \times 10^3]$
.09	1.0	4.0	.50	Does not exist	$[2.56 \times 10^2]$
.09	1.0	4.0	.75	1.044	3.76
.09	1.0	10.0	.25	Does not exist	$[1.07 \times 10^9]$
.09	1.0	10.0	.50	Does not exist	$[1.05 \times 10^6]$
.09	1.0	10.0	.75	Does not exist	$[1.82 \times 10^4]$

References

Akerlof, George A. "The Market for 'Lemons': Quality Uncertainty and the Market Mechanism." *Q.J.E.* 84 (August 1970): 488–500.

Becker, Gary S., and Stigler, George J. "Law Enforcement, Malfeasance, and Compensation of Enforcers." *J. Legal Studies* 3 (January 1974): 1–18.

Chamberlin, Edward H. *The Theory of Monopolistic Competition: A Re-Orientation of the Theory of Value.* 8th ed. Cambridge, Mass.: Harvard Univ. Press, 1965.

Darby, Michael R., and Karni, Edi. "Free Competition and the Optimal Amount of Fraud." *J. Law and Econ.* 16 (April 1973): 67–88.

Demsetz, Harold. "The Nature of Equilibrium in Monopolistic Competition." *J.P.E.* 67, no. 1 (February 1959): 21–30.

———. "Do Competition and Monopolistic Competition Differ?" *J.P.E.* 76, no. 1 (January/February 1968): 146–48.

Federal Trade Commission, Office of the Federal Registrar. *Guides concerning Use of Endorsements and Testimonials in Advertising.* 16 CFR, pt. 255. Washington: Government Printing Office, 1980.

Goldberg, Victor P. "Toward an Expanded Theory of Contract." *J. Econ. Issues* 10 (March 1976): 45–61.

Hayek, Friedrich A. "The Meaning of Competition." In *Individualism and Economic Order.* Chicago: Univ. Chicago Press, 1948.

Hobbes, Thomas. *Leviathan.* Oxford: Blackwell, 1955, first published 1651.

IMS America, Ltd. *U.S. Pharmaceutical Market, Drug Stores and Hospitals, Audit of Purchases.* Bergen, N.J.: IMS America, 1978.

Klein, Benjamin. "The Competitive Supply of Money." *J. Money, Credit and Banking* 6 (November 1974): 423–53.

———. "Borderlines of Law and Economic Theory: Transaction Cost Determinants of 'Unfair' Contractual Arrangements." *A.E.R. Papers and Proc.* 70 (May 1980): 356–62.

Klein, Benjamin; Crawford, Robert G.; and Alchian, Armen A. "Vertical Integration, Appropriable Rents, and the Competitive Contracting Process." *J. Law and Econ.* 21 (October 1978): 297–326.

Klein, Benjamin; McLaughlin, Andrew; and Murphy, Kevin M. "Resale Price Maintenance, Exclusive Territories, and Franchise Termination: The Coors Case." Working Paper, UCLA, 1980.

Leffler, Keith B. "The Role of Price in Guaranteeing Quality." Working Paper no. CPB77-5, Univ. Rochester, June 1977.

Luce, R. Duncan, and Raiffa, Howard. *Games and Decisions: Introduction and Critical Survey.* New York: Wiley, 1957.

Macaulay, Stewart, "Non-contractual Relations in Business: A Preliminary Study." *American Soc. Rev.* 28 (February 1963): 55–67.

Macneil, Ian. "The Many Futures of Contracts." *Southern California Law Rev.* 47 (May 1974): 691–816.

Marshall, Alfred. *Principles of Economics: An Introductory Volume.* 8th ed. New York: Macmillan, 1949.

Mishan, Edward J. *21 Popular Economic Fallacies.* New York: Praeger, 1970.

Nelson, Phillip. "Information and Consumer Behavior." *J.P.E.* 78, no. 2 (March/April 1970): 311–29.

———. "Advertising as Information." *J.P.E.* 82, no. 4 (July/August 1974): 729–54.

Schmalensee, Richard. "A Model of Advertising and Product Quality." *J.P.E.* 86, no. 3 (June 1978): 485–503.

Scitovsky, Tibor. "Some Consequences of the Habit of Judging Quality by Price." *Rev. Econ. Studies* 12, no. 2 (1945): 100–105.

Smith, Adam. *An Inquiry into the Nature and Causes of the Wealth of Nations.* New York: Modern Library, 1937, first published 1776.

Spence, A. Michael. "Job Market Signaling." *Q.J.E.* 87 (August 1973): 355–74.

Telser, Lester G. "A Theory of Self-enforcing Agreements." *J. Bus.* 22, no. 1 (January 1980): 27–44.

Williamson, Oliver E. "Transaction-Cost Economics: The Governance of Contractual Relations." *J. Law and Econ.* 22 (October 1979): 233–61.

[19]

Contract Law and the State of Nature

ANTHONY T. KRONMAN
Yale University

1. INTRODUCTION

> If a covenant be made, wherein neither of the parties perform presently, but trust one another, in the condition of mere nature, which is a condition of war of every man against every man, upon any reasonable suspicion, it is void: but if there be a common power set over them both, with right and force sufficient to compel performance, it is not void. For he that performeth first, has no assurance the other will perform after; because the bonds of words are too weak to bridle men's ambition, avarice, anger, and other passions, without the fear of some coercive power; which in the condition of mere nature, where all men are equal, and judges of the justness of their own fears, cannot possibly be supposed. And therefore he which performeth first, does but betray himself to his enemy; contrary to the right, he can never abandon, of defending his life, and means of living.
>
> —Thomas Hobbes, *Leviathan*

A contract is a legally enforceable agreement, one the state will enforce by placing its coercive powers at the disposal of either party if the other fails to perform. The rules that specify when the state will do so constitute our law of contracts. From the point of view of the parties themselves, the law of contracts is a valuable and important institution because it enables them to harness the state's powers of coercion for their own private ends. The state may be thought of as a kind of machine (an enforcement machine). There is no other like it; within its own territory, the state possesses matchless powers of compulsion. If this machine were privately owned, contracting parties would pay for its use, and the taxes the state collects to support its monopoly of violence in part represent disguised payments of exactly this sort.

Suppose the state did not exist. Would people still make agreements, even though they could no longer make contracts? Another way of putting this is to ask whether people would make agreements in what philosophers have traditionally referred to as a "state of nature." This is a question of general significance that has been of interest not only to philosophers such as

Journal of Law, Economics, and Organization vol. 1, no. 1 Fall 1985

6 / JOURNAL OF LAW, ECONOMICS, AND ORGANIZATION   I:1, 1985

Scanlon (1) and Nozick (3–25), who explicitly invoke the concept of a state of
nature, but also to many economists and lawyers who do not use the term itself. As examples I would mention Thomas Schelling's work on the strategy
of bargaining (1956: 281); Oliver Williamson's analysis of transaction-specific
capital investments as a form of economic hostage-giving (1983: 519); the account that Klein, Crawford, and Alchian have offered of vertical integration
as a response to certain types of contractual opportunism (1978:297); Telser's
work on self-enforcing agreements (27); the theory of bonding costs proposed by Jensen and Meckling (305), together with its recent applications in
corporate and commercial law (Kraakman: 857; Jackson and Kronman, 1979:
1143; Levmore: 49); Peter Reuter's book on the organization of illegal markets; Posner's economic analysis of primitive society (146); and Stewart
Macaulay's well-known account of what he terms the "non-contractual" element in exchange relations (55).

In style, method, and content, this is a diverse literature, but one with a
common theme. Each of the writers I have mentioned is interested in the
opportunities that individuals exploit, and the arrangements they invent, to
enhance the security of their agreements where no legal remedies for breach
exist (or where those that do are plainly inadequate). One can describe the
work of these writers in various ways—Williamson, for example, refers to it
as "the law and economics of private ordering" (1983: 520)—but I prefer to
characterize it somewhat differently, as a contribution to our understanding
of the techniques of agreement in the state of nature. This way of putting
things, which may at first seem rather odd, has the advantages of emphasizing the easily overlooked connection between a very new intellectual tradition and a much older one and of drawing our attention to the relevance
each may have for the other.

There is, of course, some risk in using an expression like "the state of nature," which comes with so much historical baggage and calls to mind so
many suggestive images. It may help, therefore, if I indicate at the outset
how I propose to use the term in the essay that follows.

In Hobbes's classical account, the state of nature is described as a "war of
every man against every man" and conceived as a condition of radical insecurity. The insecurity that Hobbes associates with the state of nature is of two
different sorts. The first we might call "vulnerability of possession": in a state
of nature, according to Hobbes, whatever an individual already happens to
possess at any given moment is subject to attack and expropriation by others,
so that even the things he now controls are not securely his. The second we
might call "transactional insecurity": in a state of nature, any exchange which
requires one party to perform before the other exposes the party who performs first to the danger that after completing his side of the exchange, he
will be denied whatever it was he bargained for in return. In his description
of the state of nature, Hobbes tends to treat these two forms of insecurity as
if they were inseparable, ascribing both to the same cause (the absence of a

CONTRACT LAW AND THE STATE OF NATURE / 7

sovereign power able to enforce proprietary and contractual claims) and recommending for both an identical cure. The link between them does seem, however, to be looser than Hobbes supposed, for relative invulnerability of possession may be accompained by an absence of transactional security as, for example, in the kind of defensive stand-off that Hobbes thought characteristic of relations between states. If two states are evenly matched in strength and each is well protected geographically, neither may be able to expropriate the possessions of the other, and yet the transactional insecurity to which they are subject in their voluntary dealing need not, for that reason, be at all diminished. The same may be true of relations between small groups, or even individuals, depending upon their relative ability to hide, shield, or otherwise protect themselves; there is, in short, a range of plausible, indeed familiar, situations in which a considerable degree of possessory security is accompanied by a very large measure of transactional insecurity. It would appear, in fact, that the two forms of insecurity which Hobbes associates with the state of nature are not only separable, but that the second of the two—transactional insecurity—is more deeply entrenched and less easily eliminable than the first, for it is hard to imagine how this form of insecurity could be eliminated without eliminating the other as well (although the reverse, as I have just suggested, seems not to be the case). In any event, the situations in which I am most interested are those that combine possessory security with transactional insecurity, and I shall define the state of nature, in a more limited way than Hobbes, to cover only situations of this sort.

When two individuals (or groups) exchange promises and neither has the power to compel the other to perform, and there is also no third party powerful enough to enforce the agreement on their behalf, I shall speak of them as being in a state of nature vis-à-vis one another, even where both parties are able to protect whatever they presently possess from attack or expropriation by the other. When I say that neither has the power to compel the other's performance, I mean that neither possesses such power on his own or can acquire it without the other's cooperation (for example, by the voluntary transfer of a hostage). In a state of nature, the parties to an agreement must establish, by themselves, the conditions of whatever enforcement powers they hope to enjoy—these powers do not exist by nature and, more important, they do not exist by virtue of the effective guarantees of a dominant third party. This last point is the one I want to stress: in "the condition of mere nature," as Hobbes called it, those who make covenants are not subject to any "common power" with the "right and force sufficient to compel performance" (89). This characteristic, which has often been taken to be a symptom of the state of nature, I shall treat as its definition.

Three points should be emphasized. First, my idea of the state of nature is a relational one: to say that two persons or groups are in a state of nature is to assert something about the relationship between them. It follows that no one can be in a state of nature by himself. Even Crusoe is not in a state of

8 / JOURNAL OF LAW, ECONOMICS, AND ORGANIZATION   I:1, 1985

nature, at least not until he discovers Friday and makes or attempts to make his first agreement with him. A state of nature is therefore not a condition of radical isolation, as Rousseau at times implies in his essay on the origins of inequality (104–11), but a social state, a condition defined by the dealings men have (or can have) with one another.[1]

Second, the term "state of nature," as I shall use it is not intended to suggest any specific level of moral or cultural development on the part of those to whom the term is applied. The attainment of a high level of cultural refinement, the existence of shared moral beliefs, and general agreement in matters of taste are all consistent with the absence of a "common power" strong enough to enforce agreements between the parties. It would be wrong, therefore, to conceive the state of nature as a condition of backwardness or to associate it exclusively with historically primitive societies.

Third, my deliberately vague definition of the state of nature is also not meant to imply anything about the nature or source of the "common power" whose absence is its distinguishing characteristic. We tend to equate this common power with preeminent physical force (having always before us the example of the modern nation state), but nothing in my definition requires us to do so. Suppose two villagers agree to an exchange and agree, in addition, that any dispute between them shall be arbitrated by a village elder respected for his wisdom and regarded by everyone in the community as the supreme bearer of traditional authority. Though the compulsion that he exercises over the parties is entirely psychological and rests exclusively upon an appeal to their convictions and beliefs, my imaginary village elder may be as much a "common power," from the standpoint of the parties themselves, as any modern state apparatus enjoying a monopoly of physical violence.[2] It would be a mistake, therefore, to equate the existence of a state of nature, as I have defined it, with the absence of such an apparatus, the absence of those specific arrangements that we associate, both conceptually and historically, with the modern state.[3]

---

1. For the expression of a similar idea, see Marx (84).

2. I am using the concept of power in the way Max Weber did, to mean "the probability that one actor within a social relationship will be in a position to carry out his own will despite resistance, regardless of the basis on which this probability rests" (53).

3. If two individuals belong to a mutual protection association which is willing and able to enforce any agreements its members make with one another, then the individuals in question are not in state of nature vis-à-vis one another (though it is obvious that they may still be in a state of nature with regard to nonmembers). However, if we adopt Max Weber's definition of a state as "a human community that (successfully) claims the *monopoly of the legitimate use of physical force* within a given territory," then the mutual protection association need not necessarily be a state. It will not be a state, for example, if it is indifferent to, or unable to control, the use of physical force by nonmembers living interstitially within the territory of its members. Nozick describes the forces that drive an association of this sort in the direction of a fully developed Weberian state (22–25; 88–119).

As these remarks suggest, my concept of the state of nature is a broad one, broad enough to include any situation in which individuals and groups must arrange their transactions (if they are to transact at all) without the aid of an independent enforcement mechanism whose powers are significantly greater than their own. As I conceive it, the state of nature is neither a philosophical fantasy nor a primitive stage of life that we have permanently transcended. On the contrary—nothing could be more familiar or more real. Consider, for example, the predicament of two warring countries attempting to conclude a peace treaty—or, for that matter, two friendly countries negotiating an arms control agreement (Schelling, 1966; Gauthier: 207–12). In the absence of a global sovereign capable of enforcing such an agreement, the parties remain in a state of nature and must provide for their own protection. To this extent, they face the same problem as the California gold miners who in the 1850s had to establish workable agreements to govern their joint projects despite the political vacuum left by the collapse of local Spanish rule (Umbeck: 421). The Norse invasions of Western Europe created comparable conditions in the early Middle Ages and the small, self-protective associations that emerged (which we associate with the idea of feudalism) represent another example of how people have dealt with the difficulties of establishing reliable agreements in a state of nature (Bloch: 443). And because outlaws have had to find a way of conducting business without the assistance of the state, they have at all times faced similar problems in their dealings with one another (Reuter: 119–23).

These examples are deliberately eclectic, and I have chosen them to convey some sense of how broad a range of situations I mean to include within the scope of my discussion. It is the breadth of this approach that recommends it: widening our conception of the state of nature in the way I have proposed encourages us to search for the structural features these situations have in common and gives us a fuller appreciation of the techniques available to those who, for one reason or another, must make their agreements without the security afforded by Hobbes's "common power."

2. SECURITY AND INSECURITY IN THE STATE OF NATURE

We ought to begin, perhaps, by noting what is obvious: even in a state of nature, two individuals will have an incentive to exchange resources whenever both can be made better off by the trade (the same incentive they would have in any other setting). Suppose I have an orange and you have an apple. If we each want what the other has, we can simply meet and make the exchange. When the exchange is simultaneous, neither of us needs to worry about enforcing the other's performance. Of course, if I am worried that your apple may have hidden defects—that it may be rotten at the core—the fact that we are trading in a state of nature will cause me greater concern. In this case, I have not really gotten what I want until the apple is consumed, and if we simply exchange fruits and walk away I run the risk that you may have done me a harm I have no power to repair. This illustrates a general point: whenever the full performance of an exchange requires time (on one side or both), a situation may arise in which one party receives what he has bargained for before the other does, leaving the latter to rely on the promise of his trading partner to complete a still-unfinished job. Where one of the parties is put in an asymmetrically disadvantageous position of this sort—where the exchange cannot be made perfectly simultaneous at every step—the absence of a centralized enforcement mechanism increases the risk and hence the cost of the exchange for the disadvantaged trader. If the risk is great enough, it may kill the exchange entirely, even though both parties would be better off were it completed.

There will be pressure, therefore, to make exchanges in the state of nature as simultaneous as possible (even if this must be arranged artificially) so as to reduce the risk that the party who finishes first will be deprived of his agreed return (Kronman and Posner, 1979: 1–4). You and I might agree, for example, to eat our fruit, bite by bite, in one another's presence. Or, to take another case, instead of giving you my horse in return for the promise of an unborn calf, I might insist that the calf be *in esse* and that you deliver it to me at the same moment I relinquish possession of the horse. In a state of nature one would expect to observe, in general, the widespread substitution of barter for contract as a method of exchange and a tendency to make all transactions as instantaneous as possible, since perfect simultaneity becomes more difficult to sustain as the time required for performance increases.[4]

But this push toward simultaneity has its costs; after all, we probably have better things to do than watch each other eat, and you may need my horse

4. One might also expect to observe the opposite phenomenon: the systematic transformation of one-shot transactions into long-term relationships based upon a repetitive pattern of exchange. If I grow most of the wheat in a particular area, and you catch most of the fish, you may be willing to give me fish on credit until my annual harvest; knowing I shall want more fish afterwards, you are confident I will keep my promise and deliver a portion of the wheat crop as payment for the fish I have already received. If we cannot arrange to exchange our goods simultaneously, the next best thing is to make our relationship a permanent and cyclical one, so that at any given moment the party who has extended credit by performing first knows he can withhold some desired future benefit as a punishment for cheating on the other's part. Rather than reducing our exchange to an instant, we may adopt the opposite strategy and try to avoid the risk of opportunism by stretching it out forever; our aim, in this case, will be *never* to complete the transaction.

One of the conditions for our initiating a long-term transaction of this sort, however, is that we not know, in advance, which round of exchanges will be our last. "If two parties are in a sequence of transactions such that both know for sure which transaction is the last, then each also knows that violating the terms of the agreement on the last transaction cannot evoke a sacrifice of the net gains thereafter. Consequently, each party would be under no compulsion to abide by the terms at the last transaction. Since the same argument applies to the next to the last transaction and so on to the first, we would be driven to the conclusion that no finite sequence of transactions can be self-enforcing if both parties know for sure which transaction is that last one" (Telser: 29).

right now—to plow a field—and consider even a two-week wait catastrophic. If the cost of altering our conduct to assure simultaneity is high enough, and if there are no other means by which we can reduce the risk of exploitation created by our temporally disjunct perfomances, the exchange we both would like to make may never materialize. The exchange of my horse (which you need immediately) for your unborn calf can take place only if I am prepared to part with my property in reliance on your promise to perform. Will I agree to make such a trade where there is no dominant third party with sufficient strength to compel your performance if you breach? If the risk is great enough, I may be prepared to go forward only if there are private mechanisms that I can substitute for the missing guarantees of a coercive "common power." The introduction of money might seeem to be the simplest way to eliminate the risks associated with nonsimultaneous exchange: if I transfer my horse to you and you pay me for it immediately, then in a later, simultaneous exchange I can use the money to buy your calf or someone else's. This may, however, be a less satisfactory solution than at first appears. In the state of nature an object can function as a medium of exchange only by virtue of its real or intrinsic worth, since the establishment of a currency system in which the nominal value of money exceeds it real value itself requires the effective guarantee of some centralized institution or common power. This necessarily limits the money supply in any state of nature situation and makes it more likely that the parties to a particular exchange will have to choose between barter and no exchange at all; thus, you may simply not have enought money to buy my horse or enough disposable assets to sell to obtain the money. Second, even if you have given me the money to pay for the horse, there is no guarantee that you will take the money back in exchange for your calf when the time comes; in the meantime, for example, you may have received a better offer. If others have equally suitable calves, this need not concern me, since I can use the money you have given me to buy a calf from someone else. But if your calf is the only one I want, then even the introduction of money cannot assure that I will realize the full benefits of our proposed exchange; having been paid for my horse, I am no worse off than I was before, but unless I can compel you to transfer the calf I am no better off, either—and thus, from my perspective at least, the purpose of our exchange has been frustrated.

In the state of nature, where there is no coercive common power, those contemplating a nonsimultaneous exchange must rely for their security on devices of their own construction. There are at least four different devices or techniques of this sort, and although in reality the lines between them are often blurred, for the sake of analytic clarity I shall treat them as ideal types and emphasize the features that distinguish each from the others. The first technique involves the use of hostages and the second the use of collateral (an important difference). The third technique aims to make agreements self-enforcing by means of what Williamson (following Schelling) has called

12 / JOURNAL OF LAW, ECONOMICS, AND ORGANIZATION   I:1, 1985

"hands-tying" (1983: 73), and the fourth technique seeks to overcome the tensions that create insecurity by encouraging (or compelling) an emotional and psychological union between the parties, so that neither is able to distinguish his own interest from that of the other. Each of these techniques has its advantages and disadvantages; each brings benefits and none is costless. In some cases, it is helpful to view one technique as an attempted solution to the problems of another, and I have arranged my discussion of the four to bring out these relationships where they exist.

2.1 HOSTAGES

Suppose that I agree to trade my horse for your unborn calf, the exchange to take place immediately. If I want to increase the likelihood that you will deliver your calf as promised, I may insist that you give me a hostage to hold until your performance is completed. The hostage can be anything (or anyone) of value to you; knowing that I can destroy the hostage if you fail to perform, you have an incentive to keep your end of the bargain and I, knowing this, am made more secure.

The intended effect can be achieved even if the hostage is of no value, even resale value, to me, so long as it is of value to you. (As we shall see, this is what distinguishes a hostage from collateral.) Suppose, for example, that you have an heirloom of great sentimental but no market value—a skillet that has been in your family for three generations (too short a time to be a valuable antique). If you give me the skillet as a hostage, I can influence your behavior by threatening to destroy it, even though its destruction will do me no good at all. Consider a less far-fetched and more important example: the antiballistic missile (ABM) treaty of 1972. By forswearing the use of certain defensive measures against one another's offensive nuclear forces, the United States and the Soviet Union gave each other the power to destroy their respective populations. The actual destruction of 100 million Soviet citizens would do us no good whatsoever, but the threat to destroy them is of considerable value as a deterrent. As Schelling has suggested (1960: 136–37), an antidefensive treaty of this sort constitutes, in effect, a mutual exchange of hostages—an exchange intended to enhance the confidence of each side that the other will keep its word and refrain from starting a nuclear war.

The ABM treaty dramatizes another important feature of hostage-giving: in order to give your trading partner a hostage, it is not always necessary that the hostage be delivered into his possession.[5] It is sufficient that you give up

---

5. "Reciprocal trading supported by separate but concurrent investments in specific assets provides a mutual safeguard against [the risk of breach by the other party]. The hostages that are thereby created have the interesting property, moreover, that they are *never exchanged*. Instead, each party retains possession of its dedicated assets should the contract be prematurely terminated" (Williamson, 1983: 532). What Williamson describes as a mutual exchange of hostages I would classify, under the scheme proposed in this essay, as a form of bilateral hands-tying.

your ability to prevent the hostage from being harmed; if this can be done without actually relinquishing the hostage, it may be to the advantage of all concerned that the hostage remain with its original possessor.

Naturally, the hostage-giver will want his hostage to be returned when he performs his promise; indeed, these two things must occur simultaneously, for otherwise there is nothing to prevent the recipient from keeping the hostage and insisting that it be ransomed back. When you deliver your calf to me, I must return the skillet. There may be some technical difficulties in arranging the exchange so that it is perfectly simultaneous, but these will, in most cases, be the same difficulties we would have had in arranging a simultaneous horse-calf exchange if your calf had been in a deliverable state at the time of our original agreement. Hostage-giving is, in fact, simply a means for achieving a simultaneity that would otherwise be unattainable; the hostage acts as a bridge between two temporally distant moments of performance and brings them into an artificial union with one another. In this sense, the function of hostage-giving is to transform exchange back into barter. If, for some reason, his hostage cannot be given back at the time he performs, the hostage-giver will have to rely on the recipient's promise to return it later on and therefore will be in the same position the recipient was in at the outset of their exchange. In this event, the use of a hostage will not have eliminated the risk of opportunism inherent in the original situation but merely transferred it from one party to the other. If, to protect himself, the hostage-giver then demands a hostage for his hostage—a mutual exchange of hostages—the other party will be no better off than he was to begin with before any hostage had been given at all.[6] To avoid these problems, the hostage he gives must be the kind of thing that *can* be returned to the hostage-giver at the time of his performance: only things of this sort make suitable hostages because only they can be used to achieve the artificial simultaneity which is the aim of all hostage-giving.

The essential characteristic of a hostage is that it is valued by the hostage-giver but not necessarily by the recipient or anyone else. The purest example of a hostage, therefore, would be something that had worth to the hostage-giver but no market value at all or, even more strongly, something that anyone other than the hostage-giver would consider a positive liability

6. If, upon receiving my horse, you promise to give me your calf and, in addition, a hostage to hold until your promise is fulfilled, and I give *you* a hostage of some sort to stand as security for my promise to return your hostage after the calf has been delivered to me, what is to prevent you from keeping the horse and then offering to ransom back your hostage by returning mine, in a simultaneous swap? This may or may not work, depending upon the relative value that each of us attaches to the hostages we have given and the knowledge we have of one another's (true) valuations. As the first mover, however, I recognize that a mutual exchange of hostages leaves me vulnerable, perhaps as vulnerable as I was to begin with, because it is self-neutralizing and therefore fails to counterbalance the risks created by the nonsimultaneity in the underlying exchange. This gives me a reason to insist on a unilateral arrangement and to resist any suggestion that I give you a hostage in return; only an arrangement of the former sort can offset the risk associated with being the first to perform.

14 / JOURNAL OF LAW, ECONOMICS, AND ORGANIZATION   I:1, 1985

and pay to have taken off his hands. It is precisely this characteristic that makes hostage-giving so appealing from the perspective of the hostage-giver; if a hostage has no independent value to the recipient, he will always prefer the performance he has been promised to the hostage he holds and therefore be happy to exchange the one for the other. The hostage-giver need not worry that when the time comes to complete the transaction, the other party will want to keep what he has already received as a substitute for the hostage-giver's performance (unless, of course, the recipient's tastes have changed or the hostage has acquired a market value it previously did not have).

From the recipient's point of view, however, this same characteristic constitutes the most important defect that hostage-giving has as a method for increasing transactional security. Let us assume, to fix ideas, that the skillet you have given me to secure your promise to deliver the calf after it is born is in fact worth nothing to anyone but yourself. In taking a hostage of this sort, I run the obvious risk that you have deceived me regarding its (idiosyncratic) value to you. I must take your word, supported by whatever circumstantial evidence is available, that you do indeed care as much about the skillet as you claim;[7] I must, in other words, trust you, and that is just what my insistence on a hostage suggests that I am *not* prepared to do. If you have lied and do not care about the skillet, I will lack the means of coercing you to keep your original promise; I will, in effect, have sold you my horse for a worthless piece of junk. (The same is true, though to a lesser degree, if the skillet has some small resale value and you have only lied to me about the strength of your attachment to it.)

Even if you have not lied to me but do, in truth, care as much about the skillet as you say, the fact that its value is personal or idiosyncratic compromises its usefulness to me as a form of security. Suppose that you disavow our original agreement and refuse to deliver your calf after it is born. I am now free to use or sell or destroy the hostage you have given me, as I please. But if the hostage has no value to anyone but yourself, its worth to me is wholly a function of my ability to coerce you by threatening to destroy it. Destroying the skillet, however, will do me no good; if I do destroy it, I will have lost the only thing that gives me any hope of coercing your performance. So I must threaten destruction of the hostage, and do so in a believable way, but without ever following through if I am to get what I want. Since you are aware that actual destruction of the hostage can do me no good, you are in a position to bargain for an advantageous compromise. "Return my skillet," you will say, "and I will give you some small amount in exchange" (an amount that represents a fraction of the value of my horse). *You* know that I

---

7. This is a good example of what Williamson calls "impacted" information. See Williamson, (1975: 31–37).

CONTRACT LAW AND THE STATE OF NATURE / 15

am better off agreeing to the exchange, no matter how small the sum, and *I* know that you are willing—if necessary—to pay a great deal more or, indeed, to give me your calf, in order to get the skillet back. What kind of bargain we eventually strike depends upon many things—the value you attach to the hostage, your ability to persuade me that you value it less highly than you actually do, my ability to persuade you that I am prepared to destroy the hostage unless I get what I want in return (even though doing so would be self-destructive from my own point of view), and so forth. Where we settle in this "bargain space," however, is less important than the fact that the space exists, that there is something to bargain over. The space exists because the hostage you have given is worth more to you than to me. Whenever this is true, the party who receives the hostage has reason to fear that he will be forced to engage in a bargaining process he would rather avoid, because the process itself is costly and the outcome potentially disadvantageous. The more convinced a hostage-giver is that any postbreach bargaining will go in his favor, the weaker will be his incentive to perform. These are risks which, from the recipient's point of view, are necessarily connected with the use of hostages, as I have defined the term. Seeing all this in advance, anyone who agrees to an exchange in the state of nature and is required to make the first move will have an incentive to consider other methods for enhancing his transactional security.[8]

2.2. COLLATERAL

When I ask for a hostage, I am asking for something that *you* value, something you want back badly enough to fulfill your original promise, if that is

---

8. Since hostage-giving is an important method for reducing transactional insecurity, where such insecurity is especially great, as it is in the state of nature, the task of supplying hostages may be taken over by enterprising third parties and turned into a profitable business. Consider Mario Puzo's description in *The Godfather* (279–80) of the Bocchicchio clan, a group whose "one asset was a closely knit structure of blood relationships, a family loyalty severe even for a society where family loyalty came before loyalty to a wife."

A Bocchicchio never lied, never committed an act of treachery. Such behavior was too complicated. Also, a Bocchicchio never forgot an injury and never left it unavenged no matter what the cost. And so by accident they stumbled into what would prove to be their most lucrative profession.

When warring families wanted to make peace and arrange a parley, the Bocchicchio clan was contacted. The head of the clan would handle the initial negotiations and arrange for the necessary hostages. For instance, when Michael had gone to meet Sollozzo, a Bocchicchio had been left with the Corleone Family as surety for Michael's safety, the service paid for by Sollozzo. If Michael were killed by Sollozzo, then the Bocchicchio male hostage held by the Corleone Family would be killed by the Corleones. In this case the Bocchicchios would take their vengeance on Sollozzo as the cause of their clansman's death. Since the Bocchicchios were so primitive, they never let anything, any kind of punishment, stand in their way of vengeance. They would give up their own lives and there was no protection against them if they were betrayed. A Bocchicchio hostage was gilt-edged insurance.

the only condition under which I will return the hostage to you. From my point of view, however, any hostage-giving arrangement involves an irreducible risk of opportunism, for the reasons just indicated. I may be tempted, therefore, to take a different approach to the problem of assuring my own security in the state of nature and instead of demanding a hostage (something you value) insist on being given collateral (something that has a direct use or exchange value to me). Suppose, for example, that you have a golden goblet as well as an heirloom skillet. If you give me the goblet as security for your promise to deliver the calf, I now hold something that is of value to me, because either it gives me pleasure or it can be exchanged for something else that I want. To be sure, the goblet is of value to you, too, but that is not what I care about. What matters to me is that I now have an asset which is a direct substitute for the performance you have promised, an asset whose value I can realize through use or trade and (most important) without having to deal with you at all—in contrast to a hostage, which gives me a power that can only be realized by means of threats and cajolery and therefore requires our continued interaction following breach. My possession of the goblet frees me from the need to engage in any postbreach negotiations with you whatsoever and thus eliminates the peculiar form of opportunism to which those who take a hostage as security are always vulnerable.

In any particular exchange, the asset that is offered as collateral to secure the second-mover's promise to perform will probably not be worth a great deal more to the recipient than to its original possessor, since any asset of that sort is likely to have been traded away beforehand. But whatever the relative value of the collateral to the two parties, one thing seems clear: if it is to provide complete protection from the recipient's point of view, the property in question must be worth as much to him as the performance he has been promised. To the extent that it is not, the party who has received the collateral is either unsecured or secured only by whatever threat-advantage possession of the asset gives him (assuming it has a higher value to its original possessor than to the party who now holds it and therefore also functions as a hostage). Someone who wants to avoid entirely the risks associated with hostage-giving must demand collateral that is worth as much, to him, as the performance it secures, so that if the other party threatens breach he will be indifferent, or nearly so, between keeping what he already has and exchanging it for what he was originally promised.

Unfortunately, this creates a risk of opportunism on the recipient's part which is the mirror-image of the risk created by hostage-giving. Suppose that you have now given me a golden goblet as collateral to secure your promise to deliver the calf once it is born. The goblet, let us assume, is worth as much to me as the calf—it is, therefore, a perfect form of collateral. We can also assume that the goblet is worth at least as much to you (it may be worth more), since otherwise you would already have sold or traded it to me. Furthermore, we can assume that you value the goblet more than the calf. This last assumption follows from two premises: first, that the goblet is worth as much to me as the calf (that it is a complete substitute for the calf and hence a perfect form of collateral), and second, that the calf is worth more to me than to you, as it must be, or we would not have agreed to our original exchange.

To summarize, if the goblet is worth as much to me as the calf, we can confidently assume that you value the goblet more highly than the calf. You will therefore have an incentive to redeem the goblet by performing, by giving me the calf when it is born. If, however, I am indifferent between getting the calf and keeping the goblet, I can credibly threaten to keep the goblet unless you give me something more than you originally promised (say, the calf plus a month's supply of hay). It will be to your advantage to accept any such proposal so long as the additional benefit I demand costs you less than the difference between the value, to you, of the goblet and the calf, respectively. Knowing this, I can extract from you the full benefits (the "profits") you would have realized if our original horse-calf exchange had been completed and the collateral returned to you. By giving me collateral that is equal in value to the performance I have been promised, you create an opportunity for bargaining that I can exploit, if I am skillful enough, to appropriate the gain you expected to realize from our transaction.

Seeing this in advance, you have a powerful incentive to resist any demand, on my part, for complete collateralization. The most you will agree to give me is an asset (a brass goblet, perhaps) that is worth as much to me as the calf is to you, whatever the worth of the goblet itself to you may be. If I place the same value on a brass goblet that you place on your calf, I cannot make a credible threat to keep the goblet as a substitute for the calf, since the calf is worth more to me than to you and is therefore also worth more to me than the goblet. The most that I can do is threaten to destroy the goblet, if you happen to place a higher value on it than I (in which case the goblet also functions as a hostage), but this threat is inherently incredible. The actual destruction of a hostage never does the party holding the hostage any good; quite to the contrary, it harms him by extinguishing the coercive power which possession of the hostage confers. Where the hostage also has some direct use or exchange value to the party holding it, however, its destruction means the loss of this value as well as the loss of its usefulness as an instrument of blackmail. Hence, the more a hostage takes on the attributes of collateral, the more costly its destruction becomes to the hostage-holder (and the more incredible his threat to destroy it). Even if you care about the brass goblet more than I do, the higher the value I place on it, the harder it will be for me to exploit the goblet's potential as a hostage. At the same time, if I am undercollateralized—if I value your brass goblet less highly than I value the calf—I have no choice but to exploit whatever hostage potential

18 / JOURNAL OF LAW, ECONOMICS, AND ORGANIZATION   I:1, 1985

the goblet may possess. You, on the other hand, have an incentive to exploit *my* predicament by insisting that I give you back the goblet plus a premium of some sort in return for the calf—which it is in my interest to do unless I can threaten or cajole you into keeping our original agreement.

Once again, who prevails in this contest of wits and nerves depends on many factors. But the contest itself is costly (because of the risks it entails), and I would as soon avoid it altogether. To do so, however, I must be fully collateralized, and this creates a different but comparable set of risks from your point of view. Either I have adequate collateral, in which case you are at risk, or I am undercollateralized and to that extent still subject to the risks associated with hostage-giving. The interlocking and symmetrical disadvantages involved in the use of these two techniques give the parties to an exchange in the state of nature an incentive to search for an arrangement that will balance, and ideally neutralize, the risks that each technique creates. It also gives them an incentive to search for something better.

2.3. HANDS-TYING

A third method for reducing the insecurity of transactions in the state of nature takes the form of what Williamson and Schelling call "hands-tying"— actions that make a promise more credible by putting it out of the promisor's power to breach without incurring costs he could otherwise have avoided. Hands-tying is similar to hostage-giving in one general way: in each case the promisor does something at the outset that has the effect of making a subsequent breach on his part more costly. As a result, his own incentive to perform is strengthened and the confidence of the other party increased. There is, however, an important difference between these two techniques. In the case of hostage-giving, punishment for breach requires that the promisee himself do something—namely, destroy the hostage he holds as security. By contrast, hands-tying schemes are designed in such a way that the promisor's punishment is self-executing. Indeed, this is their distinctive feature; if the promisor breaches, a hands-tying arrangement guarantees that he will pay the added cost of doing so even if the promisee does nothing in response.

One example of hands-tying might be following. Let us assume (what does not seem at all unreasonable) that you are interested in preserving your reputation as a person who keeps his promises, since this will increase your opportunities for other favorable exchanges in the future (Klein and Leffler, 1981:615–16). To persuade me that you really mean to deliver the calf after it is born and will not renege, you offer to declare your commitment in a public forum, in the presence of our neighbors who have assembled for the occasion. By making a public declaration of this sort, you substantially increase the harm that will be done to your reputation if you breach. In effect, you have given your reputation in the community as security for your promise to perform. The security in question (your reputation) resembles a hostage: I cannot appropriate it for my own benefit but its destruction will do you considerable harm. There is, however, one important difference between this arrangement and the hostage-giving schemes considered earlier. If you break your promise and refuse to give me the calf, the damage to your reputation will follow automatically, or nearly so; there is nothing that *I* need to do to insure that in the future you are treated as an unreliable cheat (except, perhaps, to spread the word, and even this may be unnecessary if we have arranged to complete our exchange in public as well). By contrast, if you have given me your heirloom skillet as a hostage (rather than your reputation), an affirmative act on my part is required to deprive you of the hostage as a penalty for failing to keep your promise.

Consider another example of hands-tying. Suppose that I agree to give you my horse and in exchange you agree to make me a suit of clothes. You need the horse immediately, but the suit will take time to complete, and in the interim I must rely on your promise to perform. To make the promise credible, you take a bolt of cloth and cut from it the pieces you will need to construct my suit (you do this at the same time that I give you the horse). It is, of course, still possible for you to break your promise if you choose. But you have considerably less to gain from breach now that you have taken the first decisive step of cutting the cloth to my dimensions. To use these same pieces for someone else will now require more work (additional cutting, stitching pieces back together, etc.)—if, indeed, they can be made to fit anyone else at all. By cutting the cloth, you have increased the cost of using it for any purpose other than to complete my suit; this gives me added confidence that the reputational harm you will suffer if you break your promise is likely to be greater, in your own eyes, than any potential advantage to be gained from doing so. Most important, you have now made it certain, by your actions, that in the event of breach you will automatically incur certain additional costs that would otherwise have been avoidable. Again, there is no need for me to intervene, to do something *to* you; you have arranged things so that whatever wounds you suffer will be self-inflicted.

It is this element of automaticity that distinguishes hands-tying from the other forms of hostage-giving described earlier.[9] From the promisee's point of view, it is the automatic or self-enforcing nature of such arrangements that recommends them. Whenever the promisee is required to *do* something to make the promisor bear the consequences of his own breach, the promisor is

9. Nuclear deterrence rests upon each side's threat to retaliate against the other's undefended population. It is based, as I remarked earlier, on a form of mutual hostage-giving. If one side built a doomsday machine irreversibly programmed to destroy the world in the event that side were attacked, its hands would now be tied and it could no longer be subjected to opportunistic bargaining by its adversary. For a discussion of the strategic implications of a doomsday machine, see Kahn (175).

20 / JOURNAL OF LAW, ECONOMICS, AND ORGANIZATION   I:1, 1985

in a position to exploit the situation because both parties know it is not in the promisee's self-interest to carry through. This is the source of the opportunism inherent in all hostage-giving schemes whose enforcement depends upon the independent action of the hostage-holder. Hands-tying eliminates the condition that makes such opportunism possible by giving the promisor sole power to determine the fate of his own hostage. From the promisor's point of view, hands-tying has appeal because it provides security to the other party without the use of collateral (as I have defined the term) and therefore avoids the symmetrical form of opportunism that collateralization makes possible. Consequently, if a hands-tying scheme can be devised—and there is nothing to guarantee that it can in every transaction— the parties may each have a reason for preferring it to the two alternatives considered earlier.

But even hands-tying has its limitations. There is nothing to prevent the promisor who has tied his hands from breaking his promise anyway, if the benefits of doing so are large enough. Hands-tying can affect the promisor's calculation of costs and benefits, but it cannot stop him from calculating or from abandoning an earlier commitment when he thinks it is in his own self-interest to do so. This is, of course, a limitation on each of the three techniques that I have discussed. It might accurately be described as a *fundamental* limitation, and as such it is likely to stimulate the search for a more radical solution to the problem of transactional security than any I have considered so far.

2.4. UNION

A fourth method for reducing the risks of nonsimultaneous exchange in a state of nature where there is no Hobbesian "common power" might be described as the method of union. It is important to remember that these risks exist only because the parties perceive their interests to be divergent; absent such divergence, there would be no danger of opportunism on either side. This is reflected in the fact that we have difficulty even imagining how a single person—the limiting case of perfect union—could cheat or defraud himself, without implicitly assuming the existence of independent faculties within the individual.[10] The parties to an exchange in the state of nature can therefore reduce the risk of opportunism by taking steps to increase the likelihood that each will see his own self-interest as being internally connected to the welfare of the other.

In a broad sense, all of the strategies I have described are meant to have this effect. If one party to an exchange gives the other a hostage, or pledges

10. An assumption that both Plato and Freud appear to have made, at one time or another. See Plato (114–25) and Freud (3–29).

collateral, or ties his hands, their respective interests will be more tightly linked; this is indeed the general aim of every security-enhancing arrangement. It seems useful, however, to have a special term for those arrangements that seek to reduce divergence and competition by encouraging the parties to develop sympathy, affection, or love for one another. One could say, I suppose, that a mother refrains from exploiting her children because of the psychic price she would pay for doing so. But this misses the central fact of motherhood: to the extent a mother truly loves her children, her welfare and theirs are indistinguishable from her own point of view and she could no more exploit them than she could exploit herself.[11] In this respect, she differs from the calculating buyer or seller who easily distinguishes his own interests from those of the other party and who elects to perform because he wishes, quite self-consciously, to spare himself the expected costs of breach. By "union" I mean any arrangement that seeks to reduce divergence by promoting a spirit of identification or fellow-feeling between the parties, and I shall use the term in this somewhat specialized sense.

Thus, for example, if the members of a community deliberately establish routines, designed to reinforce in one another the altruistic habit of subordinating their own individual welfare to the welfare of others, if they make a conscious effort to instill similar habits in their children as they mature, and if they do all this, in part, to reduce the tensions that would otherwise accompany their efforts to establish exchange relationships among themselves, they are pursuing the strategy of union as I have defined it. Marriage is another example of an arrangement aimed at cultivating a spirit of solidarity on the part of those involved which may, in certain circumstances, be an effective instrument for reducing transactional insecurity (Klein et al., 1978: 323). Unlike the bond between parents and children, the marriage bond does not exist by nature and must therefore be artificially created. But the object of marriage, and its effect, is to establish between the parties an identity of interest that makes it increasingly difficult for either to view the other at arm's length. This process of identification is consummated in the procreation and rearing of children who, as Hegel observed (117), strengthen their parents' union by giving it an "objective" or "external" form. (Children, it should be noted, can also be an effective means of mutual hostage-giving, since the interdependency of the contributions which the parents of a child make to his or her development often prevent either parent from withdrawing from the marriage without incurring a substantial investment loss, regardless of who retains the child.) In a state of nature, the identification that marriage brings about can be an important resource in the search for transactional security. Warring clans and commercial competitors, for example, may through inter-

---

11. "Parents love their children as themselves: offspring is, as it were, another self, 'other' because it exists separately" (Aristotle: 237).

22 / JOURNAL OF LAW, ECONOMICS, AND ORGANIZATION I:1, 1985

marriage be able to increase each other's confidence in their future willingness to abide by the terms of whatever cooperative agreements they have made.[12] Eventually, it is hoped, the distrust and suspicion inevitable in an arm's-length relationship will be replaced by the solidarity of a household community, making breach unthinkable. In a state of nature, intermarriage is one way to tap the springs of intimacy for the sake of contractual exchange.[13]

The ceremony of homage that accompanied the feudal contract between lord and vassal could be described in similar terms (Bloch, :145-47). The parties to the contract agreed to exchange land and protection for periodic military services, seeking in this way to achieve some measure of common security under otherwise anarchic conditions. But they did something else as well: they pledged their personal loyalty to one another in a dramatic and emotionally powerful manner intended less to evidence such feelings than to awaken them. The feudal bond was contractual, but it was more than that, for it represented a lifelong commitment of a quasi-familial kind (Bloch: 224–25), predicated upon admission of the vassal to his lord's table and a willingness to serve him unto death. This latter aspect of feudalism—the one we associate with the institution of homage—underscores the value of intimacy in a world without Hobbes's "common power."

As a method for combatting opportunism, union operates at a different and deeper level than the other methods I have described. Arrangements that make use of hostages and collateral, or that exploit the advantages of hands-tying, all assume an opposition of interests on the part of those involved; their aim is to moderate the effects of this opposition by altering the costs and benefits of breach, but the existence of the opposition is a fact that each of these techniques takes for granted. Union does not. It seeks, instead, to eliminate the condition of separateness that makes an opposition of interests possible in the first place. To the extent it is successful in doing this, the parties can no longer be said to be in a state of nature vis-à-vis one another. The state of nature is a relational concept and therefore presupposes the parties' independence; one man cannot be in a state of nature by himself, nor can his physical or mental parts be in a state of nature with regard to one

---

12. "Family partnerships seem to have existed in early Roman times, but they had become obsolete by the Byzantine period. Possibly they owe their rebirth to conditions of the feudal and early communal Middle Ages, which stressed the need for solidarity of the family in the political, military, economic and social life" (Lopez and Raymond: 185–86). See also Lane (179).

13. "Another response to market transaction costs [in primitive societies] is the transformation of an arm's-length contract relationship into an intimate status relationship. In some primitive societies if you trade repeatedly with the same man he becomes your blood brother and you owe him the same duty of generous and fair dealing that you would owe a kinsman. This 'barter friendship' is a way of bringing reciprocity into the exchange process and thereby increasing the likelihood that promises will be honored despite the absence of a public enforcement authority" (Posner: 172).

another—they simply lack the requisite degree of independence. Because it combats transactional opportunism by annulling the independence of the parties, union (where it is successful) actually replaces the state of nature with something altogether different. Hands-tying, hostage-giving, and the use of collateral are methods for transacting within the state of nature; union is a method for abolishing it.

Of course, like the other techniques, union also has its limitations. First, it can rarely, if ever, be achieved completely; there appears to be a deep impediment to our attaining the condition of perfect identification at which the technique of union aims, although we can approach it by degrees. To the extent that we fall short of this condition, however, we retain our independence and thus remain subject to the risk of opportunism, which gives us an incentive to supplement our partially successful union with one of the other techniques I have described. Second, as a method for enhancing transactional security, union poses special dangers in the short-run; until the bonds of intimacy have taken hold and grown strong, the relaxation of defenses that it requires can increase the risks of exploitation rather than diminish them. For this reason, too, the parties may feel a need, at least in the early stages of their relationship, for the additional security of a hostage or collateral (which of course itself bespeaks a lack of trust and hence makes the achievement of union more difficult).

I have now described a number of different, though related, techniques that individuals in a state of nature might employ to reduce the risks created by the absence of an independent power strong enough to enforce the promises they make to one another. In the state of nature, the parties to a transaction have a choice, generally speaking, between the following four alternatives: they can make their exchange simultaneously; they can simply accept the risks which nonsimultaneity implies and go forward without any security at all; they can forgo the exchange completely; or they can adopt one (or some combination) of the techniques I have described. Which alternative they choose will depend, in any particular case, upon its relative cost. If it is very costly to achieve simultaneity, for example, the parties may have to choose between an extremely risky exchange, no exchange at all, and an exchange supported by hostage-giving or some other form of security. If they choose the latter alternative, the parties must also select from among the various techniques available to them—again, on the basis of their relative cost. None of these techniques is costless and each has its own specific limitations. Indeed, they may all be too costly, given the expected benefits of a particular exchange, in which case the exchange itself will either be made without security or simply fail.

I shall offer no opinion as to which technique (if any) is likely to predominate in the state of nature or hazard a guess regarding the frequency with which we migh expect them all to be inadequate. The point I want to em-

24 / JOURNAL OF LAW, ECONOMICS, AND ORGANIZATION   I:1, 1985

phasize is that individuals in a state of nature have available to them a variety of methods for creating, on their own, at least some measure of security to replace the security they would enjoy were their promises legally enforceable. There is no reason to think that exchange, even nonsimultaneous exchange, must end where the state and the law of contracts do.

In the next section, I shall argue that the reverse is also true: the existence of the state and an enforceable law of contracts do not put an end to the risks that parties transacting in a state of nature face, and in this sense they do not put an end to the state of nature itself. Nor could they—except, perhaps, at a cost we would never accept.

3. Contract Law and the Limits of Security

It may seem strange to some man, that has not well weighed these things; that nature should thus dissociate, and render men apt to invade, and destroy one another: and he may therefore, not trusting to this inference, made from the passions, desire perhaps to have the same confirmed by experience. Let him therefore consider with himself, when taking a journey, he arms himself, and seeks to go well accompanied; when going to sleep, he locks his doors; when even in his house he locks his chests; and this when he knows there be laws, and public officers, armed, to revenge all injuries shall be done him; what opinion he has of his fellow-subjects, when he rides armed; of his fellow citizens, when he locks his doors; and of his children, and servants, when he locks his chests. Does he not there as much accuse mankind by his actions, as I do by my words?

—Thomas Hobbes, *Leviathan*

The existence of the state and its enforcement machinery make it unnecessary, one might think, to rely on any of those devices which in a state of nature are the only source of transactional security. But the most casual observations are enough to suggest that this is not the case. Indeed, even where there is a developed law of contracts underwritten by a public authority with awesome powers of coercion, private parties contracting with one another continue to make use of each of the four techniques discussed in the previous section. Despite the fact that their claims are legally enforceable, creditors, for example, often demand some valuable property as collateral to secure their loans. The arrangement may be a simple one (a pledge of stock certificates or jewelry) or more complex (a field warehouse),[14] but its objective in each case is the same: to assure that the creditor will have in his possession at the time of his borrower's default property of sufficient worth to compensate him for the loss. Alternatively, a creditor may insist that he be given physical control of some small piece of equipment, critical to the borrower's business, until the loan is repaid. If the equipment has little use or exchange value to anyone other than the borrower but can only be replaced

---

14. For a description of what a field warehouse is and how it works, see Gilmore (146–95).

by him at great expense because it is specialized to his own operations, the security held by the creditor is clearly a hostage in the sense defined above. Hands-tying also continues to play an important role in the exchange process, despite the existence of a developed system of enforceable contract rights. The investments that firms make in transaction-specific equipment, in fancy shops that cannot easily be converted to another use, and even in their own advertising programs—whose function often is simply to increase a firm's reputational commitment to the advertised product (Klein and Leffler, 1981: 627–33); Williamson, 1983: 528–33)—are all examples of hands-tying that exhibit the automaticity peculiar to this method of enhancing transactional security. Even union, the most radical of the four techniques I have described, has a continuing utility despite the parties' ability to invoke the state as the guarantor of whatever contractual agreements they choose to make; where the interests of the parties are sharply divergent and the risk of opportunism especially great, their integration into a single enterprise with a common profit-maximizing goal—the commercial analog to intermarriage—may be preferable, from the parties' point of view, to continued exchange under a legally enforceable contract, as Ronald Coase suggested in his famous article on the nature of the firm (386).

What explains the fact that these techniques, designed to provide some measure of security in a state of nature where there is no centralized mechanism for the enforcement of promises, continue to be used even after such a mechanism is in place? Only one answer seems possible: the legal right to enforce a promise can reduce but never eliminate the insecurity associated with all temporally asymmetrical exchanges, and the parties to such an exchange will therefore always have some use for the techniques I have described. Even the parties to a legally enforceable contract remain, to one degree or another, in a state of nature and hence must rely, for security, on their own devices. Although the extent to which they must do so will vary from one legal system to another depending upon the nature of the protection which the law affords disappointed promisees, an irreducible quantum of insecurity always remains. Of course, the parties to any particular contract may conclude that whatever special arrangements might be made to produce a marginal increase in their security are too costly to be worthwhile, especially if certain of these arrangements—the use of human hostages, for example—have themselves been outlawed and the cost of their (now illegal) use increased as a result. But we should not infer from this that no residuum of insecurity exists or assume that the law of contracts puts an end to the state of nature.

To understand why this cannot be the case, it may help to reflect briefly on the nature of contract remedies and their necessary limitations. When someone makes an enforceable promise, the person to whom the promise is made acquires the right to sue for relief if the promisor fails to perform. In

26 / JOURNAL OF LAW, ECONOMICS, AND ORGANIZATION   I:1, 1985

most cases, "relief" means money damages but in certain circumstances a promisee may sue for specific perfomance. If a promisee is entitled to money damages only, there is always some risk that he will not be fully compensated for the losses caused by the other party's breach (even on the assumption that he is reimbursed for all expenses incurred in prosecuting his lawsuit—attorney's fees, court costs, etc.). This is so for two reasons. First, the legal rules that define compensable harm limit the promisee's recovery by denying him the right to compensation for losses that are considered too remote or speculative. Losses of this sort may be quite real insofar as the promisee is concerned; he will not be compensated for them, however, unless he has taken precautions to make them less speculative—for example, by insisting on the inclusion of a liquidated damages clause in his original contract. But even this may not be enough, as long as the third party empowered to enforce the contract retains final authority to pass on the validity of this or any other private term purporting to modify the general rules of compensation that would otherwise be applicable.

Second, even assuming that a particular loss falls within the limited domain of harms which the law of contracts acknowledges to be compensable, it must still be measured before damages can be awarded. In many cases, the magnitude of the loss will be controversial and where it is, someone other than the disappointed promisee (either judge or jury) must resolve the dispute. But there is always some risk that a third party's estimate of the harm suffered will diverge from the promisee's own and thus a risk that the damages he receives will be undercompensatory. No contractual provision can give the promisee ironclad protection against this danger. Nor, more important, can the problem be remedied simply by rewriting the law of contracts. However broadly we define the class of compensable harms, any court-administered damages remedy carries with it a risk of undercompensation. No refinement of doctrine can eliminate this risk, which is bound to arise whenever someone other than the promisee is empowered to determine the value of the promise made by the party in breach.

This explains why we grant a right of specific performance in cases where the idiosyncratic nature of the contract makes the risk of undercompensation especially great (Kronman, 1978: 351). If the promisee is entitled to insist on actual performance of the contract, he may himself set the price for releasing the other party from his obligation and thereby avoid the risk of undercompensation that arises whenever the price is set by someone else, as it is in an action for damages. Because the calculation of money damages always involves some risk of this sort, it has been argued that every promisee ought to have a right of specific enforcement, unless the parties have provided otherwise in their contract (Schwartz: 271). I shall not take a stand on this issue; what I wish to emphasize, instead, is the inevitable limitation (from the promisee's point of view) even of specific performance, the law's most powerful remedy for breach of promise.

To begin with, specific performance clearly involves an element of moral hazard. A promisor who has been ordered to perform may have little incentive to do a good or even adequate job; instead, he is likely to shirk and cut corners, shifting resources (disposable time, imagination, raw materials, etc.) from the other party to himself. He may even do so out of spite. Of course, if the court discovers that the promisor is shirking, it can order him to upgrade his performance or risk imprisonment for contempt. But a court may lack the ability to distinguish adequate from inadequate performances and be unpersuaded by any evidence of shirking that the promisee brings before it. If the promisee had a hostage or collateral, *he* would be the arbiter of the promisor's performance and would be spared the burdensome, and risky, task of having to justify his own assessment to some third party.

Specific performance may prove inadequate for an additional reason. Suppose that a person makes, and breaches, several contracts. If it is impossible for him to perform all of them at once, some of his creditors will have to accept money damages in lieu of specific performance or agree to the postponement of their claims; in either case, they risk undercompensation. Of course, the promisor's creditors might agree to divide their common debtor's time and other resources on a pro rata basis, each receiving (let us imagine) an hour a day from the debtor until his claim has been satisfied in full. But while there might be reasons for the promisor's creditors to cooperate in this way (Jackson, 1982: 857), such an arrangement would not itself eliminate the risk that the debtor may die or disappear—become irrevocably judgment-proof—before all of his debts have been paid. Even a right to specific performance cannot guarantee the promisor's solvency, his *ability* to complete performance when ordered to do so. To protect himself against the risk of his debtor's insolvency, a creditor needs something more than his legal remedies for breach of promise: he needs collateral, an independent fund that he controls and may appropriate to satisfy whatever claims he has against the debtor. Because the risk of insolvency is attributable to the debtor's inability, rather than unwillingness, to perform, it cannot be eliminated by means of hostage-giving or hands-tying. These techniques achieve their intended aim through the effect they have on the promisor's incentives, and where the promisor lacks the ability to perform, behavioral effects of this sort do the promisee no good; hence only collateral provides protection against the risk of insolvency. (By which I mean something different from and more basic thaan the risk of bankruptcy. The debtor's right to a discharge in bankruptcy is a legal artifact, an entitlement which itself is enforceable by the state. The existence of such an entitlement may increase the risk that the debtor's creditors will be undercompensated as a result of his inability to pay, but it does not create this risk, which would remain even if the institution of bankruptcy were abolished.)

I have been arguing that a promisee's legal remedies for breach of contract—his right to money damages and, in some cases, specific perform-

28 / JOURNAL OF LAW, ECONOMICS, AND ORGANIZATION I:1, 1985

ance—give him only limited protection and do not eliminate the need for those security-enhancing devices which in a state of nature provide the only substitute for the enforcement powers of the state. What needs to be stressed is that these limitations cannot be overcome simply by making the promisee's legal remedies stronger or more far-reaching. Suppose, for example, that the sanction for nonperformance of a contract was raised from money damages or specific performance to imprisonment or physical punishment or even death. So long as the promisee does not himself have full control over the administration of whatever sanction is adopted, he runs the risk of being unable to persuade the official charged with responsibility for monitoring the promisor's performance that the promisor is indeed doing less than he has been ordered to do. And even if we take the final, awful step of giving the promisee sole power to judge the adequacy of the promisor's performance and allow him to use the coercive machinery of the state (including the electric chair) in whatever way he wishes, the promisee's contractual expectations may still be frustrated, for if the promisor is too old or weak or crazy to perform, no threat of harm can effectively be used against him. Knowing this in advance, the promisee still has reason to demand collateral as security for his contract rights—even though the state has given him the power of life and death over his contractual partner.

But while no system of legal remedies—even the harshest one we can imagine—could ever eliminate entirely the risk to which every contracting party is subject, it is undeniable that the existence of a centralized mechanism for the enforcement of promises does greatly increase the security of the parties and at a comparatively low cost (at least up to a point). Where no such mechanism exists, a measure of security can be obtained in other ways, but generally speaking, only at a higher price. It can therefore truly be said that we would have a reason to invent the state if it did not already exist: the state is (among other things) a device for reducing the transaction costs of exchange, one whose own marginal cost is, *at the outset,* almost certainly lower than the marginal cost of alternative methods for achieving the same end. On this view, the difference between the state and the various private techniques described in the preceding section should be thought of not as a difference in kind but as a difference in relative cost (which, to be sure, may be considerable depending upon the circumstances).

It is misleading, however, to speak of the state as if the concept had a single definite meaning. A centralized institution for the enforcement of contracts may, in fact, assume many different shapes, depending upon the nature and content of the remedies it offers disappointed promisees. The concept of the state encompasses a variety of remedial systems which differ in the degree of coercion they apply to those who break, or threaten to break, their contracts; it is a concept, we might say, that has scale or intensity. As we move up the scale, in imagination, from the comparatively mild systems that we actually have in the West today to the harsher ones we might have (and, to some degree, have had in the past), two general points should be kept in mind. First, as I have already emphasized, no remedial system can ever eliminate entirely the sources of contractual insecurity. Second, the marginal cost of obtaining additional increments of security through the state's remedial system is likely to increase as the remedies themselves become more painful and intrusive. Consider, for example, a rule giving all disappointed promisees the right to sue for specific performance. Adopting such a rule might enhance the security of contractual relationships, but only at a price. In the first place, a generalized regime of specific enforcement would be more costly to administer because of the moral hazard problem noted earlier. And since specific performance deprives the promisor of the power to depersonalize his relationship with the promisee, a regime of this sort would have moral costs as well: where a contract calls for personal services, loss of the right to put the other party at a distance by substituting damages for performance can be demoralizing to the promisor and undermine his self-respect for reasons I have elaborated elsewhere (Kronman, 1983: 763). Thus, while a decision to make specific performance universally available might enhance contractual security by eliminating the risk of undercompensation inherent in the calculation of money damages, it would also have moral and administrative consequences that must be weighed in deciding whether the benefits of such a rule exceed its cost. The same would obviously be true of a decision to increase the severity of the sanction for breach of contract from damages to corporal punishment. A regime of this sort would probably discourage people from contracting and—if carried to extremes—brutalize us all; moral externalities of this sort must also be taken into account in weighing the advantages of implementing such a program.

These last remarks suggest a general rule: where the marginal cost of increasing transactional security by strengthening the parties' legal remedies exceeds the marginal benefit of doing so, the law will leave the task of further enhancing their security to the parties themselves. Beyond this point, the relationship of the parties is as it was before the establishment of the state and its law of contracts; unlike the original state of nature, however, the one that now remains cannot be reduced, at an acceptable cost, by a further increase in state power.

To reduce the inevitable residue of insecurity that remains, beyond the limits of the law, the parties to a contract must adopt one or another of the strategies described here. But each of these, as I have stressed, has its costs as well. Both hostages and collateral create their own special forms of opportunism and are costly, too, because they may require the temporary transfer of an asset that is less valuable to the recipient than to the party who origi-

30 / JOURNAL OF LAW, ECONOMICS, AND ORGANIZATION I:1, 1985

nally possessed it.[15] Hands-tying frequently requires an expensive, transaction-specific investment which the promisor has no reason to make apart from the added credibility it gives him. And union, when it leads to the expansion of a firm or family beyond some indefinite optimal size, is likely to result in the internal replication of those same conflicts it was intended to overcome (Klein et al., 1978: 299; Knight: 254).

In any particular case, the comparative marginal costs of these different methods for reducing risk will determine which (or what combination) the contracting parties choose. It may be that none can provide additional security at a reasonable cost, in which case the parties must decide whether to go ahead with their exchange despite the risks it entails. Often they will do so, since there are many risks worth taking. But under no circumstances can risk be banished from exchange, at least in all those cases where one of the parties must perform before the other: neither by the existence of a legal system (however painful its penalties for breach) nor by the private devices that function in a state of nature as a substitute for state power and in civil society as a supplement to it. How little risk remains depends upon how much the parties are willing to pay for security. But some risk is unavoidable. To this extent, the parties to an agreement—whether or not it is legally enforceable and however it has been secured by additional devices of their own construction—always remain in a state of nature with regard to one another. The state of nature is an inescapable condition and the problems that it poses can never be dissolved or completely overcome, no more than we can overcome our finitude (of which the state of nature is, in some sense, the badge or emblem).

There is only one condition under which it might be said that the state of nature has indeed been overcome, and that is where the possibility of conflict itself no longer exists. In *The Book of Laughter and Forgetting* (62–68), Milan Kundera describes the ideal collectivist society as a great fugue in which each individual is a single note, related to the other notes and to the work as a whole in a perfectly harmonious way. In such a society there could, by definition, be no conflict because each person would see his own interest as identical to the interests of everyone else, all being merged in a single, indivisible melody; indeed, the very notion of self-interest would disappear, together with the institution of the state, which is required only so long as there is conflict between individuals. By removing the source of all

---

15. Hostage-giving need not involve the actual transfer of the hostage so long as the hostage-giver puts it out of his power to protect the hostage from destruction by the other party. Collateral, on the other hand, must be in the possession of the promisee, or within his power to appropriate upon breach by the promisor. If the property which the promisor offers as collateral plays an economically important role in his own enterprise, an arrangement must be devised that will allow the promisor to retain possession of the property while adequately protecting the promisee. The entire modern law of nonpossessory security interests in personal property may be viewed as a response to this same problem. See Gilmore (24–26).

CONTRACT LAW AND THE STATE OF NATURE / 31

exploitative behavior, the abolition of self-interest would put an end to the state of nature: the members of such a society could no more be in a state of nature vis-à-vis one another than the limbs of a body can, and for the same reason—too much unity makes conflict impossible.

A society of the sort Kundera describes would be a monstrosity, and even if it were attainable—which happily it is not, except, perhaps, for small groups and short periods of time—we should resist the temptation to remake ourselves in its image. The great fugue would indeed remove us from the state of nature, but it would also deprive us of the sense of separateness that underlies our notions of moral duty and personal achievement (and much else besides). Were we faced with such a choice, it would be right to embrace the state of nature as a condition better suited to the qualities we value in ourselves. The state of nature is the human condition. It is—to carry the theme of these concluding remarks one step further—the price we pay for the mixed blessing of being who we are.

REFERENCES

Aristotle. 1962. *Nicomachean Ethics*, trans M. Ostwald. New York: Bobbs-Merrill.
Bloch, Marc. 1964. *Feudal Society*, trans. L.A. Manyon. Chicago: University of Chicago Press.
Coase, Ronald. 1937. "The Nature of the Firm," 4 *Economica* 386.
Freud, Sigmund. [1923] 1962. *The Ego and the Id*, trans. J. Riviere. New York: Norton.
Gauthier, David. 1969. *The Logic of Leviathan*. Oxford: Oxford University Press.
Gilmore, Grant. 1965. *Security Interests in Personal Property*. Boston: Little, Brown and Co.
Hegel, G. W. F. [1821] 1952. *Philosphy of Right*, trans. T. M. Knox. Oxford: Oxford University Press.
Hobbes, Thomas. [1651] 1955. *Leviathan*, ed. M. Oakeshott. Oxford: Basil Blackwell.
Jackson, Thomas. 1982. "Bankruptcy, Non-Bankruptcy Entitlements, and the Creditors' Bargain," 91 *Yale Law Journal* 857.
———, and Anthony Kronman. 1979. "Secured Financing and Priorities among Creditors," 88 *Yale Law Journal* 1143.
Jensen, Michael, and William Meckling. 1976. "Theory of the Firm: Managerial Behavior, Agency Costs, and Capital Structure," 3 *Journal of Financial Economics* 305.
Kahn, Herman. 1960. *On Thermonuclear War*. Princeton: Princeton University Press.
Klein, Benjamin, and Keith Leffler. 1981. "The Role of Market Forces in Assuring Contractual Performance," 89 *Journal of Political Economy* 615.
———, Robert G. Crawford, and Armen Alchian. 1978. "Vertical Integration, Appropriable Rents, and the Competitive Contracting Process," 21 *Journal of Law and Economics* 297.
Knight, Frank. 1965. *Risk, Uncertainty and Profit*. New York: Harper and Row.
Kraakman, Reinier. 1984. "Corporate Liability Strategies and the Costs of Legal Controls," 93 *Yale Law Journal* 857.

32 / JOURNAL OF LAW, ECONOMICS, AND ORGANIZATION I:1, 1985

Kronman, Anthony. 1978. "Specific Performance," 45 *University of Chicago Law Review* 351.

———. 1983. "Paternalism and the Law of Contracts," 92 *Yale Law Journal* 763.

———, and Richard Posner. 1979. *The Economics of Contract Law*. Boston: Little, Brown and Co.

Kundera, Milan. 1981. *The Book of Laughter and Forgetting*, trans. M. Heim. New York: Penguin.

Lane, Frederic. 1944. "Partnerships and Joint Ventures in the Venetian Republic," 4 *Journal of Economic History* 178.

Levmore, Saul. 1982. "Monitors and Freeriders in Commercial and Corporate Settings," 92 *Yale Law Journal* 49.

Lopez, Robert, and Irving Raymond. 1955. *Medieval Trade in the Mediterranean World*. New York: Columbia University Press.

Macaulay, Stewart. 1963. "Non-Contractual Relations in Business," 28 *American Sociological Review* 55.

Marx, Karl. [1953] 1973. *Grundrisse*, trans. M. Nicolaus. Baltimore: Penguin.

Nozick, Robert. 1974. *Anarchy, State and Utopia*. New York: Basic Books.

Plato. 1968. *Republic*, trans. A. Bloom. New York: Basic Books.

Posner, Richard. 1981. *The Economics of Justice*. Cambridge: Harvard University Press.

Puzo, Mario. 1969. *The Godfather*. New York: G. P. Putnam's Sons.

Reuter, Peter. 1983. *Disorganized Crime: The Economics of the Visible Hand*. Cambridge: MIT Press.

Rousseau, Jean-Jacques. [1750; 1755] 1964. *The First and Second Discourses*, trans. Roger and Judith Masters. New York: St. Martin's Press.

Scanlon, Thomas. 1984. "Is Promising a Social Practice?" Unpublished manuscript.

Schelling, Thomas. 1956. "An Essay on Bargaining," 46 *American Economic Review* 281.

———. 1960. *The Strategy of Conflict*. New York: Oxford University Press.

———. 1966. *Arms and Influence*. New Haven: Yale University Press.

Schwartz, Alan. 1979. "The Case for Specific Performance," 89 *Yale Law Journal* 271.

Telser, L. G. 1980. "A Theory of Self-Enforcing Agreements," 53 *Journal of Business* 27.

Umbeck, John. 1978. "A Theory of Contract Choice and the California Gold Rush," 20 *Journal of Law and Economics* 421.

Weber, Max. [1922] 1968. *Economy and Society*, trans. E. Fischoff et al. New York: Bedminster Press.

Williamson, Oliver. 1975. *Markets and Hierarchies: Analysis and Antitrust Implications*. New York: Free Press.

———. 1983. "Credible Commitments: Using Hostages to Support Exchange," 73 *American Economic Review* 519.

[20]

PRIVATE ORDER UNDER DYSFUNCTIONAL PUBLIC ORDER

John McMillan*
Christopher Woodruff**

The freedom and extent of human commerce depend entirely on a
fidelity with regard to promises.[1]

INTRODUCTION

Businesspeople need contractual assurance. Most transactions are
less straightforward than a cash sale of an easily identifiable item.
Buyers need assurance of the quality of what they are purchasing, and
sellers need assurance that bills will be paid. The legal system may not
always be available to provide contractual assurance — and when the
law is dysfunctional, private order might arise in its place.

Many developing and transition economies have dysfunctional legal systems, either because the laws do not exist or because the machinery for enforcing them is inadequate. In such countries, bilateral
relationships, communal norms, trade associations, or market intermediaries may work in place of the legal system.[2] In this Article, we
use data obtained from surveys of firms in five transition economies in
Eastern Europe and the former Soviet Union as well as Vietnam to
show that, at least in these economies, social networks and informal
gossip substitute for the formal legal system, while business networks

* Professor of International Management and Economics, Stanford Graduate School of
Business; B.Sc. 1971, M.Com. 1973, University of Canterbury (New Zealand); Ph.D. 1978,
University of New South Wales (Australia). Professor McMillan can be contacted at
mcmillan_john@gsb.stanford.edu. — Ed. We thank the participants in the conference on
"Empirical Research in Commercial Transactions" at the University of Michigan Law
School for valuable comments, Jeffrey Baker for research assistance, and the Stanford
Graduate School of Business for research support.

** Assistant Professor of Economics, Graduate School of International Relations and
Pacific Studies, University of California at San Diego. B.A. 1980, University of Chicago;
M.A. (Economics) 1984, University of California at Los Angeles; Ph.D. (Economics) 1994,
University of Texas. Professor Woodruff can be contacted at cwoodruff@ucsd.edu. — Ed.

1. DAVID HUME, A TREATISE ON HUMAN NATURE 546 (Oxford University Press, 1978
& 1739).

2. Even in countries where the legal system works well, there is still often a need for private order, as we discuss later. For example, market players may prefer private-order
mechanisms to the courts, either because certain kinds of agreement are not susceptible to
court enforcement or because the transaction costs of using private order are smaller than
those of using the courts.

2422   *Michigan Law Review*   [Vol. 98:2421

and trade associations work in conjunction with it.[3] These transition countries provide an informative place to examine the interaction between the formal legal system and private-order mechanisms because both are in a state of flux. Although market-oriented laws have begun to replace the bureaucratic controls of the old planned economy, private firms' access to the courts varies, from almost no access in Vietnam to considerable access in Poland and Romania. Even within these countries, the transitional state of the legal system means that managers vary in their perceptions of the courts' usefulness, and ultimately it is their willingness or unwillingness to utilize the formal legal system that shapes the development of private order.[4] Because the data from these economies contain more variation than would be found in a steady-state economy, we can run meaningful regressions relating firms' behavior to their perceptions of the courts' workability.

Many types of private-order mechanisms arise in market economies. Sometimes parties directly involved in the transaction arrange the private order. For example, if a buyer is locked in with a particular seller, either because the seller is a monopolist or because the buyer would face high costs of locating an alternative seller, the seller can make the contract self-enforcing by cutting off further dealings. Self-enforcement in these lock-in situations sometimes takes more imaginative forms. A New York cable television company, Paragon Cable, has a novel strategy to get its customers to pay their overdue bills.[5] It does not unhook the cable. Instead, using what is supposedly a far more effective bill-collection measure, Paragon runs C-SPAN, with its political speeches, debates, and hearings, on all seventy-seven channels.

In close-knit communities, where people interact with each other frequently and information flows freely, people may adhere to social norms of cooperation because it is in their long-term interest to do so. For example, this type of relational contracting has arisen spontaneously within groups such as whalers and neighboring cattle farmers, as Robert Ellickson has shown.[6] In Asia, especially among the ethnic Chinese, contracting typically rests on personal relationships, or

---

3. The surveys in Eastern Europe and the former Soviet Union were done in collaboration with Simon Johnson. They are described in more detail in Simon Johnson et al., *Entrepreneurs and the Ordering of Institutional Reform: Poland, Slovakia, Romania, Russia, and Ukraine Compared*, 8:1 ECON. TRANSITION 1 (2000) [hereinafter Johnson et al., *Entrepreneurs*].

4. We asked our survey respondents (managers of recently started firms) whether they believed they could use the courts to enforce contracts with customers or suppliers. In Vietnam, just 9% said they could. In Romania, 87% said the courts were usable, in Poland 73%, in Slovakia 68%, in Russia 56%, and in Ukraine 55%.

5. *See Telecommunications Policy Review* 8 October 1995, p. 9.

6. *See* ROBERT C. ELLICKSON, ORDER WITHOUT LAW (1991).

guanxi.[7] In Japan, according to Ronald Dore, firms' opportunism is limited by "moralized trading relationships of mutual goodwill. The stability of the relationship is the key. Both sides recognize an obligation to try to maintain it."[8]

In the right circumstances, then, private order can be achieved *spontaneously.* In large, anonymous communities, however, where people can enter and leave and where alternative trading partners are readily accessible, spontaneous private order may not be feasible. Anonymity strips reputational constraints of their power; more is needed than social norms or self-enforcing dealings. Private order, if it is to operate at all, needs to be *organized.*

Market participants thus sometimes form themselves into groups such as trade associations to support contracting and create private order. Profit-seeking firms also sometimes provide private order: market intermediaries such as wholesalers and trading companies on occasion supply, among other services, contractual assurance for buyers and sellers. We argue below that private-order organizations of either kind have two roles in sustaining contracting: first, providing information about breaches, and second, organizing the responses to those breaches. Historical studies of notably diverse settings, from medieval Europe to present-day Mexico, demonstrate a consistency in this functioning of private-order organizations: a private organization (such as a market intermediary or a trade association) disseminates information about contractual breaches, and then coordinates the community's response to them. The usual sanction is to boycott the offender. These private-order organizations provide contract-enforcement mechanisms that lie between formal, state-supported order and informal, spontaneous order.

Private order unfortunately also has a down side. It sometimes harms efficiency by excluding new entrants from trading or by achieving price collusion. Private order also can cause or perpetuate racial or gender discrimination. Additionally, some private-order organizations' enforcement techniques overflow into criminal violence. Because of these disadvantages, private order can usefully supplement public law, but cannot replace it.

Our evidence comes from two sources. First, we review published descriptions of private-order practices in various countries. In reviewing this anecdotal evidence we aim to show how similar private-order mechanisms have arisen in quite diverse settings, from medieval Europe to present-day Mexico. Second, we analyze data from the surveys of entrepreneurs we conducted in countries in the process of transition to a market economy from central planning: Vietnam,

---

7. *See* Yao Souchou, *The Fetish of Relationships: Chinese Business Transactions in Singapore,* SOJOURN 2, 1, 89-111 (1987).

8. RONALD DORE, TAKING JAPAN SERIOUSLY 173 (1987).

2424   *Michigan Law Review*   [Vol. 98:2421

Russia, the Ukraine, Romania, Slovakia, and Poland. In using this statistical evidence, we aim to examine, in depth, how the legal system affects the operation of private-order mechanisms, both spontaneous and organized.

In Part I, we discuss why private order is needed and why it sometimes needs to be organized, and argue that private organizations serve two functions — to disseminate information about contractual breaches and to coordinate the responses of multiple parties. We then provide evidence in Part II to demonstrate when private order works spontaneously and when it does not. In Part III, we present evidence regarding the information provision and coordination roles of private-order organizations. In Part IV, we discuss evidence demonstrating how private-order mechanisms interact with the formal legal system. We conclude in Part V with a discussion of the downside of private order, and argue consequently that public order sometimes is preferable to private order.

I.   REPEATED GAMES AND THE LAW

In this Part, we describe the role and emergence of relational, informal contracting (private order) in relation to the relative adequacy of the existing legal system (public order). As a preliminary matter, we then describe the different types of private order (spontaneous and organized), the functioning of each, and, correlatively, when each type arises. In the subsequent parts, we explore more fully when and how these two types of private order function.

A.   *The Law versus Relational Contracting*

Many business dealings have the character of the prisoner's dilemma. A seller can cheat by supplying inferior merchandise, and a buyer can cheat by not paying its bills. The best outcome for both, of course, is that neither cheats. In an isolated transaction, however, both parties may have an incentive to cheat, leading to an outcome that benefits neither.

There are two ways to counter the self-defeating incentives of the prisoner's dilemma. One is the law. If the players can write binding contracts in advance promising not to cheat, with a sufficiently severe sanction for cheating, then it is rational not to cheat. The other countermeasure arises from repetition of the game, or relational contracting. Players may refrain from squeezing the last cent out of the current deal because they wish to do business in the future, either with this particular trading partner or with others who could learn of this behavior. Contracting thus becomes self-enforcing through the threat of retaliation and consequent loss of business. In other words, the shadow of the future can induce the trading partners to cooperate.

If the legal system functioned perfectly, contracts would never need to be self-enforcing. A frictionless legal system would always work at least as well as relational contracting. In practice, however, laws meant to provide contractual assurance sometimes do not exist, and even when they exist, their application and enforcement may not be cost-effective or even possible.

Some countries, especially developing and transition countries, have inadequate legal systems. Writing good laws does not automatically solve the problem, for it takes years to create the institutions of a functioning court system and to train judges and lawyers. Indeed, in some countries rampant corruption renders the courts entirely unreliable.

Even in countries with sophisticated legal systems, the law may not work smoothly. For example, the transaction costs of appealing to the law sometimes exceed the transaction costs of using relational contracting. Market participants have some advantages over judges in deciding whether commitments have been fulfilled.[9] First, market participants possess greater expertise than courts in the monitoring of other participants' conduct. Second, their decisions and actions can be more nuanced than the binary decision that a court must make — that of liability or no liability.[10] Third, they can consider information that cannot be introduced in court, such as impressionistic evidence about business trends or judgments about the quality of items sold. They can base their decisions on a firm's behavior over time, on probabilistic patterns that would not be admissible evidence in court.

In countries with functioning legal systems, then, relational contracting can supplement the law by mitigating the transaction costs of investigation and enforcement. In countries with dysfunctional legal systems, on the other hand, relational contracting may replace the law altogether. We shall investigate both situations.[11]

B. *Spontaneous versus Organized Contracting*

The size of a community and the adequacy of existing market institutions influences whether spontaneous order can arise, or whether

---

9. *See* David Charny, *Nonlegal Sanctions in Commercial Relationships*, 104 HARV. L. REV. 373, 415-17 (1990). There are, of course, good reasons why certain kinds of evidence are inadmissible. A cost of achieving the economic efficiencies that, on average, such probabilistic evidence produces is that sometimes in specific instances the outcome is unjust. The law is designed to avoid specific injustices more than to produce outcomes that on average promote efficiency.

10. For example, a finding of liability in one lawsuit may not have the same far-reaching effects of a boycott by other market players, or of consequently restrained or narrowly tailored dealings with a party found guilty of breach.

11. *See infra* Part IV.

2426   *Michigan Law Review*   [Vol. 98:2421

spontaneous order is rendered ineffective and the order must therefore be organized.

1. *Spontaneous Contracting*

If a buyer and seller expect to deal with each other repeatedly, each might refrain from cheating the other in order to maintain the relationship. Whether the prospect of future business suffices to overcome the immediate incentive to cheat depends on the value attached to any future returns. For cooperation to be consistent with self-interest, the interactions must be sufficiently frequent and future returns must not be discounted too heavily.

Spontaneous cooperation between two trading partners also requires them to be locked in with each other. If the buyer can easily find another seller to deal with, the seller's threat to cut off future business carries little weight.[12] On the other hand, if firms are locked in with their current trading partners, perhaps because they trade a unique product or because of the difficulty of locating alternative trading partners, the firms will make efforts to sustain their existing relationships. This implies, incidentally, that spontaneous cooperation is easier to achieve when market institutions are inadequate. Lock-in prevails in underdeveloped economies with poor market information or high transport costs. As the economy develops and market frictions fall, the cost of breaking a relationship will also fall and firms will become less willing to cooperate with each other. Thus, more sophisticated economies can rely less on this type of spontaneous, lock-in relational contracting.

2. *Organized Relational Contracting*

If no lock-in exists and the two parties deal with each other only infrequently, then cooperation will not further their interests. The shadow of the future can still come into play in such a situation, however, if the retaliation for a breach comes not only from the affected party but also from other firms — that is, if community sanctions apply.[13] A firm will more likely pay its bills if it knows that its other trading partners, current or potential, would otherwise refuse to do business with it.

---

12. *See* Rachel Kranton, *Reciprocal Exchange: A Self-Sustaining System*, 89 AM. ECON. REV. 830 (1996) for a model of the effects of lock-in on cooperation.

13. *See* Avner Greif, *Contract Enforceability and Economic Institutions in Early Trade: The Maghribi Traders' Coalition*, 83 AM. ECON. REV. 525 (1993) [hereinafter Greif, *Contract Enforceability*]; Avner Greif, *Cultural Beliefs and the Organization of Society: A Historical and Theoretical Reflection on Collectivist and Individualist Societies*, 102 J. POL. ECON. 912 (1994); Michihiro Kandori, *Social Norms and Community Enforcement*, 59 REV. ECON. STUD. 63 (1992).

Although community sanctions sometimes can be invoked spontaneously, they often need to be managed.[14] For example, even in markets with adequate information flow, the sheer size of the market may mean that some players may not even learn about third-party contractual breaches, and therefore not know when to enact sanctions. Or, even where informational problems do not exist, the application of differential sanctions by uncoordinated market players may provide outs for the breacher. In these situations, community sanctions do not work without formal organization. This organization might be an independent third party, such as a wholesaler or some other kind of market intermediary, or it might be the firms themselves in combination, like a trade association. These organizations serve to provide both information about breaches and coordination of the community response.

a. Providing Information. As a first matter, then, the enactment of community sanctions requires the provision of information because firms must know when a breach has occurred and who caused it. Private organizations can serve as convenient and effective repositories of this information. In addition, by providing formal channels of communication, an organization can reduce the likelihood of mistakes in the transmission of this information. As anyone who has played the children's "telephone game" can attest, stories change when they are orally transmitted through a chain of people.[15] As a result, reliable information transmission depends on having only a few links between the original source of the information and each recipient. This would require every member of the group to communicate frequently with every other member. This type of spontaneous communication may be unlikely or even impossible in a large group, and organizations therefore provide the most reliable means of information transmission.[16] These organizations may take the form of trade associations formed by the actual market players, or of market intermediaries, such as wholesalers.

14. We posit here that organized private order arises when market characteristics foreclose effective functioning (or even development) of spontaneous order. Of course, there are situations where organized private order exists but may be dysfunctional, *see infra* Section II.A, and market players therefore revert to (or maintain) spontaneous order as the primary mechanism for enforcing contracts. This phenomenon is unsurprising when one considers the existence of private order in the face of an existing but dysfunctional formal legal system.

15. In the telephone game, a long sentence is whispered from one person to another in a group. The second person repeats the sentence to a third, the third to a fourth, and so on, until everyone has heard the sentence. The last member then repeats what he or she heard, usually uttering a sentence entirely unrelated to the original. On the idea that a formal organizational structure reduces the likelihood of mistakes, see Joel Sobel, *How to Count to One Thousand*, 102 ECON. J. 1 (1992).

16. This problem with the transmission of information provides another explanation for the inability of relational contracting to be effective in larger groups.

A trade association can effectively serve as a repository of information. A buyer, say, considering dealing with a new seller can go to the information repository and check whether the seller has a history of reneging on deals. In addition, a trustworthy party may be needed to investigate any reports of cheating and assess which party to the transaction actually cheated. A trade association (or other type of information provider) can perform this task, and can also check the veracity of the offended firm's claim that it has been cheated (for example, claims of unpaid debts or delivery of low-quality goods). Otherwise, sellers could use the threat of reporting to hold up innocent buyers, or vice versa.[17]

In the examples provided below,[18] we will show that trade associations must inspect their own members as well as those on the other side of the transaction. If they imperfectly police their own members, then those members may use the threat of multilateral sanctions in bargaining with their customers, thus undermining their own incentives. The key lies in verification of the claims of cheating. Having verified, the organization might just publicize the cheating, or it might take a more active role in generating punishment by community sanctions or some other route.

A wholesaler or market intermediary that deals with several customers can also have an effect similar to that of an information repository. If a seller produces a low-quality item, it risks losing not just the customer who bought the good, but also other customers, if the wholesaler that handled the purchase ceases dealing with the seller. In addition, if the wholesaler stocks multiple product lines, it has an incentive to drop a reneging seller; otherwise its own reputation will suffer, with consequent loss of sales in its other product lines.[19]

Moreover, the benefit of intermediaries as information-providers goes beyond the implementation of community sanctions. By inspecting the quality of a product and certifying it, intermediaries resolve problems generated by asymmetric information about trading partners' capabilities. The fact that intermediaries are prominent in the marketplace and themselves have a reputation to maintain gives them an incentive to carry out this certification honestly. Trading through intermediaries generates a better match of buyers to sellers than does unintermediated trade.[20] If the intermediary is a monopo-

---

17. *See* Ronald J. Mann, *Verification Institutions in Financing Transactions*, 87 GEO. L.J. 2225, 2267-69 (1999); Paul R. Milgrom et al., *The Role of Institutions in the Revival of Trade: The Law Merchant, Private Judges, and the Champagne Fairs*, 2 ECON. & POL. 21 (1990) *reprinted in* REPUTATION 243 (Daniel B. Klein ed., 1994).

18. *See infra* notes 74 to 80 and accompanying text.

19. *See* Gary Biglaiser & James Friedman, *Middlemen as Guarantors of Quality*, 12 INT'L J. INDUS. ORG. 509 (1994).

20. *See* Gary Biglaiser & James W. Friedman, *Adverse Selection with Competitive Inspection*, 8 J. ECON. & MGMT. STRATEGY 1 (Spring 1999).

list, this information provision and certification role may be attenuated; the monopolist might choose to reveal only partial information. If sufficient competition exists among intermediaries, on the other hand, complete information might be revealed.[21]

    b. Coordination of Community Response. As well as information, coordination is sometimes needed in enacting community sanctions. Information and coordination are separable in principle though not in practice: without information, coordination obviously cannot occur. For private order to work, the issue is whether it suffices for market participants to be informed of a breach, or whether, in addition, effective sanctioning requires some coordination of their responses.

    Coordination has two aspects. First, the repeated game has multiple equilibria; as in the standard prisoner's dilemma, many different outcomes are consistent with everyone behaving rationally. Cooperation supported by the threat of community sanctions is not the only possible outcome. Another equilibrium has everyone cheating. This rests on a self-confirming prophecy: each player expects everyone else to cheat, so each cheats, and everyone's expectations are fulfilled. An effective initiation of cooperation faces an obstacle: it does not pay to act in a trustworthy way unless you believe that everyone else will act in a trustworthy way. Escape from an untrusting equilibrium requires everyone to change his beliefs about others, and his own behavior, simultaneously. Such a coordinated change is unlikely to occur spontaneously if there is more than a handful of players; someone will have to organize it.

    Moreover, because most economic interactions can be more complicated than the standard prisoner's dilemma, there is an aspect to this multiplicity of equilibria beyond the issue of achieving *cooperative* outcomes. Complicated economic interactions indeed have a range of *efficient* outcomes that can be achieved. So in addition to achieving cooperation, there must also be a resolution of the issue of how to share the gains from that cooperation. Squabbling over the division of the spoils frequently causes agreements to break down. By developing customary rules to govern exchanges, and perhaps even by offering formal arbitration procedures, an organization can help prevent these costly bargaining breakdowns.

    The second aspect of coordination involves the resolution of the free-rider problem. After a seller has cheated a buyer, other potential buyers may have little incentive to join in the sanctioning of the cheater. It furthers each individual's interest to let bygones be bygones.[22] But if all do that, there is no sanction. A formal organization

---

    21. *See* Alessandro Lizzeri, *Information Revelation and Certification Intermediaries*, 30 RAND J. ECON. 214 (1999).

    22. *See* Dilip Abreu, *On the Theory of Infinitely Repeated Games with Discounting*, 56 ECONOMETRICA 383 (1988).

may be needed to provide the discipline to prevent this free-riding over punishment.

How, then, do private-order organizations address these two problems? Organized private order means that any individual trader need not have frequent (or any) contact with any other particular trader in order for reliable information to be transmitted between the two. Hence, more open groups are workable. Furthermore, an organization increases the force of economic sanctions because it eliminates the need for future dealings to occur between any single pair of traders. To sustain cooperation it is only necessary that a firm foresee future dealings with *some* members of the group.

II. When Spontaneous Order Does, and Does Not, Work

Spontaneous cooperation may arise between two transactors or among many. In this Part, we review anecdotal and empirical evidence on bilateral relational contracting.

A. *Bilateral Relational Contracting*

Long-term bilateral relations are pervasive in less-developed countries. In Moroccan bazaars, for example, the lack of an organized market for information means that the "search for information one lacks and the protection of information one has is the name of the game."[23] The result is a "clientalization" of the market where, for the sake of assurance against being cheated, buyers habitually return to the sellers they know, even if other sellers offer lower prices. In rural Thailand, rice and rubber are marketed in different ways.[24] Rice is sold in impersonal auction markets, while rubber is traded via longstanding bilateral relationships between growers and buyers. The difference between these two formats lies in the ability of the buyer to assess the quality of the product. Whereas a buyer can immediately assess the quality of rice, the quality of rubber becomes apparent only several months later when it is processed. The buyer must trust the grower to have carefully removed impurities; this trust rests on the relationship.[25]

Vietnam's transitional economy provides a stringent test of the workability of spontaneous private order because the legal system is inadequate (or at least is perceived as such by market players) and the economy is not yet far enough developed for private-order organiza-

---

23. Clifford Geertz, *The Bazaar Economy: Information and Search in Peasant Marketing*, 90 AM. ECON. REV. 28, 28-30 (1978).

24. *See* Ammar Siamwalla, *Farmers and Middlemen: Aspects of Agricultural Marketing in Thailand*, 29 ECON. BULL. FOR ASIA & PAC. 38, 41-44 (1978).

25. *See id.* at 44.

tions to have been built. A survey of managers of small start-up firms in Vietnam we conducted in 1995 showed the inadequacy of formal contract-supporting institutions, both public and private.[26] The managers we interviewed said that they did not believe the courts could help them. "They normally just create more problems," said one.[27] "[I]n Vietnam no one believes we have a good legal system."[28] According to another, "[t]he court is weak and no entrepreneurs use it."[29] In responding to the inquiry on whether third parties exist that can enforce agreements with customers or suppliers, only 9% of those interviewed thought that a court or other government agency could help.[30] Third parties provide even less help for disputes over the quality of goods; only 2% of the managers said they would take such disputes to court or appeal to local authorities.[31] Moreover, trade associations do not seem to play a major contracting role. While 47% of the surveyed firms belong to a trade association, only 28% of these (or 13% of the total) say that the association provides "information about the trustworthiness of customers or suppliers," and only 13% (or 6% of the total) say that the association provides "contract and/or dispute resolution."[32] Most deals among Vietnam's firms, therefore, rest on unorganized bilateral relational contracting.

Because bilateral relationships require some degree of lock-in between the two parties,[33] our survey also asked a series of questions about the surveyed firms' first and newest customer relationship.[34] These data provide evidence regarding the relevance of customer lock-in for relational contracting. Using, as our measure of lock-in, the number of sellers of similar products located within one kilometer of the seller in question, we found that a seller's willingness to grant trade credit to a customer is significantly related to the buyer's degree of lock-in. A seller that has competitors nearby offers its customers about fifteen percentage points less trade credit than one with no nearby competitors.[35]

---

26. *See* John McMillan & Christopher Woodruff, *Dispute Prevention Without Courts in Vietnam*, 15 J.L. ECON. & ORG. 637 (1999) [hereinafter McMillan & Woodruff, *Dispute Prevention*].

27. *Id.* at 640.

28. *Id.*

29. *Id.*

30. *See id.* at 641.

31. *See id.*

32. *Id.* at 649.

33. *See supra* text accompanying note 5.

34. *See* John McMillan & Christopher Woodruff, *Interfirm Relationships and Informal Credit in Vietnam*, 114 Q.J. ECON. 1285 (1999) [hereinafter McMillan & Woodruff, *Interfirm Relationships*].

35. *See id.* at 1299.

Given that they are locked together, people can learn to trust each other. Bilateral cooperation may evolve in relationships via a process in which the potential loss from having a trading partner defect is kept small in initial transactions and allowed to increase as the relationship progresses. Our Vietnamese managers described such a process. They said that they investigated potential trading partners before starting a trading relationship by talking with the customer's neighbors or other trading partners. But even with this pre-trading research, it is difficult for managers to identify trustworthy customers at the outset. Early in the relationship, the two sides of the trading relationship test each other. As trading continues, experience with the trading partner provides information. One manager explained that "[p]eople show their personality through their actions in difficult times," so after a few transactions this manager selected a few customers to concentrate on.[36] The data show that longer-lasting relationships involve significantly more trust. After two years of dealings, the amount of trade credit offered is on average fourteen percentage points higher than at the start of the relationship.[37]

Also, given that they are locked in, the firms may be able to design the terms of each transaction so as to reduce the reliance on the shadow of the future by reducing either party's immediate temptation to renege. Setting the timing of payments right might achieve this, for example. If a manufacturer must make some initial specific investment in order to meet a buyer's needs, the gains from defection can be balanced by having the buyer pay part or all of the bill in advance of delivery. There is evidence that the Vietnamese firms structure their transactions in this way.[38]

B. *Multilateral Relational Contracting*

Bilateral relational contracting is not reliable if lock-in does not exist between the two trading partners. Relational contracting may still develop spontaneously, however, if community ties are strong enough.

Communities of traders may derive social norms that encourage cooperation between any two of their members. Interviewing ranchers in Shasta County, California, Robert Ellickson found that "most residents resolve trespass disputes not according to formal law, but rather, according to workday norms that are consistent with an overarching norm of cooperation among neighbors."[39] Among the rural

---

36. McMillan & Woodruff, *Dispute Prevention*, supra note 26, at 652.

37. *See* McMillan & Woodruff, *Interfirm Relationships*, supra note 34, at 1306.

38. *See* McMillan & Woodruff, *Dispute Prevention*, supra note 26, at 644-48.

39. ELLICKSON, *supra* note 6, at 48.

residents, interactions are frequent and residents expect them to continue indefinitely into the future. The conditions for cooperation in a repeated game are thus met. Similarly, merchants in Mexican California of the 1830s and 1840s, dealing with one another repetitively, enhanced the effect of reputation by communicating their experiences with one another.[40] Given the small size of the community and the frequency of interactions, gossip sufficed to keep traders honest. Among New York City garment-manufacturing firms, interfirm relationships promote cooperation, and thus reduce transactional uncertainty, facilitate the exchange of goods that are difficult to price, and enable the creation of agreements that are difficult to enforce contractually. These relationships often start from third-party referrals, and often are based on social relationships outside business.[41]

Our data on Vietnamese firms show that network links among firms engender cooperation.[42] We asked managers how they first learned about a customer before beginning to trade with it. If they responded that they found the customer through "other similar producers," "other suppliers," or business associations, we interpreted the two firms to be connected by a business network. One-quarter of the ongoing customer relationships in the sample were initiated through such business links. Connections significantly increased cooperation: a customer identified through a business network on average paid 10% to 20% more of its bills after delivery than did a customer identified by other means.[43] Similarly, in Africa, "firms that rely on information sharing to screen prospective credit recipients sell an additional 36% to 39% of their output on credit relative to others."[44]

Social sanctions can add to, or replace, economic sanctions in helping to ensure cooperative behavior. Social norms and sanctions have particular force in ethnic networks — linked by ties of culture, language, or religion — because these networks possess the advantage of having a wider range of methods of influence at their disposal than do groups of merchants connected only by their commercial interests. For example, an ethnic network provided the backbone for the elev-

40. *See* Karen Clay, *Trade without Law: Private-Order Institutions in Mexican California*, 13 J.L. ECON. & ORG. 202 (1997). Arguably the fact that trade was based on the missions facilitated this process by limiting the number of sites for trade.

41. *See* Brian Uzzi, *The Sources and Consequences of Embeddedness for the Economic Performance of Organizations: The Network Effect*, 61 AM. SOC. REV. 674 (1996).

42. *See* McMillan & Woodruff, *Interfirm Relationships*, *supra* note 34, at 1298.

43. *See* McMillan & Woodruff, *Interfirm Relationships*, *supra* note 34, at 1306.

44. Marcel Fafchamps, *Ethnicity and Credit in African Manufacturing*, 61 J. DEV. ECON 205, 229 (2000).

enth-century Maghribi traders' coalition.[45] In Asia and Africa, firms use ethnic ties to support transactions.[46]

In the precommunist Vietnam of the 1960s, business among the merchants who were ethnic-Chinese (a well-defined category in Vietnam) "was based upon personal relationships and word-of-mouth agreements."[47] If a merchant was untrustworthy, "it would be impossible for him to do business. Once the fact that a merchant had failed to honour his word became known, other merchants would simply refuse to do business with him."[48] These relationships were specifically ethnic-Chinese, and the inability of the ethnic-Vietnamese merchants to establish trust among themselves was alleged to explain their "lack of success in competing with the Chinese."[49]

Among the present-day Vietnamese firms we surveyed, however, ethnic ties seemed less important. When asked how they first learned about a customer before beginning to trade with it, 17% identified family connections (a surprisingly small number given the conventional views about the dependence of Asian business on family), but there was no significant extra amount of trust (as measured by trade credit) in those trading relationships. Furthermore, 18% of the managers we interviewed said they could speak Chinese.[50] If the existence of a Chinese ethnic network depends on this language ability along with the use of family connections, we found no significant tendency for family-based contracting to be used in transactions with a higher-than-average risk of reneging.[51]

Table 1 summarizes some studies of spontaneous cooperation. These groups have several characteristics in common. They lack the ability to implement formal sanctions, such as fines, although they may, and generally do, rely on social sanctions as an enforcement mechanism. These social sanctions usually operate through ostracizing or excluding members from the group. If this threat of exclusion is to shape behavior, there must be "social profits" from future interaction with the group, just as there must be economic profits for the threat of exclusion to have pecuniary penalties. This may be one reason that almost all of the groups on Table 1 are "closed" to the extent that membership is limited by ethnicity or geography.

---

45. *See* Greif, *Contract Enforceability, supra* note 13, at 535-41.

46. *See generally* JANET TAI LANDA, TRUST, ETHNICITY, AND IDENTITY (1994); Fafchamps, *supra* note 44.

47. Clifton A. Barton, *Trust and Credit: Some Observations Regarding Business Strategies of Overseas Chinese Traders in South Vietnam, in* 1 THE CHINESE IN SOUTH VIETNAM 53, 49 (Lim & Gosling eds., 1983).

48. *Id.*

49. *Id.*

50. *See* McMillan & Woodruff, *Dispute Prevention, supra* note 26, at 651.

51. *See id.* at 650-51.

TABLE 1: SPONTANEOUS ORDERING

Group	Author	Reference Footnote	Open or closed	One sided or two?	Information or coordination?
Maghribi	Greif (1994)	13	Closed	One	Information
Vietnam manufacturers	McMillan/ Woodruff (1999)				
Social networks		26	Closed	Two	Information
Business networks			Open	Two	Information
California merchants	Clay (1997)	41	Closed	Two	Information
Shasta ranchers	Ellickson (1991)	6	Closed	Two	Information
Singapore/Malaysia Ethnic networks	Landa (1994)	47	Closed	Two	Information

In sum, then, spontaneous relational contracting can work bilaterally if the two trading partners are locked in with each other. In the absence of lock-in, relational contracting requires the involvement, not just of the two parties to the transaction, but of a community of traders. Such community-based contracting can work spontaneously, based on social norms or on social or business networks, in close-knit communities with free flows of information. The market friction needed to support spontaneous relational contracting exists in transition economies such as Vietnam, which are characterized by thin markets and high transportation costs. As the private sector develops and infrastructure is improved, however, market friction decreases, making spontaneous order harder to sustain. As this occurs, more formal systems of private ordering are necessary to sustain cooperation between trading partners.

III. Organizing Private Order

In this Part, we review evidence from published anecdotes and from our own empirical studies that demonstrate how market players organize private order. As discussed above, private organizations serve two main functions in providing contract assurance: providing information about breaches, and coordinating responses (that is, sanctions) to those breaches.

A. *Information Provision*

In open communities of traders where entry and exit are frequent, reliable information exchange is critical. How can new traders become quickly informed about the reliability of trading partners? How can word about newcomers who cheat be spread quickly so that the gains of cheating are minimized?[52] Numerous examples from diverse settings show how organized ordering increases the effectiveness of reputation in controlling behavior.

Wholesalers of fresh fish in the United States used to suffer from buyers' failure to pay their bills.[53] Relationships consequently developed, so much so that one observer identified long-lasting bilateral relationships as the defining characteristic of the industry: "[D]ealers, wholesale firms and retail firms maintain longstanding ties to ensure steady supplies and customers."[54] Nevertheless, despite the prevalence of long-term relationships, "sharp practices are rife," according to a 1984 study by James Acheson.

> There are many stories in the industry about firms that have sent shipments of lobsters to distant parts of the country and then have had great difficulties collecting their money. Other firms have sold lobsters to out-of-state trucking firms for a good price only to find that the check was no good.[55]

The buyers could easily find other wholesalers to buy from, so they could get away without paying. Observing this, Neal Workman, an entrepreneur in Portland, Maine, formed a firm called GoFish to act as a debt-collection agency for the wholesalers. He soon realized that there was unused value in the information that he was gathering. "You can collect the bill once," he said. "You can sell the information about the guy that doesn't pay over and over and over."[56] GoFish began using the internet to provide fish wholesalers with credit information about deadbeat buyers. This changed the industry. According to fish dealers, buyers now must pay their bills if they want to continue to buy fish.

Two trade associations of footwear manufacturers in Mexico perform a similar role in regulating trade between manufacturers and retailers. The associations are located in the cities of Leon and Guadalajara, which together account for three-quarters of the coun-

---

52. In an open network with no pre-screening, a trader will always be able to enter and cheat once. This could be prevented in two ways. First, there might be some profit from future trade within the network, giving an incentive for those who enter to remain after entering. Alternatively, it may be profitable for the network to use courts to sanction cheaters even when the cost of doing so exceeds the recovery. That is, business networks or trade associations may gain a reputation for punishing defectors as a means of preventing defections. This could explain why (as shown in Part IV *infra*) business networks complement, rather than replace, courts in Eastern Europe.

53. *See* James M. Acheson, *The Social Organization of the Maine Lobster Market*, *in* MARKETS AND MARKETING 105-51 (Stuart Plattner ed., 1990).

54. *Id.* at 128.

55. *Id.* at 117.

56. The GoFish story is on National Public Radio, Morning Edition, January 29, 1999, available at <http://npr.org/news/business/1999/Jan/990129.fish.html> (visited September 21, 2000).

try's manufacturing.[57] They offer two related services. First, each regional association maintains a database of information on the past behavior of retail clients of their members. Did the retailers pay their bills on time? Did they return an excessive amount of the merchandise, claiming it was defective? Did they cancel orders at the last minute, after goods had already been produced to fill them? A member receiving an order from a retailer with whom he has never worked can call the association and obtain a report on the retailer within 48 hours. Communication among manufacturers is made easier because they are geographically agglomerated. Second, both trade associations intervene to resolve disputes between manufacturers and retailers. Lawyers working for the associations travel regular routes throughout Mexico, visiting the retailers who owe money, and filing court cases if necessary.[58] Representatives of the association in Leon, however, claim that most disputes are resolved with a telephone call to the retailer. The association's power comes from its threat to put the retailer on a "clients in default" list that is sent to association members every two months. These collection services complement the information gathering, since manufacturers gain directly from reporting delinquent clients. Also, association lawyers traveling to collect accounts from one client will often gather information on other clients. This information is kept on file at the association and made available to members.

In nineteenth-century Japan, contract-supporting information provision was one of the main functions of trade associations.[59] The names of firms that reneged on agreements were posted on a blackboard for everyone to see, so cheating resulted in immediate loss of business. The courts were less effective then than they are now,[60] but organized information gathering is not limited to environments in which courts are ineffective, and Japanese trade associations still perform the same function. During the recession of the early 1990s, wholesalers of heat-insulation materials faced an increase in fraudu-

---

57. *See* Christopher Woodruff, *Contract Enforcement and Trade Liberalization in Mexico's Footwear Industry*, 26 WORLD DEV. 979, 982 (1998). The associations were most effective when the market was closed to imports. For further discussion of this phenomenon, see *id.* at 984-86.

58. Using the courts in Mexico is possible, but problematic, according to manufacturers. First, the action must be filed in the city where the retailer does business. This makes delay tactics used by retailers' lawyers more costly. Second, judgments may be difficult to collect. One manufacturer recounted that he had been awarded the retailer's automobile by the court. However, since automobile titles were not registered electronically, there was no way to put a lien on the car. The retailer sold the car before he could take possession of it. The association representative reported that the most important role of the courts was to provide certification of the loss for tax purposes.

59. *See* ULRIKE SCHAEDE, COOPERATIVE CAPITALISM: SELF-REGULATION, TRADE ASSOCIATIONS, AND THE ANTIMONOPOLY LAW IN JAPAN at chs. 5 & 7 (2000).

60. *See id.* at ch. 7.

lent activity, with checks bouncing and customers disappearing after receiving merchandise. To protect its members, the wholesalers' trade association created a list of all its members' potential customers, indicating each one's creditworthiness. Dishonest companies were boycotted.

Credit bureaus similarly function as information repositories. For most consumers, the knowledge that failure to pay a bill would damage their credit rating is sufficient incentive to ensure they pay their bills.[61]

In the present-day Taiwanese footwear industry, trading companies act as a "hub of information regarding the managerial and financial condition" of manufacturers.[62] The trading companies gather similar information about the demands and reliability of buyers in the United States and in Europe. Employees of a trading company often stay in the factories to monitor quality while an order is being produced. If disputes later arise between seller and buyer, the trading company then has the information it needs to judge which party is at fault. Are the goods defective, or is the buyer claiming a quality defect to avoid paying for goods she has decided she doesn't want? The trading companies increase the effectiveness of reputation in two ways. First, since each trading company works with many manufacturers and many buyers, a manufacturer delivering merchandise late or of low quality will lose business with many clients all at once. Second, other players in the industry learn which party was at fault in the dispute (so long as the trading company can be trusted to be a fair judge). Wholesalers and similar intermediaries perform similar functions in other markets as well.[63]

B. *Coordination*

The separation of the two roles of private-order organizations — information and coordination — is somewhat artificial. Since coordination requires information in the first place, organizations often do both. One can nonetheless independently assess whether the organization engages in coordination as well as information provision. In

---

61. *See generally* Daniel B. Klein, *Promise Keeping in the Great Society: A Model of Credit Information Sharing*, 4 ECON. & POL. 117 (1992).

62. You-tien Hsing, *Trading Companies in Taiwan's Fashion Shoe Networks*, 48 J. INT'L ECON. 101, 106 (1998). Hubert Schmitz describes a similar role for wholesalers in Brazil's footwear industry. *See* Hubert Schmitz, *Small Shoemakers and Fordist Giants: Tales of a Supercluster*, 23 WORLD DEV. 9, 14 (1995).

63. Banks appear to operate in a similar manner in the market for Letters of Credit ("LOCs"). According to Ronald Mann, sellers rarely comply strictly with the terms of LOCs. The buyer's bank, however, will pressure the buyer to pay so long as the breach is not material. Thus, payment through LOCs rests on the reputation of the bank rather than on the formal legal system. *See* Ronald J. Mann, *The Role of Letters of Credit in Payment Transactions*, 98 MICH. L. REV. 2494, 2525 (2000).

Section III.A, we discussed organizations whose functions seem limited to information provision. We now discuss organizations that actively coordinate their members' responses to breaches of agreements.

Cooperation depends on history. If players have cheated each other in the past, they will tend to continue to cheat each other. Thus, cooperation requires coordinated action by all of the players to break out of a low-level equilibrium. The European car industry provides an example of a persistent inefficient equilibrium, and a coordinated attempt to break out of it. A report sponsored by the U.K. government noted: "The mistrust which is in evidence is the result of many years of broken promises, abuse of confidence, and general acrimony in the industry."[64] This was seen as raising the European industry's costs and harming its competitiveness against U.S. and Japanese imports. In 1994, the two European trade associations, representing the car makers and the components suppliers, launched an initiative "aimed at improving the often hostile relations between the two sides of the motor industry."[65] The guidelines sought more transparency in negotiations over prices, greater cooperation in design and technology, and quality improvement. While it was accepted that the guidelines "could not give a legal or contractual definition to the relationship between vehicle-makers and component suppliers," they were intended to provide a "framework for cooperation."[66]

Providing information about those who cheat may not suffice to deter cheating when punishment is costly — coordination may be required to prevent free riding.[67] For example, in interviews conducted as part of our study of manufacturers in Vietnam, managers expressed some hesitancy to use their full arsenal of sanctions, in part because doing so would give them a reputation among their other customers of being difficult to deal with. "[K]eeping a good reputation is the most important thing," noted one manager.[68] "[I]n Vietnam if you treat customers fairly when they have difficulties you will have that reputation. People will do business with you because they think you will not kill them when they have difficulties."[69] It is apparently not enough for the offended manager to determine whether the customer deliberately defected; it must also be clear to his other customers or potential customers that the customer cheated. Managers expressed a similar concern about hiring private agencies to collect unpaid bills. When a

64. K. Done & G. Tett, *Peace Move in European Motor Industry*, FIN. TIMES, Apr. 13, 1994, at 2.

65. *Id.*

66. *Id.*

67. *See supra* Section I.B.2(a).

68. McMillan & Woodruff, *Dispute Prevention*, *supra* note 26, at 643.

69. *Id.*

wholesaler owed one of our interviewees 60 million dong ($5,500), the interviewee considered hiring outside agents to collect his debt, but decided against it because it would have harmed his relationship with his other customers. He said, "in order to keep long-term relationships with other customers, the firm must be very careful in dealing with disputes."[70]

In the absence of an incentive to participate in sanctioning, free riding by traders weakens the ex ante incentive for cooperation. Private organizations can coordinate sanctioning by punishing those who fail to carry out required punishments. An early mechanism for doing this was the medieval law merchant.[71] Law merchants had the power to adjudicate disputes between trading partners, and set restitution to be paid by the party at fault. They kept records of defecting traders who had not made the payments set by the law merchant. This facilitated information transmission by providing a central location in which the past behavior of any potential trading partner could be checked. But this system is effective only if the traders stay informed by checking the status of each trading partner before trading with them and refusing to deal with those not in good standing. Otherwise, those who defect will not be fully sanctioned. Since checking on the status of each potential trading partner is a costly activity, traders had to be given an incentive not to free ride. Law merchants did this by establishing the rule that traders who failed to check on the status of a trading partner before transacting could not bring a case before the judge. This gave traders an incentive to stay informed, and ensured that the reputation of being a trader in good standing had more currency.

Japanese banks use a clearinghouse to deter default.[72] If a person or firm dishonors a note or check twice during a six-month period, all the financial institutions participating in the clearinghouse are required, by the rules of the clearinghouse, to suspend transactions with the defaulter for two years. Before the system was established in 1894, banks had a loose understanding that they would inform each other of defaults. The creation of the clearinghouse led to a substantial decline in default rates, showing that the spontaneous order that had prevailed evidently did not work as well as the organized private order of the

---

70. *Id.* at 644.

71. *See* Milgrom et al., *supra* note 17.

72. *See* J. Mark Ramseyer, *Legal Rules in Repeated Deals: Banking in the Shadow of Defection in Japan*, 20 J. LEGAL STUD. 91, 110-11 (1991); Marc Ryser, *Sanctions without Law: The Japanese Financial Clearinghouse Guillotine and Its Impact on Default Rates*, in REPUTATION 225 (Daniel B. Klein ed., 1997). Ramseyer views the role of the clearinghouse as providing a commitment that the banks would actually carry out the prescribed punishments (that is, in our terms, its role is coordination). Ryser views it as a repository of data about defaulters (that is, its role is information). As we have noted, the two roles are not mutually exclusive.

clearinghouse. The creation of the clearinghouse coordinated a shift to a new equilibrium, involving increased cooperation among the banks. The clearinghouse also helps address the free-rider problem involved in punishment by making it harder for banks to continue dealing with defaulters. Further, it serves as a repository of information about defaulters.[73]

Industry trade associations may coordinate the actions of their own members as well. The Fur Dressers' and Fur Dyers' Association provides one example of this.[74] Operating in the United States in the early 1900s, the association consisted of thirty members who performed 70% of the cleaning and dyeing of fur pelts used in the manufacture of garments. Association members complained it was "general practice" for their clients (fur garment manufacturers) to claim that furs had been damaged in the dressing and dyeing process, and the damage claims were used to justify reductions in payments to dressers and dyers.[75] The small size of the transactions and the difficulty in describing the agreed-upon quality level made use of the courts impractical in resolving the disputes.

According to association bylaws, any manufacturer who did not pay the full amount demanded by a dresser and dyer after delivery of the merchandise was blacklisted directly by the harmed dresser/dyer. Association members agreed not to do business with a blacklisted client unless they were paid in advance for services.[76] Members of the trade association, who had to post bonds of $500 upon joining, were fined for any transactions with manufacturers currently blacklisted. These fines helped overcome free-rider problems and strengthened the enforcement mechanism.[77]

The ability of an individual member to blacklist, however, admits the possibility of extortion: a dresser and dyer could force a garment

---

73. In its early days, the New York Stock Exchange certified the creditworthiness of traders on the exchange and judged disputes involving members and suspended members found at fault, according to Stuart Banner. It also filled a gap in the formal laws. Traders frequently engaged in "time bargains," or futures contracts, even though, until 1858, contracts for the sale of stock that the seller did not own on the contract date were legally void in the state of New York, so these futures contracts were unenforceable in New York courts. The stock exchange took on the role of forcing traders to comply with their futures contracts, with the penalty for breach being suspension or expulsion of members. *See generally* Stuart Banner, *The Origin of the New York Stock Exchange, 1791-1860*, 27 J. LEGAL STUD. 113 (1998).

74. The association's activities are discussed in *United States v. Fur Dressers' & Fur Dyers' Ass'n*, 5 F.2d 869 (1925). This, and other similar cases, are also discussed in GEORGE P. LAMB & SUMNER S. KITTELLE, TRADE ASSOCIATION LAW AND PRACTICE 96-105 (1956).

75. *See* LAMB & KITTELLE, *supra* note 74, at 100.

76. In this case, the manufacturer could make no ex post claim even if it were legitimate.

77. In a closed community, norms might be used to overcome problems with proper enforcement by members of the group. In Shasta County, Ellickson notes that "persons who respond [to transgressions] with excessive force" are themselves punished by the community. ELLICKSON, *supra* note 39, at 253.

2442 *Michigan Law Review* [Vol. 98:2421

manufacturer to pay in full even when there were legitimate reasons for a discount. Such an action, which would work to the detriment of the overall association, suggests the need for the association to monitor its own membership as well. The monitoring might even be conducted informally. For example, in Mexico, footwear manufacturers reportedly ignore complaints against retailers made by certain manufacturers because those manufacturers are themselves viewed as unreliable by the manufacturing community.[78]

Some trade associations use more formal methods of monitoring their own members. The Popular Priced Dress Manufacturers Association, for example, formed a subsidiary called the Dress Control Returns Bureau. The Bureau employed investigators to inspect all merchandise returned to manufacturers by retailers and certify that each return was made because of legitimate quality defects.[79] Retailers (clients) who returned merchandise for any reason other than legitimate quality defects, and who refused to pay for that merchandise, were blacklisted by the manufacturers' association. The members of the association themselves were "coerced and compelled ... to abide by rules and regulations ... under penalty of being required to pay ... fines in a substantial amount of money."[80]

Arbitration may also provide a method of enforcing standards and coordinating equilibria. For example, the New York Diamond Dealer's Club "facilitates the transmission of information about dealers' reputations and, at least with respect to members, serves both a reputation-signaling and reputation-monitoring function."[81] A typical transaction in the diamond industry involves the transfer between traders of bags of diamonds worth millions of dollars, but without any written contract. Upon joining the association, members must sign an agreement that they will submit all disputes to arbitration. The "Floor Committee" (the arbitral body) can exact a fine up to $1,000 and suspend a member's trading privileges for twenty days. Both the amount of the fine and the rationale for reaching the decision are kept secret,

---

78. *See* Woodruff, *supra* note 57, at 986.

79. *See* Popular Priced Dress Mfg. Group, Inc., 47 F.T.C. 1608 (1951). The association "employed and now employ[s], investigators to investigate the return by retailers of all ladies' dresses to the manufacturers thereof and to ascertain whether or not said returns are in accordance with the rules and regulations promulgated by ... [the] Popular Priced Dress Manufacturers Group, Inc. ..." *Id.* at 1612.

80. *In re* Nat'l Coat & Suit Recovery Bd. 47 F.T.C. 1552 (1950). The Film Board of Trade carried out similar monitoring of their members. *See* United States v. First Nat'l Pictures, Inc., 34 F.2d 815 (S.D.N.Y. 1929), *rev'd,* 282 U.S. 44 (1930). The monitoring of members in these cases may have extended beyond that needed for contract enforcement. Actions by these and other associations allowed under the National Industrial Recovery Act were later deemed to constitute restraint of trade.

81. Lisa Bernstein, *Opting Out of the Legal System: Extralegal Contractual Relations in the Diamond Industry,* 21 J. LEGAL STUD. 115, 121 (1992).

but unpaid fines are posted.[82]   The arbitration board also has the power to suspend or expel a member from the association.[83]

In the grain industry, the arbitration board of the National Grain and Feed Association indeed provides more effective enforcement of contracts (than do courts) for a novel reason, argues Lisa Bernstein. While courts search for "immanent business norms" to guide dispute settlements, the trade association arbitrators strictly apply the terms of the contract. This allows trading partners to structure contracts on two levels, with a set of rules ("norms") governing relationships in the cooperative phase, and a set of rules (contracts, or "end-game norms") governing relationships in the defection phase. These two sets of rules allow trading partners to sustain cooperation under a broader set of circumstances. The failure of the courts to more strictly enforce the contracts, on the other hand, undermines cooperation. In this example, private ordering substitutes for the formal legal system not because it has a better understanding of industry practices, but because it has a better understanding of the theory of contract.

* * *

Table 2 summarizes cases of organized private ordering from the literature. The organized institutions divide along several characteristics. Some institutions provide only information, while others sanction their own members for failure to sanction defectors. Those providing only information allow their members' trading partners more latitude to maintain strong relationships with some members even while they cheat others. Those that sanction their own members provide a stronger incentive for cooperation.

---

82. According to Bernstein, the secrecy of the arbitration rulings enables a trader to "minimize the reputation cost of his breach." *Id.* at 126. Thus the fine imposed by the arbitrator is the sanction against defecting. Traders are not doubly punished by reputation sanctions as well.

83. *See generally id.* Numerous other trade associations provide arbitration services to their members. These associations generally have memberships comprised of traders on both sides of the transaction. Among these are the American Spice Trade Association and the National Grain and Feed Association. *See* HANDBOOK, BY-LAWS, AND CONTRACT RULES OF THE AMERICAN SPICE TRADE ASSOCIATION (1936). *See also* Lisa Bernstein, *Merchant Law in a Merchant Court: Rethinking the Code's Search for Immanent Business Norms,* 144 U. PA. L. REV. 1765, 1771 (1996).

TABLE 2: ORGANIZED INSTITUTIONS

Group	Author	Reference Footnote	Open or closed	One sided or two?	Information or coordination?
NGFA	Bernstein (1996)	84	Open	Two	Coordination
Diamonds	Bernstein (1992)	82	Closed	Two	Coordination
Mexican footwear	Woodruff (1998)	58	Open	One	Information
Taiwan footwear	Hsing (1998)	63	Open	Independent	Information
Japan mafia	Milhaupt/ West (1999)	115	Closed	Independent	Coordination
Law merchant	Milgrom/ North/ Weingast (1990)	17	Open	Independent	Coordination
Merchant Guild	Greif/ Milgrom/ Weingast	115	Open	One	Coordination
NYSE	Banner (1998)	74	Open	Two	Coordination
Japanese banking clearinghouse	Ryser (1997)	73	Open	One	Coordination
US trade associations (not previously published)					
Fur dressers/dyers		75	Open	One	Coordination
Popular Priced Dress Association		80	Open	One	Coordination
GoFish		57	Open	One	Information

Note: Open means there are no significant restrictions to becoming a member of the institution; closed means there are significant restrictions.

A second way in which the organized institutions differ is that some are primarily interested in actions that are *verifiable*, while others are interested in actions that are *observable* to the parties involved in the transaction, but which are not verifiable by those outside the transaction. Credit bureaus and some trade associations, for example, are interested primarily in whether or not sellers actually deliver goods and buyers pay for them. Once the information is gathered, third parties can verify these actions by examining shipping receipts, canceled checks, and so on. Where courts function poorly, the trade associations reduce the cost of transmitting information about such behavior.

The trading companies in Taiwan and the arbitration boards at trade associations provide examples of institutions involved in disputes that are observable but not verifiable. The Taiwanese trading companies, for instance, certify the quality of footwear delivered. Since the precise quality level agreed upon proves very difficult to write down, trading companies cannot provide information which allows third parties not involved in the transaction to verify which party is at fault in a dispute. To be effective, then, the trading companies must have some incentive to be impartial in their judgments — and their own reputation in the market provides this. Two-sided membership in trade association (that is, both buyers and sellers) may provide a similar incentive for fairness.

IV. INTERACTIONS BETWEEN PRIVATE AND PUBLIC ORDER

How does the presence of the legal system, or its absence, affect the operation of private-order mechanisms? In advanced economies with well-functioning legal systems, courts underpin existing private-order mechanisms. Bargaining occurs in the shadow of the law; the law shapes agreements even if they operate without appealing to it. Even when it does not work well, a formal legal system can sometimes help spontaneous private order work. The ability to damage a trader's reputation works as a sanction even if the court's coercive enforcement powers are weak.

In China in the early 1990s, for example, lawyers who specialized in debt collection maintained good relations with the local press and would then threaten debtors with publicity.[84] The unworkability of official enforcement mechanisms meant that even the courts sometimes did this. Courts in the province of Heilongjiang, for example, threatened newspaper exposure of debtors who failed to pay. This apparently worked in the big cities, and particularly with enterprises wishing to protect a reputation they had built through expending huge sums of advertising money.[85]

Private order can serve as either a complement to or a substitute for public order. Private order provides a complement (or a substitute) to the law if an improvement in the law generates an increase (or a decrease) in the marginal value of private order. An improvement in the law will increase the use of complementary private-order mechanisms; it will similarly decrease the use of substituting private-order mechanisms. Which type of private order exists in any given system is an empirical question.

---

84. Private conversation with Donald C. Clarke, Professor of Law, University of Washington.

85. *Id.*

Countries making a transition from a centrally planned to a market economy provide an experimental forum to study how the various contract-assurance mechanisms interact. Certainly legal systems have been created there, and many companies indeed express faith in them, but trade associations, informal networks, wholesalers, and reputation also still have a profound effect on contracting. In this Part, we turn to evidence from a survey of manufacturing companies carried out in Poland, Slovakia, Romania, Russia, and the Ukraine.[86] We use these survey data to determine whether a manager's use of social networks, business networks, wholesalers, and/or reputation depends on his faith in the ability of courts to enforce contracts with trading partners.

A. *The Data*

As determined by managers' perceptions, the courts in Eastern Europe and the former Soviet Union are more effective than those in Vietnam. The survey asked the managers about the ability of courts, other government agencies, or private parties to enforce contracts with customers and suppliers. Overall, just over two-thirds (68%) of those surveyed said courts could enforce contracts with customers. (Eighty-seven percent of the Romanian managers, 73% of the Polish managers, 68% of the Slovakian managers, 56% of the Russian managers, and 55% of the Ukrainian managers said the courts were effective.)[87] This reflects a much higher confidence in the court system in these countries than exists in Vietnam.[88]

Similarly, trade associations seem to underpin contracting in these countries more than they do in Vietnam. Although the survey gave us little direct indication of the role of organizations other than courts in contracting, overall two-fifths[89] of the managers said they belong to trade associations that provide important services: information about the location of new suppliers and/or customers; information about the trustworthiness of suppliers and/or customers; or arbitration services. In Vietnam, by comparison, 26% of the firms belong to trade associations that offer some sort of contracting support.[90] Wholesalers inter-

---

86. This survey asks questions similar to those asked in the Vietnam survey discussed above. *See supra* Part II.

87. *See* Simon Johnson et al., Courts and Relational Contracts (Sept. 2000) (unpublished manuscript, on file with authors) [hereinafter Johnson et al., Courts and Contracts].

88. *See supra* text accompanying notes 26 to 29.

89. The actual numbers, by country, were 44% in Romania, 21% in Poland, 23% in Slovakia, 60% in Russia, and 64% in the Ukraine.

90. The membership percentage for Vietnam given here differs from that given in Section II.A because we have included "information about new customers and suppliers" as contracting support. Just over 12% of the Vietnamese firms belong to a trade association providing information about new trading partners without providing the other contracting services.

mediate more a higher percentage of sales (10%) in Vietnam than in Romania (7%), Russia (5%), or Ukraine (4%). They are much more likely to intermediate transactions in the most advanced or the Eastern European economies — Poland (26%) and Slovakia (19%). With the possible exception of Vietnam, this ranking coincides with these countries' relative degrees of institutional development.[91]

We find that both the courts and trade associations have a significant effect on business trust in Eastern Europe. A firm that finds courts effective is on average 9% more likely to grant its customers trade credit than one that says the courts are ineffective. A firm that belongs to a trade association providing contract-supporting services is 6% more likely to offer trade credit than one that does not.[92] These numbers demonstrate the relevant role that these institutions play in providing contractual assurance.

Spontaneous relational contracting also plays a significant role. From our data we can identify two types of relational contracting — the use of *social networks* and the use of *business networks*. The survey asked a series of questions about the firms' longest-running and newest customer relationships, and also identified how the manufacturer first made contact with the customers identified in the survey. In particular, we know whether the trading partners are managed by family members or by people who were friends of the manufacturer before their trading relationship began. In both these scenarios we identify the relationship as one that arose from a social network. About 17% of the customer relationships arose from social networks.[93] Almost half (45%) of the time, however, initial information about customers came from business networks — suppliers, other customers, or competitors of the manufacturer.[94] Both social and business networks increase information flow and make sanctions possible.

In addition to providing information about the ability to use formal institutions and to rely on networks for contractual assurance, the survey gives some indication about how well reputation functions. With respect to customers, manufacturers were asked: "If your company had a dispute with this customer, would other suppliers of this customer find out about it?" and "If this customer had a dispute with another firm, would your company find out about it?"[95]

---

91. For evidence of these countries' relative institutional development by a variety of criteria, see Johnson et al., *Entrepreneurs, supra* note 3, at 4-13.

92. *See* Johnson et al., Courts and Contracts, *supra* note 87.

93. *See id.*

94. Regardless of the initial source of information, 14% of the customers are identified as wholesalers. *See id.*

95. Word gets around. In 28% of the relationships for which we have complete data (618 of 2184), the manager said a customer's other suppliers would hear about a dispute. In 39% (854 of 2184), managers said they would hear about any transgressions of their customers.

2448   *Michigan Law Review*   [Vol. 98:2421]

We find that these forms of relational contracting, like the courts and trade associations, also have a significant effect on business trust. Customer lock-in matters: having one fewer competitor located nearby raises the probability of offering credit by 3%. More trust exists in longer-lasting relationships: three years after the start of a relationship, the probability of credit increases by 18%. Customers identified through business networks are 13% more likely to receive credit, and those identified through social networks are 14% more likely to receive credit, than customers identified without the help of networks.[96]

B. *The Interaction of Public and Private: Analyzing the Data*

We now use these data to ask how the courts, trade associations, informal networks, and reputation interact in supporting contracting. We do this with a series of regressions (reported in Table 3). We asked firms about both their oldest and newest customers, so the sample includes two observations per firm. The questions indicating membership in a trade association and belief in the effectiveness of courts relate to characteristics of the firm rather than of the individual relationships between the manufacturers and their customers. To correct for the biases in the standard errors created by the mismatched aggregation of data, we use a random-effects probit model. In addition to the variables of interest reported in Table 3, all the regressions include a set of variables which control for firm and manager characteristics, and a series of dummy variables for each of eight industries in each of the five countries. These variables are described in the notes to Table 3.

---

96. Johnson et al., Courts and Contracts, *supra* note 87.

TABLE 3: INTERACTIONS OF USE OF NETWORKS

	Random Effects Probits					
	Customer identified by business network	Customer identified by social network	Customer is wholesaler	Manufacturer learns about customer's other disputes	Customer's other suppliers learn about disputes	Customer is located in a different city
Courts are effective	0.172 (2.57)	-0.157 (1.93)	-0.035 (0.42)	-0.27 (3.59)	-0.073 (0.91)	-0.101 (1.38)
Member of trade association	0.009 (0.14)	0.073 (0.92)	-0.188 (2.18)	0.227 (3.04)	-0.005 (0.07)	0.042 (0.58)
Customer identified through business network				0.318 (5.06)	0.124 (1.92)	-0.195 (2.99)
Customer identified through social network				0.295 (3.42)	-0.099 (1.08)	-0.436 (4.62)
Customer is wholesaler				-0.088 (1.02)	0.02 (0.23)	0.542 (6.25)
Number of observations	2381	2381	2381	2184	2184	2231

Note: Regressions also include three variables measuring characteristics of the firm's manager (age, years of schooling, and a variable indicating that the manager previously worked as a high-level manager in a state-owned enterprise), three variables measuring characteristics of the firm (log age of firm, log of the number of employees, and an indicator that the firm was started from scratch rather than spun off from a state-owned firm), and 39 industry/country dummy variables.

Taking the manager's attitude toward the effectiveness of courts and membership in trade associations as given, we first ask how these affect the use of business networks, social networks, and wholesalers.[97] Managers who express confidence in the courts are more likely to use business networks and less likely to use social networks to identify customers. The first effect is significant at the 0.01 level, the second at the 0.10 level. Trade association members are less likely to have customers who are wholesalers. There is also a negative relationship between confidence in courts and the use of wholesalers, though this effect is

97. Whether the manufacturer is a member of a trade association might also be taken as an endogenous variable, dependent on the ability to use courts. Given that a trade association providing customer/supplier services exists in the manufacturer's industry, the manufacturer can choose whether to join or not. We find no significant relationship from belief in courts to membership in a trade association in the data (β= 0.019, t= 0.60, result not shown on table). It is also possible that belief in the effectiveness of courts is itself affected by membership in trade associations, or the use of business or social networks. We are unable to identify appropriate instruments in the survey to address this possibility. But the regressions do include controls for variables that affect the ability to use courts, including the size and age of the firm, the age and education of the manager, and the industry and country in which the firm is located.

not statistically significant. These results suggest that firms use social networks and perhaps wholesalers as substitutes for courts, but use business networks in conjunction with courts.

The amount of information a manufacturer possesses about his customers depends on how much effort the manufacturer expends on information gathering and on the difficulty of gathering that information. Institutions like trade associations make information gathering less costly, leading to traders who are better informed about their trading partners' past behavior. We find that both trade associations and networks result in manufacturers' being better informed. Members of trade associations are more likely to say that they would learn about their customers' disputes with other manufacturers, although not that the customers' other suppliers would learn about disputes. Manufacturers are also more likely to be better informed when the customers came from business or social networks. Manufacturers who believe that courts are effective, however, are less likely to say that they would know if their customers had disputes with other trading partners.

Together, these results present a coherent picture. Trade associations and networks lower the cost of information gathering, resulting in better-informed manufacturers. Effective courts, on the other hand, lower the benefit of information gathering, resulting in less well-informed manufacturers. Social networks and reputation appear therefore to serve as substitutes for functioning legal systems, while business networks function better when courts are effective.

Whether the customers are located in the manufacturer's same city, in a different city in the same country, or in another country might affect contracting. Geographic distance adds to the complexity of relationships, making shipping, payment, quality inspection, and other issues more difficult. The last regression in Table 3 explores the use of public and private ordering to support trade over long distance. Both business and social networks are strongly and significantly associated with trading locally, suggesting that geographic proximity makes reputation easier to communicate.

We find no evidence that either courts or trade associations support long-distance trade. Those who believe courts are effective are more likely to trade locally, and those who are members of trade associations are more likely to sell to distant buyers, but neither effect is significant. Long-distance trade is instead supported by wholesalers. Customers located in distant cities are much more likely to be wholesalers than are local customers.[98] Our data likely underestimate the

---

98. The regressions use data for only two of the manufacturer's customers. Other data from the survey support the role of wholesalers in long-distance trade as well. We find a very strong positive correlation between the percentage of the manufacturer's overall sales that are made to wholesalers and the percentage of overall sales that are made outside the manufacturer's city (= 0.21, p < 0.0001).

importance of wholesalers in supporting trade over distance, since wholesale customers located in the manufacturer's city likely sell some part of their purchases in distant cities. These sales would not show up as sales in distant cities in our data. Hence, while we find no correlation between courts and trade associations, on the one hand, and selling over long distances on the other, we do find evidence of a strong role of wholesalers in supporting trade over long distances. This is the case even though wholesalers have not yet become a significant force in the five surveyed countries. Overall only 12% of manufacturers' sales are made through wholesalers.

Finally, we consider what the data illustrate about when firms take their customers to court. The survey asked firms if a customer had ever failed to pay them or if a supplier had ever refused to accept the return of defective merchandise. The majority of firms (80%) reported having had at least one such dispute with a trading partner, most of which (86%) involved a dispute with a customer. We focus here on the manufacturer-customer disputes.[99] Courts were used in the resolution of 37% of these disputes.[100] In 86% of the cases where the court was used, the relationship with the customer ended; the relationship ended only 53% of the time when the court was not used. This difference may reflect the severity of the dispute. Manufacturers reported that the debt owed by the customer was collected in full in 28% of the cases in which the court was involved and in 40% of the cases when the court was not used. On the other hand, the debt was written off completely 26% of the time when courts were used and only 12% of the time when courts were not used. This suggests either that courts are so ineffective as to be detrimental to recovery, or that the court was more likely to be used for more difficult disputes.

Table 4 shows the results of probit regressions with actual use of the courts as the dependent variable. Here, we are most interested in knowing whether membership in a trade association, reliance on business and social networks, use of wholesalers, and belief in the reputation mechanism are correlated with the decision to use courts. The results indicate that firms that are members of trade associations use courts more often, but the effect is not statistically significant. We do find evidence (consistent with the Table 3 results) that courts and reputation substitute for one another. Court use is less likely among firms who say that other suppliers of the customer would hear about disputes. (It is not clear in which direction the causation runs here.)

---

99. The survey instrument used in Russia and the Ukraine does not allow us to determine whether the reported dispute was with a customer or a supplier. We therefore exclude the data from these two countries from the sample used in the regressions reported in Table 4.

100. The survey did not ask for what purpose courts were used. Thus, we do not know if courts helped resolve disputes, or simply certified losses.

Neither networks nor wholesalers have significant associations with court use.[101]

The probit regressions in Table 4 include several other control variables. Not surprisingly, we find that court use is more likely among firms expressing a belief that courts are effective. The regressions also control for how long the two firms had traded before the dispute arose, where the trading partner is located (in the same city as the manufacturer or not), and whether the trading partner is a private firm or a state-owned enterprise, as well as a set of manager and firm controls described in the notes to Table 4. Among these additional variables (which are not shown in the table), only the size of the interviewed firm and the duration of the relationship before the dispute occurred are significant. Larger firms are more likely to have used courts. Disputes are also more likely to end in court when the two trading partners had dealt with each other for a longer period of time before the dispute occurred, perhaps reflecting an increase in the complexity of trading relationships over time. The first regression controls for whether or not the two firms are still trading partners; the second regression removes this control.

---

101. The lack of a significant association between networks and the use of courts may reflect the indirectness of our measure. We do not know how the customer involved in the dispute was identified, or whether this customer is a wholesaler. We know only whether the surveyed manufacturer used social and business networks to identify his oldest and newest customer, and the percentage of his sales that is made to wholesalers. Thus, our measures provide a noisy indication of the interaction between use of courts on the one hand and networks and wholesalers on the other.

TABLE 4: PROBIT FOR USE OF COURT

Did manufacturer use courts in
most recent dispute with customer?

Member of trade association	0.063	0.048
	(1.11)	(0.88)
Reliance on business networks	0.002	0.016
	(0.05)	(0.47)
Reliance on social networks	-0.055	-0.065
	(1.06)	(1.30)
Percent of sales through whole-salers	-0.0003	-0.0001
	(0.33)	(0.10)
Manufacturer knows if customer has a dispute with another trading partner	0.023	0.021
	(0.60)	(0.57)
Customer's other suppliers learn of disputes	-0.081	-0.064
	(2.04)	(1.70)
Courts are effective	0.161	0.167
	(2.69)	(2.84)
Relationship ended	0.421	
	(7.86)	
Number of observations	499	499
pseudo R-square	0.243	0.136

Notes: Data for Poland, Slovakia and Romania only. Regressions also include 3 manager and 3 firm characteristics variables (see the note to Table 3 for a description), and variables measuring the duration of the relationship before the dispute occurred, a dummy indicating the trading partner is located in the same city, or is an SOE, and 23 country/industry dummies. Reliance on social (business) networks is measured from 0 to 4 — the number of the 4 trading partners identified in the survey. The survey identifies the oldest and newest customer and the oldest and newest supplier. The three reputation measures are based on responses to questions related to the oldest and newest customer.

* * *

In sum, we find evidence from our survey of small-firm managers in Poland, Slovakia, Romania, the Ukraine, and Russia that social networks and reputation act as substitutes for effective courts. Manufacturers who reportedly find courts ineffective are more likely to use social networks to locate trading partners, and more likely to remain informed about the behavior of their trading partners. Trade associations and business networks are also associated with a better flow of information about the behavior of trading partners. But rather than acting as substitutes for courts, business networks are more often used in concert with the legal system.

V.   THE DOWNSIDE OF PRIVATE ORDER

Private-order mechanisms have costs as well as benefits. Their disadvantages range from economic inefficiencies of exclusion and collusion to social costs of racial discrimination and criminal violence.

We have seen that private order can support exchanges when market players cannot rely on the courts. Private order therefore promotes economic efficiency by giving businesspeople the confidence to transact. But it also creates economic inefficiencies in two ways. First, spontaneous private order necessitates exclusion. The corollary of ongoing relationships is a reluctance to deal with firms outside the relationship, and exclusion clearly can result in inefficiencies. Second, organized private order, changing the relative bargaining powers of buyers and sellers, can create the inefficiencies of monopolistic pricing.

Consider first the exclusion costs of spontaneous private order. Closed networks have an obvious drawback. Dealing only with a limited group limits private-sector growth. Entrepreneurial talent is wasted, as potentially productive entrepreneurs are prevented from setting up firms. Even if they can get started, efficient firms may be unable to grow, since potential new customers would not look beyond their current suppliers.

The managers we interviewed in Vietnam and Eastern Europe expressed a hesitancy to deal with trading partners with whom they had never dealt. Regarding both their longest-term supplier and their newest supplier, manufacturers were asked: "If another firm you have never purchased from offered to supply this input for a price 10% less than your current supplier, would you purchase from the new firm?" Three possible answers were offered: buy entirely from the new supplier, reject the new supplier, and buy from the new supplier but continue buying from the existing supplier as well. In Eastern Europe (Vietnam), only 38% (29%) of our respondents gave the response that simple economics would suggest, saying they would accept the bargain; 45% (53%) said they would buy from the new supplier while continuing to buy at the higher price from their accustomed supplier; and 17% (19%) said they would reject the lower-priced offer outright.

In evaluating these responses, the success of the relationship must be weighed against the failure of the market. In a (hypothetical) market with perfect information and complete contracting, the buyer would have no reason to be suspicious of a low-priced offer, and would always accept it. If there is uncertainty about the reliability of the new supplier, however, it could be rational to reject the apparently better deal. This situation could arise in any economy, but is especially likely when the law is dysfunctional. Firms' unwillingness to take the risk of working with a new supplier, even for a much lower price, however, sometimes means foregoing a genuinely better deal. The fact that only 29% of our respondents said they would switch to buying from a new supplier offering a 10% lower price implies that considerable inefficiencies exist in this market.

How do courts and informal contract enforcement affect a firm's willingness to switch suppliers? Controlling for the complexity of the good produced, regressions using the data discussed in Part IV show that those who find courts effective are 6% less likely to reject the deal outright, and those who are members of trade associations are 9% less likely to reject the deal outright. Business networks have no significant effect on the propensity to switch. But where the initial contact came through social networks, we find some evidence that manufacturers are more likely to reject the new deal completely. Rejecting the deal is also more likely when the manufacturer's "other suppliers would learn about a dispute with this supplier."[102] We conclude that social networks and reputation have a dampening effect on market forces.

How does public order or organized private order affect the exclusionary costs of spontaneous private order? We showed in the regressions reported in Table 3 that market players will more likely use social networks and reputation when they cannot rely on the courts. These mechanisms, however, exact the highest cost in terms of excluding potentially efficient new entrants. Trade associations have favorable effects, and informal business networks negligible effects, on exclusion. But the evidence in Tables 3 and 4 indicates that firms use business networks and, to a lesser extent, trade associations in conjunction with courts. Thus, while firms may find substitutes for dysfunctional legal systems, public policy should not equally encourage all of these substitutes.

The exclusion costs of spontaneous private order arise in bilateral relationships with lock-in or in closed networks, such as ethnic or social groups, where entry and exit are inherently difficult or impossible. Exclusion costs do not exist in open networks that allow entry and exit, such as networks of firms in a similar line of business. But in open networks, private order must be organized. Organized private order can give rise to another kind of economic inefficiency by pushing the bargaining power of sellers and buyers out of balance.

Exclusion obtained through continued dealings with the same trading partners and reliance on social connections sometimes results

---

102. McMillan & Woodruff, *Interfirm Relationships, supra* note 34, at 1308; Johnson et al., Courts and Contracts, *supra* note 87, at Table 6.

in more than missed business opportunities; it can result in discrimination against certain groups in society.[103] In Kenya and Zimbabwe, firms' reliance on the existing networks, while arguably done simply to facilitate contracting and not to express any preference for discrimination, nevertheless creates ethnic and gender bias.[104] In the white-dominated New York construction industry, African-American contractors attempting to break in are reportedly hindered by the existing social ties.[105] One entrepreneur complained that he could not win contracts because he was "not in the social circles where those kinds of deals are made"; he could not "play golf or go on boats with people."[106]

In addition, the ability to organize contract enforcement sometimes becomes the ability to collude. "Merchants of the same trade seldom meet together, even for merriment or diversion, but the conversation ends in a conspiracy against the public, or in some contrivance to raise prices," according to Adam Smith's famous dictum.[107] Private-order organizations that share information about customers and coordinate firms' actions will find it relatively easy to fix prices. In Japan, for example, firms regularly use trade associations to organize price-fixing conspiracies, to the cost of their customers.[108]

The extent of price-fixing power depends on the nature of the private-order organization. Some private-order organizations are neutral intermediaries, favoring neither buyers nor sellers. The medieval law merchants,[109] the Taiwanese trading companies,[110] and the New York diamond-traders association[111] provide examples of this. These include both buyers and sellers as members or as clients. Some of these are constrained, moreover, by facing competition from other organizations performing similar functions; the Taiwanese trading companies provide an example of this. Other private-order organizations, however, are one-sided, favoring (usually) sellers over buyers. The medie-

---

103. *See* Jean Tirole, *A Theory of Collective Reputations (with Applications to the Persistence of Corruption and to Firm Quality)*, 63 REV. ECON. STUD. 1 (1996).

104. *See* Fafchamps, *supra* note 44, at 205.

105. *See* Alejandro Portes & Patrica Lanolt, *The Downside of Social Capital*, AM. PROSPECT, May-June 1996, at 18.

106. *Id.* at 20.

107. ADAM SMITH, 1 AN ENQUIRY INTO THE NATURE AND CAUSES OF THE WEALTH OF NATIONS 144 (1976).

108. *See* Schaede, *supra* note 59, at ch. 3 & ch. 5; John McMillan, *Dango: Japan's Price-Fixing Conspiracies*, 3 ECON. & POL. 201 (1991).

109. *See* Milgrom et al., *supra* note 17.

110. *See* Hsing, *supra* note 62.

111. *See* Bernstein, *supra* note 81.

val guilds,[112] the Japanese bank clearinghouse, the Fur Dressers' and Fur Dyers' Association, and other US trade associations discussed in Section III.B above, and the Mexican shoe-industry association provide examples of this.

In one sense, a one-sided association has an incentive to promote contracting efficiency because it furthers the interest of even a one-sided association for its members to be able to credibly make promises. Firms can generally structure contracts so that either side receives most of the gain from defecting. In Mexican footwear, for example, retailers could pay at the time orders are placed. This would put the burden of cooperation on the manufacturer rather than the retailer. Since the manufacturers are organized, and a retailer's reputation spreads more quickly, having the retailer move last (that is, pay after delivery) makes cooperation easier to sustain.

That industry associations may go beyond contract enforcement to coalitional bargaining helps answer a puzzle: Why might wholesalers replace trade associations in ensuring cooperation? At first glance, wholesalers are at a disadvantage. They have no direct sanctions. Moreover, because they represent only a portion of the buyers and sellers, they are less effective in transmitting information than an association comprised solely of one side of the transaction. But competition among wholesalers gives them an incentive to be fair and honest. Those with reputations for fairly arbitrating disputes between buyers and sellers will see their business grow and their profits increase. Competition gives the middlemen stronger incentives than a monopolistic trade association to monitor the suppliers and clients they deal with (their "members") and to be honest in arbitrating disputes between suppliers and clients.

The downside of private order goes farther than discrimination or mere economic inefficiencies. A corollary of private order in some cases is socially destructive activities. Private-order organizations usually limit their sanctioning techniques to boycotting offenders, but sometimes effective contract enforcement needs stronger sanctions. In situations involving a large initial investment with a long-delayed return, for example, the shadow of the future may not be strong enough to deter reneging. In the absence of a functioning legal system, then, private-order organizations might be tempted to expand their enforcement techniques. Some private-order organizations use threats of physical violence. The Sicilian and Russian Mafias, for example, offer contract-supporting services, but a lot else besides.[113] Or-

---

112. *See* Avner Greif et al., *Coordination, Commitment, and Enforcement: The Case of the Merchant Guild*, 102 J. POL. ECON. 745 (1994).

113. *See generally* DIEGO GAMBETTA, THE SICILIAN MAFIA (1993); Avner Greif & Eugene Kandel, *Contract Enforcement Institutions: Historical Perspective and Current Status in Russia, in* ECONOMIC TRANSITION IN EASTERN EUROPE AND RUSSIA: REALITIES OF

2458   *Michigan Law Review*   [Vol. 98:2421]

ganized crime, according to Curtis Milhaupt and Mark West, "is the dark side of private ordering — an entrepreneurial response to inefficiencies in the property rights and enforcement framework supplied by the state."[114] We thus need public order to limit these abuses of private order.

VI. SUMMARY

People's concern for their own reputation can support contracting between a pair of trading partners when one or both are locked in, and among multiple trading partners in close-knit communities where information flows freely. In countries making a transition from planned to market economies, such spontaneous private ordering substitutes for the lack of functioning legal systems. The underdevelopment of the private sector makes cooperation easier to sustain by locking trading partners together. The market frictions fall as the private sector develops, creating the need for more formal contract enforcement.

In communities where people can hide behind their anonymity, private order, if it is to operate at all, must be organized. Private-order organizations in notably diverse settings, from medieval Europe to present-day Mexico, work in similar ways. An organization such as a market intermediary or a trade association disseminates information about contractual breaches and coordinates the community's response to breaches. The usual sanction is to boycott the offender.

The data from our survey of firms in five transition economies in Eastern Europe and the former Soviet Union show that social networks and informal gossip substitute for the formal legal system, while business networks and trade associations work in conjunction with the formal legal system.

While private order fosters economic efficiency by making gains from trade realizable, it sometimes also harms efficiency by excluding new entrants from trading or by achieving price collusion. Private order can cause racial or gender discrimination. Some private-order organizations' enforcement techniques overflow into criminal violence. Private order can usefully supplement public law, but cannot replace it.

REFORM (Edward P. Lazear ed., 1995); Ekaterina Zhuravskaya & Timothy Frye, *The Rise of the Racket in Russia* (1998) (unpublished manuscript) (on file with authors).

114. Curtis J. Milhaupt & Mark D. West, *The Dark Side of Private Ordering: An Institutional and Empirical Analysis of Organized Crime*, 67 U. CHI. L. REV. 41, 43 (2000).

[21]

ECONOMICS AND POLITICS   0954-1985

Volume 2   March 1990   No. 1

THE ROLE OF INSTITUTIONS IN THE REVIVAL OF TRADE: THE LAW MERCHANT, PRIVATE JUDGES, AND THE CHAMPAGNE FAIRS

PAUL R. MILGROM, DOUGLASS C. NORTH AND
BARRY R. WEINGAST*

A good reputation can be an effective bond for honest behavior in a community of traders if members of the community know how others have behaved in the past — even if any particular pair of traders meets only infrequently. In a large community, it would be impossibly costly for traders to be perfectly informed about each other's behavior, but there exist institutions that can restore the effectiveness of a reputation system using much less extensive information. The system of judges used to enforce commercial law before the rise of the state was such an institution, and it successfully encouraged merchants (1) to behave honestly, (2) to impose sanctions on violators, (3) to become adequately informed about how others had behaved, (4) to provide evidence against violators of the code, and (5) to pay any judgments assessed against them, even though each of these behaviors might be personally costly.

How can people promote the trust necessary for efficient exchange when individuals have short run temptations to cheat? The same question arises whether the traders are legislators swapping votes, medieval merchants exchanging goods, or modern businesspeople trading promises about future deliveries. In each of these situations, one of the important ways in which individuals ensure one another's honest behavior is by establishing a continuing relationship. In the language of economics, if the relationship itself is a valuable asset that a party could lose by dishonest behavior, then the relationship serves as a *bond*: a trader would be unwilling to surrender this bond unless the gain from dishonest behavior was large.

Variants on this basic idea are found throughout the literatures of economics (Klein and Leffler, 1981; Shapiro, 1983; Shapiro and Stiglitz, 1984), politics (Axelrod, 1984, 1986; Calvert, 1986) and game theory (Abreu, 1988; Aumann, 1985; and Fudenberg and Maskin, 1986). Even in a community in which any particular pair of people meet rarely, it is still possible (as we show) for an individual's reputation in the group as a whole to serve as a bond for his good and honest behavior toward each individual member. This illustrates the important fact that a reputation system may sometimes work only when it encompasses

*Department of Economics, Stanford University; Department of Economics, Washington University; Hoover Institution, Stanford University. The authors thank Robert Aumann, Gary Becker, Peter DeMarzo, Avner Greif, Michihiro Kandori, Bart Lipson, Uwe Schimack and the participants at numerous workshops for helpful conversations. Mr Milgrom and Mr Weingast thank the National Science Foundation for partial support.

2   MILGROM, NORTH AND WEINGAST

sufficiently many traders and trades, that is, there are economies of scale and
scope in reputation systems.

These conclusions about the potential effectiveness of a reputation system,
however, leave us with a puzzle: If informal arrangements based on reputations
can effectively bond good behavior, then what is the role of formal institutions
in helping to support honest exchange? The legal apparatus for enforcing business
contracts in many ages and many parts of the world, the suppliers' organizations
that negotiate contracting patterns among modern Japanese firms, the complex
institutional structure that facilitates agreements among US Congressmen,[1] the
notaries that recorded agreements in the Italian city-states in the middle ages,
and the organization of international trade via the Champagne fairs are all examples
of institutionalized arrangements to support trade and contracting. All involve
the creation of specialized roles which would not be necessary if reputations alone
could be an adequate bond for trade. But, why can't a simple system of reputations
motivate honest trade in these various settings? And, what role do formal
institutions play when simple reputational mechanisms fail?

We embed our study of these questions in the time of the revival of trade in
Europe during the early middle ages. At that time, without the benefit of state
enforcement of contracts or an established body of commercial law, merchants
evolved their own private code of laws (the *Law Merchant*) with disputes
adjudicated by a judge who might be a local official or a private merchant. While
hearings were held to resolve disputes under the code, the judges had only limited
powers to enforce judgments against merchants from distant places. For example,
if a dispute arose after the conclusion of the Champagne Fair about the quality
of the goods delivered or if agreements made at the Fair for future delivery or
for acceptance of future delivery were not honored, no physical sanction or seizure
of goods could then be applied.

The evolution and survival for a considerable period of a system of private
adjudication raises both particular versions of our general questions and new
questions about the details of the mechanism. What was the purpose of the private
adjudication system? Was it a substitute for the reputation mechanism that had
worked effectively in earlier periods (Greif, 1989)? Also, if there was no state
to enforce judgments, how did they have any effect? How could a system of
adjudication function without substantial police powers?

The practice and evolution of the Law Merchant in medieval Europe was so
rich and varied that no single model can hope to capture all the relevant variations
and details. Our simple model is intended to represent certain universal incentive
problems that any successful system would have to solve. It abstracts from many
of the interesting variations that are found across time and space as well as from
other general problems, such as the spatial diversion of traders and trading centers
and the interactions among competing trading systems.

---

[1] Either by facilitating coordination (Banks and Calvert, 1989) or by preventing reneging on
agreements (Weingast and Marshall, 1988).

INSTITUTIONS IN THE REVIVAL OF TRADE 3

We begin in section 1 with a discussion of the medieval Law Merchant and related institutions. We set the theoretical context for our analysis in section 2. It is well known, as we have explained above, that in long-term, frequent bilateral exchange, the value of the relationship itself may serve as an adequate bond to ensure honest behavior and promote trust between the parties. We argue in section 2 that even if no pair of traders come together frequently, if each individual trades frequently enough within the community of traders, then transferable reputations for honesty can serve as an adequate bond for honest behavior *if members of the trading community can be kept informed about each other's past behavior*. Well informed traders could boycott those who have violated community norms of honesty, if only they knew who the violators were. It is the costliness of generating and communicating information — rather than the infrequency of trade in any particular bilateral relationship — that, we argue, is the problem that the system of private enforcement was designed to overcome.

In section 3, we introduce our basic model of a system of private enforcement and develop our core thesis that the role of the judges in the system, far from being substitutes for the reputation mechanism, is to make the reputation system more effective as a means of promoting honest trade. The formal system is more complex than the simple informal system of reputations that preceded it, but that was a natural outcome of the growing extent of trade. In a large community, we argue, it would be too costly to keep everyone informed about what transpires in all trading relationships, as a simple reputation system might require. So the system of private judges is designed to promote private resolution of disputes and otherwise to transmit *just enough* information to the right people in the right circumstances to enable the reputation mechanism to function effectively for enforcement. In order to succeed, such a system must solve a number of inter-connected incentive problems: Individual members of the community must be induced to behave honestly, to boycott those who have behaved dishonestly, to keep informed about who has been dishonest, to provide evidence against those who have cheated, and to honor the decisions of the judges. All of these problems can be resolved by the system if certain institutional constraints are satisfied, as we show in section 3. Briefly, the costs of making queries, providing evidence, adjudicating disputes, and making transfer payments must not be too high relative to the frequency and profitability of trade if the system is to function successfully.

Intuitively, the system of private judges accomplishes its objectives by *bundling* the services which are valuable to the individual trader with services that are valuable to the community, so that a trader pursuing his individual interest serves the community's interest as well. Unless a trader makes appropriate queries, he cannot use the system to resolve disputes. The requirement that the traders make queries provides an opportunity for the judge to collect payments for his services even if no actual disputes arise. As applied to the Champagne Fairs, the local lord or his agents could appoint honest judges, register transactions, and tax them.

In section 4, we make a brief digression to assess how *efficiently* the system of private judges accomplishes its task. We argue that no system can restore the

4   MILGROM, NORTH AND WEINGAST

effectiveness of the community reputation mechanism without incurring costs that are qualitatively similar to those incurred by the system of private judges, and moreover that the latter system seems to have been designed in a way that kept these transaction costs low.

Our analysis in section 3 gives the judge a passive role only. In section 5, we study the possibility that the judge may threaten to sully the reputations of honest traders unless they pay bribes. We show how the system can survive some such threats, though we do not attempt a comprehensive evaluation of all the kinds of bribes and extortion that might be tried in such a system.

Concluding remarks, relating our model to a broader institutional perspective, are given in section 6.

1. THE MEDIEVAL LAW MERCHANT

The history of long-distance trade in medieval and early modern Europe is the story of sequentially more complex organization that eventually led to the "Rise of the Western World." In order to capture the gains associated with geographic specialization, a system had to be established that lowered information costs and provided for the enforcement of agreements across space and time. Prior to the revival of trade in the early middle ages, few institutions underpinned commercial activity; there was no state to enforce contracts, let alone to protect merchants from pirates and brigands. In contrast, modern Western economies possess highly specialized systems of enforcing contracts and protecting merchants, resulting in widespread geographic specialization and impersonal exchange. The story of this evolution has been told elsewhere (e.g., Lopez, 1976; North and Thomas, 1973). Our purpose in this section is to suggest the outlines of an important step in this evolution, namely the early development of commercial law prior to the rise of large-scale third-party enforcement of legal codes by the nation-state.

A large number of problems had to be resolved in order to support the expansion of trade. First, as trading communities grew larger, it became harder within each community for merchants to monitor one another's behavior. New institutions were required to mitigate the types of cheating afforded by the new situation. Second, as trade grew among different regions, institutions were needed to prevent reneging by merchants who might cheat in one location, never to be seen again.

In response to these problems, a host of institutions arose and evolved over time. Towns with their own governments became homes for merchants who developed their own law separate from the traditional feudal order (Pirenne, 1925; Rorig, 1967). Merchant gilds arose to provide protection to foreign merchants away from their homes, but also protection to local merchants against fly-by-night foreign merchants who might never be seen again (DeRoover, 1963; Thrupp, 1948). Key to understanding the ability of merchants from widely varying regions to enforce contracts was the evolution of the *Lex Mercatoria* or Law Merchant — the legal codes governing commercial transactions and administered by private judges drawn from the commercial ranks. While practice varied across time and space, by the end of the 11th century, the Law Merchant came to govern most commercial transactions in Europe, providing a uniform set of standards across large numbers of locations (Benson, 1989). It thereby provided a means for reducing the uncertainty associated with variations in local practices and limited the ability of localities to discriminate against alien merchants (Berman, 1983; Trakman, 1983). Thus, "commercial law can be conceived of as coordinating the self-interested actions of merchants, but perhaps an equally valuable insight is gained by *viewing it as coordinating the actions of people with limited knowledge and trust*" (Benson, 1989, p. 648, emphasis added).

While the governments of towns supported the development of markets and were intimately involved in developing merchant law (Pirenne, 1925; Rorig, 1967), they often could not provide merchants protection outside their immediate area.[2] Nor could they enforce judgments against foreign merchants who had left town prior to a case being heard. Thus, merchant law developed prior to the rise of a geographically extensive nation-state. But this raises a key problem in the theory of enforcement, for what made these judgments credible if they were not backed up by the state? Ostracism played an important role here, for merchants that failed to abide by the decisions of the judges would not be merchants for long (Benson, 1989; DeRoover, 1963; Trakman, 1983).

The Law Merchant and related legal codes evolved considerably over time. In addition to providing a court of law especially suited for merchants, it fostered significant legal developments that reduced the transaction costs of exchange (North, 1989, ch. 13). As agency relationships became common — whether between partners in different locations or between a sedentary merchant who financed a traveling one — a new set of rules governing these agreements was required. The same also held for the new practices of credit agreements and insurance. Here, we note the development of law covering agency relations (DeRoover, 1963; Greif, 1989), bills of exchange, and insurance (North, 1989, ch. 13).

The benefits of all these developments, however, could only be enjoyed as long as merchants obeyed the Law Merchant. Moreover, since disputes arise even among honest merchants, there needed to be a system for hearing and settling these disputes. To see how these feats of coordination might have been accomplished, we develop a game theoretic model of the judicial enforcement system — a model inspired by the Law Merchant and by the Champagne Fairs. The latter played a central role in trade in the 12th and 13th centuries (DeRoover, 1963; North and Thomas, 1973; Verlinden, 1963), and included a legal system in which merchants could bring grievances against their trading partners. However, it is not clear why such a system would be effective. What prevents a merchant from cheating by supplying lower quality goods than promised, and then leaving the

---

[2]Of course, considerable variation existed across locations, especially between northern and southern Europe. In the latter area, city-states arose, providing law and protection beyond the immediate area of the city. Further, over time, as the nature of governments changed, so too did their involvement in the legal and enforcement process.

Fairs before being detected? In these circumstances the cheated merchant might be able to get a judgment against his supplier, but what good would it do if the supplier never returned to the Fairs? Perhaps ostracism by the other merchants might be an effective way to enforce the payment of judgments. However, if that is so, why was a legal system needed at all?

Another part of the inspiration for our formal model is the system of notaries that was widely used to register the existence of certain types of contracts and obligations. Typically, notaries were used for long-term contracts such as those for apprenticeships, sales of land, and partnerships (Lopez and Raymond, 1955). The extensive use of notaries in certain areas to register agreements suggests that reputation via word of mouth alone was insufficient to support honest behavior and that a third party without any binding authority to enforce obligations was nonetheless quite valuable for promoting honest exchange.

2. COMMUNITY ENFORCEMENT WITHOUT INSTITUTIONS

With the exception of barter transactions, in which physical commodities are exchanged on the spot, virtually all economic transactions leave open the possibility of cheating. In the Champagne Fairs, where merchants brought samples of their goods to trade, the quantities they brought were not always sufficient to supply all the potential demand. Then, the merchants sometimes exchanged promises — to deliver goods of like quality at a particular time and place, or to make payment in a certain form. Promises, however, can be broken.

To represent the idea that cheating may be profitable in a simple exchange, we use the Prisoners' Dilemma (PD) game as our model of a single exchange transaction. Although this PD model is too simple to portray the richness of even simple contracts, it has the advantage that it is very well known and its characteristics in the absence of institutions have been thoroughly studied, so that the incremental contribution made by the Law Merchant system will be quite clear. Moreover, the PD game represents in an uncluttered way the basic facts that traders have opportunities and temptations to cheat and that there are gains possible if the traders can suppress these temptations and find a way to cooperate.

The Prisoners' Dilemma game that we employ is shown below, where $\alpha > 1$ and $\alpha - \beta < 2$.

	Honest	Cheat
Honest	1, 1	$-\beta, \alpha$
Cheat	$\alpha, -\beta$	0, 0

Each player can choose to play one of two strategies: Honest or Cheat. As is well known, Honest behavior maximizes the total profits of the two parties. However, a trader profits by cheating an honest partner ($\alpha > 1$) even though cheating imposes a still larger loss on his honest partner $(1 - (-\beta) > \alpha - 1)$.

It is clear that if this game is played only once, it is in each player's separate interest to play Cheat, since that play maximizes the player's individual utility regardless of the play chosen by the competitor. Consequently, the only *Nash equilibrium* of the game is for both to play Cheat. Then both are worse off than if they could somehow agree to play Honest.

Now suppose that the players trade repeatedly. Let a_{it} represent the action taken by player i in period t; let $\pi_i(a_{1t}, a_{2t})$ represent the resulting payoff earned by player i in period t; and let δ be the discount factor applied to compute the present value of a stream of payoffs. If trade is frequent, then δ is close to one; if trade occurs only once (or is quite infrequent), then δ is (close to) zero. A player's time weighted average payoff over the whole sequence of trades is given by:

$$\bar{\pi}_i = (1 - \delta) \sum_{t=0}^{\infty} \delta^t \pi_i(a_{1t}, a_{2t}) \tag{1}$$

In this repeated trading relationship, if the players can condition their actions in each period on what has transpired in the past, then they have an instrument to reward past honest behavior and to punish cheating. For the PD game, Axelrod (1984) has shown that for δ close enough to 1 there is a Nash equilibrium in which each player adopts the Tit-for-Tat (TFT) strategy — according to which the player chooses honest play at $t = 0$ and for any later t plays whatever his partner played in the immediately preceding period (that is, at $t - 1$).

The central idea that frequent trading with the same partner, or "clientization," makes it possible to find an equilibrium with efficient trading applies even for more refined solution concepts, such as subgame perfect equilibrium. It has been shown to hold for virtually all repeated games, regardless of the number of players, the number of strategies available to each, or the magnitudes of the payoffs (Fudenberg and Maskin, 1986). What is less fully appreciated is that the same conclusion holds in a community of traders in which players change partners often and cheaters may never again have to face the cheated partner — provided that information about the behavior of the traders is widely shared in the community.

To see this, suppose that there are N traders and that there is some rule M that matches them at each stage. Let h_t be the history of trade through date t and let $M(h_t, i)$ be the identity of the trader who is matched with trader i at date $t + 1$ at history h_t. Consider the Adjusted Tit-for-Tat (ATFT) strategy according to which player i plays Honest at date 0 and then plays Cheat at date $t + 1$ if two conditions hold: (1) i made the play at date t that was specified by his equilibrium strategy and (2) $M(h_t, i)$ did not make the play at date t that was specified by his equilibrium strategy. If either condition fails, then the ATFT strategy calls for i to play Honest. The ATFT strategy formalizes the idea that a trader who cheats will be punished by the next merchant he meets if that merchant is honest, even if that merchant is not the one who was cheated.

One might wonder what reason the merchant who was not cheated has to carry

8   MILGROM, NORTH AND WEINGAST

out the punishment. Within the PD model, the answer is twofold: First, punishing the cheater is directly profitable, because the punishment is delivered by playing Cheat. Second — and this is the reason that applies even in more general models — a merchant who fails to deliver a punishment, say by participating in a boycott, when he is supposed to do so is himself subject to punishment by the community of merchants. The community, in its turn, will carry out the punishment, for the very same reasons. Theorem 1 below verifies that this system is in fact sometimes an equilibrium, that is, no merchant could gain at any time by deviating from its rules provided he expects other merchants to adhere to the rules in all future play.

Theorem 1. For δ near enough to one — specifically if

$$\delta \geq \text{Max}[\beta/(1 + \beta), (\alpha - 1)/(1 + \beta)] \tag{2}$$

— the Adjusted Tit-for-Tat strategies are a subgame perfect equilibrium in the community trading game for *any* matching rule M.

Proof. By the Optimality Principle of dynamic programming, it suffices to show that there is no point at which player i can make a one-time play different from the equilibrium play that raises his total payoff. By inspection of the strategies, it is clear that the player may face one of four decision situations according to whether condition (1) only is satisfied, condition (2) only is satisfied, or both or neither of (1) and (2) are satisfied. If just condition (1) or condition (2) (not both) is satisfied, then a current period deviation by player i is unprofitable if:

$$(1 - \delta)[\alpha - \delta\beta] + \delta^2 \cdot 1 \leq (1 - \delta) \cdot 1 + \delta \cdot 1 \tag{3}$$

which holds if and only if $\delta \geq (\alpha - 1)/(1 + \beta)$. If (1) and (2) are both satisfied, deviation is unprofitable if:

$$(1 - \delta)[0 - \delta\beta] + \delta^2 \cdot 1 \leq (1 - \delta) \cdot \alpha + \delta \cdot 1 \tag{4}$$

and this is satisfied for all $\delta \geq 0$. If neither (1) nor (2) is satisfied, then deviation is unprofitable if:

$$(1 - \delta)[0 - \delta\beta] + \delta^2 \cdot 1 \leq -(1 - \delta) \cdot \beta + \delta \cdot 1 \tag{5}$$

which holds if and only if $\delta \geq \beta/(1 + \beta)$.   ∎

Our formal analysis verifies that it is not necessary for any pair of traders to interact frequently — that is, for traders to establish client relationships — in order for the boycott mechanism to be effective. However, that simple conclusion relies on the condition that the members of the community are well enough informed to know whom to boycott. This condition is probably satisfied in some communities, but it is more problematical in others. For example, merchants engaged in long-distance trade could not be expected to know, of their own knowledge, whether another pair of merchants had honored their mutual obligations. Unless social and economic institutions developed to fill in the knowledge gap or unless other means of enforcement were established, honest behavior in

INSTITUTIONS IN THE REVIVAL OF TRADE 9

a community of self-interested traders could not be maintained. Our model in
the next section shows how a particular institution could have resolved this
problem.

3. THE LAW MERCHANT ENFORCEMENT SYSTEM

We now consider in more detail a model of trade in which outsiders cannot readily
observe what has transpired in a given bilateral trade. While "disputes" may arise
in which one party accuses the other of cheating, none of the other players have
a method of freely verifying the parties' claims. Even if the dispute itself can
be observed by others, they cannot costlessly determine whether cheating by one
has actually occurred or whether the other is opportunistically claiming that it did.

In our model, we suppose that choices in each bilateral exchange are known
only to the trading pair, so that each individual possesses direct information *solely
about his own past trading experiences.*[3] To capture the idea that traders know
little of their partners' past trading behavior, we use an extreme model of matching
due to Townsend (1981). In Townsend's matching model, there is an infinity of
traders indexed by ij where $i = 1$ or 2 and j is an integer which may be positive
or negative. At period t, trader $1j$ is matched with trader $2, j + t$.[4] In particular,
no two traders ever meet twice and no trader's behavior can directly or indirectly
influence the behavior of his future trading partners. In the absence of institutions,
players possess *no information* about their current partner's past behavior.

Under these conditions, the opportunities available to a player in any period
cannot depend in any way on his past behavior. Strategies such as TFT and ATFT
become ineffective. So, in our Prisoners' Dilemma game, it can never be in the
players' interest to be honest. We have established the following:

Theorem 2. In the incomplete information Prisoners' Dilemma with the
Townsend matching rule, the outcome at any Nash equilibrium is that each trader
plays Cheat at every opportunity.[5]

With limited information about the past behavior of trading partners and no
institution to compensate, there are no incentives for honest behavior. It is evident
that incentives could be restored by introducing an institution that provides full
information to each trader about how each other has behaved. Such an institution,
however, would be costly to operate. Moreover, efficient trade does not require
that every trader know the full history of the behavior of each other trader. For

---

[3]This is also the premise of the game-theoretic analysis of Kandori (1989).

[4]This matching rule is often called the "Townsend Turnpike," for Townsend suggested that one
way to think of it is as two infinitely long sets of traders moving in opposite directions.

[5]Kandori (1989) has shown that there exist other matching rules for which, despite the absence
of sufficient bilateral trade and each player's ignorance about what has happened in trades among
other players, there may nevertheless be a code of behavior that supports efficient exchange. However,
as Kandori argues, the resulting system is "brittle" and leads to a breakdown of honest trade when
there are even minor disturbances to the system. Both Kandori (1989) and Okuno and Postlewaite
(1989) consider other institutional solutions to this problem.

10   MILGROM, NORTH AND WEINGAST

example, in the ATFT strategy considered in the preceding section, a trader need only know his own history of behavior and whether his partner has defected in the immediately preceding period to determine his own current behavior. One part of the problem is to arrange that the traders are *adequately* well informed so that they can sanction a Cheater when that is required.

However, there is a second problem that the institutions must overcome: Traders may not find it in their individual interests to participate in punishing those who cheat. As one simple example, if trade is expected to be profitable, a trader will be reluctant to engage in a trade boycott. The institutions must be designed both to keep the traders adequately informed of their responsibilities and to motivate them to do their duties.

In the model we develop below, this second problem has multiple aspects. First, traders must be motivated to execute sanctions against Cheaters when that is a personally costly activity. Second, traders must be motivated to keep well enough informed to know when sanctions are required, even though information gathering activities may be personally costly and difficult to monitor. In effect, one who keeps informed about who should be punished for past transgressions is supplying a public good; he deters the traders from cheating against *others*. Moreover, in our model, no other trader except his current partner will ever know if a trader does not check his partner's past history, so the trader could avoid supplying the public good without facing any sanction from future traders. Third, traders who are cheated must be motivated to document the episode, even though providing documentation may be personally costly. After all, from the cheated trader's perspective, what's lost is lost, and there may be little point in "throwing good money after bad." But if players who are cheated are unwilling to invest in informing their neighbors, then, just as surely as if the neighbors are unwilling to invest in being informed, the Cheater will profit from his action and Honest trade will suffer. These are the problems that the trading institution in our model must solve.

The institution that we model as the resolution of these problems is based on the presence of a specialized actor — a "judge" or "law merchant" (LM) who serves both as a repository of information and as an adjudicator of disputes. The core version of our model is based on the following assumptions. After any exchange, each party can accuse the other of cheating and appeal to the LM. Any dispute appealed to the LM is perfectly and honestly adjudicated at cost C to the plaintiff. (We consider the case of a dishonest LM later.) The LM's pronouncements include the ability to award damages if the defendant is found to have cheated the plaintiff. However, payment of the damage award is *voluntary* in the sense that there is no state to enforce payment. Finally, we assume that any party can visit the LM prior to finalizing a contract. At that time, for a cost of Q, the party can *query* the LM for the records of previous judgments about any other player. Without querying the LM, players have *no* information about their current partners' trading history.

By structuring this sequence of events around the basic trade transaction, we create an "extended" stage game called the *LM system stage game* with the following sequence of play:

(a) Players may query the LM about their current partner at utility cost $Q > 0$. In response to a query, the LM reports to the traders whether a party has any "unpaid judgments." Whatever transpires at this stage becomes common knowledge among the LM and the two partners.

(b) The two traders play the (Prisoners' Dilemma) game and learn the outcome.

(c) Either may appeal to the LM at personal cost $C > 0$, but only if he has queried the LM.

(d) If either party makes an appeal, then the LM awards a judgment, J, to the plaintiff if he has been Honest and his trading partner has Cheated (we call this a *valid appeal*); otherwise, no award is made.

(e) If a judgment J is awarded, the defendant may pay it, at personal cost $f(J)$, or he may refuse to pay, at cost zero.

(f) Any unpaid judgments are recorded by the LM and become part of the LM's permanent record.

The players' utilities for the extended stage game are determined as the sum of the payments received less those made. For example, a player who queries, plays Honest, is Cheated, and appeals, receives $-Q - \beta + -CJ$ if the other party pays the judgment and $-Q - \beta - C$ if he does not.

The function $f: \mathcal{R}^+ \to \mathcal{R}^+$ represents the utility cost of paying a given judgment. We naturally assume that f is increasing and continuous. Thus, the greater the size of the judgment, the greater the cost to the defendant. We also assume that $f(x) \geq x$: The cost of paying a judgment is never less than the judgment itself. This excludes the possibility that the payment of judgments adds to the total utility of the players.

The desired behavior of the parties in various contingencies under the Law Merchant system is fully described by the *Law Merchant System Strategy* (LMSS) as follows.

At substage (a), a trader queries the Law Merchant if he has no unpaid judgments on record, but not otherwise.

At substage (b), if either player has failed to query the Law Merchant or if the query establishes that at least one player has an outstanding judgment, then both traders play Cheat (which we may interpret as a refusal by the honest trader to trade); otherwise, both play Honest.

At substage (c), if both parties queried at substage (a) and exactly one of the two players Cheated at substage (b), then the victim appeals to the LM; otherwise, no appeal is filed.

At substage (d), if a valid appeal was filed, the LM awards damages of J to the aggrieved party.

At substage (e), the defendant pays the judgment J if and only if he has no other outstanding judgments.

Theorem 3. The Law Merchant System Strategy is a symmetric sequential equilibrium strategy of the LM system game if and only if the following inequality holds.

$$(1 - Q)\delta/(1 - \delta) \geq f(J) \geq \max[(\alpha - 1), f(C)] \tag{6}$$

If this condition is satisfied, then the average payoff per period for each player (at the equilibrium) is $1 - Q$.

Remark. The condition in Theorem 3 can be satisfied only if $1 - Q$ is positive (because the right-hand-side is at least $\alpha - 1 > 0$).

Proof. To establish that the LMSS is a symmetric sequential equilibrium strategy, we again appeal to the Optimality Principle of Dynamic Programming. If we show that there is no point at which a single change in the trader's current action only (followed by later adherence to the LMSS) can raise the trader's expected payoff at that point, then there is no point at which some more complicated deviation can be profitable, either.

In evaluating his expected payoffs, the player must make certain conjectures about what other players have done in the past in order to forecast what they will do in the future. To verify the equilibrium, we may assume that the trader believes that all other traders have played according to the LMSS in all past plays except those where the trader has actually observed a deviation. We may also assume that the trader believes that all others will adhere to the LMSS in all future plays. To derive the conditions under which the LMSS is an equilibrium strategy, we work backward through a typical extended stage game.

First, we check when it "pays to pay judgments," that is, under what conditions a player will find it more profitable to pay any judgment rendered against him than to refuse to pay. (We ignore the sunk portion of the payoff which is unaffected by later behavior.) Paying the judgment J yields an additional payoff of $-f(J)$ in the current period. In future periods, the player will spend Q to query the LM and earn a trading payoff of 1, for a total of $1 - Q$. In terms of lifetime average payoff, paying the judgment leads to $-(1 - \delta)f(J) + \delta(1 - Q)$. If the trader refuses to pay the judgment, then his current period payoff is zero and, given the system, his payoff is also zero in every subsequent period. Therefore, it "pays to pay judgments" if and only if $-(1 - \delta)f(J) + \delta(1 - Q) \geq 0$, or equivalently,

$$f(J) \leq (1 - Q)\delta/(1 - \delta). \tag{7}$$

Second, does it pay the victim to appeal at substage (c), incurring personal cost C? Given the strategies, the trader expects the judgment to be paid. So he will appeal if and only if $J \geq C$. It is convenient to write this condition as:

$$f(J) \geq f(C). \tag{8}$$

If there are no unpaid judgments and the LM has been queried, does it pay the trader to play Honest? If he does, then his current period payoff will be $1 - Q$. If he Cheats and later adheres to the strategy (which entails paying the

INSTITUTIONS IN THE REVIVAL OF TRADE 13

judgment), then his payoff will be $-Q + \alpha - f(J)$. Equilibrium requires that the former is larger, that is:

$$f(J) \geq \alpha - 1. \tag{9}$$

Does it pay the trader otherwise to play Cheat? With the given strategy, his future opportunities do not depend on his play in this case, and Cheat always maximizes the payoffs for the current period, so the answer is that it does pay, regardless of parameter values.

Does it pay the players to query the LM if neither has an outstanding judgment? If a player does so, his current period payoff is expected to be $1 - Q$. If not, it will be zero. In both cases, his payoffs per period for subsequent periods are expected to be $1 - Q$. So, it pays if and only if

$$Q \leq 1. \tag{10}$$

However, condition (10) is redundant in view of conditions (7) and (9).

Does it pay a party with an outstanding judgment to query? No, because the party's expected payoff is $-Q$ if he queries and 0 if he does not.

Thus, regardless of the circumstances wrought by past play, there is no situation in which a one-time deviation from the Law Merchant System Strategy that is profitable for a trader provided that conditions (7)–(9) hold. These are the conditions summarized in formula (6). ■

Corollary. There is a judgment amount J which makes the LMSS a symmetric sequential equilibrium strategy (that is, satisfying formula (6)) if and only if

$$(1 - Q)\delta/(1 - \delta) \geq \max[(\alpha - 1), f(C)]. \tag{11}$$

Conditions (7)–(10) show the relationship among the various parameters for the LM system to support the efficient cooperation. Each corresponds to one of the problems we described in introducing the model. Condition (7) requires that Cheating and then paying a judgment not be profitable; put simply, the judgment must be large enough to deter Cheating. Condition (8) requires that judgments exceed the cost of an appeal, that is, the judgment must also be large enough to encourage the injured party to appeal. Otherwise, information about Cheating will never reach the LM and Cheating will go unpunished. The two previous conditions require that the judgment be large enough, but condition (9) requires that it not be so large that the Cheater would refuse to pay, for then the injured party would not expect to collect, and so would find it unprofitable to appeal. Notice that the feasibility of satisfying all these conditions simultaneously depends on the technology of wealth transfer summarized by f. If the traders live at great distances from one another and if their principal asset holdings are illiquid (such as land and fixed capital, or reputation and family connections), then wealth transfers may be quite costly ($f(J)/J$ may be large) and the fines required by the LM system then will not work.

Finally, condition (10) requires that it be worthwhile for the traders to query the LM. In our model, this condition is implied by the others, but that need not be true for extensions of the model. If traders do not query the LM, then they will have insufficient information to administer punishments, so once again Cheating will go unpunished. The LM institution encourages queries by making them a condition for appealing to the LM, and, as we have seen, querying deters Cheating. At equilibrium, traders who fail to query are constantly Cheated by their trading partners.

If condition (6) fails, then the LMSS is not an equilibrium strategy. However, the condition is satisfied for a wide range of plausible parameter values. Table 1 below gives some acceptable values for the parameters. In it, we assume that $f(x) = x/(1 - p)$ where p is the percentage of value that is lost when assets are transferred. The LMSS is an equilibrium strategy for some J with the given combinations of parameters and for any other combination with lower transaction costs (lower p, Q, and C), less temptation to cheat (lower α), and more frequent trade (higher δ). In the table, $J = C/(1 - p) = \alpha - 1$ is the judgment which is just sufficient to provide the incentives for not cheating and for complaining about being cheated.

For example, in the last line of Table 1, Cheating is seven times more profitable than playing Honest at each current round, the cost of querying the LM consumes one-third of the profits of Honest venturers, the cost of complaining is three times the profits of the venture, and half of any assets transferred in settlement of a judgment are lost. The judgment itself is six times what the Cheater could expect to earn from Honest trade with his next partner (nine times net of transaction costs). Nevertheless, if the inter-trade discount factor is at least 0.9, the LM system is in equilibrium and supports honest behavior, filing of valid complaints, and payment of judgments.

4. MINIMIZING TRANSACTION COSTS

Theorem 3 shows that the LM system restores cooperation even when the players know little about their partners' histories. There are transaction costs necessary to maintain this system, however: That the average payoff per period is $1 - Q$ reflects the transaction cost of Q per period incurred by each trader to support the Law Merchant system.

TABLE 1 SAMPLE PARAMETERS FOR WHICH THE LAW MERCHANT STRATEGY IS A SEQUENTIAL EQUILIBRIUM STRATEGY

Transaction Costs Parameters			Temptation to Cheat	Discount Factor	Penalty or Judgment
Q	C	p	α	δ	J
0.50	0.5	50%	2.0	0.67	1.0
0.50	1.0	50%	3.0	0.80	2.0
0.33	3.0	50%	7.0	0.90	6.0

Notice that the cost, C, of making and investigating a claim and the cost $f(J) - J$ of making the transfer do not appear in the expression for the average payoff. These costs do appear in condition (6): The Law Merchant system is not viable if the cost of making and investigating a claim or the cost of paying a judgment is too high, for then the traders cannot reasonably expect that the others will make claims and pay judgments when they should. However, once these costs are low enough that the threat to file claims with the Law Merchant is credible, they act only as a deterrent: These costs are never actually incurred at equilibrium in our model of the Law Merchant system.

Is the Law Merchant system the least expensive way to induce Honest behavior from rational traders at every stage? Theoretically, any institution that restores incentives for Honest trading by restoring the effectiveness of decentralized enforcement must inform a player when his partner has cheated in the past. If the temptation to Cheat is small and the value of continued trading is high, then this information need not be perfect, as in our model. So it may be possible to induce honest behavior using a less costly information system — one that costs only $q < Q$ to inform a trader adequately well — and correspondingly to increase the traders' average payoffs from $1 - Q$ to $1 - q$.[6] However, using imperfect information to economize on information costs calls merely for a refinement of the Law Merchant system — not for something fundamentally different. It is not possible to provide correct incentives without incurring some information cost of this kind and, as we have seen, the LM system avoids the unnecessary costs of dispute resolution and loss on transfers.

In operation, the Law Merchant system would appear to be a low cost way to disseminate information, for two reasons. First, the LM system centralizes the information system so that, for information about any partner, a player need only go to one place. He need not incur costs trying (i) to establish who was his current partner's previous partner, and (ii) to find the partner to make the relevant inquiry. Second, for the Prisoners' Dilemma, it is not sufficient to know only one period's history, but several.[7] The LM system not only centralizes this information but provides it in a very simple form: all that needs to be communicated is whether there are any outstanding judgments. For large communities, locating each of one's partner's previous partners and asking them for information is likely to be more expensive than the centralized record-keeping system of the Law Merchant.

Given the lack of quantitative evidence about the full costs of running different kinds of institutions, it is not possible to write down a convincing formal model to establish that the LM system minimizes costs in the class of feasible institutions.

---

[6] And, given that our model has a fixed starting date, there is really nothing to be learned from the initial query, so that could be eliminated with some small cost savings. However, this is just an artifact of our desire for modeling simplicity and not an inherent extra cost of the system.

[7] Kandori (1989) shows that in the repeated Prisoners' Dilemma, players must know at least two periods of history for each partner to sustain an equilibrium with Honest behavior.

What we can say confidently is that the *kind* of costs incurred by the LM system are inevitable if Honest trade is to be sustained in the face of self-interested behavior and that the system seems well designed to keep those costs as low as possible.

5. DISHONEST LAW MERCHANTS

Our analysis in section 2 proceeded on the assumption that the Law Merchant has no independent interest in the outcome of his decision. In addition, he is diligent, honest, and fair.

One need not look far in history (or, for that matter, in the modern world) to see that judges are not always so perfect. Within our model, there are many small amendments that could be made to insert opportunities for bribery and extortion. Although we do not provide a systematic treatment of these, we shall give a brief development of one of them to emphasize the simple idea that the Law Merchant business is itself valuable and that LMs may wish to maintain their reputation for honesty and diligence in order to keep the business active.

The most obvious problem with this reputation based account is that it seems to presume that a trader who is extorted by the Law Merchant can somehow make his injury widely known to the community of traders. It might be that the Law Merchant is a more sedentary merchant than the long-distance traders whom he serves, so that idea is perhaps not so far-fetched. Nevertheless, we shall argue that even if, in the spirit of our earlier analysis, there is no way for the trader to inform others about his injury, it may still be an equilibrium for the LM to behave honestly, due to the "client" incentives in the long-term relationship between the LM and each individual trader. More precisely, we will show that there is an equilibrium of the system in which every trader expects that if he pays a bribe he will be subjected to repeated attempts at extortion in the future; this dissuades the trader from paying any bribe. Then, a Law Merchant who commits to his threat to damage the reputation of a trader succeeds only in losing business, so he does not profit from making the threat.

To set the context for the formal extension, we modify the Law Merchant system stage game to regard the Law Merchant as a player. In the original version, the LM was allowed no choices, but let us nevertheless suppose that the LM earned a payoff of $2\epsilon > 0$ per contract, which is paid for as part of the $2Q$ that the parties spend to query the LM.

Next, we create a Modified Law Merchant System game in which our basic model is altered to allow the LM to solicit bribes. Initially, we consider only one kind of bribe — that extorted from a trader with no unpaid judgments by an LM who threatens to report falsely that there *are* unpaid judgments. Thus, we assume that before the traders make their queries, the LM may demand that one of the traders who has no unpaid judgment pay a bribe, $B \geq 0$. The amount B demanded is chosen by the LM. If the bribe is not paid and a query is made, the LM is committed to report falsely that the trader has an unpaid judgment.[8] The trader next decides whether to pay the bribe. The stage game then continues as previously described. When a bribe of B is paid, the LM's payoff is increased by B and the victim's payoff is reduced by an equal amount.[9]

Now consider the following variation of the Law Merchant System Strategy for the traders. If a player has no unpaid judgments and no bribe is solicited from him at the current stage, then he plays the LMSS as previously described. If the player has never before paid a bribe and a bribe is solicited, then he refuses to pay the bribe and does not query the LM in the current period. If the player has ever before paid a bribe, then he pays any bribe up to $\alpha - Q$ that is demanded of him. A player who has paid a bribe at the current round plays Cheat at that round and refuses to pay any judgment made against him. We call this specification the Extended Law Merchant System Strategy (ELMSS).

The Law Merchant's expected behavior is specified by the LM's Bribe Solicitation Strategy (BSS). If one of the present traders has no unpaid judgment but has previously paid a bribe, then the LM demands a payment of $\alpha - Q$. Otherwise, the LM does not demand any payment.

Theorem 4. If condition (6) holds and, in addition,

$$\alpha \leq 1 + (1 - Q)(2\delta - 1)/(1 - \delta), \tag{12}$$

then there is a sequential equilibrium of the Modified Law Merchant System game in which each trader adopts the strategy ELMSS and the Law Merchant adopts the strategy BSS.

Proof. Once again, we check that there is no contingency after which a one-time deviation by any player is profitable, when each player expects that the others have adhered to the strategy except where deviations have been explicitly observed, and each expects that all will adhere to it in the future. As before, we begin again from the last stage and work forward.

Consider a trader who has paid a bribe and cheated, and been assessed a judgment of $J > 0$. He expects a zero future payoff in each future period if he pays the judgment (because he will be extorted again and again). He expects the same zero payoff if he does not pay, since he will then have an unpaid judgment on his record. Since $-f(J) < 0$, he will find it most profitable to refuse to pay the judgment.

Having paid a bribe B, a trader expects to earn α this period and zero in the

---

[8]If the Law Merchant cannot commit to this action, then it is easy to show that there is an equilibrium in which the trader ignores the threat and the LM does not carry it out. It is no doubt true that some threats are disposed of in just this way — the victim simply calls the LM's bluff. We are interested in showing that the reputation mechanism can sometimes function even when the LM's threat must be taken at face value.

[9]If we assumed that transfers are costly here, as in the case of judgments, then the victim would become more reluctant to pay and bribery would be less likely to succeed.

future if he cheats today, or 1 this period and zero in the future if he does not. Since $\alpha > 1$, cheating is most profitable.

Given that a player has paid a bribe before, if a bribe B is demanded today, then the profits from paying the bribe, querying, and cheating are expected to be $\alpha - Q - B$; not paying leads to profits of zero. Hence, it is at least as profitable to pay the bribe whenever $B \leq \alpha - Q$.

If a trader has paid a bribe before, the strategy specifies that he will pay any bribe up to $\alpha - Q$ in the current period. In this case, according to the strategics, no trader's play in future periods will depend on whether the LM demands a bribe or on the amount of the bribe, so his most profitable play is to demand $\alpha - Q$.

Suppose a trader has not paid a bribe before and a bribe, B, is demanded currently. If the trader pays the bribe then, according to the strategy, he will cheat and refuse to pay the judgment. The resulting payoff is $\alpha - B - Q$ in the current period and, as a trader with an unpaid judgment, zero in future periods. If he refuses to pay the bribe, then his expected payoff is zero in the current period and $1 - Q$ in subsequent periods. So, it is most profitable for him to refuse to pay if

$$(1 - \delta)(\alpha - B - Q) + \delta \cdot 0 \leq (1 - \delta) \cdot 0 + \delta \cdot (1 - Q),$$

which is equivalent to condition (12).

Finally, when facing a trader who has never before paid a bribe, the LM expects that any demand for a bribe will be refused and that the trader will also not query in the current period, leading to a loss of revenues of ϵ, with no effect on play in future periods. Hence, it is most profitable for the LM not to demand any bribe in this case.   ■

Theorem 4 pertains to a model in which only one kind of dishonest behavior by the LM is possible. The problem of discouraging other kinds of dishonest behavior may require other strategies. From our preliminary analysis, it appears that the most difficult problem is to deter the LM from soliciting or accepting bribes from traders who have an unpaid judgment but wish to conceal that fact. By concealing the judgment, cheating, and refusing to pay the new judgment, the trader could "earn" $\alpha - Q$ and a portion of that might be offered as a bribe to the LM. As we add richness to the possibilities for cheating, it is natural to expect that the necessary institutions and strategies must respond in a correspondingly rich way.

6. CONCLUSION

We began our analysis by studying an environment in which private information about behavior in exchanges is a potential impediment to trade. Under complete information, even if meetings among particular pairs of traders are infrequent, informal norms of behavior are theoretically sufficient to police deviations. But when information is costly, the equilibrium may potentially break down and informal means may not be sufficient to police deviations.

The Law Merchant enforcement system that we have studied restores the equilibrium status of Honest behavior. It succeeds even though there is no state with police power and authority over a wide geographical realm to enforce contracts. Instead, the system works by making the reputation system of enforcement work better. The institutions we have studied provide people with the information they need to recognize those who have cheated, and it provides incentives for those who have been cheated to provide evidence of their injuries. Then, the reputation system itself provides the incentives for honest behavior and for payment by those who are found to have violated the code, and it encourages traders to boycott those who have flouted the system. Neither the reputation mechanism nor the institutions can be effective by themselves. They are complementary parts of a total system that works together to enforce honest behavior.

Our account of the Law Merchant system is, of course, incomplete. Once disputes came to be resolved in a centralized way, the merchants in Western Europe enhanced and refined their private legal code to serve the needs of the merchant trade — all prior to the rise of the nation-state. Without this code and the system for enforcement, trade among virtual strangers would have been much more cumbersome, or even impossible.[10] Remarkably, the Law Merchant institution appears to have been structured to support trade in a way that minimizes transaction costs, or at least incurs costs only in categories that are indispensable to any system that relies on boycotts as sanctions.

Our model is a stylization, not set in a particular locality at a particular date. Necessarily, then, it omits many important elements that some historians will argue are essential to understanding the institutions that are found there and then. However, our core contention that institutions sometimes arise to make reputation mechanisms more effective by communicating information seems almost beyond dispute. The Mishipora, described in the Hebrew Talmud, according to which those who failed to keep promises were punished by being publicly denounced; the use of the "hue and cry" to identify cheaters in medieval England; the famed "Scarlet Letter," described in Hawthorne's famous story; and the public stocks and pillories of 17th century New England, which were sometimes used to punish errant local merchants, are all examples of institutions and practices in which a principal aim is to convey information to the community about who has violated its norms.

It is our contention that an enduring pattern of trade over a wide geographical area cannot be sustained if it is profitable for merchants to renege on promises or repudiate agreements. In the larger trading towns and cities of northern Europe in the 10th through 13th centuries, it was not possible for every merchant to know

---

[10]Of course, merchants could and did communicate extensively, writing letters, engaging in trial relations, and checking the credentials of their trading partners. Where possible, they also relied on family members and client relationships to provide reliable services. But with geographic specialization in production, these devices alone could not allow merchants to escape the need to rely on the promises of individuals with whom they were not well acquainted.

the reputations of all others, so extensive trade required the development of some system like the Law Merchant system to fill in the gap.

Many of the key characteristics of our model correspond to practices found at the Champagne Fairs. While merchants at the Fairs were not required to query prior to any contract, the institutions of the Fair provided this information in another manner. As noted above, the Fairs closely controlled entry and exit. A merchant could not enter the Fair without being in good standing with those who controlled entry, and any merchant caught cheating at the Fair would be incarcerated and brought to justice under the rules of the Fair. So anyone a merchant met at the Fair could be presumed to have a "good reputation" in precisely the sense of our model. It did not indicate that all free merchants had never cheated in the past; but it did indicate that anyone who had been convicted of cheating had made good on the judgment against him. Moreover, because merchants might disappear rather than pay their judgments, judges at the Fairs had to balance the size of their judgment so that the value of being able to attend future Fairs exceeded the award.

According to Verlinden (1963, p. 132): "At the end of the 12th century and during the first half of the 13th, the Champagne Fairs were indeed the centre of international commercial activity of the western world." This is a long time for a single fair to maintain such dominance, but the Champagne Fair had two advantages over its potential competitors. First, it had an effective system for enforcing exchange contracts. Second, as we observed earlier, there are important economies of scope and scale in reputation mechanisms. Other, smaller fairs that tried to compete with the Champagne Fairs on an equal footing would have to contend with merchants who participated only long enough to make a profitable cheating transaction and then return to the Champagne Fairs where their participation rights were intact.

Despite this observation, it must be counted a weakness of the model that it does not fully account for trade outside of a single trading center. Even if the Law Merchant and related systems were effective underpinnings for local trade, how was information about a trader's dishonesty in one location transmitted to another? The model in this paper is too simple to handle this problem, but we hope to extend our approach to the institutions that developed during the middle ages to protect against the added problems raised by spatial separation. This includes the merchant gilds in northern Europe, the consulates of the Italian city states, and the organization of alien merchants into colonies (like the Steelyard in medieval London) with local privileges and duties. These institutions can also be understood from the perspective developed in this paper — they are designed to reinforce reputation mechanisms that alone are insufficient to support trade.

The Law Merchant system of judges and reputations was eventually replaced by a system of state enforcement, typically in the late middle ages or the early modern era in Western Europe. Enforcement of the private codes by the state added a new dimension to enforcement, especially in later periods when nation-states exercised extensive geographic control. Rather than depend for punishment upon the decentralized behavior of merchants, state enforcement could seize the property of individuals who resisted paying judgments, or put them into jail. If judgments could be enforced this way, then, in principle, the costs of keeping the merchants well informed about one another's past behavior could be saved. To the extent that the costs of running state adjudication and enforcement were roughly similar to the costs of running the private system and to the extent that taxes can be efficiently collected, a comprehensive state-run system would have the advantage that it eliminates the need for each individual to pay Q each period. As the volume of trade increased in the late middle ages, the cost saving from that source would have been substantial.[11] Thus our approach suggests that the importance of the role of the state enforcement of contracts was not that it provided a means of enforcing contracts where one previously did not exist. Rather, it was to reduce the transaction costs of policing exchange.[12]

In closing, we return to the broader implications of our work for the study of institutions. In complete information settings, institutions are frequently unnecessary because decentralized enforcement is sufficient to police deviations. However, this conclusion fails in environments where information is incomplete or costly. In the context of our model, the Adjusted Tit-for-Tat strategy requires that a trader know his current partner's previous history. When such information is difficult or costly to obtain, decentralized enforcement mechanisms break down. Institutions like those of the Law Merchant system resolve the fundamental problems of restoring the information that underpins an effective reputation system while both economizing on information and overcoming a whole array of incentive problems that obstruct the gathering and dissemination of that information.

PAUL R. MILGROM
Department of Economics
Stanford University
Stanford
CA 94305

DOUGLASS C. NORTH
Department of Economics
Washington University
St. Louis, MO 63130

BARRY R. WEINGAST
Hoover Institution on War,
Revolution and Peace
Stanford University
Stanford
CA 94305

REFERENCES

Abreu, Dilip, 1988, On the Theory of Infinitely Repeated Games with Discounting, *Econometrica* 39, 383–96.
Aumann, Robert, 1985, Repeated Games, in George Feiwel (ed.), *Issues in Contemporary Microeconomics and Welfare*, Macmillan Press, London, 209–42.
Axelrod, Robert, 1984, *The Evolution of Cooperation*, Basic Books, New York.

[11]Historically, the successful state enforcement came in a series of stages. As suggested above, state enforcement began with the adoption of the legal codes by a wide range of cities and towns. Some of these evolved over time into large city-states (e.g., Venice or Genoa) or, later, became part of a larger nation-state (e.g., London). For a discussion of the evolution of legal codes underpinning merchant trade, see North (1987).

[12]As we emphasized in section 4, however, a full evaluation of state enforcement must also assess the potential for corruption in the enforcement mechanisms of state enforcement.

Axelrod, Robert, 1986, An Evolutionary Approach to Social Norms, *American Political Science Review* 80, 1095–1111.

Banks, Jeffrey and Randall Calvert, 1989, Equilibria in Coordination Games. MS, University of Rochester.

Benson, Bruce, 1989, The Spontaneous Evolution of Commercial Law, *Southern Economic Journal*: 644–61.

Berman, Harold, 1983, *Law and Revolution: The Formation of Western Legal Tradition*, Harvard University Press.

Calvert, Randall, 1989. Reciprocity Among Self-interested Actors, in Peter C. Ordeshook, ed., *Models of Strategic Choice in Politics*, Michigan University Press.

Fudenberg, Drew and Eric Maskin, 1986, The Folk Theorem in Repeated Games with Discounting or with Incomplete Information, *Econometrica* 54, 533–554.

DeRoover, Raymond, 1963, The Organization of Trade, *Cambridge Economic History of Europe*, Vol. III.

Greif, Avner, 1989, Reputation and Coalitions in Medieval Trade: *Journal of Economic History*, 49, 857–82.

Jones, William Catron, 1961, *The Settlement of Merchants' Disputes by Merchants: An Approach to the Study of the History of Commercial Law*, PhD dissertation, University of Chicago.

Kandori, Michihiro, 1989, *Information and Coordination in Strategic Interaction Over Time*, PhD dissertation, Stanford University.

Klein, Benjamin and Keith Leffler, 1981, The Role of Market Forces in Assuring Contractual Performance, *Journal of Political Economy*. 89, 615–41.

Lopez, Robert S., 1976, *Commercial Revolution of the Middle Ages, 950–1350*, Cambridge University Press, Cambridge.

Lopez, Robert S. and Irving W. Raymond, 1955, *Medieval Trade in the Mediterranean World*, Columbia University Press, New York.

Mitchell, W., 1904, *Essay on the Early History of the Law Merchant*, Cambridge University Press, Cambridge.

North, Douglass, 1987, Institutions, Transactions Costs, and the Rise of Merchant Empires, in James Tracey (ed.), *The Economics of the Rise of Merchant Empires*, Vol. 2.

North, Douglass, 1989, *Institutions, Institutional Change, and Economic Performance*, Book MS, Washington University.

North, Douglass and Robert Thomas, 1973, *Rise of the Western World*, Cambridge University Press, Cambridge.

Okuno-Fujiwara, M. and Andrew Postlewaite. 1989, Social Norms in Random Matching Games, mimeo, University of Pennsylvania.

Pirenne, Henri, 1925, *Medieval Cities: Their Origins and the Revival of Trade*, Princeton University Press.

Rorig, Fritz, 1967, *The Medieval Town*, University of California Press, Berkeley.

Scutton, Thomas E., 1909, General Survey of the History of the Law Merchant, in *Select Essays in Anglo American Legal History*, compiled by the Association of American Law Schools.

Shapiro, Carl, 1983, Premiums for High Quality Products as Returns to Reputations, *Quarterly Journal of Economics* 98(4), 659–679.

Shapiro, Carl and Joseph Stiglitz, 1984, Equilibrium Unemployment as a Worker Discipline Device, *American Economic Review* 74(3), 433–444.

Thrupp, Silvia, 1948, *The Merchant Class of Medieval London*, University of Chicago Press, Chicago.

Townsend, Robert M., 1981, Models of Money with Spatially Separated Agents, in J.H. Kareken and Neil Wallace (eds.), *Models of Monetary Economies*, Federal Reserve Bank, Minneapolis.

Trakman, L., 1983, *The Law Merchant*, Littleton, Rothman and Co.

Verlinden, C., 1963, Markets and Fairs, *Cambridge Economic History of Europe*, Vol. III.

Weingast, Barry R. and William Marshall, 1988, 'The Industrial Organization of Congress; or Why Legislatures, like Firms, are not Organized as Markets, *Journal of Political Economy* 96, 132–163.

[22]

L. G. Telser

University of Chicago

A Theory of Self-enforcing Agreements*

. . . a prudent ruler ought not to keep faith when by so doing it would be against his interest, and when the reasons which made him bind himself no longer exist. If men were all good, this precept would not be a good one; but as they are bad, and would not observe their faith with you, so you are not bound to keep faith with them. Nor have legitimate grounds ever failed a prince who wished to show colourable excuse for the nonfulfillment of his promise. [NICCOLO MACHIAVELLI, *The Prince*]

I. Introduction

A self-enforcing agreement between two parties remains in force as long as each party believes himself to be better off by continuing the agreement than he would be by ending it. It is left to the judgment of the parties concerned to determine whether or not there has been a violation of the agreement. If one party violates the terms then the only recourse of the other party is to terminate the agreement after he discovers the violation. No third party intervenes to determine whether a violation has taken place or to estimate the damages that result from such violation. No

In a self-enforcing agreement each party decides unilaterally whether he is better off continuing or stopping his relation with the other parties. He stops if and only if the current gain from stopping exceeds the expected present value of his gains from continuing. No outside party intervenes to enforce the agreement, to determine whether there has been violations, to assess damages, and to impose penalties. The theory gives a solution of the Prisoners' Dilemma. Application of the theory to transactions between a buyer and a seller gives limits on the sequence of prices that induces repeated transactions. Applied to a group of sellers, the theory describes the conditions under which competition is more profitable than collusion.

* I am grateful to Jack Gould, Sam Peltzman, and the members of the Seminar on Applied Price Theory, University of Chicago, for their helpful comments and criticism. All responsibility for any errors that may be present in this paper is mine.

(*Journal of Business*, 1980, vol. 53, no. 1)

third party decides whether a violation has been "willful" or "accidental." A party to a self-enforcing agreement calculates whether his gain from violating the agreement is greater or less than the loss of future net benefits that he would incur as a result of detection of his violation and the consequent termination of the agreement by the other party. If the violator gains more than he loses from the violation, then he will violate the agreement. Hence both parties continue to adhere to an agreement if and only if each gains more from adherence to, than from violations of, its terms.

Many economic transactions illustrate self-enforcing agreements. Since it is costly to rely on the intervention of third parties such as the courts to enforce agreements and to assess damages when they are violated, the parties to an agreement devise its terms to make it self-enforcing, if this can be done cheaply enough. Thus, one of the strongest incentives for honesty of a seller is his desire to obtain the continued patronage of his customer. In cases where a similar transaction between the two parties is unlikely to be repeated in the future so that a loss of future business is not an effective penalty, substitutes for self-enforcing agreements will appear. These substitutes often can avoid the use of third parties as a means of enforcing agreements. A prudent person avoids making a transaction with someone he suspects will be unreliable. Therefore, people seek information about the reliability of those with whom they deal. Reliability, however, is not an inherent personality trait. A person is reliable only if it is more advantageous to him than being unreliable. Therefore, the information about someone's return to being reliable is pertinent in judging the likelihood of his being reliable. For example, an itinerant is less likely to be reliable if it is more costly to impose penalties on him.[1]

1. Information about the reliability of purchasers may be one of the reasons for the success of credit cards. The argument is as follows. Most firms do not offer a lower price to customers who pay in cash or by check than to those who use credit cards, although a firm retains from 95% to 97% of its receipts from a credit card transaction and pays the remainder as a fee to the bank issuing the credit card. It would appear that the net return to the seller is lower on a credit card sale than on a sale paid by check or in cash, yet it charges all of its customers the same price regardless of their mode of payment. (It may accept payment by check from its well-known customers.) Those who use credit cards can pay by check to the bank issuing the credit card, and they do not incur finance charges except for payments deferred for more than 1 month. What services does a credit card give? The answer is that the bank keeps a record of the purchases and payments of the credit card user that enables it to judge the financial reliability of the user. Hence a person who has a valid credit card is certified as reliable to a firm who knows nothing else about him. Therefore, the credit card enables a stranger to buy something and pay for it without using cash as a means of payment. Even so, the customer may offer to pay by check after showing the seller his credit card in order to establish his reliability if the firm will charge him a lower price for his purchase. One objection to this practice is that it would not assure the seller that the buyer's check would clear. A stronger objection is that such a practice would create a free-rider problem. The bank would be certifying the reliability of its credit card holders and would be unable to be remunerated for doing so. In order to solve this free-rider problem, the

A basic hypothesis of this approach is that someone is honest only if honesty, or the appearance of honesty, pays more than dishonesty. Hence, if someone thinks he can gain by dishonesty with impunity then he will be dishonest. This hypothesis leads to important conclusions. For example, if two parties are in a sequence of transactions such that both know for sure which transaction is the last, then each also knows that violating the terms of the agreement on the last transaction cannot evoke a sacrifice of the net gains thereafter. Consequently, each party would be under no compulsion to abide by the terms at the last transaction. Since the same argument applies to the next to the last transaction and so on to the first, we would be driven to the conclusion that no finite sequence of transactions can be self-enforcing if both parties know for sure which transaction is the last one. Therefore, assuming that every sequence of transactions must be finite, a sequence of self-enforcing transactions must have no last one. How can this be? A sequence has no last term if there is always a positive probability of continuing. As long as this is true, anyone who violates the terms at one time incurs the risk of losses in the future. Therefore, there is no certainty of gain from a violation of the agreement on any transaction because there is always a positive probability of continuing to another transaction. Owing to this, there is a positive probability that current violations are punished later.[2]

A theological argument helps illustrate the importance of a finite uncertain horizon. Suppose that after a sinful life on earth, the punishment after death is the torment of the soul in hell. Assume that a sinner can obtain forgiveness by taking various actions before death such as good works, confession to a priest, and so on. If the time of death is uncertain, then a potential sinner incurs the risk of being unable before he dies to perform the good works or take the other appropriate actions that can avoid punishment in hell. If the date of death were certain, then he could allow some time before his death for those actions that would remove the consequences of the sinning that follows his death.

---

bank issuing the credit card often requires that those sellers who will accept its credit card not charge a higher price to those of its customers who use its credit card as a means of payment.

2. The cartel's dilemma illustrates this argument. Let two firms contemplate collusion in order to increase their return. If one sells the agreed upon quantity while the other, relying on this, sells the quantity giving him the maximal net return, then the cheating firm can get a higher net return than he would under collusion. Assuming both firms are equally intelligent and avaricious, Cournot (1960) concludes that collusion is not a stable equilibrium even with only two firms. For an application to the Prisoners' Dilemma, see Luce and Raiffa (1957). These authors also suggest that an uncertain finite horizon can lead to a resolution of the Dilemma (p. 102 and appendix 8). For a detailed analysis of whether collusion is more profitable than competition using the theory of a finite horizon which is a random variable, see Telser (1972, chap. 3, sec. 5; chap. 5, sec. 5). The relation between the number of competing firms and the profitability of collusion compared to competition is discussed in Telser (1978, chap. 1, sec. 10).

Even a nonbeliever in the existence of hell can accept this argument provided he is willing to concede there is a small positive probability that hell exists and that the disutility of the torments of hell is unboundedly large. Given the uncertainty of the date of death, although the short-term gain of sinning exceeds that from a good life, one should lead a good life all of the time because of the large expected long term penalty of sinning.[3]

We shall study two situations in which self-enforcing agreements may occur. First, there is an exchange between two parties such that one sells a good or a service to the other for which he receives a payment. Second, two or more parties seek an agreement among themselves under which they propose to undertake a common venture. In both situations there is a sequence of transactions over time such that the ending date is unknown and uncertain. The penalty for failure to abide by the terms of the agreement is to stop the sequence of transactions so there would be no future relations among the parties. The problem is to see under what circumstances there are mutually satisfactory terms for a self-enforcing agreement.

II. A Formal Theory

Assume two parties are considering whether or not to begin a sequence of transactions that is equivalent to a self-enforcing agreement. We calculate the expected gain to each party of such a sequence.

Let u_j denote the net gain to a party during time period j if a transaction occurs at time j. The sequence terminates either because one of the parties stops it or because an event occurs which neither party can prevent. This makes a distinction between the stopping that is the result of an action taken by one of the parties and which one of them induces, and the stopping that is fortuitous, and, therefore, autonomous, which is equivalent to the result of a random event. We shall confine our attention at the outset to fortuitous stopping.

Let T denote the time of stopping, which is a random variable for the stopping that is autonomous. Let p_t denote the probability that T equals t so that p_t is the probability of a horizon of duration t. Since the stopping time is autonomous, p_t does not depend on current or past gains. We may assume that the parties know the sequence of stopping

---

3. This argument may also explain why some organized religions oppose suicide. Suicide makes the date of death more certain and would lower the risk of inadequate preparation for preventing the punishment of the soul after death (I am indebted to J. A. Telser for this point). The argument in the text also explains why the old are more likely to be virtuous than the young even if the taste for sinning is independent of age. The old have less time left for repentance than the young and therefore have a smaller expected return from sinning. It also follows that a position of trust is more likely to be given to an older than a younger person.

probabilities. It is certain that the process comes to a halt sooner or later so that

$$\sum_{0}^{\infty} p_t = 1. \tag{1}$$

Let q_t denote the probability of a horizon lasting for more than t periods.

$$q_t = \sum_{t+1}^{\infty} p_j. \tag{2}$$

The expected duration of the horizon, denoted by $E(T)$, satisfies

$$E(T) = \sum_{0}^{\infty} t p_t = \sum_{0}^{\infty} q_t. \tag{3}$$

Notwithstanding (1), $E(T)$ can be infinite.[4]

Given the possibility of stopping at time t, there is the question of whether the gain at time $j < t$, namely u_j, should also depend on t. It should not. Since the horizon is a random variable, the return at an earlier time cannot depend on the value of a random variable at a later time.

There are other possible complications. One we consider below is whether fortuitous events that cause the process to stop for one or both of them are independent of each other. Another is whether the probability of stopping depends on the age of the agreement, that is, on how long it has gone on. As we shall see, the present formulation is general enough to accommodate these factors.

Putting aside these considerations for the moment, we now calculate the expected gain to one of the parties. Define s_t as follows:

$$s_t = \sum_{j=0}^{t} u_j, \tag{4}$$

so that s_t gives the sum of the net gains to a party for a sequence of transactions lasting for $t + 1$ periods. Observe that this allows for discounting, since u_j has a time subscript, j, and the present value of a given u_j can decrease as j increases. The probability of s_t is p_{t+1} so that $p_{t+1} s_t$ is the contribution to the expected value of a horizon of length t. Summing over horizons of all possible durations gives the expected value of the gain, denoted by $E(u)$, as follows:

$$E(u) = \sum_{0}^{\infty} p_{t+1} s_t. \tag{5}$$

Another way of writing $E(u)$ which uses (2) and (4) is given by

$$E(u) = \sum_{0}^{\infty} q_t u_t. \tag{6}$$

4. See Feller (1962, vol. 1, chap. 11, sec. 1, theorem 2).

We now consider some complications. A self-enforcing agreement refers to a sequence of transactions between at least two parties, and fortuitous events can affect at least one of them bringing their relation to an end. A relation can continue between two parties if and only if no fortuitous event stops the process for either one of them. The length of the horizon, t, satisfies

$$t = \min \, <t_1, t_2>, \tag{7}$$

where t_i is the time when some event would occur that would prevent the continued participation of the ith party. Therefore, p_t is the probability of $T = t$ with t as defined by (7). Consequently, it does not matter in this formulation whether the fortuitous events stopping a relation among the parties are independent or dependent.

The age of the relation between the two parties does not affect the probability of ending their agreement if and only if the conditional probability of stopping is the same at all points in time. In particular, the conditional probability of stopping at time t must be the same as the probability of never starting, which is p_0. This holds if and only if

$$p_t = (1 - p_0)^t p_0 \tag{8}$$

(Feller 1962, vol. 1, chap. 13, sec. 9). We note for future reference that in this case

$$q_t = (1 - p_0)^{t+1}. \tag{9}$$

Also, from (3) and (9), we obtain

$$E(T) = (1 - p_0)/p_0. \tag{10}$$

The sequence of transactions can stop because one of the parties believes this would make him better off. Let δu_t denote the increment in the net gain to a party who stops the sequence at time t. We now refer to induced stopping and not to fortuitous stopping that is beyond the control of either party. Write the sequence δu^t so that $\delta u^t = \, < 0$, $\ldots, 0, \delta u_t, -u_{t+1}, -u_{t+2}, \ldots >$. Using this notation, the sequence of net gains to a party who takes an action bringing the transactions to a halt from period $t + 1$ onward is given by $u + \delta u^t$ (the superscript shows when the violation occurs). Therefore,

$$E(u + \delta u^t) = E(u) + q_t \delta u_t - \sum_{t+1}^{\infty} q_j u_j. \tag{11}$$

We may conclude from (11) that the gain from continuing the sequence of transactions exceeds the gain from stopping at time t if and only if for all t,

$$E(u + \delta u^t) - E(u) = q_t \delta u_t - \sum_{t+1}^{\infty} q_j u_j \leq 0. \tag{12}$$

In applications, the net gain u_t depends on the terms of the transaction at time t and δu_t depends on how much the party can gain from a violation of these terms. Therefore, the problem of finding terms that can give a self-enforcing agreement reduces to determining whether there is a sequence $\{u_t\}$ that can satisfy (12) for the implied δu_t so that $E(u)$ would give the maximum.

It is convenient to pause at this point and consider whether this theory captures the important aspects of the problem under study. If one party takes an action giving him a net gain of δu_t at time t which is an unfavorable surprise to the other party and constitutes a violation of the agreement, then the theory assumes that the victim responds by terminating the agreement. This gives the maximum penalty that the victim can impose on the violator of the self-enforcing agreement. If the maximum penalty cannot deter a violation because $E(u + \delta u^t) - E(u) > 0$, then no smaller one suffices. Hence (12) is both necessary and sufficient for a self-enforcing agreement.

Second, the victim may not immediately discover the violation. If he makes the discovery after violations have been going on for k periods, the gains to the violator would be $\delta u_t, \delta u_{t+1}, \ldots, \delta u_{t+k-1}$. Slowness in the detection of violations raises the gains to the violator. In order to simplify the algebra, the preceding formulation assumes discovery with a minimum delay ($k = 1$). This does not change the validity of the analysis in any important way.

Third, the reader may object that the theory fails to allow for deviations from the expected gains and seems to require rigid and continuously perfect adherence to expectations. Here, too, nothing essential is lost with this approach. To see why, consider how we would take deviations into account. Assume there is a band around the expected gains such that actual gains falling within the band are admissible. Gains outside these bands imply a violation of the agreement. The deviation between the actual and the expected gain should behave like a sequence of independent and identically distributed random variables if the parties are in compliance with the agreement. There is a violation either when the actual gains go outside the limits or remain too close to one of them for too long. It follows that the parties would pay careful attention to those gains which are close to the limits. Consequently, the limits themselves have a role in the analysis allowing for deviations just like u_t in the present theory. Therefore, without loss of generality we may proceed with our analysis.

Since δu_t is the increment of gain to a party who stops the sequence at time t, $\delta u_t > 0$ is a weak necessary condition for stopping.

In order to describe the properties of a sequence $\{u_t\}$ capable of sustaining a self-enforcing agreement, it is necessary to make assumptions about the relation between δu_t and u_t. Assume first that δu_t and u_t

vary inversely. Thus, the simplest relation of this kind would be linear so that

$$\delta u_t = a_0 - a_1 u_t, \qquad a_0, a_1 > 0.$$

But then, $u_t \geq a_0/a_1$ would make δu_t negative. Hence if u_t exceeds this lower bound, the sequence would be self-enforcing. In general, a sequence would be self-enforcing whenever u_t is large enough if δu_t and u_t vary inversely.

Alternatively, assume that δu_t is proportional to u_t. Thus, let

$$\delta u_t = \beta u_t, \quad \beta > 0. \tag{13}$$

By virtue of (12), the necessary and sufficient condition for continuing becomes

$$\beta q_t u_t \leq \sum_{t+1}^{\infty} q_j u_j \tag{14}$$

Before giving a general result for this case, it is helpful to consider two examples. First, assume that $q_t u_t = r^t$ with $0 < r < 1$. Condition (14) is equivalent to $\beta \leq r/(1 - r)$. If $\beta = 1$, then $r > \frac{1}{2}$. If $\beta = 2$, then $r > \frac{2}{3}$. In the second example, let $q_t u_t = t^{-\alpha}$ with $\alpha > 1$. The series on the right side of (14) is approximately $[1/(\alpha - 1)][1/(t + 1)^{\alpha-1}]$. In order to satisfy (14), conditions on β and α are required. Write $\alpha = 1 + \sigma$. Then (14) holds if and only if

$$\beta(t + 1)^{\sigma}/t^{1+\sigma} \leq 1/\sigma \text{ for all } t \geq 1. \tag{15}$$

The function on the left decreases monotonically with t and has a maximum at $t = 1$. Therefore, to satisfy (15) it is necessary and sufficient that

$$\beta 2^{\sigma} \leq 1/\sigma. \tag{16}$$

For $\beta = 1$, it can be shown that (16) holds for all $\sigma < 0.64115$. More generally, (16) gives the implication of an inverse relation between β and σ. Both examples share the property that the series $\Sigma q_j u_j$ must not converge too rapidly in order to satisfy (14). This means that an agreement is self-enforcing if and only if the expected horizon is long enough.

Treating time as a continuous parameter gives convenient expressions for the necessary and sufficient condition of a self-enforcing agreement. Let $f(t)$ denote a probability density function so that

$$F(t) = \int_0^t f(s) \, ds \to 1 \text{ as } t \to \infty.$$

The probability of going on longer than t is $1 - F(t)$. Let $u(s)$ denote the gain at time s. Then

$$E(u) = \int_0^\infty u(s)[1 - F(s)]ds \qquad (17)$$

corresponds to (6). The necessary and sufficient condition for continuing is

$$\delta u(t)[1 - F(t)] \leq \int_t^\infty u(s)[1 - F(s)]ds, \qquad (18)$$

where $\delta u(t)$ is the gain from cheating. Define the function $H(t)$ as follows:

$$H(t) = \int_t^\infty u(s)[1 - F(s)]ds \qquad (19)$$

so that $H'(t) = -u(t)[1 - F(t)] < 0$. If $\delta u(t)$ is proportional to $u(t)$, $\delta u(t) = \beta u(t)$, $\beta > 0$, then (18) becomes

$$0 < -\beta H'(t) \leq H(t) \text{ for all } t \geq 0. \qquad (20)$$

Rearranging terms in (20) gives an interesting condition on $H(t)$. It follows that $0 < -\beta dH/H \leq dt \rightarrow -\beta \log H \leq t + c$, where c is a constant. Consequently,

$$H(t) \geq e^{-(t+c)/\beta} \qquad (21)$$

gives a lower bound on H.

In this theory each party compares his current gain from cheating the other party to his expected gain from continuing his relation honestly with the other party. The probability of continuing does not depend on the past record of transactions the parties have had with each other though it may vary with time. Some may wish to argue that previous favorable experience raises the probability of continuing while previous unfavorable experience lowers this probability. Equivalently, assume that a party to an agreement accumulates a stock of goodwill toward the other party that depends on his past experience with the other party. Favorable past experience raises and unfavorable past experience lowers this stock of goodwill. He terminates his relation with the other party when he has no remaining stock of goodwill.

The argument postulating a stock of goodwill based on past experience faces a fatal objection because it is inconsistent with rational behavior. To see why, suppose that a buyer accumulates goodwill toward a seller based on the excess of his favorable over his unfavorable experiences with that seller. Each past favorable experience raises and each past unfavorable experience lowers the buyer's goodwill. A seller who knows that the buyer behaves in this way has various tempting ways of cheating the buyer. Such a seller dealing with a new customer may deliberately behave honestly toward him at first to gain his confidence so that he can cheat him more profitably later. Moreover, he need only maintain the stock of goodwill of his old customers at a level just high enough to obtain their continued patronage. In the process he can cheat them, but not too often. The accumulation of a fund of goodwill of a buyer toward a seller that depends on past experience stands as a temptation to the seller to cheat the buyers and convert their goodwill into ready cash. It is the prospect of the loss of future gain that deters and the existence of past goodwill that invites cheating. Therefore, rational behavior by the parties to an agreement requires that the probability of continuing their relation does not depend on their past experience with each other. We recognize this condition as equivalent to an efficient market with rational traders.

III. Self-enforcing Agreements between a Buyer and Seller

Before giving the theory it is helpful to give an example. Consider a firm as a buyer and a worker as a seller to it. Assume that the worker initially accepts a lower wage rate in order to acquire skills that will be useful as long as he remains with that employer. The sacrifice in his current earnings during the training period is equivalent to an investment by the worker in firm specific human capital upon which he expects to receive a return subsequently. This return comes in the form of a higher wage rate later on in compensation for the lower wage during the earlier period of employment. If the firm does not pay the higher wage rate subsequently then it violates the agreement and the worker can quit. The firm also incurs part of the cost of investment in firm specific human capital if it pays the worker a wage rate during the training period above the value of his marginal product at that time. The firm expects to obtain a return on its investment subsequently if it pays the worker a wage rate below the then current value of the worker's marginal product. If the worker quits, then the firm stands to lose the investment that it has made in the worker. Therefore, these circumstances raise the problem of seeing whether it is possible to have a self-enforcing agreement.[5]

A formal statement of the situation is as follows. The buyer expects a benefit in period t of b_t^* for which he expects to pay x_t^*. The seller expects to incur a cost of a_t^* in period t for which he expects to receive x_t^*. The gain the buyer expects is $u_t^* = b_t^* - x_t^*$. The gain the seller expects is $v_t^* = x_t^* - a_t^*$. The expected benefit of the buyer, b_t^*, depends on the expected cost incurred by the seller, a_t^*. The lower is a_t^*, the

---

5. For an empirical analysis of firm specific human capital, see Telser (1972, chap. 8).

lower is b_t^*. The buyer is said to violate the agreement if he gets b_t^* and pays $x_t < x_t^*$. Hence

$$u_t = b_t^* - x_t > u_t^* = b_t^* - x_t^*, \tag{22}$$

and

$$\delta u_t = u_t - u_t^* = x_t^* - x_t \leqslant x_t^*. \tag{23}$$

The maximal gain of the buyer occurs when $x_t = 0$. The seller is said to violate the agreement if he incurs the cost $a_t < a_t^*$ and gets x_t^* from the seller. Hence the seller obtains

$$v_t = x_t^* - a_t > x_t^* - a_t^*, \tag{24}$$

and the gain to the seller is δv_t where

$$\delta v_t = v_t - v_t^* = a_t^* - a_t \leqslant a_t^*. \tag{25}$$

If the buyer violates the agreement in period t, then the seller detects the violation afterward and, in a self-enforcing agreement, imposes the penalty of stopping the transactions with the buyer. Therefore, the buyer would gain δu_t and would sacrifice the expected gains that he would obtain by faithful adherence to the expectations. Similarly, if the seller violates the agreement by furnishing a commodity that proves to be less beneficial to the buyer than the buyer expected, then the penalty that the buyer imposes in a self-enforcing agreement is termination of future transactions with the seller.

Condition (12) applies in the present situation. The buyer obtains a maximal gain by continuing the sequence of transactions if and only if for all t, it is true that $E(u + \delta u) \leqslant E(u)$. Therefore, taking the upper bound for δu_t given by (23), we obtain a sufficient condition for the buyer to continue the sequence of transactions which is given as follows:

$$q_t x_t^* \leqslant \sum_{t+1}^{\infty} q_j u_j^* = \sum_{t+1}^{\infty} q_j (b_j^* - x_j^*). \tag{26}$$

We may conclude that the buyer is willing to continue the sequence of transactions if there is a sequence $\{x_t^*\}$ such that

$$\sum_{t}^{\infty} q_j x_j^* \leqslant \sum_{t+1}^{\infty} q_j b_j^*. \tag{27}$$

The equivalent sufficient condition for the seller is that

$$q_t x_t^* \leqslant \sum_{t+1}^{\infty} q_j v_j^* = \sum_{t+1}^{\infty} q_j (x_j^* - a_j^*). \tag{28}$$

Rearranging terms in this expression gives

$$\sum_{t+1}^{\infty} q_j a_j^* \le \sum_{t+1}^{\infty} q_j x_j^* - q_t x_t^*. \tag{29}$$

Hence there is a self-enforcing agreement if there is an $\{x_t^*\}$ that can satisfy (27) and (29).

To illustrate these conditions, consider the important special case where $a_t^* = a$, $b_t^* = b$, and $p_t = (1 - p_0)^t p_0$ so that $q_t = (1 - p_0)^{t+1}$ (cf.[8]). Then (27) is equivalent to $x(1 - p_0)^{t+1} \le b(1 - p_0)^{t+2}$, which reduces to

$$x \le b(1 - p_0) < b. \tag{30}$$

Condition (29) is equivalent to $a(1 - p_0)^{t+2}/p_0 \le x(1 - p_0)^{t+2}/p_0 - x(1 - p_0)^{t+1}$. This becomes

$$a(1 - p_0) \le x[(1 - p_0) - p_0]. \tag{31}$$

The inequality in (31) can be satisfied only if $p_0 < \frac{1}{2}$. This means that the expected horizon must exceed one period (cf. [10]). Let $\theta = p_0/(1 - p_0) = 1/E(T)$. Then we can rewrite (31) in the shape as follows:

$$a/(1 - \theta) \le x. \tag{32}$$

If $p_0 < \frac{1}{2}$ then $\theta < 1$. Hence we have $a < a/(1 - \theta)$. Combining (30) and (32), we may conclude that there is a self-enforcing agreement if

$$a < a/(1 - \theta) < x < b(1 - p_0) < b. \tag{33}$$

We must necessarily have

$$a/b < (1 - p_0)/(1 - \theta) = 1 - 2p_0, \tag{34}$$

or (33) cannot hold. Notice that the presence of uncertainty about continuing the sequence of transactions narrows the range in which an admissible x can fall.[6]

---

6. The argument in the text does not require either $u_t^* = b_t^* - x_t^* > 0$ or $v_t^* = x_t^* - a_t^* > 0$. Hence the upper bounds for δu_t given by (23) and for δv_t given by (25) are valid even if either u_t^* or v_t^* is negative. We obtain different results by assuming $x_t^* \le b_t^*$ so that $\delta u_t \le b_t^*$ in place of (23). A sufficient condition for the buyer to continue now becomes as follows:

$$q_t b_t^* \le \sum_{t+1}^{\infty} q_j u_j^* = \sum_{t+1}^{\infty} q_j (b_j^* - x_j^*)$$

which reduces to

$$\sum_{t+1}^{\infty} q_j x_j^* \le \sum_{t+1}^{\infty} q_j b_j^* - q_t b_t^*. \tag{a}$$

For the seller, a sufficient condition for continuing is given by

$$\sum_{t}^{\infty} q_j a_j^* \le \sum_{t+1}^{\infty} q_j x_j^*. \tag{b}$$

Together these give sufficient conditions for a self-enforcing agreement between the buyer and the seller. We can see the difference between this situation and the one in the

The analytic formulation in Section 2 is useful in giving sufficient conditions for continuing the series of transactions between the buyer and the seller. Corresponding to (26), there is

$$x^*(t)[1 - F(t)] \leq \int_0^\infty [b^*(s) - x^*(s)][1 - F(s)]ds \qquad (35)$$

which becomes

$$x^*(t)[1 - F(t)] + \int_t^\infty x^*(s)[1 - F(s)]ds \leq \int_t^\infty b^*(s)[1 - F(s)]ds. \quad (36)$$

For the seller, corresponding to (28), there is

$$a^*(t)[1 - F(t)] \leq \int_t^\infty [x^*(s) - a^*(s)][1 - F(s)]ds$$

which becomes

$$a^*(t)[1 - F(t)] + \int_t^\infty a^*(s)[1 - F(s)]ds \leq \int_t^\infty x^*(s)[1 - F(s)]ds. \quad (37)$$

Define

$$A(t) = \int_t^\infty a^*(s)[1 - F(s)]ds$$

so that $A'(t) = -a(t)[1 - F(t)]$. Using a similar notation for $B(t)$ and $X(t)$ we can obtain a sufficient condition for a self-enforcing agreement. Thus, (36) becomes

$$-X'(t) + X(t) \leq B(t) \qquad (38)$$

and (37) becomes

$$-A'(t) + A(t) \leq X(t). \qquad (39)$$

A necessary condition for (38) and (39) is that

$$A(t) - A'(t) \leq B(t) + X'(t). \qquad (40)$$

Consequently, (40) imposes conditions on $X'(t)$ in terms of the given functions $A(.)$ and $B(.)$ that are necessary for (38) and (39). Any function $X(.)$ that satisfies (38) and (39) implies a self-enforcing agreement between the buyer and the seller.

---

text most easily for the special case where $a_j^* = a, b_j^* = b, x_j^* = x$ and $q_j = (1 - p_0)^{j+1}$. For this case (a) and (b) reduce to

$$a \leq x(1 - p_0) \leq b[(1 - p_0) - p_0]. \qquad (c)$$

Necessarily, $p_0/(1 - p_0) < 1$ which holds if and only if $p_0 < \frac{1}{2}$. The limits in (c) are wider than the limits in (33) as is readily verified. However, it remains true that the bounds for x sufficient for a self-enforcing agreement are narrowed because $a < a/(1 - p_0)$ and $b > 1 - \theta$.

IV. Self-enforcing Cooperative Agreements

The preceding section analyzes a sequence of transactions between two parties who trade goods for money. Another important application is to a situation where the two parties can cooperate in some venture which does not involve a direct exchange between them. A leading example would be collusion between two firms, say the two sellers of mineral water in Cournot's theory, who can choose the same policy as a monopoly that obtains a maximal net return. The alternative to cooperation is the noncooperative equilibrium that results if each firm acting independently chooses the policy giving it the maximal net return for a given policy of the other firm. Cournot's theory states there is never collusion because one party to a collusive agreement can always gain more by violating it than by adhering to it, although together the firms gain more from collusion than competition. In the present formulation, Cournot asserts that a self-enforcing collusive agreement is impossible even if there are only two firms. This conclusion is correct if the firms operate over a finite certain horizon so that punishment of departures from the agreement is not possible after the last period. However, the presence of uncertainty about the length of the horizon giving the implication that there is no last period, implies different results. Such uncertainty may enable a self-enforcing cooperative agreement to be an equilibrium.

As above, let u_j denote the expected gain to a firm in period j if it cooperates with the other firm.

$$E(u) = \sum_{0}^{\infty} q_j u_j \tag{41}$$

gives the expected net return if there is cooperation. Let v_j denote the gain in period j if the firms do not cooperate. Hence $v_j < u_j$ and

$$E(v) = \sum_{0}^{\infty} q_j v_j \tag{42}$$

gives the expected net return to a firm in the noncooperative equilibrium. Assume there is cooperation until period $t - 1$ and that the firm, counting on the adherence of the other to the cooperative agreement, violates the agreement in period t so that its gain in that period is $u_t + \delta u_t > u_t$. The punishment is a cessation of the cooperative agreement thereafter, which means a sequence of net returns given by v_{t+1}, $v_{t+2}, \ldots$. Denote the expected return from a violation of the cooperative agreement by $E(u + \delta u^t)$, and we have

$$E(u + \delta u^t) - E(u) = E(v)_{t+1} - E(u)_{t+1} + q_t \delta u_t, \tag{43}$$

where $E(u)_{t+1}$ and $E(v)_{t+1}$ are defined as follows:

$$E(v)_{t+1} = \sum_{t+1}^{\infty} q_j v_j \quad \text{and} \quad E(u)_{t+1} = \sum_{t+1}^{\infty} q_j u_j.$$

A self-enforcing cooperative agreement gives the maximal expected net return if and only if for all t, $E(u + \delta u^t) - E(u) \le 0$, which by virtue of (43), is equivalent to

$$0 < q_t \delta u_t \le E(u - v)_{t+1}, \tag{44}$$

for all t. Take the special case where the probability of a horizon longer than t periods is given by $q_t = (1 - p_0)^{t+1}$. Let $\delta u_t = \delta_2$, a constant, and let $u_t - v_t = \delta_1 > 0$, a constant. The necessary and sufficient condition for a self-enforcing cooperative agreement given by (44) implies that $0 < (1 - p_0)^{t+1}\delta_2 \le \delta_1(1 - p_0)^{t+2}/p_0$, which simplifies to

$$\delta_2 \le \delta_1(1 - p_0)/p_0 = \delta_1 E(T). \tag{45}$$

Thus, given δ_2 and δ_1, the longer is the expected horizon, the greater is the dominance of the self-enforcing cooperative agreement over the alternative, noncooperation. The values of the parameters δ_1 and δ_2 depend on the underlying cost and demand conditions.

This theory also has interesting implications for multiproduct firms. Let u_{itk} denote the net return to firm i in period t from product k if it colludes with the other firm on this product. Assume the products are independent so that autonomous stopping for any product is a random event independent of autonomous stopping for any of the other products. These assumptions raise the question of whether linkage among such independent products by the two firms can result in a self-enforcing cooperative agreement on all of the products. The point is this. It may be that collusion on one product does not satisfy (44) so that noncooperation gives the highest expected return. On another independent product (44) may be satisfied so that cooperation gives the highest expected return on this product. By linking the two products together, it may be that cooperation on the two may satisfy (44). Thus, the higher expected return on the one product, where collusion would be more profitable in its own right, is a hostage to the other product, where competition would be more profitable in its own right. In place of (44) holding product by product, linkage gives a necessary and sufficient condition for cooperation on all n products as follows:

$$\sum_{k=1}^{n} q_{tk} \delta u_{t,k} \le \sum_{k=1}^{n} E(u - v)_{t+1,k}. \tag{46}$$

Plainly, (46) can hold although some of the components do not satisfy (44). This argument assumes that if there is a violation of the cooperative agreement on one product by one firm, then punishment takes the form of noncooperation on all of the products. Otherwise, of course, there would be no linkage.

For substitutable products, linkage is no luxury but a necessity so that there can be a successful self-enforcing agreement on them. Dependence refers to two aspects; relations among the net gains of the products and relations among the autonomous events that cause stopping for a product. Relations among the net gains means that there may be a direct effect on the net gains of one product as a result of actions taken on the other products. Thus, the net return to collusion on one product depends on whether there is cooperation on the related products. Relations among stopping probabilities means that if the sequence for one product terminates, this affects the probability of termination of the other products. Consequently, in contrast to the situation with independent products, it may not be possible to sustain an agreement on one product unless there is agreement on related products. A rigorous analysis would require a more elaborate description of how the products are related.[7]

V.   Alternatives to a Self-enforcing Agreement

A self-enforcing agreement is possible if and only if the expected future gains from adherence to it exceeds the current gain from a violation of the agreement. Therefore, given a sequence of gains $\{u_t\}$, a self-enforcing agreement is not possible when the expected horizon is too short or when δu_t is too large. In these cases a third party may intervene to enforce an agreement so that the agreement is not self-

---

7. Space constraints do not permit an elaborate description of how this can be done. A sketch of the theory is as follows. Define a commodity in terms of its characteristics so that it has m characteristics given by the coordinates of the m-vector, x. Measure the distance between two products, x and y, by a norm, denoted by $||x - y||$. A norm is a convex function homogeneous of degree one. Assume that the difference in unit value between x and y, denoted by $p(x) - p(y)$, that consumers are willing to pay satisfies

$$|p(x) - p(y)| = ||x - y||. \tag{d}$$

Let $q(x)$ denote the quantity demanded of type x and write the demand function

$$q(x) = G[p(x), s(x)], \tag{e}$$

where $s(x)$ is the number of customers who prefer type x. Assume that $q(x)$ varies inversely with $p(x)$ and directly with $s(x)$. Customers who prefer type x and buy type y instead do so because alternatives to y are more costly. The price they pay to the sellers of y is $p(y)$ and their implicit price is

$$p(x) - p(y) = ||x - y||. \tag{f}$$

The quantity they buy satisfies (e). Customers who prefer type x are indifferent among all other types that are equidistant from x as measured by the norm, which is in money terms. Proceeding in this way leads to a theory of the relations among substitutable products with many useful implications. It turns out that uncertainty and product change are conducive to competition because they tend to shorten the expected horizon and to decrease the punishment for a violation of a potential self-enforcing agreement.

enforcing. There are situations where the parties have an involuntary relation and the intervention of a third party may be necessary to protect the weaker members of the relation. For instance, small children cannot be said to enter into a voluntary agreement with their parents, and the state intervenes to protect them from parental abuse. The domain of the theory of self-enforcing agreement is the cases where there is voluntary consent among the parties. Even so, it may well happen that the probability of a continuing relation is too low to sustain a self-enforcing agreement. This will incline the parties to seek less costly alternatives if there are any. In the absence of such alternatives, no agreement will occur.

Many alternatives to a self-enforcing agreement have a common feature—a sum of money that will be paid or not depending on whether there is fulfillment of the terms. Thus, each party may deposit a sum of money or give an equivalent guarantee of that sum with the understanding that either stands to lose it to the other as a result of failure to abide by the agreement. There is the problem, however, that one party may claim, falsely, that the other has violated the agreement so that it can obtain the sum of money that is subject to forfeiture. Alternatively, there may be deferred payment. The party who would make the payment at the appropriate time may claim, falsely, that the other party has violated the agreement so that it should not receive the deferred payment. In these cases it may be necessary for a third party to intervene in order to settle disputes. A self-enforcing agreement has an object that is equivalent to a deferred payment or bond. This is the expected value of the future gains that is lost by the party who violates the implicit terms of a self-enforcing agreement.[8]

Deferred rebates, deferred wage or salary compensations, stock options, money back guarantees, security deposits in rentals, and posting bonds are among the alternatives to a self-enforcing agreement. Advertising outlays are another important example of an alternative. Such outlays create public awareness of a firm's products and are firm-specific capital that it can lose if the consumers believe that its products are unsatisfactory. Thus, the capital value of the advertising outlays are approximately equivalent to posting a bond as an assurance of satisfactory products.

VI. Conclusions

No one would enter an agreement expecting the other parties to violate it. In a self-enforcing agreement the only penalty that can be imposed on the violator is stopping the agreement. Therefore, aware of this, a

---

8. Becker and Stigler (1974) discuss alternatives to self-enforcing agreements apparently under the assumption that one of the parties to the agreement is honest and seeks ways to deter the dishonesty of the other party.

44   **Journal of Business**

potential violator compares the current gain from a violation with the sacrifice of future gains that will result in response to his current violation. These future gains would accrue to him were he to remain faithful to the agreement. He chooses the more profitable alternative. It follows that the parties to a self-enforcing agreement do not expect any violations of it. The terms of the agreement are such that adherence is more advantageous than violation. Were they to expect violations to be more profitable than adherence, they would not embark on the agreement in the first place.

From these premises follow important conclusions. First, self-enforcing agreements are not feasible if the sequence of occasions for transactions has a definite known last element. Although termination is certain to occur sooner or later, when this happens must be uncertain in order to sustain a self-enforcing agreement. Second, for a given sequence of gains, the expected horizon must be long enough or there can be no self-enforcing agreement. Equivalently, the longer is the expected horizon, the greater is the return to the parties from adherence to the terms of the agreement. Third, parties who have a self-enforcing agreement do not expect violations to occur. The theory explains violations of a self-enforcing agreement as the response to unexpected changes in the underlying factors that determine the terms of the agreement. Owing to these unexpected changes, there may be violations if the parties cannot find' mutually acceptable terms appropriate for the new conditions. This is to say that highly uncertain conditions are not conducive to self-enforcing agreements.

References

Becker, G. S., and Stigler, G. J. 1974. Law enforcement, malfeasance and compensation of enforcers. *Journal of Legal Studies* 3 (January): 1–18.

Cournot, A. 1960. *Researches into the Mathematical Principles of the Theory of Wealth.* Translated by Nathaniel Bacon from 1838 French ed., introductory essay by Irving Fisher. New York: Kelley.

Feller, W. 1962. *An Introduction to Probability Theory and Its Applications.* 2 vols. Vol. 1, 2d. ed. New York: Wiley.

Luce, R. D., and Raiffa, H. 1957. *Games and Decisions.* New York: Wiley.

Telser, L. G. 1972. *Competition, Collusion and Game Theory.* Chicago: Aldine-Atherton.

Telser, L. G. 1978. *Economic Theory and the Core.* Chicago: University of Chicago Press.

[23]

Journal of Institutional and Theoretical Economics (JITE) 149/1 (1993), 286–311
Zeitschrift für die gesamte Staatswissenschaft

Constitutions as Governance Structures:
The Political Foundations of Secure Markets

by

BARRY R. WEINGAST *

Thriving markets require not only an appropriately designed economic system, but a secure political foundation that places strong limits on the ability of the state to confiscate wealth. This requires a form of *limited government*, i.e., a state whose institutions credibly commit it to honor economic and political rights. To learn something about how this may be accomplished, this paper studies how limited government arose in states of the developed west. It focuses on the critical role of federalism for protecting markets in both England and the United States. Federalism proved fundamental to the impressive economic rise of England in the 18th century and the United States in the 19th and early 20th centuries. (JEL: N 2, N 4, O 2)

1. Introduction

Among the expanding frontiers of the New Institutional Economics (NIE) are a series of applications to politics and political choice. In the past decade, scholarship on two political problems has considerably profited from application of ideas from the NIE. The first is the study of bureaucratic and regulatory agency policymaking. Viewed in part as a problem of the delegation of political authority from elected officials to bureaucrats, creating a new bureau results in a variant on a problem familiar to the NIE, the separation of ownership and control. Once elected officials have delegated authority to bureaucrats, how are they to be assured that the latter will make decisions that are, in some sense, related to those they desire?[1] The second is the study of legislatures, asking how

---

* The author is senior fellow at the Hoover Institution and Professor of Political Science, Stanford University. He gratefully acknowledges Robert Bates, Peter Bernholz, Thomas Gilligan, Victor Goldberg, Gabrielle Montinola, Douglass North, Richard Posner, Douglas Rivers, Kenny Schultz, Urs Schweizer, and Kenneth Shepsle for helpful conversations and Paulina Favela for editorial assistance. This paper draws substantially on his recent work, WEINGAST [1992a] and especially [1992b].

[1] See, e.g., MOE [1990], KIEWIET and McCUBBINS [1991], McNOLLGAST [1989], and WEINGAST [1984].

149/1 (1993)   *Constitutions as Governance Structures*   287

the delegation of information collection and decisionmaking authority will be allocated and what effect this has on policy outcomes.[2]

My purpose in this article is to discuss a recent addition to the application of techniques from the NIE to politics, namely, questions concerning the role of political institutions in a society, and especially the constitution. The importance of this question is easily seen in the context of the predominant advice proffered by economists to the emerging democracies of Eastern Europe and the former Soviet Union. Focusing on economic reform, this advice charges the new states to "get prices right." This is a critical aspect of economic reform and cannot be neglected. Yet it alone cannot ensure success. Something is missing, for that advice ignores the way in which the economy is lodged in the political system. Though receiving considerably less attention than the form of the economic system, the relationship between the economic and political systems is equally critical for economic and democratic success.

Juxtaposed to the problem of "getting prices right" is what I call the *fundamental political dilemma of an economic system:* a government strong enough to protect property rights is also strong enough to confiscate the wealth of its citizens (WEINGAST [1992 b]). Thriving markets require not only the appropriate property rights system, an unfettered price mechanism, and a law of contracts, but a secure political foundation that limits the ability to the state to confiscate wealth by altering those rights and systems. How is this to be accomplished?

On the one hand, these are old problems. As BERNHOLZ [1993] observes, these were central concerns for Hobbes, Locke, and Montesquieu. On the other, little of this knowledge has been integrated into modern economics and seems to have had little impact on the advice being offered by economists to the emerging democracies.[3] In what follows, I suggest how this integration may take place by relying on the NIE.

Economic actors are concerned not only about the form of the economic system today, but about its form tomorrow. Even if a state begins with an appropriately specified set of economic mechanisms, the economy might fail due to the political risk generated by the possibility that the state will alter economic rights in the future. Historically, the problem was generated by a sovereign facing hard times (NORTH [1981, ch. 11], and SCHUMPETER [1919]). In Eastern Europe, it may well be a "democratic" state facing unexpected financial difficulties during the reform process (McKINNON [1991], LITWACK

---

[2] Cox and McCubbins [1992], Krehbiel [1991], and Weingast and Marshall [1988]. For a review, see Gilligan [1993].

[3] For example, of the eleven contributions by economists to the *Journal of Economic Perspective's* "Symposium on Economic Transition in the Soviet Union and Eastern Europe," (Fall 1991), this question is studied by only one scholar (Litwack [1991]) and raised by only one other (McKinnon [1991]). A small literature in political science and economic history raises these issue, e.g., North [1991], Ordeshook [1992], Przeworski [1991].

[1991]). The problem is that, as always, because markets create concentrations of wealth, that wealth is tempting for others to take, confiscate, or redistribute.

This implies that not only is the specification of the economy important, so too are its political foundations. The degree to which the new economic policies are durable is an essential component of the success of economic reform. Unless there is appropriate and credible protection against a major change in economic policy, economic reform may fail because the gains of economic agents are inadequately protected.

Inadequate attention to securing the political foundations of reform can create a form of *equilibrium trap* in which economic reform fails despite the apparently "correct" economic policies. The equilibrium trap may occur when the state cannot assure its citizens that it will stick to the reforms. This equilibrium trap is especially likely in the face of revenue problems combined with a citizenry clamoring for solutions to these problems – now. As McKINNON [1991] observes, such states will be pressured into a major "reintervention" into the economy to generate new revenues. Reinterventions may allow the state to address immediate problems, but they comprise long-run economic success. Of course, economic actors can anticipate this in advance, so that the uncertainty over economic policy generates *political risk*.

The problem is one of *credible commitment*, i.e., whether the restrictions on the state preventing massive economic intervention are binding in practice. The political risk underlying the equilibrium trap is generated by the inability of the state to credibly commit to its policies. Lacking such a commitment, citizens will not believe they are durable. The necessity to create a credible commitment to markets provides for the role of political institutions, and in particular, the constitution. Appropriately specified political institutions are the principal way in which states create credible limits on their own authority. These limits are absolutely critical to the success of markets. Because political institutions affect the degree to which economic markets are durable, they influence the level of political risk faced by economic actors. Attention to political institutions is thus essential to the success of an economic system.

In important respects the logic of politic institutions parallels that of economic institutions. To borrow Williamson's phrase, the political institutions of society create a "governance structure" that at once allows the society to deal with on-going problems as they arise and yet provides a degree of durability to economic and political rights. Importantly, these help limit the ability of the state to act opportunistically by confiscating wealth it had previously attempted to protect.

Understanding these issues requires a positive theory of constitutionalism.[4] For this purpose, I offer three principles of positive constitutionalism. The first

---

[4] Though no coherent, widely accepted approach exists to the positive theory of constitutionalism, many substantial contributions have been made. What follows draws on BRENNAN and BUCHANAN [1984], HARDIN [1989], NORTH [1991], ORDESHOOK [1992], and WEINGAST [1992b].

149/1 (1993)   *Constitutions as Governance Structures*   289

is that a constitution must provide for its own preservation, i.e., it must provide a set of incentives that address the question of why its constraints are observed. This requires that the constitution be *self-enforcing,* i.e., that its constraints provide credible commitments that political actors find it in their interests to respect.

The second principle of positive constitutionalism is that democracy alone is not enough. As positive political theorists have long shown, there are a large set of problems with unconstrained majority rule.[5] Most notably, the absence of a majority rule equilibrium means that no policy is stable. This implies that markets are not politically stable under majority rule. In and of itself, instituting democracy alone is insufficient to protect markets.[6]

The third principle puts the second one in a more positive light: institutions that limit majority choices are a necessary component to establishing and maintaining guarantees for economic and political rights.[7] As we study below, the problem is not simply inventing constraints on politics, but doing so in a way that makes them credible.

To learn something about how constitutions provide credible commitments in practice, I turn to an examination of how a subset of nations have done so in the past. In what follows, I focus on the institution of federalism.[8] The first observation to make about federalism is that, for the past 300 years, the richest state in the world has had a federal structure: the Netherlands from the late 16th century through the mid-17th century; England from the late 17th century or early 18th through the mid-19th century; and the United States from the late 19th century through the mid to late 20th century. This association is not accidental.

To demonstrate this, this paper studies a subset of federal systems called *market-preserving federalism.* These systems are characterized by the decentral-

---

[5] See ORDESHOOK [1992] and RIKER [1980], [1982]. This result has a long history and involves four decades of results from social choice theory. Starting with Arrow and Black in the late 1940s and early 1950s, important contributions have been made by Cohen, Hinich, Kramer, McKelvey, Ordeshook, Riker, Schofield, and Schwartz. Specific references may be found in the above citations.

[6] This holds even if nearly all citizens not only support economic reform but wish to maintain it. The problem is that, in the context of revenue problems, different citizens have different tradeoffs between solving today's problems and the long-term economic success. Those whose wealth is tied up in the latter will prefer little sacrifice of long-term growth. But those with little wealth and who are hungry will be more willing to redistribute the wealth of others, particular in the context of a crisis.

[7] This result has a long history. For the case of theories of majority rule, see RIKER [1980]; for Congress, SHEPSLE and WEINGAST [1987]; for the judiciary, LANDES and POSNER [1975]; for policy in general, McNOLLGAST [1989] and MOE [1990]; and for constitutions, HOLMES [1988], ORDESHOOK [1992], and WEINGAST [1992b]. Of course, restrictions on majority sovereignty was a major theme of the Federalists (see HAMMOND and MILLER [1989]).

[8] This does not imply that federalism is the only institution that will serve this purpose, nor that it alone provides a complete credible commitment.

ization of regulatory authority over the market and the absence of prohibitions against goods and services from other jurisdictions. The effects of market-preserving federalism have been known for some time.[9] These include the now familiar argument about the decentralization of political power: because no government or jurisdiction has a monopoly over regulation of the market, it induces political competition among jurisdictions, competition that limits the ability of any one state to impose debilitating regulation. If one state tries, then mobile resources will move. This not only implies that jurisdiction loses population, resources and tax base, but it gives firms in other jurisdictions a competitive advantage.

Although the effects of market-preserving federalism are well-known, less well-understood is the central problem of this paper. How does federalism survive? Given market-preserving federalism's strong effect, what prevents the federal government from over-awing the states, i.e., from overturning or ignoring the restrictions of federalism and then intervening? Paradoxically, federalism creates pressure for its own destruction. After all, if under federalism it is nearly impossible for an interest group to capture a majority in all fifty states of the United States (as OSTROM [1987] observes), then what prevents that group from appealing to the federal government? What is it that makes the federal government unresponsive to these political appeals, whereas, a unitary or nonfederal government presumably would? The answer must go beyond the "parchment barrier," i.e., that the constitution prohibits this, since constitutional provisions can be ignored or altered.

To address these issues, this essay proceeds as follows. Section 2 describes the political theory of market-preserving federalism. Section 3 discusses the role of market-preserving federalism in the economic development of Great Britain and the United States. Section 4 takes the first step toward answering the deeper question of the political foundations of federalism – i.e., what made it and its restrictions credible? It does so by describing a model of the forces that help a state observe a given set of constraints on its power. The approach is then applied to England before and after the Glorious Revolution of 1688–89. Section 5 analyzes how federalism was sustained in England. This section also explores the evolution of a civil society and the rule of law. My conclusions follow.

2. A Political Theory of Federalism[10]

The essence of federalism is that it provides a viable system of political decentralization. In his seminal work on the political theory of federalism, RIKER

---

[9] See, e.g., ARANSON [1991], CASELLA and FREY [1992] and SCOTCHMER [1990].

[10] This section draws on the work of ARANSON [1991], RIKER [1964] and WEINGAST [1992a].

[1964, 11] defines a political system as federal if it has three characteristics: a *hierarchy* of governments, i.e., "two levels of governments rule the same land and people"; a *delineated scope of authority* so that each level of government is autonomous in its own, well-defined sphere of political authority; and a *guarantee of autonomy* of each government in its own sphere of authority. In what follows, I focus on a subset of federal systems called *market-preserving federalism*. A federal system is market-preserving if it has a fourth characteristic, called the *locus of economic regulatory authority*, which requires, first, that the authority to regulate markets is not vested with the highest political government in the hierarchy; and second, that the lower governments are prevented from using their regulatory authority to erect trade barriers against the goods and services from other political units.

All four characteristics play an important part in federalism's market-preserving role. The first two are clearly defining characteristics that establish minimal or necessary conditions for a federal system. But they alone are not sufficient. The reason is that federal systems are not generally viable if they are based solely on the discretion of the highest political authority since that delegation of power can always be reversed. As Riker observes, a central problem for federal systems is that the highest or central government may *overawe* the lower units. A viable system of federalism must therefore prevent this. The first three characteristics define a system of political decentralization. They say nothing about the authority over economic issues, however. To have market-preserving economic effects, federalism must also limit the central government's authority to make economic policy; this authority must be placed in the hands of the lower political units.

2.1 Economic Consequences of Market-Preserving Federalism

The economic consequences of market-preserving federalism, explored by HAYEK [1939], [1960] and made famous by TIEBOUT [1956], are sufficiently well-known that they need only be briefly described here.[11] The first effect of market-preserving federalism is that the prohibition on economic regulation at the highest level implies that privately valuable, politically created monopoly rights and restrictions cannot be established for the entire economy all at once. The second, and perhaps the best studied effect of market-preserving federalism, is the induced competition among lower units of the federal structure. As long as capital and labor are mobile, market-preserving federalism constrains the lower units in their attempts to place political limits on economic activity since resources will move to other jurisdictions.

The literature on the economic effects of federalism yields two principal conclusions about public policy choice. First, political competition implies that

---

[11] ARANSON [1991] provides the statement of the economic effects of federalism. For summaries of recent models, see CASELLA and FREY [1992] and SCOTCHMER [1990].

only those economic restrictions that citizens are willing to pay-for will survive. Were a jurisdiction to respond to political pressure by attempting to cartelize an industry, the mobility of labor implies that it will relocate in more compatible jurisdictions. If a jurisdiction attempts to confiscate the wealth of an industry, the mobility of capital implies that firms will relocate. The mobility of resources thus provides an economic cost to those jurisdictions that attempt to establish certain policies. Jurisdictions will therefore do so only if the political benefits are worth these and other costs.

Political competition implies that jurisdictions will compete for residents and economic activities via their menus of public policies. Residents and economic actors make location decisions based on those menus. This yields a diversity of public goods with some jurisdictions providing lower taxes and lower level of public goods and others with higher taxes and higher level of public goods.[12]

Federalism thus greatly diminishes the level and pervasiveness of economic rent-seeking and hence the formation of distributional coalitions. Competition among the lower units limits the success from rent-seeking. Because rent-seeking type regulation can only be local, it provides firms outside that locale with a competition advantage over those being regulated.

2.2 Sustaining Market-Preserving Federalism

Economic analysis of federalism take the structure of federalism's division of political authority as given (WEINGAST [1992a]). For purposes of understanding the effects of an on-going and viable system of federalism, that assumption is reasonable as it bypasses the question of why the system of federalism is viable. In terms of the political theory of federalism, the economic analysis of federalism ignores how Riker's third characteristic is achieved. While I postpone until section 4 the discussion of how it is achieved in practice, the above discussion can be used to demonstrate why it is necessary.

The beneficial economic consequences of federalism result from the political decentralization of economic authority that induces competition among the lower political units. Some guarantee to the central government's lack of political authority to regulate is essential to this system's success. Were the structure of political authority solely the consequence of a discretionary decision by the higher authority, the beneficial effect could not be realized. Because the forces of competition limit the efficaciousness of rent-seeking strategies at the lower political levels, if the central political authorities have the discretion to remove the authority from the lower levels, those interests seeking intervention will appeal to the central government. Rent-seeking under these circumstances would proceed in a two-step process. The central government would first assert power over the issue, and then change the relevant economic regulation.

---

[12] Here too, qualifications to the general results have appeared, see, notably, ARANSON [1991].

Without a mechanism to prevent this action at the central level, federalism would be neither viable nor market-preserving. In order for market-preserving federalism to have its intended economic consequences, the third condition is essential: something must guarantee the limits on the central government's authority to regulate directly, to usurp that authority, or to simply remove its earlier grant of that authority to the lower levels.

3. Market-Preserving Federalism in Practice

3.1 England

Federalism is rarely used to describe the British system, in large part because it lacks political divisions corresponding to states, lander or cantons. Nonetheless, by the criteria provided in section 2, it was a *de facto*, federal system. First, the national and local governments were important and distinct sources of political authority. Second, by the beginning of the 18th century, the national government was limited in its ability to regulate the domestic economy.[13] The constitutional changes made over the previous century and solidified in the Glorious Revolution (1688–89) abolished, greatly restricted – or granted jointly to parliament and the crown – many of the powers used by the deposed Stuart kings. Throughout the Stuarts' reign, rent-seeking activity was prevalent (EKELUND and TOLLISON [1981]), and part of these constitutional changes were aimed at preventing it.

The independent power of local governments over economic matters – and hence federalism – played a critical role in fostering the industrial revolution. The importance of the induced competition among localities is revealed by its effects on the pattern of local economic controls. In nearly all the established commercial centers of England, production was controlled via local regulatory laws. Various industries and professions, for example, were governed by gilds whose regulatory controls limited competition, pricing, entry, and training. These constraints handicapped potential entrants, including those attempting to devise new forms of economic activity or to promote significant innovation for existing activities.

As economic historians emphasize, one of the central factors underlying the industrial revolution was the absence of enforcement of these restrictions (see MOKYR [1988]). Yet that absence was neither uniform nor accidental (see HARTWELL [1971] and esp. NORTH [1981, ch. 12]). As is well-known, industrialization did not proceed in the established commercial centers but in the north instead. This pattern of economic activity occurred because local political officials in the north were willing to ignore, evade, or remove regulatory restric-

---

[13] The international economy was heavily controlled, as the well-known corn laws attest, but that is another matter.

tions in force elsewhere.[14] In an effort to evade local economic restrictions, many of the new entrepreneurs so critical to the industrial revolution located in areas traditionally outside the commercial orbit.

England's market-preserving federalism fostered economic growth during the industrial revolution in two ways. First, precluding the national government's authority to regulate economic activity prevented it from responding to efforts by the established economic interests to provide national controls that would have effectively prevented many of the new industrial activities. In this sense, 18th century England differed considerably from Stuart England of the 17th century.[15] Second, the induced political competition among local jurisdictions implied that some localities were willing to take on the extra burdens in exchange for the prospects of generating new forms of economic activity, local employment, and taxes. The absence of this politically-induced avenue of economic innovation would have significantly hindered the industrial revolution. Federalism thus played a crucial role in the *political* foundation of the industrial revolution.

3.2 The United States

The U.S. Constitution granted the states the power to provide their citizens with various forms of public goods. The historical record shows they took advantage of these powers in different ways (HANDLIN and HANDLIN [1947], HARTZ [1948], HUGHES [1977]). The Constitution also allowed states to respond to interest groups and distributional coalitions, but limited their influence to particular states. Federalism provided strong limits on the degree to which these coalitions could impose uniform national regulations.

One of the Constitution's central pillars in its protection of markets was the commerce clause.[16] This clause prevented states from regulating interstate markets and from erecting various forms of trade barriers. It also limited federal regulation to problems truly national in scope, an authority not exer-

---

[14] As one of the foremost scholars of the industrial revolution, T. S. Ashton, concludes: "It is beyond doubt that employers often transferred their activities from corporate towns in order to escape from restrictions imposed by privileged groups of workers, or from municipal regulations as to labour... [T]he movement of industry was rarely induced by the prospect of lower wages in the new area. Quite the reverse: 'we daily see manufacturers leaving the places where wages are low and removing to others where they are high,' it was said in 1752." (ASHTON [1955, 94]).

[15] Indeed, as ROOT [1992] shows, the reaction of French political institutions was exactly the opposite of that in England. French courts, for example, helped the gilds extend their reach into the countryside. In contrast, local justices of the peace refused to do so in England.

[16] For a discussion of this issue, see ARANSON [1991]. The commerce clause was not the sole clause designed for this purpose (e.g., the privileges and immunities clause).

cised via direct intervention in domestic markets for the first 100 years of the Constitution.

With its provision for the strong protection of property rights and an absence of regulation, the Constitution created one of the largest common markets in the world. The Constitutional limits on state and federal governments served as the critical political foundation for the enormous expansion of the economy during the 19th century. By mid-century, the pattern of interregional trade had transformed the nation from one of largely self-sufficient farmers at the time of the Constitution to one of striking regional – and international – economic specialization (NORTH [1961], FOGEL [1989]). The growth in national wealth reflected this pattern of specialization.

The pattern of specialization produced a tripartite economy (NORTH [1961], FOGEL [1989]). The South specialized in the production of cotton and other exports. During the early part of the century, strong and growing international demand for cotton proved the "engine of American economic growth" (NORTH [1961], LEE and PASSELL [1979]). The Northeast specialized in providing commercial services, e.g., transporting cotton to European markets. It also provided insurance, marketing, and other financial services attending the growth and delivery of these exports. The Northwest, largely self-sufficient at first, increasingly came to specialize in growing food. These crops were shipped south along the water routes and, increasingly over time, east via canals and railroads for eastern markets. On the eve of the Civil War, a large portion of midwestern farmers were specialists in international markets, producing grain bound for Europe (BOGUE [1963], FOGEL [1989]). After the interruption of the Civil War, this growth and specialization continued. By century's end, the United States was the richest nation in the world.

Economic historians have, by and large, taken the relatively unregulated aspect of the thriving markets of the 19th century for granted (see, e.g., LEE and PASSELL [1979] and FOGEL [1989]; an important exception is TEMIN [1991]). Neoclassical economics, taking property rights as given, proceeds as if the secure economic rights in the 19th century were inevitable or immutable characteristics of the United States. This presumption is false. The striking degree to which they proved immutable in practice demands, instead, an explanation.

American economic growth reflected the absence of regulatory controls that would have hindered the growth of interstate trade and regional specialization. The absence of such controls was not due to lack of demand for intervention, however. Just as today we observe a host of displaced economic interests providing political support for intervention to halt or reverse the economic changes accompanying economic growth, so too did such groups advocate political intervention to limit economic change. Thus, commercial agents along the traditional water transportation routes fought the growth of the railroads. Cattle producers in upstate New York sought relief from cheaper producers farther west. Nascent manufacturers in the Northeast fought cheap land policy at the federal level because lower prices increased westward migration rates.

The New Institutional Economics of Markets

Barry R. Weingast JITE

Although the reasons varied from case to case, these interests were by and large unsuccessful in their attempts to gain beneficial legislation.[17]

The American common market's secure political foundation limited the ability of state and federal governments from responding to distributional coalitions. The absence of debilitating regulatory intervention critically depended on this foundation. For well over a century, interregional markets were not only unregulated but *protected from regulation* by the Constitution's constraints. As emphasized above, federalism played a central role in these constraints.[18]

4. The Evolution of a Civil Society in England

England's decentralized political authority over local economic regulation proved critical to the industrial revolution. This section examines a critical aspect of the English system that helps account for the absence of national controls. A range of elements contributed to this result. First, among all states in early modern Europe, England had the strongest tradition of private property rights. Second, after the Glorious Revolution, Parliament served as a political counterbalance to the crown, by and large opposing national economic intervention. Third and most important from our standpoint, was the rise of a civil society and the rule of law at the end of the 17th century whereby a consensus emerged opposing national economic intervention.

Our central concern is the limits on sovereign or state power. We assume that all citizens have opinions and views about these limits and hence about what acts violate them. In other words, citizens have views about what state actions are legitimate and what constitute a fundamental transgression of their rights. These concepts are defined here for an individual, not for the society. No automatic mechanism is assumed to create a societal consensus about such views. Citizens may have widely different beliefs about these limits and about fundamental transgressions.

4.1 The Model

The model is developed more fully in WEINGAST [1992c]. It is based on two assumptions about the relationship between a sovereign and his citizens. First, a necessary condition for an individual citizen to support the sovereign is that

---

[17] On the railroads, see MILLER [1971]; on northeastern interests and immigration policy, see PASSELL and SCHMUNDT [1971]; more generally, see CHANDLER [1977] for a systematic study of these in the second half of the 19th century.

[18] This form of the constitutional underpinning of the common market has not lasted until the present, changing dramatically during the 1930s. Those changes – and their effects – are another story.

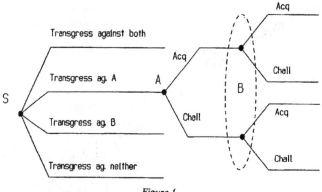

Figure 1

he not transgress that citizen's rights. Second, remaining in power requires that the sovereign retains a sufficient degree of support among the citizenry. Without the necessary support, the sovereign loses power. Suppose there is a single sovereign, S, and two groups of citizens, A and B. The groups of citizens have different views about the legitimate boundaries of the state and hence what actions by the sovereign are considered a fundamental violation of their rights. To survive, the sovereign needs to retain the support of at least one of the two groups in order to retain power.

The sequence of actions in this game is shown in figure 1. S moves first and may choose to attempt to transgress against both A and B,-against A alone, against B alone, or against neither. After S moves, A and B move simultaneously.[19] Each may choose to acquiesce or to challenge the sovereign. Challenging is costly; moreover, each may challenge even if the sovereign has not transgressed. If both A and B challenge, the sovereign is deposed. Any transgression attempted by the sovereign is rebuffed. If only one group of citizens challenges S, the challenge fails and any transgression attempt by S succeeds. Of course, if both A and B acquiesce, any attempted transgression succeeds.

The payoffs from this game are given in table 1. Power is valuable to the sovereign, and he loses 1 if he is deposed. Successful transgressions are also valuable to him and are worth 2 each. A transgression against either group costs that group 3, reflecting the fact that there are economic costs associated with transgressions, e.g., a loss of wealth. Challenging costs each challenger 1 regardless of whether it is successful.

---

[19] The simultaneous move between A and B is shown in the figure as A moving first followed by B, but, as indicated by the dashed ellipse or "information set" around B's two nodes, where B does not know A's decision when he must choose.

Table 1

Payoffs for the Sovereign-Constituency Transgression Game.

S chooses		Induced subgame between A & B (payoffs: S, A, B)

transgress against both

			B acq	B chall
A	acq		5, 1, 1	5, 1, 0
	chall		5, 0, 1	0, 3, 3

transgress against A

			B acq	B chall
A	acq		3, 1, 4	3, 1, 3
	chall		3, 0, 4	0, 3, 3

transgress against B

			B acq	B chall
A	acq		3, 4, 1	3, 4, 0
	chall		3, 3, 1	0, 3, 3

transgress against neither

			B acq	B chall
A	acq		1, 4, 4	1, 4, 3
	chall		1, 3, 4	0, 3, 3

Outcomes are determined by the strategy combinations chosen by the three players. If S attempts to transgress against both A and B and both acquiesce, the transgression succeeds and the payoffs are: 5 to S, 1 to A, and 1 to B. If S attempts to transgress against both A and B and both challenge, the transgression fails and the king loses power, resulting in payoffs of 0, 3, 3. The Pareto optimal outcome for society occurs when no transgressions or challenges are attempted (the parties obtain 1, 4, and 4, respectively).

The structure of this game resembles that of the prisoner's dilemma, in part because responding to transgressions is costly to each citizen group. Consider the set of incentives facing the citizens if S attempts to transgress against B. Naturally, B prefers that both challenge. On the other hand, A has a dominant strategy: no matter what strategy B plays, A prefers to acquiesce. Knowing this, B will acquiesce.

This structure of interaction allows the sovereign to transgress some citizens' rights and survive.[20] In the one-shot game, there are three pure strategy equilibria. Which equilibria occurs depends in part upon the reaction functions of the citizens groups to a transgression. The worst outcome for the citizens – where the sovereign transgresses against both – is an equilibrium; the Pareto optimal strategy combination with no transgressions is not. The former holds because citizens acquiesce whenever they are the target of a transgression: acting alone and taking the behavior of the others as given, each citizen group can only increase its costs by challenging but it cannot change the outcome.

In two other equilibria (depending upon which citizen group S chooses as a target), A and B challenge S if and only if both are the targets of a transgression. Suppose that S chooses to target B in every period and that A and B respond as just suggested. Then S has no incentive to deviate: transgressing against both leads to being deposed; transgressing against A instead of B is no better; and transgressing against neither leaves him worse off. Furthermore, neither citizen group has an incentive to deviate. For A this conclusion has already been demonstrated. For B, it follows because it can do no better. Given that it alone is the target and thus that A will not challenge, challenging will not change the outcome but will increase its costs. Hence B is better off acquiescing if it alone is the target.

The situation is more complicated when this game is repeated, i.e., when the interaction between the sovereign and citizens is on-going. Given the structure of payoffs, the "folk-theorem" applies, implying that virtually any outcome can be sustained as an equilibrium of the repeated game (FUDENBERG and MASKIN [1986]). Any of the equilibria of the one-shot game is an equilibrium of the repeated game. Moreover, the folk-theorem implies that the Pareto optimal outcome can be sustained. The reason concerns the behavior of each citizen group when the sovereign attempts to transgress against the other. Repetition provides the opportunity for citizens not only to punish the sovereign, but to punish one-another. The Pareto optimal outcome is supported by both groups challenging the sovereign when the sovereign attempts to transgress against either. That behavior can be supported under repeat play because players can use "trigger" strategies to punish one another for failure to cooperate. If, say, A fails to challenge the sovereign when the latter attempts to transgress against B, then B can retaliate by failing in the future to challenge the sovereign whenever the sovereign attempts to transgress against A. This behavior by B allows the sovereign to transgress successfully against A. B's trigger strategy provides A with the following strategy choice. It can acquiesce today, avoiding

---

[20] Throughout we use the concept of subgame perfection as the equilibrium concept, defined as follows. A *strategy* is a specification of the action a player will take at every branch of the game tree. An *equilibrium* is a set of strategy combinations such that no player has an incentive to deviate given the strategies of others. The equilibrium is *subgame perfect* if it remains an equilibrium when restricted to every subgame.

the cost of 1, and then face losing 3 in all future periods; or it can challenge today, costing 1 but maintaining 3 in all future periods. Clearly, when A does not discount the future too heavily, it will prefer the latter, so that B's threat strategy induces A to challenge the sovereign when the latter attempts to transgress against B alone.

The existence of multiple equilibrium implies that the Pareto optimal outcome is not the only equilibrium. Although normatively attractive, that equilibrium will not inevitably occur. The game might instead yield any of the three equilibria of the one-shot game, allowing successful transgressions against some or all citizens. In these equilibria, the sovereign may transgress the rights of some citizens while retaining the support of others. This is a stable pattern, and none of the players, acting alone, can change it.

The implications of multiple equilibria are as follows (see FEREJOHN [1990] and WEINGAST [1992c]). Suppose there is a diversity of preferences over outcomes, especially if citizens' economic circumstances differ considerably – some might be wealthy elites; others, successful commercial agents or economic entrepreneurs; others, farmers who own their land; still others, peasants who work land they do not own. Under these circumstances, the range of opinions about the appropriate role of the state and what actions constitute a transgression is likely to be quite broad. Because there is no natural mechanism to produce a consensus on these issues, the most natural equilibrium of the game is the asymmetric one. Put another way, the diversity of interests provides an impediment to the development of the pareto optimal equilibrium, making it more likely that the game will result in one of the asymmetric equilibrium in which the sovereign transgresses the rights of some and retains the support of others.

Substantial impediments hinder the ability of citizens to police the sovereign. When their views about the nature of the state and of citizen duty diverge, it is possible for the sovereign to form a coalition with one group of citizens against another, allowing the sovereign to transgress boundaries considered fundamental by other citizens. Policing a state or sovereign is thus a form of a coordination problem, i.e., of coordinating citizens' views about the appropriate role and limits of the states. In this setting, it is possible for a constitution to serve as a coordinating device, i.e., to help coordinate citizens' strategy choices so that they can attain the Pareto optimal outcome.[21] Problems of this type can be solved by a coordinating device because citizens understand that the outcome depends upon mutually compatible expectation (see, e.g., MILGROM and ROBERTS [1992]). When the problem is deciding on what those may be, an appropriately chosen set of public rules can play that role. Of course, the availability of such a device in principle does not tell us what circumstances may be used in practice.

---

[21] This point is made generally by HARDIN [1989] and, in the current context, by WEINGAST [1992b].

This argument also implies that, for those issues over which citizens agree about the nature of a transgression, the Pareto optimal outcome can be supported. When the state of agreement in society is large, producing something approaching a consensus, a sovereign who attempts to transgress against citizens cannot survive.

4.2 Application of the Model to the Glorious Revolution

To see the value of this approach to the problems of policing the state, we turn to a brief discussion of the constitutional changes following the Glorious Revolution in England and the rise of a national consensus about the appropriate boundaries of the state (see WEINGAST [1992 d] for greater details). The 17th century was one of considerable political turmoil. Within a decade of the accession of the Stuarts in 1603, problems emerged between the sovereign and a subset of citizens. This century also included a Civil War and the beheading of the king (1640s), a restoration of the monarchy (1660), and the Glorious Revolution (1688–89) which deposed the last of the Stuart kings, James II, in favor of William and Mary.

Citizens were deeply divided throughout this century over the role of the sovereign, the appropriate limits on state behavior, and the benefits of various public policies. By century's end, two political coalitions, the Tories and the Whigs, had emerged. Whigs tended to focus on commercial activities, favoring secure property rights, low and stable taxes on economic activity, and an activist profile in international relations to promote and defend their economic claims around the world. They also sought explicit limits on sovereign behavior. Tories, on the other hand, cared much less about commercial activity, wanted a low international presence, and preferred low and stable taxes on land, their primary source of wealth. They also strongly supported the Church of England and opposed explicit limits on the crown. The two factions also differed in their views over citizens duties in the face of undesirable acts by the sovereign. Whigs held a Lockean notion, arguing that sovereign power was granted by citizens and that therefore it could be withheld. Tories, in contrast, argued for the notion of passive obedience to the sovereign.[22]

Throughout the era of the late Stuarts (from the Restoration to the Glorious Revolution) and especially by the mid-1670s, the Tories supported the crown while the Whigs opposed it. Moreover, the late Stuarts transgressed significant rights of the Whigs while retaining support of the Tories. In its campaign to "pack the constituencies," the crown attempted to disenfranchise the major sources of Whig opposition. JONES [1972, 47], for example, reports that of the

---

[22] As MILLER [1992, 64] suggests, "Tories argued (conventionally enough) that, as the powers of kings came from God, resistance to kingly authority could never be justified: if a king maltreated his subjects, they should accept that maltreatment with the same fortitude as the primitive Christians under the pagan Roman emperors."

104 former Whig strongholds rechartered between 1681 and 1685, only one returned a Whig to the next parliament in 1685. By the mid-1680s, the king had successfully violated the Whigs' rights of representation while retaining the support of the Tories.

In the mid-1680s, however, King James II became embroiled in a dispute with his own constituents. In reaction, he attempted to use the same political weapons against the Tories that he had used against the Whigs. While this attempt nearly succeeded, it ended in dismal failure. The result was a united political nation against James II, forcing him to flee.

Going far beyond a simple coup, the Glorious Revolution also resulted in significant constitutional change. In particular, the Tories came to agree with the Whigs that explicit limits on the sovereign and the state were required. While the two coalitions disagreed about the content and role of these limits, they agreed that not only were limits necessary, but so too was a consensus about those limits. The result was the Revolution Settlement passed by Parliament in early 1689. From our standpoint, the key is the Bill of Rights. This document both identified those actions of the previous sovereign that constituted fundamental violations of citizens rights and provided a list of activities the sovereign could no longer undertake.

A new consensus also emerged on the notion of citizen duty. With its conditional grant of authority to the crown, the Revolution Settlement implied a fundamentally different view of that duty. The new consensus held that support for the sovereign could be withdrawn if the sovereign violated the Revolution Settlement's terms.

The model described above provides a useful way to understand these events. Prior to the Revolution, citizens fundamentally disagreed not only about what actions they considered fundamental violations of their rights, but about citizen duty in the face of such violations. Marked divisions in 17th century England reflected the absence of consensus about critical matters such as the role of the state, the limit of sovereign power, citizen duty, and the appropriate definition of economic and political rights. The diversity of interests and preferences allowed the crown to transgress rights held as fundamental by the Whigs as long as the Tories were willing to acquiesce. This described the situation from at least the mid-1670s through the mid-1680s. This situation was seemingly stable, reflecting the nature of the asymmetric equilibrium of the game. James's move against his own constituents broke this pattern, losing him the support required to retain power. Not only was he removed from power, but his actions caused a wholesale and speedy revision in opinions about fundamental issues. This led to the construction of a new consensus that provided a clearer and nearly uniformly held definition of the legitimate actions of the state and of citizen duty.

In terms of the Revolution Settlement served as a device coordinating not only citizens' views about the legitimate boundaries of the state, but about their expectations of one-anothers' behavior. The model helps us interpret the implied changes in behavior. The new consensus was critical to preventing further transgressions. The constitutional changes in the form of the Bill of Rights defined what actions constituted a fundamental transgression. Despite contentious arguments over what should be included, the Bill of Rights received overwhelming support within Parliament from both Whigs and Tories. The effect of coordination among the English citizenry is reflected in the words of the 19th century American Supreme Court Justice, Joseph Bradley. He observed that a constitutional violation "would produce a revolution in an hour." [23] This is precisely the reaction predicted by the model.

The new boundaries on the state were both explicit and consensual. As such they fundamentally altered the game among the citizenry and the new sovereign. For many of the most central political issues of the era, a single set of limits on sovereign behavior had emerged. This process resulted in a set of shared beliefs about what constituted a fundamental transgression by the state and about what citizens should do in the face of these transgressions. These shared beliefs implied that citizens would react in concert against any future sovereign transgression, thus ensuring that their political and economic rights were more secure.

5. Market-Preserving "Federalism" and the Rule of Law in England

The approach described in the previous section helps explain what preserved federalism in 18th century England. It also helps us understand the rise of a civil society and hence of the rule of law. These are considered in turn.

Market-Preserving Federalism. Given the distinct hierarchy in English government, the main question as to whether post-Glorious Revolution England was characterized by market-preserving federalism concerns the limits on national regulatory authority. Because of the experiences with the Stuarts, especially with the campaign to pack the constituencies, national decisions with respect to regulation were dramatically altered after the Glorious Revolution. Citizens more closely guarded local power, authority, and autonomy. Looking backward, English citizens jealously guarded their local powers as a means of preserving their rights of representation in Parliament. Because violating local political liberty had been a principal factor in the Revolution, citizens throughout England were wary of national changes in their authority. MILLER [1992, 53] reports that:

"The right, in most towns, to practice a particular trade or take part in municipal government was confined to a comparatively restricted group of craftsmen and traders possessing the 'freedom' of their town or craft guild which gave them rights denied to other citizens. Municipal and other corporations (including colleges and universities) had been granted (usually by the Crown) the right to a measure of control over their own affairs: here 'freedom' meant immunity from outside intervention."

---

[23] Bradley's dissent in *The Slaughter House Cases* (1873).

As argued above, this local liberty proved critical to the economic changes of the 18th century.[24] The consequence was not only a consensus about the limits of national regulatory authority and the importance of local autonomy, but the freedom to embrace the new, enterprising entrepreneurs and, hence, to help facilitate the industrial revolution.

The rule of law. The notions of legitimacy and transgressions were defined above only for individuals. In contrast, most discussions of legitimacy and the civil society focus on the societal level, i.e., on the collectivity (ALMOND and VERBA [1963], HUNTINGTON [1969], PRZEWORSKI [1990], RABUSHKA and SHEPSLE [1972]; see also HAYEK [1960]). For example, ALMOND and VERBA [1963] and RABUSHKA and SHEPSLE [1972] investigate the question, how do stable democracies differ from both unstable ones and non-democracies? Almond and Verba's answer is, in part, that the former societies are characterized by a set of shared attitudes or beliefs which they call the "civic culture." These beliefs centered on the role of government, legitimacy, and the duty of citizens. Unstable and non-democracies were characterized by an absence of a system of shared beliefs and opinions.[25]

Our approach provides an explanation for these findings. The equilibria of the game correspond closely to the phenomena studied by ALMOND and VERBA [1963] and RABUSHKA and SHEPSLE [1972]. When citizens have diverse views about the nature of transgressions, it is difficult to police sovereign or state behavior. On the other hand, when they hold similar notions about the appropriate boundaries of the state, state behavior can be policed. As illustrated by the discussion of the Glorious Revolution, citizens cannot protect political rights against encroachment if their notion of those rights fundamentally differ. In those circumstances the state can undermine the fundamental pillars of a democratic society – e.g., the right of some or all citizens to vote – and still survive. The model thus shows why the set of common attitudes and understandings about legitimacy is crucial to the success and maintenance of democracy. As ALMOND and VERBA [1963] showed, they are intimately related.

Our model provides an approach to the microfoundations of the *rule of law*, i.e., a stable society of laws, not of discretionary political power. Respecting

---

[24] Two other factors also influenced these limits (WEINGAST [1992c]). First, the clear and final elevation of the common law courts as the protector and promoter of private property rights effectively removed many of these decisions from the political realm. The history of these courts under the Stuarts reveal them as staunch defenders of private rights against intervention by the state. Second, the changing political relationships among the state, the Whigs, and the Tories also played a role. The Whigs retained their views about limits on the state. As the Tories became the political minority, they also became the chief proponents of limits on sovereign authority in order to protect themselves (BREWER [1989]). This helped solidify the national consensus about limits on the state.

[25] A range of other scholars present similar conclusions. RABUSHKA and SHEPSLE [1972], e.g., focus on "plural societies," i.e., those characterized by a diversity of ethnic, religious or racial groups. See WEINGAST [1992c].

agreed upon limits on the state is clearly a central aspect of the rule of law. Like culture, the rule of law is a societal characteristic. And yet, as our approach suggests, whether a society is characterized by the rule of law depends upon the attitude and behavior of individuals.

Most works studying it emphasize that it depends on a set of institutions (e.g., HAYEK [1960]) or that it reflects specific components of a larger set of cultural attitudes making up the civil society (e.g., ALMOND and VERBA [1963]). Our approach shows that the rule of law depends on both (see also NORTH [1992]). Institutions (such as federalism and the constitution as a coordinating device) and the attitudes and opinions of citizens (such as a consensus that the constitution represents the legitimate boundaries of the state) are both essential. As emphasized throughout this paper, the appropriate set of political institutions is important for maintaining boundaries on state behavior. But they alone are incapable of producing a government that adheres to them. Because rules can be disobeyed or ignored, something must be added to police deviations. Our approach argues that the foundation for institutional restriction fundamentally rests on the attitudes of citizens.

Put another way, the approach shows that a society characterized by the rule of law has two interrelated characteristics. First, it possesses institutions that limit and define the legitimate boundaries of state action. Second, these institutions are themselves maintained in part by a set of shared beliefs among citizens who react against the state when the latter attempts to transgress the boundaries defined by those institutions.

The social mechanisms underpinning the rule of law provided the means by which the English secured their political and economic rights. Developing the consensus about the legitimate boundaries of the state seemed crucial to policing the state and hence in preserving a constitution protecting individual rights.

6. Conclusions

The political foundations of economic markets are critical to their success. The fundamental political dilemma of an economic system is that a state strong enough to protect private markets is strong enough to confiscate the wealth of its citizens. The dilemma implies that attention must be given to the question, what guides the state down the former path? As NORTH [1993, 11–12] argues:

"Throughout most of history and in much of the present world[,] institutions have not provided the credible commitment necessary for the development of low cost transacting in capital and other markets. There is, therefore, little evidence to support the view (apparently implicitly held by many economists doctoring the ailing economies of central and eastern Europe) that the necessary institutions will be the automatic outcome of getting the prices right through elimination of price and exchange controls."

Markets cannot survive without strong political protections from the state itself. This provides for the role of the constitution, the set of institutions governing political decisionmaking. By placing an appropriate set of constraints on the state, the constitution can limit the state's actions in desirable ways.

One of the key questions of this paper concerns the potential beneficial limits on state action: what makes those limits credible, i.e., what makes them binding on political actors? To address this question, this paper has studied how England and the United States grappled with these problems in the past. In each case, a range of factors played important roles. This paper focused on one factor, the institution of federalism.

The history of market-preserving federalism in England and the United States illustrates variations on the same theme. In England it provided the political foundation for the success of the industrial revolution in the North. In the United States, it provided the basis for the common market, fostering first regional and then international specialization and underpinning the great growth in American wealth.[26]

Federalism thus played a central role in protecting the growth of economic markets. Both aspects of federalism – political competition among lower political authorities and the prohibitions on national regulation – proved critical to its success. For both the United States and England, federalism proved an essential component of the political foundations of secure markets. Though the details differ considerably, both cases reveal that federalism's success in practice relied on a mix of formal and informal constraints. I conclude by emphasizing this mix of formal institutions and informal norms.

For both England and the United States, the success of constitutional constraints depended on the emergence of a civil society and the rule of law. A civil society not only requires the appropriate combination of citizen views about the limits of the state and about their duty in the face of state violation of those limits, it requires a societal consensus about these limits. Binding limits do not depend on a constraint being explicit, nor that it might have been agreed upon at some time in the past – though both may play a role. Binding limits instead depend on a sufficient portion of the citizens believing that it is fundamental to the society and who are thus willing to police those limits by withdrawing their support from a government that fails to abide by them.

This yields a critical implication that distinguishes societies characterized by the rule of law from those which are not. The requisite social consensus about the legitimate boundaries of the state implies that those citizens who stand to gain from a violation of the limits nonetheless participate in an attempt to punish those who proposed it. The failure of the latter allows a host of constitutional violations in Latin America and other parts of the third world (see, e.g.,

---

[26] I should also add that it has played a central role in the success of China's economic reform since 1978. This success, founded on a credible political decentralization via federalism, presents a striking contrast to the lack of success with economic reform in the former Soviet Union and its satellites. See WEINGAST [1992 b] for greater details.

MONTINOLA's [1992] discussion of Marcos's rejection of the Philippine Constitution). Notice, in contrast, the reaction to Roosevelt's famous court packing scheme in the 1930s. Although proposed at a time of unprecedented political support for Roosevelt and the New Deal – approaching constitutional-sized supramajorities after the 1936 elections – and although it was an institutional change clearly designed to benefit his constituents, it was deemed illegitimate by a sufficient number of his supporters that its future was highly questionable.

For both England and the United States, the decentralization of political authority implied by federalism was the product of a historical process resulting in a strong consensus supporting these limits. In post-Glorious Revolution England, limits on the national government's authority were part of the increased reliance on the common law courts, the increased attention to the security of property rights, and concern for the maintenance of local political authority.[27]

In sum, constitutional limits must not only seek to constrain governmental decisions, but citizens must agree that these ways are appropriate and necessary.

---

[27] Of course, this raises the question of why explicit constraints are needed at all. The reason concerns unanticipated contingencies in which there are multiple interpretations of how to expand the current set of norms to the new situation. Such problems create a lack of equilibrium, and hence the strong potential for failure due to the resulting heterogeneity of attitudes. Hence explicit institutions are needed. Put another way, explicit institutions, themselves supported by norms, are more effective than norms alone (GREIF, MILGROM and WEINGAST [1992]).

References

ALMOND, Gabriel A. and VERBA, Sidney [1963], *The Civic Culture: Political Attitudes and Democracy in Five Nations*, Newbury Park: Sage Publications.

ARANSON, Peter [1991], "Federalism: Doctrine Against Balance," MS, Emory University.

ASHTON. T. S. [1955], *An Economic History of England: The 18th Century*, London: Methuen and Co.

BERNHOLZ, Peter [1993], "Constitutions as Governance Structures Comment," *Journal of Institutional and Theoretical Economics*, 149 (1), 312–320.

BOGUE, Allen [1963], *From Prairie to Corn Belt: Farming on the Illinois and Iowa Prairies in the Nineteenth Century*, Chicago: University of Chicago Press.

BRENNAN, Geoffrey and BUCHANAN, James M. [1984], *Reason of the Rules*, New York: Cambridge University Press.

BREWER, John [1989], *The Sinews of Power*, New York: Alfred A. Knopf.

CASELLA, Alessandra and FREY, Bruno [1992], "Federalism and Clubs: Towards an Economic Theory of Overlapping Political Jurisdictions," *European Economic Review*. Papers and Proceedings. 36, 639–646.

CHANDLER, Alfred D. [1977], *The Visible Hand*, Cambridge: Harvard University Press.

COASE, Ronald H. [1937], "The Nature of the Firm," *Economica N.S.*, 4, 386–405.

–– [1960], "The Problem of Social Cost," *Journal of Law and Economics*, 3, 1–44.

COX. Gary W. and McCUBBINS, Mathew D. [1992], *Legislative Leviathan: Party Government in the House*, Berkeley: University of California Press, (forthcoming).

DEANE, Phyllis [1979], *The First Industrial Revolution*, New York: Cambridge University Press.

EKELUND, Robert and TOLLISON. Robert [1981], *Mercantilism as a Rent-Seeking Society*, College Station: Texas A & M Press.

ELSTER, Jon and SLAGSTAD, Rune [1988], *Constitutionalism and Democracy*, New York: Cambridge University Press.

FEREJOHN, John [1990], "Rationality and Interpretation: Parliamentary Elections in Early Stuart England," MS, Hoover Institution.

FOGEL, Robert W. [1989], *Without Consent or Contract: The Rise and Fall of American Slavery*, New York: Norton.

FUDENBERG, Drew and MASKIN, Eric [1986], "Folk Theorems in Repeated Games with Discounting and Incomplete Information," *Econometrica*, 54, 553–554.

GELY, Raphael and SPILLER, Pablo T. [1992], "The Political Economy of Supreme Court Constitutional Decisions: The Case of Roosevelt's Court Packing Plan," *International Review of Law and Economics*, forthcoming.

GEORGETOWN LAW JOURNAL [1992], "Symposium on Positive Political Theory and Public Law," *Georgetown Law Journal*.

GILLIGAN, Thomas W. [1993], "Information and the Allocation of Legislative Authority," *Journal of Institutional and Theoretical Economics*, 149 (1), 321–341.

GREIF, Avner [1992], "Cultural Beliefs and the Rise of the West," MS, Stanford University.

––, MILGROM, Paul and WEINGAST, Barry R. [1992], "The Merchant Gild as a Nexus of Contracts," MS, Hoover Institution, Stanford University.

GROFMAN, Bernie and WITTMAN, Donald [1989], *The Federalist Papers and the New Institutionalism*, New York: Agathon Press.

HAMMOND, Tom and MILLER, Gary [1989], "Stability and Efficiency in a Separation-of-Powers Constitutional System." pp. 85–99 in: Bernie Grofman and Donald Wittmann (eds.), *The Federalist Papers and the New Institutionalism*, New York: Agathon Press.

HANDLIN, Oscar and HANDLIN, Mary [1947], *Commonwealth: A Study of the Role of Government in the American Economy, Massachusetts, 1774–1861*, New York: New York University Press.

HARDIN, Russell [1989], "Why a Constitution?," pp. 100–120 in: Bernie Grofman and Donald Wittmann (eds.), *The Federalist Papers and the New Institutionalism*, New York: Agathon Press.

HARTWELL, R. M. [1971], *The Industrial Revolution and Economic Growth*, London: Meuthen.

HARTZ, Louis [1948], *Economic Policy and Democratic Thought: Pennsylvania, 1776–1860*, Harvard: Cambridge University Press.

HAYEK, Friedrich A. [1939], "The Economic Conditions of Interstate Federalism," reprinted in: *Individualism and the Economic Order*, ch. XII, Chicago: University of Chicago Press.

—— [1960], *Constitution of Liberty*, Chicago: University of Chicago Press.

HILL, Christopher [1980], *The Century of Revolution: 1603–1714*, New York: W. W. Norton.

HIRST, Derek [1986], *Authority and Conflict: England, 1603–1658*, Cambridge: Harvard University Press.

HOLMES, Stephen [1988], "Precommitment and the Paradox of Democracy," pp. 195–240 in: Jon Elster and Rune Slagstad (eds.), *Constitutionalism and Democracy*, New York: Cambridge University Press.

HUGHES, Jonathan [1977], *The Governmental Habit*, New York: Basic.

HUNTINGTON, Samuel [1969], *Political Order in Changing Societies*, New Haven: Yale University Press.

JONES, J. R. [1972], *The Revolution of 1688 in England*, New York: W. W. Norton.

KIEWIET, D. RODERICK and McCUBBINS, Mathew D. [1991], *The Logic of Delegation*, Chicago: University of Chicago Press.

KLEIN, Benjamin, CRAWFORD, Robert G. and ALCHIAN, Armen A. [1978], "Vertical Integration, Appropriable Rents, and the Competitive Contracting Process," *Journal of Law and Economics*, 21, 615–641.

KREHBIEL, Keith [1991], *Information and Legislative Organization*, Ann Arbor: University of Michigan Press.

KREPS, David [1990], "Corporate Culture," pp. 90–143 in: James A. Alt and Kenneth A. Shepsle (eds.), *Perspectives on Positive Political Economy*, New York: Cambridge University Press.

LANDES, William and POSNER, Richard [1975], "The Independent Judiciary in an Interest-Group Perspective," *Journal of Law and Economics*, 875.

LEE, Susan Previant and PASSELL, Peter [1979], *A New Economic View of American History*, New York: W. W. Norton.

LITWACK, John M. [1991], "Legality and Market Reform in Soviet-Type Economies," *Journal of Economic Perspectives*, 5, 77–90.

McKINNON, Ronald I. [1991], "Financial Control in the Transition From Classical Socialism to a Market Economy," *Journal of Economic Perspectives*, 5, 107–122.

McNOLLGAST [1989], "Structure and Process, Politics and Policy," *Virginia Law Review*, 75, 431–482.

MILGROM, Paul and ROBERTS, John [1992], *Economics, Organization, and Management*, Englewood Cliffs: Prentice Hall.

MILLER, George [1971], *Railroads and the Granger Laws*, Madison: University of Wisconsin Press.

MILLER, John [1992], "Crown, Parliament, and People," pp. 53–87 in: J. R. Jones (ed.), *Liberty Secured?*, Stanford: Stanford University Press.

Moe, Terry [1990], "The Politics of Structural Choice: Toward a Theory of Public Bureaucracy," pp. 116–153 in: Oliver E. Williamson (ed.), *Organization Theory: From Chester Barnard to the Present and Beyond*, NY: Oxford University Press.

Mokyr, Joel [1988], "The Industrial Revolution and the New Economic History," in: Joel Mokyr (ed.), *The Economics of the Industrial Revolution*, Totowa, NJ: Rowman and Allanheld.

Montinola, Gabriella [1992], "Institutional Foundations of Crony Capitalism: The Rise and Fall of the Marcos Regime in the Philippines," MS, Department of Political Science, Stanford University.

North, Douglass C. [1961], *The Economic Growth of the United States: 1790–1860*, New York: W. W. Norton.

– – [1981], *Structure and Change in Economic History*, New York: W. W. Norton.

– – [1991], *Institutions, Institutional Change, and Economic Performance*, New York: Cambridge University Press.

– – [1993], "Institutions and Credible Commitment," *Journal of Institutional and Theoretical Economis*, 149(1), 11–23.

– – and Weingast, Barry R. [1989], "Constitutions and Credible Commitments: The Evolution of the Institutions of Public Choice in 17th Century England," *Journal of Economic History*, 49, 803–832.

Offe, Claus [1991], "Capitalism by Democratic Design? Democratic Theory Facing the Triple Transition in East Central Europe," *Social Research*, 58, 865–892.

Ordeshook, Peter [1992], "Constitutional Stability," *Constitutional Political Economy*, 3, 137–175.

Ostrom, Vincent [1987], *The Political Theory of a Compound Republic*, Lincoln: University of Nebraska Press.

Passell, Peter and Schmundt, Maria [1971], "Pre-Civil War Land Policy and the Growth of Manufacturing," *Explorations in Economic History*, 9, 35–48.

Przeworski, Adam [1990], *Democracy and the Market*, New York: Cambridge University Press.

Rabushka, Alvin and Shepsle, Kenneth A. [1972], *Politics in Plural Societies*, Columbus: Charles E. Merrill.

Riker, William H. [1964], *Federalism: Origin, Operation, and Significance*, Boston: Little Brown.

– – [1980], "Implications From the Disequilibrium of Majority Rule for the Study of Institutions," *American Political Science Review*, 74, 432–447.

– – [1982], *Liberalism Against Populism*, San Francisco: W. H. Freeman.

Root, Hilton L. [1992], *The Fountain of Privilege: Institutional Innovation and Social Choices in Old Regime France and England*, Berkeley, University of California Press, forthcoming.

Schumpeter, Joseph A. [1918], "The Crisis of the Tax State," reprinted in Richard Swedberg (ed.), *Joseph A. Schumpeter*, (1991), Princeton: Princeton University Press.

Schwoerer, Lois [1981], *The Declaration of Rights, 1689*, Baltimore: Johns Hopkins University Press.

Scotchmer, Suzanne [1990], "Public Goods and the Invisible Hand," MS, UC Berkeley.

Shepsle, Kenneth A. and Weingast, Barry R. [1987], "The Institutional Foundations of Committee Power," *American Political Science Review*, 81, 85–104.

Taylor, George R. [1951], *The Transportation Revolution: 1815–1860*, New York: Holt, Rinehart, and Winston.

Temin, Peter [1991], "Free Land and Federalism: A Synoptic View of American Economic Development," *Journal of Interdisciplinary History*, 21, 371–389.

Tiebout, Charles [1956], "A Pure Theory of Local Expenditures," *Journal of Political Economy*, 64, 416–424.

WEINGAST, Barry R. [1984], "The Congressional-Bureaucratic System: A Principal-Agent Perspective (With Applications to the SEC)," *Public Choice*, 44, 147–192.
–– [1992a], "Federalism and the Political Commitment to Sustain Markets," MS, Hoover Institution, Stanford University.
–– [1992b], "The Economic Role of Political Institutions," MS, Hoover Institution, Stanford University.
–– [1992c], "The Political Foundations of Democracy: The Evolution and Maintenance of a Civil Society and the Rule of Law," MS, Hoover Institution, Stanford University.
–– and MARSHALL, William J. [1988], "The Industrial Organization of Congress," *Journal of Political Economy*, 96, 132–163.
WILLIAMSON, Oliver [1985], *The Economic Institutions of Capitalism*, New York: Free Press.

Professor Barry R. Weingast
Hoover Institution
Stanford University
Stanford, CA 94305-6010
U.S.A.